King of the Court

THE GEORGE GUND FOUNDATION
IMPRINT IN AFRICAN AMERICAN STUDIES

The George Gund Foundation has endowed
this imprint to advance understanding of
the history, culture, and current issues
of African Americans.

King of the Court

Bill Russell and the Basketball Revolution

Aram Goudsouzian

With a Foreword by Harry Edwards

UNIVERSITY OF CALIFORNIA PRESS
Berkeley   Los Angeles   London

University of California Press, one of the most distinguished
university presses in the United States, enriches lives around the
world by advancing scholarship in the humanities, social sciences,
and natural sciences. Its activities are supported by the UC Press
Foundation and by philanthropic contributions from individuals
and institutions. For more information, visit www.ucpress.edu.

University of California Press
Berkeley and Los Angeles, California

University of California Press, Ltd.
London, England

Library of Congress Cataloging-in-Publication Data

Goudsouzian, Aram.
   King of the court : Bill Russell and the basketball revolution /
Aram Goudsouzian with a foreword by Harry Edwards.
      p.   cm.
   Includes bibliographical references and index.
   ISBN 978-0-520-25887-7 (cloth : alk. paper)
   1. Russell, Bill, 1934–2.   Basketball players—United States—Biography.
3. Basketball—United States—History.   I. Title.
GV884.R86G68   2010
323′092—dc22   2009031100

Manufactured in the United States of America

19   18   17   16   15   14   13   12   11   10
10   9   8   7   6   5   4   3   2   1

This book is printed on Cascades Enviro 100, a 100% post-consumer-
waste, recycled, de-inked fiber. FSC recycled certified and processed
chlorine free. It is acid free, Ecologo certified, and manufactured by
BioGas energy.

May 2010

For my dad

To Bill Russell

I have never seen
an eagle with a beard
but if there is
in some strange
corner of the world
and the Hindu
belief is true,
you will return
and beat your wings
violently
over my grave.

—TOM MESCHERY, *OVER THE RIM* (1968)

CONTENTS

ILLUSTRATIONS

Following page 106.

FOREWORD

I have known Bill Russell for more than forty years, and for the past thirty years, I have featured aspects of his life and career as study segments in my sociology of sports classes. So when I was asked to write the Foreword to the present book, my initial reaction was that, based on the title, the author had undertaken a daunting, if not impossible task—to elucidate in a single volume the life *and* the basketball legacy of the most illustrious icon in team sports history. Such would be the challenge of judiciously exploring the understated intellectual brilliance, the profound psychological dexterity, the athletic mastery, and the strength of character underpinning the incomparable basketball career and myriad life contributions of William Felton Russell. Nonetheless, particularly when considered in combination with Russell's own autobiographical books—*Go Up for Glory, Second Wind,* and *Red and Me*—and the scores of more limited profile articles and interviews published over the years, I judge *King of the Court: Bill Russell and the Basketball Revolution* to be an exceedingly rewarding and superbly complementary contribution toward broadening our understanding of this truly extraordinary man and athlete.

It is said that "a picture is worth a thousand words," to which might arguably be added "except in the case of Bill Russell." Neither dramatic action photos nor the grainy black-and-white films from Russell's basketball career have the capacity to capture or depict, much less to encompass, his unique mastery of and contribution to the game. The images of Russell rebounding and running the court—gazelle-like in his agility, in his jumping ability, and in the pace and grace of his stride—seem all but off-set by the practiced adequacy of his left-handed field goal and free-throw shooting. Relative to "style points" and the usual array of individual statistical measures of basketball performance and proficiency, he neither exhibited the scoring flash, jaw-dropping body control, and outright levitating skills of Elgin Baylor, nor the combination of assists, scoring, and rebounding prowess that enabled the great Oscar Robertson to *average* a triple-double in one entire season. Even in comparison to the man typically posed as his chief foil and archrival for dominance at the center position, Wilt Chamberlain, Russell comes up short in terms of individual statistics. In the 143 games in which they met, Chamberlain typically outscored Russell and either matched or exceeded his totals in rebounds and blocked shots. Not only did Chamberlain once garner fifty-five rebounds against the Celtics, but over the course of his professional basketball career, he averaged twenty-nine points and twenty-eight rebounds per game. Russell, by comparison, averaged only half as many points, fourteen, and twenty-four rebounds. When considered within the context of the National Basketball Association's showcase talent event, the All-Star Game, one would be even more hard put to find statistical rationale for ranking Russell a preeminent player. He is not in the top five in number of All-Star appearances or in minutes played when he was selected to All-Star teams. He does not rank in the top ten among All-Star Game players in field goals attempted or made, or even in rebounds or blocked shots. And he was selected to the All-NBA first team a mere three times, ranking him twenty-sixth among players in league history.

Juxtaposed against these statistical facts are other, more telling realities. From his days as a student-athlete at the University of San Francisco, where he guided his team to fifty-five straight victories and two consecutive National Collegiate Athletic Association championship basketball titles, through his performance as leader and captain of the 1956 gold-medal-winning U.S. Olympic basketball team, to his roles as captain, player-coach, anchor, and defining personality in a Boston Celtics dynasty that won eleven NBA championships in thirteen seasons, it has not been the tangibles and measurables so much as the *intangibles* that have set Russell apart from and ahead of even the greatest players of his or any other era. Quite simply, Russell has demonstrated an unparalleled, ubiquitous, and sustained capacity for *winning*. Indeed, in Russell's case the one instance where a picture might be worth a thousand words would be if his picture were placed next to the word "winner" in the dictionary. No other athlete in the history of basketball has so effectively developed and deployed his own unique vision and version of how to play his position while cultivating and fully immersing himself in the imperatives of team success— an abiding respect for the game and unwavering commitment to the concepts of team strategy, preparation, and execution, and to a locker-room "culture of winning." For Russell, the challenge never existed in the guise of a personal duel, never as him against Chamberlain, or him against Wayne Embry, or him against Bob Pettit, or against Ed Mcauley, or Walt Bellamy, or Nate Thurmond, or any of the other outstanding players he faced. It was always the Celtics against the opposing team. And in most cases, Bill Russell's Celtics won those matchups, particularly during the play-offs—all individual statistical comparisons notwithstanding.

It was largely in recognition of his irrepressible penchant for winning through-out his professional career that prompted the National Basketball Writers Association of America in 1980 to name Russell "The Greatest Player in NBA History." In 2009, the NBA named the award for the Most Valuable Player of the NBA Finals after Bill Russell. Still, to portend an understanding of Bill Russell even after the most rigorous and exhaustive analysis of his career and achievements as a basketball player would be to presume to know him too soon. After exploring his life and impact beyond the basketball arena, one could justifiably conclude that his principal identity should not be that of a basketball player at all, but rather that of a man, who, while not without his share of human faults and frailties, has evinced unwavering principles and progressive sentiments, had a disarming intellect and capacity for insight, was possessed of uncommon commitment and courage, and, among other things, also happened to play one hell of a great game of basketball.

In some ways, as *King of the Court* makes clear, Russell's life outside of basketball has been even more layered, nuanced, and intensely complex than his career on the court. His experiences as a child in Louisiana and as an adolescent and young adult growing up and attending school in the Oakland and San Francisco Bay Area in California conditioned and contoured his disposition toward life circumstances and events he subsequently encountered, particularly during the turbulent 1960s. Unlike most of the black professional athletes of the time, Russell was actively and openly supportive of the civil rights movement, contributing financially to a spectrum of causes and supporting both local and national events, boycotts, rallies, and marches.

He was vociferous in his backing of legislation such as the Civil Rights Act of 1964 and the Voting Rights Act of 1965. In 1964, he organized basketball camps in Mississippi during the height of that state's deadly and violent "Freedom Summer." And he did not limit his outspokenness and activism to racial issues and problems in the South. Much to the chagrin and frequently to the outrage of many Celtics fans and citizens of both Boston and his residential town of Reading, Massachusetts, the local situation did not escape his attention and scathing critique. Not even the NBA received a pass from Russell when it came to issues of racism and injustice.

By the middle of the 1960s, Russell had established himself as one of two highly visible and influential superstar black athletes—the other being Jim Brown of the National Football League's Cleveland Browns. These were the two most transformative sports figures of the era, bridging the generational and social-political gap between Joe Louis and Muhammad Ali, between Jesse Owens and Tommie Smith and John Carlos, and between Jackie Robinson and Curt Flood. It was a time of seminal change and challenge relative to developments at the interface of race, sports, and society. A new, more militant generation of elite black athletes was emerging, a generation that was far less inclined than its predecessors to feign the "happy-go-lucky," passive, smiling visage that the white mainstream media had come to expect, if not insist on, from the "colored" athlete. Confronted with black athletes whom they neither understood culturally nor felt comfortable with polit-ically, establishment sports reporters frequently employed a "trap-and-gotcha" technique during interviews. (As Russell confided to me at the time, "There is al-ways the prospect that what a black athlete says can and will be used against him, against other black athletes, or against black people.") For instance, shortly after he was named player-coach of the Boston Celtics, a reporter asked him a "trap ques-tion": What is the right number of black players to play? (The "trap" is that what-ever the number suggested, it would be a controversial answer: unavoidably, the implication would be that a franchise having fewer than that number of black play-ers on the floor at the same game would be guilty of discrimination, a franchise playing more would be inappropriately privileging black players, while playing the number of blacks cited as "right" by Russell, the NBA's first black head coach, could be creating an artificial ceiling on black players' opportunities.) With characteris-tic perceptiveness and intellectual acuity, Russell avoided the trap, answered the question, and addressed head-on a league problem evident in the fact that the ques-tion had been asked in the first place: "I don't know that there is a right number, but in the NBA the tradition is to play two black players at home, three on the road, and five when you get behind."

Bill Russell was not the most bombastic or radically outspoken black athlete of the day—Muhammad Ali easily took the prize in that category. He was not the most dramatically demonstrative in opposition to racism—Tommie Smith and John Carlos stand alone in that regard with their protest on the victory stand at the 1968 Mexico City Olympics. He was not the most analytically expressive—Arthur Ashe standing at a country club podium extrapolating on the legitimacy of anti-apartheid politics in sports and entertainment prevails here. Nor was he viewed as the most intimidating black sports figure of the time—that honor would have gone to Jim Brown. Rather, as was the case with Russell and his approach to the game of basketball, it was the intangibles that distinguished his iconoclastic activist style outside the arena. He never ceased his intellectual and political explorations of the philosophies, goals, and strategies of the various leadership and activist compo-nents of the "Movement." While he rejected black orthodoxy as much as white racism, his openness, honesty, and deeply rooted sincerity of commitment to the struggle for racial justice earned him the abiding respect, admiration, and allegiance of all those privileged to have worked with him and experienced firsthand his as-tute eye for political propriety and promise.

In 1968, when I was organizing the Olympic Project for Human Rights (OPHR)—

at the outset, long before the twenty-four-foot statue was erected on the campus of San José State University honoring the OPHR and Tommie Smith and John Carlos, and long before the flood of honorary doctorates and other recognition awards—some of us associated with the effort were turned into villains and were pilloried by the mainstream media and the sports establishment as ungrateful, unpatriotic traitors to both the civil rights cause and our country, and worse. In the face of all this, two black professional athletes came out politically in our support. One was Jim Brown. The first was Bill Russell. Russell had just won an NBA title as player-coach of the Boston Celtics, and he would soon be named *Sports Illustrated*'s "Sportsman of the Year." Following the Smith-Carlos Olympic victory stand demonstration, he was asked "as a past great Olympian," if he had a problem with the Smith-Carlos gesture. His answer: "Yeah, I have a problem with it. I didn't think of it first." The answer was quintessentially and characteristically Russell, consistent with the man and the athlete, the life and the career probed and profiled in *King of the Court*. Aside from presenting Russell's own words and writings, the pages that follow offer the most penetrating and broad-spectrum perspective to date on this complex, driven, and inspiring personality, on this warrior prince of an athlete, on this winner, on this man.

Harry Edwards
Professor Emeritus
Department of Sociology
University of California, Berkeley

ACKNOWLEDGMENTS

The Department of History at the University of Memphis has been my academic home throughout the research and writing of this book, and I owe big thanks to my colleagues for their personal and professional support. Furthermore, the students in my classes on "The Black Athlete and American History" helped clarify my ideas, while the graduate students in a variety of seminars provoked in me a more sophisticated understanding of African American history. In support of this project, the School of Liberal Arts and Sciences awarded me a Faculty Research Grant, a Donovan Travel Award, an Early Career Research Award, and a Professional Development Assignment.

On the research trail, I encountered many generous souls. David Youngblood was a gracious tour guide in Monroe, Louisiana. Larry Foreman led me through Special Collections at the Ouachita Parish Public Library. At the University of San Francisco, I depended on the resources of Peter Simon in Sports Information, the feedback of amateur historian Bernie Schneider, and especially the good graces of Father Michael Kotlanger, director of the University of San Francisco Archive Room. The staff at the Urban Archives at Temple University and at the Spencer Research Library at the University of Kansas aided some related research on Wilt Chamberlain. The staff at the Widener Library at Harvard University and the Microtext Department at the Boston Public Library hosted my research through Boston's newspapers. Jodee Fenton and the staff at the Seattle Public Library, as well as Don Lee and Kristine Krueger of the Margaret Herrick Library, helped with Russell's post-playing days. Matt Zeysing at the Naismith Memorial Basketball Hall of Fame clued me into the indispensable Bill Mokray Scrapbook Collection.

Interviews with Bill Russell's teammates, friends, associates, relatives, and political allies enriched my understanding of a complicated man and his times. Talia Bargil at the National Basketball Retired Players Association kindly passed along my countless letters to Russell's NBA contemporaries. Jenny Koltnow of the Memphis Grizzlies also helped me with interview contacts. Thanks to the interviewees for their generosity of time and spirit: Al Attles, Steve Balchios, Warren Baxter, Dave Bing, Eugene Brown, Stan Buchanan, Bill Bush, Bud Collins, Gene Conley, Mel Counts, Bob Cousy, John Cunningham, Frank Deford, Ron Downey, Harry Edwards, Charles Evers, Mike Farmer, Harold Furash, Ross Giudice, Elijah "Pumpsie" Green, Gene Guarilia, Cliff Hagan, Burdette Haldorson, John Hollingsworth, Bob Hopkins, Tim Horgan, Bailey Howell, Mel King, Earl Lloyd, John LoSchiavo, Ed Macauley, Leigh Montville, Tom Nelson, Hal Perry, Mike Preaseau, Frank Ramsey, Arnie Risen, Reverend John Russell, Tom "Satch" Sanders, Dolph Schayes, Larry Siegfried, Nate Thurmond, Ron Tomsic, Jerry West, Peggy White, John Wooten, and Magdalean Young.

A slew of historians of sport and American culture have connections to my graduate alma mater, Purdue University. Many of them read chapters and provided trusty advice. Deep thanks to Carson Cunningham, Elliott Gorn, Jamal Ratchford, Randy Roberts, David Welky, and especially Johnny Smith, who read every chapter carefully and thoughtfully.

Thomas Whalen and David Wiggins read the manuscript for the University of California Press, and I thank them for their expert opinions and generous support. I further depended on a large community of historians who read chapters, gave feedback at conferences, answered my e-mails about their research specialties, and even let me crash on their couch during research trips. Thanks to John Carroll, Chris Chekuri, Anne Choi, Emilye Crosby, John Dittmer, Charles McKinney, Chris Messenger, Murry Nelson, Michael Smith, Jeanne Theoharis, Damion Thomas, and Russ Wigginton. Special thanks to Peggy White, who exceeded the normal boundaries of kindness in finding material on Russell's life in Reading, Massachusetts.

Portions of this book appeared in *American Studies* and *California History*, and I thank the editors for allowing those sections to be reprinted here. Tra Angelos at Getty Images, Kevin Grace at the University of Cincinnati, Richard Johnson at the Sports Museum of New England, Nick Lammers at the *Oakland Tribune*, Steven Lavoie at the Oakland History Room of the Oakland Public Library, Jim Mahoney at the *Boston Herald*, Holly Reed at the National Archives, and Kathy Struss at the Dwight D. Eisenhower Library all helped me procure photographs. In this regard, special thanks to Aaron Schmidt at the Boston Public Library.

Matt McGowan is a smart and supportive agent, and I owe a lot to him. Further thanks to my editor, Naomi Schneider, and the staff at the University of California Press.

My father, Nishan Goudsouzian, to whom this book is dedicated, is my role model for his humility, work ethic, and compassion. I am equally thankful for my kind and generous mother, Mary Goudsouzian. Thanks, as always, to my brothers- and sisters-in-law, Steve, Haig, Lara, and Jarka.

Finally, thanks to my wife, Chrystal. I saved her for last, because she is the best.

Introduction

Bill Russell first stepped on an NBA court against the St. Louis Hawks on December 22, 1956. Boston Garden quivered with anticipation. Tucked under the clattering trains of North Station, the smoky, creaky arena filled with more than eleven thousand spectators, almost double the typical Sunday afternoon crowd. The fans were excited but curious, unsure what to expect. Russell had piloted the University of San Francisco to a fifty-five-game winning streak and two NCAA championships, and he joined the NBA after winning a gold medal at the Melbourne Olympics. The Harlem Globetrotters had offered him riches. The Boston Celtics secured him after a complicated trade. Yet he had never appeared on national television, and he looked nothing like a conventional center. Most of professional basketball's big men possessed sturdy frames and sound offensive fundamentals. Russell was spindly, all elbows and knees, a huge string puppet in the hands of a clumsy child.

By conventional measures, that first game lent ammunition to Russell's doubters. He did not start, played less than half the game, and scored only six points. His stomach churned with anxiety. He missed eight shots, and he flubbed all four of his free throws. "We've got boys on our high school team who shoot better than he does," sniffed one woman from a small New Hampshire town.[1]

Yet clues to Russell's impact surfaced. He sprang off the floor and sucked in missed shots, grabbing sixteen rebounds in only twenty-one minutes. More than the number of rebounds, it was *how* he rebounded: collecting the ball off the glass and whipping an outlet pass in one motion, igniting a fast break. On defense, he covered the burly center Charlie Share, but he ranged all around the basket, displaying the agility of a nimble guard. St. Louis forward Ed Macauley dribbled around

1

a pick and pulled up for an eighteen-foot jump shot. "There was no reason for Russell to be anywhere near me," he recalled. "He was someplace else guarding Share. So I went up for the shot and there was no problem. Except that Russell came out of nowhere and slapped that ball directly over my head." By the time Macauley landed and turned around, Russell was gliding to the opposite basket and stuffing the ball with two hands.[2]

Russell defended the way Picasso painted, the way Hemingway wrote: in time, he changed how people understood the craft. Until Russell, the game stayed close to the floor. No longer. Twice Bob Pettit drove past his defender for presumably easy layups. Twice Russell pounced, redirecting Pettit's efforts toward a Boston teammate. "I think we just witnessed the birth of a star and the start of a bright new era in Celtics history," proclaimed radio announcer Johnny Most. "I just saw Bob Pettit shaking his head in total disgust—and that is a great sight for every Celtics fan." Bob Cousy marveled at Russell's explosive quickness, his radical disruptions of established patterns. As Boston's star guard walked off the Garden's parquet floor, he thought that the future had arrived.[3]

Professional basketball needed that glimpse of a brighter future. When Russell joined the Celtics, the National Basketball Association owned a sweaty, scuffling, small-time reputation. The league had only eight teams—none further west than St. Louis, none in such major markets as Chicago or Detroit, and three in the small-potatoes, industrial-belt cities of Rochester, Syracuse, and Fort Wayne. A cabal of paternalistic owners struggled to keep their teams afloat. NBC's "Game of the Week" generated little revenue. Many players earned under $5,000 a year. A nascent Players Association had to beg for such concessions as a twenty-game limit on the exhibition season. Scenes of screaming coaches, incompetent referees, and brawling players sullied the NBA's reputation. Its critics called it a "bush league."[4]

The NBA was also a white league. Russell was the sole African American on the Celtics' roster, and the Hawks were lily-white. Only fifteen blacks appeared on professional rosters that season. Here, too, Russell initiated a sea change in the character of professional basketball. More than any contemporary, he acted as his sport's Jackie Robinson. Though not the NBA's first black player, he became its first black superstar—the first to generate copious publicity, the first to alter the sport's texture, the first to shape a team's championship destiny.[5]

Arriving in the wake of *Brown v. Board of Education* and the Montgomery Bus Boycott, Russell radiated this integrationist spirit. The two-time NCAA champion and Olympic gold medalist exuded a deft combination of humility and confidence. Traveling in the footsteps of racial ambassadors such as Joe Louis, Jesse Owens, and Jackie Robinson, he had encountered bigotry, but he had transcended that hatred with soaring grace. In 1956, Russell embodied the myth that sport fostered racial progress. In cultural politics, as in basketball, he offered an icon of black possibility.[6]

. . .

Bill Russell last stepped on an NBA court against the Los Angeles Lakers on May 5, 1969. The Fabulous Forum showcased basketball at its swankiest. Rimmed by eighty columns, the $16.25 million edifice featured ushers in togas guiding Hollywood stars to wide, cushioned, theater-style courtside seats. The arena epitomized professional basketball's transformation from a marginal, regional endeavor into the nation's third major team sport. Lucrative television contracts now attracted interest and investors. Fourteen NBA teams occupied major markets across the country, and the American Basketball Association competed for players and fans. NBA players earned lucrative salaries, flew first class, stayed in luxury hotels, and sparred with a new generation of wealthy owners. The sport had acquired a distinctly modern ethic.[7]

Russell had grown thicker in the midsection, more grizzled, weathered by physical and emotional campaigns. He relied more than ever on guile and experience. The game had changed, too. Almost paradoxically, Russell had fed the sport's offensive transformation. Because of his rebounding, the Celtics operated their fast break with vicious efficiency. Because of his defense, every team adapted. His leaping ability and timing had corroded basketball's older, earthbound patterns. After Russell, one needed to play faster, stretch the court, shoot from new spots, jump higher. The game rose above the rim. It demanded agility and speed, and it valued all-around skill. In Russell's wake came a new generation of dynamic stars including Jerry West, Elgin Baylor, and Wilt Chamberlain—all of them, by Russell's last season, members of the Los Angeles Lakers.[8]

Russell's last contest was the decisive seventh game of the 1969 NBA Finals. The series had collected his greatest foils: six times before his Celtics had beaten the Lakers in the NBA Finals, and six times before he had vanquished his great nemesis Chamberlain. Los Angeles owner Jack Kent Cooke expected his superstars to carry the day. He ordered a spectacular victory celebration: the USC marching band, balloons released from the rafters, and an elaborate presentation of the championship trophy.[9]

The band stayed silent, the balloons stayed on the ceiling, and the Celtics stayed champions. Boston won, 108–106. The victory polished Russell's reputation as the greatest winner in the history of team sports. In his thirteen seasons, the Boston Celtics won eleven NBA championships. Russell provided the common thread for the greatest dynasty in the history of professional basketball. He had lent the critical element to the talent-choked Celtics teams of the late 1950s and early 1960s, spearheaded the defense-oriented squads of the mid-1960s, and player-coached a band of veterans in the late 1960s. During the league's emergence from obscurity, Russell was its greatest representative, especially as his compelling rivalry with Chamberlain became the sport's preeminent narrative.[10]

In many ways, Russell had fulfilled the political optimism of his early career. By 1969 the NBA had a black majority, and fifteen of the twenty-four All-Stars were black. Basketball had incorporated an African American aesthetic: a grace, a swagger, a flourish of individuality and physicality. Young black men embraced the sport as an arena of cultural expression. Basketball and blackness had established links in the American imagination.[11]

Moreover, as the civil rights movement triggered the destruction of Jim Crow laws and practices throughout the American South, Russell broke basketball's racial barriers. He earned prodigious respect. He transmitted messages of black equality. He protested when he faced segregation, and he became an international symbol of American democracy, earning admiration from Australia to Europe to Africa. He developed friendships with teammates, both white and black. He lauded his coach and general manager Red Auerbach. In 1966 Russell became the first black coach of any major professional team sport. The Boston Celtics served as professional sport's finest model of racial integration, and Russell led this athletic crusade.[12]

Yet Russell rejected any easy political characterization. As his sport's most respected star, the leader of a racially integrated outfit, and a key public face as basketball established its financial and cultural moorings, he refused the outlaw image embodied by such boxers as Jack Johnson and Muhammad Ali. But he snapped the fetters of the established icon represented by Joe Louis, Jesse Owens, and Jackie Robinson. The civil rights movement had shaped a generation with rising expectations, a generation seeking equality beyond access to a lunch counter. For Russell, the political climate prompted a personal crisis. He pondered his own worth and searched for fulfillment, sometimes sleeping only two hours a night. Off the court, he remained a black man in a racist society. Sport had delivered him fame and fortune, but he chafed at its hypocrisies, and he refused to let sport define him.[13]

So Russell shaped a unique persona. Even as his athletic accomplishments bolstered integrationist ideals, he attacked the racial double standards of the sports establishment. He adopted a scowling, regal demeanor that contradicted expectations of black humility. He distrusted the nonviolent strategy of the civil rights movement. He denounced the racial climate of Boston. Well before the "Revolt of the Black Athlete" in the late 1960s, he questioned the liberal assumptions guiding black participation in sport.[14]

Historically, black athletes had adopted a gracious, grateful public persona that engendered good will among the broader public. By the era of Black Power, black athletes often embodied a greater rejection of American ideals and institutions. Russell stepped into neither skin. Instead, he revealed both the possibilities and limitations of racial change through sport. In so doing, he provoked people to consider his complicated individuality.[15]

. . .

"I should epitomize the American Dream," Russell wrote in *Sports Illustrated*, one year after the 1969 NBA Finals. He rose from the destitute segregation of Depression-era Louisiana, from the ghetto bleakness of West Oakland, California. Despite such desperate beginnings, he earned wealth and fame. He altered his sport. Led by Russell, the University of San Francisco Dons, the U.S. Olympic team, and the Boston Celtics established new standards of basketball excellence. Sports fans respected him, and many African Americans idolized him.

But Russell wrote that he *should* embody the spirit of democracy. Instead, bitterness crept through him. Sport provided a "sugarcoated fantasy," masking hatred and greed. Myths of "character" and "community" and "loyalty" cloaked the exploitation of athletes and the inattention to racial injustice. He could not rest on his sporting laurels. He continued a journey that began in his mind, in his understanding of himself and his history. His athletic greatness sprung from these intellectual impulses. They drove his understanding of American racial politics. More than any other athlete, he expressed the dreams of Martin Luther King while echoing the warnings of Malcolm X.[16]

Russell's story thus reveals the brilliance of the black freedom struggle, refracted through the prism of a commercial sports boom. The game's most respected figure was also its public intellectual. He prodded beyond the status quo, embracing American ideals yet articulating personal anger at the nation's persistent racism. During his reign, basketball underwent meaningful changes: a stylistic evolution, a financial expansion, a new standard of team excellence, and a racial upheaval. These changes arrived gradually and imperfectly, but together they transformed the sport's meaning in American culture. Call it the basketball revolution—and place Bill Russell at its center.

Russell Moves

Every man draws a line inside himself, according to Charlie Russell. A black man in the Jim Crow South needed that line. From childhood he absorbed cruel lessons about the potency of white power, the futility of black ambition, the hovering menace of violence, the intricate codes of racial behavior. A man survived by acquiescing to the system. But a man's soul survived by defending his dignity. When pushed too far, a man pushed back.[1]

Charlie's father Jake once drew his line while sharecropping in the northeastern Louisiana delta. After one harvest, Jake told his landlord that he would not farm the next year. "Nigger," said the boss, "don't tell me what you ain't gonna do. I'll *make* you do it." That proclamation captured the essence of Jim Crow: the white man claimed dominion over not only the black man's labor but also his spirit. According to racial etiquette, the black worker backed down. Jake knew this code. To survive, he deferred to whites and limited his own aspirations. But this time, he pushed back. "Sir," he answered, "you and who else?" That defiance enraged the white man. After a scuffle, Jake scared the landlord off his own property. Jake then packed his children into his truck, deposited them at a friend's home, and returned home for the inevitable reprisal. When the Ku Klux Klan arrived, he delivered a volley of shotgun shells, scattering the whites away, intimidating his intimidators.

Charlie drew his own line while working construction. His white boss had just slapped, berated, and humiliated a black mule-team driver. Charlie started laughing. He proclaimed that in the same circumstance, he would run or fight, but never just suffer a beating. Like his father, he challenged one white man and an entire system of white power. The boss needed to save face. He promised to next whip Charlie. "Naaaw, Mr. George," drawled Charlie. "I don't think so." Their faces neared, their stares locked. Finally, the white man huffed away. Passing down the story, Charlie explained that he could lose a fight or get fired. He could not, however, let his boss assume absolute control. "What good would it do to let him beat me bloody to make me make my own living?" He repeated that last part, bellowing with confident fury: "*to make me make my own living!*"[2]

William Felton Russell grew up hearing these stories, delighting in the embellishments, the back-and-forth clarifications, the laughter, and the pride. He learned their lessons. He spent a lifetime drawing these same lines, articulating his own manhood. His journey transcended the South. It coursed along the path of black migration, pushing him north and west, into schools and onto basketball courts that opened new possibilities. But it began on February 12, 1934, in West Monroe, Louisiana. Russell's childhood textured his future principles. In the interstices of racial limitations, he learned the values that framed his later ideology. He also built a powerful sense of self-pride—sharpened by these lessons about manhood, and bathed in the memories of a mother's love.

. . .

In the 1930s West Monroe straddled Louisiana's past and future. The rich delta soil of the outlying regions nourished cotton fields, grim poverty, and racial tyranny. Just across the Ouachita River lay Monroe, the trade center of northeastern Louisiana. Since the 1916 discovery there of natural gas, Monroe had attracted thousands of migrants to work its petroleum refineries, lumber mills, and service jobs. Tax revenues funded paved roads, streetlights, and schools. Downtown Monroe had its heyday during Bill Russell's childhood; department stores and hotels lined the blocks from Fourth Street to South Grand. By the standards of northern Louisiana, anyway, Monroe was a beacon of progress.[3]

Less congested than its sister city, West Monroe had a small black population, including the Russells, who lived in a four-block quarter called Trenton. West Monroe had relatively peaceful race relations, yet the surrounding farm and mill regions bore threats of overt racial hatred. In the preceding decades, Ouachita Parish had suffered a quantity of lynchings comparable to any county in the South. Such attacks ebbed by the 1930s, although in 1938, in nearby Ruston, a mob lynched a nineteen-year-old black man accused of murdering a white man and beating his girlfriend. The throng attacked its victim, hanged him from an oak tree, and pumped bullets into his corpse for ten minutes. The sheriff drove away upon hearing the shots. Before the body came down, thousands visited the scene, foraging for such souvenirs as a shotgun shell or a bloody oak leaf.[4]

Blacks in Monroe evaded the rope and torch, but they possessed little power. Color bars restricted them from skilled jobs as electricians, machinists, or printers. Poll taxes and intimidation prevented them from voting. In 1936, a candidate for city office promised to hire exclusively white labor for skilled work. Only the local NAACP president Charles H. Myers agitated with uncompromising resolve. Despite struggling for members and funds, he forged the state's most active branch, challenging police brutality, discrimination by railroad unions, and unjust imprisonment of black citizens. But most of Monroe's black elite of doctors, funeral directors, and restaurateurs acquiesced to segregation. Russell later criticized this leadership class. "They did what the white community wanted," he said in 1963. He lamented the constant pleas for blacks to stay patient, to stay in their place.[5]

Education opened one path to marketable skills, critical-thinking abilities, and slipping the fetters of Jim Crow. But after World War One, local whites burned down the original black schoolhouse in West Monroe. Charlie Russell went to school in a church, funded by parents who paid a teacher one dollar a week. During the Depression, Governor Huey Long discoursed about educating Louisiana blacks, but parish school boards hoarded state funds for white schools. Bill attended school in a ramshackle barn propped up by poles.[6]

The Russell family nevertheless implanted values of self-improvement, upward mobility, and independence. Neither middle-class hoity-toities nor dirt-shack poor—just "average-type people," according to one cousin—they earned the esteem of Monroe's black community. The Old Man, as Bill called his grandfather, was something of a community patriarch. Choosing jobs that preserved his independence, he worked as a farmhand, drayman, and trader. Mister Charlie, as Bill called his father, worked at the Brown Paper Mill Company. This large, imposing, gregarious man commanded respect. He built Bill's sense of dignity. He said that it was fine to dig ditches, so long as you became the best ditchdigger in Louisiana. Bill had role models in his father, grandfather, and also his brother Chuck, who was two years older.[7]

But no one shaped Bill's early life more than his mother, Katie Russell. "When I think about my mother for any reason," he recalled, "what first jumps to mind are memories of her telling me that she loved me more than anyone in the world." She doted on him, washed him in affection. She also told him that some people would always hate him for his black skin. Her integrity complemented her warmth— once, when Charlie got too drunk and rowdy, she bashed him with an iron pipe. Bill felt safe around her. Katie Russell embodied the resistance of black women in the Jim Crow South: women who endured the double prejudice of race and gender, who worked and raised children, who envisioned a better life for their families. Katie insisted that Mister Charlie open college funds when the boys were still babies. Charlie and Katie also resisted the custom of large families, so they could properly feed and educate their two sons.[8]

Bill's world further encompassed the extended kin networks that marked black life in the South. His Grandpa King drifted in and out of Monroe. This quirky, perhaps insane man prone to supernatural visions fathered five daughters besides Katie, including Kammie, the family's secret lesbian transvestite. Charlie's brother Bob had an enduring effect on Bill. Convinced that a tall left-handed pitcher would attract the attention of the Negro Leagues, he insisted that his nephew develop his left hand. As the story went, if Bill fell asleep holding a turkey drumstick in his right hand, Uncle Bob switched it into his left hand. Bill never knew if he was a natural lefty. His baseball career stalled out, but in the decades to come, he blocked countless shots with that left hand.[9]

In family gatherings, after dinner, Bill heard countless folk tales about slavery, about ghosts and spirits called "haints," about the heroic resistance of The Old Man and Mister Charlie, about the foibles of white folks, about the lynching in Ruston. Sundays belonged to God, to two versions of Sunday school and two church services, to thudding lectures with fire-and-brimstone bluster. In August, his extended family gathered for weeklong revivals. "About the only thing that was fun for us kids was the huge amount of food," recalled a cousin. "We just ate and ate the whole week."[10]

Kids like Bill had time, however, for playing in the fields and fishing. Bill was a happy child, prone to making jokes and mischief. Once, as a superstitious, ghost-obsessed neighbor couple walked home at night, Bill and his brother surprised them. The boys dressed in sheets and made spooky sounds. To their delight, the neighbors panicked and sprinted away—the wife jiggling with fat, the husband speed-hobbling on a wooden leg.[11]

Too young to internalize all the racial patterns of behavior, Bill nonetheless shaped an understanding of American society. He had no white friends or acquaintances. In Monroe, he heard taunts and slurs from white children. One time, he and Chuck lobbed pebbles at each other—until one struck a passing car, driven by a white man. The outraged adult chased them along the back roads. He called Bill a "nigger" and threatened to hang him. "I ran off, half angry, half laughing," Bill recalled. "Much later in life, I can laugh more." He understood how black people accommodated white power, but bitterness infiltrated his recollections.[12]

Two emblematic instances illustrated the agony of the South. One Saturday afternoon, Bill found his mother at home sobbing. She had gone into downtown Monroe dressed in a new suit modeled after a riding habit, with a trim coat and pants. A policeman chided her for dressing like a white woman, and he ordered her home. The sight of his crying mother shook Bill. He, too, broke into sobs.

Not long after, in the spring of 1942, Charlie and his two sons waited at a gas station while the white attendant gabbed with a friend. When a white customer arrived, the attendant pumped the man's gas and then resumed his conversation. Bursting with frustration, Charlie started his car. The attendant, brandishing a rifle, raged at the insult: "Boy, don't you *ever* do what you just started to do!" He sputtered a stream of cuss-laden invective, emasculating Charlie in front of his children—until Charlie emerged from the car carrying a tire iron. Caught between shock and fear, the attendant ran away.[13]

Pushed out by Jim Crow, pulled away by the promise of jobs and better schools, the Russells soon participated in the Great Migration. The massive demographic shift of black people from the rural South to the urban North had begun during World War One. Bill remembered visitors home to Louisiana, sporting new cars and tales of urban freedoms. At the time, however, more than three-fourths of blacks still lived in the South. The onset of World War Two spurred new demands for labor in the industrial North and West. In the next thirty years, five million black people left the South. In 1942, Charlie rode alone to Detroit, where he made war equipment at the Ford Motor Plant. He despised the Michigan weather, however, and caught a life-threatening cold. So he moved west to Oakland, California, and worked at the Moore Dry Dock shipyards before sending for his family.

In 1943 Katie, Chuck, and Bill boarded a train themselves. Confined to the rear, they carried wrapped-up fried chicken for the ride through Little Rock, since the dining cars refused service to blacks. When they reached St. Louis they moved forward. Once out of the South, they could sit wherever they wanted.[14]

· · ·

The Russells settled in West Oakland, along with tens of thousands of other migrants. "It was like a parade," said one resident, remembering the scene at the Southern Pacific's Sixteenth Street station. "You just couldn't believe that many people would come in, and some didn't even have any luggage, they would come with boxes, with three or four children with no place to stay." During the war years, Oakland's African American population tripled.[15]

They came for jobs. The Southern Pacific railroad yards and the Oakland Inner Harbor needed longshoremen, Pullman porters, cooks, freight loaders, redcaps, waiters, and truck drivers. Working-class families packed into blocks dense with turn-of-the-century cottages and bungalows. The West Oakland flatlands also featured small factories and commercial districts of restaurants, bars, laundries, groceries, and barbershops catering to the black influx. The Great Migration had created vibrant urban spaces that illustrated the range of African American life, mixing professionals with the poor, respectable women's clubs with randy gentlemen's clubs, hot jazz with heavenly gospel, Saturday night sin with Sunday morning salvation.[16]

But the surge of southern migrants—both black and white—brought Jim Crow to the East Bay. "The Negro newcomer," complained a 1944 editorial in the *Oakland Observer,* "does not concede that the white man has the right to be alone with his kind." A recent confrontation between black workers and white policemen stirred anxieties about the "what might be called socially-liberated or uninhibited Negroes . . . butting into white civilization instead of keeping in the perfectly ordered and convenient Negro civilization of Oakland." The editorial warned that more violence loomed.[17]

West Oakland whites fled a previously comfortable, middle-class neighborhood. Shipyards, loading docks, and factories restricted blacks from skilled or administrative work. Many unions and local employers excluded blacks. Downtown hotels and restaurants brandished signs proclaiming "We Refuse Service to Negroes." Discrimination by residents and real estate agents prevented blacks from spreading beyond West and North Oakland, so blacks packed into overcrowded homes and apartments, even as rents remained high. The Russells first lived in an eight-room house shared by eight families, with another family in the garage. Pigs, sheep, and chickens roamed the backyard.[18]

Charlie Russell insisted that they were broke, not poor. That little axiom rejected the fatalistic mind-set inflicted by poverty, and it reflected Charlie's resolve to provide for his family. Both he and Katie worked in the shipyards, one during days and the other nights. The Oakland City Housing Authority had put him on a waiting list. Every day for four months, Charlie stopped at the city office to ask about his application status. Thanks to Charlie's perseverance, the Russells moved into a project near the intersection of Tenth and Union Streets, despite the wartime housing crunch. The public housing implied a rising status—the project was racially integrated, though whites and blacks occupied separate sections.[19]

Katie Russell remained the anchor in Bill's life. Once, a neighborhood boy slapped Bill across the mouth, harassing the new kid on the block. Katie rushed outside, grabbed her son, and chased down the bully. She made Bill fight him. Bill then challenged another boy who had insulted him during the first fight. Katie insisted that Bill learn self-respect. She further required that he think for himself. He now attended Cole Elementary School, a real school with real desks in a real building. Each class had its own teacher, and the curriculum pushed students beyond rote learning. Bill absorbed his mother's passion for education. Katie asked about his lessons, answered his questions, and took him to the library. "Every morning I felt I was going out to slay a big dragon for her," he remembered, "and I'd come home from school to tell her how it hadn't stood a chance, just like we'd figured."[20]

The Russells scraped, but their emphasis on hard work and education suggested a future security. When the war ended in 1945, Charlie lost his job in the shipyards. The postwar demobilization devastated industrial centers such as Oakland, slicing black workers the deepest. By 1950, Bay Area blacks suffered 20 percent unemployment, twice the rate of whites. Charlie survived with ingenuity. He bought a surplus army truck, and every morning at dawn, he waited at the corner of Eighth and Center Streets. Then he ferried crops and fruit pickers to the surrounding farm country. He soon operated a healthy business with a small fleet of trucks.[21]

Then, in the fall of 1946, Katie Russell died. Charlie Russell had come home from the hospital, woken his children in the darkness, and simply told them, "Your mother died tonight." She had been hospitalized for two weeks with a mysterious flu-like sickness, and then her kidneys failed. Her death surprised her doctors. "We'll all have to stick together now," said Charlie.[22]

Bill was twelve years old. For months afterward he dreamed of his mother hugging him, rocking him awake in the morning, telling him that she would never leave. During the funeral back in Louisiana, he refused to look at her corpse. He could not accept her absence. No instance in Bill Russell's life molded him more his mother's death. She had implanted him with his sense of self and a sense of security. Even as an adult, he sought to protect himself from the pain of personal loss.[23]

After the funeral, Katie's sisters debated the fate of her sons. In the African American tradition, kin networks provided necessary safety nets. During slavery, fathers often lived apart from their families, and masters constantly sold away family members. Webs of aunts, uncles, cousins, and grandparents thus assumed necessary child-rearing roles. These practices lasted after emancipation. Black people often relied on extended families for support through the ravages of Jim Crow, the struggles of poverty, and the upheavals of the Great Migration. When Katie died, her husband could have returned to Oakland while her sisters reared their boys.[24]

Mister Charlie bucked tradition. He had promised Katie that their children would attend college—a more likely prospect outside Louisiana. So they returned to Oakland, and Charlie ran a unique all-male household. "We gonna live like *people*," he announced. Bill and his brother cooked, cleaned, and even signed each other's report cards. Charlie relinquished his trucking business, which required long hours away from home. He took a job with regular hours, pouring molten iron in a foundry. Although handsome and virile, he remained single until his boys matured. He accepted responsibility for his family, stood as a beacon of integrity, and shaped his own destiny. He demonstrated the meaning of manhood.[25]

But Bill's own confidence crumpled. Once a sociable jokester, he withdrew into solitary melancholy. "I was held back by serious doubts that I could ever become anything without my mother," he remembered. His peers exploited his dwindling self-assurance. They mocked his awkward efforts at sports, driving him to tears. He even struggled in class, almost failing the eighth grade at Hoover Junior High School. As a split-year student, which meant that he started a new grade every January, he felt like an outsider. His older brother excelled at athletics and attended Oakland Tech, a prestigious and mostly white school. Bill idolized his brother, who would later play basketball for Santa Rosa Junior College and serve in the Korean War.[26]

Upon entering McClymonds High School, Bill could not fill Chuck's shoes. He once overheard a coach grumble, "Why is it that Tech gets all the good ones and McClymonds gets all the stiffs on these brother combinations?" Awkward and skinny, Bill stood only 5'10". He loved football and tried to play defensive end, but he got cut. He then got cut from varsity basketball. A lack of rhythm doomed his attempt to play clarinet in the band. When he ran for sergeant-at-arms in the student government, he finished last. He instead served as the McClymonds Warriors' mascot, donning an Indian costume to rally the crowd at football games On the totem pole of teenage status, he laid low.[27]

Over time, Bill drew inspiration from his father. Mister Charlie arrived home from the foundry to spin tales, boom with laughter, and play whist, dominoes, and Monopoly with his boys. He provided for food and education. He insisted that their family would survive. "Gradually," Bill recalled, "I became sure he'd never crack." Despite their collective tragedy, however, Charlie refused to mollycoddle his sons. He inculcated values of hard work and personal responsibility. Bill could not drive, for instance, until he could afford his own car, gasoline, and insurance. Despite their frequent clashes, Bill gained strength from this cooperative, all-male environment, foreshadowing his experience in basketball.[28]

Bill nevertheless remained a classic introvert. He spent most afternoons at the Oakland Public Library. He pored through art collections, absorbing the tiniest details of masterpieces by Da Vinci or Michelangelo. He also loved history, though his psyche jarred upon reading one passage that claimed American slaves possessed better living standards than blacks in "primitive" Africa. "I was repulsed by the idea that life could be better without freedom," he recalled. "To me, being a slave meant you had to buckle under." Russell understood that identity hinged upon history, and this claim seemed like a personal attack.

With much greater satisfaction, he happened upon Richard Halliburton's *Complete Book of Marvels,* a swashbuckling account of one man's world travels. A chapter described Henri Christophe's Citadel in Haiti, the first free black country in the Western Hemisphere. Russell grew fascinated with Christophe, who rose from slave to general to iron-fisted emperor. Despite Christophe's bloodthirsty despotism, Russell considered him a hero. "He was just the opposite of a slave: *he would not be one,*" remembered Russell. "His life brought home to me for the first time that being black was not just a limiting feeling."[29]

Russell learned to question assumptions, to look beyond the surface. After seeing *King Kong* with his friends, he wondered why the giant ape lusted after a white woman. He resented the fear, greed, and racism that underlay such a fantasy. In his daily life, Russell experienced a more tangible bias, the kind that threatened a young man's self-worth. As whites abandoned West Oakland, his neighborhood seemed invisible to outsiders, a ghetto. When he went to downtown Oakland, police chased him and called him "nigger."[30]

McClymonds High School exacerbated this bleakness. Technically, the school was racially integrated. In 1938, the school had 684 white students and 272 minorities, including 115 blacks. By the late 1940s, it had 797 black students, with only 50 whites and a handful of Mexicans, Chinese, Filipinos, and Puerto Ricans. Most of the teachers, Russell believed, deflated student ambition. His counselor tried enrolling him in shop courses, and she ignored his questions about college. Despite his intelligence, he possessed few prospects.[31]

The shroud of clumsy alienation weighed heavy. His pathetic efforts to woo girls flopped. One girl brought her boyfriend on their "date." When he asked out another girl, she grimaced, "What would I want to talk to *you* for?" But by his junior year, Russell had undergone an epiphany—an actual, physical, quasi-religious experience. He once claimed that it occurred while waking up, and another time while walking down the hall at McClymonds. In any case, he remembered feeling a warm surge of self-pride. No longer would he internalize the scorn of teachers, coaches, policemen, or classmates. No longer would he consider himself ungainly or cringing. His upbringing had laid the foundation for this attitude, but his emotions crystallized in this one moment. "From that day on," he believed, "whenever I've felt hostility from someone, I've assumed it was their problem rather than mine."[32]

Russell still needed a means of self-expression, and he ultimately found it in basketball. But that discovery never occurred during high school. He played the sport, but without distinction, and only by the good graces of a stern, thickset, buzz-cut white man named George Powles. With a knack for fostering children's self-esteem, Powles coached sandlot and semipro baseball teams, supervised youth leagues, and invited gaggles of kids to raid his wife's refrigerator. He coached an astounding number of future professional athletes, including baseball major leaguers Vada Pinson, Billy Martin, and Joe Morgan, professional football players Ollie Matson and John Brodie, and Bobby Woods of the Harlem Magicians. Powles also coached three extraordinary barrier-breakers: Frank Robinson, the first black manager in the Major Leagues; Curt Flood, who challenged baseball's reserve clause; and Bill Russell.[33]

Powles had been Russell's junior high homeroom instructor, and he transferred to McClymonds when Russell was in tenth grade. Despite no basketball experience, Powles coached the junior varsity. He found a place for Russell on the end of the bench. The sixteenth player on a squad of fifteen, Russell shared a uniform with the second-worst player. "We want Russell!" fans would chant at the end of blowouts, only to hoot and jeer at his awkward efforts.[34]

Yet Powles recognized something in Russell—maybe potential, maybe desperation. He mentored the benchwarmer, insisting that Russell would improve. Powles urged team members to challenge Russell in practice, stirring Russell's competitive juices. Powles even lent him two dollars to join the Boys Club and play pickup games. Russell remained so awkward that senior members of the Boys Club excluded him. The 6'2" high schooler thus endured the humiliation of playing with younger children.[35]

Powles got promoted to varsity coach before Russell's junior year. He knew little about basketball fundamentals or strategy, so he coached a fast, free-flowing style that exploited his players' creativity and athleticism. The players appreciated his trust, care, and honesty about the racial politics of sport. "You've got an all-Negro team here," he told them. "If another team has a fight, it will be called a melee. If you get into a fight, it's a riot." The players learned not only self-discipline, but also that black athletes lived by higher standards. Their on-court actions had off-court implications.[36]

Meanwhile, Powles kept an eye on his pet project. Russell had sprouted four inches in one year, and though his height later paid dividends, it now made him even clumsier. Powles encouraged Russell to believe in himself. He also lent an unorthodox coaching tip, suggesting that Russell improve his coordination by playing table tennis. The new jayvee coach cut him, but Powles had him practice with the varsity team. That promotion validated the sensitive young man. "The very fact that I made the high-school squad changed my whole outlook on life," he reflected. Joining a team delivered a sense of belonging.[37]

Only 160 pounds, Russell struggled with overwhelming gawkiness. But he possessed great speed, practiced with enthusiasm, and kept growing. "I was afraid to get up in the morning because I would be taller than I was when I went to sleep," he joked. He bought a suit in September and outgrew it by January. By senior year he reached 6'5" and started at center, concentrating on rebounds and defense. Unschooled in fundamentals, he shot the ball with his palm instead of his fingertips, a bad habit that he never shook. But Powles had inspired a drive for self-improvement. "Russell always was a battler," recalled Pinson. "If there was some kind of a play giving him trouble, he'd spend hours on the court practicing until he had it down."[38]

His career scoring high—only fourteen points—came in January 1952 against rival Oakland High School. It was Russell's last game. Along with forty-seven others at McClymonds, he began and ended the school year in January. He graduated in the middle of basketball season, just as the team entered the heart of its league schedule. McClymonds captured the city championship without him. At the end of the season, the erstwhile center qualified for none of the first, second, or third all-star teams in the Oakland Athletic League. Upon graduating high school, he had every reason to believe that he had played his last organized basketball game.[39]

. . .

"The American boy or man," opined one basketball manual of the 1940s, "does not adapt himself easily or cheerfully to a formal program designed for physical development. He prefers to express himself freely, without domination, and is most interested when his physical needs can be satisfied by recreation or competition." Bill Russell first played basketball in the West Oakland projects. On playgrounds, at the Boys Club, and in school gymnasiums, he participated in a sport undergoing constant evolution since its 1891 birth. Basketball experienced an acutely American metamorphosis. Driven "by recreation or competition," individuals continually refigured the sport to fit their visions.[40]

James Naismith invented basketball to suit his practical and moral purposes. An instructor at the YMCA in Springfield, Massachusetts, he sought an indoor sport for the winter months, something more appealing than monotonous calisthenics and gymnastics. But he also sought to inculcate the values of Progressive reformers: moral character, social order, individual sacrifice for collective ends, and vigorous physicality fused with Protestant spirituality—a "muscular Christianity." So he composed a game that rewarded self-control and cooperation. He drafted thirteen rules that promoted passing (no running with the ball), health (no holding, no pushing, no tripping), and order (point penalties for fouls). To encourage movement, he placed goals at the long ends of the court. To reduce roughness, he raised the goals high, nailing peach baskets to the overhanging balcony. "Basketball was thus made in the office," Naismith later wrote, "and was a direct adaptation of certain means to accomplish certain ends."[41]

Players, coaches, entrepreneurs, and fans immediately propelled the game beyond Naismith's objectives. None of the original rules considered dribbling, but players freed themselves from defenders by rolling, batting, and bouncing the ball. Scoring increased as players obsessed over shooting. Naismith had designed basketball for amateur recreation, but universities soon established squads of hired guns with spurious connections to academia. In northern industrial cities, rowdy fans watched professional teams engage in brutal clashes—until the 1920s, wire cages encased the court (hence the nickname "cagers" for basketball players). A host of professional leagues rose and fell over the first half of the twentieth century. Basketball also spread nationwide through YMCAs, schools, clubs, churches, settlement houses, and other urban institutions. By 1941, 95 percent of high schools had basketball programs.[42]

The ingenuity of players and coaches generated a faster, more appealing spectacle. The earliest teams assigned a few defensive-minded players to hang back on offense, so most games were rugged, slogging affairs. In different regions, in different ways, basketball grew more democratic. On the East Coast, teams played a "give and go" style associated with professionals: quick passes, screens, fakes, and cuts toward the basket. In the Midwest and the South, players often tried long passes for easy layups, but in the half-court they pounded the ball inside. West Coast basketball featured more up-and-down action.[43]

In the 1930s, rules changes adjusted to the new pace. Instead of a jump ball at center court after each basket, teams had ten seconds to cross half-court, further speeding the game. Players also began using a "one-hand push shot" instead of a two-hand set shot. In December 1936, Stanford University played Long Island University (LIU) at the Mecca of college basketball, Madison Square Garden. Hank Luisetti introduced New York to a one-hand runner that prefigured the jump shot. East Coast fans gaped as Stanford, led by Luisetti's offensive creativity, snapped LIU's forty-one-game winning streak. The much-ballyhooed match indicated that regional styles were cross-fertilizing. Players throughout the country soon introduced their own versions of the jump shot. When Bill Russell first stepped onto a court, he played a game in stylistic flux, a game full of individual innovators, regional traditions, and an emerging national network.[44]

As basketball evolved, it drifted from its original ideological underpinnings. "Games demanding team play are played by the Anglo-Saxon peoples, and by these peoples alone," declared Luther Gulick, who ran the Springfield YMCA and trained James Naismith. But the new immigrants of the late nineteenth and early twentieth centuries embraced basketball. The Original Celtics, the greatest professional team of the 1920s, contained an ethnic hodgepodge led by the Jewish star Nat Holman. By the 1930s basketball was "the Jewish game." The South Philadelphia Hebrew Association, known as the SPHAs, captured copious league and tournament championships. Basketball provided a vehicle of assimilation, contradicting stereotypes of Jews as weak intellectuals. Into the early 1950s, Jews still composed a significant percentage of professional basketball players.[45]

African Americans played basketball, too, but the sport did not always occupy a central place in black culture. Basketball was rooted in patterns of city life, and when Naismith invented the sport, blacks were the least urban group in America. The Great Migration quite literally changed basketball's complexion. Black urban areas became centers of sporting life. Elite clubs steeped in the ideals of Muscular Christianity, such as St. Christopher in New York and Loendi's Big Five in Pittsburgh, staged games on Friday and Saturday nights, often followed by dances. Black youths could play in YMCAs, athletic clubs, and schools. Washington, DC, established the first black high school athletic association in 1906, and a national black high school tournament began in 1929. Basketball teams at prestigious schools featured African Americans, including Paul Robeson at Princeton and Ralph Bunche at UCLA.[46]

Black basketball became big business, led by two legendary clubs. The Harlem Renaissance Five, better known as the Rens, were a sharp-passing, pivot-oriented, quick-cutting squad. Owned by black entrepreneur Bob Douglas, the "World's Colored Champions" earned fame by the late 1920s and thrived through the Depression, even winning eighty-eight straight games in 1932–33. They attracted good crowds on long barnstorming tours, especially against their great rivals, the Original Celtics.[47]

By 1940 the Rens had acquired another rival: the Harlem Globetrotters. The Globetrotters combined pivot play with more individualistic flair. On their own Depression-era barnstorming tours, encouraged by white owner Abe Saperstein, they lured customers with "clowning" routines that satisfied black stereotypes as jesters. In the inaugural World Professional Tournament in 1939, the Rens edged the Globetrotters in the semifinals and won the title. The next year, the Globetrotters prevailed. As these squads suggested disparate ethics of black style, they proved equal to the world's best.[48]

African Americans placed their own cultural stamp on basketball. By 1950, 62 percent of black people lived in cities, and basketball fit the space and temperament of urban life. Especially on outdoor courts, the sport adopted a more experimental flair, with audacious jump shots and flamboyant dribble drives. "It was a learning process on the playground, picking up different things you didn't learn being coached in the YMCA," recalled Pop Gates, a black professional of the 1940s. Blacks, like Jews and other ethnic groups, were embracing "the city game." Russell's team at McClymonds High School absorbed this exuberant, free-form style, barreling downcourt and launching jump shots. Critics accustomed to set patterns and earthbound offense belittled it as "playground" or "Negro" basketball.[49]

Throughout the nation, black players adopted some version of this sporting ethic. But no one pattern defined "Negro basketball." As Russell graduated from high school with a fuzzy sense of his own future, a 6'11" teenager named Wilt Chamberlain honed his remarkable combination of size, speed, and power in constant pickup basketball games at the Haddington Recreational Center in West Philadelphia, while also playing at YMCAs, in police leagues, at churches, in summer leagues, and on outdoor courts in Philadelphia and New York. In Indianapolis, Oscar Robertson forged his perfect fundamentals near a housing project, on some dirty clay courts known as the Dust Bowl. In Washington, DC, Elgin Baylor grew up near two parks with well-kept athletic facilities—but he had to play on the street because the parks excluded blacks. Not until attending Phelps Vocational High School did Baylor polish his sweeping, bullishly graceful drives to the basket.[50]

City life launched constant challenges at African Americans: it confined them, it limited their economic possibilities, it stoked their anger. Basketball provided young men with a means of self-expression—a type of freedom. "When I play basketball I'm not doing it simply to score points or to win," said John Edgar Wideman. He linked his creativity as a writer to his moves on the court, and he placed them both within a larger black artistic tradition: a "need to find the space to express what I am, who I am." Playgrounds served as havens, little arenas to win attention and status. Men engaged in rituals of bonding, but they proved their distinctiveness in the heat of competition. Basketball lent order amidst anarchy, brotherly fellowship amidst urban anonymity, individual humanity amidst concrete bleakness.[51]

Most players discovered their particular style on city courts, with the ball in their hands. But Bill Russell crafted his idiom when he left the city, with the ball in the hands of his opponent.

. . .

A petty entrepreneur named Brick Swegle organized a tour through the Pacific Northwest with players who graduated high school midyear. His sponsors, the Oakland Jaycees and the Mohawk Athletic Club, insisted that he include someone from

McClymonds. As the school's only graduating "splitter," Russell won a spot. He relished every moment traveling by Greyhound, rolling through Oregon, Washington, Idaho, and British Columbia, playing games and waiting at bus stations and barely sleeping. He had already awakened to his self-worth. Now, in the winter of 1952, he had his basketball epiphany.[52]

Though the team had only two blacks, Swegle's all-stars played "Negro basketball." Bill Treu, a white Mormon, dribbled in wheels and weaves, using spin moves to shake defenders. The whole team ran fast breaks and took jump shots. Rival coaches muttered at the undisciplined style, but Swegle's team kept winning. Russell, in particular, benefited from a convivial atmosphere. As the bus wound across mountain roads, he peppered Treu and others with questions. He realized that, just as he could picture the details of a Michelangelo masterpiece, he could replicate his teammates' moves in his mental camera. Then he could apply it on court. This imagination fed his sense of personal possibilities. "It seemed so easy," he recalled. "My first dose of athletic confidence was coming to me when I was eighteen years old."[53]

On offense, Russell could imitate others. On defense, however, he could innovate. He reached with his left hand, which lined up with most players' shooting hands. So when Russell visualized Treu's spin moves and dribble drives, he envisioned himself as the mirror image, performing a nimble defensive fandango. Employing this visualization in a game, he suffocated opponents with his defense. He also leaped to block shots. Most coaches warned that if you left your feet, opponents could drive past you or draw a foul. But Swegle let his players experiment, and Russell's teammates appreciated his high-flying swats. They called his blocks "Russell Moves."[54]

Russell now found affirmation in basketball. "Hey, you can jump," a teammate remarked. When a pack sprung off the floor for a rebound, Russell hovered an extra second, his chest above others' chins. The feeling exhilarated him. He later tabbed it as a universal impulse, "jumping for joy" in a flash of delight. But it also captured a particular African American aesthetic. Like the "jump blues" played in the same dance halls that hosted the Harlem Rens, it was a vigorous physical demonstration, a pronouncement of individual style, a flamboyant sense of possibility. Russell fused this emotional expression to his process of cerebral deduction.[55]

He returned to Oakland with newfound confidence. "I can play now," he told his father. Mister Charlie had good news in return. Hal DeJulio, a scout for the University of San Francisco (USF), had called asking about him. DeJulio had learned about Russell from Dick Lawless, a USF forward who had faced Russell in a three-on-three pickup game. Lawless marveled at how Russell bounded above the rim, soaring for rebounds and blocked shots. "Everything I tried to put up, he'd slam it down my throat," Lawless remembered.[56]

So DeJulio checked out Russell's last game against Oakland High. He left the game intrigued: Russell got tangled in his own arms and legs, but he also challenged shots with perfect timing. DeJulio confirmed his instinct with Coach Powles, who lauded Russell's athleticism and intelligence. When Russell returned from the tour, DeJulio called again and praised his performance. "I was trying to interrupt him to say that he hadn't seen anything," Russell recalled. "I wanted to tell him about what had happened to me on the tour, but I didn't even know how to begin." The scout invited him to campus for a workout with USF head coach Phil Woolpert.[57]

Until DeJulio's call, Russell had never heard of the University of San Francisco. Though just across the bay, San Francisco seemed a foreign world, and USF lacked the public profile of UCLA, Cal, or Stanford. On the day of his workout, Russell got lost. After arriving late, he performed drills for Woolpert. "I couldn't believe my eyes," the coach recalled. "He could jump—oh, how he could jump—but he was *so* ungainly." Still, Woolpert noticed the effects of Russell's awakening: a self-possession, an aplomb. Russell took an entrance examination. Woolpert neither promised a scholarship nor dismissed the possibility.[58]

So Russell worked days hauling steel at a shipyard, spent nights in pickup games on the West Oakland courts, and wondered days and nights about this singular opportunity. He had considered enlisting in the army, but when he took a physical he measured just over 6'6"—above the military limit, tall enough to be declared 4-F. He could keep working and enroll at junior college. But to surpass the confines of West Oakland, he believed, "San Francisco was my one chance. The one chance I'd ever get." That prospect had nothing to do with professional sports—it meant a college education, the development of his intellectual skills, and a better job than carrying steel or pouring iron.[59]

When the scholarship offer arrived, it represented an improbable fortune for a role player on his high school team, a potential escape from the West Oakland ghetto, and the continuation of an intellectual and physical journey. Best of all, it fulfilled a promise to Katie Russell. Her son was going to college.

2

Big Man on Campus

In September 1952, Bill Russell trekked across the Bay Bridge to the University of San Francisco. Though only fifteen miles from home, the gangly eighteen year old entered an alien universe. Incoming freshmen had to wear initiation sweaters, perform tasks for upperclassmen, and don "dink" hats until the Freshman Smoker at the end of the month. Russell stuck out—in its first issue the student newspaper labeled him "a potential Globetrotter." Some Hispanics and Filipinos dotted the sea of white faces, but Russell and fellow basketball recruit Hal Perry represented the entire black population of the freshman class.[1]

Russell arrived at USF as a curious combination of raw physical gifts, frightful clumsiness, and curious confidence. Upon arriving on campus, he visited Phil Woolpert's office. Woolpert and assistant Ross Giudice gaped as Russell ducked his head through the door. In six months, Russell had grown nearly two inches. Giudice knew that he had a special project: he could teach basketball fundamentals, but he could not teach height or leaping ability. "Gentlemen," Russell soon announced to the coaching staff, "I want you to know that I am going to be the University of San Francisco's next All-American."[2]

Yet during the team's first official practice, Russell could not perform a warmup callisthenic of walking while squatting. Some teammates grumbled that Woolpert had wasted a scholarship on an awkward freak. The older players disparaged him. Once, an upperclassman tried teasing him with an ironic, insulting nickname: "Snowball." Russell warned him. His tormentor persisted. So Russell walloped him.[3]

He delivered a lesson to his upperclassman foe, and in time he shaped a new understanding of college basketball. But in those same USF years, Russell received his own education—in academics, athletics, and the politics of race and sport.

22

. . .

St. Ignatius College, founded in 1855, moved its campus atop a hill north of Fulton Street, just east of Golden Gate Park, soon after the city's famous earthquake and fire of 1906. In 1930 it changed its name to the University of San Francisco. When Russell arrived, the university had only about eleven hundred full-time students. "The Barracks," a set of Quonset huts built by the army, housed the residential students. The campus boasted an impressive cathedral and new library, but it lacked the cachet of Cal's Strawberry Canyon or Stanford's graceful, palm-shaded grounds. USF seemed scattered and empty, and it lacked a gymnasium. The basketball team got nicknamed "The Homeless Dons."[4]

The university provided a Jesuit education, which combined instruction in rigorous logic with universal Christian truths. Priests composed most of the administration and many of the faculty. They taught democratic values grounded in the Gospels, advocating principles that included individual rights, social conscience, and racial tolerance. Russell studied how to distinguish truth through rational deduction. He learned to not only interpret the meaning of a statement but also consider its source, and thus understand its motivations and subjectivities—a valuable discipline for a future public figure.[5]

Exposure to white students of different backgrounds widened Russell's viewpoint. USF had only a handful of black students. Many students came from the rural, all-white towns of the San Joaquin Valley, and they brought their prejudices to campus.

Russell felt like an outsider. He compensated with brash humor, alienating his detractors to the point that the student body president complained to Woolpert. Russell also neglected his schoolwork, at least until Woolpert notified Mister Charlie of the problem. After withstanding his father's fury, Russell studied harder. In other ways, too, Russell learned lessons. In one bull session in his dormitory, he laughed at an anti-Italian crack. "Do you think it's funny?" asked his classmate. "I'm Italian. What are you?" Ashamed that he lacked a complete answer, Russell resolved to better grasp his own people's history.[6]

Russell also received a basketball education. Because NCAA regulations deemed first-year students ineligible for varsity athletics, he played on the freshman team for Giudice, who nurtured his center's development. Giudice taught precise fundamentals backed by logical explanation. He not only explained the correct technique; he explained *why* it was correct. He patiently taught Russell how to set a screen, fire a chest pass, shoot a hook, spin on a pivot, lay it in with either hand, and other basic fundamentals.[7]

"We gave him a foundation," Giudice recalled, "but make no mistake, he taught himself how to play like a champion." He marveled at how quickly Russell improved, how deeply he desired to become a great player. Russell was still envisioning new techniques and then sharpening his muscle memory. For instance, he learned to land with flexed knees after challenging a shot, so that he could recover and block another attempt. He drilled himself by leaping to touch the rim thirty-five times in succession. In late-night gym sessions, he spent long hours practicing swooping hook shots with both hands, crafting a basic offensive repertoire. He possessed a particular self-confidence, his ambition matched by his work ethic.[8]

If Giudice cultivated Russell's physical skills, his black teammates provided a sense of community. A black person's arrival at USF, Russell later reflected, "was a real cultural shock." In Oakland, he lived, learned, and played among other African Americans. At USF, he felt misunderstood, as if he sometimes spoke an alien language. As he reflected with mock wonderment, the white students "thought mother was a word all by itself."[9]

Russell befriended Hal Perry, a standout athlete with an expansive, engaging personality. Perry adjusted quickly to USF. The single African American in his high school in the northern California timberlands, he had won election as student body president. He studied philosophy, drilled himself on new vocabulary, quoted Shakespeare and the Bible, and played six instruments. He lent Russell a model of achievement and confidence, and he helped Russell steer through life as a black athlete on a white campus. Russell, meanwhile, brought Perry back to Oakland for pickup games and a more substantial black community.[10]

Russell's friendship with K. C. Jones developed more slowly, though they shared similar backgrounds. Jones had grown up in racially segregated Texas. His father left when he was nine years old, and his family migrated to San Francisco. The oldest of five children, Jones became the man of the house, even taking over cooking duties. He earned a basketball scholarship to USF one year before Russell. He may have been the most popular student on campus. He had a sense of humor, good looks, and deep intelligence. "He was so nice, and so quiet," remembered teammate Mike Preaseau. "But what a leader!" Jones related to all types of people with a certain moral clarity. Yet in more private circumstances he exhibited painful shyness, perhaps stemming from insecurity over his functional illiteracy as a young child. At first, Jones communicated little more than grunting nods to pass the saltshaker.[11]

Then, as if someone flipped a switch, Jones started talking. Linked to Russell by sports and skin color, he adopted a big brother role. Varsity athletes got a monthly scholarship allotment of thirty dollars, so Jones treated him to movies and ice cream, and he even bought Russell a new pair of shoes. Just as important, back-and-forth discussions replaced the weird silences. They mostly talked about basketball, their mutual passion. Jones had exceptional quickness and intelligence, but upon spurting three inches after high school, his shooting touch had abandoned him. So Jones, like Russell, developed a fascination with basketball that transcended jump shots and fancy dribbles.[12]

The more Russell talked to Jones, the more he saw basketball as a team enterprise, a series of collective contingencies and adjustments. Together they analyzed the sport as "a game of geometry—of lines, points, and distances." Getting rebounds relied on controlling space. Defense demanded action rather than reaction, attacking an opponent's comfort zone. "We didn't get much sleep," Jones recalled. "Russell had a gift for mapping out plays and strategies. He focused on the details: how to position your body, how to find a player's blind spot, how to anticipate the shot. The details made up the big picture."[13]

Yet with Russell still an ineligible freshman, USF finished 11–12 overall and 6–2 in the newly formed California Basketball Association, a second-tier conference that included St. Mary's, Santa Clara, San Jose State, and the College of the Pacific. Driven by Russell's evolution, the freshman team offered hope of a promising future, going 19–4. Russell now stood 6'8", and he averaged twenty points a game. At a Pacific Association tournament that included varsity and semiprofessional clubs, the USF freshman won two games. The Olympic Club, which had various college and Amateur Athletic Union (AAU) All-Americans, edged USF, 65–59, but not before Russell blocked numerous shots, scored twenty-five points, and won the "Most Promising Player" award. One reporter called him "the Goose Tatum of the future," referring to the great Harlem Globetrotter. Russell now declined various schools' offers to transfer, sweetened with promises of cash bonuses.[14]

Russell displayed this same athletic promise in track and field. He had never jumped higher than 5'4" for the McClymonds junior varsity, but he wanted the natty USF button sweater awarded to varsity lettermen. In the interim, he had sprouted, packed on lean muscle, developed some coordination, and trained through a basketball season. In his first meet, he jumped 6'4". He would have cleared 6'6" but his elbow scraped the bar. He rarely practiced and possessed crude form, rolling over the bar headfirst with his hands out and knees bent. Still, he kept clearing 6'4".[15]

His prowess prompted an early lesson in the hazards of the black athlete. The track team operated on a shoestring budget, often sending its athletes to meets with bare-bones expense money. Russell drove to St. Louis for an AAU meet. USF paid his expenses and made his reservation at the Chase Hotel. When he arrived at the reception desk, the clerk turned him away. Only nineteen years old, alone in a strange city, humiliated by a racial insult, and too proud to wander St. Louis looking for lodging, he slept in his car.[16]

Russell rejoined the track and field team as a sophomore. That year he jumped 6'7½", only 4⅛ inches off the world record. Johnny Mathis, the future singing star who jumped for San Francisco State, remembered thinking that Russell could be the world's best. A rival coach agreed. "There's the man who could be the first to clear seven feet," he marveled. "He's got the spring and he's got the legs. His gams begin where his neck ends." Russell, who now stood 6'9", also placed in the 120-

meter high hurdles, the broad jump, and the javelin. Running the last lap for the mile relay team, he covered a quarter mile in 49.6 seconds.[17]

How would these extraordinary gifts translate against elite basketball talent? Rampant speculation accompanied Russell's varsity debut on December 1, 1953, against the University of California, whose All-American center Bob McKeen stood 6'7", weighed 225 pounds, and combined rugged pivot play with a deft shooting touch. Many figured that McKeen would outsmart and outmuscle the skinny sophomore. An overflow crowd of sixty-four hundred, packing every nook in San Francisco's Kezar Pavilion, watched McKeen try a hook from the right wing. Russell swatted it into the third row. "Ooooooooooh," the crowd hummed. McKeen next tried a hook from the left side, and Russell again blocked him. He redirected shots all game; once he simply plucked a shot out of the air and flipped it downcourt for a USF fast break. The *San Francisco Chronicle* conjectured that this "aerial with arms" would become one of the Bay Area's all-time basketball greats. He also scored twenty-three points. USF won 51–33, and the team looked like a contender for the CBA championship.[18]

But USF's 1953–54 campaign never fulfilled the promise of that idyllic debut. The next night, in the locker room at Fresno State, K. C. Jones collapsed from a burst appendix. Doctors later determined that the organ had ruptured about ten days earlier. Jones spent four days unconscious, barely sidestepping death. Weak and twenty-five pounds lighter, he missed the rest of the season. Injuries plagued other starters, and the Dons finished 14–7 overall and 8–4 in the CBA, good enough for second place.[19]

Riddled with jealousies and egos, the team never equaled the sum of its parts. "We ran into the racial issue," admitted Hal Perry. "They didn't see the need to have us in the school." The older players refused to accept the African Americans. According to Perry, prejudiced and resentful white players had already driven off Carl Lawson. They all underachieved. Looking back, Russell blamed both himself and his teammates: none possessed the fortitude to challenge the team's poisonous culture.[20]

Moreover, Russell butted heads with Woolpert. Despite Russell's self-driven improvement, Woolpert fumed that he loafed through practices. "He was a lazy player," the coach recalled. "I kicked him out of the gym many, many times." Woolpert offered little praise for his outwardly confident star. But Russell fumed that when USF won, the coach lauded the whole squad, never singling out his center. Russell craved respect. Once he stormed out of practice after Woolpert insisted that he shoot free throws underhanded, which made him look foolish.[21]

Russell further smoldered over Woolpert's conventional defensive philosophy geared to slower, stouter centers. He recalled the first game against Cal, when he approached the bench after blocking multiple shots by Bob McKeen. "You can't play defense that way," Woolpert admonished. "A defensive player never leaves his feet."

But Russell envisioned new possibilities in his airborne, shot-blocking defensive style. He perceived Woolpert's coaching as shortsighted and small-minded.[22]

Russell did have individual accomplishments. He established himself as a star, averaging a team-high 19.8 points and 18.8 rebounds a game. He scored 32, 31, and 28 points in a consecutive stretch. He appeared on various league and regional all-star teams. One opposing coach even called him "the most valuable player to any one team I've ever seen." He had been the quiet mama's boy, the gangling teenager, the goofy bookworm in the shadow of his older brother. Now he was a Big Man on Campus.[23]

"My inferiority complex had disappeared, to be replaced by an insufferably big head," Russell later wrote. Love nevertheless grounded him. While attending a dance in Berkeley, he spied Rose Swisher. He later learned that she was the niece of one of his favorite high school teachers and an eighteen-year-old freshman at West Contra Costa Junior College. He cut in on a dance, and she made polite conversation. But she had never heard of Bill Russell. That taught him a lesson. She liked him as a person, not as a basketball player. They soon began a serious relationship. A demure and traditional woman, Rose offered a haven of warmth and constancy, the type of love missing since his mother died.[24]

Despite the team's struggles, Russell's early years at USF laid a foundation for his future success. He was studying basketball, devouring sports magazines to deduce ways to defend the best players. He also earned a B average as a business administration major studying accounting. He then switched his major to transportation. Furthermore, he experienced a world beyond West Oakland, frequenting the North Beach coffee houses that featured cutting-edge comedians such as Mort Sahl or radical folk singers such as Pete Seeger. There he met beatniks who contradicted his stereotype of white people as hopelessly straitlaced.[25]

College life inspired and stimulated Russell. When K. C. Jones fell ill, hundreds of students attended a special prayer vigil in his honor. When Jones recovered consciousness, they resumed their basketball discourses. When Jones recovered health, they traveled as far as Los Angeles to test themselves against the best competition. Despite the season's frustrations, the game still provided them with challenges, passion, craftsmanship, solidarity—a higher meaning.[26]

. . .

After World War Two, as the economy surged and college enrollments skyrocketed, the business of college sports boomed. Universities discovered new revenue streams through sports, though sometimes at a cost. USF suffered a scandal in 1948, after news broke that football coach Ed McKeever had paid twenty-two players. Three years later, the squad featured a 9–0 record and three future Hall of Famers in Bob St. Clair, Gino Marchetti, and Ollie Matson, but the Dons received no bowl invitations—officially because of a soft schedule, but really because Matson and Burl

Toler were black. Their prospective bowl games were in the South. Unable to schedule high-profile teams, USF was losing money, and it dropped football.[27]

The university found a more lucrative public profile in basketball. Like urban Catholic schools such as St. John's, Marquette, and St. Louis, USF reasoned that a basketball program could offer fewer scholarships and more games than a big-time football operation. College basketball had already set its commercial and cultural moorings during the Great Depression. Ned Irish, a young reporter for the *New York World-Telegram*, realized the entrepreneurial possibilities after helping organize a sold-out charity tripleheader. By 1934, Irish was booking eight doubleheaders a year, offering travel expenses and ticket revenue to the nation's best teams. In 1938 he started the National Invitational Tournament (NIT), which drew sixteen thousand customers to the final. Fan interest grew, media coverage escalated, and Irish got rich.[28]

Irish's tournaments and doubleheaders only surged in popularity after World War Two. The NCAA had established its own tournament in 1939, but the NIT remained the most prestigious postseason championship. USF first gained national attention, in fact, when it improbably won the 1949 NIT. Pete Newell's team, which included Ross Giudice and Hal DeJulio, entered the tournament as 20-1 underdogs. They charmed New York with a series of dramatic upsets. The Dons won in Madison Square Garden—"the prime showcase for basketball," according to *Life*, where "college teams draw the biggest gates and get the greatest prestige."[29]

"But here also the biggest money is bet," *Life* added, warning of the temptations begat by riches. "The interest of Garden spectators is less in the game's winner or loser than in the point spread, the margin of points by which a team wins and on which all basketball betting is based." Bettors waged an estimated $10,000,000 a day during the season. As gambling encouraged fan interest, it created a new problem: point shaving. The unpaid players saw promoters, universities, and coaches pocketing the spoils of paying customers, and some accepted bribes—not necessarily to lose, but to win by fewer points than the spread. Point shaving was difficult to detect: a shot can drift astray, a pass could wander off-target, a dribble might bounce off a knee. Seasoned fans realized its prevalence, but until 1951, point shaving remained an underground activity.[30]

Then the scandal broke. A Manhattan College sophomore named Junius Kellogg reported in January 1951 that gamblers had offered him a $1,000 bribe. America soon learned that an endemic corruption infested college basketball. By March 1951, New York district attorney Frank Hogan had discovered twenty-three fixed games involving nineteen players from four New York schools, including CCNY, which had captured both the NIT and NCAA titles in 1950. As Hogan announced each arrest, it kept the scandals in the headlines, swelling a sense of disillusionment. At CCNY, four players were proven guilty of fixing. A campus rally celebrated Floyd

Lane, the sole innocent on the starting five. Days later, the authorities implicated Lane.[31]

In the eyes of Middle America, the players were whores to greed, and Madison Square Garden was the house of ill repute. "The city game" belonged to urban slicks and ethnic minorities. Italian immigrant Salvatore Sollazzo masterminded the operation, Jews populated an organized gambling web, and all the CCNY players were Jewish or black. Bradley University declined an NIT bid, lest Madison Square Garden stain its moral purity. "Gamblers couldn't get at my boys with a ten-foot pole," proclaimed Adolph Rupp, coach at the University of Kentucky. But by April 1953, a Grand Jury investigation had fingered thirty-two players for fixing eighty-six games in seventeen states. Seven fixers played for Bradley University. All-Americans and two-time NCAA champions Ralph Beard, Alex Groza, and Bill Spivey shaved points under Rupp at Kentucky.[32]

The basketball scandals struck during the McCarthy era, a time of widespread hand-wringing about American culture. With a communist threat looming even on American shores, hysteria seemed to accompany any evidence of loose moral character, whether a cheating scandal at West Point, a surge in juvenile delinquency, or this stain on college athletics. "The tall children of basketball have been consumed by the slot machine racket of sports," mourned the *New York Post*. "They have forfeited honor at an age when the dream of life should be beautiful." The *Chicago Herald-American* called it "a sick and dying game." The *New York Herald Tribune* proclaimed that "basketball is through as a big-time sport."[33]

But college basketball survived. In fact, it thrived. Despite their possible complicity, prominent coaches such as Nat Holman at CCNY, Clair Bee at Long Island University, and Adolph Rupp at Kentucky distanced themselves from the scandal. Madison Square Garden remained the basketball Mecca, even as the NIT's prestige dulled. After penalizing guilty schools, the NCAA emerged as the sport's key governing authority. It clamped down on illegal recruiting and player payments, even as it signed a lucrative television contract for college football. The NCAA built its reputation on this enforcement of amateurism, and its basketball tournament supplanted the NIT as the legitimate national championship.[34]

In this context, Phil Woolpert engineered the resurgence of USF basketball. A former prison guard, social worker, and army veteran, Woolpert had been coaching the USF freshmen and the varsity at St. Ignatius, a prep school with strong ties to the university. He replaced Newell in 1950. A sharp-witted chain-smoker with a long, angular face and a thin mustache, Woolpert's anxieties lay on the surface. "Phil would make coffee nervous," remarked former player Mike Farmer. Before games, Woolpert suffered from facial tics and a roiling stomach. With a gentle soul and an intellectual's self-awareness, he fretted about the pressures of his job, and he worried about his own coaching abilities. In his first three years, the team went

31–42. Alumni bellyached. One called him "a lousy coach" to his face. Woolpert almost quit.[35]

Woolpert rebuilt the program by recruiting northern California. Depending on volunteer scouts like DeJulio, he unearthed gems where others failed to mine—especially by enlisting African Americans. Only 10 percent of basketball programs at predominantly white schools had black players. "You could count the number of black players on west coast teams on the fingers of one hand," remembered Newell. Only one African American, Carl Lawson, had played for USF before 1951. But thanks to a politically forthright father and a childhood in an integrated Los Angeles neighborhood, Woolpert embraced a liberal outlook. Woolpert recruited Jones, Russell, and Hal Perry, the core of his greatest teams. Before most schools, USF developed black athletes as valuable resources in the postwar college sports boom.[36]

Woolpert's teams would propel college basketball into its modern form. The sport would have a truly national profile. It would have a more dynamic style of play, a touchstone of team greatness, and compelling individual stars. It would also have black players who reshaped the game and rewrote its cultural meaning. No one saw it coming.

. . .

Woolpert hankered for the start of the 1954–55 season. The players had won a Berkeley summer league and held early workouts. Forward Jerry Mullen possessed a sharp shooting eye, and a healthy K. C. Jones supplied defense, passing, and leadership. Russell now had a decent hook shot, moved around the post when denied entry passes, stopped taking unnecessary dribbles, and stood almost 6'10". He could also back down his defender, crouch low, and spring for a two-handed, back-to-the-basket dunk. "His shooting eye has improved, his timing is better, and his floor play savvy has shown up as well," marveled one reporter after the season opener, an 84–55 steamrolling of Chico State. Russell scored thirty-nine points, a school record. The Dons then beat Loyola 54–45. Blocked shots were not yet an official statistic, but the opposing coach guessed that Russell swatted away at least twenty attempts.[37]

Although fan interest in the Bay Area was growing and the CBA signed its first local television contract, West Coast basketball had a marginal national profile. *Sports Illustrated* dismissed the Pacific Coast, the region's main conference, and predicted only UCLA in the Top Ten. It mentioned only Ken Sears of Santa Clara and Bob McKeen of California among seventeen "Players to Watch." Most sportswriters and fans had no expectations for the University of San Francisco, and they knew nothing about Bill Russell.[38]

Even the USF players could not imagine national glory. They played the third game of the season at UCLA. The Bruins had crushed Santa Clara—the favorite for the CBA title—by forty points. "We went in there expecting to be beaten by 20 or 25," recalled K. C. Jones. Instead, UCLA edged USF in a tight defensive struggle, 47–40. Russell looked impressive. When celebrated Bruins center Willie Naulls blocked him out and leaped for a rebound, Russell bounded over him and tipped in the ball. UCLA coach John Wooden had never seen a better defender in the post.[39]

Once torn by racial tension and personal jealousy, the Dons now embodied harmony. Before the opening weekend at home against Oregon State and UCLA, Hal Perry took over the starting guard position from Bill Bush. According to Perry, Bush voluntarily ceded his position. Neither Bush nor others remembered such a gesture, but Perry's skewed recollection suggested the team's new spirit. Even Bush, after all, recalled that Perry deserved to start. Already a quick dribbler and able defender, Perry had improved his shooting since arriving at USF. He modeled his game and demeanor after K. C. Jones.[40]

Perry made USF a faster, more aggressive team. Jones and Perry pressured their opposing guards from half-court. The Dons stayed in their opponents' chests, taking away the outside shot and challenging them to drive the lane, where Russell loomed to block and rebound. Russell keyed fast breaks with smart outlet passes, and in the half-court they ran Woolpert's pattern offense. Jerry Mullen supplied extra scoring punch. That Friday USF beat Oregon State 60–34. The Beavers' center Swede Halbrook could not play, and Russell rested for all but six minutes. The next night USF avenged its loss to UCLA, triumphing 56–44. The Bruins did not score a field goal for the first ten minutes of the game. Russell sped around and leaped over Naulls for twenty-eight points.[41]

The insertion of Perry into the starting lineup had political as well as athletic consequences. San Francisco was imbued with the myth of racial tolerance. Blacks attended integrated schools and faced little overt violence. In 1953 Collier's ran an article titled "Racial Prejudice—How San Francisco Squelched It." But the black migration during and after World War Two had altered the city's racial texture. San Francisco blacks, too, faced discrimination in housing, public accommodations, and jobs. In its 1954 Brown v. Board of Education decision, the Supreme Court deemed the racial segregation of schools unconstitutional, but the contours of American race relations remained stagnant. As elsewhere throughout the nation, true racial equality remained distant, a hopeful dream for African Americans.[42]

Russell, Jones, and Perry thus represented a black invasion onto historically white territory. Most major college programs had nothing more than token integration, and USF started three blacks. A fourth African American, Warren Baxter, came off the bench. This on-court majority violated many whites' sense of propriety. "It was never said," recalled Woolpert, "but you knew as a coach that you had to be aware of the quota thing." According to Perry, the local Catholic high schools had already objected that Woolpert gave scholarships to blacks instead of their students. The USF athletic director had even threatened to strip Perry's scholarship after his sophomore year unless he improved. For all the racial enlighten-ment of a Jesuit school in San Francisco, black players endured more barriers and higher expectations.[43]

When USF started winning games, it surfaced a racist resentment. Woolpert re-ceived hate mail. "It was really awful, awful stuff," recalled Russell. "He never said anything to us about it, but we knew about it." They saw the pressure on Woolpert's face. Russell and the other players considered their coach a fair, decent, and coura-geous man.[44]

Though some players do not recall hearing racist jibes during games, backup center Tom Nelson remembered race-baiting from fans throughout northern California, even at Santa Clara, another Jesuit school just forty-five miles away. Nel-son also faced teasing from high school friends in his hometown of San Mateo, who saw the team's racial mixing as abominable. Stan Buchanan thought his old friends seemed "a little goofy" when the subject of his black teammates arose. Even on the USF campus, students delivered nasty cracks. Alumni complained. "They are scarcely representative of the school," said one. Sticking to his liberal principles, Woolpert played the best team regardless of skin color. Anyone who voiced such bigotry, he suggested, "is not representative of this school either."[45]

A trip to the Oklahoma City All-College Tourney cemented USF's racial mean-ing and athletic excellence. Upon arrival, the team learned that the downtown ho-tels excluded blacks. At a players-only meeting, Perry suggested that they room in university dormitories vacated during the Christmas break. Rudy Zannini seconded the idea. They stayed together, and someone even procured some beer. Stan Buchanan recalls the tiny, tipsy Zannini, walking around the dormitory dressed in Russell's topcoat and homburg. In this understated way, the Dons let race unite rather than divide them.[46]

The day before the tournament, the Dons practiced on the game court, which was raised like a stage. Local fans called them "Globetrotters," taunted them with racist barbs, and threw coins at them. Russell erected defenses of dignity and hu-mor. He scooped up the coins. "Coach," he asked Woolpert, "can you hold these for me?"[47]

USF then staged an astounding display of high-powered basketball. Seeded eighth out of eight teams, the Dons drew Wichita State. Before the game, a scout had reported that USF shot poorly, played unsound defense, and started a center with no discernible talent besides leaping ability. USF went ahead 25–3 and won 94–75. They next routed Oklahoma City, 75–51, and overcame nationally ranked George Washington with a second-half flurry, 73–57. Russell won the tournament MVP but affected nonchalance. "I've heard so much about these Midwestern teams that I expected to see a lot more class at Oklahoma City," he said. "Frankly I was very disappointed. They don't play much defense." USF now knew it had a special team.[48]

Heading into 1955 and the CBA conference schedule, the Associated Press ranked the Dons fifth in the country. Yet the emerging powerhouse operated on a shoe-string budget. They practiced at St. Ignatius whenever the high school team allowed them. Other times, they drilled at the San Francisco Boys Club. Kezar Pavilion—a smallish, squalid structure with seats obscured by rusting steel beams—hosted most home games. The team sometimes took private cars to play nearby games and scrimped on longer trips. According to legend, the manager once hid in the bath-room while the train conductor collected tickets.[49]

After a tune-up win over San Diego State, USF opened the CBA schedule at St. Mary's on January 4. The team surmounted a transportation snafu, a slow start, a collapsing zone on Russell, and a 19 percent shooting percentage to prevail 51–37—only to find their locker room burglarized at the end of the game. Even when their shots missed, USF won games. Their defense never slumped. The winning streak reached ten games after successive victories against San Jose State, Santa Clara, and the College of the Pacific.[50]

USF climbed to #3 in the national polls before a weekend twin bill at the Cow Palace, a cavernous arena originally built for livestock expositions. The first game against Stanford drew 13,824 fans, the largest audience in the history of West Coast college basketball. USF won 76–60. Stanford's Ron Tomsic, who grew up in Fre-mont, remembered Russell as a "pretty mediocre" center at McClymonds. Now, he thought, "we didn't have anybody that could compete with him." Russell's height and athleticism controlled the contest. At one point George Selleck stole the ball and ran downcourt for a presumably uncontested layup, only for Russell to swoop across the court, leap from the top of the key, and block the ball off the backboard. The next night, USF scored the first twenty points in an 84–62 victory over Cali-fornia. The polls bumped the Dons to #2 in the country.[51]

"Just How Good is Bill Russell?" asked a newspaper headline. Radio broadcaster Cat Wooden had once opined, "USF is simply a one-man team and that man—Bill Russell—is not tremendous." But Russell had since prompted comparisons to the West Coast's two All-American big men, Bob McKeen and Ken Sears. Russell lacked their shooting, dribbling, and passing skills, and he looked nothing like a conven-tional pivotman. His body remained pathetically skinny. He ran hunched over—one writer compared him to a pretzel. Yet no one had a bigger impact on his team or, ultimately, the sport.[52]

"Don't leave your feet should your opponent set himself for an outside shot," declared one contemporary basketball manual. "Your opponent may fake the shot and drive in for a basket. Furthermore, a guard who has leaped into the air will be in no position to turn to help on the defensive rebounding if the drive-in shot has been missed." Russell defied this convention by leaping, reaching, and swat-ting away shots. He succeeded through relentless athleticism. In the Stanford game, for instance, Russell had leaped at a Russ Lawler fake. Lawler drove left in three long strides, stopped, and hooked. In that time Russell had landed, sprinted back, and leaped so high that his chin reached rim height. He redirected the shot at Lawler's face.[53]

Russell had occasioned no preseason hype and played only in California and Oklahoma City. But local coaches gauged his faculties. Stanford's Howie Dallmar thought he could cover the best professional centers. "He'll be the greatest defensive player in the history of the game," predicted Cal's Pete Newell. In a *Sporting News* feature highlighting the team's emerging success, Woolpert called Russell "the greatest defensive center I have ever seen."[54]

After another win over Loyola, USF continued its conference schedule. Russell embodied the confident, athletic, defense-oriented squad's march toward greatness. The Dons beat St. Mary's, Pacific, San Jose State, and Santa Clara two times each to finish the regular season 23–1. They allowed only 52.1 points a game, the fewest in the country. In early February the University of Kentucky dropped a game to Georgia Tech, so the University of San Francisco took over the #1 ranking. They entered the NCAA tournament on a twenty-one-game winning streak.[55]

As black newspapers trumpeted nationwide, a team starting three African Americans reigned supreme over college basketball. The game now featured other black stars such as Dick Ricketts and Sihugo Green of Duquesne, Maurice Stokes of St. Francis College, and the UCLA trio of Willie Naulls, Morrie Taft, and Johnny Moore. Marion Jackson of the *Atlanta Daily World* suggested that such triumphs reflected new opportunities for black achievement, a shift in public attitude toward racial integration, and even a response to communist propaganda. Although Southern newspapers omitted photographs or racial identifications when reporting All-America teams, the new black basketball stars "should not be overlooked by troubleshooters in our state department who need answers to the charges of suppression of exploitation of minorities as leveled by the Soviet conspiracy."[56]

Russell averaged 21.4 points and 20.5 rebounds a game, and he made first-team All-American for both the United Press (UP) and Associated Press (AP) squads. No other West Coast player made either team, except Ken Sears, who made the UP's third team. Yet local writers named Sears Player of the Year for the CBA and all of northern California. Russell burned with hurt. He blamed Woolpert. Santa Clara coach Bob Feerick had lobbied for Sears, while Woolpert withheld public praise. Woolpert knew Russell's ego, clashed with him over playing style and practice habits, and feared elevating an individual at the team's expense. Russell saw a racial double standard. He already resented that Woolpert had appointed Jerry Mullen to captain when the players would have voted for K. C. Jones. Now he threatened to skip an awards banquet for Sears. "Bill, that'll demean you as a man," warned Woolpert. "That's beneath you." In the end, Russell gave Sears a warm, gracious speech.[57]

Russell's reaction revealed the complexities of his personality and politics. His speech for Sears suggested his self-awareness as a public representative of his team, his school, and all African Americans. Yet he chafed at Woolpert, the era's most liberal white coach. Even though Woolpert cared for his players as people, recruited and played African Americans, and weathered alumni pressure and hate mail, Russell saw racism beyond crude epithets and "White Only" signs. Out of some combination of sensitivity and intelligence, his bitterness festered not just when bigots launched pennies or insults at him, but when race clouded the eyes of well-meaning whites.

. . .

USF had entered the NCAA tournament as the top-ranked team in the country, but throughout its title run it overcame internal hardships and external doubts. Because the CBA was a second-rate conference, the Dons did not receive an automatic bid for the Western Regionals. They first hosted Border Conference champions West Texas State, which employed intimidation tactics. With the score 2–2, a West Texas defender undercut a leaping Russell, who spun in midair and landed on his back, with his leg folded under him. The crowd hushed for an uncertain moment. Russell picked himself up, gingerly. Then, with the score 8–8, another defender crashed into the leaping center. This time the referee assessed a technical foul, the crowd booed, and USF got angry. Russell notched ten straight first-half field goals on the way to twenty-nine points. The Dons won the game, 89–66, and gained more admirers. "I saw it, I was hit by it, I still don't believe it," said West Texas coach Gus Miller.[58]

Three days later USF faced its stiffest test yet. Fourth-ranked Utah University won the Skyline Conference and arrived confident: their scouting report labeled forward Stan Buchanan an "Achilles' Heel," Hal Perry a "man who shouldn't be on the starting team," and Russell a player with one offensive weapon, the "tip-in." USF, meanwhile, looked drained from the extra game. Russell had a cold, fever, and pregame stomachache. Luckily, newspapers published the scouting report, providing a little extra inspiration. The Dons led 41–20 at halftime.[59]

Walking into the locker room, however, Russell started hacking coughs and spitting up blood. A local doctor determined that Russell had improperly digested a steak, needed a complete medical examination, and could not play. Five minutes into the second half, Utah had cut the lead to eight points. Russell pleaded that he felt fine. Still, Woolpert refused to endanger his health. Then a soused USF alumnus stormed over to the bench, demanding that Russell get a second opinion—from a San Francisco doctor that he had found in the stands. The new doctor cleared him to play. Russell reentered the game and reenergized his teammates. Jones and Perry could now press the speedy Utah guards, knowing that their defensive lynchpin stood behind them. Russell returned to the bench with eight minutes left in a 78–59 rout.[60]

The next morning a doctor thoroughly examined Russell. He may have caught a flu bug, but he had recovered his health. Now, the team faced Oregon State on its home court. The Beavers featured 7'3" Swede Halbrook, who in the semifinal had scored twenty-one points in only twenty-three minutes. Most experts expected Oregon State to prevail, since Russell could not dominate the behemoth. But Russell had confidence. Upon arrival in Corvallis, Halbrook and Russell had posed for a photographer. Halbrook held a basketball at the top of his outstretched arm. Then Russell reached up, and his fingers cupped the top of the ball. His teammates exhaled. "Needless to say, that picture never was shown in any Corvallis newspapers," said Woolpert. "And as our players later said, we had beaten Oregon State right there."[61]

Actually, USF needed a dramatic, wire-to-wire effort to beat Oregon State. Jerry Mullen twisted his ankle after two seconds of play. He returned after a heavy tape job but managed no field goals. Oregon State double-teamed Russell, leaving Stan Buchanan open, but Buchanan kept passing the ball. Woolpert had to call timeout and insist that Buchanan shoot. Oregon State played a nearly perfect game, biting at USF's heels the whole game—down 56–49 with one minute left, they scored six unanswered points and put Jerry Mullen on the line for two free throws. The first barely touched the front rim, and Mullen buckled in pain. He gutted the second one into the hoop. Then, when Woolpert called over K. C. Jones, Jones accidentally barreled into Oregon State's Jim O'Toole. The referee awarded a technical foul. With seconds left, the lead again shrunk to one point, and Oregon State had the ball. Jones redeemed himself twice—first tying up Halbrook in a wild scramble for a rebound, and then somehow guiding the ensuing jump ball toward Hal Perry, who dove under a scrum as the final whistle sounded. USF won 57–56.[62]

Now the Dons headed to the NCAA Finals in Kansas City. As in Oklahoma, racial segregation marred the event: though the team stayed together, a number of establishments refused service to the black players. The location also reflected the legacy of the point-shaving investigations. The NCAA tournament abandoned Madison Square Garden in the 1950s. Although half the players preferred entering the NIT, USF administrators steered clear of New York City, where the NIT absorbed the stench of the scandals.[63]

The NCAA now attracted the better teams. To protect its status, the organization depended upon an image of moral rectitude, and it warned teams to beware of suspicious characters seeking inside dope. One morning, a nervous Russell pulled Woolpert outside the Continental Hotel. A man had been peppering the USF star with questions about the team's morale, health, and preparation. Just then Russell saw the man walking down the street. Woolpert sighed. It was a reporter from *Sports Illustrated*.[64]

In the semifinal, USF played Colorado, the rugged champions of the Big Seven. USF fans worried about Jerry Mullen's weak ankle, and their angst multiplied in the early going, as Mullen sat on the bench and Colorado slowed down the game. "Shake Russell and Roll!" chanted the Colorado fans, but in the second half, it was Russell who shook Colorado and the Dons who rolled. Colorado center Burdette Haldorson stood 6'9", but he had never faced anyone with Russell's leaping ability and timing. Haldorson planned to prevent lobs to the rim by staying behind Russell, letting him shoot. Russell hit his first five shots, and Haldorson fouled out with the score 30–21. The Dons never looked back. At one point Jones whipped a no-look pass to Russell, who stepped under the hoop and thundered down a two-fisted reverse slam dunk. The Municipal Auditorium crowd roared. "Did you ever see that before?" asked a Midwesterner on press row. "No," answered an awed East Coast reporter. The USF reserves finished the 62–50 runaway.[65]

The victory set up a dream final against defending champion LaSalle, led by Tom Gola. To the sporting cognoscenti, Gola embodied basketball perfection. The 6'7" forward could pass, dribble, shoot, defend, and rebound with equal aplomb, and he glided around the court with effortless grace. He had won MVP in both the NIT and NCAA tournaments. Granted freshman eligibility because LaSalle was so small, he made All-America for four straight years. He also listened to his coach, loved his mother, and acted nice to schoolchildren. Like Russell, he had launched a small Catholic school into national prominence. But Gola played in basketball-mad Philadelphia, near the nation's media center, and he had traditional skills. He was also white. Reporters fawned over him with dreamy reverence.[66]

The papers trumpeted "A Gola-Russell Duel." The day of the final, Russell and Ross Giudice encountered Gola and his coach, Ken Loeffler, in the hotel lobby. "Well, we're honored," smiled Russell. "Here comes MISTER Gola." Loeffler grumbled back a boast about Gola. The exchange captured the final's essential tension: Russell resented Gola's star treatment, and Loeffler's bluster betrayed anxiety about Russell.[67]

Meanwhile, Phil Woolpert fretted about Gola. He first planned to have Russell guard him. Then he huddled with some friends, including old teammate Scotty McDonald, who suggested that K. C. Jones cover Gola. Though he gave up six inches, Jones played relentless defense. This strategy also freed Russell to rebound and block shots. In the pregame meeting, Woolpert told Jones his assignment. "That just about blew my dinner," remembered Jones.[68]

Jones hounded Gola, shadowing him chest-to-chest, nose-to-nose, up and down the court, jabbing and poking whenever Gola had the ball. The LaSalle star never established a rhythm, finishing with sixteen points. Jones notched twenty-four points and Russell added twenty-three, mostly on tip-ins of missed outside shots. LaSalle tried using a sliding zone to collapse on the center, but it could not contain his perfectly timed aerial twists to guide in errant shots. The capacity crowd of 10,500 grew more amazed with each display of Russell's agility. The Dons coasted to a 77–63 win. When the buzzer sounded, Russell's teammates and fans swamped him, lifted him to their shoulders, and carried him off like a victorious gladiator.[69]

· · ·

"I've never seen anything like this team," said Doc Carlson, the longtime coach at Pittsburgh. "They make you grope for words." Coaches across the country echoed him. USF won the national championship, finished the season 28–1, and owned a twenty-six-game winning streak. No team had ever displayed such astonishing athleticism or stifling defense.[70]

Nor had any team ever boasted a presence such as Bill Russell. He set a five-game tourney mark with 118 points, won the tournament MVP award, and captured the Helms Foundation award for the nation's best player. "Nobody had really seen that shot-blocking technique," remembered Pete Newell. "You were never ready for that hand coming out of the air. He made coaches look at big men in a different way." Coaches at the NCAA Tournament took mental notes, wondering how they could instruct their own centers in Russell's style.[71]

USF's success had stemmed not only from Russell's springy legs and elongated arms, but also from his flights of intellect—his analytical emulations of others, his passionate discourses with K.C. Jones, his creative imaginings of his own possibilities. By weaving his individual virtuosity into the fabric of team excellence, he had become the unlikely centerpiece to the best team in college basketball.

3

Russell Rules

"We want the Dons! We want the Dons!" chanted six hundred fans as the NCAA champions landed at San Francisco International Airport. The team, clad in green blazers, descended onto the tarmac. A pep band wearing mariachi uniforms— "The Tooter Rooters"—belted out the USF fight song, while a middle-aged woman banged a drum with her purse. Russell emerged last, wearing a bowler hat and a huge grin, holding the game ball high in his left hand. Kids encircled him. He called the celebration "the greatest experience ever." Then horns blared as cars, festooned with green and gold streamers, followed the team bus up the Bayshore Freeway. The exultant party continued on campus.[1]

The title sparked unprecedented fervor in the Bay Area and beyond. USF had overcome a perceived disregard for West Coast basketball, rendering the college game a truly national enterprise. "The Dons," wrote Bob Brachman of the *San Francisco Examiner*, "brought fame not only to themselves and their school, their city and their state, but to an entire Pacific Coast area starved for recognition." Sport was shaping regional identity. "Now, the rest of the country has to respect us!" he wrote. "USF is OUR champion!"[2]

The day after their return, a ticker-tape parade showered the champions. The USF band fronted the procession, which included a fire engine dressed in green bunting. "San Francisco's Finest Buries LaSalle" proclaimed a baby-blue hearse. Each player rode in his own convertible, accompanied by a girlfriend holding a bouquet of green and gold daffodils. One hundred thousand San Franciscans cheered Russell and Rose Swisher as they rolled to City Hall and then turned north toward the Fairmont Hotel. One thousand people attended a civic luncheon. Phil Woolpert introduced each player with a personal tribute.[3]

Woolpert called up Russell last, and the great center won the loudest ovation. "With all this tremendous pressure, with all this unaccustomed adulation, he has carried himself so modestly he has become a wonderful public relations man for USF and for San Francisco," Woolpert beamed. "He has done a magnificent job for you, for me, for all of us." Such praise from his reserved, anxious coach touched Russell, who dabbed at his moist eyes with his knuckles.[4]

Woolpert's tribute exposed the emerging public perception of Russell. National magazines such as *Time* and *Sports Illustrated* had published his self-effacing, team-oriented quotes. They noted his affable, gregarious personality. His interviews combined humility with enthusiasm. "I'm not as good on defense as people think," he said. "In fact, I am the worst defensive man on the team." In Kansas City, basketball fans of every size and stripe shook his hand, engaged him in conversation, and got his autograph. In the wake of *Brown v. Board of Education*, Russell suggested the hopeful contours of an integrated America. Black newspapers such as the *Chicago Defender* and *Pittsburgh Courier* trumpeted his accomplishments. His team succeeded through the cooperation of blacks and whites. More than anyone else in college basketball, he embodied a liberal optimism about American race relations.[5]

Yet anger simmered beneath the surface. That summer Russell visited Louisiana with his father. They stopped for gas in Mississippi. Defying Jim Crow, Mister Charlie used the station's restroom rather than the "Colored" outhouse. The furious attendant started asking sharp-edged questions. Mister Charlie answered tersely, eschewing the obsequious "yes sirs" and "no sirs" expected of Southern blacks. But they avoided confrontation when the attendant noticed a USF sticker on the car window. He assumed it meant "United States Federal," and his anger softened into deference. When the Russells reached West Monroe, they told the tale again and again, laughing at their defiance of racial etiquette.[6]

Russell had escaped the depredations of West Monroe and West Oakland. He had lost his mother. He had suffered racist indignities and arrogant dismissals. When celebrated by *Time* and *Sports Illustrated,* he had been nevertheless pigeonholed into black stereotype, called "a happy-go-lucky Oakland Negro" and "something of a clown." For all his achievements, race shackled his possibilities. That frustration, that rage, that pessimism stimulated his greatness. "I decided in college to win," he later said. "Then it's a historical fact, and nobody can take it away from me."[7]

Russell led USF from anonymous underachievers in a weak-sister conference to the reigning titans of college basketball. As the Dons won, they effected a fundamental transformation. Before their winning streak, a snapshot of big-time college basketball revealed white players focused on deliberate, earthbound offensive patterns. After the streak, that picture showed a racially integrated unit, placing a premium on speed and aggressive defense, controlling not just horizontal but vertical space. If one man was the avatar of this transformation, it was Bill Russell.[8]

. . .

"Height has caught up with the rules committee," fulminated Phog Allen during the 1955 NCAA Finals, "and are their faces red." The eccentric, honey-tongued coach at the University of Kansas had long clamored to raise the basket to twelve feet, and he delivered copious diatribes bemoaning the growing dominance of big men. In the 1920s and 1930s, basketball had been a small man's game, based on quick passes and sharp cuts. Most people considered tall men too slow and awkward. Joe Lapchick of the Original Celtics seemed a giant at 6'5".[9]

The 1937 elimination of the jump ball after every basket changed the center position. As the pace grew faster, big men started transcending the image of the clumsy galoot. Tall boys who might have avoided competitive sports found opportunities in basketball. The sport now valued centers that could rebound, defend the entire lane, and score easy baskets. But this development bred distance between fans and players, who assumed that big men lacked skill. Players mourned the constant jokes and stares when they appeared in public. It so bothered Bob Pettit, a 6'9" forward for the NBA's St. Louis Hawks, that he wrote a *Saturday Evening Post* article entitled "Don't Call Us Freaks!"[10]

Numerous journalists and coaches now echoed Allen, painting basketball as a sport under assault by leviathans. *Life* published a photo essay called "The Giants of Schoolboy Basketball," featuring a swarm of high school players 6'10" and over, including Philadelphia's Wilt Chamberlain. Fear spread that such monsters would destroy basketball's cooperative ethic and that smaller men would abandon the game. "These fellows are biological accidents who ought to be more usefully employed, like hiring out as rainmakers and going to sow a few clouds," wrote Shirley Povich in a *Sports Illustrated* diatribe called "Basketball Is for the Birds." Other writers, too, had trouble relating to big men. Red Smith, the influential columnist syndicated to more than one hundred newspapers, almost never wrote about basketball. He was 5'8".[11]

Russell's ascendancy in Kansas City spotlighted attention on Allen's pet cause. When the National Association of Basketball Coaches met during the NCAA Finals, they envisioned a generation of Russells driving little men out of the sport. They discussed rules changes targeted at basketball behemoths. After watching Russell guide in shot after shot with his hands above the rim, Allen lobbied to outlaw "offensive goaltending," railing that "Russell put a funnel and sideboards on the basket." The coaches decided to still allow offensive goaltending. But they widened the lane from six to twelve feet, hoping to free congestion under the basket, opening space for smaller men to drive. They approved the change as USF concluded its title run, so the decree earned a nickname: the Russell Rule.[12]

The wider lane actually helped Russell; it punished heavy-footed centers anchored in the post, not those with the quickness and agility to range across the court. His team ranked first in the country's preseason polls. The schedule featured high-profile tournaments in Chicago and New York. Fresno State, Loyola, and Pepperdine joined the California Basketball Association, and the NCAA now granted the conference champion an automatic tournament berth. Although forwards Jerry Mullen and Stan Buchanan had graduated, the position received an upgrade with Carl Boldt, a junior college All-American, and Mike Farmer, a California high school all-star. The CBA had awarded K. C. Jones an extra year of eligibility after his one-game season in 1953–54, so he and Hal Perry constituted the best backcourt in the country. Russell, of course, headed the list of preseason All-Americans.[13]

The opening games at Kezar Pavilion confirmed the preseason prognostications. Decked in modish new warm-ups with gold capes, USF stretched its winning streak to twenty-nine games by dismantling Chico State, University of Southern California, and San Francisco State. Russell looked dominant. On offense, he operated more from the high post, opening space for drives through the wider lane. He averaged nearly a point per minute played, and Woolpert pulled him out halfway through each rout. On defense, he delighted the hometown fans with effortless swats. "It was like a big boy playing keep-away with small boys," marveled *Sports Illustrated.* USF seemed nearly invincible.[14]

After final exams the team embarked on a sixteen-day, seven-game tour across the country. It began in Chicago at the DePaul Invitational Tournament, the old stomping grounds of George Mikan. The great center had attended DePaul from 1941 to 1945 before joining the pros. When Russell was a fifteen-year-old third-string center for the McClymonds junior varsity, he watched his first professional game, an exhibition featuring the Minneapolis Lakers. After the game, Mikan saw the gangly black kid outside the locker room. "How ya' doin', big fella?" asked Mikan. He talked to Russell for fifteen minutes, urging him to keep playing basketball. From that day on, Russell idolized Mikan.[15]

Mikan had established the prevailing definition of the pivotman. The child of Croatian tavern-keepers in Joliet, Illinois, he stood 6'10", about four inches taller than the average center of his era. Bulky, brawny, and begoggled, he had a distinctive stature. Over and over, he muscled his way into the low post, took the entry pass, drop-stepped with a protruding elbow, and sank a baby hook shot. A three-time All-American, he guided DePaul to an 81–17 record and the 1945 NIT championship. A 1955 panel voted him the greatest player in college basketball history.[16]

By the time he met Russell, Mikan had led the Minneapolis Lakers to the 1948 title in the National Basketball League and the 1949 title in the Basketball Association of America. After those two leagues merged into the National Basketball Association, Mikan piloted the first NBA dynasty, capturing four titles between 1950 and 1954. As his interaction with Russell indicated, Mikan was also his sport's greatest representative. Fans gravitated to the gregarious center, and he pitched gum, televisions, deodorant, airlines, and apples. The Madison Square Garden marquee once advertised an upcoming game as "Mikan vs. Knicks."[17]

Now Russell treaded on Mikan's territory. After first cruising past Marquette, 65–58, his Dons met the host team in the final. More than eleven thousand DePaul fans left disappointed—or maybe awestruck—as USF won 82–59. The 1955–56 Dons had even more speed, shooting ability, and depth. "They could name the score against any college team in the country," said one coach. Russell led the way. He blocked about fifteen shots, caught one shot attempt in midair, and forced a variety of feeble attempts from his psyched-out opponents. He won the tournament MVP award.[18]

DePaul coach Ray Meyer compared Russell to Mikan. He conceded that Russell's defense allowed USF to hawk every ballhandler and challenge every shot. But Meyer remained wedded to the conventional perception of the center position, embodied by his former meal ticket. "I think Mikan was easier to hit on the post," he said. "He backed his defensive man under the basket and always had such good position." Mikan could grind out baskets, and he depended on bulk and power for his rebounds. Russell, by contrast, relied on athleticism and angles. He leaped, he reached, he moved his feet. That style contradicted prevailing principles. For traditionalists like Meyer, Russell remained an anomaly, not the herald of a stylistic transformation. That larger appreciation of his talents would arrive only as USF kept spreading its gospel, appearing on bigger stages, and facing challenges that transcended basketball.[19]

. . .

The Dons next beat Wichita State in Kansas, 75–65. Fueled by racial resentment, many of the 10,500 fans booed Russell and Hal Perry when they shot free throws. After the game, Wichita coach Ralph Miller apologized to Woolpert for the crowd's behavior. Thanks to the 1955 championship, the Dons had a national reputation, and their black stars fused a popular association of the team with racial integration.[20]

USF now had five black players. Along with Russell, Jones, Perry, and Warren Baxter, the team added Eugene Brown, a 6'3" sophomore with superb all-around skills. Brown substituted in at guard. He had never considered himself as a forward, and Carl Boldt was bigger and stronger. Still, despite Woolpert's well-deserved reputation for courage and open-mindedness, a few teammates believed that Brown deserved to start at forward—"no ifs, ands, or buts about it," according to Tom Nelson. But if Brown took Carl Boldt's place, the Dons would start four African Americans, perhaps pushing a taboo too far.[21]

The Dons nevertheless upset sport's racial traditions, especially as their road trip continued southward, into Russell's home state of Louisiana, for a December 23 game against Loyola University in New Orleans. After the *Brown* decision, the Deep

South's resistance to integration had thickened. College sports proved a popular battlefront, and that month, Louisiana sat in the spotlight. The upcoming Sugar Bowl in New Orleans slated all-white Georgia Tech against the University of Pittsburgh, which had a black backup fullback.

Forget adding blacks to their own teams—in Dixie, even playing *against* a black person signaled some acquiescence to integration. "The South stands at Armageddon," thundered Georgia governor Marvin Griffin. "There is no more difference in compromising the integrity of race on the playing field than doing so in the classroom." Soon after, the Georgia Board of Regents restricted state schools from future bowl games against integrated competition, and Louisiana passed a law outlawing interracial athletics.[22]

At the time, however, Loyola's teams competed against black athletes, and its five-thousand-seat field house had integrated seating. A Jesuit institution like USF, Loyola had eliminated sporting segregation in 1954 to promote racial tolerance. USF scheduled the game to cultivate this progress. "I guess it was something of a small crusade on our part," said Woolpert. Unfortunately, as USF was beating Wichita, Loyola was hosting Bradley University, whose black forward Shellie McMillon fouled out of the game. The *New Orleans Times Picayune* charged that McMillon had first "showboated" and then "lost all of his poise and started fouling intentionally." As McMillon left the court, the Loyola band played "Dixie" and fans shouted "Bye Bye Blackbird!" McMillon got angry. He brushed away his opponents' back pats. One report claimed that he stuck out his tongue. Others maintain that he stuck out his middle finger. The incident revealed how the Deep South subjected black athletes to enormous pressures. Any bad publicity reflected on the larger quest for racial integration.[23]

Now USF's black players faced that burden. Even at home, they banded together, sitting at the same cafeteria tables and socializing in each other's rooms. They were the school's racial pioneers—as Brown said, "USF was more or less integrating itself through basketball." The black players went to the same parties, dated their own women, and walked together down to Fillmore Street for barbecue ribs and red soda. They pledged to their own all-black fraternity, Kappa Alpha Psi. They liked their white teammates, but skin color, background, and religion separated them from the Catholic majority. "We used to get buckets of hate mail every week," said Russell. Before they traveled south, they steadied each other, resolving to be strong upon entering hostile territory.[24]

"We got off the plane and saw the restroom signs for 'white' and 'colored,'" recalled K. C. Jones. "That shook some of the guys up." The white players and coaches stayed at the downtown Jung Hotel, while the black players lodged at Xavier University. On public buses, the black players rode in the back. Some restaurants forced the black players to enter through the side door. Everyone seemed edgy, especially

Russell. The stress of competition strained him enough, let alone the anxiety of political experimentation. Moreover, he hated any acquiescence to segregation.[25]

Yet the Dons had arrived in Louisiana to foster racial goodwill. When a local black restaurant owner threw a banquet, each player gave a short speech. As his teammates spoke, Russell hunched over, scribbling notes. He stood up last. "I was pretty worried about what he might say," Woolpert later admitted. Stone-faced, Russell surveyed his teammates, the locals, and the media. The room got quiet. "Ladies and gentlemen," he began, "the greatest place to be from in America is New Orleans." He then delivered a deft, warmhearted speech, neutralizing the tension.[26]

During the game, the spirit of liberal tolerance clashed with the context of racial bigotry. Officials from both schools expressed confidence that no controversies would mar the game, and the black players drew polite ovations during pregame introductions. At the tip-off, however, the referee boorishly mimicked a black dialect, right in front of Russell. During the game, fans taunted the black players. Again, Russell calmed the bubbling pot. Seven minutes into the game, he grabbed a rebound as two Loyola players crashed to the floor. Russell dropped the ball and lent his white opponents a hand. This time, the crowd cheered. USF also provided a furious spectacle of denied entry passes and blocked shots, winning 61–43. In contrast to the Bradley game—and to the relief of the black press—the players received ovations as they substituted out. Russell, Jones, Perry, Warren Baxter, and Eugene Brown had struck a mild blow against Jim Crow.[27]

Upon solidifying their credentials as emblems of racial integration, the Dons buttressed their athletic reputation. The previous season, they had emerged from anonymity by winning the NCAA title. Yet the Dons never played east of the Mississippi River, and the NCAA tournament was not televised until 1963. So cynics remained. West Coast writers for *Sports Illustrated* kept suggesting Russell for cover photos, but the home office in New York resisted, citing his unimpressive point totals. New Yorkers had seen Hank Luisetti and George Mikan and Tom Gola, but they had never seen this skinny, black center who presumably caught Gola on an off night. To convert the nonbelievers, USF needed the sport's biggest stage, in the beating heart of basketball: Madison Square Garden.[28]

The Holiday Festival Tournament derived from Ned Irish's popular tripleheaders. After the 1951 scandals, most New York schools had de-emphasized their basketball programs. Holiday tournaments sprang up around the country, but the New York tournament kept big-time basketball in its historic home. Playing to packed houses, it featured an array of stars. None generated more anticipation than Russell. Milton Gross of the *New York Post* had become a Russell apostle: "He is a goal tender in a time when goal tending is illegal, only Bill does it legally in a way that tries the imagination and baffles the opposition."[29]

Yet the basketball cognoscenti had long measured excellence on all-around offensive skills. When Russell stepped on the floor against LaSalle, the crowd hooted. He could not dribble or pass like Gola. His loping style looked lazy. And he missed his first three shots, all from close range. The fans jeered him, teased him, and waved handkerchiefs when he took foul shots. If Hank Luisetti had once enraptured New Yorkers with his audacious one-hand shots, Bill Russell offended their sensibilities.[30]

But soon, observed Roy Terrell of *Sports Illustrated,* "the looks of doubt and derision changed into looks of incredulity and awe." Russell guided in errant shots and scored on tip-ins, tallying twenty-six points. Springing so high that his chin reached the rim, he plucked twenty-two rebounds. True, he lacked a jump shot. True, he looked awkward. But only Russell could leave his man on the weakside perimeter, take two long strides, extend an antenna-like arm, and block a driving layup on the other side of the court. USF won the game 79–62, and Russell won more acolytes. "All the words they had read," Terrell wrote, "had not really prepared the crowd for Bill Russell."[31]

Whether people appreciated Russell depended on whether they looked to basketball's past or its future. New York sportswriter Leonard Koppett later likened watching Russell to first seeing Willie Mays or Cassius Clay, men of such extraordinary ability that they rewrote popular expectations. Yet to basketball purists, Russell lacked skills and strength. "We'd have to doubt that he'd do well in the pro league," opined the *New York Journal American,* noting his deficient shooting touch. "Walter Dukes was a better all-around basketball player in college," said Ken Norton of Manhattan College. "Gola played every phase of the game well and did more than Russell can do," argued Fran O'Malley of LaSalle. "This guy's got size, that's all," added O'Malley's teammate Charley Greenberg. The media further described Russell's rail-thin frame, simian arms, and "turkey neck."[32]

Russell chafed at this sardonic tenor. "Don't you think I read the papers?" he said. "It's like knives. It hurts." He drew extra motivation for the semifinal against Holy Cross, led by Tom Heinsohn—a white, 6'7", slick-shooting bulldog revered by the New York papers. Russell fumed at the disrespect. "At the hotel, he felt pretty bad," said K. C. Jones. "Everybody building up Tommy Heinsohn in the papers and knocking Bill down. He's just a big fellow. He's no freak. He didn't like that kind of reading." Most experts assumed that Russell would guard another player to avoid foul trouble. But Woolpert had him cover Heinsohn. When told of his assignment, Russell smiled with relish.[33]

In pregame warm-ups, as eighteen thousand fans filed into sold-out Madison Square Garden, Heinsohn's teammates fumbled with nervousness. "Don't be afraid of Russell! Don't be afraid of him!" Heinsohn exhorted. The Holy Cross star embraced the challenge. Operating out of a 3–2 spread offense, he pulled Russell away from the basket, sank perimeter shots, and fed cutting teammates for layups. On defense, he countered Russell's quickness with brute force, even planting an elbow into Russell's stomach during a break in the action. (Russell waited a few minutes, then landed his own cheap shot while the referees looked elsewhere.) At halftime Holy Cross led 32–29. In the locker room, Woolpert chided Russell for letting Heinsohn score twelve points.

But Heinsohn also had three fouls, so Holy Cross moved sophomore Pete Houston into the pivot. Russell dominated the second half, finishing with twenty-four points and twenty-two rebounds in a 67–51 rout. Heinsohn never scored after halftime, as Russell thwarted his efforts near the hoop. The postgame conversations revolved around Russell's superiority. Even Heinsohn agreed. "I didn't get my 30, did I?" he growled to reporters. Russell reveled in the moment. "Heinsohn's a great ballplayer," he said. "Everybody wrote that in the papers. I wanted to prove that I'm as good as he is. Can you blame me for wanting to prove that?"[34]

The final against UCLA proved more a coronation than a contest, though it illustrated the shifts in college basketball embodied by Russell. Both teams hailed from the West Coast. Willie Naulls, Morrie Taft, and Johnny Moore all started for UCLA—the only other major college program to start three blacks. In Russell's mind, USF won the game before it started. The teams stayed at the same hotel, and they ate their pregame meals in the same dining room. As the Bruins ate in studied silence, the Dons whooped it up. They giggled, tossed dinner rolls, and stuffed food down their throats. USF advertised the confidence of a champion. "The game that followed wasn't much," Russell recalled. "The *meal* was one of America's great moments in sports."[35]

The game did feature a revealing moment when Naulls rose for a powerful two-hand dunk. Russell reached over the cylinder and blocked it, even though the ball never left Naulls's hands. UCLA coach John Wooden cried goaltending, but the amazing block "surprised everyone so much that no one knew what to call." That play spoke to Russell's revolutionary influence, and it sparked a USF win, 70–53. Russell left the game to a huge ovation. In three games he had accumulated sixty-seven points and sixty-two rebounds. He won the MVP award, his fifth consecutive tournament honor.[36]

Joe Lapchick—a thirty-five-year veteran of competitive basketball, the former star of the Original Celtics, the current coach of the New York Knicks, and the personification of the sport's urban East Coast legacy—called USF "the best college basketball team I have ever seen." Some teams had better shooters, but none played defense like the Dons. "That's because no team ever had a player like Bill Russell." USF had won seven road games in sixteen days, stretching their winning streak to thirty-six games. As the calendar flipped to 1956, the Dons returned to California. Along with their conference schedule, they faced the burden of basketball history.[37]

. . .

Long Island University had set an NCAA record with thirty-nine consecutive wins from 1935 to 1937, and Seton Hall tied the mark from 1939 to 1941. After opening its CBA schedule with easy wins over Pepperdine, Santa Clara, and Fresno State, USF shared the record. Because San Francisco had only one professional franchise, the 49ers of the National Football League, the Dons became the city's darlings. Capacity crowds packed Kezar Pavilion. Coaches across the country raved about Russell. Local television specials glorified them. College presidents, professors, and politicians visited the locker room to bask in their glory. Alumni boosters offered invitations, favors, cash. Players faced temptations to cheat in school. Winning created a sense of civic satisfaction, but it also brewed new tensions.[38]

Russell attracted national attention: photo essays in *Life, Look,* and *Ebony,* profiles in *Time,* the *New York Times,* and the *Chicago Tribune.* The black press breathlessly followed his exploits, highlighting his statistics, awards, and respect within the basketball world. He became a Bay Area celebrity. The local media painted him as proud, "with a deep sense of personal dignity," but also humble, selfless, and happy. When the Federation of Catholic High Schools presented him an award, five thousand students and teachers thundered with cheers. Carl Boldt joked that if the team plane crashed, the headlines would read "BILL RUSSELL KILLED" and the back page would list his teammates as "also dead."[39]

Russell resented such teasing because he worked to establish the team's cooperative spirit. "I was in awe of the guy," recalled teammate Mike Preaseau. "He knew who he was." K. C. Jones lauded his intelligence, his insistence on detail, his on-court communication skills, and his supreme confidence. Hal Perry recalled how Russell would insist on one-on-one games to test himself against a quick dribbler. Tom Nelson marveled at his sharp mind and verbal facility, Bill Bush at his selflessness and competitive spirit. Mike Farmer remembered Russell as intellectually curious and opinionated, but always deriving his conclusions after research and careful thought. He believed that the team adopted Russell's character: analyzing the game's larger patterns, studying their opponents, and taking confidence in their abilities. "Don't ever do what you CAN'T do," Russell said. "Just do what you CAN do—and do it well."[40]

Phil Woolpert celebrated Russell as a "good citizen" who absorbed strong values from his father. His teammates found him affable and outgoing, "one of the boys." In front of crowds, he shone with charisma, making people laugh and feel at ease. John Cunningham forever appreciated that the All-American center invited him, a lowly freshman from San Diego, home for Thanksgiving. Few players saw any resentment within Russell. Instead they enjoyed his wit and enthusiasm. When Warren Baxter first transferred from City College of San Francisco, he kept to himself until Russell called him prejudiced—"prejudiced against tall guys." They shared a laugh and thereafter developed a friendship.[41]

Russell revealed his prodigious competitive fire only in bursts of angst. "I never, ever experienced pressure like I did during the streak," Russell later reflected. Before games, he became a hypochondriac, complaining about skin irritations, swollen tongues, shoulder pain, eye tics, appendicitis, and other disorders. He often vomited in the locker room. Then the game began, and the illnesses dissolved.[42]

The Dons survived the stress. The constant winning smoothed over personality conflicts, and cross-country travel bonded them. Often rooming whites and blacks together on the road, the team created friendships across the racial divide. For instance, one night during a school break, K. C. Jones took Mike Preaseau to a black nightclub. With the racial proportions reversed, Preaseau glimpsed the difficulties of African American life at USF. In general, the players traded jokes, played poker, and shrugged off the outside pressures. Living by the cliché of "one game at a time," they possessed extraordinary confidence in their collective excellence. At times they seemed preternaturally loose. "Luckily," Russell said, "we had players who were kinda hep."[43]

Phil Woolpert was not "hep" whatsoever. He worried about the costs of winning: a flawed value system that overemphasizes victory, psychological scars from the continued pressures. He stopped eating, snapped at his wife, and developed a twitch. His hair grew gray. In one game, Woolpert jumped up to protest a foul. His lips moved, but no words emerged. The strain was grinding his nerves.[44]

His anxiety built to a crescendo for the January 28 game against California, a chance for an NCAA record forty straight wins. The game, sold out since mid-December, riveted the region. Scalpers fetched $25 for $1.50 tickets. During the two-week break in mid-January for final exams, fans clamored to move the game to the Cow Palace, which seated almost six thousand more people than Berkeley's Harmon Gymnasium. They further moaned that no stations were televising the game. Though the game remained in Berkeley, a civic-minded USF alumnus sponsored a telecast.[45]

USF set the record, but only after the ugliest, weirdest game of their historic streak. USF shot 21 percent, and Cal 22 percent. Most points came on free throws. Early in the second half, after Cal center Duane Asplund fouled out, coach Pete Newell figured that he needed to draw Russell away from the basket. Even though his team trailed 26–21, Newell ordered substitute Joe Hagler to hold the ball on the perimeter. Hagler was a terrible shooter, so Russell stayed in the lane. For over eight minutes, Hagler held the ball. The crowd hooted. Hagler looked forlorn. Jones and Boldt talked to their Cal counterparts. Hal Perry shadowboxed, trying to stay loose. Gene Brown sat at midcourt, waiting to check in, for a seeming eternity. Finally, with six minutes left, Newell called time-out, sent in a substitute, and tried a shot. It missed. The Dons won the grim affair, 33–24.[46]

The Berkeley game provoked unease about the state of basketball. Woolpert and some reporters defended Newell, but fans called his freeze tactics "cowardly" and "un-American." The game also revisited concerns about the dominance of big men. "Saturday night's farce at Berkeley was caused by Bill Russell," claimed one fan. Newell stalled the game only to neutralize Russell, whose height, timing, and ability were overturning protocol. "Already, by his antics at Kansas City last year, he forced the rules committee to approve the 12-foot lane." Further rules would have to neutralize future Russells, such as a shot clock and a ban on "offensive goaltending."[47]

The Dons now faced the meat of their conference schedule, and they chewed up the CBA. San José State, Loyola, College of the Pacific, Fresno State, Santa Clara, Pepperdine, and St. Mary's all fell before USF, some of them twice. No games were even close, even though Woolpert refused to run up the score. At Pepperdine on March 2, USF led 23–0 midway through the first half. "We were a great team," Russell recalled, "but once we got this terrible 'unbeatable' monster idea loose, all we had to do a lot of times was show up at the gym and we had the game won." The wins fed the swelling enthusiasm for basketball in northern California. USF booked more dates in the Cow Palace, and some opponents moved games to larger venues. The Cow Palace set an attendance record of 14,297 for a January 31 dismantling of San José State, and it topped the record when 15,732 customers watched a March 6 win over St. Mary's.[48]

As the streak persisted, basketball historians unearthed new challenges. Seton Hall and Long Island University had each won four games against alumni teams and junior colleges during their strings, so some claimed that the record was forty-three wins. USF bested that mark against Fresno State on February 10. Then someone dug up that Kansas State Teachers College of Pittsburg won forty-seven straight games from 1929 to 1932. USF surpassed that record on February 28 against the College of the Pacific. Then it surfaced that Peru State Teachers College in Nebraska won fifty-five consecutive games from 1922 to 1926. To match that unofficial mark, the Dons needed to win another NCAA championship.[49]

USF entered the tournament with impeccable credentials. Deemed a first team All-American by every major media outlet, Russell had averaged 20.5 points and twenty-one rebounds a game. Woolpert again won United Press Coach of the Year. The team was 25–0. They had overcome doubts about their weak conference schedule, and some already proclaimed them the best team in college basketball history.[50]

But a specter had hung over the Dons all season: they would defend the championship without K. C. Jones. Although the CBA had granted Jones an extra year of eligibility, the NCAA had declared him ineligible for its postseason tournament. "USF's hopes of putting a second national title back to back just about flew out the window yesterday," mourned the *Foghorn* after the ruling. At its annual meeting in December 1955, the governing board had stubbornly refused to hear Jones's appeal. Although USF could have instead entered the NIT, that tournament now attracted second-tier teams. The Dons' decision reflected the NCAA's successful power grab after the gambling scandals.[51]

Could they win without Jones? His reputation had soared during the streak. A first-team UP and second-team AP All-American, the floor general and defensive spark plug earned respect for his quiet determination, level head, and friendly demeanor. He played his last game against St. Mary's at the Cow Palace. When he left the game, the crowd stood and cheered for three minutes. His teammates showered him with handshakes and thanks. Jones had kindled the team's defensive press and offensive production. Now he served as an informal assistant coach. "No man will miss K. C. during the tournament as much as I will," said Russell. They had formed a powerful partnership based on their common histories, cerebral approaches, and complementary playing styles. For this final act, Russell stood alone at center stage.[52]

. . .

Accompanied by 250 fans, the Dons rode an overnight train to Corvallis, Oregon, to begin their NCAA title defense. Pessimists worried that USF needed Jones's superlative all-around skills. Optimists pointed to Russell's game-altering defensive impact. The players said that his replacement, talented sophomore Eugene Brown, only needed confidence. Reporters asked how he felt about filling Jones's shoes. "Scared," Brown replied.[53]

USF opened against UCLA, the last team to beat the Dons. Led by Willie Naulls, the Bruins averaged eighty-three points a game. Some neutral coaches believed that UCLA would crush a Jones-less USF team. They were wrong. USF absolutely stifled UCLA. "A strong wind couldn't have penetrated the Dons' defensive net through the opening minutes," reported the *San Francisco Chronicle*. USF established a twenty-point lead and coasted to a 72–61 win.[54]

USF next faced Utah, another fast-breaking team. This game provided a sterner test, as Russell accumulated three fouls with four minutes left in the first half. Without K. C. Jones and fearful of fouling out, Russell "walked on eggs the rest of the way," allowing Utah to maintain a breakneck pace. More than any previous game, the Dons relied on offensive firepower. They finally pulled away with about ten minutes left and won 93–77, the most points they had scored or allowed all season. Russell netted fifty points in two games, winning the regional's MVP award. Eugene Brown joined him on the All-Tourney team.[55]

Heading to the NCAA Finals in Evanston, Illinois, Woolpert's anxieties again bubbled. He had never scouted Southern Methodist University, which boasted a nineteen-game winning streak and sweet-shooting center Jim Krebs. Russell had sprained a finger, and Brown suffered from an upset stomach and painful foot blisters. But SMU never stood a chance. After twelve minutes USF led by twenty points, and Woolpert substituted freely throughout the 86–68 victory. Afterward, Russell seemed almost solemn, disappointed with his seventeen-point, twenty-three-rebound performance amidst constant double teams. Mike Farmer had picked up

the scoring slack, finishing with twenty-six points. "San Francisco can beat any basketball team I know of," said SMU coach Doc Hayes. "San Francisco can beat the
Russians."[56]

The next morning, before their final showdown against Iowa, Russell slept until 11:00. He walked downstairs to pick up a good-luck telegram from Rose Swisher.
Then he and his teammates lounged around the hotel, joking and laughing. Excited USF fans chatted with them as they boarded the bus, and on the ride to Mc-
Gaw Memorial Hall they belted out songs to a rock-and-roll beat, changing the lyrics
to tease their trainer. Even in the locker room, they jabbered and giggled until game
time. A relaxed attitude had served them well throughout the streak, but Woolpert's
stomach tied into ever-tighter knots. He feared overconfidence.[57]

Those fears seemed realized in the opening minutes, when Iowa grabbed a 15–
4 lead. The Hawkeyes scored on fast breaks and back-door cuts as their lone black
player, the versatile forward Carl "Sugar" Cain, amassed ten quick points on fake-
right, go-left dribble drives. Thousands of fans from neighboring Iowa whipped
into a frenzy. USF clearly missed K. C. Jones, and the new unpaid assistant coach
fumed. "You guys have the fat head," he lectured during a time-out. "You're choking, really swallowing the olive. You lose this one and the winning string you're
gloating about won't mean a thing." The Dons broke the huddle with a clap. They
had overcome deficits before, but the streak and championship lent extra pressure.
"Nervous? No, I wasn't nervous," Russell later said. "I was just flat scared."[58]

Yet one final time, Russell and the Dons submitted a bravura performance. They
clamped down defensively. Eugene Brown shifted to forward and shut down Carl
Cain. Warren Baxter took his guard spot, putting four blacks on the floor in the
NCAA Final. Six minutes before halftime, USF regained the lead. The Dons forced
turnovers throughout the second half. During one possession, Russell blocked a
shot, blocked another, and scared a Hawkeye into a wild miss. Iowa shot only 33
percent, and Russell finished with twenty-six points and twenty-seven rebounds.
Time and again, he received the ball on the right wing and swept across the court
for a left-handed hook. He also scored three baskets with his patented "steer" shot,
guiding in errant shots above the rim. When the final buzzer sounded on the 83–
71 victory, USF owned a fifty-five-game winning streak and two consecutive
NCAA titles. "This," marveled the *San Francisco Chronicle*, "must be the finest un-
dergraduate team since Naismith first hung the peach basket."

Woolpert had withheld that highest praise during the season, but now he
agreed with the assessment. "The difference—without a doubt—was Russell."[59]

· · ·

The Rules Committee again saw Bill Russell firsthand, and it approved more "Russell Rules." During free throws, two defensive players now occupied the inside positions, instead of one player from each team. Also, players could not enter the lane

until the foul shot hit the rim or backboard. These rules curtailed offensive rebounds, decreasing the reward for missed shots. Most dramatically, the Rules Committee banned "offensive goaltending," a direct result of Russell's steer shot. The best basketball teams had long depended on cuts, screens, and ball movement. USF had instead relied on speed and quickness, height and agility, defense and rebounds. Russell augured the sport's future. The legends had begun circulating about Wilt Chamberlain, a seven-foot freshman at the University of Kansas. ("Twelve-foot baskets?" KU coach Phog Allen now grinned to *Time*. "What are you talking about? I've developed amnesia.")[60]

Russell observed the rules changes with bemusement, as his college career had ended. But a disappointment festered: after winning MVP in six consecutive tournaments, he lost the NCAA tournament's honor to Hal "King" Lear of Temple, a 5'10" guard who had scored forty-eight points in the consolation game. Russell handled it diplomatically: "It's all part of the game," he shrugged to reporters. But in private—even after two national titles, two awards for national player of the year from the Helms Athletic Foundation, and buckets of praise from sportswriters—he remained excruciatingly sensitive to any perceived disrespect. He stored away his pain, motivating himself for future victories.[61]

Those victories included the annual Shrine Game, a charity match just days after the NCAA final. As two thousand fans greeted the other Dons at San Francisco International Airport, Russell, Jones, and Woolpert flew to the All-Star Game in Kansas City. Russell scored a game-high eighteen points and led the West All-Stars to a 74–62 win over the East, once again besting Tom Heinsohn. Russell and Jones then returned to Madison Square Garden for the East-West College All-Star Game. Russell again led all scorers with nineteen points, and the West won 103–72. Besides demonstrating the firepower of Russell and West Coast basketball, the games illustrated the emergence of African American stars in college basketball: Russell, Jones, Cain, Lear, Willie Naulls of UCLA, Sihugo Green of Duquesne, and Julius McCoy of Michigan State. The black press celebrated this new fame. It lauded the athletes as role models for black youth, illustrations of black achievement on a level playing field.[62]

Meanwhile, *Newsweek* noted how just five years after the 1951 scandals, fans were embracing college basketball with unprecedented gusto. Attendance records toppled from California to Chicago, North Carolina to New York. USF had presented the most compelling story of those years. The Dons were the fulcrum upon which college basketball pivoted—they made the sport faster, more vertical, more athletic, more dynamic, more black. No African Americans made the *Look* All-American team until 1952, and by 1958 four of the five All-Stars were black. USF injected "Negro basketball" into the sport's traditions.[63]

As another triumphant motorcade rolled down Market Street, led by fire trucks with sirens wailing, the citizens of San Francisco cheered the phoenix emerging from the ashes of the gambling scandals. Possessors of a fifty-five-game winning streak and two national titles, pioneers of their sport's cultural revolution, they boasted the greatest team in the history of college basketball.

The ensuing reception at City Hall raised money for a gymnasium on the USF campus. A fifty-eight-person committee had initiated an eighteen-day fund-raising drive during the 1955 title run. The campaign had rallied the community around the "Homeless Dons," revealing the civic benefits of athletic success. But it raised only half the required amount. The committee filed an extension, and as the Dons rewrote the record book, the donations streamed in. After another championship, the committee raised more than $700,000. In December 1956 the University of San Francisco broke ground on an eight-thousand-seat on-campus arena named War Memorial Gymnasium.[64]

It could have been called the House That Russell Built.

4

The Amateur

The summer before his senior year, Russell received an invitation from Dwight Eisenhower. The president asked him to a luncheon with a galaxy of sports stars, including Willie Mays, Gene Tunney, Hank Greenberg, and Bob Cousy. In July 1955 the athletes—selected to represent various sports, different racial and ethnic groups, and both professionals and amateurs—heard a presentation about the deficient physical fitness of American youth. The ceremony suggested the cold war implications of sports. Eisenhower bemoaned a "very serious" crisis: children who shunned athletics might become juvenile delinquents, and the military rejected the physically unfit. The president suggested that sports incubated democratic values. Then he shook hands with the athletes. "You all look bigger on television," said Ike, "all but Mr. Russell."[1]

The media later reported that Eisenhower urged Russell to participate in the 1956 Olympic Games at Melbourne. "I promise, Mr. President," Russell supposedly responded, "that I won't do anything to hurt my amateur standing. I'll be on that Olympic team if I can make it." Indeed, the Olympics had long enchanted Russell. He loved the creed of competition for its own sake, and he had always wanted to attend the international sports festival, even as a spectator. Representing his country in Melbourne would fulfill a childhood dream.[2]

But that conversation never happened. Russell just listened to Eisenhower's presentation like everyone else, and he performed the usual rituals associated with presidential luncheons. The legend of his Olympic promise, which originated a year later, illustrated popular notions about amateurism, patriotism, and the democratic function of sports. In the aftermath of his college career, Russell passed through this thicket of myths.[3]

. . .

"Being an amateur is like being a virgin," Russell later reflected. "It is an old idea that has some innocence and charm, celebrated mostly by people to whom it doesn't apply. It doesn't look as good on old people as on young ones. It is impossible to keep partially, though many try to do so. It is associated with deception and pretense. And even if you love the idea, you still can't help being suspicious when you see the pious members of the U.S. Chastity Committee charging the public money to peep at their soiled virgins." Approaching the Olympics with exuberant innocence, Russell maintained that ideal through his time in Melbourne. But his amateur experiences birthed this cynicism.[4]

Selection for the Olympic basketball team revolved around politics and power. The Amateur Athletic Union (AAU) blacklisted teams outside its organizational umbrella, and it established domain over various amateur groups, including industrial basketball leagues. Companies such as Phillips, Caterpillar, and Goodyear hired college basketball stars for lucrative full-time jobs, with basketball their primary duty. These teams provided valuable company advertising. The National Industrial Basketball League (NIBL) recruited prime "amateur" talent into the postwar years, including Oklahoma A&M center Bob Kurland, a giant rival to George Mikan, who joined the Phillips 66ers.[5]

As the NCAA established control of college basketball, the AAU governed much of American participation in international sports. In April 1956, the national AAU champion Buchan Bakers, the AAU runner-up Phillips 66ers, and the Armed Forces All-Stars attended a tournament in Kansas City, vying for the highest proportional representation on the Olympic squad. In past Olympiads the NCAA and NIT champions had joined this tournament, but the Melbourne Olympics would be held in November, during college basketball season. So the colleges sent a fourteen-man squad of senior All-Stars that included Russell, K. C. Jones, Willie Naulls, Carl Cain, and Hal Lear.[6]

Russell's College All-Stars beat the Buchan Bakers and Armed Forces, but on the final day the Phillips 66ers edged them 79–75, winning the round-robin tournament on a tiebreaker. Five players from Phillips went to Melbourne, as did three from the Armed Forces and one from the Bakers. Russell led the tournament in scoring and rebounding, and he made the Olympic team along with K. C. Jones and Carl Cain. But his team lost for the first time since December 1954. He suspected that officials rigged the final contests for the AAU teams.[7]

That spring Russell witnessed more hypocrisy, as AAU officials offered him exorbitant appearance fees for amateur track and field meets. He had rejoined the USF track team after a two-year layoff. He had become a world-class high jumper. He never went to track practice, and in his bastardized version of the "Western Roll," he kicked his bent legs sideways, stretched out his arms, and sailed face-first over the bar. Despite a sore heel, he routinely jumped 6'8", and at the Fresno Relays he jumped 6'9¼". On his third try he almost cleared seven feet—on the way down, his ankle nudged the bar off the standards.[8]

Yet Russell retired from track after a June 5 meet in Stockton. He never jumped at the Olympic trials, when Charlie Dumas first surpassed the seven-foot barrier. With his basketball spot already won, he resisted taking a spot from another high-jumper, and schedule conflicts in Melbourne might have prevented him from competing in both sports. Anyway, track and field was a lark. He drove to meets in his 1941 Packard, often ferrying along Johnny Mathis. He arrived in a golf cap, letter jacket, sunglasses, and elongated woolen scarf. He chatted up his opponents, and he carried himself with a swagger. At one meet with thirty-four contestants, he insisted that they set the bar at 6'4" instead of 5'8". Unlike his experience with basketball, he never got nervous, never vomited beforehand, never invested meaning in this individual sport.[9]

His goofy jumping style nevertheless exposed his sensitivity to criticism. He received some hurtful letters. "One guy wrote me that I was turning out to be just as bad at high jumping as I was bad at basketball," recalled Russell, descending into gloom. "Another told me I jumped like a goat." Such cruelties still stabbed him like a hot poker.[10]

In any case, Russell was in Latin America during the Olympic trials. The State Department had sponsored a tour for his USF squad. This trip, like hundreds of other government excursions, was supposed to demonstrate American achievement, foster international goodwill, and champion the democratic, capitalistic system of the United States—especially since its communist enemies trumpeted the United States' lack of racial equality. The issue had assumed greater visibility with the stirrings of a national civil rights movement, evidenced by the 1954 *Brown v. Board of Education* decision, the outcry over the 1955 murder of fourteen-year-old Emmett Till, and the ongoing Montgomery Bus Boycott led by Martin Luther King Jr. So the State Department showcased black athletes. Willie Mays, Althea Gibson, and Jesse Owens had all participated in these international tours. The racially integrated USF team seemed ideal emissaries of American democracy.[11]

The NCAA barred undergraduates from participating, so Phil Woolpert took a team of recent USF graduates, augmented by UCLA's Willie Naulls. They marveled at the Panama Canal, and they shuddered at the widespread poverty. In about thirty games from San Salvador to Caracas to Santiago to Buenos Aires, they played to large and enthusiastic crowds. The Dons won every game, despite some comically corrupt officiating. In Bogota they won only 30–22, but that game occurred at midnight, in an open-air bullfight arena, during a rainstorm.[12]

The Dons visited Latin American dignitaries, performed interviews on local television, and demonstrated sportsmanship. American officials reported that they "exemplified true democratic principles applied to the field of sports" and made "great quantities of friends for the United States." Fans and reporters gravitated to the black athletes. The Public Affairs Officer in Ecuador noted that the team's camaraderie was "worth more than hundreds of thousands of printed words" on race relations in the United States, and another embassy dispatch described how Latin Americans "saw for themselves how Americans, Caucasian and Negro, can live and travel together." To the State Department's delight, the tour contrasted with a recent visit to Brazil by the Soviet Union's basketball team, who alienated the locals with rude behavior and mediocre performances.[13]

Russell hit the road again in October, this time with the Olympic squad. After training camp at an air force base in Peru, Indiana, the team embarked on a month-long, cross-country fund-raising tour. It swept ten games against AAU and college All-Star teams. The Olympic Committee, meanwhile, pleaded for contributions to counter the state-sponsored teams of foreign regimes. Russell later complained that the money only benefited the officials and cronies of amateur organizations.[14]

The Olympic Committee instructed the players to avoid disparaging remarks about the United States. "Then," Russell recalled, "they proceeded to place us in situation after situation where we were segregated or embarrassed." In Dallas, the black players faced Jim Crow in hotels, restaurants, and even elevators. The situation enraged Russell, who considered boycotting the exhibition. Though he showed enthusiastic team spirit, never complained when coming off the bench, and even played with a hernia, Russell described this second-class citizenship as "another scar, another slice."[15]

Russell then got enmeshed in a controversy with International Olympic Committee president Avery Brundage. An American millionaire obsessed with the European aristocracy, Brundage crammed antique ideals into modern sports. The amateur concept—playing sport for its own sake, not material gain—arose among the elite in Victorian England. It should have stayed there. Now the NCAA, AAU, and IOC harvested the fruits of the athletes' labors, and Brundage built the Olympic movement on self-serving definitions of amateurism. Olympic athletes from communist nations got paid by their governments. AAU players got paid by their employers. But athletes like Russell got held to different standards. In August 1956, Brundage insisted that Olympians pledge to remain amateurs *after* the Melbourne games.[16]

In Russell's case, that was silly. Every sports fan in America knew that he would play professional basketball. Russell willingly delayed a professional career, but he refused Brundage's oath on principle, neither surrendering his future nor lying to the public. One columnist imagined a farcical Russell response to the professionals: "How dare you have the effrontery to offer me $50,000 to play basketball? As you well know, I promised Avery Brundage I would not permit the Russell escutcheon to be smirched by the taint of professionalism. Besides, I like working down here in the sewer." He may have embraced the powerful mythology of athletes and democracy, but even before arriving in Melbourne, Russell witnessed its hypocrisies.[17]

· · ·

Avery Brundage insisted that the Olympics transcend politics. He believed that they showcase competition among individuals, not governments. Yet the Olympics rest on a paradox. The spectacle compels international fascination because the athletes compete for international bragging rights, trading on myths of national character. The Olympics and politics are thus inherently intertwined.[18]

The prelude to the Melbourne Olympics demonstrated the political consequences of international sport. Lebanon and Iraq boycotted in protest after Israel, · Great Britain, and France invaded Egypt. Communist China boycotted after the IOC invited Nationalist China. Just weeks before the Games, the Soviet army crushed an incipient rebellion in Hungary, killing 40,000 freedom fighters and displacing 150,000 refugees. Spain, Switzerland, and the Netherlands objected by boycotting the Olympics. The IOC, however, truckled before the Soviets. "Every civilized person recoils in horror at the savage slaughter in Hungary," Brundage said. "But that is no reason for destroying the nucleus of international cooperation."[19]

In Melbourne, crowds jeered the Soviets and cheered the Hungarians. A water polo match ended early after a Russian head-butted a Hungarian, staining the pool with blood. American politicians and reporters obsessed over winning more medals than the Soviets; Senator John Marshall Butler fulminated that communists would use "the spirit of sportsmanship itself as a velvet-gloved iron fist to ruthlessly hammer out their godless propaganda." Other Americans criticized the regimented training system of the "Russian machine." "It's like taking a man apart on a scientific basis and putting him back together again," said one American athlete. "We would never allow ourselves to be subjected to anything like that." American gold medals reflected the virtues of American freedom.[20]

That notion bore particular resonance for black Olympians. African Americans had participated in track and field since the 1904 St. Louis Games. When Jesse Owens won four gold medals at the 1936 "Nazi Olympics" in Berlin, it smashed the doctrine of Aryan supremacy, inspired a generation of African Americans, and fused black achievement to democratic ideals. In those same Olympics, basketball debuted. But prior to 1956, the only black members were Don Barksdale and Jack Robinson, who played on the 1948 team.[21]

Now Russell, Jones, and Cain represented the United States—though not without complications. Walking through downtown Melbourne, they noticed a crowd hovering behind them. "They must be Zulus from Africa!" whispered some enthralled Aussies. Russell played along, spouting the stereotypical gibberish of

"Africans" in Tarzan movies. This young man under the spell of Olympic benevo-
lence could laugh off the crowd's ignorance. To participate in the Olympics was to
lay claim to the American dream, to the full fruit of democratic hope.[22]

Indeed, Russell reveled in the pageantry, patriotism, and goodwill of Melbourne.
He got chills during the elaborate opening ceremonies before 102,000 spectators
at the Melbourne Cricket Ground. "When they light that Olympic torch," he said,
raising his hand in demonstration, "it's like lighting a fire in our hearts." Australia
hosted a feisty, well-organized exhibition. Despite the various diplomatic crises,
some cold war frost had thawed. In between Olympiads, Josef Stalin had died, Joe
McCarthy's anticommunist hysteria had been discredited, and Dwight Eisenhower and Nikita Khruschev had opened talks at the Geneva Convention. The
Olympics remained what George Orwell called "war minus the shooting," but
Brundage's cooperative ideals wafted through Melbourne.[23]

In this context, Russell possessed a potent symbolism. At the 1952 Olympics in
Helsinki, Finland, the communist nations had established their own camp—an
Olympic Village with an Iron Curtain. Now all the athletes stayed together in an
elaborate, state-of-the-art housing facility, creating a friendly ethnic hodgepodge.
They talked, joked, flirted, and played Ping-Pong. The thirty-six African American
athletes—all from track and field, boxing, and basketball—received warm welcomes.
Russell loved it. "It was one of the biggest thrills of my life," he recalled. "We all
mingled together, even the Russians." Belying their stone-faced reputations, the
Soviets gravitated toward the Americans. One Russian with a permanent goofy grin
kept reaching his hand far above his head, illustrating Russell's height.[24]

The United States had never lost an Olympic game, and it was the overwhelming favorite in Melbourne. Basketball had spread to Asia and Europe through mis-
sionaries and the armed forces, but the Americans' first opponent, Japan, had only
one player over six feet. The United States had only one player under six feet. In
thirteen minutes of action, Russell scored twenty points and held Japan to three.
The Americans won 98–40. The next two preliminary round-robin games offered
similarly comical contrasts of height and ability. Thailand's tallest man stood 5'9".
The United States won 101–29 and then beat the Philippines 121–53, setting a one-
game Olympic point record.[25]

"Russell was really something then, full of pride and satisfaction," recalled assistant coach Bruce Drake. "He couldn't do enough for that team." His teammates
remembered him as laughing, cracking jokes, and reveling in the Olympic experience. He cheered from the bench, and he energized his squad upon entering the
game. He watched over sixteen-year-old sprinter Wilma Rudolph like a friendly
big brother. The *New York Times* reported how he charmed everyone "with his clev-
erness and likeable qualities." His shotblocking inspired awe. When he dunked,
the crowd howled with glee.[26]

The Americans' style revolved around Russell: they pressed and gambled for steals, since Russell neutralized drives to the basket. In the opening game of the quarterfinal round robin, an 85–44 win over Bulgaria, Russell converted a lob pass with a tip-in dunk. The Singaporean referee disallowed the basket, contending that Russell illegally touched the ball on the rim. At halftime coach Gerald Tucker protested, explaining the structure and timing of a dunk. Only then did officials rule it legal. The maneuver exemplified the dynamic American style and how Russell was rocking the international scene.[27]

The United States then topped Brazil 113–51, setting up a ballyhooed match against the USSR, which possessed the best chance of conquering the Americans, given its athlete pool and state-sponsored sports programs. The Soviets had first entered the Olympics in 1952, as Stalin realized the propaganda value of international sports. Training athletes in the entire range of Olympic sports, the Soviets almost won the overall medal count in Helsinki. "Each new victory is a victory for the Soviet form of society," proclaimed one official. "It provides irrefutable proof of the superiority of socialist culture over the decaying culture of the capitalist states."[28]

Soon after organizing a national basketball team in 1947, the Soviets dominated European competition, and in 1952 they earned an Olympic silver medal. Upon facing huge American centers Bob Kurland and Clyde Lovellette, the USSR's Sports Committee issued a nationwide call for tall players. By 1956 the organization had unearthed a 360-pound lumberjack named Jan Kruminsh. He generated much rumor and speculation—over his height, reported from 7'2" to 7'8", and his name, which reporters spelled Yanis Kruminsh, Yan Krouminch, Ivan Krumminch, and Ian Krouminch. He never touched a basketball until age twenty-four and was nursing a sore foot, but his mystique permeated the impending showdown against the United States.[29]

The Americans won before the game started. Rather than begin their own stretching and shooting routines, the Soviets stared across the court. Some snapped photographs. When Russell slammed the ball, the crowd oohed and aahed, and so did the Soviets. A few tried mimicking the dunk. Kruminsh clambered toward the hoop and rose about three inches. The ball squirmed off the rim. Then the game began, and one Russian accumulated three quick fouls. "He wants to get out," surmised Tucker, "so he can take some more pictures of Bill Russell."[30]

The full-court pressing, fast-breaking, jump-shooting, shot-blocking, Russell-dunking United States won 85–55. Their flair, creativity, and adaptability fed the team's overall strength. "It showed the rest of the world just how America lives," said Tucker. That democratic approach contrasted to the deliberate patterns of the Soviet Union. There were no Russian Russells. Kruminsh, reported the wire services, "is poorly coordinated and possesses nothing resembling the agility, brains or talent of Russell." Russell scored twenty points, and "it was almost impossible to shoot past him." This product of Jim Crow Louisiana and an Oakland ghetto had become basketball's foremost representative of the American system.[31]

The Yankees stampeded through the medal round. The United States beat Uruguay 101–38 in the semifinal. In the other bracket, Kruminsh muscled in twenty-seven points, and the USSR beat France. But the Soviets basically conceded the gold medal. They had watched with dropped jaws when the United States crushed Uruguay. When the Americans gave them new sneakers as pregame gifts, the Soviets seemed satisfied with their Olympic experience.[32]

The United States owned too many scorers, too much speed, too suffocating a defense, too much Russell. The Americans led 16–2 within minutes and 56–27 at halftime. Kruminsh never scored a field goal. The USSR stalled rather than concede 100 points, and the United States won 89–55. The Soviets converged upon Russell, congratulating him with warm embraces. "My proudest moment," he proclaimed upon winning the gold medal.[33]

Just as the Soviet Union had recruited behemoths after facing Kurland and Lovellette, it soon followed the Bill Russell model, pursuing players that jumped high and ran the open floor. In time the Soviets featured more agile big men, and at the 1959 world basketball championships, they crushed a team of air force amateurs. They also looked impressive while touring against NIBL teams. African American stars remained their touchstones. When a United States team toured Moscow, the Russians asked about collegians Wilt Chamberlain and Oscar Robertson, and they mourned that Russell had turned professional.[34]

The Soviets revealed a more general sporting progress in Melbourne. The USSR won the overall medal count, leading to hysterical rationalizations from the American media. While the United States lived by the amateur code, reporters suggested, the Soviet Union created cold-blooded athletic specimens. How could honest democratic nations compete with state-sponsored sports machines? Yet as commentators read political supremacy into gold medals, the athletes embraced Avery Brundage's idealism. At the closing ceremonies on December 8, they marched into the Olympic stadium en masse, singing and laughing, establishing a tradition that celebrated peace and unity. Also, American hammer thrower Hal Connolly and Czechoslovakian discus thrower Olga Fitokova got romantically acquainted in Melbourne. They later married. For this couple, anyway, love transcended politics.[35]

Love caused Russell to miss the closing ceremonies. He was marrying Rose Swisher on December 9. "I was twenty-two, fresh from the Olympics, and didn't have the slightest idea what I was doing," he recalled. "I knew only that Rose accepted and cared for me apart from basketball, which was a great breakthrough for me." Basketball had lent him confidence, notoriety, and exhilaration. But only Rose gave him a special security, the same feeling once imparted by his mother. He loved Rose with complete, dedicated, romantic enthusiasm.[36]

Russell almost missed his own wedding. Until he raised a stink, Olympic officials had bumped him off his December 6 flight. His disillusionment with the amateur sports establishment continued. The administrators threw parties with the fund-raising money, and the Olympic committee refused to pay the doctors' bills for his hernia after he turned professional. Although Brundage rescinded his proposed clause that athletes remain amateurs after the Olympics, Russell still treaded carefully. "I have no plans at this time for a professional career," he said after the final game.[37]

Rose, his family, and reporters greeted him as he disembarked at San Francisco Airport. The homecoming hero touched Rose's hand, stared into her eyes, spun her around, and planted a theatrical kiss. He then gave her his gold medal. Two days later they married at Taylor Memorial Methodist Church. Hal Perry was best man, and eight hundred people attended the ceremony, including the entire Olympic basketball team, who served as "honorary best men." Boston Celtics owner Walter Brown also attended, hinting at Russell's future plans.[38]

At the airport a reporter had asked Russell if he had "done any business with the Boston Celtics." After a pregnant pause, Russell stared down from his elevated perch. "Man," he deadpanned, "that would be dishonest." Beneath that crack lay a sage awareness of his career decision and its political implications.[39]

. . .

Russell's first professional offer had come from Abe Saperstein of the Harlem Globetrotters. A 5'3" pumpkin in a rumpled suit with flood-level pants, Saperstein had seized control of the all-black, small-town barnstormers by 1930. By the mid-1950s his Globetrotters had three units touring the United States, Europe, South America, Asia, and the Middle East. They had battled college All-Stars and the Minneapolis Lakers in ballyhooed exhibitions. They had played in dilapidated haylofts and Berlin's Olympic Stadium, where seventy-five thousand fans cheered them. They had met Pope Pius XII in the Vatican, performing their "Magic Circle" routine while whistling "Sweet Georgia Brown." This premier outlet for black talent was also the most popular basketball team in the world.[40]

Yet the Globetrotters won popularity as clowning showmen, not steely competitors. They sank trick shots and pulled madcap stunts, such as when someone fainted until a teammate waved a sweaty sneaker by his nose, causing him to spring up and cakewalk across the court. Such gags reinforced black stereotypes—basketball's version of the lazy, bug-eyed "coons" and "darkies" played by Stepin Fetchit in the movies. White audiences embraced the comforting caricature of a black athlete with natural talent but no real competitive drive. Saperstein encouraged this comic sensibility, and he manipulated his players to curb their egos. He also warned them to uphold racial taboos. Never contradict white men, he told them. Never drive a Cadillac. Never get caught with white women.[41]

Saperstein started courting Russell in 1954, when he invited the USF center to sit on the Globetrotters' bench at the Cow Palace. A local newspaper reported that Russell "nearly convulsed with laughter on several occasions." Saperstein began actual negotiations in December 1955, during the DePaul Invitational in Chicago. Bolstered by his soaring reputation, Russell believed that Saperstein would offer a huge contract.[42]

Instead, Saperstein's patronizing attitude repelled him. When Russell arrived at his office, Saperstein pulled out pornographic photographs. "If you sign with the Globetrotters," he said, "you can have all this and more." Russell recoiled, disgusted by the implication of black hypersexuality. Then Saperstein lauded the "social advantages" of playing with the Globetrotters. Now Russell scoffed. He knew his principles and his history. He understood image politics from the recent media attention, and he listened when Hal Perry had criticized the Globetrotters. He possessed no inclination to play the shuffling Negro. He might laugh and joke, but he was no clown.[43]

That evening, Saperstein came to his hotel. He suggested Russell bring his coaches, so they could negotiate on the "up and up." Then Saperstein spoke only to Phil Woolpert, while assistant Harry Hannin joked with Russell and Ross Giudice. Russell got insulted. He interpreted Saperstein's approach: "As one Great White Father to Another Great White Father this is what we'll do for this poor dumb Negro boy." Moreover, Saperstein offered just $15,000, and he moved to only $17,000. That figure trumped most NBA salaries, but the Globetrotters traveled three hundred nights a year. Russell kept his options open. "I hold some things more important than money," he said. "Of course, if the Trotters offered me a fantastic deal, I'd sign."[44]

Russell's price rose as USF won its second national championship. Former Globetrotters Marques Haynes and Goose Tatum now co-owned the Harlem Magicians, a competitor to Saperstein's squad. In March 1956, they promised to top any offer for Russell, proposing a package deal of Russell, Willie Naulls, and Morrie Taft for $100,000. Now Saperstein responded. Since Haynes and Tatum had quit the Globetrotters, he had lacked a superstar drawing card. Saperstein suggested a contract between $20,000 and $25,000.[45]

At the end of April, the Boston Celtics drafted Russell. In the ensuing thirteen years, Russell and the Celtics would forge the sport's greatest dynasty, pioneer the NBA's commercial and cultural emergence, and suggest powerful models of racial integration and the modern black athlete. But the pairing depended on lucky twists, backroom deals, and battling visions of the future. The story—slathered in revisionist boasts and justifications—begins with the retirement of Russell's boyhood hero, George Mikan.

The Minneapolis dynasty had ended with Mikan's 1954 departure. In the spring of 1955, Lakers executive Sid Hartman offered star forward Vern Mikkelson for three players drafted by the Celtics: Cliff Hagan, Frank Ramsey, and Lou Tsioropoulos. Since all three were serving in the armed forces, Minneapolis-minus-

Mikkelson would probably have finished last, drafted first, and rebuilt the squad around Russell. According to Hartman, the Celtics agreed to the deal, but the Lakers ownership nixed it. Starring Mikkelson, Minneapolis finished second in the Western Division. The Rochester Royals finished last instead.[46]

Before the 1956 draft, Rochester owner Lester Harrison met with Russell. Harrison had built a civic institution, but as big-market teams paid for college stars, the Royals struggled to compete. Losing an average of $20,000 a year, he could not afford big risks. He feared that Russell would sign with the Globetrotters. He worried that Russell would miss the early season while at the Olympics. And he had seen Russell just once, at the East-West College All-Star Game in Madison Square Garden. "One New York sportswriter did an article saying the guy would be lucky to make the league," Harrison recounted, "and I was supposed to make him the No. 1 pick?" For his part, Russell dreaded winters in snowy, gray, industrial Rochester. Harrison offended his intelligence, moreover, by bringing along his former player Dolly King, who was black. So Russell demanded $25,000, a salary commanded by only Mikan and Bob Cousy.[47]

As the scuttlebutt swirled that Rochester could not afford Russell, the New York Knicks offered Walter Dukes and $15,000 for the first draft pick. Some likened the two tall black centers, a comparison rooted in ignorance: the mediocre Dukes possessed none of Russell's athleticism or drive. Harrison nevertheless agreed to the trade. Then Knicks owner Ned Irish caught wind, and he balked. Irish had erected an entertainment empire through Madison Square Garden; he ran the Knicks as an afterthought. Russell was an expensive, uncertain drawing card. Irish would part with Dukes, but not $15,000. "Tell them to shove it," he said.[48]

Despite his accomplishments, Russell remained a curiosity among NBA types. Based in the East and Midwest, they saw few of his games. Accustomed to skilled offensive stars, they ignored his defensive impact. Judging centers by the Mikan standard, they shortchanged his athleticism. They failed, finally, to grasp a future dominated by black superstars. Maybe Russell would end up a Globetrotter, maybe another Walter Dukes. Who knew?

Others stored doubts. Arnold "Red" Auerbach envisioned possibilities.

· · ·

Auerbach, in some respects, embodied basketball's past. The son of a Jewish immigrant dry cleaner, he grew up in Brooklyn. His neighborhood of Williamsburg was an ethnic stew of Irish, Poles, Jews, Italians, and blacks. Hyman Auerbach considered sports a waste of time, but in those concrete-infested blocks near the East River, his son discovered the perfect outlet for his savvy, competitive nature. The school president, solid student, and second-team All-Brooklyn point guard spent a year at Seth Low Junior College before winning a basketball scholarship to George Washington University in 1936. There he found a mentor in coach Bill Reinhart, who ran efficient practices, emphasized discipline, and taught fast-break tactics.[49]

Auerbach applied Reinhart's vision on a grander scale, shaping basketball's future. After teaching and coaching in high schools, Auerbach got stationed at a naval base in Norfolk, Virginia, during World War Two. As chief petty officer in charge of recreation, he organized countless sports tournaments. He further absorbed the cross-fertilization of basketball styles, watching ballhandlers from the Northeast, runners from the Midwest, jump shooters from the South, rebounders from the West. He assembled a team that won two of three from the all-black Washington Bears. When the Basketball Association of America (BAA) formed in 1946, he convinced Washington Capitols owner Mike Uline to hire him as coach. Only twenty-eight years old, he came cheap, a self-described "punk kid competing against proven coaches."[50]

A pugnacious proponent of fast breaks and referee baiting, Auerbach went 115–53 in three seasons with Washington. He never won the title, however, and Uline replaced him with a cheaper player-coach. By then the BAA had absorbed the remnants of its rival, the National Basketball League (NBL), and renamed itself the National Basketball Association. In 1949, Ben Kerner hired Auerbach to coach the Tri-Cities Blackhawks, an NBL holdover representing Moline, Illinois; Rock Island, Illinois; and Davenport, Iowa. When Kerner traded players without his consent, Auerbach quit. Still a relative greenhorn, he exhibited a gritty independent streak rooted in confidence and competitiveness.[51]

In 1950 Auerbach became coach of the Boston Celtics. In six years the Celtics went 241–181, scored the most points in the NBA, and played an entertaining style built around the All-Star backcourt of Bob Cousy and Bill Sharman. Meanwhile, Auerbach feuded with coaches, referees, and reporters. He scoffed at overhyped college stars. He employed forward Bob Brannum as a bruising enforcer. His coaching manual, published in 1953, included a section that advocated grabbing an opponent's shirt, inciting the home crowd, jockeying from the bench, faking fouls, staying extra-long in the huddle, delaying the halftime break, and manipulating the schedule.[52]

But Boston never sniffed an NBA championship. For all their skill, the Celtics lacked defensive and rebounding toughness. In the 1955–56 season they scored an NBA-record 106 points a game, but also allowed an NBA-record 105 points a game. In the play-offs, they bent before powerful center-forward combinations such as Harry Gallatin and Sweetwater Clifton of the New York Knicks, or Johnny Kerr and Dolph Schayes of the Syracuse Nationals. "Damn it," Auerbach grumbled after Syracuse eliminated Boston in 1956. "With the talent we've got on this ball club, if we can just come up with one big man to get us the ball, we'll win everything in sight."[53]

Auerbach coveted Russell. An informal network of former players and associates fed him scouting reports. Bill Reinhart coached against Russell at the 1954 Oklahoma City All-College Tourney. Auerbach watched Russell himself at the 1955 Holiday Festival Tournament. "Don't be a leaper, diver or jumper," his own coaching manual advocated as its first defensive principle. Russell defied those very tenets, but he provided a new athletic model for defense and rebounding. Auerbach started calling California. Phil Woolpert emphasized Russell's speed. Pete Newell lauded his rebounding. "Red, this kid can't shoot to save his ass. He can't hit the side of a barn," said retired Celtic Fred Scolari. "He's only the greatest basketball player I've ever seen."[54]

The Celtics had the seventh pick in the draft. How could they land Russell? First, Auerbach needed assurance that Russell would reject the Globetrotters. He contacted Don Barksdale. One of basketball's black pioneers, Barksdale was the first consensus All-American (UCLA, 1947), the first Olympian (London, 1948), and the first NBA All-Star (Tri-Cities, 1953). After playing with the Celtics, he retired to the Bay Area, where he befriended Russell and his father. He praised Auerbach, warned about the Globetrotters' travel, and confirmed Russell's opinion of Saperstein. Russell, according to Barksdale, "was not the kind of person you could overwhelm with a bunch of bull. He was smart, and his personality would not be right for the Globetrotters, and I told the Celtics that."[55]

Next, Boston needed confirmation that Rochester would pass on Russell. Boston owner Walter Brown called Lester Harrison. They shared professional interests— Brown owned part of the Ice Capades, for instance, and both men booked the show in their arenas. Harrison confirmed that he would draft Duquesne forward Sihugo Green, who would spend his middling nine-year career with four NBA franchises. Harrison's blunder became the stuff of legend. Auerbach later bragged that Harrison gave up Russell for a two-week Ice Capades booking. In fact, Harrison had been showcasing the Ice Capades for years. But as Russell won MVP awards and NBA titles, paranoia infected Harrison's recollections. "You ever hear about a horse race where a 3-to-5 favorite finishes last?" he said. "I was cheated out of Russell." He started claiming that Russell tanked the East-West All-Star Game to avoid getting picked by Rochester. In fact, Harrison already harbored serious doubts about Russell's talents, availability, and price.[56]

Auerbach now offered Ed Macauley for the second pick in the draft, owned by the St. Louis Hawks. Macauley embodied both the Celtics' merits and flaws. A perfect offensive complement to Cousy and Sharman, "Easy Ed" ran the floor and sank gliding hook shots—but he played center at 6"8", 185 pounds. He provided more speed and finesse, not defense and rebounding. Still, Walter Brown cleared the offer with Macauley. The owner adored the earnest, hardworking center. Macauley reciprocated that loyalty, but he and his wife grew up in St. Louis, and their infant son had just been diagnosed with spinal meningitis. He endorsed the trade to his hometown, near family and doctors.[57]

Ben Kerner owned the Hawks. Since his break with Auerbach, he had moved his franchise from Tri-Cities to Milwaukee to St. Louis, where it earned its first profit. He craved economic stability. Macauley was a hometown hero, and Russell was a risk. If he drafted Russell, Kerner would bid against the Globetrotters and wait through the Olympics. Also, St. Louis had no black players. The most southern city in the NBA had ordinances that enforced racial segregation. "In 1956, St. Louis was an antiblack city," recalled referee Norm Drucker. When black visitors played there, "all you heard was 'nigger . . . monkey . . . coon.'" Kerner feared that Russell might destroy his last chance for an NBA franchise.[58]

Kerner approved the trade—if Auerbach threw in Cliff Hagan, the star Kentucky forward then serving in the army. That ultimatum raised the stakes. "For an untested defensive specialist," Auerbach summarized, "I was offering Ben a high-scoring seven-time All-Star who would also be a natural for him at the gate. And Ben wanted the package sweetened with nothing less than the six-foot-five solid-rock Kentucky All-American, a sure-bet corner man for any NBA club." Auerbach nevertheless agreed. One final hurdle remained: the NBA barred the trading of first-round draft picks. The board of governors overrode the ban, since the swap fortified both teams.[59]

On April 30, 1956, the NBA held its draft. With its territorial pick, Boston selected Tommy Heinsohn, the Holy Cross star once humbled by Russell. The territorial draft allowed teams to draft players from colleges in a fifty-mile radius, providing local gate attractions. By drafting Heinsohn, the Celtics relinquished their seventh pick. No other team exercised its territorial option. After Rochester took Sihugo Green, Boston chose Russell. In the second round, the Celtics took K. C. Jones. From the hindsight of history, the Celtics dynasty started on that day.[60]

But would Russell even join the NBA? Professional basketball beckoned through most of 1956, as he high-jumped for USF, traveled through Latin America, toured cross-country with the Olympic team, and won the gold medal in Melbourne. As Avery Brundage insisted, he had remained an amateur.

. . .

Just before Labor Day, Walter Brown walked down Tremont Street past King's Chapel. He bumped into John B. Hynes. "Walter, do you think you can get Russell to play with the Celtics?" asked the Boston mayor. The encounter struck Brown. For years, Bostonians had paid little attention to his team. "What convinced me Boston is pro basketball-conscious was that Mayor Hynes was interested in August about our chances of landing Russell," Brown said. "That to me was positive proof the Celtics had arrived."[61]

If Red Auerbach was the franchise's brain, then Walter Brown was its heart. His father George had been general manager of Boston Arena and Boston Garden. An expansive, emotional Irishman with blue eyes and sandy hair, Walter manned every job from ticket-taker to carpenter. He inherited his father's job in 1937 and soon took over the Garden-Arena Corporation. He also directed the Boston Marathon and ran the Boston Bruins, his financial bread and butter. He filled arena dates with the Beanpot hockey tournament, track meets, the Ice Capades, boxing matches, political rallies, the rodeo, the circus, War Bond shows, Liberace concerts, Catholic masses, steel-cage wrestling, dance contests, the Shriners Ball, and a winter carnival with an indoor ski jump.[62]

Still, after World War Two, Boston Garden sat dark half the year. The arena cost $1 million a year to operate, with rising taxes and wages. Brown knew little about basketball, which had never progressed beyond barnstorming teams and scattershot regional leagues. But to fill empty dates, Brown helped start the eleven-member Basketball Association of America in June 1946. Ten of the founders owned arenas, and ten controlled professional hockey teams. Trading on his city's Irish population and the legacy of the Original Celtics, Brown named his squad and dressed them in green.[63]

The Celtics proceeded to hemorrhage money. The team went 89–151 in its first four years. Some newspapers refused to carry box scores, and attendance flagged. Brown kept faith. He took personal ownership when the Boston Garden Corporation abandoned its investment. He brought in Providence promoter Lou Pieri as partner. He hired Auerbach. A generous father figure, he indulged Cousy, Sharman, and Macauley with the league's highest payroll, all while performing charitable favors that sabotaged his bottom line. The IRS threatened to seize the team's assets. Brown sold his home and investments but kept the Celtics. Sometimes he delayed play-off bonus checks, but everyone trusted his handshake. Slowly, the team built a following. The Celtics finally pulled a profit in 1955, rewarding Brown's faith.[64]

Brown joined Auerbach in October 1956 at the University of Maryland Field House to see the Olympic team on its fund-raising tour. Bothered by his hernia, Russell looked terrible. After the game, he came to dinner at Auerbach's home in Chevy Chase with K. C. Jones and Carl Cain. Russell immediately apologized. But Auerbach and many trusted associates had already lauded his abilities. So both Brown and Auerbach told Russell to relax. In fact, his humility impressed them.[65]

Russell had to maintain his amateur standing, but they agreed that Brown would pay the richest contract ever awarded an NBA rookie: $19,500 (a salary of $22,500, prorated for two missed months). Russell signed nothing, but he asked Brown to order him a new, fully loaded Chrysler Imperial as an advance. He trusted the forthright professionals, especially after his interactions with amateur organizations. "Auerbach made a heckova more honest impression than some of the people I'd been meeting the past few years," he recalled. "I had a hunch he was more interested in people than just hunks of beef in short pants."[66]

Both sides upheld the gentleman's agreement. Russell declined an Italian team's offer of $15,000 plus expenses. In Melbourne, he played coy regarding his professional plans, leaving the media to speculate. Some assumed that he would jump at Abe Saperstein's riches. Others noted his preference for "legitimate basketball." One unfounded rumor suggested that an NBA team would pay him $40,000. Meanwhile, Walter Brown rebuffed George Mikan, now the Minneapolis general manager, who offered $10,000 just to negotiate with Russell.[67]

The morning after returning to San Francisco, Russell met Globetrotters representative Bill Miller. Still groggy, he listened to Miller's pitch. Saperstein had authorized a contract of $32,000, more than double the original offer. He would further excuse the newlywed from an impending European tour. Miller expected Russell to ponder the tempting proposal. Russell answered in five seconds. "Tell Mr. Saperstein thanks," he said, "but no dice!"[68]

Russell had one more amateur commitment. After a brief honeymoon with Rose in Carmel, he reunited with the Olympians at the Chicago Invitational Tournament on December 13. The "joyous giraffe," as one newspaper called Russell, joined his teammates in receiving congratulations from the mayor. Then, in an ironic twist, after beating Santa Clara 97–57, they met the University of San Francisco. The Dons had won their first five games, but Russell and K. C. Jones beat their former teammates, 83–52, unofficially halting the USF win streak at sixty games. (USF lost its next game to Illinois, officially ending the streak). Tournament title in hand, "the greatest amateur team ever assembled" disbanded for good.[69]

Bill and Rose Russell flew to Boston, where Walter Brown and Bill Sharman greeted them with a huge key to the city. "I have agreed to terms with Mr. Brown," Bill announced, his hand clasping Rose's. He signed a contract on December 19 in a brief ceremony at Boston Garden. The Celtics assigned him the number six for his December 22 professional debut, a nationally televised home game against the St. Louis Hawks. *Sports Illustrated* burnished the Russell myth, once again circulating the story that he had fulfilled a promise to President Eisenhower by joining the Olympic team, and then marveling at how Russell had, through dint of "sweaty, bone-wearying work" and "becoming modesty," become an athletic hero. "Basketball—in fact, all sport—is better off because of Bill Russell."[70]

Until signing his contract, Russell had subscribed to the dictates of amateurism, if not the spirit of the amateur myth. He had delayed professional basketball until fulfilling his Olympic dream. The interval had reinforced the ramifications of his career decision. When he told Saperstein "no dice," he rejected a stereotype buried in America's tortured racial history. Now the Globetrotters had to be considered first as comic entertainment, and second as legitimate basketball. Russell wanted acceptance on his own terms. "I wanted to erase that barrier," he later said. "I wanted to open up basketball so there would be no limits for the black player." He chose the NBA. Instead of sticking to past patterns, he pioneered basketball's future.[71]

5

Big League, Bush League

"These boys are real big, ain't they?" said Russell while watching the St. Louis
Hawks and Fort Wayne Pistons. "I don't mean in height. I mean in width." Before signing with the Celtics, he and Rose had attended a December 18 doubleheader at Madison Square Garden. The game was both rough and fast. While absorbing poundings, the players raced up and down the court. St. Louis scored
thirty-one points in the first quarter. "This ain't possession basketball," he said. "This
sure ain't."[1]

Russell had seen an NBA doubleheader during USF's 1955 trip to New York.
This time, however, he studied players and patterns. He kept glancing at his program, repeating players' names while absorbing their tendencies. Red Auerbach
sat nearby. Watch Mel Hutchins of the Hawks, he said. "See him block that big
man out? See him tap that ball?" asked Auerbach. Russell picked the coach's brain.
Would defenders chop his exposed arm on a hook shot? Would they undercut him
on rebounds? Auerbach assured him of the players' professional ethics, but he also
lent fervent, detailed advice on the Hawks' strengths and weaknesses. Bob Pettit
faked to set up jump shots and dribble drives. Larry Foust had no left hand or hook
shot. Charlie Share relied on bulk and power. Here was a crash course in NBA basketball, with the first exam in three days, during Russell's professional debut.[2]

Before the second game of the doubleheader, Auerbach asked if Russell could
sit on the Boston bench, despite not having yet signed a contract. "Why not?" answered NBA president Maurice Podoloff. Russell would generate good publicity.
"Every once in a while point out to the court and then point your finger at him,"
Podoloff instructed. "It will look good." He added a jibe for Auerbach: "You won't
mind, of course, if I fine you $25 for the privilege."[3]

Auerbach figured that Russell was worth it. The rookie sat on the bench as the Knicks prevailed 110–99, despite Bob Cousy's thirty-five points. Soon, Russell would apply his analytical approach. More than simply adjust to the physical style and breakneck speed, he would employ his skills to devastating effect. Despite doubts about his unique style, he would draw fans to the NBA. His visit to Madison Square Garden illustrated the character of his new league. The NBA showcased the best basketball in the world, meshing power with speed, brutality with grace, cooperative synchronicity with individual transcendence. But the league also had a scrappy personality, regional profile, and small-time mentality.[4]

. . .

Podoloff personified both the NBA's dogged emergence and its continued image problem. Born in a Jewish settlement outside Kiev, he immigrated to New York City as a young child. His father first made sneakers in an East Side shop. Respectful of hard work and passionate about education, the Podoloffs moved to New Haven, Connecticut, where Maurice obtained bachelor and law degrees from Yale University. He then joined his father's real estate business. Despite little interest in sports, they purchased an ice arena and minor-league hockey franchise. In 1935 Podoloff became president of the American Hockey League. Voluble, intelligent, and hardworking, he established contacts with hockey entrepreneurs and arena owners. When eleven of those men started the Basketball Association of America in 1946, they hired him as president. At that point, he had seen one basketball game in his entire life.[5]

Podoloff shepherded the league's climb to financial stability. In 1948, he lured the marquee teams from the rival National Basketball League. When the NBL crumbled the next year, the BAA absorbed its remnants and adopted its new name. After the 1949–50 season—featuring an unwieldy seventeen teams in such podunk cities as Anderson, Sheboygan, and Waterloo—the NBA winnowed down to eight stable franchises. Podoloff orchestrated the entire process. He filibustered during conflicts among squabbling owners. He cajoled and bluffed. He weaved compromises out of equivocation, misdirection, and self-contradiction. But he commanded little respect. In print, his backroom blustering seemed comical. In person, he cut a ridiculous figure. Partial to big red suspenders and bow ties, the sad-eyed, roly-poly president stood only five feet tall. At league headquarters in the Empire State Building, visitors craned their necks to see him over his mammoth desk.[6]

Furthermore, Podoloff possessed little actual power. NBA owners had built their clubs from scratch, outlasted the shakeout of unprofitable franchises, and needed the continued clicks of arena turnstiles. They showed singular concern for their own bottom lines. In the NBA, unlike in other leagues, the home team kept all gate receipts. Podoloff often announced grand plans for future expansion, such as in 1957, when he predicted seven new teams in four years. But the owners rejected every new franchise applicant. They resisted sacrificing players for an expansion draft, and they demanded inflated entrance fees. "I've spent years, and lost money too, trying to build a winning team," complained an owner after one expansion proposal. "Why should I help him by hurting myself?"[7]

As lords of small fiefdoms, the owners took a paternalistic approach to labor relations. They knew their players well, and they involved themselves in all aspects of team management. The players signed annual contracts without any bargaining power. A standard reserve clause bound their rights to one team. Salaries averaged $6,500. In 1954 Bob Cousy of the Boston Celtics started a Players Association. Fort Wayne owner Fred Zollner intimidated his players from joining, and Podoloff first ignored Cousy's pleas for negotiation. When Russell joined the NBA, the Players Association was asking for narrow concessions, including a twenty-game limit on exhibitions, an arbitration board to settle labor disputes, minor fees for public appearances, and a stop to referees levying in-game cash penalties (a practice known as the "whispering fine").[8]

Yet the NBA lurched toward respectability. An annual All-Star Game, first proposed by Walter Brown in 1951, had become an important marketing tool. The NBA also benefited from the college scandals of 1951. The league aspired to the popularity of the college game, and during the temporary disillusion over amateurs' corrupted morals, the professionals fed the popular appetite for basketball. The NBA distanced itself from the scandals. In 1951 Podoloff banned referee Sol Levy, who had allegedly fixed six games. In 1954 he exiled Jack Molinas, a brilliant forward who had dumped games with the Fort Wayne Pistons. Rumors of point shaving persisted, but a major scandal never tarnished the league.[9]

Television further promoted the NBA, though most owners feared that broadcasts would spoil attendance. In 1953 the league signed a one-year contract with the short-lived Dumont Television Network. The next year, NBC started paying nominal fees to televise twenty Sunday afternoon games per season. As the middle class flocked to the suburbs, television grew critical to the development of modern sports. By 1956 more than three-fourths of American families owned a television set. Still, Podoloff had to keep assuring the owners of their independence from the networks, even as they required television for national exposure.[10]

The NBA would have crashed, however, if the game was slow and boring. In the early 1950s, coaches often resorted to fouling and stalling—most infamously in November 1950, when Fort Wayne beat Minneapolis 19–18. Everyone hated the tedious hatchet jobs. Many proposed changes. Philadelphia Warriors owner Eddie Gottlieb advocated "innings," whereby teams alternated possession for twelve two-minute periods. Others proposed to save all foul shots until the end of the half, when one team shot the difference in free throws awarded.[11]

After years of minor tinkering, the NBA took drastic action in 1954. Coach Howard Hobson, reporter Dick Young, referee Eddie Boyle, and player Ed Macauley had all suggested a time limit on offensive possessions. But it was Danny Biasone, owner of the Syracuse Nationals, who proposed the twenty-four-second shot clock. A small, soft-spoken Italian immigrant prone to Borsalino hats and filter cigarettes, he had arrived at the idea of allocating twenty-four seconds by dividing the somewhat arbitrary figure of 120 shots a game into forty-eight minutes of play. In August the league powers convened at a Syracuse high school to watch a sweaty, experimental pickup game. "It certainly changed the tempo of play," recalled Dolph Schayes, who participated that day. "It was all running. No standing around. It made the game more fun to play." Upon implementation of the shot clock, the average score rocketed from 79 to 93.[12]

Offensive skills had been dramatically improving. Once a two-hand set shot had sufficed. Now a player needed a jumper, a hook, or at least a one-hand push shot. The new generation had better coaching, superior equipment, and exposure to more techniques. When the BAA began, the entire league shot 28 percent. By 1956, NBA players shot 39 percent. The twenty-four-second clock spotlighted these skills. Fans enjoyed the back-and-forth style, which encouraged scoring sprees and come-from-behind finishes.[13]

Yet despite exciting games and star players, national magazines printed articles such as "Is the N.B.A. Big League?", "The Trouble with Pro Basketball," and "Does Pro Basketball Have a Future?" The NBA still had a ramshackle feel. Everyone bullied the referees, sullying the league's long-term reputation. Eddie Gottlieb organized the entire schedule, sending teams on crisscrossing overnight train journeys to fill available dates. Arenas were cold. "Home" games took place in remote locations. Fights were common. Players, coaches, and owners moaned about the hectic schedule, rule changes, the territorial draft, and the generally "bush-league" conditions.[14]

The NBA still smelled of its urban-ethnic roots, of improvised hucksterism, of vaudeville in high tops. Its entrepreneurs acted with petty self-preservation, and the league lacked a consistent vision for administration, marketing, or expansion. But the forces of modern basketball were emerging, including a faster, higher, more exciting on-court product. Russell embodied that trend.

. . .

"Bill Russell's Buildup Rivals that of Ted Williams," boomed a December 19 headline in the *Boston Globe*. The comparison to the iconic baseball star might have been hyperbole, but it revealed the hopes and doubts surrounding Russell. The USF winning streak, Olympic gold medal, and professional bidding war heightened the scrutiny. "No basketball player in recent years has received so much nation-wide attention," described the *Boston Herald*. "No newcomer to professional ranks has ever been asked to launch his career under such pressure."[15]

Russell was a bundle of nerves. "How do you do, Mr. Cousy?" he asked his star teammate in New York, even though they had met the previous year. He had touched a basketball once in the past three weeks, and he lacked the offensive repertoire of most professionals. In three practices with his new team, he seemed unsure with the ball.[16]

He had plenty of doubters. He stood 6'9" and weighed only 215 pounds. Bulky seven-footers like Ray Felix and Charlie Share possessed more rebounding tricks and post moves. When Willie Naulls lauded Russell to New York teammates and sportswriters, they were skeptical. Eddie Gottlieb thought Russell was overpaid. Arthur Daley of the *New York Times* figured that veterans would spring his bony frame with subtle hip checks, or launch him into the stratosphere with cagey shot fakes. "We've all heard about Russell's greatness," said George Yardley of the Fort Wayne Pistons, "but I'm not so sure that he'll be the sensation that a lot of people predict."[17]

The Celtics did not need a sensation—they needed a missing puzzle piece. Russell had entered a perfect situation, where he could ease into a specific role. Boston had already set a club-record nine-game winning streak, and it led the Eastern Conference by three games. Bob Cousy had reached the pinnacle of his talents. Bill Sharman had just returned from injury. Rookie Tom Heinsohn provided a third scoring option. Veteran Arnie Risen kept the center position warm, and second-year forward Jim Loscutoff supplied defense and rebounding.

Could Russell lend the championship edge? His teammates had no idea. They had never seen him play, and they assumed that his college reputation had overhyped his abilities. But in his first practice, remembered Risen, "he almost jumped over the backboard!" Russell grabbed rebounds and sprinted downcourt, triggering the Boston fast break. "I'm sold," Sharman said before the St. Louis game. "I feel better about the season already. Russell has my confidence."[18]

Risen started at center on December 22 against St. Louis. Russell checked in after 5:31 played. His stomach churned. He immediately missed a jump shot. He converted a right-handed hook three minutes later, but he went 3–11 from the field and 0–4 from the free-throw line. He was sitting on the bench when Sharman sank a fifteen-foot buzzer-beater for a 95–93 win. But Russell also grabbed sixteen rebounds in only twenty-one minutes, and his defense won raves. "Did you see those two shots of mine he blocked?" said Bob Pettit, referring to a pair of layups erased by Russell. "He's as good as they said and will be better with experience." President Podoloff proclaimed, "They'll love him everywhere in the league."[19]

Podoloff was right. The Celtics next traveled to Fort Wayne, and though Russell scored only five points in twenty minutes, he drew almost triple the average crowd. During his first swing through the pro circuit, the Celtics played to sold-out arenas in New York City, Minneapolis, Philadelphia, and St. Louis. The NBA set a new attendance record in Madison Square Garden. Double the normal crowd arrived in Syracuse despite a blizzard. Even in second trips to rival cities, Russell attracted sellout crowds. Neither George Mikan nor Bob Cousy had ever compelled such curiosity. Boston crushed its home attendance record for one season. "Bill Russell is the first real gate attraction the National Basketball Association ever had," pronounced Walter Brown.[20]

Much of the fascination stemmed from Russell's revolutionary defense, encapsulated by his mastery of Neil Johnston, a lanky, narrow-faced, sharp-elbowed, 6'8" center for the Philadelphia Warriors. Besides an awkwardly effective one-hand push shot from long range, Johnston delivered a line drive, half-hook, half-runner with metronomic accuracy. He established post position with dogged, stoic resolve. The three-time scoring champion remained an All-Star, ranking third in scoring average that season. He exemplified the skilled, if slow, professional pivotman of the 1950s.[21]

Russell first faced Johnston during a Christmas doubleheader at Madison Square Garden. Johnston could not score for forty-two minutes. The next night in Boston, Johnston scored only one field goal in the first half. Johnston kept offering right-handed, low-trajectory flips. Russell kept springing up and tipping them with his left hand. "I figured I could block nine out of 10 of them," he later recalled. Russell even started conceding certain shots, keeping Johnston from making adjustments. "I guess I just have to figure out something to do," Johnston shrugged after the second game, when Russell had also snatched a record-setting sixteen first-quarter rebounds. Johnston owned an effective style within basketball's historically earthbound patterns. Suddenly, Russell had rendered him obsolete.[22]

Russell so disrupted convention that Philadelphia owner Eddie Gottlieb accused him of "goaltending" and playing a "one-man zone." The comments sparked a minor media frenzy. "I think its bush and that he owes the young man an apology," thundered Walter Brown. He fumed that Gottlieb would smear the sport's new attraction, and he accused Gottlieb of manipulating the league—first by controlling the schedule, and now by influencing the referees. Auerbach attributed the "big bunch of sour grapes" to Russell's defiance of his doubters.[23]

Yet Russell also adjusted to the NBA. In college he scored on tip-ins, put-backs, and driving hooks with sheer athleticism. But without the polished footwork and soft hands of his professional peers, he fretted about his reputation and future contracts. NBA stars all had high scoring averages. As Joe Lapchick wrote, "It's fine to be known as a great defensive player, but the owners forget it when it comes time to talk salary. They say, 'Defense—Wahhhh!'" Red Auerbach had to assure Russell to forget about scoring. His contracts would reflect his contributions to victory, not his statistics.[24]

Russell still endured "The Treatment." During a rookie's first tour through the league, opponents administered a ritual of flying elbows, driving forearms, stomped-on toes, and tugged shorts. If the veteran fraternity bullied the rookie, the news spread through locker rooms, train cars, and hotel lobbies. Russell recalled that when he entered the lane, "the opposition walked all over me. I got pushed, pulled, pinched, punched, bumped, and stepped on." The massive, physical seven-foot Walter Dukes overpowered Russell during his first visit to Minneapolis.[25]

Harry "The Horse" Gallatin best illustrated Russell's growing pains. The rugged New York Knicks forward, playing in his record 628th consecutive game, first faced Russell on January 8 in Madison Square Garden. On offense, Gallatin knocked down perimeter shots. On defense, he kneed, grabbed, and pushed Russell. Gallatin scored twenty-six points and got seventeen rebounds. Russell looked like a "novice," according to the *Boston Globe*: "Gallatin was giving Russell a man-sized physical whipping and tugging at the lad's silks to embarrass him even further." Because the game occurred in the nation's media capital, the legend of Gallatin's mastery inflated.[26]

The debacle offended Russell's sense of self. Auerbach had planned on using Heinsohn against Gallatin for the Knicks game on January 20. But Russell asked for the assignment. "I said okay," Auerbach recalled, "and as I watched him walking onto the court I knew that this was a momentous occasion. He *killed* Gallatin." Russell blocked four shots and seized six rebounds in the first six minutes. Gallatin scored nine quiet points, and the Celtics won a rout.[27]

As a rookie—especially one who represented his fellow African Americans—Russell tried to embody humility and restraint. But Auerbach urged him to assert himself. Later that season, Ray Felix was swinging elbows at him. Auerbach called time out. He needled Russell to stop taking the punishment and to start fighting back. The game resumed, and when Felix next elbowed him, Russell shoved back. The referee called the foul on Russell. While complaining to the referees, Russell spied Felix winding up for a punch. Russell snuck in a left hook first. The giant New York Knick crashed to the ground. He needed six stitches. Russell was no fighter or cheap-shot artist, but he would not be bullied.[28]

"He is a fellow with fabulous pride," Auerbach advertised. "He's made a lot of critics eat their words." A master motivator, the coach realized Russell's sensitive nature. His meager offensive output and terrible free-throw shooting scalded his pride. But Auerbach jammed praise for Russell down the media's throats. He listed the barriers to Russell's success: his midseason arrival, his lack of conditioning, his recent marriage, and the copious attention. Yet Russell had invigorated the NBA fan base and altered the strategies of opposing coaches. If Russell never scored a basket, he could still win games by snaring rebounds and intimidating shooters. "In a month's time Bill has commanded the respect and fear of the entire league," Auerbach said. "Already he's shown that he's the greatest defensive big man in the game."[29]

By January 1957 sports columnists called Russell "a dominant figure in the NBA" and someone "who could change the entire pattern of play in professional basketball." Others remarked how he had focused attention on defense, the reliable but ugly sister to shooting. *Los Angeles Times* columnist Ned Cronin likened Russell to carbon monoxide: almost imperceptibly, he retarded, disoriented, and exterminated his opponents.[30]

Players around the NBA shared that regard. Arnie Risen remarked how Russell could block any conventional shot—an opponent needed to fake and move before shooting. Earl Lloyd noted that Russell not only blocked shots but also altered the trajectory of countless others. Most defenders played their own man. Russell ranged across the lane, blocking *any* opponent's shot near the rim. That physical talent had psychological manifestations. "Understand, I'm a shooter," explained Ed Macauley. "Carl Braun is a shooter. George Yardley is a shooter. Neil Johnston is a shooter. That's our main function. Shoot the ball." Shooters needed concentration—a single-mindedness for the task at hand. But in the age of Bill Russell, a second thought infiltrated their brain waves: "*Where is he?*"[31]

. . .

The fans of rival teams had other considerations. They called Russell "nigger," "coon," and every other imaginable vile racial epithet. St. Louis was the worst. "Go back to Africa, you baboon!" they yelled. "Watch out Pettit, you'll get covered with chocolate." The insults bruised Russell, but they also hardened him. Professional basketball was a lonely and traumatic undertaking. Off the court, too, he developed his own particular defense.[32]

Russell entered the NBA as the consummate outsider. "I was the only black player on the Celtics," he recalled, "and I was excluded from almost everything except practice and the games." His first time in St. Louis, Russell bunked with Tom Heinsohn. After the game, the coffee shop at the Melbourne Hotel was closed. Heinsohn suggested crossing the street to a late-night greasy spoon. Russell declined. The diner refused to serve blacks. He stayed in his room, alone and hungry.[33]

Russell nevertheless drew sustenance from the team's atmosphere. "I liked him," recalled Risen. "I think we all did." They considered him a good-natured teammate with a loud, cackling laugh. But Russell sometimes arrived late for practice, which could be annoying. Heinsohn thought him curiously cocky. Indeed, Russell sometimes carried himself with aloof self-assurance. "I would not be unfriendly," he remembered, "but at the same time I did not want the reputation of being just a joking, laughing Negro." He would prove himself—as a player, and as a man.[34]

That determination molded his complex, competitive relationship with Heinsohn. The powerful 6'7" forward had replaced Ed Macauley's production beyond expectations, averaging sixteen points and ten rebounds. He won a place in the All-Star Game alongside Bob Cousy and Bill Sharman. He also carpooled with Cousy from their homes in Worcester. A super-sized puppy dog, Heinsohn heaved up and down the court, pouring his heart into the game (he had already sprained Auerbach's neck after crashing into the Boston bench). He shot without conscience. His teammates called him "Ack-Ack" and "Gunner." "In his defense," quipped Cousy, "he shoots only when he has the ball."[35]

Heinsohn's affable personality also made him the team whipping boy. Even before training camp, Auerbach told the press that Heinsohn needed to lose weight. He harped on Heinsohn's inconsistent hustle. He singled out Heinsohn for poor play. These tactics not only fired up Heinsohn but also spared sensitive stars such as Cousy, Sharman, and Russell from direct criticism. When Russell joined the Celtics, Heinsohn still endured Auerbach's cracks. Heinsohn still carried the ball bag. Heinsohn still fetched sodas for the veterans, while Russell avoided the typical rookie hazing. "When you have a player who is setting attendance records all around the league," explained Cousy, "you tend to think twice before you send him down to the corner for a coke."[36]

Russell nevertheless resented that Heinsohn had established himself, befriended his teammates, and got recognized for scoring. He remembered, as well, how New York reporters fawned over Heinsohn before their duel at the 1955 Holiday Tournament. Heinsohn also bore grudges from that game because his coach then benched and humiliated him. When he joined the Celtics, moreover, reporters probed him about Russell. Yet Heinsohn respected Russell. Growing up in Union City, New Jersey, he had never questioned the racial myths circulating through his neighborhood: blacks are lazy, blacks are weak in the stomach, blacks cannot handle pressure. But now Russell handled his publicity-charged midseason arrival with aplomb, played basketball with extraordinary skill, and shouldered racism with dignity. For Heinsohn, it was a period of racial enlightenment.[37]

Russell, for his part, appreciated the friendly welcome of his new teammates, including Heinsohn. Arnie Risen felt too old for prolonged minutes in Boston's up-tempo offense, and he tutored his understudy on the tendencies of rival big men. Though a Milton Gross column had suggested that teammates might resent Russell's rich contract, they appreciated him. On defense, they gambled for steals, knowing Russell loomed behind them. When an opponent shot, they boxed out, let Russell rebound, and released downcourt an instant earlier, accelerating the fast break. They had catapulted from contenders to front-runners.[38]

The rich got richer when Frank Ramsey rejoined the Celtics in January. The University of Kentucky star had played the 1954–55 season with Boston and then served in the armed forces. The 6'3" swingman marveled at how Russell and Heinsohn had improved the team. "The boys can go out and shoot the eyes out of the ball," he said, "and they can play that defense." Scrambling, aggressive defense keyed a faster pace, more points, and a stretching lead in the standings. Boston set a single-game scoring record with 140 points in a January 23 win over Syracuse. They again won eight straight games. Reporters and fans debated if they were the greatest team ever assembled. By February, the *Boston Globe* was surmising that the Celtics owned the best playmaker (Cousy), shooter (Sharman), and rebounder (Rus-

sell) in NBA history. "What a joke," exclaimed Dick McGuire. Boston had shel-
lacked his Knicks even though Cousy sat out with an injury. "Who's gonna stop
Russell and the rest of those guys? That Sharman got only 33. That Russell got 29
rebounds. Oiks!"[39]

The Celtics clinched their first Eastern Conference title in early March and
finished 44–28, six games ahead of Syracuse. Walter Brown now characterized the
Russell trade as "the most daring gamble in the history of the NBA." He risked re-
linquishing Ed Macauley and Cliff Hagan. "If Russell hadn't wanted to play NBA
ball we were sunk," said Brown. "If Russell proved to be a bum—we were also sunk."
Instead, Russell had blended in perfectly. In limited minutes, he averaged nearly
fifteen points and twenty rebounds a game. When Risen got hurt in January, Russell joined the starting lineup. His defense and rebounding accentuated the fast-
breaking, quick-shooting skills of his teammates, and he fed his individual ego
through his team's success.[40]

Yet Russell still bubbled with self-pride. In the locker room at Boston Garden,
Heinsohn received a check and congratulatory letter for winning Rookie of the
Year. Russell peered over his shoulder. "I think you ought to give me half of that
check," he said. "If I had been here from the beginning of the year you never would
have gotten it." Heinsohn sat dumbfounded at Russell's rudeness. For all his team-
oriented play, Russell craved validation. His competitive embers hissed, awaiting
the spark of championship basketball.[41]

• • •

The 1957 play-offs showcased Russell's extraordinary impact, launched the Boston
Celtics dynasty, and proved a watershed for professional basketball. Yet these same
play-offs exhibited the silly, squabbling small-mindedness that tarnished the
league's reputation. The NBA had arrived at its crossroads, both big league and bush
league.

Six teams made the play-offs, relegating little value to the regular season. The
Celtics waited while the second-place Syracuse Nationals swept the third-place
Philadelphia Warriors in a best-of-three series. Boston's veterans relished the opportunity. "I want to play them for strictly sentimental reasons," said Bob Cousy.
"If we play just normal ball against them, we'll whip them good." Syracuse had
eliminated Boston in three of the last four play-off series, and the teams hated each
other.[42]

Russell dominated his play-off debut, a 108–90 cakewalk before a full house at
Boston Garden. "He was everywhere," said Dolph Schayes after the game. "He was
the difference." The Nationals marveled at how Russell could jump at a fake, recover, and block the next try. He guarded the rim as much as his man. "Against
any other team in the league, once I get in close I've got it made," said Schayes. "I
can take a layup, or pass off. Usually I can count on a free throw at worst. But noth-

ing's sure when Russell's around. Even when he's not guarding you, he always manages to get near the hoop and put that hand in the way."[43]

The Celtics swept the best-of-five series. Schayes submitted three gritty games, but Russell had shaped the Syracuse lineup. Coach Paul Seymour sat starting center Johnny Kerr for long stretches, since Russell so easily blocked his hook shot. Seymour instead used Earl Lloyd, who could launch set shots from the perimeter, and Bob Hopkins, a cousin of Russell's who had attended Grambling State. Russell snatched more than thirty rebounds in every contest, and his counterparts offered continually diminishing resistance. Boston reached its first-ever NBA Finals, and longtime Celtics such as Auerbach, Cousy, and Sharman savored victory over their nemeses.[44]

Now Boston faced the St. Louis Hawks. Ben Kerner's team had undergone a turbulent season. After starting 14–19, Kerner fired coach Red Holzman and installed Slater Martin as player-coach. The veteran guard spent two unhappy weeks in double-duty before convincing Kerner to hire Alex Hannum, a bright and burly benchwarmer. The players respected Hannum's enthusiasm and toughness, and Hannum loved his new job. He started Cliff Hagan at forward, urged a faster style, and survived a wrist injury to superstar Bob Pettit. St. Louis finished 34–38, landing in a three-way tie for first place with Minneapolis and Fort Wayne. From this middling milieu, the Hawks emerged as the improbable representative of the Western Conference.[45]

The series attracted more national attention than any previous NBA Finals. Unlike Syracuse, Fort Wayne, or Rochester, Boston and St. Louis had the "major league" imprimatur, thanks to long-standing baseball franchises. For the first time, both finalists' home arenas accommodated more than ten thousand fans. The schedule ensured home dates at Boston Garden and Kiel Auditorium, rather than smaller secondary arenas. The series also featured exciting teams and compelling story lines. Cousy, Sharman, and Pettit ranked among the game's most dazzling stars, and the previous summer's trade had intertwined the two franchises: St. Louis gave up Russell, Ed Macauley joined the Hawks, and college teammates Ramsey and Hagan were now rivals. The March 30 opener appeared on national television.[46]

The Hawks shocked the Celtics in a double-overtime thrill ride, 125–123. Bob Pettit played fifty-four minutes and scored thirty-seven points, and Slater Martin battled Bob Cousy to a standstill. Tom Heinsohn tied the game with five seconds left in regulation, and Cousy hit a twenty-footer at the end of the first overtime. Then, after Jack Coleman sank a fifteen-foot quasi-hook "desperation heave" to put the Hawks ahead, Cousy missed another twenty-footer with three seconds left. The next afternoon, seven Celtics scored in double figures, Cousy dominated Martin, and Jim Loscutoff muscled around Pettit. The Celtics led by thirty before winning, 119–99, and squaring the series.[47]

In the weeklong layoff until the next game, the NBA reinforced its reputation for petty scuffling. The Celtics cried about poor officiating, and Alex Hannum called the Celtics "a bunch of butchers, so taught by Red Auerbach." The Boston coach blew his top. "Who is he to talk?" asked Auerbach, dismissing Hannum as an old "hatchet man." Walter Brown added that Hannum is "lucky he's in the league. He's always been a real butcher."[48]

The bickering then reached carnivalesque proportions. Kiel Auditorium was a snake pit. The fans sat exceptionally close, and they acted exceptionally nasty. Launching continual insults (and reserving their worst for blacks like Russell), they even slurred Mendy Rudolph, a dark-skinned Jewish referee whom they thought was Puerto Rican. Visiting players ran a vicious gauntlet of fans between the locker room and the court. That season, a number of visiting Celtics had dodged projectile eggs.[49]

Auerbach escalated the hysteria before Game Three. After Bob Cousy noted that one rim seemed below regulation height, Auerbach kicked up a fuss. The referees measured the basket at exactly ten feet. Ben Kerner marched onto the court, accusing Auerbach of dirty tricks. According to Auerbach, Kerner used a dirty word. Auerbach threw a roundhouse, bloodying Kerner's lip, and walked away. Remarkably, the referees ignored the fight, and Auerbach never even received a technical foul. "He just cussed me out, and I didn't want to take it," Auerbach explained. "All I called him was a busher," objected Kerner. "Look, I took his best punch and nothing happened. That's real bush."[50]

The game turned into a tense, sloppy struggle. In the final minute, Pettit hit a long jump shot to put the Hawks up 100–98. Three different Celtics then missed, and when Heinsohn slipped a pass to Russell, it caromed out of bounds off his chest. The Celtics again trailed the series. Rubbing salt in the wound, Podoloff fined Auerbach $300 for the pregame punch. Jerry Nason of the *Boston Globe* ridiculed the whole affair. He smirked at Walter Brown's laughable claim that Kerner deserved an equal fine for foul language. He scoffed at Kerner's bullying of the league's referees. He snorted at some inconceivable equivalent in baseball, such as New York Yankee manager Casey Stengel attacking Boston Red Sox owner Tom Yawkey at home plate at Fenway Park. "Bush league?" Nason wrote. "The NBA is cluttered with twigs."[51]

Meanwhile, Russell despaired. He had been playing below par, and he hurt his back in Game Three. But the next afternoon, during the first period, Russell suddenly burst with anger. He scored a quick basket, and he ultimately sparked the Celtics with seventeen points and twenty rebounds, powering a 123–118 win. After the game, Russell refused to divulge his provocation. But given the fanaticism within Kiel Auditorium, the racial climate of St. Louis, and the sensitivity of Russell, he had probably weathered one insult too many.[52]

Given their healthy starters and deep bench, the Celtics believed that the momentum had shifted. Indeed, back in Boston Garden on Tuesday night, they won

124–109. Sharman scored thirty-two points, Cousy set a play-off record with nineteen assists, and Russell had twenty-three rebounds. They overwhelmed another Herculean effort by Pettit, who collected thirty-three points and fifteen rebounds. En route to St. Louis, the Celtics oozed confidence.[53]

The pesky Hawks persevered. In Game Six, the teams dueled to another last-second finish. The score was deadlocked at 94 for the final minute and a half. With seven seconds left, Pettit missed a shot from the corner. Cliff Hagan emerged from a scrum and scored. Two seconds remained when Cousy signaled time out, but the final buzzer sounded before the referees acknowledged him. The Hawks won 96–94, tying the series at three.[54]

Now the Celtics tensed. Despite gliding through three victories, they had dropped three close games. They faced the pressure of their disappointing history and current expectations. After the game, Ramsey and Heinsohn argued about Hagan's last-second basket. Others fumed that the officials awarded St. Louis more free throws. The Celtics thought that Sid Borgia, who had refereed five of the six games, bore a grudge against them. At the St. Louis airport, Auerbach harangued Podoloff about the officials for the final game. Auerbach then accused Bob Duffy, the official timekeeper in St. Louis, of cowardice by letting the clock run out. "Don't say that to me you phony," snapped back Duffy. "You always were a phony." They neared blows.[55]

On Saturday, April 13, Boston hosted the deciding game. The exciting contests, filled with passionate performances by the sport's greatest stars, had captivated both cities. They had shattered league records for gate receipts. In a touch of serendipity, Game Seven took place as reporters returned from baseball's spring training, awaiting the season opener and looking for sports stories. The NBA won new national publicity.[56]

The pressure ratcheted up. Before the final game, Russell stayed awake all night, praying. The next day, his competitive anxieties kept bubbling. He invested so much in competition. His life contained obstacles: childhood loss, racism and poverty, prejudice and doubt, inner shyness and outer exclusivity. If he proved himself through basketball, he also feared potential failure. That anxiety boiled his stomach, sent him jittering, and filled his eyes with tears. Then it all spilled out in one vomitous mess. Even after the other Celtics took the floor, Russell sat in the locker room, plagued by worry. The door swung open, and he heard a snippet of excited chatter. He collected himself, walked onto the Boston Garden floor, and played his part in NBA history.[57]

It started with some poignant sportsmanship. "Sorry about it Ben," said Auerbach. "Forget it," replied Kerner. They had shared a history since Auerbach coached Tri-Cities, so they shook hands and put their earlier fiasco behind them. Then the Celtics and Hawks once again battled. St. Louis led 28–26 after one quarter and 53–51 at halftime. Boston tied it seven times in the third quarter before surging ahead, 83–77. The Hawks clawed back in the fourth quarter, and with 1:10 to play, Boston trailed 101–97. Bob Pettit, Slater Martin, and Cliff Hagan had all played brilliantly.[58]

Cousy and Sharman, by contrast, wilted under the pressure. Winding tighter and tighter, they combined to hit only five of forty shots. The rookies saved them. As Tom Heinsohn shot with confidence and passion, Russell played demonic defense, driving Boston's charge at the end of regulation. He pulled the Celtics ahead 102–101 on a clever pivot move. Then Jack Coleman drove for the game-winning basket, and Russell made a spectacular block. With twelve seconds left, St. Louis fouled Cousy.[59]

Cousy hit the first shot, and St. Louis called time-out. "When Cooz hits the next one," Auerbach reminded, "make sure we don't foul anyone." Another free throw iced the title. Cousy stepped to the line. Rather than just shoot, he reminded himself to maintain form. He short-armed a pathetic air ball. Bob Pettit then evened the game with two free throws. At the end, Sharman took a potential game-winner. It hit the front rim.[60]

Overtime. The game now filtered through a haze of emotions and strains, frenzied joy and deflating disappointment in every undulation of momentum. "I remember very little of it," Russell later recalled. "Just a sea of voices washing over like waves and impressions of arms reaching past and bodies bumping." The Hawks never caved, even as Frank Ramsey netted two jumpers and a breakaway layup. In the closing seconds, with the score tied at 113, Sharman took another potential game-winner. It hit the front rim.[61]

Double overtime. It had become a war of attrition. Heinsohn, pushed beyond exhaustion, fouled out with thirty-seven points and twenty-three rebounds. Blubbering with tears, he wobbled away until teammates steered him to the bench. His head, covered with a towel, dropped between his knees. On the St. Louis side, Pettit had aggravated his wrist injury, and Cliff Hagan, Jack Coleman, Jack McMahon, and Ed Macauley all fouled out. With 2:30 left, Hannum inserted himself into the game. He had not played in three weeks, but he still wore a uniform, and few options survived on his bench.[62]

Russell and Ramsey kept leading the Celtics. Russell blocked a shot, and Ramsey sank another twenty-footer. In the final minute, as the Garden alternately shook with roars and shrieks and moans, the Hawks refused to succumb. St. Louis trailed by just one with seventeen seconds left. Then Hannum got called for traveling, and Jim Loscutoff hit one of two free throws, giving the Celtics a 125–123 edge. The Hawks had the ball under their basket with one second left. They called time-out.[63]

Hannum drew up an audacious plan—a fitting end to a championship series with pressure-packed circumstances, four down-to-the-wire games, heroic and frustrated stars, myriad controversies, and a winner-take-all contest in its second overtime. He told Pettit to stand at the opposite foul line. Hannum would throw the ball the length of the court, *off the backboard* and into his hands. Hannum seemed so confident that the Hawks just nodded. But they wondered, too. "Alex had a hard time hitting the backboard from 15 feet," remembered Macauley. "How was he going to do it from 94 feet?"[64]

Somehow, he did it. He heaved a perfect strike. "No," thought Auerbach. "It's impossible." The ball rocketed off the glass and skipped off the rim, right to a leaping Pettit. The 6'9" third-year forward from Louisiana State University could score on jumpers, one-hand pushes, tap-ins, and hooks. He had powerful hands, rigorous practice habits, a studied grace, and a gift for offensive rebounds. The league's scoring and rebounding champion had already tallied thirty-nine points and nineteen rebounds in another magnificent effort. No one in the universe was better suited to converting this basket. "Pettit misses this kind of shot," wrote Herbert Warren Wind, "about as frequently as destiny touches a comparative unknown like Hannum." Pettit shot before his feet touched the ground. The ball bounced on the rim. It swirled around. It toppled out.[65]

"It's all over! It's over! It's over!" screamed a hoarse, sweat-soaked Johnny Most to the radio audience. The Celtics had won their first NBA championship. The fans enveloped the victors. Russell jumped for joy, his legs giddily splayed, and landed in the arms of Celtics' publicist Howie McHugh. He and Arnie Risen then put Auerbach on their shoulders. They paraded off the court, threw the coach into the shower, swilled beers, and traded compliments. Cousy and Sharman heaved mammoth sighs of relief. "I could have ended up an awful bum," said Sharman.[66]

"Who's got a razor?" cried out Russell. He had been wearing a goatee. At the time few professional athletes had facial hair, and after a teammate had asked him about it, he had promised to shave it when they won the NBA title. As the beer cans popped, Russell laughed at his own nervousness, and he praised everyone from Heinsohn to Pettit. Auerbach and Heinsohn jubilantly shaved off his beard. "Well, there it is boys," Russell yelled. "Or I mean there it isn't. No more goatee. It's gone down the drain. I promised to do it, and now nobody can ask me about that thing any more."[67]

In thirteen months, Russell had won an NCAA championship, an Olympic gold medal, and an NBA title. He had expunged any lingering doubts about his ability. He had earned the fellowship of his coach and teammates. The Celtics had won his trust and brotherhood.

So why the beard? He recognized that it marked him as unusual, subtly defiant. He faced unique doubts, bore distinct sensitivities, and possessed a special anger. For Bill Russell, the bright sea of victory often masked a dark undercurrent.[68]

6

The Man Who Must Be Different

"Boston has been wonderful," proclaimed Russell after the 1957 championship. "I feel as if I'm home." He owned a new status and security. The Celtics split $18,500 in play-off money. Russell then earned extra cash on an All-Star barnstorming tour. One day after Game Seven, the players boarded a train headed west. They played in Des Moines, Denver, Provo, Salt Lake City, and Spokane on consecutive days. The tour ended in California.[1]

Because he had left USF sixteen credits short of graduation, Russell had planned on staying in the Bay Area for summer classes. He intended to waive his scholarship "as a gesture of good will." But when the treasurer billed him, Russell considered it a symbol of ingratitude—an exploitation of an athlete, another perversion of the amateur ideal; one more personal injustice. So he stormed off campus, and he never finished his degree. Instead he enjoyed his first summer with disposable income. He practiced with his brother, who was home from Korea and a student at USF. He and Rose also drove cross-country in their Chrysler Imperial, outfitted with air conditioning, a hi-fi set, and the license plate "Celtics 6." He later picked up a part-time gig as a disc jockey.[2]

Russell was living the 1950s ideal as consumer and citizen. He and Rose had first stayed at the Hotel Lenox and then rented an apartment. In late 1957 they bought a ranch-style home at 1361 Main Street in suburban Reading. The day that they moved in, Rose delivered their first son, Bill Jr., nicknamed "Buddha." A pack of neighbors soon arrived to welcome them. "Get out the shotgun," Bill joked, "we may have to fight for our home."[3]

Tasting the fruits of middle-class stability, Russell built a huge record collection and bought an elaborate electric-train set, with manifold bridges and switches and stations. As a boy in Louisiana, whenever he had heard a train whistle, he had sprinted to the tracks and waved at the engineers, enraptured by the cars rolling to destinations beyond Monroe. He begged his mother for a set, but she could never afford one. Now those clattering, whistling toy trains gave him deep satisfaction.[4]

Russell signed another lucrative contract with the Celtics, the league's marquee attraction. The NBA had also exchanged two small cities for "big league" markets; the Rochester Royals moved to Cincinnati, and the Fort Wayne Pistons to Detroit. Los Angeles, San Francisco, Chicago, and Washington had all exhibited interest in franchises. The televised "Game of the Week" and the dramatic 1957 play-offs had boosted the league's profile. So as Russell won new esteem, he found new opportunities for public expression. His stardom initiated a new era for black basketball: a growth in numbers, an influence of style, and a challenge to the racial order.[5]

. . .

With the eighth pick in the 1957 NBA draft, Red Auerbach drafted Sam Jones. "Who the hell is Sam Jones?" someone shouted. Auerbach had no good answer. Jones had attended small, all-black North Carolina College and then served in the armed forces. Auerbach drafted the 6'4" guard on the recommendation of Bones McKinney, a former Celtic coaching at Wake Forest. Auerbach also asked Russell about Jones, since both were black. Russell had never heard of him. "Look, Red," he said, a bit perturbed, "I really don't know all of them."[6]

Russell nevertheless took Jones under his wing. "Sad Sam" struggled with his confidence. Before the season opener in Madison Square Garden, the arena went dark, a spotlight shone, and the Knicks burst through a paper hoop. Then the lights flashed on. Jones had never played before five thousand people, let alone twenty thousand. He returned every pass without dribbling or shooting. Russell teased him with the nickname "Right Back," but throughout the season he prodded Jones to assert himself. He even invited Jones to stay with him. Jones was in Reading, in fact, when Rose had contractions before Buddha's birth. Bill was driving their only car, and while Rose swayed in her rocking chair, Jones panicked. "Please, please wait till Bill gets back," he begged. "He'll know what to do . . . he can handle anything."[7]

Jones offered minimal contributions that year, but Boston already possessed a full arsenal. *Sport* proclaimed that "The Celtics Look Better Than Ever." *Sports Illustrated* promoted the "matchless opportunity this year of seeing one of the all-time great combinations in basketball playing together for a full season." *Newsweek* marveled that "after almost a month of competition, the Celtics were still unbeaten and seemed unbeatable." Boston's average winning margin was more than ten points. Frank Ramsey scored thirty-five against Detroit; Bob Cousy scored thirty-six against Philadelphia; Bill Sharman scored forty-one against Minneapolis and forty-four against New York. On January 31, 1959, Russell got thirty-two points and thirty-three rebounds against Philadelphia. Boston finished the season 49–23, three games better than the club record.[8]

In this sophomore campaign, Russell established himself as an NBA star—the first with defense as his calling card. On November 16, 1957, he plucked forty-nine rebounds against Philadelphia, shattering the single-game record. While watching Russell break his old record of thirty-nine rebounds, Neil Johnston suffered another heap of humiliation. The Warriors center was averaging a league-best twenty-six points a game. On the first possession, Russell blocked his hook, sprinted downcourt, and dunked. Russell scored twenty-eight points. Johnston missed eleven of his twelve shots. He also kneed Bob Cousy in the thigh. Cousy claimed that the frustrated center acted intentionally, leading to blustery justifications by Johnston and Eddie Gottlieb.[9]

Russell inspired another small tempest when St. Louis coach Alex Hannum accused him of traveling before every layup or dunk. The Celtics dismissed the complaint as a cheap ploy. Walter Brown called Hannum a "basketball accident" whose primary skill "was his ability to clobber a guy." Cousy added, "If Russell is walking, so is everyone in the league. The other teams don't know how else to beat Russell, so they're trying to upset him."[10]

Neither Hannum's head games nor rival pivotmen threatened Russell's supremacy. The Knicks' Ray Felix and the Nationals' Johnny Kerr often sat rather than watch Russell block their hook shots. If Russell rested on the bench, recalled Ed Macauley, "the game changed dramatically." Teams could set picks on perimeter defenders, but they had no recourse for Russell's shotblocking. His offensive confidence had also improved, and he averaged nearly seventeen points and twenty-three rebounds over the season. He broke the single-season rebound record by mid-February. At season's end, his peers voted him the NBA's Most Valuable Player.[11]

The writers then placed Russell on the league's second team. Bob Pettit, fourth in MVP balloting, made the first team. The writers picked no centers. Russell's teammates called it an outrage. How could the MVP not be all-league? Did they only measure point totals? Did race influence their appraisals? "How can I begrudge anything to Pettit?" instead asked Russell. "He murders me whenever we face each other, and nobody else in the league can handle him much better. I'd pick him for the first team myself if I had a choice between him and me."[12]

That graceful discretion revealed an awareness of the black athlete's historic burden. But inside, Russell fumed at the insult, considering it petty prejudice. That boiling sense of injustice shaped an evolving reevaluation of his responsibilities as an African American icon.[13]

· · ·

In August 1935, the colored Elks of Washington, DC, feted Joe Louis and Jesse Owens. Crowds thronged as the heroes strolled the city's black neighborhoods. By then Louis had knocked out former champion Primo Carnera, and Owens had beat or matched four world records at one track meet. Both athletes understood their significance to American race relations. "When white folks see that we dance as well as they, when they see that we eat and drink the same things, and laugh and cry over the same things, they begin to realize we are human beings," said Owens. "All this bleating about being downtrodden doesn't do any good."[14]

Louis and Owens served as symbols of black America. But just as their achievement reflected on the race, so too did any embarrassment. Black celebrities lived with limitations. Louis's trainers set specific guidelines: no pictures with white women, no unsupervised nightclub appearances, no soft fights, no fixed fights, no dirty fighting, and no public gloating, smiling, or clowning. Louis and Owens bolstered their standing by prevailing over symbols of Nazi Germany, establishing democratic bulwarks against a fascist menace. Owens won four gold medals at the 1936 "Nazi Olympics" in Berlin, and Louis defended his heavyweight championship in a celebrated 1938 rematch against Germany's Max Schmeling.[15]

When Jackie Robinson reintegrated Major League Baseball in 1947, he subscribed to similar image politics. The college-educated veteran contradicted black stereotypes of laziness, silliness, or delinquency. He suppressed his fiery personality. He weathered death threats, racist baiting from opponents, the humiliations of Jim Crow, and a threatened player strike after he joined the Brooklyn Dodgers. In turn he inspired African American devotion, pioneered baseball's black influx, and represented racial equality in the national pastime.[16]

Sports offered a particular potential for racial progress. Despite such dramatic instances as the Montgomery Bus Boycott and the 1957 Little Rock Crisis, the civil rights movement had not yet sustained public momentum. Moreover, television shows presented blacks only as stock characters. But televised sports, news programs, magazine features, and newspaper articles could uphold black athletes as heroes. Narratives of humble, hardworking blacks could open white liberals to new racial possibilities.[17]

The mythology of black athletes nevertheless reflected futility. It implied that one individual could represent all African Americans. It suggested that blacks needed athletic superiority to gain equality. It further insinuated that blacks must possess exceptional moral character. This code of behavior unduly burdened athletes, and it obscured their individual personalities and politics. When Robinson broke this code in the 1950s by decrying racism, he inflamed the baseball establishment. Black athletes could symbolize equality, but they could not protest inequality.[18]

Until Bill Russell, professional basketball lacked a galvanizing emblem of African American excellence. Basketball lacked the status or history of baseball, so blacks had entered the NBA without the publicity, controversy, or metaphoric significance of Jackie Robinson. Most of the urban, college-educated whites populating "the city game" accepted blacks. Pop Gates and Dolly King joined the NBL in 1946, and six others enlisted with the Chicago Stags of the BAA in 1948.[19]

But the NBA began without blacks. Abe Saperstein possessed a stranglehold on black talent, and the league owners hosted profitable doubleheaders with the Globetrotters. When Ned Irish of the Knicks tried signing Nat "Sweetwater" Clifton from the Globetrotters, most owners balked. Philadelphia's Eddie Gottlieb also feared a racial floodgate. He predicted that "in five years, it'll be seventy-five percent black and nobody will be coming to the games."[20]

So when Walter Brown drafted Chuck Cooper in 1950, it provoked consternation. "Walter, don't you know he's a colored boy?" someone asked. Brown replied, "I don't give a damn if he's striped or plaid or polka dot. Boston takes Charles Cooper of Duquesne!" The hardworking 6'6" forward played four years with the Celtics. Cooper endured segregation in Washington and Baltimore, as well as some on-court tussles after racial slurs. Don Barksdale had similar experiences during his Boston tenure from 1953 to 1955. Yet both men formed friendships with teammates, their bonds forged by travel and teamwork.[21]

Blacks trickled into the NBA. After Boston drafted Cooper, Irish bought Clifton from the Globetrotters. Clifton became the first African American to sign an NBA contract. Earl Lloyd, drafted by the Syracuse Nationals, was the first to step on an NBA court. These players founded the fraternity of black professionals that Russell joined in 1956. Hosts looked out for visiting players. For instance, Lloyd and Russell advised each other on restaurants, clubs, and other amenities that welcomed blacks. Black players also shared stories about their particular hardships: eating room service in St. Louis, getting targeted for debris and spit from Fort Wayne fans, competing against other blacks for limited roster spots. As late as 1958, no team had more than two blacks, and St. Louis remained all white.[22]

The pioneer generation consisted of role players: bulky centers like Walter Dukes or Ray Felix, complementary forwards like Chuck Cooper or Earl Lloyd, decent guards like Dick Ricketts or Sihugo Green. "At that time they weren't making any black stars," recalled Clifton. No African Americans made first or second team all-league until 1956. Clifton consciously exorcised his Globetrotter flourishes, concentrating on defense and rebounding out of racial responsibility. "Being the first in something," he reflected, "you don't want to do anything that'll mess it up for somebody else."[23]

Prior to Russell, only one potential star emerged. Maurice Stokes, a 6'7", 240-pound center from tiny St. Francis College, was Rookie of the Year in 1956. The Rochester Royal "was built like a bull and played with the grace of an antelope," according to one contemporary. For three years Stokes was an All-Star who averaged more than fifteen points, seventeen rebounds, and five assists. Then tragedy struck. During the final regular season game of 1958, Stokes fell hard and briefly lost consciousness. Three days later, during a flight, he began vomiting. His breathing grew labored. He sweated through his tweed sport coat. He had contracted en- cephalitis: the original jolt had swelled his brain, and the change in air pressure had triggered an attack. Stokes spent six weeks in a coma and was paralyzed for the rest of his life.[24]

Russell was the NBA's most prominent African American during the 1950s. Black newspapers across the country delighted in his stardom. A *New York Ams- terdam News* item on Negro History Week in 1958 gloried in black contributions to American culture: "Can we imagine baseball without Jackie Robinson, track with- out Jesse Owens, basketball without Bill Russell?" He might not have *desegregated* the NBA, but he *integrated* it. No other black player had starred on a championship team. No one else had reshaped the game's patterns. No one else had magnetized such attention. So given the historic mission of black athletes, Russell's persona pos- sessed broad ramifications. He represented something bigger than himself.[25]

That burden was laden with complications. The *Sporting News* noted that Rus- sell "has the kind of voice, personality, and facial expressions which make him a natural for situation comedy." *Sport* portrayed "Big Bill" as "a friendly, gregarious, good-natured, humorous fellow" who cracked one-liners and ate ice cream for breakfast. The magazine described how Red Auerbach alternately teased and prod- ded him, especially when Russell was lazy or late. Russell did save his competitive energy for games, and he possessed a genuine conviviality. But if a black athlete re- inforced a public perception as a slothful joker, he risked the same "Sambo" stereo- type as the Harlem Globetrotters.[26]

When Russell controlled his image, he instead embodied restraint. He originally refrained from fighting back against dirty play. In an "as told to" article in the *Sat- urday Evening Post,* he chronicled the difficult adjustments of his rookie year. In press conferences, he detailed plans for self-improvement. He also tried cultivat- ing relationships with the media. "I want to be friends," he told reporters at his ini- tial Boston press conference.[27]

Yet Russell laid initial brushstrokes on a complex self-portrait. At the time, *Sports Illustrated* considered the NBA an afterthought. Frank Deford, who joined the staff in the early 1960s, remembered a general perception of pro basketball as "sweaty," beneath the "class" audience that preferred upscale sports. Yet the mag- azine lent writers freedom to delve into personalities and social issues. In 1958, it assigned Jeremiah Tax to profile Russell. Tax and Russell struck up a lasting friend- ship, and Russell judged the subsequent article as particularly perceptive. Titled "The Man Who Must Be Different," it captured the tensions driving the sport's new phenomenon.[28]

"There is a constant warring within him," Tax wrote, "between the man who wants to run away and hide so no one will ever again call him a goon or insult his race, and the man who glories in the remarkable feats he can accomplish with his long, elastic body and who wears his color like a banner." Russell cackled with his teammates, but he also chafed at every skeptic of his talents, every gawker of his height, every spouter of racial insensitivity. He demanded recognition of his intellect. He analyzed basketball's psychology of intimidation. He dissected his strengths and weaknesses. He learned from teammates. He came across as thoughtful, intelligent, likable.

Russell also distinguished himself as an individual. "I don't want people to stereotype me ever," he said. He explained why he spurned the Harlem Globetrotters, and he refused to satisfy any racial typecast. He liked Cadillacs, but he drove a Chrysler, because "they think that every time a colored man goes places, the first thing he does is get himself a Cadillac." The fashion among hip black men was tight suits with short sleeves and pant legs, so he custom-made oversized suits with extralong arms and legs. "I *always* try to do things people say I won't do or can't do," he said.[29]

Russell shouldered the black athlete's historic responsibility. But just as his aerial style prefigured basketball's future, his insistent distinctiveness poked the boundaries of the integrationist icon.

. . .

The Celtics opened the 1958 play-offs by crushing the Philadelphia Warriors. Despite headaches and congestion from a case of tonsillitis, Russell registered eighteen points and twenty-five rebounds in the opening 107–98 win. Philadelphia coach George Senesky benched Neil Johnston, who was helpless against Russell, but the strategy disrupted the Warriors' rhythm. Russell got twenty-eight rebounds in a 109–87 Game Two victory, and forty more in a 106–92 Game Three win. The Warriors then salvaged a 112–97 victory, but Boston finished them in Game Five, 93–88, setting up a championship rematch against the St. Louis Hawks.[30]

The series promised to match the excitement of the 1957 Finals. In the nationally televised Saturday afternoon opener at Boston Garden, the Hawks surprised the Celtics 104–102. The next day, Boston played to near-perfection and won 136–112. The series then shifted to Kiel Auditorium. The Celtics could have tied Game Three with seventeen seconds left, but Bill Sharman botched an inbounds pass, and St. Louis won 111–108. The game spelled double disaster for Boston. Halfway through the third quarter, Russell jumped to block a shot. By the time the referee called goaltending, Russell lay crumpled on the ground, clutching his throbbing right ankle. He tried to reenter the game but lasted only forty-five seconds. He had torn tendons and chipped his ankle.[31]

Russell spent the next three days in St. Louis on crutches, taking constant whirlpool and diathermy treatments. Still, doctors could not bandage-wrap the tender ankle. Attending the next game in street clothes, he watched Bob Cousy overcome a pulled tendon in his instep and a bashed nose from a collision. Without Russell, the Boston fast break decelerated. Cousy took turns in the pivot, quarterbacked a deliberate half-court offense, and finished with twenty-four points, thirteen assists, and thirteen rebounds. During player introductions, the crowd had so expected a Hawks victory that they applauded the Celtics. Instead, Boston evened the series with a 109–98 triumph.[32]

Russell's injury required three weeks to heal, and the team announced that his season was over. Then the Celtics dropped another heartbreaker at Boston Garden, 102–100. Bill Sharman had a bad knee, Arnie Risen had debilitating sinus trouble, and Jim Loscutoff had torn up his knee in the regular season. Meanwhile, Russell insisted that continuing whirlpool and heat treatments had helped him. He rejoined his club in St. Louis for Game Six, his ankle immobilized in a plaster cast.[33]

Russell played twenty-four minutes, scoring eight points and getting eight rebounds. He lacked his explosive quickness. Meanwhile, Tom Heinsohn missed time with an upset stomach, Bob Cousy got hit in the mouth, and Frank Ramsey caught a sharp elbow with his forehead. In the final minute, the weary Celtics missed two chances to pull ahead. The day instead belonged to Bob Pettit. Fighting through double and triple teams, he scored on long jumpers, twisting layups, powerful drives, and free throws. He soared over Arnie Risen for rebounds and tip-ins. At every break in the action, the Celtics wondered how to stop Pettit. Whatever they tried, failed. "I don't remember any of the individual shots or plays," Pettit recalled. "I just knew I wanted the ball because I didn't think they could do anything to stop me." He scored fifty points, including nineteen of the Hawks' final twenty-one. With sixteen seconds left, his tip-in gave St. Louis a three-point edge.[34]

After a Boston basket, the Hawks inbounded to Ed Macauley with thirteen seconds left. He never crossed half-court. But the shrieking crowd cowed the referees from calling a ten-second violation, and the Hawks won 110–109. After four wins by a total margin of eight points, the St. Louis title rewarded Ben Kerner's years of scraping and clawing. In the final thirty seconds of the championship game, the overexcited owner blacked out. After winning the title, Kerner crowed that trading away Bill Russell was justified.[35]

In hindsight, that claim seemed ridiculous. Russell would pilot a Celtics dynasty, and the Hawks were the last all-white champion in NBA history.

. . .

While Russell rehabilitated his ankle in St. Louis, burglars ransacked his Reading home, stealing property worth $1,500. Two weeks later, thieves pinched another $1,300 in electronic equipment. Although both robberies occurred in daylight, no neighbors reported any suspicious activity. The crimes fed Russell's developing disillusion with the Boston area.[36]

On their first day in Boston in December 1956, Bill and Rose took a taxi to the Registry of Motor Vehicles, accompanied by Harold Furash, an insurance executive and longtime season-ticket holder. On the ride, the driver lectured Russell to treat people nicely, to avoid a swelled head. His advice smacked of racial conde-scension. It implied that Boston blacks had a place, and they should not step out-side it. Russell's perceptions intensified when buying his home in Reading. Furash and his friend Hyman Horwitz had canvassed neighborhoods, knocking on doors and gauging reactions to a potential black neighbor. The Russells ended up buying a modest ranch house near a restaurant, a bank, and a busy commercial intersec-tion. Despite having only one real neighbor, Russell felt under surveillance. When driving late at night, he noticed cars following his Chrysler through town.[37]

Russell further bristled at the media. Provincialism tainted the sports pages, even though Boston had five daily newspapers, as well as reporters from suburbs and nearby cities. They ignored national news, and they obsessed over local figures. Unlike in New York or Los Angeles, moreover, sports provided most of the city's celebrities. Influential columnists thus dictated public opinion, such as when "Colonel" Dave Egan of the *Record* feuded with Red Sox star Ted Williams. Racism polluted the sports scene. The Red Sox had passed on signing Jackie Robinson in 1945 and Willie Mays in 1949, but few reporters challenged this exclusion. The last professional baseball team to integrate finally promoted Elijah "Pumpsie" Green in 1959. [38]

Bostonians also exhibited indifference for basketball, even as the Celtics drew hys-terical crowds in Philadelphia, Syracuse, or St. Louis. Though average attendance at Boston Garden spiked during Russell's rookie year to 10,517, it plummeted the next year to 8,308, and it continued falling in subsequent years. That same season the fourth-place, devoid-of-stars Bruins often sold out Boston Garden. While the Bru-ins received the arena's prime dates, the Celtics paired games with Globetrotter ex-hibitions, tennis matches, the Ice Follies, fashion shows, or donkey basketball.[39]

The Bruins owned a loyal, passionate fan base because hockey was woven into the New England sports fabric. The Bruins won Stanley Cups in 1929, 1939, and 1941, featuring such stars as defenseman Eddie Shore and the "Kraut Line" of Woody Dumart, Milt Schmidt, and Bobby Bauer. The region contained some of American hockey's deepest talent pools. By contrast, early professional basketball teams in New England possessed little stability and limited appeal. The Eastern Mas-sachusetts high school "Tech Tourney" struggled to attract teams and fans, and Boston's city schools lacked basketball programs from the mid-1920s to the mid-1940s. Besides Holy Cross in Worcester, New England lacked college basketball powerhouses.[40]

Throughout the 1950s, the Celtics battled this apathy. Publicist Howie McHugh buttered up reporters, invited celebrities to games, and kept the Celtics in the pa-pers. Radio announcer Johnny Most painted opponents as scoundrels. The Celtics crushed local teams during preseason tours. They held charity matches, attended promotional events, and gave demonstrations in small-town gymnasiums and park-ing lots. These seeds bore some fruit. By Russell's arrival, all Massachusetts high schools had basketball teams, Boston Garden filled up for the Tech Tourney, and an annual Celtics clinic drew legions of youngsters.[41]

Yet the Boston press often resented the Celtics, especially Red Auerbach, a man constitutionally incapable of tact. Upon taking the job in 1950, Auerbach drafted seven-foot center Charlie Share. Reporters howled that he snubbed Bob Cousy, the razzle-dazzle All-American from Holy Cross. Since winning the NCAA championship in 1947, Holy Cross had captured the region's fancy, even selling out Boston Garden. Some New Englanders assumed Holy Cross could beat the Celtics. Auerbach bristled at that parochial outlook: three of Cousy's teammates had failed as professionals, and the Celtics needed a center. "Look," he barked, "am I supposed to win or worry about the local yokels?"[42]

Auerbach would never forget that crack. That offseason, "local yokel" Cousy followed a byzantine path to Boston. Tri-Cities drafted him, then traded him to Chicago. The Stags subsequently folded. At a meeting to disperse Chicago's commodities, Boston, New York, and Philadelphia all desired high-scoring All-Star Max Zaslofsky. Auerbach also preferred savvy guard Andy Phillip to Cousy. Team owners selected the three names out of a hat. Walter Brown picked Cousy. Auerbach soon maligned Cousy for his fancy passes, poor defense, and flashy dribbling. The press speculated on a feud. In 1953, Cousy demanded a trade after public criticism from Brown and Auerbach.[43]

Like Russell, Cousy smothered bubbling anxieties under a steely confidence. The lone child of French immigrants, Cousy grew up sensitive about his lisp and accent. He found assurance playing basketball in Queens. Neither tall nor strong, he nevertheless had peripheral vision, sloping shoulders, elongated arms, and huge hands—perfect for dribbling and passing. He captained New York City's all-scholastic team and performed heroics at Holy Cross. But he felt a consistent compulsion to prove himself. He almost transferred after conflicts with Doggie Julian, his first college coach. He grew weary with the NBA's constant pressure, yet he needed that stimulation. During frequent nightmares he punched pillows, crashed bedside lamps, and babbled in French.[44]

In 1953 Cousy scored fifty points in a triple-overtime play-off victory over Syracuse, and he soon became the NBA's most charismatic superstar. No one matched his imagination, daring, and flair. He dribbled at breakneck speed and sliced delicate passes through a maze of arms. He passed behind his back, over his head, through his legs. He flipped in floaters, hook shots, one-hand sets. The "Houdini of the Hardwood" engendered such fascination that *Sports Illustrated* published illustrated, frame-by-frame sequences of his moves. Cousy was also articulate, smart, and honest. Reporters flocked to him. Players respected him. Fans adored him.[45]

Cousy also meshed with Bill Sharman, establishing the Celtics' dynamic, high-scoring identity in the pre-Russell years. A five-sport high school letterman, Sharman starred in basketball and baseball at the University of Southern California, and he played five years in the Brooklyn Dodgers organization. With the Celtics, Sharman displayed machinelike precision. Fastidious to the point of absurdity, he ate the same meals, took the same naps, and performed the same pregame calisthenics at the same time. He also kept notebooks on opponents' tendencies, and he carried an index card with shooting fundamentals. In games he wheeled around picks, opening space for his pure one-hander. As Cousy led the NBA in assists eight times, Sharman led in free-throw percentage seven times. From 1956 to 1959, he led the Celtics in scoring.[46]

By the late 1950s, young players around New England imitated Sharman's shooting stroke and Cousy's behind-the-back dribble. Cousy was 6'1" and Sharman 6'2", so fans related to them—especially as anxiety spread that "Frankensteins" dominated basketball. The small guard seemed a vanishing breed. Only Slater Martin of St. Louis stood under six feet. "In five years I doubt if there'll be anyone left under six-four, with the possible exception of a few holdovers who are playing now," said Cousy in 1959. "And the six-four guys will all be in the backcourt."[47]

Bill Russell thus seemed the big black menace driving out the little white man. He attracted fewer emulators, fewer admirers. Who copied a 6'9" man with tentacle arms and springboard legs? Who revered a spidery giant that blocked shots? Who, among Boston's predominantly white fan base, identified with a black man? Fans and reporters valued Russell, and his peers deemed him MVP. But Cousy looked like he might step out of a South Boston convenience store carrying a newspaper and a cup of coffee. Only Cousy received the hero worship.[48]

It bothered Russell. "There might have been an unspoken rivalry," admitted Cousy. They respected each other. They never argued. They complemented each other. But both men burned with competitive ardor, craving not only wins, but also recognition. As Cousy noted, Russell drove the Celtics to championships, "and I was the darling of the media." Russell hated that a fan might say, "Let me shake your hand. I've just shaken the hand of the greatest basketball player in the world, Bob Cousy. Now, I want to shake the hand of the second greatest." Their uneven ranks in Boston's sports pantheon created a gulf, preventing a profound friendship.[49]

In the coming decade Russell would be showered with respect, surrounded by black teammates, and catapulted into celebrity. But he never shed the sensibility of the lone black outsider, looming in the shadow of the spotlight.

· · ·

By Russell's third year, the NBA confronted a racially integrated future, with all its bounties and complexities. The crop of black rookies included Wayne Embry in Cincinnati, Guy Rodgers in Philadelphia, and Hal Greer in Syracuse. Another rookie, Elgin Baylor of Minnesota, joined Russell as a bona fide superstar. The 6'5", 225-pound forward combined brute strength, springboard jumping, and balletic grace. "He never broke the law of gravity," one writer reflected, "but he's awfully slow about obeying it."[50]

Baylor had followed a roundabout path to the pros. Poor grades prevented major scholarship offers, so he left Washington, DC, for the College of Idaho, where he played basketball and football. During his freshman year, Baylor kept reading about Bill Russell and the University of San Francisco. Listening to the radio broadcast of the 1955 NCAA title game against Tom Gola and LaSalle, Baylor got excited about playing big-time college basketball. He soon transferred to Seattle University, which he vaulted into national prominence. He won the NCAA tournament MVP in 1958, even though Seattle lost to Kentucky. *Sport* called him the "probably the best basketball player in the world." He was certainly the most exciting. Minneapolis owner Bob Short rebuffed New York's $100,000 offer for his rights. Baylor rescued the floundering franchise, nearly doubling its revenue while averaging twenty-five points and fifteen rebounds.[51]

Meanwhile, the Celtics added black players as veteran reserves Arnie Risen, Jack Nichols, and Andy Phillip retired. K. C. Jones joined the team after two years in the armed forces. He had first tried out for the Los Angeles Rams of the NFL, despite never playing college football. Jones had a knack for grabbing interceptions, but he got cut after aggravating a muscle injury during an exhibition game. So he returned to basketball. Rusty from his layoff, he played terribly on a seventeen-game, eighteen-day exhibition tour through New England. Cousy and Sharman urged Auerbach to dump him. When Auerbach signed him anyway, Boston reporters assumed that he made the team as "Russell's little buddy." Indeed, Russell lauded Jones and hosted him in Reading, as he had Sam Jones. But Auerbach insisted that K. C. Jones provided tough defense, savvy passing, and a winning habit from his USF years.[52]

That off-season Boston drafted another African American, Bennie Swain from Texas Southern. No other NBA team had more than three blacks. One reporter predicted that neither owners nor fans would accept this breach of an implicit quota. In fact, Russell, Sam Jones, K. C. Jones, and Swain all remained with the Celtics, but the reporter's matter-of-fact opinion aggravated Russell's sense that sport lacked genuine equality. Those persistent barriers appeared most obvious in the South. While in Dallas during another All-Star exhibition tour, Russell learned that the promoter arranged lodging at a segregated hotel. Russell decided to leave Dallas immediately. When the promoter tried to shake his hand, Russell spat at it.[53]

That November Boston and Minneapolis staged a regular season game in Charlotte, North Carolina. When Russell heard that the black players were staying at a Jim Crow hotel, he fumed that Auerbach had misled him. After the game, Baylor decried the "decrepit" conditions. Russell vowed to avoid future games in the South. "I don't believe in segregation," he said. "It's against my principles. I came down here with my team and had to eat and sleep apart from them. I was shocked and hurt." Walter Brown and Bob Short promised to avert such incidents in the future.[54]

Two months later, however, Baylor met Jim Crow in Charleston, West Virginia, where the Cincinnati Royals had moved a home game. The hotel refused to admit blacks. No restaurants served them, either, so they ate sandwiches from a grocery store. Baylor sat in his room, head in his hands, insisting that he was "torn up inside" and would not play. He watched his team lose that night, 95–91. The incident earned considerable publicity, especially after the Charleston mayor refused to apologize. The NBA soon resolved to reject segregated accommodations, but assigned the responsibility to individual teams.[55]

As the NBA's two major black stars, Russell and Baylor possessed a unique leverage to challenge the racial order. While Baylor enthralled fans with his acrobatic drives, Russell earned a ripening respect. He was redefining his position, as his shot-blocking negated the patterned offenses of every NBA opponent. This Russell Revolution shaped the entire game. Boston could run fast break after fast break, earning high-percentage shots. Coaches now valued athletes who sprinted downcourt before defenses got set. Jump shooters found more opportunities. The overall pace accelerated. Now basketball barely resembled George Mikan's game. A *Boston Globe* reporter speculated on a game between Mikan's Lakers and Russell's Celtics. "The 'old Lakers' couldn't run with the Celtics, couldn't shoot with the Celtics," he wrote. "Mikan would be so pooped trying to catch Russell that he couldn't reach high enough to comb his hair by the time the fourth quarter arrived."[56]

The Celtics applied the gas pedal throughout the 1958–59 season, constantly cracking one hundred points. They won eleven straight in December. An NBA-record 18,386 watched them beat New York during a Christmas doubleheader at Madison Square Garden. In January, they beat Minneapolis in San Francisco and Seattle during an exploratory junket for West Coast expansion. Then, on February 27, 1959, with Russell on the bench nursing a sore leg, they smashed the single-game scoring record, beating Minneapolis 173–139. Cousy had twenty-six assists, another record. When Podoloff heard the score, he wondered aloud if the teams were playing legitimate defense. "This guy is our president," yowled Auerbach. "He's supposed to be boosting our sport—not knocking it!" Scoring had become so prolific that coaches were proposing a longer shot clock, zone defenses, or even a smaller basket.[57]

Boston finished the season a league-best 52–20. Frank Ramsey again deserved to be an All-Star alongside Cousy, Sharman, and Russell. Heinsohn remained a potent weapon, Jim Loscutoff recovered from his knee injury, and Sam Jones earned more playing time. Also, Gene Conley had returned. Conley also pitched in the major leagues. He had played with the Celtics in 1952–53, but when the Boston Braves moved to Milwaukee, so did Conley. He struck out the side in the twelfth

inning of the 1955 All-Star Game and helped Milwaukee win the 1957 World Series. But after a salary cut in 1958, he picked up his old part-time job. Conley often
covered centers, allowing Russell more defensive freedom. That spring, thanks to
a Walter Brown bonus, Conley chose the NBA play-offs over spring training.[58]

Boston opened the 1959 play-offs against Syracuse. Russell had upended the rivalry. "I play different against Boston," admitted center Johnny Kerr. "I play 60
games in the hole during the season; 12 outside against Russell." Kerr, Dolph
Schayes, and Bob Hopkins either avoided the post or faced Russell's shotblocking.
Once the bullying big brother, now Syracuse hoped that Boston would carelessly
coast until it was too late. The Nationals joked that unless you had a girlfriend there,
Boston was an unpleasant trip.[59]

Despite their 35–37 record, however, Syracuse posed a hazard. The Nationals
now boasted the league's best 1–2 scoring punch. Schayes personified the game's
urban, ethnic roots: a child of Jewish immigrants, a boy in the Bronx, a star at NYU.
When not launching long-range two-hand set shots, the big forward relentlessly
cut, faked, and slashed to the basket. He would have signed with the Knicks of the
BAA in 1948, but Ned Irish refused to pony up an extra $1,000. Instead he joined
the Nationals of the NBL, and he became the NBA's all-time leading scorer. The
people of Syracuse revered the handsome, friendly star.[60]

They were less familiar with George Yardley, who arrived via trade from Detroit that February. The bald, skinny, part-time engineer hated the NBA life and
constantly threatened to retire, but in 1958 he set the single-season scoring record.
The 6'5" forward hit jump shots despite a cast on his left, nonshooting hand. His
talent elevated the Nationals, who swept a preliminary round against New York.
Schayes played for fourteen years and won the NBA title in 1955, but he called the
1959 team "the best we ever had in Syracuse."[61]

The Celtics won in Boston, 131–109. The next game in Syracuse promised a
greater challenge. War Memorial Auditorium was the most hostile, intimidating
venue in the NBA. Its fans had an inferiority complex. The Nationals stayed in
cold, industrial Syracuse as other franchises moved to big cities, magnifying the
upstaters' antipathy of urban slicks. Fans all over central New York braved ice-
covered roads for games. The Nationals helped define their civic identity. They resented Cousy's suggestions that the team relocate. They threw paper cups, glass
bottles, and punches. They spit at players entering the locker room, jiggled the guy
wires holding the basket, and shone lights into the faces of free-throw shooters.
A man called "The Strangler" heckled from behind the opponents' bench. That
season, fans scuffled with various Celtics and referee Sid Borgia. Boston lost its
last four games there.[62]

The pattern held for the play-offs. Behind thirty-four points from Schayes and
a fourth-quarter spree from Yardley, Syracuse evened the series 120–118. Neither
side ceded home-court advantage. The Celtics won in Boston, 133–111, and lost

in Syracuse, 119–107. Boston won at home, 129–108, and lost on the road, 133–121. The tight, physical series took a toll. Cousy and Schayes had stomach viruses. Ramsey sprained his finger, Schayes sprained his ankle. Both sides complained that the referees favored the home team. Borgia ejected Tom Heinsohn after a "verbal lambasting" in Game Six. Red Auerbach wound tighter and tighter.[63]

Syracuse almost triumphed in Game Seven at Boston Garden, opening a sixteen-point lead in the second quarter. Schayes and Yardley both scored more than thirty points. Boston, however, possessed resolve and balance. Five Celtics scored at least eighteen points. Russell got thirty-two rebounds before fouling out in the closing minutes. Gene Conley took his place and grabbed some clutch rebounds. In the final minute, with Boston clinging to a three-point lead, Cousy beat the twenty-four-second clock with a flipped-up one-hander, delighting the crowd. When Boston won 130–125, the fans carried Cousy off on their shoulders. The diminutive Boston hero splayed out on a training table in the dressing room, spent from the pressure-packed circumstances and his own twenty-five-point, ten-assist effort.[64]

All season, the Celtics had expected a rubber match against St. Louis in the finals. The past two champions owned the two best records, and their enmity had thickened. Walter Brown lambasted Podoloff for allowing lopsided trades that netted Clyde Lovellette and Sihugo Green. After the Hawks' fourth straight win over the Celtics in mid-January, Auerbach complained that St. Louis fans threw a towel in his face, booed an injured Cousy, and included a disproportionate number of drunken idiots and uncouth women. Eight days later, the Boston Garden balcony rained raw eggs upon the Hawks. Every one of their contests featured extraordinary passion.[65]

But St. Louis lost the Western Division Finals to the 33–39 Minneapolis Lakers. The Lakers never stood a chance. Boston had beaten them eighteen straight times—every game of the past two seasons. The trend continued. Boston won 118–115 and 128–108 at home, then won 123–110 and 118–113 in Minneapolis. The Celtics became the first team to sweep the NBA Finals. Every game featured balanced scoring, fast breaks, and clamp-down defense. Russell registered twenty-eight, thirty, thirty, and thirty rebounds, breaking his play-off record from 1957. Minneapolis coach John Kundla marveled at how Russell ignited the Boston fast break, and he admitted that his team had no answer. Boston's prowess might have inspired vitriol and violence in St. Louis or Syracuse, but in Minneapolis they offered loud applause, a polite appreciation of basketball perfection.[66]

· · ·

The Celtics held their traditional breakup dinner at a small banquet room in the Lenox Hotel. Each player offered a brief testimonial, lauding the harmony that suffused the organization. Ileana Sharman spoke on behalf of the wives. Then they all went home. It seemed quaint, even surreal, to Gene Conley. When Milwaukee won the World Series, the celebration included a ticker-tape parade, a huge banquet, an orchestra, political proclamations, and extensive media coverage. The Celtics invited a few reporters who cared more about the Bruins or Red Sox.[67]

By 1959 Bill Russell had won two NBA titles, an MVP award, and the esteem of every knowledgeable basketball fan. But he had yet to capture the public imagination. His sport struggled for "big league" status, his arts of defense and rebounding remained underappreciated, and he was alienated from Boston's sporting mores. To define his place in American culture, Russell needed the challenges of the 1960s. He needed a black revolution in society and sport, crises over his personal and political identity, and popular recognition of his extraordinary talent.

He needed Wilt Chamberlain.

7

Goliath's Shadow

The rare sellout of Boston Garden on November 11, 1958, had little to do with the Celtics' game against Minneapolis. Most arrived for the first half of the double-header, featuring the Harlem Globetrotters and starring Wilt Chamberlain. The Celtics watched, too. They oohed and aahed by the first minute, when Chamberlain elevated for a thunderous slam. They watched him score fifty effortless points, and they predicted greatness. "What are you trembling for?" someone joked to Bill Russell. The Boston center tried summoning words to describe Chamberlain: "How do they say it, devastating?"[1]

Russell and Chamberlain were already linked in the public imagination. While at the University of Kansas, reports called Chamberlain the "new Russell" and "heir to Bill Russell's collegiate laurels." Fans often confused them. "I'd sure like to meet that Chamberlain," laughed Russell during USF's 1956 trip to Kansas City for the NCAA Finals. "People have been calling me Wilt the Stilt ever since I got here." Later that year, when Kansas took a West Coast road trip, people assumed Chamberlain was Russell. That infuriated Chamberlain, who, like everyone else, anticipated their professional clashes.[2]

Russell or Chamberlain? That debate, too, preceded their first matchup. Most college coaches ranked Chamberlain first. He possessed extraordinary power, speed, grace, and height. Even Phil Woolpert admitted that the 1957 Dons "are just as flabbergasted by him as I, and they played with Russell." But Red Auerbach riled up the Philadelphia press by deeming Russell superior, based on his defense and rebounding.[3]

"It all depends on how you want to die," said Pete Newell. "One beats the life out of you. The other stabs you to death."[4]

. . .

At first glance, Russell and Chamberlain seem mirror images: two black giants of unparalleled athleticism, one an unstoppable offensive force, the other an immovable defensive object. But a longer look reveals divergent histories, offering clues to their distinct styles and philosophies.

While Russell had powerful male role models, Chamberlain grew up among strong women. The fifth of nine children, he lived in a tree-lined section of West Philadelphia. His father, a janitor, was kind but passive. His mother, a housekeeper, dominated their home with a warm, outgoing personality. Wilt had six sisters, including one enrolled in the same grade. He had his own sensitivities: he lost a school year to pneumonia, his shins throbbed from mosquito bites, he stuttered and sucked his thumb, and he was freakishly tall. But he directed his energies outward, zealously applying himself to odd jobs such as shoveling snow and cleaning gutters.[5]

While Russell tripped over his own feet, Chamberlain displayed astonishing athleticism. As a teenager he high-jumped 6'6", shot-putted 47 feet, and ran the 440 in 48.6 seconds. He had uncommon strength, broad shoulders, and a skinny waist. His giraffe legs swallowed up the basketball court, and his elongated arms guided in finger rolls, hooks, and jump shots. His Overbrook High School team won the Public League three times and the city championship twice. Chamberlain averaged 44.5 points as a senior.[6]

While Russell floated in adolescent anonymity, Chamberlain achieved celebrity. A Philadelphia sportswriter tabbed him "Wilt the Stilt." *Life* proclaimed him the nation's best high school player. As the publicity escalated, so did Chamberlain's self-regard. Affecting a haughty boredom, he ignored coaches when convenient. He could not ignore Red Auerbach, however. They both spent a summer at Kutsher's, a Catskills resort that sponsored basketball teams to entertain guests. Auerbach challenged and berated the headstrong star. But he also urged Walter Brown to bribe Chamberlain toward a New England college, so that Boston could pick him in the territorial draft. Auerbach suggested Harvard.[7]

While Russell bloomed late, *Sport* tabbed Chamberlain "The High-School Kid Who Could Play Pro Now." In 1955 the NBA allowed Eddie Gottlieb to use his territorial pick on Chamberlain, then still at Overbrook. But with Chamberlain ineligible to join the Warriors until his college class graduated, he inspired the first national recruiting campaign in college basketball history. More than two hundred schools vied for his services. Chamberlain chose the University of Kansas, sparking accusations of illegal inducements. "I feel sorry for the Stilt," wrote one columnist. "When he enters the NBA four years from now, he'll have to take a cut in salary."[8]

So while Russell entered sports as an enthusiastic innocent, Chamberlain always understood himself as a commodity. The burden of fame, the engorgement of ego, the glorious stench of potential profit—he experienced it all before graduating high school. Questions about his amateur status continued during college. "Wilt Chamberlain should be barred from the NBA," thundered Walter Brown in 1957. "He has proselytized himself at Kansas. No NBA team can afford to pay him what he gets at Kansas." Brown was pricking Gottlieb, who had just accused the rookie Russell of playing a "one-man zone." But he also articulated a popular revulsion of Chamberlain's cynical, greed-coated aura.[9]

And while Russell led USF to two NCAA titles, Chamberlain left Kansas with dashed expectations. Even more than Russell, Chamberlain threatened basketball convention. He was too big, too good, too black. "Can Basketball Survive Chamberlain?" asked the *Saturday Evening Post,* just as Wilt began his varsity career. His prodigious hype promised a national title, and Chamberlain led Kansas to the 1957 NCAA Final against undefeated North Carolina. But the Jayhawks lost by one point in triple overtime. The next season, Kansas failed to qualify for the NCAA tournament. Chamberlain then skipped his senior year, defying the taboo of leaving college early. He announced his decision in *Look,* which paid him $10,000. He felt buried under the weight of unfair expectations, constant triple-teaming, and hounding reporters.[10]

Finally, while Russell rejected paternalist exploitation and racial stereotypes, Chamberlain signed a $65,000 contract with the Harlem Globetrotters. He loved the unfettered display of his greatness. No coach constructed game plans to negate him. He even played guard, which placated Meadowlark Lemon, the grinning, droopy-eyed center of their comedy routines. Chamberlain further enjoyed a superstar's adoration and sexual attention, especially on European tours. He called his year with the Globetrotters "the happiest of my life," a lucrative and stress-free vacation from genuine competition.[11]

Chamberlain thus entered the NBA knowing only the pressure-cooker of sporting celebrity. If he wanted validation, he pointed to public adulation, not private self-pride. If he perceived injustice, he did so purely as an individual. If he measured greatness, he looked to personal accomplishments. "I don't have to prove anything," he said in 1959. "When I first played in junior high school, I proved to myself that I could play ball. After that, I never played another game to prove anything. If I can't make the NBA, that won't bother me. If I go in, it will be for material gain."[12]

. . .

Eddie Gottlieb needed Wilt Chamberlain. The balding, pudgy, Ukraine-born Jew from South Philadelphia had clawed his place into professional basketball. From the 1920s through the 1940s, his Philadelphia SPHAs won various professional leagues, barnstormed through the Midwest, and battled the Harlem Rens and Original Celtics. Saturday night games and dances at the Broadwood Hotel—a staple of Philadelphia's Jewish life—attracted patrons who might win a suit, a salami, or a lady's heart. Gottlieb then founded the Philadelphia Warriors in the BAA. But even with his legendary economizing, he lost money. Rival owners let Gottlieb pick Chamberlain in the 1955 territorial draft because they feared his franchise's dissolution.[13]

Four years later, those owners offered help with Chamberlain's NBA salary, figuring that he would boost revenues. Chamberlain possessed a rare bargaining strength: Abe Saperstein offered another contract, and the surefire star profited from exclusive magazine articles and a "Chamberlain" basketball. But Gottlieb passed on their offer. The Warriors had won the 1956 NBA championship and achieved stability. They boasted Paul Arizin, an All-Star forward with a deadly jump shot; Tom Gola, the multitalented local hero; and Guy Rodgers, a speedy dribbler and pinpoint passer. Gottlieb signed Chamberlain for at least $30,000, $5,000 more than Bob Cousy or Bob Pettit.[14]

"He's going to drive coaches to the nuthouse," cracked Auerbach after watching Chamberlain dominate a charity game in the Catskills. He mulled special defenses for the league's new behemoth. Thanks to Russell, the NBA had already considered a "three-seconds" rule to keep shotblockers from planting themselves in the lane. With Chamberlain's arrival, the owners drafted the rule.[15]

In Chamberlain's shadow, Russell seemed an underdog. They first faced each other at a fund-raising exhibition in Minneapolis. Chamberlain, one report stated, made Russell "look like an ordinary basketball player." Four inches taller, fifty pounds heavier, significantly stronger, with huge hands and a diverse offensive repertoire, the Warriors rookie represented the evolution of the athletic center. Russell had never guarded this concoction of size, speed, and coordination. "He's never been challenged this way," said Bill Sharman. "Wilt will push him to his limit."[16]

Before their first official clash on November 7, 1959, Russell acted uncharacteristically reserved. He spent the day playing with Buddha and repairing a bathroom shelf. After an early steak dinner, he played poker with K. C. Jones and rookie Maurice King. Although King had roomed with Chamberlain at Kansas, they avoided talk about basketball. "He didn't say much about Wilt today," reported Rose. "Some of the things sportswriters have said about Bill have hurt him. He's a proud man." Chamberlain posed not only an epic challenge but also a special opportunity to gain respect.[17]

The game generated a new fervor for the NBA. Although a stenographers' strike had halted the printing of Boston newspapers, basketball chatter bounced along the city's sidewalks, stores, and saloons. Boston Garden sold out months in advance. Scalpers hawked three-dollar tickets for ten dollars. The arena filled up before warmups. Chamberlain strolled out wearing a confident smile, and fans squeezed close to watch his pregame dunks. At the other end, Russell looked grimly determined. No longer would massive, lumbering giants define basketball's central position. "The age of the dinosaurs has ended," wrote Leonard Koppett. "It's hard to tell what the new age will bring—but it starts now."[18]

Their first collision foreshadowed their rivalry. Chamberlain expected Russell to mirror his moves. Instead, Chamberlain said, "he played my shots—and he seemed to know every time I was going to shoot." Chamberlain often used an indefensible fall-away jump shot. But Russell slapped and poked at the ball, disrupting any low-post rhythm, and he challenged every shot attempt, sticking his long fingers into Chamberlain's vision. Once, Russell blocked the ball straight down, an impossible feat for many defenders. Chamberlain grew frustrated by the second half, when he attempted some flat-footed hook shots. None went in. The statistics reflected reporters' characterizations of a "standoff" or "standstill": Chamberlain got thirty points and twenty-eight rebounds, and Russell had twenty-two points and thirty-five rebounds. But Russell had pierced Chamberlain's armor of invincibility. The Warrior took thirty-eight shots, and he scored only four baskets head-to-head against Russell. The Celtics won, 115–106.[19]

Despite that setback, Chamberlain drove Philadelphia's challenge to Boston's supremacy. He scored forty-five points in their second matchup, a Warriors win. Russell missed their next game with a sprained ankle, and Chamberlain scored forty-nine points in another Philadelphia victory. But the Celtics, despite losing Jim Loscutoff to another season-ending injury, set a record seventeen-game winning streak. After snapping the Warriors' ten-game streak in mid-January, they beat Philadelphia again two days later on national television. Russell submitted his finest overall season. He broke his own record by grabbing fifty-one rebounds against Syracuse, and he had career-best scoring and rebounding averages. Philadelphia trailed by only three games in early February, but Boston pulled away, capturing the Eastern Division by ten games. The Celtics finished 59–16, smashing their own record for victories.[20]

The headlines nonetheless belonged to Chamberlain. "Wilt has become the NBA's biggest problem and its foremost topic of conversation," wrote Milton Gross. New York coach Fuzzy Levane called him "the monster." When asked how to defend Chamberlain, St. Louis coach Ed Macauley said, "I'd lock the door of the dressing room before he comes out." Others marveled at his expanding catalog of dunks, fall-aways, and finger rolls. Chamberlain averaged 37.6 points and 26.9 rebounds a game. He broke the single-season scoring record before Valentine's Day, and he set additional records for field goals, free-throw attempts, and rebounds. He won Rookie of the Year, All-Star Game MVP, and league MVP.[21]

Chamberlain was the Babe Ruth of basketball, a larger-than-life superstar reshaping the sport's landscape. Leonard Koppett said that if Russell was the Lenin of basketball's revolution, then Chamberlain was its Stalin—a figure of uncompromising, overarching power. National magazines marveled at his feats. NBA attendance surged 23 percent. The Warriors broke their attendance record by mid-January. Despite complaining about the gapes and silly questions in public, Chamberlain exploited his celebrity, even cutting a rock-and-roll single called "By

Figure 1. Scarred by his mother's death, the awkward young migrant from Louisiana struggled to find his place in West Oakland. Unable to match his older brother's athletic accomplishments, Russell lacked social status. He served as team mascot for the McClymonds High School Warriors. (Courtesy Oakland Tribune)

Figure 2. By the time he graduated from high school in January 1952, Russell had found intellectual inspiration and a strong sense of self-worth. Yet his unremarkable stint in organized basketball seemed over. (Courtesy Oakland Public Library)

Figure 3. By his college years, Russell not only developed physically but also realized his gifts as a leaping shotblocker and rebounder. This "aerial with arms" shattered conventional perceptions of the lumbering, earthbound center, so upsetting his sport's conventions that the National Association of Basketball Coaches widened the lane and banned offensive goaltending—changes known as "Russell Rules." (Courtesy University of San Francisco Archive Room)

Figure 4. By the 1955–56 season, when most college teams had no more than token racial integration, USF started three blacks and played five. Led by Russell, USF won two NCAA titles and had a fifty-five-game winning streak. Front row, left to right: Warren Baxter, Hal Payne, Jack King, Hal Perry, Steve Balchios; Middle row: Phil Woolpert (coach), Vince Boyle, John Koljian, Bill Russell, Bill Bush, K. C. Jones, Bill Mulholland (manager); Back row: Tom Nelson, Gene Brown, Mike Farmer, Carl Boldt, Mike Preaseau. Not pictured: Ross Giudice (assistant coach). (Courtesy University of San Francisco Archive Room)

Figure 5. "With all this tremendous pressure, with all this unaccustomed adulation, he has carried himself so modestly he has become a wonderful public relations man for USF and for San Francisco," beamed coach Phil Woolpert about Russell, soon after this 1955 landing at San Francisco International Airport. The Dons had just won their first NCAA championship. (Courtesy University of San Francisco Archive Room)

Figure 6. At this 1955 White House gathering with other sports stars such as Willie Mays and Bob Cousy, Russell supposedly promised President Dwight Eisenhower that he would maintain his amateur standing for the 1956 Olympics. Although Russell reveled in winning gold in Melbourne, the experience also spawned his disillusion with the hypocrisies of amateurism. (National Park Service Photo, courtesy Dwight D. Eisenhower Library)

Figure 7. When Russell turned professional in December 1956, the NBA was struggling for "big league" status, while the Boston Celtics sought to lure an indifferent fan base. Here, flanked by coach Red Auerbach and owner Walter Brown, Russell attends a 1958 banquet of an American Legion Post. (Courtesy Boston Public Library)

Figure 8. The small, flashy, and white Bob Cousy dribbled and dished with artistic flair, and he won the affection of Boston fans. Though he and Russell possessed deep respect for each other, the two stars also had an unspoken rivalry, preventing a genuine friendship. (Courtesy Boston Public Library)

Figure 9. After battling Russell during a college tournament at Madison Square Garden, Tom Heinsohn partnered with him on the Celtics. They were opposites in temperament and style: Heinsohn wore his emotions on his sleeve, and he shot with abandon. On the court, however, their skills proved perfect complements. (Courtesy Boston Public Library)

Figure 10. Russell once called his wife Rose "the finest person I've ever met." She loved him independent of his basketball fame, and her steady personality balanced his moodiness. But Bill grew restless with traditional marriage, widening the chasm between them. (Courtesy Boston Public Library)

Figure 11. Karen, Jacob, Bill Jr. ("Buddha"), Rose, and Booma greet Russell at Logan Airport in the spring of 1965. Ultimately, his separation from Rose forced Russell to become more than a detached patriarch. (Courtesy Boston Public Library)

Figure 12. Wilt Chamberlain possessed an unprecedented combination of size, strength, speed, stamina, and skill. His threat only elevated Russell. Throughout the 1960s, Chamberlain acquired the reputation of the selfish loser, and Russell of the consummate defensive hero. (Courtesy Boston Public Library)

Figure 13. The Los Angeles Lakers starred Elgin Baylor and Jerry West. Baylor was the prototype for the modern forward, a graceful leaper and explosive scorer. West was basketball's tragic hero, a grim-faced sharpshooter whose greatness kept escalating, only for his Lakers to fall, again and again, before Russell and the Celtics. (Hollywood Citizen News, courtesy Los Angeles Public Library)

Figure 14. No one ever possessed greater all-around skills than Oscar Robertson the Cincinnati Royals. His competitive ardor fed not only his basketball dominance but also his leadership of the National Basketball Players Association. (Courtesy Kevin Grace Collection)

Figure 15. A June 18, 1963, boycott of Boston schools, organized by the NAACP, protested the inferior conditions of the system's de facto segregation. Here Russell stands outside St. Marks Church, where he instructed students at a freedom school to "wear your color like a badge." His outspokenness foreshadowed the "Revolt of the Black Athlete." (Courtesy Boston Public Library)

Figure 16. "The fire that consumes Roxbury will also consume Boston. The fire will spread," Russell told students at the Patrick T. Campbell Junior High School "Freedom Graduation." Both an activist and a celebrity, Russell proved an important liaison between Boston's black community and its political powers. (Courtesy Boston Public Library)

Figure 17. Under Red Auerbach, the Boston Celtics stood at the forefront of NBA's racial revolution, incorporating winning players without regard to skin color. Here he poses with the starting lineup from the 1963–64 season: K. C. Jones, Russell, Tom Heinsohn, Satch Sanders, and Sam Jones. (Courtesy Boston Public Library)

Figure 18. "Of all the men I know in life, K. C. is the one I would like one of my sons to be like," Russell said upon Jones's retirement in 1967. Jones had been his mentor during his difficult adjustment to USF. Together they won two NCAA titles, an Olympic gold medal, and nine NBA championships. (Courtesy Boston Public Library)

◄ Figure 19. Satch Sanders, John Havlicek, and Sam Jones walk off the court with Russell during the 1966 NBA Finals. Each teammate proved an indispensable ingredient in Boston's continuing success. Sanders embraced his role as a suffocating defender, Havlicek progressed from the consummate "Sixth Man" into a superstar, and Sam Jones sank countless clutch shots in the play-offs. (Courtesy Getty Images)

Figure 20. The evolving relationship between Red Auerbach and Bill Russell occupied the core of the Boston Celtics dynasty. A shrewd observer of human nature, Auerbach accepted Russell on Russell's own terms. Russell rewarded him with respect and a deepening friendship. (Courtesy Getty Images)

Figure 21. In 1966 Russell became the first black coach of any major professional team sport. The double duty of playing and coaching layered additional responsibilities on him, but the challenge inspired him to new accomplishments. (Courtesy Boston Public Library)

1967-68 Boston Celtics

Standing, left to right: Trainer Joe DeLauri, Rick Weitzman, Tom Thacker, Tom Sanders, Bailey Howell, Wayne Embry, Don Nelson, John Jones & Mel Graham
Sitting: Sam Jones, Larry Siegfried, Gen. Mgr. Red Auerbach, Marvin Kratter (Chairman of Board), President Clarence Adams, Coach Bill Russell and John Havlicek

BOSTON *Celtics* BASKETBALL CLUB

Figure 22. Russell led the 1967–68 Celtics to the NBA championship, making him made the first player-coach to win a major professional sports title since 1948. (Courtesy Boston Public Library)

Figure 23. In 1969, Russell improbably led the fourth-place Celtics to their eleventh championship in thirteen seasons. In the finals, they overcame the star-studded Los Angeles Lakers, who had added Wilt Chamberlain. The larger-than-life superstar had long served as Russell's foil, but his celebrity also opened new possibilities for Russell. (Courtesy Boston Public Library)

◄ Figure 24. By the late 1960s, Russell's provocative persona included a distinctive wardrobe that featured such items as opera capes, love beads, and Nehru jackets. Here he signs a two-year, $400,000 contract at a 1968 Hotel Lenox press conference, while wearing a black mohair suit with three-quarter sleeves, a turtleneck, flared pants, and a gold peace medallion. (Courtesy Boston Public Library)

Figure 25. Russell's first television part was a guest spot opposite Chuck Connors on the ABC program *Cowboy in Africa*. After his 1969 retirement, Russell moved to Hollywood and became a compelling public figure: touring on the college lecture circuit, hosting his own television talk show and a drive-time radio program, guest starring on variety shows, and appearing in popular advertisements. (Courtesy Boston Public Library)

Figure 26. Russell kept a relatively low profile after stints running the Seattle Supersonics, working as a television broadcaster, and leading the Sacramento Kings. But by 2000, he reemerged as a public figure, cementing his legacy as the greatest winner in American sports history. He had quieted his inner turmoil and established a peace with himself. Here, he accepts an honorary degree from Harvard University in 2007. (Courtesy Boston Herald)

the River." Dressed in a five-button tweed Chesterfield with black satin lapels, he appeared on "American Bandstand"—shuffling, snapping his fingers, crooning doo-wop in his low baritone before squealing schoolgirls.[22]

But Chamberlain ruptured team harmony. He insisted on a private room for road trips. He carped when a Detroit scorekeeper shortchanged his rebound total. He stopped hustling when he received fewer passes. He alienated teammates with his monopoly on shots. The white and black Warriors, moreover, shared little camaraderie. Some blacks hated that light-skinned, straight-haired Guy Rodgers socialized more with whites. Some whites privately called Chamberlain "nigger."[23]

Neil Johnston—once tormented by Russell—was now tortured by Chamberlain. Gottlieb had hired his erstwhile pivotman as coach, an act of loyalty after Johnston suffered a career-ending knee injury. When Johnston tried teaching his hook shot, Chamberlain resisted. When Johnston fined Chamberlain for a preseason indiscretion, Gottlieb waived the penalty. When Johnston barked instructions, the players ignored him. One night in Syracuse, Chamberlain erupted in anger at his coach's criticisms.[24]

Chamberlain also pursued attention to the point of self-sabotage. He moaned to the press about his opponents' physical tactics, rather than dealing it back. In another *Look* article, called "Pro Basketball Has Ganged Up on Me," he whined about dirty play, triple teams, rule changes, and the shortcomings of Rodgers and Gola. Chamberlain also cooperated for a five-part series in the *Philadelphia Daily News*. The first installment revealed that he might quit the NBA. He kept his name in the papers, but he also annoyed his team, his opponents, and the referees.[25]

Dolph Schayes once said that his ambition was to be recognized as the greatest basketball player in the world. "Well, that's not mine," said Chamberlain. "My ambition is to walk down the street and have nobody pay attention to me." That statement spoke to the burdens of stardom, but it also smacked of absurdity. Whether singing rock and roll, issuing outlandish statements, or crushing basketball's records, Wilt Chamberlain existed for public consumption.[26]

· · ·

Once, after Chamberlain racked up forty-nine points, Russell entered the locker room and sobbed. He would always give up size and strength. To contain this nimble giant, he needed guile.[27]

All season, Russell fed Chamberlain barrels of honey. While others treated him like a freak, Russell lauded him: "I only wish I could have been that good as a rookie"; "By the end of the season, everybody will be saying Wilt's the greatest!"; "He could be the greatest basketball player of all time." While others looked for shortcomings, he called Chamberlain a superior rebounder and scorer. While others jostled and jabbed at him, Russell played clean defense. And while others considered him an egotistical loner, Russell struck up a friendship.[28]

The 1960 play-offs displayed both Chamberlain's physical magnificence and mental vulnerability. Chamberlain led Philadelphia past Syracuse in the opening series, swelling enthusiasm for a showdown with Boston. But Russell ignited the Celtics' opening 111–105 win. He started the game with a three-point play and sealed it with a spectacular, end-to-end, soaring block of Guy Rodgers' fast-break layup.[29]

The second game lent the series its signature moment. Auerbach had hatched a new strategy: after the Warriors shot free throws, Tom Heinsohn set cheeky picks on Chamberlain, freeing Russell to sprint downcourt. Chamberlain clattered to a boil. He threatened Heinsohn. Twice he shoved Heinsohn away. "Arnie, he's tossing me around the block!" Heinsohn complained to the referee. In the second period, Chamberlain burst. He knocked Heinsohn to the floor, and he cocked his fist. Just then Gola rushed in, trying to keep the peace. Chamberlain hit his teammate in the back of the head. As haymakers flew across the ensuing melee, Chamberlain winced. His hand was throbbing.[30]

Chamberlain picked the worst moment to finally fight back. The Warriors won 115–110, but he had severe contusions and bruises on his knuckles. For the next afternoon's game in Boston, doctors wrapped his hand in bandages. He managed only twelve points and fifteen rebounds, and Boston won 120–90. Adding insult to injury, when Chamberlain received a lob pass over Russell in the low post, Heinsohn rushed over and accidentally punched the swollen hand, further enraging the Colossus. After the game, Chamberlain complained that the announcer had celebrated Russell's twenty-six points and thirty-nine rebounds. Russell just wished Chamberlain a speedy recovery.[31]

With Chamberlain still in pain, Boston won the next game in Philadelphia, 112–104. The Warriors seemed squashed, except that Chamberlain recovered by the fifth game, scoring fifty points as his team prevailed, 128–107. Boston finally clinched upon the return to Convention Hall. On the final possession, with the score tied at 117, Chamberlain blocked Bill Sharman's drive, but Heinsohn tapped in the rebound. The series had ebbed and flowed on Chamberlain's psyche and hand. Russell, by contrast, had offered consistent defense and rebounding, allowing his teammates to sparkle. "Wilt Chamberlain may be fabulous, fantastic, and phenomenal, but Boston's Bill Russell is solid," judged the *Boston Globe*. "For that reason the Celtics are in the National Basketball Assn final as defending champions."[32]

A familiar nemesis awaited in the Finals, though the St. Louis Hawks had only nine healthy players, and Ben Kerner was again meddling with his coaches. After the 1958 championship, Alex Hannum had wanted a raise and a two-year contract. Kerner instead let Hannum resign, fired Andy Phillip after ten games, and replaced him with Ed Macauley. Then, with St. Louis down 3–2 in the 1960 Western Division play-offs, Kerner secretly hired Paul Seymour to coach the next season. Macauley promptly led his squad to two gritty victories. As the Finals began, the Hawks heard distracting rumors of the premature coaching change.[33]

Meanwhile, the Celtics rejoiced: no more Wilt Chamberlain! "It's great to be able to drive through that key and not worry about that 7–2 giant in my way," said Heinsohn. In the opener, the emancipated Celtic shooters connected from outside, midrange, and in the lane. Boston shattered six play-off scoring records while winning 140–122. Some called it "the greatest team in 25 years." Bookmakers made them eleven-point favorites for Game Two, but Macauley ordered a slower pace, Bob Pettit led a second-half charge, and St. Louis stole a game, 113–103. Now Boston Garden rang with boos.[34]

The Jekyll-and-Hyde nature of the Finals continued for weekend games in St. Louis. Boston's balanced scoring, hustling defense, and Russell's furious fourth-quarter shotblocking drove a 102–86 win on Saturday. On Sunday, the Celtics managed only five assists—a team low in the entire history of the NBA—and lost 106–96. The rivals again got testy. Auerbach yelped that Pettit milked sympathy by exaggerating injuries, and he accused Clyde Lovellette of manhandling Russell. Kerner snapped back, "If Lovellette was holding Russell, the only one sore was Auerbach!" Heinsohn vowed revenge on "that big goon" Lovellette for elbowing him in the face; Bob Cousy was angrier with himself—he swore to bench himself if his shooting slump continued.[35]

Heinsohn got revenge in Game Five by scoring thirty points, and when Cousy walked to the bench, it was to a standing ovation, as he finished with twenty-one points and ten assists in a 127–102 rout. But the Celtics failed to clinch the title in Game Six at St. Louis, falling behind by twenty-six points before succumbing 105–102.[36]

With the climactic Game Seven looming, the NBA again embarrassed itself with petty politics. Kerner insisted that Jim Duffy not referee the finale because he lived in Rhode Island and might be a "homer," even though Duffy had worked all six previous games. Maurice Podoloff did assign Duffy to Game Seven, but not before further shaming the league. "I wanted Sid Borgia in this series, but he walked out on me when he didn't get the first game," said the league president.[37]

The Celtics acted frustrated and antsy. After winning fifty-nine regular season games and surviving Wilt Chamberlain, they could not purge their pesky, undermanned rivals. Auerbach walked into the locker room, unsure what to say. Then he saw Russell drinking a pregame cup of tea. "Before we start on the intricacies of this ball game, I want you all to look at Russell," Auerbach said. "He thinks this is a tea party. Will you all look at Russell's little pinky? Isn't he delicate? Aren't we lucky to get his lesson in etiquette?" The players laughed, the tension broke, and Boston promptly annihilated St. Louis 122–103, capturing a third NBA title in four years.[38]

At the end, fans paraded Cousy around Boston Garden. Others tried to lift Russell, but they could not prop him up. They settled for pounding him on the back. Later, Russell wandered through the locker room, a solitary and proud figure, happy yet restrained. While microphones surrounded Cousy and beer showered upon

Auerbach, Russell sat on a training table in a quiet corner. "This gang, it's really special," he said. "I've won all these titles, and some men never win nothing. I'm lucky. People always helped me win so much." He projected modesty, dignity, selflessness.[39]

In the other dressing room, an unlikely source emphasized Russell's significance. Bob Pettit was not just a white man from Louisiana, but one whom the Celtics had kept from multiple NBA championships. Moreover, he insisted, "I'm not much for this talking about other players." But Russell had controlled the last game, set a new play-off rebounding record, shaped every possession with his defense, and "played the game like a gentleman." He was a credit to the NBA. "I'll take off my hat to Bill Russell as a basketball player and man any time I'm asked to," Pettit said. "He's a lot of man in my book."[40]

· · ·

Meanwhile, Chamberlain stood in the center ring of a media circus. "I'll never play basketball in the NBA again," he announced after the loss to Boston. He had hinted at quitting since the *Daily News* series in February, but few imagined that he would reject Eddie Gottlieb's three-year contract offer for about $180,000. Chamberlain insisted that his decision was final.[41]

Chamberlain claimed that he faced too much pressure, too much harassment. His attempt to punch Heinsohn augured poorly for the future. "If I continue I feel it may be bad for me and bad for my race," he said. "I may have to punch eight or nine guys in the face. I may lose my poise. I don't want to." Chamberlain also worried about scoring fewer points in upcoming seasons, which would diminish his leverage. Into this stew of self-righteous self-marketing, Chamberlain sprinkled in some self-centered self-justification: "I have achieved everything a man can achieve in pro basketball."[42]

The alleged retirement won publicity and ridicule. Photographers snapped away as Chamberlain and Gottlieb met at a sportswriters' banquet. Reporters followed Chamberlain to Chicago, where he played in a Globetrotter exhibition. He then joined the Globetrotters' European summer tour, and Saperstein offered $150,000 for his full-time services. As Gottlieb fumed that Saperstein was stealing his meal ticket, sportswriters called Chamberlain's decision foolish and illogical.[43]

Many NBA veterans resented Chamberlain's rationalizations. "Well," sniffed Cousy, "if Wilt quits the league we can all go back to playing basketball again." Besides taking that potshot at his singular talent, Cousy objected to Chamberlain's suggestion of racial prejudice. ("Any opponent or referee who discriminates against a Negro player dishonors sport," echoed a *Sports Illustrated* editorial, but "a Negro who makes exaggerated claims of prejudice does a disservice to his own people.") Others mocked Chamberlain's claim that he had nothing left to prove, since he possessed neither an NCAA nor an NBA title. Auerbach said that the rookie Russell weathered dirtier tactics, but "Bill took his lumps, fought back, and kept his mouth shut."[44]

In *Sport*, Dolph Schayes wrote that referees actually protected Chamberlain, and they never called offensive charges when he plowed toward the rim. Chamberlain used his elbows, too. Schayes essentially labeled Chamberlain a crybaby: "Wilt's retirement statement should be accepted for what it was—a statement chock-full of immature remarks, made in anger and disappointment in a losing team's locker room." A mature person would retract such comments, but not Chamberlain.[45]

Chamberlain resented the attacks, and he dismissed his own suggestions that he was a racial symbol. "I'm not crusading for anyone," he insisted. "I'm no Jackie Robinson." Anyway, his "retirement" proved short-lived. He signed a three-year contract worth at least $300,000. Gottlieb boasted that the contract made Chamberlain "the highest paid athlete in sports history." Indeed, Chamberlain sold tickets, and his contract elevated the league's status—at the expense of his own good name.[46]

Chamberlain's return coincided with the arrival of Oscar Robertson, who immediately joined Russell, Chamberlain, and Elgin Baylor in the pantheon of African American superstars. "The Big O" approached basketball perfection. The 6'5", 200-pound guard filled every line on the stat sheet. He overpowered smaller defenders, bullying close for high-percentage shots. He possessed deceptive speed, sliding through traffic. He saw the whole court, whipping perfect passes out of double-teams. He had uncommon stamina and grace. With absolute economy of motion, he dictated a game's texture.[47]

Like Russell, Robertson felt compelled to prove himself, to win retribution for insults and inequalities. From 1954 to 1956, as Russell drove USF to fifty-five straight wins and two NCAA titles, Robertson led Crispus Attucks High School to forty-five straight wins and two Indiana state titles. The smart, introspective teenager took satisfaction in his team's glories, which promoted black achievement and pride. Yet his large, all-black high school also reflected the stubborn segregation of Indianapolis. Like Russell, Robertson remembered every slight, such as insufficient recognition from city authorities or racist assumptions that he wanted money from college recruiters.[48]

Robertson attended the University of Cincinnati, where from 1957 to 1960, he won three national player of the year awards, set the NCAA scoring record, and led the Bearcats to a 79–9 record. Even before scoring fifty-six points in his Madison Square Garden debut, he received droves of press attention. After graduating in 1960, he won a gold medal at the Rome Olympics, headlining a team that included Jerry West, Jerry Lucas, and Walt Bellamy. But "Basketball's Moody Marvel" erected a sullen, intense shell to protect himself from exploitation and bigotry. The university had a handful of black students—all athletes—and two campus hangouts refused to serve them. On road trips to Texas and North Carolina, he endured segregation and fan abuse.[49]

The Cincinnati Royals' selection of Robertson in the territorial draft quite literally saved the franchise. Since moving from Rochester, the cellar-dwellers had been plagued by institutional negligence, the paralysis of Maurice Stokes, and fan apathy. But Robertson packed Cincinnati Gardens, and the Rookie of the Year averaged 30.5 points, 10.1 rebounds, and 9.7 assists a game. A cover feature in *Time* considered him the exemplar of the NBA's emerging trends: high scores, fluid patterns, excellent athletes, and commercial popularity. Robertson, many surmised, had already supplanted Cousy as the world's greatest guard.[50]

What Chamberlain represented to Russell, Robertson meant to Cousy: a physically superior nemesis, impossible to transcend individually, requiring a deeper summons of pride and will. Yet Robertson needed to hoard the basketball, to boss his veteran teammates, to dominate. Cousy, conversely, just revved up the Celtic machine. The 1960–61 team had enough talent, depth, and balance to be the best in NBA history. Anyway, Boston's greater challenge lay in Philadelphia. In December 1960, Auerbach predicted that the Celtics and Warriors would finish first and second in the Eastern Division. "Red," a friend replied, "I have a six year-old boy and he said the same thing before the season started."[51]

. . .

Philadelphia opened the season with nine straight wins, staking a claim as legitimate contenders for Boston's throne. The Warriors even crushed the Celtics in Boston, 131–103. In one early season game, Chamberlain earned forty-four points, thirty-nine rebounds, and twenty-two blocked shots. He had somehow improved: his defense grew more energetic, his stamina even stronger, his demeanor more composed.[52]

But Boston recovered first place with a 132–129 Thanksgiving Day win at Convention Hall, overcoming a fourth-quarter deficit and Chamberlain's fifty-five rebounds, which surpassed Russell's single-game mark. ("Let Wilt have the record," offered Russell. "I'll take the game.") In the ensuing months, before passionate crowds in both cities, the teams staged a nip-and-tuck battle for the Eastern Division crown. While Boston pulled away, finishing 57–22, the Warriors collapsed down the stretch. A growing rift between Chamberlain and Neil Johnston poisoned the team. The coach wanted a more balanced offense. Chamberlain insisted on hoarding shots, even as he complained about unfair scoring expectations. Philadelphia finished nine games behind Boston.[53]

Chamberlain broke ten records for points, shots, rebounds, and minutes, eight of which he had set the previous year. He became the first 3,000-point scorer in NBA history. Yet in the midst of Chamberlain's statistical conquest, Russell compelled league-wide respect. For one, he chose a proper moment to defend himself.

In early November, the Lakers' Jim Krebs was throwing elbows. "Krebs, put your guts where your mouth is," said Russell. As Krebs pulled his arm back, Russell popped him in the mouth. After twenty minutes in semiconsciousness, Krebs got eight stitches. Russell got a $100 fine.[54]

More important, Russell keyed Boston's frenetic pace and late-game confidence, illustrated by one representative sequence from a November game against St. Louis. With Boston down 79–76, Russell blocked Cliff Hagan. Boston scored a free throw and a put-back. Then Russell blocked Bob Pettit. Boston hit a jump shot. Then Russell stole a pass from Clyde Lovellette, sprinted downcourt, took a pass, and slammed a two-fisted dunk. After Russell rebounded the next shot, Boston scored again, establishing a six-point lead that it never relinquished. As Cousy noted, the Celtics could win without him, Sharman, or Heinsohn. They needed Russell.[55]

His peers voted Russell his second MVP award. Red Auerbach chastised the league's publicity department, which pumped out releases about Chamberlain. Auerbach had long been plugging Russell. When Chamberlain first occasioned massive hype, Auerbach insisted that he "has not had the profound effect on the thinking and theories of professional basketball that Russell had as a rookie. The NBA was prepared for Chamberlain by the advent of Russell." When Russell won MVP again, Auerbach crowed that "statistics do not fool pro basketball players." Russell embodied "a game with guts and heart, and defense and team effort."[56]

Russell valued the honor over his 1958 MVP because he beat new stars such as Baylor, Robertson, and Chamberlain. He motivated himself with self-pride, met the challenge of this next generation, and elevated his status. "Bill Russell Is Better than Ever," proclaimed *Sport*.[57]

Yet Russell's award also reflected animosity against Chamberlain, who finished behind Pettit and Baylor in the balloting. "Don't like the guy, personally," said one New York Knick about Chamberlain. "I wouldn't vote for him for anything." Many resented his ego. His rich contract benefited all players, but they found his off-season retirement distasteful. They also ridiculed his 50 percent free-throw shooting. "Any high school kid could do better," scoffed Dolph Schayes.[58]

According to Chamberlain's detractors, his incredible statistics resulted from his freakish size. St. Louis coach Paul Seymour called him "tall but without talent." Auerbach lobbied to regulate Chamberlain by banning "offensive goaltending" (the NCAA had banned the practice in 1956, one of the "Russell Rules"). Fans heckled him, players analyzed his shortcomings, coaches devised gimmick defenses. The media treated him like a cartoon giant villain. Bud Collins of the *Boston Globe* facetiously suggested that the Celtics hire a giraffe: "His presence would be no more of a travesty than Chamberlain's."[59]

As others rained scorn upon Chamberlain, however, Russell kept offering an ego-shielding umbrella. "He's No. 1—the best," said Russell, praising Chamberlain's work ethic and fall-away shot. If he started a basketball team, he would pick

Chamberlain first. When sportswriters voted Chamberlain the first-team All-Star center, Auerbach was apoplectic. But Russell praised the selection. Not once did he criticize his counterpart. Instead he joked about his "three-part defense." One, he tried denying Chamberlain the ball. Two, he tried staying between him and the basket. "Three is when everything else fails," he said. "I panic."[60]

Russell needed his rival's complacency. If Chamberlain built a personal animus against him, then Russell was doomed. If Chamberlain cared about scoring points and setting records, then Russell could concentrate on winning. So Russell lauded him. If the Celtics were blowing out the Warriors in the fourth quarter, he even allowed Chamberlain to rack up points. Russell could never match Chamberlain's awesome statistical production. So he disciplined himself, sharpened his strengths, and fed his ego through team-oriented contributions.[61]

Russell also nurtured their complicated friendship. When the Warriors came to Boston, Chamberlain ate dinner in Reading with Bill and Rose. When the Celtics visited Philadelphia on Thanksgiving, Russell ate turkey with Wilt and his parents. Then he napped in Wilt's bed ("My mother always thought that was kind of rude," recalled Chamberlain). Chamberlain's friends and coaches warned that Russell was manipulating him. But the two men considered their friendship genuine. Together they laughed at perceptions of a rivalry, even if, privately, Russell knew that he was softening Chamberlain's competitiveness.[62]

No story line in the NBA generated more fascination than Russell versus Chamberlain. "Never before have so many people taken an active interest in professional basketball," marveled *Sport*. "Suddenly, housewives and college coeds who generally avoid athletic events with a passion are taking sides in this battle between the giants. The names of Chamberlain and Russell have given new life to the game, even to the world of sport." If lumbering giants like Ray Felix or Walter Dukes were Model Ts, Russell and Chamberlain were Corvettes. A photo spread in *Life* featured the two graceful stars leaning into each other, soaring high together, scrambling for a ball. Russell compared facing Chamberlain to fighting a war, and Chamberlain compared Russell to a Roman gladiator. Linked by size and agility and race, marked by distinct talents and reputations and values, Russell and Chamberlain had established professional basketball's defining rivalry for the coming generation.[63]

· · ·

The rivalry took a hiatus for the 1961 play-offs, because Syracuse swept Philadelphia in the best-of-five preliminary round. Neil Johnston resigned as coach, lambasting Chamberlain on the way out: "It is tough to coach a team when one player is given so many privileges." He also blamed Chamberlain's inept foul shooting for the team's failure.[64]

The ensuing play-offs revealed two things: the solidification of the Boston Celtics dynasty, and the stickiness of the NBA's squabbling, slapdash reputation.

In Boston's opening 128–115 victory over Syracuse, the referee's whistle blew as Russell jumped for a rebound. Russell gave an incredulous double take. A black dog had wandered onto the court and stopped underneath his legs. Before the Nationals evened the series in Syracuse, 115–98, the coaches quibbled over the selection of referees. The Celtics won the next two games, 133–110 and 120–107, but during the fourth game in Syracuse, three fans stormed the court, jawed with Auerbach, and got pounded in the Celtics huddle. (The next winter, the offending fans actually tried to sue Auerbach and four Celtics—newspapers pictured Auerbach getting served a subpoena in a Syracuse hotel, clad only in underpants). The Celtics closed out the series in Game Five, 123–101, behind Russell's twenty-five points and thirty-three rebounds.[65]

For the fourth time in five years, Boston faced St. Louis in the NBA Finals. Their regular season games had again indicated their animosity. In one game, a St. Louis fan stepped six feet in front of Auerbach and bruised his forehead with a yolky missile. "This is a bush town," cried Auerbach, "and you can quote me on that." When the Hawks next visited Boston, an egg shower delayed the start a half-hour. In the play-offs, the coaches' histrionics against the referees diminished the games, especially when broadcast on television. "Their endless bickering, screaming, moaning and complaining, their raging rushes onto the court to play the victimized leader is a boring and offensive act," judged one sportswriter.[66]

Boston took the first two games at Boston Garden, 129–95 and 116–108. St. Louis had Bob Pettit and Cliff Hagan, but Boston had depth. "How can you depend on two men to beat us?" bragged Cousy. Even before the series ended, he called this outfit "the greatest basketball team ever assembled." The Celtics let Game Three slip away, 124–120, but they won Game Four in St. Louis, 119–104. Then, in Game Five at Boston Garden, Cousy offered heroic leadership, overcoming sinus problems that left him gasping. Russell delivered a spectacular thirty-point, thirty-eight-rebound performance. Boston won 121–112, capturing its third consecutive NBA championship, its fourth in five years.[67]

The now-familiar scene ensued: fans stormed the court, the heroes got carried off, the beer-soaked Celtics hugged and laughed and celebrated, the dejected Hawks praised Bill Russell. The MVP deflected credit to his teammates—not just to veteran stars like Cousy but also to role players such as Jim Loscutoff. The Celtics had talent, heart, and chemistry. "It's going to be awful hard to beat us for some time," said Russell. "We like this winning feeling."[68]

8

The Mystique

Russell once called sports a mixture of art and war. They adopt political and spiritual dimensions. They stir the passions of participants and observers. They provide heroes and villains, rules and rituals, insurmountable obstacles and improbable triumphs. Sometimes, Russell recalled, a few men played with such beauty and passion that "the feeling would spread to the other guys, and we'd all levitate. Then the game would just take off, and there'd be a natural ebb and flow that reminded you how rhythmic and musical basketball is supposed to be." These moments of transcendence suggest basketball's larger appeal. More than baseball or football, basketball is the American game. Invented on American soil, it fuses individual freedom with communal enterprise. Its solo feints, flair, and bursts—managed through collective patterns—compare to another American art form: jazz.[1]

The Boston Celtics offered basketball in its highest form, merging individual and team, white and black. They also lent the sport its archetype. "The Celtics are the aristocrats of basketball—arrogant perfectionists who play with almost insulting contempt," wrote Jim Murray. "They come on court with the Emperor of Basketball, Bill Russell, and the score is psychologically 20–0 before the tip-off." The players often referred to their "pride," a quality built on mutual trust and quiet confidence. Their aura of invincibility became known as the "Celtic Mystique."[2]

This character stemmed from a cooperative dedication to winning, but it was rooted in one man. "Forget about the stories of magic leprechauns in the rafters of Boston Garden and how the cramped visitors' dressing room and psychological games created some sort of Celtics' mystique," insisted Oscar Robertson. "No matter how good the players surrounding him were, no matter how competitive his coach was, Bill Russell *was* the Celtics' mystique."[3]

. . .

"You big shvartzeh sonofabitch!" Auerbach screamed, while Russell loafed through practice. The needling typically provoked a scowl, but Russell never challenged his coach, and he always worked harder. The exchanges illustrated how Auerbach, behind an abrasive image, combined authority and democracy. His use of "shvartzeh"—a derogatory Yiddish term for a black person—revealed insensitivity, but it also suggested comfort with his star center. Their evolving relationship fueled Boston's dynasty.[4]

Auerbach's personality blended combativeness, garishness, miserliness, and bad manners. He stalked the sideline with a rolled-up program, barking at referees. Maurice Podoloff levied fines on him. Reporters considered him arrogant. Rival crowds hated him. When the Celtics opened a comfortable lead, Auerbach pulled out a fat cigar, sat back with a satisfied grin, and puffed away. He dodged eggs, rotten tomatoes, beer cans, spitballs, lit cigars, popcorn, peanuts, and snowballs, as well as a swinging woman's handbag and a few drunken men's fists. He was a sore loser and a sore winner.[5]

If other coaches were ex-jocks whose idea of practice involved rolling out the ball for a scrimmage, Auerbach gave coaching his single-minded devotion, like some loudmouthed monk. Uncomfortable around women and inept at small talk, he banned players' wives on road trips. He stayed at the Hotel Lenox while his family resided in Washington, DC. His wardrobe contained discount-rack plaid sport coats, and his diet consisted of junk food, Chinese take-out, soda, and cigars.[6]

Yet Auerbach created an enduringly loyal culture for the Celtics. On scouting trips he looked for intelligent men who hustled, communicated well, and knew fundamentals. He ignored statistics. He earned trust by helping with off-season jobs, potential endorsements, and investments. He avoided playing cards or drinking beers with players, but his office had an open door.[7]

The Celtic philosophy depended on collective responsibility: ball movement on offense, swarming effort on defense. Russell's shotblocking made that defense possible. Even when shooting poorly, the Celtics won with defense. But as the season's grind dulled the competitive edge, Auerbach instinctually realized when the team needed tongue-lashings, blunt reminders, teasing jokes, or silence. He also tailored individual approaches. He shamed Tom Heinsohn and Jim Loscutoff into furious effort. He left Frank Ramsey alone, trusting his sharp focus. He massaged Cousy, Sharman, and Russell with effusive praise. He indulged the pregame hypochondria of Russell and Sam Jones, who had nervous stomachs.[8]

Auerbach focused on his players' strengths, installing a modern system of specialized functions. Russell was the rebounder and shotblocker, Cousy the ballhandler, Sharman and Heinsohn the shooters, Loscutoff and Gene Conley the bruisers. For Ramsey, Auerbach invented the "Sixth Man" role, substituting the sharpshooter and clever defender to lend a boost. Ramsey could have been a leading scorer and perennial All-Star, but he embraced his particular responsibility because Auerbach crafted him a special status.[9]

Auerbach enforced basic principles and empowered his players. In half-court sets, they ran only seven different plays, though each stratagem involved multiple options. For instance, the "3" play gave Russell the ball on the high post, while a guard and forward cleared out the left side, allowing Russell to drive past a slower center. If his defender overplayed the entry pass, Russell could cut back toward the basket. He could also dish off, since his teammates were cutting and setting screens. The players read the defense and adjusted accordingly. Everyone in the NBA knew their plays, but their skills, intelligence, and unselfishness created baskets.[10]

Boston's success sprung from this ethos of democratic collaboration. The team's hyperkinetic pace balanced out minutes and points. Russell played most of the game, but the others averaged between twenty-five and thirty-five minutes a game. Rarely did a Celtic rank among the top ten scorers. Despite Auerbach's image as a belligerent autocrat, he valued his players' input. During practices or time-outs, he solicited their opinions on matchups, patterns, and plays. Then he delivered instructions, which they accepted without questioning, because Auerbach had invested them in the process.[11]

African Americans folded into this cooperative unit. By the early 1960s, Sam Jones and K. C. Jones had progressed into essential reserves. Perhaps the league's fastest player, Sam Jones scored at a growing clip. He slid toward the basket for one-hand scoops, popped midrange bank shots, and converted deep two-handers. K. C. Jones set up shooters with deft dribbling and passing, and his chest-to-chest defense frazzled opponents. National publications touted "The Jones Boys" as a viable starting backcourt for most NBA teams.[12]

In the 1960 draft, Boston added Tom "Satch" Sanders. Auerbach revamped the high-scoring 6'6" center from New York University into a defense-oriented forward. Sanders had quick feet, long arms, and good timing. While covering Elgin Baylor, Dolph Schayes, or Bob Pettit, he performed such nitty-gritty duties as setting picks, boxing out, diving for loose balls, and delivering hard fouls. Like Sam and K. C. Jones, Sanders accepted his complementary role, following the tradition of most black professionals from the 1950s.[13]

Yet if Auerbach plugged blacks into customary slots, he lacked prejudice. "Red confined his world and his efforts to basketball," explained Sanders. "Race was never an issue." The coach berated, tutored, or bantered with all his players. To reporters he praised the underrated blacks on the bench. On other NBA teams, blacks felt alienated from their white coach and teammates, but Auerbach crushed that possibility in the Celtics. As they congregated in hotel lobbies, for instance, he assigned people to taxicabs without regard to race. Reporter Clif Keane despised Auerbach, but he marveled how the coach "has blended the white and black athletes on his team brilliantly."[14]

That seamless integration centered on Auerbach's partnership with Russell. In Russell's eyes, Phil Woolpert had withheld praise and Abe Saperstein had disrespected him. But when a referee called the rookie Russell for goaltending, Auerbach stomped onto the floor, earning a technical foul. Russell considered that a sign of loyalty. Auerbach also engaged him in long private conversations, which renewed his competitive drive, and lauded him to reporters, which stoked his pride. "Red's the best," Russell said. "He's versatile, intelligent, astute, flexible, and he has me on the team. He's made the most out of it. He's getting the maximum out of me." Throughout his career, Russell commended his coach.[15]

Auerbach granted Russell unique considerations. When Russell missed a plane, Auerbach just teased him. Sometimes Russell traveled separately from the team. And Auerbach indulged Russell's hatred of practice. If Russell needed a break between games, Auerbach let him disappear. When Russell came to practice, Auerbach often assigned him to just referee scrimmages. In one representative scene, as Auerbach snarled "Elbows straight!" during a warm-up drill, Russell limply flapped his arms and broke into a mischievous grin. Auerbach stared past him. "Elbows straight!" he yelled at the others.[16]

Most important, Auerbach accepted Russell on Russell's own terms. Auerbach never displayed fatherly affection, knowing that such paternalism would offend Russell. Instead he quenched Russell's thirst for respect. He asked Russell for his basketball opinions. He ran plays for Russell. He never interfered with Russell's off-court endeavors. In turn, Russell trusted his coach's decisions, knowing that Auerbach possessed a total commitment to their mutual success. They built a professional partnership, and even a particular friendship, based on mutual esteem.[17]

Their alliance made Auerbach more racially sensitive. Before Russell, Auerbach banned fraternization with opposing players, but Russell befriended blacks throughout the NBA. Auerbach also learned that his leadership necessitated support against racial discrimination. Back in 1958, when Russell had condemned segregation in Charlotte, Auerbach had pleaded patience, insisting that he understood prejudice because he was Jewish. "Oh yeah?" asked Russell. "Well, what hotel are you staying in, Red?"[18]

So Auerbach's cries of "big shvartzeh sonofabitch" had an element of calculation. He sometimes warned Russell before these rare scoldings. Russell knew that it inspired his teammates, and his teammates knew that Russell needed recharging between games. By conceding such indulgences, Auerbach conveyed respect for his proud, vulnerable star. The team culture revolved around their collaboration. And as Russell flourished, Boston's gradual integration fed an emerging dynasty.[19]

. . .

The same debates arose every year: Was this the greatest team ever? Would it crush the old Minneapolis Lakers? Reporters called them "The Yankees of Basketball." Like the baseball dynasty in New York, they dominated perceptions of their sport, inviting both admiration and resentment. "The Celtics were now firmly established as part of America's major-league sports scene," wrote Leonard Koppett. "The character of the Celtics had been revealed so often, in so many circumstances, that even the casual sports fan was familiar with the general outline."[20]

The franchise acquired an endearing crustiness. Owner Walter Brown earned universal affection for his integrity and generosity—especially from his players, who avoided Auerbach and searched out Brown during contract time. Radio announcer Johnny Most unabashedly painted the Celtics as heroes and opponents as villains. Only the Celtics wore black sneakers, and only Boston Garden had a parquet floor, a 247-panel checkerboard made from oak scraps.[21]

The arena underwhelmed its visitors. Densely packed and sloppily functional, it was located under North Station, in a neighborhood full of gritty bars and shady characters. The dressing room, too, belied Boston's reputation as the class of the NBA. These giant athletes dressed together in a fifteen-by-twenty-feet space. Their "lockers" were a hook or nail in the wall. The shorter players changed under a low, sloping ceiling below a staircase. The trainer worked in a tiny side room. They had one toilet, one urinal, one sink, and two showers. A clogged drain often flooded the bathroom.[22]

But Boston Garden also psyched out opponents. They complained about dead spots on the parquet floor, an alternately freezing and sweltering locker room, and tough fans. When Mike Farmer played for St. Louis, he remembered Bostonians pelting him with a variety of goods, including a fish. He finally wised up: during the national anthem, he stood next to rookies, away from the team's stars.[23]

What most defined the Celtics was how, as one writer marveled, "perhaps never in organized athletics have a group of stars worked, worried, battled and played in more perfect harmony." They valued team victory over individual statistics. They possessed a quiet confidence, an easy humor, a mutual respect. Veterans trained rookies in Celtic Pride. Walter Brown paid them well, but their egos stayed in check. The organization promoted an image as a family.[24]

"There was a chemistry there," recalled Ramsey. "We truly liked each other." That camaraderie developed through a season's rituals and rigors. Auerbach's grueling training camp often spurred early leads in the standings. They piled into cars for exhibition tours, barreling along New England's back roads, where they plucked apples to eat or lob at each other's cars. They embraced Auerbach's "kangaroo court," levying tiny fines for minor transgressions such as lateness. They teased, challenged, and sometimes fought each other in competitive practices. They played practical jokes: loosening the buttons on a dress shirt, tearing the final chapter out of a mystery novel, giving an exploding cigar.[25]

They could play six games in seven days, filling arena dates both home and away. Life on the road could become a monotonous succession of airports, hotels, train stations, coffee shops, and bars. Players soaked dirty jerseys in hotel sinks between back-to-back away games. They endured red-eye flights and overnight train rides. They had marathon card games. Their conversations ranged from sports to politics to women. Some smoked cigarettes, many tomcatted, and most drank. After a Madison Square Garden doubleheader, half the NBA might end up swilling beers in the same bar.[26]

Every team had these experiences. What made the Celtics different? Russell believed that "most of us were oddballs by society's standards," an agglomeration of strong, driven personalities. Each handled pressure distinctly: Cousy might distract himself with fan mail, Ramsey might attend to business interests, Heinsohn might paint a canvas, and Russell might fiddle with his ever-expanding train set. Yet on court, each found satisfaction in collective success.[27]

The NBA was a man's world—where men found common ground and entered a competitive crucible. Roaring crowds and media attention only sharpened that experience. Resentments could fester, conflicts could detonate. But each Celtic established a self-definition that channeled his ego. "The key to being a Celtic, if there's any one thing, is you have to be a man and accept responsibility for your actions," reflected Russell. "Every one of those guys was a man, and I don't mean just a male over 21. We took care of each other."[28]

. . .

The Boston dynasty lost its first star before the 1961–62 season, when Bill Sharman signed as coach and general manager of the Los Angeles Jets in the new American Basketball League (ABL). Sam and K. C. Jones had usurped some playing time, and Sharman had long desired to coach. By early 1961, rumors arose that he would coach an expansion team in Pittsburgh or Chicago. The potential defection angered the Boston brass. In the 1961 title-clincher, Sharman played only twelve minutes. Auerbach praised everyone except Sharman, who smiled feebly from the background of celebratory photos. But the players accepted his wishes. At the breakup banquet Russell extolled him as "a brother," "a man whom I love and respect," an embodiment of "desire, unselfishness, and will to win."[29]

When Sharman promised to retire, Walter Brown released him to coach the Jets. But the paternalistic owner also called Sharman a "quitter" who violated a "moral contract," and Maurice Podoloff withheld his $3,423 play-off bonus. Brown further raged when Sharman donned a Jets uniform to boost flagging attendance. He suspected that Sharman was recruiting players, including Russell.[30]

The ABL was the brainchild of Abe Saperstein. The Globetrotter boss had first coveted an NBA franchise. No longer able to sign elite black talent, he fumed at the ingratitude of owners who had depended on Globetrotter exhibitions during lean years. After purportedly promising him a Los Angeles team, the NBA demanded an exorbitant entry fee for a San Francisco franchise. Instead, Saperstein formed the rival ABL, with teams in Washington, Pittsburgh, Cleveland, Chicago, Kansas City, Los Angeles, San Francisco, and Hawaii. His new league helped smaller men by widening the lane to eighteen feet and introducing a three-point line.[31]

The ABL formed as another scandal struck college basketball. In 1961 investigators revealed that thirty-seven players from twenty-two schools had fixed forty-four games. Though the crimes spread wider than in 1951, they prompted less outrage, a symbol of sports' declining innocence. The scandal nevertheless shaped professional sports. The ABL accepted the implicated players, including Connie Hawkins, a super-talented, pencil-thin forward expelled from the University of Iowa after his freshman year. Hawkins had taken money from gamblers out of poverty and ignorance, but he had never played a varsity contest, let alone shaved points. Hawkins joined the Pittsburgh Rens, averaged 27.5 points, and won MVP.[32]

Unlike the ABL, the NBA distanced itself from perceived impropriety. The league had just won a lawsuit filed by Jack Molinas, who had been banned for point-shaving in 1954. The mastermind of a widespread sports gambling operation, Molinas went to prison after the 1961 scandal. "I honestly believe professional basketball is the cleanest sport of them all," Russell insisted, since the sport had good salaries and smart athletes. Yet because gamblers surrounded the game and critics fretted about sport's moral crises, Podoloff employed a professional odds-maker who alerted him to betting trends suggesting a possible fix. Podoloff also banned Hawkins and everyone else stained by scandal.[33]

Plagued by poor attendance, dilapidated arenas, and economic instability, the ABL never threatened the NBA's hegemony. Sharman's Jets disbanded within months. The ABL thus indicated both the NBA's viability and vulnerability. Cities could support professional basketball, but teams needed resourceful management and popular stars. In the early 1960s, potential new franchises in Pittsburgh and Cleveland fell through, and the owners kept blocking Podoloff's expansion plans. "Of all the leagues in professional sport," opined *Sports Illustrated,* "none is more abused by its players and followers, or more confused by its owners and officers."[34]

Two major-market teams sapped the NBA's health. The league finally returned to Chicago in 1961, adding the Zephyrs as its ninth team. Although Chicago drafted Walt Bellamy, a talented center from Indiana University, the collection of rookies and castoffs finished 18–62, last in the Western Division. In New York, meanwhile, tightfisted mismanagement crippled the league's alleged flagship. "The Knicks are nothing but a tax write-off anyway," said owner Ned Irish, whose Madison Square Garden profited more from college basketball, special events, and the NHL's New

York Rangers. By 1962 New York had finished last in the Eastern Division five of the previous six years.[35]

The NBA did reach the West Coast in 1960, when the Minneapolis Lakers moved to Los Angeles. Baseball's Dodgers and Giants had already relocated to California, commercial jets made cross-country flights feasible, and the Los Angeles Sports Arena was a first-class facility. At first the Lakers struggled to draw crowds and media coverage. But after taking St. Louis to seven games in the 1961 play-offs, they attracted fans, including celebrities such as Pat Boone and Doris Day.[36]

The Lakers developed championship aspirations during the 1961–62 season, when Jerry West and Elgin Baylor formed a devastating tandem. The intense, introverted West grew up in rural West Virginia, spending hours shooting at his neighbor's hoop, dribbling on dirt. Skinny and bony-shouldered with a tip-toed gait, he got jostled by defenders. But he shot with a quick, light-fingered release, and his self-critical obsession refined his all-around game. The two-time All-American at West Virginia University won gold at the 1960 Olympics and got picked second in the NBA draft, after Oscar Robertson.[37]

West disappointed as a rookie. He hated coming off the bench, and his transition from forward to guard sputtered. The next season, however, West asserted himself. The U.S. Army Reserve called up Baylor, who played only forty-eight regular-season games. West filled the void, delivering so many last-minute heroics that announcer Chick Hearn dubbed him "Mr. Clutch." When Baylor suited up, moreover, they formed an unstoppable duo, averaging more than sixty-nine points a game. Los Angeles ended the 1961–62 season at 54–26, tops in the Western Division. Now the franchise flourished.[38]

By pushing expansion and relocation, Podoloff sought to lure not only paying customers but also national television contracts. He manipulated play-off schedules to maximize television exposure, and during NBC telecasts, he scurried between benches, instructing coaches to call time-outs for commercial breaks. Ninety percent of American households owned at least one television set, and the Sports Broadcasting Act of 1961 allowed professional leagues to negotiate contracts without violating federal antitrust law. Yet television failed to capture basketball's inherent drama. Two or three cameras were stationed high above the court, offering few close-up shots. The games got such low ratings that after the 1962 season, NBC dropped basketball. For two seasons the NBA had no national television contract, a whopping embarrassment.[39]

Shabby officiating further bedeviled the league. Referees allowed too many rough fouls, gave stars special considerations, and got swayed by home crowds. Owners and coaches bawled them out during games, then beefed about them to the press. The best referees possessed strong personalities and instincts for a game's rhythm, but many earned reputations as petty incompetents. The NBA practically guaranteed bad officials (and made them obvious targets for point-shaving bribes) by ig-noring their security, undermining their authority, and paying them per-game with-out adequate expenses or benefits.[40]

No one tormented referees more than Red Auerbach. In November 1961 he got ejected in consecutive games, earning an automatic three-game suspension. Yet the Celtics swept the ensuing road trip through St. Louis, Cincinnati, and New York, with Bob Cousy acting as player-coach. Boston was a juggernaut. Sam Jones re-placed Sharman in the starting lineup, and former New York Knick Carl Braun added a veteran guard off the bench. The Celtics finished 60–20, breaking their own single-season win record.[41]

In January 1962, however, Boston lost four straight games—all while Russell wore a blazer and tie, sidelined with a pulled Achilles tendon. While driving to-ward the basket, he had crumpled in a heap and got carried off the court. He rested only eight days. When he hobbled back on court, the Celtics restored their win-ning ways. Russell had become even more indispensable. Gene Conley had joined the ABL, leaving Russell without a backup. He averaged career highs of 18.9 points and 45.2 minutes a game. "This year has been his best and most consistent," mar-veled Cousy. "He dribbles better than any big man. He moves better. He has no equal as a rebounder. He's the best defensive player in the league."[42]

At season's end, the players once again voted Russell MVP. His defensive mas-tery sparkled ever brighter in the glow of an offensive outburst, embodied by Wilt Chamberlain.[43]

. . .

"They are a new race of men," wrote Milton Gross in 1961. "They have swiftness, grace, strength and accuracy unmatched in our heritage. They have made basket-ball a new game in which one man scoring 100 points would not be incredible, sim-ply another giant tremor in the big explosion." The 1961–62 season surpassed any other for offensive production. Every team averaged at least 110 points. Philadel-phia once beat New York 169–147. Old timers marveled at the accuracy of jump shooters, the agility of big men, and the frenetic pace. Various players and coaches proposed rules changes such as a longer shot clock, a three-point shot, twelve-foot baskets, and eliminating the backboard.[44]

That "new race of men" did not refer only to African Americans, but black su-perstars led this onslaught. Four of the six players who averaged more than thirty points were black: Wilt Chamberlain, Elgin Baylor, Oscar Robertson, and Walt Bel-lamy. Robertson averaged a "triple double" of 30.8 points, 12.5 rebounds, and 11.4 assists. The *Pittsburgh Courier* bragged that black players "have grossly changed the NBA tradition" and "own a natural endowment for basketball."[45]

Chamberlain represented the apotheosis of this trend, both for his jaw-dropping statistics and the accompanying jeremiads. Philadelphia's new coach, Frank Mc-

Guire, curried Chamberlain's favor by encouraging more shots. Chamberlain shattered records all season. Because of overtime periods, he averaged more than forty-eight minutes a game. With power dunks, tip-ins, put-backs, fall-aways, hooks, and short jump shots, he scored seventy-eight points against Los Angeles in December, seventy-three against Chicago in January. The previous season, Chamberlain first broke the 3,000-point barrier; now he scored more than 4,000. He *averaged* 50.4 points a game.[46]

On March 2, 1962, in Hershey, Pennsylvania, against the New York Knicks, Chamberlain scored one hundred points in one game. Before only 4,124 fans, in one of the remote outposts where Gottlieb sent "home" contests, the game juxtaposed an almost-mythical feat with a small-time, ramshackle milieu. After three quarters, when Chamberlain had amassed sixty-nine points, the game entered the realm of farce: the Knicks fouled the other Warriors to stop the unsportsmanlike assault, and the Warriors fouled the Knicks to stop the clock and get Chamberlain more shots. The feat received little national attention. Its sole visual commemoration is a photograph of Chamberlain, sheepishly holding a scrap of paper scribbled with "100."[47]

The next day, the *Boston Globe* switchboard lit up with readers questioning the veracity of Chamberlain's deed. But most professionals echoed Russell, who said that "at first I was really surprised, and then as I thought it over, I wasn't." Many had speculated on the possibility, including Russell. One month earlier, he told *Newsweek* that Chamberlain "has the size, strength, and stamina to score 100 some night."[48]

Fan apathy, scoring trends, and Chamberlain's image diluted appreciation for the milestone. After years of growth, attendance had dropped everywhere except Los Angeles. Scoring had become too easy and big men too dominant, an impression personified by Chamberlain. "The More He Scores, the More He Bores," exclaimed one headline. Critics considered the Warriors' style dull, selfish, and ineffective against Russell's Celtics.[49]

Yet Chamberlain compelled a unique fascination. An icon for the television age, he never uttered platitudes when boasts, whines, or conspicuous consumption won more attention. He earned the largest salary in the NBA and got offers to join the ABL. He bought harness racing horses and a celebrated jazz club in Harlem. He drove Cadillacs and Bentleys. He wore a three-carat diamond pinky ring. He bragged about speaking four foreign languages, playing the guitar and fiddle, and investing in a new Los Angeles apartment complex. He appeared on television shows such as *I've Got a Secret, The Ed Sullivan Show,* and *What's My Line?*[50]

Still, Chamberlain felt unappreciated. People *expected* him to break records. Russell won MVP, but Chamberlain scored more. Russell earned admiration for his rebounding, but Chamberlain grabbed more rebounds. "They talk about Russell and how he's so well-liked," said Chamberlain. "I have as many personal friends in the NBA as he does. I don't think our personalities are too much different. But with the sportswriters and fans everything is because of image—the image of bigness." Russell was David to his Goliath, and "no one roots for Goliath."[51]

In the era of Chamberlain, Russell seemed a defender at the gates, preserving the game's integrity. As Chamberlain trashed the record books, statistics diminished in value, enhancing appreciation for Russell. As the Celtics won championships, Russell rivaled Chamberlain as the game's dominant figure. Games between Boston and Philadelphia allowed reporters to revisit their clashes, analyze their friendship, and consider their disparate talents. Debating their relative merits became the NBA's premier parlor game.[52]

Chamberlain's boosters argued that he dominated on both offense and defense, that he racked up points on Russell, and that Russell was a glorified role player. But most NBA players chose Russell. Given first choice in a hypothetical draft, Jack Twyman chose Russell. So did Bob Pettit, who called Russell "the greatest demoralizing influence on the court." Richie Guerin chose Russell "for his value as a team player." Alex Hannum argued, "From a coach's viewpoint, Bill's the most valuable player in the history of the game. He's proved the unheralded parts of the game—defense and rebounding—are really as important as shooting and playmaking."[53]

The debate engaged great philosophical questions. What is greatness? Is it quantitative or qualitative? Individual or communal? Forcing others to adapt, or adapting to others? Achieving celebrity or respect? Chamberlain created a personal mythology, elevating the NBA by transcending it. But Russell fostered victory. That was his talent, his greatness—his mystique.[54]

. . .

The 1962 play-offs wove together basketball's defining strands—the Russell-Chamberlain rivalry, the emergence of African American stars, the torrent of offensive production, the big league/bush league dichotomy, the rise of the Lakers, the Celtic mystique—and wrapped them in drama. They fortified Russell's stature, but they pushed him to the brink.

The play-offs promised a "new" Wilt Chamberlain. In the opening series against Syracuse, Frank McGuire convinced Chamberlain to pass more, prompting a scoring renaissance from Paul Arizin and the emergence of rookie Tom Meschery. Chamberlain accepted his declining point totals until the deciding Game Five, when he took forty-eight shots and scored fifty-six points. "All season Russell has known just which way Wilt was going to turn," said McGuire. He hoped that this new strategy would keep Russell guessing.[55]

Home-court advantage dictated the Eastern Division Finals—for the Celtics and Warriors, and for Russell and Chamberlain. At Boston Garden, Russell poked the ball, blocked shots, and bumped Chamberlain, holding him to twelve first-half points. Boston won 117–89. Two nights later at Convention Hall, however, Chamberlain got forty-two points and thirty-seven rebounds, and he led a fourth-quarter comeback with twelve points in the last six minutes. His spectacular put-back over Russell pushed Philadelphia ahead, and the Warriors won 113–106.[56]

The seesaw pattern continued. During Game Three in Boston, Russell outscored Chamberlain 31–21, out-rebounded him 14–11, and led a forty-one-point second quarter surge, spurring a 129–114 rout. During Game Four in Philadelphia, Russell accumulated four fouls by the second quarter, and Chamberlain scored most of his forty-one points against overmatched forwards, leading another comeback win, 110–106. The ill will festered. McGuire sniffed at Boston's "Globetrotter" offense. Celtics and Warriors fans brawled in Convention Hall. When Chamberlain complained about brutish defense, Loscutoff called him a "prima donna."[57]

The animosity swelled to a crescendo during Game Five, which the Celtics won easily, 119–104. Early in the fourth quarter, Sam Jones dribbled into the lane and Chamberlain stuck an arm in his face. "Don't you drive on me," Chamberlain warned. "Don't you drive on me." On the next possession, Jones switched onto Chamberlain and pushed him in the back. Chamberlain swung out his arm, flinging Jones off the court. They swore at each other. Jones put up his hands, and Chamberlain tried grabbing them. Chamberlain later claimed that he was offering a peaceful handshake, but Jones wheeled away and grabbed a photographer's stool, waving it before the giant Warrior.

Chaos ensued. Russell wrapped his arms around Chamberlain. Guy Rodgers grabbed the stool. Police arrested two fans who stormed the court, and officers shooed back hundreds of riled-up spectators. A minute later, Loscutoff fouled Rodgers, and Rodgers shoved Loscutoff. When Carl Braun interceded, Rodgers punched him in the face. A police officer held back a raging Braun while Rodgers flitted away. Then Heinsohn got ejected for pummeling Ted Luckenbill with a shoulder block and flying elbow.[58]

Chamberlain threw no punches, never got ejected, and was not among the five players fined by Podoloff. Yet in the aftermath of the April Fools' Day fiasco, he appeared the biggest villain. Newspapers ran photographs of Jones scrambling for the stool, looking terrified, and getting stalked by a huge bully. One columnist blamed the entire fracas on "Wilt Chamberlain's lack of pride." Russell, by contrast, appeared the gentleman. "I don't like this kind of stuff. We try to make this a respectable game," he said. "This is supposed to be the big leagues, isn't it?"[59]

Chamberlain was exhausting Russell. The Boston center could not keep food down. Nor could he sleep. Lying awake in bed, he envisioned buildings falling all around him, bricks burying him. He was playing every game wire-to-wire, and he was getting snappy at little mistakes. He also winced when others derided Chamberlain. "I've been telling you for three years," he said. "This man is a terrible man to be in there with when he's at his best." At the beginning of Game Six, Russell called time out, because he was having trouble breathing. The Warriors established an early lead before their home crowd. (One fan got ejected for grabbing a referee; another tried fighting Auerbach at halftime; a third brandished a stool.) Boston's comeback fell short, and Philadelphia won 109–99.[60]

It came to Game Seven in Boston Garden, a classic blend of gritty efforts and spectacular performances. Tom Gola and Frank Ramsey gutted through painful injuries. K. C. Jones covered the bigger Tom Meschery after Loscutoff and Sanders fouled out. Cousy connected on snappy passes and long set shots. Heinsohn hit an array of jumpers and hooks. Sam Jones led all scorers with twenty-eight points. Russell was magnificent, holding Chamberlain to twenty-two points. Three of his blocks led to important fourth-quarter baskets.

Yet Chamberlain was equally brilliant, especially in the final minute. After a controversial goaltending call put Boston up by five, Chamberlain converted two free throws, and after a Boston miss, he scored while getting fouled. The extra free throw tied the game at 107. The Celtics had eleven seconds. Sam Jones dribbled high on the left side, and Russell set a pick. Jones drove left, past the foul line, and pulled up for a high-arcing jump shot, over the outstretched arm of Chamberlain. It swished in. Fans rushed the court, celebrating the remarkable clutch shot and another trip to the NBA Finals.

"There is one second of play remaining," the public address announcer insisted. Slowly, the court cleared. Finally, Ed Conlin inbounded from half-court. He lobbed it high, and Chamberlain out-jumped everyone, came down, turned around, and shot. The short basket would have sent the game to overtime. But Russell extended his left hand and blocked the shot. With that poetic encapsulation of the series, season, and rivalry, Boston won. "Tonight, tonight, man," sighed Russell. "I sleep, glory be."[61]

He needed the rest. Two days later, Boston opened the NBA Finals against the Los Angeles Lakers. The army had given Elgin Baylor leave for the Western Division play-offs, and the superstar forward had a weekend pass for the first two games in Boston. The Celtics won the Saturday opener, 122–108. The next day Jerry West scored forty, Baylor added thirty-six, and Los Angeles withstood Boston's furious fourth-quarter run, evening the series with a 129–122 win. The Celtics had played six times in nine days, and Russell's exhaustion sank deeper. "I feel weak," he said on Sunday night. "It's the same feeling I had in Philly, when I couldn't catch my breath."[62]

The Lakers gained confidence when the army confirmed that Baylor could extend his leave throughout the series. Los Angeles led Game Three by twelve points with six minutes left. Again, the Celtics made a late charge, and with three seconds left, they led by two. But West tied the game with two free throws, and after a timeout, he stole the ball, raced downcourt, and scored as time expired. Los Angeles won 117–115. The fans jumped, screamed, laughed, and slapped the back of West, who called it "the greatest thrill I've ever had in basketball."[63]

Boston squared the series the next night, winning 115–103 by feeding Russell in the post. Los Angeles started 6'8" Jim Krebs, who got manhandled near the basket, and brought in 6'11" Ray Felix, a slow-footed veteran. Neither could defend Russell. At least Krebs could shoot from outside, opening space for Baylor's drives. But Russell tormented Felix, a notoriously colorful character. After Russell blocked four straight shots, Felix flipped a shot over his shoulder. It soared over the backboard. Felix pointed and yelled, "You didn't get that one, baby!"[64]

The series enthralled fans on both coasts. Los Angelinos had filled the Sports Arena, and when Bostonians packed the Garden for Game Five, they witnessed one of the signature performances in NBA history. Baylor kept gliding to open space and levitating for jump shots, scoring a play-off-record sixty-one points. When he fouled out, Boston fans gave him a huge ovation. Los Angeles won 126–121.[65]

Was it the end of the Boston dynasty? "If we win the championship this year, I think we will dominate the league for several years to come," proclaimed Lakers owner Bob Short. An anonymous Celtic agreed that this might be Boston's last chance for a title. Another sellout crowd at the Sports Arena roared as West and Baylor combined for forty-four first-half points. The Celtics looked disjointed. Their concentration was fuzzy, their passes sloppy. Los Angeles led 65–57 at halftime. But Auerbach delivered no pep talks. "We got ourselves together and decided this was it," said Russell. "The whole season, the world championship, everything was on the line." The stress-crammed stakes had crippled them, but now it inspired them. Behind swarming defense, the Celtics charged through the second half and won, 119–105. Twice, Russell called time-out. He was pushing himself beyond tired. He felt numb.[66]

The Celtics limped back to Boston. Cousy had injured his shooting hand. Heinsohn needed stitches after smacking his head on the floor. Ramsey had been undergoing constant treatment on a hurt leg. Russell's chronically injured left ankle again swelled, but he complained more about insomnia. They could have used a one-day postponement of Game Seven, as Walter Brown had proposed, in a testament to basketball's Jewish fan base. Wednesday, April 18, was the first day of Passover. But Elgin Baylor would return to the army on Thursday morning, so the game remained on Wednesday.[67]

By 3:00 a.m. on Monday, just hours after Game Six, fans had arrived at the Boston Garden box office. By the next morning an estimated 8,000 ticket-seekers snaked down Causeway Street. About 7,000 left dissatisfied. "In all my 22 years on details at the Garden I have never seen anything like this," said a policeman. The Celtics had averaged only 6,852 customers that season, the lowest of the Russell era. Even the first game of the Finals drew only 7,647. Brown himself footed the $15,000 bill to televise the final three play-off games. Until this threat to Celtic supremacy, Boston had grown ho-hum about the team's sustained excellence.[68]

The 1962 play-offs had exhibited a free-flowing, up-and-down pace, but the winner-take-all stakes in Game Seven induced a tighter, more methodical style. The teams shot under 34 percent. Neither squad mounted a sustained run. Fifteen times, the score deadlocked. Thirteen times, the lead changed hands. The first quarter ended tied at twenty-two. Boston led by six at halftime, but Los Angeles evened it at seventy-five after three quarters. Baylor scored forty-one points, West thirty-five. Baylor's relentless drives fouled out Heinsohn, Loscutoff, and Sanders. Despite their depleting ranks, the Celtics led 100–96 in the closing minute. Then Frank Selvy scored his first field goal. After West stole a pass, Selvy scored again. With five seconds left, Ramsey missed a jumper. Los Angeles called time out.[69]

Score tied at one hundred, five seconds left, Lakers ball; 13,909 fans sat hushed. Rod Hundley took the inbounds pass. With his back to the basket, he dribbled above the key. Baylor, the first option, screened and rolled—Russell was smothering him. Jerry West, the second option, came off a screen on the right side—K. C. Jones was blanketing him. So Hundley stopped, pivoted, and passed left. Selvy had popped off Baylor's screen. He was about ten feet from the basket. Cousy charged at him, but too late. Selvy was wide open.[70]

Frank Selvy already owned one place in basketball history. On February 13, 1954, he had scored one hundred points in one game, for tiny Furman College. That season he averaged forty-one points and fourteen rebounds a game, won Player of the Year awards, and was the first pick in the NBA draft. After an All-Star rookie year, Selvy spent eighteen months in the army, which crippled his timing and confidence. He bounced from team to team, a spot reserve. Both the Knicks and Nationals cut him. But upon joining the Lakers in 1960, he enjoyed an improbable renaissance. The quiet veteran nicknamed "Pops" cracked the starting lineup, played great defense, and averaged almost fifteen points. He even made the 1962 All-Star Game. Because Baylor and West attracted so many double teams, Selvy often scored on open midrange shots—just like this one, with three seconds left and an NBA championship on the line.[71]

He missed.

. . .

Selvy's shot hit the back rim, bounced high, and landed in Russell's hands. Russell had believed the shot would drop, and his anxiety disoriented him. He hugged the ball to his chest, stock-still, for twenty-five seconds. Then he stumbled toward the sideline. "I remember seeing Russell sitting on a stool near the Boston bench in the excitement of that packed dark, old Boston Garden," recalled West. "His body seemed limp. His head was hung. Sweat was just pouring off him. I figured he had nothing left." Trainer Buddy LeRoux poured water on his head, but the air around him felt thick.[72]

Then overtime began, and Russell scored on a two-fisted dunk, added two free throws, and swallowed rebounds. He had finished regulation with four small men:

Cousy, Sam Jones, K. C. Jones, and Ramsey. Early in overtime, Ramsey fouled out. Auerbach sent in Gene Guarilia, who in three seasons with Boston had never played in the NBA Finals. Now he guarded Elgin Baylor in overtime of Game Seven. Luckily, finally, Baylor missed two shots and a free throw. Then he fouled out. Boston opened a seven-point lead before winning 110–107. Cousy weaved across the parquet floor, dribbling out the waning seconds. Fans gushed past the distraught Lakers to carry off Auerbach, Cousy, and Russell, celebrating Boston's fifth title in six years.[73]

"I missed the big one," muttered Selvy in the visitors' locker room. He stared into space, unable to move. West grumbled about "the breaks," and Baylor ruminated over the missed opportunity. Tears flowed, heads bowed. One fateful bounce had separated them from the title. "Don't worry," proclaimed the bizarre Ray Felix, "we're going to get them tomorrow."[74]

In the home locker room, meanwhile, the Celtics staged their annual ritual. They threw Auerbach in the shower, poured beer on their heads, and delivered encomiums to each other. Photographers steered everyone together for a victory pose. "Hey Russ, hey Russ," some players called out. "Hey, where's Russ?" He was only a few feet away, leaning against a stall, one hand covering his forehead. These playoffs had offered the sternest tests: the goliath Chamberlain, the upstart Lakers, do-or-die stakes. The pressure had consumed him, but it also elicited his greatest exploits, especially in Game Seven, when he played fifty-three minutes, scored thirty points, and grabbed forty rebounds. He had vomited upon entering the locker room. When reporters crowded him, he insisted that they interview Guarilia—a gesture that the reserve forever appreciated. Now Russell wept. His teammates pulled him in, and he wiped away his tears. A smile began.

"Well," he said, "I'm glad that's over."[75]

9

Family Man

After the 1962 title, Russell drove his two young sons to Louisiana in his brand-new, steel-gray Lincoln convertible. He carried $2,000 in his wallet. He owned five NBA championships, three MVP awards, and one of the richest contracts in professional sports. Yet upon crossing the Mason-Dixon Line, few restaurants or hotels accommodated blacks. "Daddy, can't we stop?" the kids asked. "Daddy, I'm hungry." They slept one night in the Lincoln. Russell foamed with frustration. Whatever his wealth, whatever his fame, he lived with Jim Crow.[1]

In West Monroe, Russell avoided his mother's grave, as always. He still felt abandoned by her. He remained wary of opening himself to others. But if his history scarred him, it also buttressed him. He soaked in the care of aunts and cousins. He watched his boys follow around his still-vigorous grandfather. And he talked with the Old Man, though not about basketball. "He was interested in my career only as it affected my dignity and values," recalled Russell. "Was I away from home too much to be a good father to the kids? Did I understand money? Was I at peace with myself?"[2]

He was not. Russell soon conveyed an inner discontent. "Until today my life has been a waste," he said that December. "What does all this mean?" he cried while surrounded by autograph-seekers at Madison Square Garden. "This is without depth. This is a very shallow thing." He could have chosen a "constructive" profession, such as a doctor, architect, or politician. "I feel that playing basketball is just marking time. I don't feel that this can be it for a man. I haven't accomplished anything really. What contribution have I made of which I can be really proud?"[3]

That season Russell struggled to maintain focus on basketball, and he fretted about his contribution to society. This personal crisis spawned a pessimistic critique of the United States. "I'd have to be awful foolish to believe in what is known as 'The American Dream,'" he said. How could he embrace that dream when blacks were second-class citizens? "You show me the most downtrodden, ignorant Negro in the country, and I will tell you 'This is my brother.' You show me the most corrupt and evil Negro in this country, and I will say, 'Yes, this is my brother.'"[4]

As Russell's despair deepened, it accentuated his private and public contradictions. If his personal politics adopted a radical edge, he remained an exemplar of liberal achievement, leading a team that beautifully illustrated the possibilities within racial integration.

. . .

During the opening ceremonies at the 1960 Rome Olympics, Rafer Johnson bore the stars and stripes, proudly leading the American delegation. He then won a gold medal in the decathlon. His triumphs, both symbolic and athletic, reinforced the mythology of African American sports history: rules, records, statistics, and titles acquired meaning only with authentic competition, so athletics provided a level playing field, an opportunity for black achievement, and a visible stage for amiable, hardworking, God-fearing black individuals. "The great Negro sports stars are, perhaps, more responsible for the ever-rising tide of pride among Negroes than any other group of professionals," wrote A. S. "Doc" Young. "They dwell in a world characterized by a more nearly ideal Americanism than any other group."[5]

By the early 1960s, the sports world contained abundant narratives of black achievement. Baseball featured not just charismatic stars such as Willie Mays and Ernie Banks, but also aggressive winners such as Frank Robinson and Bob Gibson. Humble, diligent Floyd Patterson overcame childhood poverty, crippling self-doubt, and upset losses to reclaim his heavyweight boxing title in 1960. Jim Brown brought unprecedented speed and power to the National Football League, and in 1962 the Washington Redskins finally integrated their roster, succumbing to pressure from the NAACP, CORE, and the Kennedy administration. Though black women had fewer opportunities in athletics, the stoic tennis player Althea Gibson twice won Wimbledon and the U.S. Open in the late 1950s, and the sweet, attractive sprinter Wilma Rudolph charmed America while winning three gold medals at the 1960 Rome Olympics.[6]

Basketball best showcased black excellence, racial integration, and cultural brotherhood. During the 1962–63 season, forty-five African Americans comprised more than one-third of the NBA. A touching interracial story, moreover, had grown out of tragedy. After Maurice Stokes contracted encephalitis, teammate Jack Twyman assumed his legal guardianship, overseeing Stokes's finances and medical care. Stokes retained his intelligence but struggled to move or communicate. Until he died in 1970, an annual charity game in the Catskills attracted the sport's greatest stars, and thousands of inspired citizens wrote Twyman. One letter stated, "Where but in this country could I, a Jew, send money to you, a Catholic, to help a Negro?"[7]

This democratic ideal flourished among Bill Russell and the Boston Celtics. Like baseball's Brooklyn Dodgers or football's Cleveland Browns, the Celtics lent sporting parallels to the civil rights movement: blacks integrating a white institution, strengthening the team, elevating the human spirit. The players roomed, ate, and socialized together across race lines. "We were always going somewhere together—different guys in groups of three or four at different times," recalled Russell. "I once went to four different shows on four straight days with a different set of guys each time."[8]

An egalitarian spirit suffused the organization, from Walter Brown's warmheartedness to Red Auerbach's no-nonsense meritocracy. Frank Ramsey volunteered as a social worker for troubled black children in Roxbury. Bob Cousy sponsored two black youths through Big Brothers of America. Ramsey, Cousy, and Bill Sharman once left a St. Louis restaurant after it refused service to Russell. "If the world could get along like the players on our squad," said Ramsey, "we wouldn't need spacemen or nuclear weapons."[9]

On a 1961 preseason tour, the Celtics confronted racial discrimination. At an honorary banquet in Marion, Indiana, the city mayor presented them with keys to the city, painted gold and inscribed "Welcome." After a game at the local high school, the players filtered into the only open restaurant, a greasy lounge. Russell arrived with K. C. Jones, Sam Jones, and Carl Braun. The hostess informed them that the tables and bar stools were all reserved. Clearly, blacks were not welcome.[10]

Russell led a delegation to the police station. No officers accepted his complaint. So a group of Celtics, both black and white, filled two cabs. Well past midnight, they pounded on the mayor's door to protest. The next morning, they filed a formal grievance. Although the mayor read a statute about the illegality of public segregation, the restaurant suffered no consequences. "They gave us the key to the city," said Sam Jones, "but it didn't open any doors."[11]

On that same tour, the Celtics had an exhibition against the St. Louis Hawks in Lexington, Kentucky. After checking into the Phoenix Hotel, Sam Jones and Satch Sanders went to the coffee shop. The waitress refused to serve them. When they told Russell, he determined to leave. The other black players followed. Russell booked the next flight to Boston. For two hours, Red Auerbach pleaded that they should honor their commitment. He tried arranging various compromises, but his players held firm. So Auerbach drove Russell, Sanders, Sam Jones, and K. C. Jones to the airport. That evening in Boston, Russell announced that he would never acquiesce to Jim Crow. He contextualized his decision within the civil rights movement. "Negroes are in a fight for their rights—a fight for survival in a changing world," he said. "I am with these Negroes."[12]

After the black Celtics boycotted, Woody Sauldsberry and Cleo Hill of the Hawks followed suit. That night's all-white exhibition celebrated University of Kentucky alumni Frank Ramsey and Cliff Hagan, who delivered halftime speeches and received scholarships for their young children. But the game itself was sloppy. "No one felt good about playing or what had happened," recalled Tom Heinsohn.[13]

Some fans, reporters, and league personnel ignored the hotel's discrimination, instead condemning the African Americans for slighting Ramsey, Hagan, and the NBA. But the Celtics established a united front. Walter Brown condemned segregation. Cousy defended his teammates. "I was 100 percent behind Bill Russell and the other boys," said Ramsey. "No thinking man in Kentucky is a segregationist. I can't tell you how sorry I am as a human being, a friend of the players involved, and as a resident of Kentucky for the embarrassment of the incident."[14]

The camaraderie extended to the players' wives, who watched games together, shopped together, and babysat for each other. The franchise invited them to an annual luncheon at the Hotel Lenox. If reporters condescendingly marveled at their intelligence and attractiveness (one described them as "displaying poise and pulchritude"), they also conveyed how black women were part of the Celtics family. Ileana Sharman relayed how Rose Russell, Sam Jones's wife Gladys, and K. C. Jones's wife Beverly braved snow-covered roads to attend her baby shower. "Wives of Celtics Shun Race Bias," stated one headline. The women thus fostered the team's interracial spirit.[15]

Once, at an annual fellowship breakfast at Fenway Park, a succession of religious and civic leaders celebrated the virtues of cooperation in a common cause. Boston Red Sox general manager Dick O'Connell stepped to the podium. "There's a team over there in Boston Garden made up of blacks and whites, Catholics and Protestants, coached by a Jew, and they've been world champions for a long time now," he said. "Everyone's running around looking for theories and searching into history for explanations. If you want a perfect example of what we've been talking about, just look at the Celtics."[16]

The players themselves refrained from touchy-feely discussions about their sensitivities, whether racial or personal. "It sounds silly to say it, but it wasn't macho to talk about feelings," reflected Cousy. Their winning tradition muted many potential animosities. Often, when they did address race, they employed humor. "I know Frank Ramsey is drunk because he just invited me down to Kentucky during the off-season," said Russell during one breakup banquet. "I know I'm not drunk because I didn't accept the invitation."[17]

In January 1963, the Celtics met John F. Kennedy. The president learned that they were touring the White House before a game at the University of Maryland, and he invited them into the cabinet room, where they pretended to be Dean Rusk and Robert McNamara. Kennedy displayed a model of his famous PT-109 boat. He presented tie pins and posed for photographs. He even asked Auerbach and Loscutoff about their reputations for fisticuffs. Heinsohn tried calling Russell, who had remained at the hotel. But Russell had instructed the front desk to block all phone calls, so he got ribbed later for missing the historic occasion.[18]

Satch Sanders earned more grief. He was an earnest, humble man full of funny quirks. While they filed past Kennedy with thanks such as "Glad to meet you, Mr. President," and "Thank you, Mr. President," he was overcome with nerves. Sweat accumulated on his thin mustache. Even Kennedy laughed when Sanders shook the president's hand and stammered, "Take it easy, baby."[19]

. . .

Maybe Kennedy took it easy, but Russell could not. The previous season's numbness, gasping, and exhaustion presaged an era of turmoil. "I was away from home almost continuously, looking for something that my wife and kids could not satisfy," he recalled. He felt lonely. He worried about a nervous breakdown. He fretted that people considered him a "fine young animal" rather than someone who considered "social problems, philosophical concepts, deep thoughts of any kind." This personal crisis began with a political awakening.[20]

A 1959 trip to Africa helped sculpt Russell's ideology. Two years earlier, Ghana had declared independence from British rule, strengthening African American identification with an ancestral homeland. By the time of Russell's visit, liberation movements had bubbled across Africa, and given the cold war battle for spheres of influence, the State Department arranged goodwill tours of black celebrities. Russell resisted becoming a propaganda tool, however. He thought that the cold war obscured the nationalism behind African independence movements. He ignored State Department attachés who insulted their host nations and called him "boy." He similarly scoffed at communist reporters who implied that he was a spy or quizzed him about African politics.[21]

In Ethiopia, Russell chatted with Haile Selassie in a limousine (the tiny emperor refused to stand next to Russell in public). He also visited Libya, Sudan, the Ivory Coast, and Liberia. After long and bumpy Land Rover rides into the countryside, he often hiked with an interpreter and a basketball, eating and sleeping among rural people. He gave clinics, delighting in the happiness of children who spoke no English and had never seen a basketball. That childlike joy honed his racial awareness. In Africa, he said, "I found a place I was welcome because I was black instead of in spite of being black."[22]

While in the Liberian capital of Monrovia, Russell befriended the secretary of the Department of Public Works, who owned a prosperous rubber plantation. Rubber dominated the Liberian economy, and demand had skyrocketed during the auto-industry boom of the 1950s. When Russell returned home, he researched the possibility of buying his own rubber farm. The next year, after forming the Bill Russell Enterprise Corporation, he returned to Liberia with a successful black Bostonian named Clarence Holder. It cost fifty cents to purchase an acre and another fifty cents to survey it. They bought fifteen hundred acres in Salala, eighty miles northeast of Monrovia, and hired nearly one hundred workers to plant eighty-five thousand rubber trees. For tax purposes Russell arranged for Walter Brown to pay his corporation directly, and he started visiting Liberia every summer.[23]

The American connection to Liberia dated to 1821, when the American Colonization Society started sending freed American slaves there. In 1847 those settlers declared Liberian independence. Despite its reputation as the only independent African republic, however, the nation was no democratic haven. The Americo-Liberians monopolized power over the native Africans. President William Tubman built a corrupt patronage network. A hut tax forced rural Liberians into low-paying wage labor, especially in the rubber industry (Russell paid his workers only eight cents an hour for clearing farmland with knives and axes). The Liberian economy was growing, but not developing. Over time, Liberia seemed less an inspiration than an emblem of racial division, political corruption, and economic exploitation.[24]

Yet Russell embraced Liberia as a beacon of black democracy. "Know why it's easy for me to love Liberia?" he said. "That country is America in Africa. There isn't any discrimination in Liberia. The constitution is copied from the American Constitution, but it safeguards human rights." American newspapers painted Russell as a capitalist stimulating Africa's economic growth. He even tried distributing American records in Liberia. Rose, too, got captivated by the continent's optimism. They loved seeing black leaders, judges, and businessmen. "There were no restrictions, no ugly racial complications, no segregation or discrimination," she said. "It was like taking your coat off on a real hot day—we felt cool and comfortable, completely at ease for the first time in our lives." They contemplated living in Monrovia after Bill's retirement.[25]

Russell's pride in Africa stimulated his restlessness with the United States. The civil rights movement was springing from a rising generation's frustrations. The 1960 student sit-in movement ignited a new phase in black politics. Young activists organized at the grass roots, staging mass demonstrations at lunch counters, department stores, and other public facilities while overcoming harassment, arrests, and violence. When interracial bands of volunteers integrated buses and stations during the Freedom Rides of 1961, it demonstrated that same courageous commitment. These protestors staged compelling moral theater, pitting their nonviolent dignity against their oppressors' crude intimidation.[26]

The civil rights movement shaped and mirrored Russell's dissatisfaction. The activism sharpened his personal sense of injustice through lost awards, insufficient respect, bigoted sportswriters, racial segregation, and racist slurs. His emerging political outlook underlay his decision to leave segregated Kentucky. He envisioned new responsibilities for popular culture icons: "For a great number of years, colored athletes and entertainers put up with those conditions because we figured they'd see we were nice people mostly, and, in most cases, gentlemen, and they'd say, 'Those people aren't so bad.' But it was the greatest mistake we ever made because as long as you go along with it, everybody assumes it's the status quo." His political convictions, moreover, informed his self-definition. "I couldn't look my kids or myself in the face if I had played there. A man without integrity, belief, or self-respect is not a man. And a man who doesn't express his convictions has no convictions."[27]

Russell explained himself in the language of manhood, a common theme in the African American freedom struggle. A man defended himself, upheld his values, and provided for his family. He possessed authority over his destiny. Yet a racist society reviled black males. Achieving manhood took courage and conviction. Mister Charlie and the Old Man had already taught him these lessons, and now Russell applied them. In the ensuing years, in his continuing quest for respect, he returned again and again to the theme of manhood. In that struggle to define himself, he developed complex, contradictory relationships with his family, his friends, and the public.[28]

. . .

In many respects, Russell was a family man. He took great joy in fathering Buddha in 1957, Jacob in 1959, and Karen in 1962 (Karen's middle name was Kenyatta, after Jomo Kenyatta, the anticolonial rebel who became prime minister of Kenya). He was firm, but affectionate and funny. When possible, he joined them for Saturday morning cartoons. He insisted on separating fame from family, rarely bringing the children to games or shooting baskets with Buddha.[29]

Russell enjoyed the status of a patriarch. He acted as a surrogate father for Jim Hadnot, a 6'10" center from Oakland whose father had died. He convinced Hadnot to attend Providence College and offered financial support. Hadnot spent many weekends in Reading in the late 1950s and early 1960s, though Russell once restricted him to campus for a semester because of a D in American literature. Russell later took a similar interest in Bill Hewitt, an orphaned teenager and talented forward from Cambridge. Russell helped Hewitt move to California, where he attended the University of Southern California before starting a six-year NBA career.[30]

Russell also appreciated aspects of traditional matrimony. He praised his wife as "the finest person I've ever met." Rose was funny, warm, and creative. She taught the children to read before they started school. She kept an even keel when he sank into prolonged moods of deep gloom. His teasing could be cruel, but she shrugged it off. Because Bill spent money without care or discipline, she controlled the family finances—Bill, meanwhile, bought stylish clothes for both of them. Though more idealistic, she shared his interest in politics. She also sheltered her husband from domestic annoyances. "I'm very proud of my man," she said. "He makes everything seem precious." When the Celtics lost an important game, she felt "inadequate as a wife."[31]

But Bill grew dissatisfied with marriage. Traditional gender roles confined them. "It was a macho world," he said. "You married somebody, but that wasn't your friend. That was your wife." Rose usually stayed home while he traveled on road trips, visited friends and family, and went to Africa. When he returned, he retreated to his $10,000 worth of electric trains in the basement. He never revealed his anxieties about appearing a confident provider, which surfaced in two odd fears: that he could not open a jar for Rose, or that he could not answer her questions. He coped by escaping meaningful interactions with her.[32]

In his initial NBA years, the romantic surge of marriage still flowed, and he possessed sticky childhood insecurities about his height and looks. He stayed in his hotel room while his fellow Celtics chased skirts. His teammates considered him a sexual fuddy-duddy. But he soon got restless. "One night I simply told Rose that I was going out," he recalled. "Nothing more was said, and I went out on the town. On that very first occasion I ran into Iodine, who turned me every way but loose."[33]

Russell called her Iodine "because she was such strong medicine that she could clean all my wounds if I didn't mind the sting." He dropped his armor of cool detachment upon spying the copper-colored, red-haired beauty with preternatural self-possession. To her coterie of admirers in Boston's black underworld—pimps, gamblers, politicians—she added the star of the Boston Celtics. He realized new sexual passion, even shedding tears in the throes of lovemaking. He also encountered her disturbing, enchanting hot-bloodedness. Once she stabbed his arm with a pair of scissors. Another time she crashed her Mustang while chasing him through the South End. Between about 1958 and 1964, they had an on-again, off-again affair. When she moved to New York City, he visited her. When she returned to Boston, he procured her an apartment, car, and clothes. But the sting of Iodine grew only more painful, and their relationship imploded.[34]

In 1960, during an "off-again" phase with Iodine, a teammate introduced Russell to a New York City stripper named Kitty Malone. White and somewhat older, she loved books and espoused radical politics. Together they roamed Greenwich Village, slipping into The Bitter End to hear Bob Dylan or Joan Baez. They discussed slavery, McCarthyism, censorship, and colonialism. She sent him books. Then, after returning one summer from Liberia, Russell discovered that she had moved. Years later, he learned that she had died, possibly from a heroin overdose.[35]

These affairs obviously betrayed Rose. They also broadened Bill's outlook. Iodine plugged him into the inner workings of black Boston, while Kitty Malone showed him the connections between different forms of injustice. "I cared about politics before meeting Kitty," Russell recalled, "but my thoughts were generally selfish and confined to matters that affected me personally." He increasingly understood prejudice and human rights on a broader scale.[36]

Russell still lacked confidence in his looks, as well as insight into the opposite sex. But in time he established girlfriends in various cities. In June 1961, a *New York*

Amsterdam News gossip column linked him to "pretty barmaid" Stacey Jones. By his later career, according to one player, "everybody knew that Russell never slept more than four hours a night until the play-offs began." His infidelities stirred his inner tumult: he yearned to be a man of principle, yet his sexual escapades fed a perpetual adolescence. Nor could he breach the chasm between him and Rose.[37]

Yet Russell found satisfaction in the company of both women and men. To know Russell was to know his laugh—a whooping, shimmying, glass-shattering cackle. During his first preseason with the Celtics, Satch Sanders resolved to isolate himself, focusing on basketball. "Well," he recalled, "that lasted two or three seconds. Russell let loose with that big laugh in this restaurant, and I decided that anyone with that much laughter wasn't anyone to be mean and hard and cold around." Russell also loved practical jokes and sarcastic put-downs. He called friends at 4:00 a.m. and said, "I had to go to the bathroom and I thought about you. Did I wake you up?"[38]

Russell's circle included many of the NBA's African Americans. Visiting players congregated in Reading, where they played cards, listened to his huge jazz collection, and ate Rose's steaks, baked potatoes, greens, and desserts. He was something of a father figure. "You looked at him as a beacon of light," said Al Attles of the Warriors. The younger blacks admired his character, and they appreciated how his stardom opened opportunities for the next generation.[39]

His fellow superstars—Wilt Chamberlain, Oscar Robertson, and Elgin Baylor—considered him a close friend. At the Maurice Stokes benefit game in the Catskills, Russell and Chamberlain dined, exercised, and laughed together. "They were like brothers," thought Attles. After games in New York, Russell headed uptown to visit Chamberlain at his nightclub. Chamberlain once arrived at Russell's doorstep in his brand-new lavender Bentley, just to bask in his counterpart's admiration.[40]

Russell grew especially close to the black Celtics. They loved the same jazz music, and they shared the same sense of humor. They laughed together as Sam Jones took their money playing poker, K. C. Jones performed a perfect imitation of Russell's stony glare, or Satch Sanders spun another hilarious tale about his foibles, such as when he was teaching himself to drive, rolling down a Cambridge street at about five miles an hour, swiveling his head back and forth, and bumped an incredulous policeman onto his Pontiac's hood. Although they had four distinct personalities, their common culture bonded them together, strengthening their black identity.[41]

But Russell exuded warmth, generosity, and humor among *all* the Celtics. "He was fun to be around," said Gene Conley. "He was one of us." They considered him loyal and honorable. If someone was broke, he lent that person money. If someone was glum, he bought that person dinner. At the Russells' annual Christmas party, he got every teammate a gift. He ignored preseason contenders for roster spots—he hated any emotional investment in someone excluded from this second family. But once someone made the team, he embraced him as a friend, hosting him in Reading or at Slades. The Celtics cocooned Russell from an outside world that could be impersonal, exploitative, and racist.[42]

Russell's closest friends outside basketball were white, such as Harold Furash and Hy Horwitz, two older, Jewish season-ticket holders who sat near the Celtic wives. Russell even asked Furash to be godfather for Buddha. One evening Furash introduced Russell to his neighbor, a white physician named Bob Franklin. They talked all night; Franklin became the Russells' family doctor, and his children babysat the Russells. Russell built a similar friendship with his accountant Harold White. Once he trusted someone, Russell ignored their differences and offered dedicated companionship. John Hollingsworth, a math teacher and football coach at Reading Memorial High School, knew Russell through their children and wives. Russell invited Hollingsworth's entire coaching staff to shoot pool at his home, even if he was out of town.[43]

Yet to strangers, Russell acted like a jerk. Bob Cousy described him as gentle and gregarious among friends. In public, however, he underwent a "Jekyll and Hyde transformation." If someone approached him, Russell's nose stayed buried in the newspaper until the fan scurried away. He answered questions with gruff, perfunctory responses. He ignored the ushers at Boston Garden. He brushed past kids and other admirers. "I don't want to bother you," said one nervous man, hoping to shake his hand in a restaurant. "Then don't," snapped back Russell.[44]

Until proven otherwise, Russell presumed that people were hurtful, resentful, and prejudiced. His terrible manners stemmed from fear of strangers. One time the Furashes were eating dinner with friends when Russell entered and immediately stalked upstairs—he had assumed the other couple was racist, based on one look. Another time, while Russell sulked in a Philadelphia coffee shop, radio announcer Johnny Most asked what was wrong. "A white guy couldn't understand my problem," Russell responded. Most had always found him arrogant, but that day they talked about prejudice. Once Russell believed in Most's character, they became friends.[45]

Russell consciously constructed this armor of aloofness. Carl Braun called it "a kingly arrogance." It challenged the expectation that blacks express gratitude for their celebrity. If the public expected a clean-cut athlete, he wore a goatee. If the public expected a grinning jokester, he acted surly. He ignored the cheering fans, as if Boston Garden was barren. This demeanor protected him from detractors, but it also confined him. If he ignored the boos, he could not acknowledge the cheers.[46]

Contrasting impulses warred within Russell. He expressed sensitivity and kindness in private, but only stoic pride in public. He intellectually rejected the adulation of worshipful fans, but he emotionally craved that validation. He cherished the company of teammates, but he feared revealing that joy—it left him too vulnerable. He sang and laughed through pregame rituals, but minutes before tip-off, he got nervous, complained of invented illnesses, and vomited.[47]

He needed to win. Losing aggravated residual insecurities. Losing conjured up the poor, gangly boy with no mother. Losing provided ammunition for doubters, fools, and racists. Winning, however, delivered respect, trust, and status. He gave everything for victory. The Celtics, said Cousy, "were happy to be the recipients of his sustained anger at the world."[48]

. . .

Winning championships became easier when Wilt Chamberlain's Warriors moved to San Francisco. Eddie Gottlieb sold his franchise for $850,000 (he had bought the team for $25,000) and moved west to become general manager. The San Francisco Warriors struggled despite Chamberlain. Attention remained on baseball's Giants, who had taken the New York Yankees to seven games in the World Series. The Bay Area, moreover, had no professional basketball tradition—Russell's USF teams remained the sport's historical touchstone. In that initial 1962–63 season, attendance sputtered at fewer than four thousand customers, on average.[49]

Chamberlain loved his new city's cosmopolitan aura, but the Warriors went 31–49, missing the play-offs. Coach Frank McGuire and veteran Paul Arizin had declined to move, and Tom Gola got traded in midseason. Chamberlain averaged 44.8 points and 24.3 rebounds, but he could not settle on a consistent offensive style, and the team had no chemistry. It lost eleven straight early games, and ugly brawls marred some later contests, by which time Chamberlain was sulking. He heard a host of new, unfavorable comparisons to Russell, especially as the Celtics took eight straight from the Warriors. "You just can't beat those guys," he grumbled throughout one game. "You just can't beat them."[50]

Auerbach liked bolstering the Boston bench with savvy veterans hungry for a championship, such as Arnie Risen or Carl Braun. Now Auerbach traded for Clyde Lovellette, a bulky 6'9" center with an accurate one-hand push shot. Until he got slowed by an Achilles tendon injury, he, Bob Pettit, and Cliff Hagan had formed the NBA's best frontcourt for St. Louis. Lovellette owned a reputation as a lazy, goofy, stats-happy "gunner," but Auerbach wanted him only to back up Russell, hustle, and rebound. "I'd heard so much about the team spirit of the Celtics," said Lovellette, "but I never realized what it really meant until I came to the Celtics."[51]

Rookie John Havlicek exemplified this ideal. A three-sport star from small-town Ohio, Havlicek won an NCAA championship and reached two other title games at Ohio State. Yet he operated in the shadow of teammate Jerry Lucas. Havlicek had a tiny ego and a huge work ethic. He possessed incredible stamina, scored on rebounds and fast-breaks, and excelled at defense. The Cleveland Browns drafted him as a wide receiver, and he almost made the NFL despite never playing college football.[52]

Auerbach selected Havlicek with the ninth pick in the 1962 draft. The Cleveland Pipers of the ABL offered more money, but he was justifiably skeptical of the fledgling league. That summer, in fact, the NBA stole the Pipers, who had signed Lucas. Cleveland never joined the NBA, however. After shipping magnate George Steinbrenner resigned as Cleveland's president, the Pipers could not afford a large indemnification payment to the Cincinnati Royals, who held Lucas's territorial rights. The NBA owners then rejected the merger. The Pipers folded, and the ABL started the 1962–63 season with six franchises, three of which had relocated. Financial problems persisted, and on New Year's Eve in 1962, the ABL disbanded.[53]

By then Havlicek had earned his teammates' esteem. The informal culture and underwhelming facilities contrasted with his Ohio State experience, but his hustle, defense, and fundamentals fit Boston's style. Frank Ramsey groomed him as his Sixth Man successor. Auerbach lauded him. Chicago's Terry Dischinger won Rookie of the Year, but Walter Brown paid Havlicek the $200 bonus anyway. Russell made him fulfill traditional rookie duties such as fixing his tea or fetching newspapers. But he also extolled Havlicek to the press. When the rookie asked about buying a stereo, the MVP drove him around the city, testing various stores for the best deal.[54]

Boston's unity and depth explained a league-best 58–22 record. Yet the Celtics were frustrated. Foot and back injuries nagged Russell, and Bob Cousy pulled a groin muscle. More than physical ailments, however, the players complained about slipshod execution and mental miscues. "We're just not thinking the game right," worried Cousy.[55]

The Celtics also resented the expectation that the Los Angeles Lakers—with their graceful scorers, baby-blue uniforms, and cocky attitudes—were beginning basketball's next dynasty. "Sure we're mad at them," said Heinsohn. "It's that Hollywood stuff and everyone is on their bandwagon and off ours all of a sudden." The Lakers won five of nine regular season matchups. Until a late injury to Jerry West, Los Angeles threatened Boston for the league's best record.[56]

Amidst his internal turmoil, Russell still delivered special performances. In January, during his first homecoming to San Francisco, he held Chamberlain to twenty-three points. In February, he broke Dolph Schayes's all-time rebounding record, surpassing the fourteen-year veteran's total of 11,002. In March, he won his third straight MVP. Russell remained the bulwark protecting the Boston dynasty. "It'll be up to Russell," predicted Detroit coach Dick McGuire. "If he plays his best, the Celtics will be champions again."[57]

For all Russell's greatness, however, the 1962–63 season celebrated Bob Cousy. Boston College had offered him its head coaching post the previous season. Though Brown convinced him to play another year, the NBA wore Cousy down. His nerves frayed. He holed up in his hotel room, immersed in books. Now, wherever Boston played, he received gifts, ceremonial tributes, and standing ovations. His behind-the-back dribbles and no-look passes won louder roars. Reporters admired his greatness. His peers shared memories. Herbert Warren Wind wrote a long, affectionate profile in the *New Yorker*. A new generation had surpassed him, but Cousy remained the people's hero—the small, tough (and white) basketball artist.[58]

On March 17, 1963, that worship spilled into the most stirring, emotional tribute in Boston sports history. "Bob Cousy Day," before his last home game, elicited ovations and tears. Auerbach read a congratulatory letter from President Kennedy before choking up in Cousy's arms. Walter Brown, Maurice Podoloff, and Mayor John Collins eulogized his career. Rose Russell "shed a torrent of womanly tears" while presenting Marie Cousy with a bouquet from the wives. When Cousy took the microphone, he started bawling. Boston Garden fell silent with weepy reverence, at least until a leatherlung from Southie bellowed: "We love ya, Cooz!" After Cousy stammered out his speech, the contest against Syracuse began. "We didn't have a chance to win that game," said Dolph Schayes. "The referees were crying, too."[59]

. . .

If Cousy prompted fond nostalgia, Oscar Robertson earned awe for his effortless all-around game. The prototype of the modern point guard led Cincinnati past Syracuse in the preliminary round of the 1963 play-offs, and then he scored forty-three points in an upset, 135–132 opening victory over Boston. Rusty from a ten-day layoff, the Celtics squandered a twenty-two-point lead. Boston won the rematch at Cincinnati Gardens, 125–102, but still looked uninspired in Game Three, losing 121–116.[60]

"The long reign of the Boston Celtics as champions of the National Basketball Assn. appears to be ending," surmised one writer. Russell and his family attended the press luncheon that week. He admitted that the Celtics needed consistent drive, but he urged patience. "We're still the best team in basketball," he insisted. On the flight to Cincinnati, they joked and played cards. Russell wore a plastic mask of Fidel Castro. Meanwhile, the Royals' morale deflated upon learning that the circus had taken over Cincinnati Gardens, and they would play in tiny Schmidt Fieldhouse at Xavier University. Boston prevailed, 128–110.[61]

Russell and Robertson reigned over the series. After Boston took its first series lead by capturing Game Five, 125–120, Robertson kept explaining the result with a single refrain: "They got Bill." The Royals nevertheless had Oscar, who dominated a 109–99 triumph in Game Six, scoring thirty-six points. The Celtics blamed Sid Borgia as much as Robertson. Auerbach and the referee had a long-standing feud. That season Borgia had twice ejected Auerbach, Walter Brown had urged Borgia to retire, and the Celtics seemed psyched out by Borgia. Even Russell uncharacteristically complained about the officials. Auerbach raised such a stink—"I'm convinced that it would be the highlight of his career if he refereed the game in which we lost the championship"—that Borgia declined to officiate Game Seven.[62]

"I've never seen the Celtics so solemn," remarked a visitor before the winner-take-all contest. They had not dispatched the lesser Royals. Cousy had barely slept or eaten. K. C. Jones lay down in one corner, his arm covering his eyes. Sam Jones had spent the day wandering Boston's streets and watching a double feature, trying to calm his nerves. Only Russell acted relaxed, busting out his tinny cackle. Then game time approached, and he threw up.[63]

Boston won, 142–131. Russell offered sterling defense and rebounding. Heinsohn sealed the game with an audacious fourth-quarter hook. Cousy delivered his entire repertoire of bounce passes, baseball tosses, and over-the-head flips. And Sam Jones scored forty-seven points, a regulation-time franchise record. Robertson blamed the Celtic Mystique. "A lot of the Royals were gun-shy about playing them," he reflected. "It was almost as if they couldn't go forward and play aggressively against the green-and-white Celtics uniforms."[64]

The Lakers awaited. Cousy honestly believed that Los Angeles would win the 1963 championship. Forward Rudy LaRusso had improved, guard Dick Barnett added scoring punch, and rookie centers Gene Wiley and Leroy Ellis now backed up Jim Krebs. Jerry West had fully rehabilitated his leg injury, and Elgin Baylor had injected himself into the "who's greatest?" conversation with Russell and Chamberlain. When Baylor backed down his defender, Russell had to shift over, opening shots for the Lakers' pivotmen. The Celtics were declining, the Lakers ascending—Los Angeles hyped itself as "the basketball capital of the world."[65]

But the Celtics won the first two games at Boston Garden, 117–114 and 113–106, while defending with verve. Russell missed the last forty-seven seconds of the opener after his jaw caught an inadvertent elbow, dropping him to the floor. The fans hushed, envisioning a repeat of 1958, when his injury prevented a potential Boston title. "Without Russell," said one teammate, "we're like a baseball team with pitchers but not a single catcher." Yet Russell laughed off the momentary blackout, and he dominated Game Two, grabbing thirty-eight rebounds while holding his counterparts to eight points.[66]

Boston's lead failed to dampen enthusiasm on the West Coast, where more than fifteen thousand packed the Los Angeles Sports Arena for the next two contests. A comeback seemed possible after Game Three, when the Lakers won a rout, 119–99. But Russell led Boston's victory in the rematch, 108–105. He scored twenty-two points and cleared rebounds all night. On one critical possession with 1:45 left, he cut off Baylor's drive and drew a charge. How had the Celtics won? "How do you spell Russell?" quipped Lakers coach Fred Schaus.[67]

Yet the Celtics squandered the title-clincher at home, 126–119. In one fourth-quarter stretch they botched three easy chances while the Lakers converted three spectacular baskets. Cousy played poorly and fouled out. A fan charged after a referee who ejected Heinsohn. Auerbach nearly attacked a patron who claimed that Boston "dumped" the game. Afterward Russell ripped off his ankle tape, chucked it across the locker room, and glared at some underperforming teammates.[68]

As the Celtics wore down, the Lakers' confidence bulged. In Los Angeles, a mob crushed the ticket office. A six-thousand-seat theater filled for a closed-circuit broadcast. Effervescent Doris Day, bubble-blowing Pat Boone, and cigar-chomping Danny Thomas helped pack the Sports Arena. Hours before tip-off, Cousy and Ramsey sat together, already in uniform, muttering to each other. The moody, anxious veterans just made each other more moody and anxious. Yet Cousy was perversely relieved that Boston lost Game Five—he hated the idea of ending his career with a substandard game.[69]

Game Six, by contrast, showcased a vintage Cousy. "He triggered the fast break," waxed Arthur Daley. "He found openings where no openings existed and threaded them with his passes. He surreptitiously handed off underneath like a three-card monte artist. He fired one almost the length of the court and hit an onrushing teammate on the finger-tips for a brush-in basket. He dribbled in and out like a minnow flashing among salmon." Cousy piloted Boston to a 92–83 advantage by the early fourth quarter. Then, while cutting back on defense, he tripped. Pain pierced his left leg. He had sprained his ankle, and he needed support to limp off court.[70]

The momentum shifted. Baylor and West sank some beautiful shots, and the Sports Arena shook. By the time Cousy minced toward Auerbach, his ankle iced and sprayed and mummified, Boston led only 100–99. In that final two minutes and twenty-three seconds, other Celtics filled the stat sheet: Russell got rebounds, Satch Sanders and Sam Jones scored, Tom Heinsohn made a key steal and various clutch hoops. But Cousy's steady hand steered them. The Celtics prevailed, 112–109. When the buzzer sounded, Cousy launched the ball skyward. It caromed off the hardwood and landed in Russell's arms—he had leaped over a bench to catch a souvenir for the retiring maestro.[71]

One cigar-wielding coach and twelve men in green piled into the visitors' locker room, where no one had thought to store champagne or beer. "You're the most, Cousy," said Russell. Reporters asked for interviews, and Russell released his hug. "Go on, Cooz," he said. "Tell 'em how great you are." Still to come were tributes to Cousy's theatrical swan song, Mayor Collins greeting them at Logan Airport, the annual panegyrics to their excellence, and the fretting about Life After Cousy. Now, the Celtics just took pride in defying their doubters. "Good-bye, Los Angeles," proclaimed Russell as their airplane circled back over the Pacific. "Good-bye, to the basketball capital of the world."[72]

. . .

Russell played that final game with numb legs. His doctor ascribed it to "complete fatigue." Once he sat on the bench, spied a woman in a short skirt, and thought, "I wish my legs felt as good as hers look." His exhaustion derived from both the season's physical demands and his obsession with winning. Yet he mentioned nothing to the press. The attention belonged on Cousy's farewell.[73]

At the breakup dinner, Russell loosened his tie and stooped over the microphone.

He had avoided champagne. He wanted to speak with clarity, with honesty. "I admit to having an ego," he began. "I consider myself a great basketball player." He spread his hands slightly apart. "If Bob Cousy were this much less a man than he is I would have resented him." He admired Cousy's proud and generous character, his leadership of this special team. They had imbued a children's game with character. They were "a family, a brotherhood of champions, a fraternity of greatness." Russell held the room in spellbound silence. Blacks and whites wept together. Rose Russell and Marie Cousy cried in each other's arms. Bill Russell sobbed, too, and when he finished speaking, he walked away with his head bowed. This same man had mocked "The American Dream," criticized the manipulation of the black athlete, and tortured himself over basketball's social value. But Russell had invested their common endeavor with the deepest possible meaning.[74]

10

His Own Little Revolution

Hope and gloom, faith and doubt, kinship and isolation—these antithetical notions all collided within Bill Russell. His struggles for self-definition sharpened a complex political voice.

Just weeks after his homage to Bob Cousy, Russell again expressed faith in his fellow man. On May 16, 1963, five hundred residents of Reading attended a testimonial banquet for "Bill Russell Day." The town selectmen, the family pastor, club officials, Johnny Most, and many of Russell's teammates commended the Celtic superstar. Rose received a charm bracelet. Tom Heinsohn had never seen him so emotional. "One of the greatest achievements a man can attain is to be called a friend," said Russell, tears welling. "You said this to me tonight. I appreciate it. I really do." He now considered this unassuming, conservative suburb his genuine home. "I only hope I can lead a life to make you always feel this way about me."[1]

Russell's family had outgrown its small ranch house, and Main Street had grown busier since the construction of a nearby supermarket. But when he considered buying some statelier homes on the town's west side, a petition circulated. Residents objected to a black family in their neighborhood. "Bill Russell Day" now seemed like an exercise in hypocrisy.[2]

The bigotry continued after Russell bought a large brick ranch home at 701 Haverhill Street. Sitting on almost two acres, it was the nicest home in a quiet, predominantly Irish Catholic neighborhood on the east side. It reflected his burgeoning upper-middle-class status. A grand piano sat in the living room, African spears and masks decorated the walls, and volumes on politics, art, sports, and history packed a ceiling-high bookcase. The backyard had a swimming pool and myriad birdhouses, since Rose liked watching birds. Their pet dog, a boxer named Booma, had room to roam.[3]

Yet when the Celtics traveled, vandals knocked over Russell's garbage cans. The police shrugged it off, blaming raccoons. So Russell installed floodlights on the front lawn. He also bought a gun, which stopped the garbage-tipping episodes. Once, however, he came home at 4:00 a.m. to find a terrified Rose pointing the gun at him.[4]

"One ever feels his two-ness," wrote the scholar-activist W. E. B. Du Bois, "an American, a Negro; two souls, two thoughts, two unreconciled strivings, two warring ideals in one dark body, whose dogged strength alone keeps it from being torn asunder." Russell personified this "double consciousness" in the modern sports world. He reflected a spectrum of ideas and emotions. He cherished an integrated community, and he raged with separatist impulses. While flowing with the black political tide, he charted new waters for the black athlete.[5]

. . .

Four days before "Bill Russell Day," Russell led a march from Roxbury to Boston Common, site of a 10,000-person human rights rally. The Boston rally echoed the ideals of the Birmingham Campaign, the dramatic civil rights demonstrations in Alabama led by Martin Luther King Jr. The speakers included Governor Endicott Peabody, State Attorney General Edward Brooke, and civil rights leaders James Bevel, James Farmer, and Charles Evers. The march initiated a new era in Boston politics. A few speakers connected discrimination in Birmingham to that in Boston. Activist Mel King remembered a boy telling his father, "Daddy, I'm no longer ashamed to be a Negro."[6]

Boston was undergoing a larger racial transformation. As late as 1940, African Americans formed only 3 percent of the city's population. The South End and Lower Roxbury composed a small "colored district," centered on jazz clubs, barbecue restaurants, and local ward boss "Shag" Taylor, who curried small favors from James Michael Curley's political machine. By 1960, however, an influx of southern migrants had increased the black population to 9 percent. African Americans pushed deeper into Roxbury, Dorchester, and Mattapan. As middle-class whites fled to suburbs, the black community suffered from overcrowded homes, absentee landlords, high tuberculosis rates, reputations for criminality, and inferior schools. Middle-class blacks and West Indians resented the migrants, and black Boston stayed politically passive.[7]

But the condition of Boston schools stimulated a new generation of activists, including Russell. He got involved through Thomas Atkins, chairman of the Boston NAACP. Russell became a lifetime member of the city's chapter, and Rose served on its board. The NAACP soon documented thirteen schools with predominantly black enrollments, dilapidated buildings, and insufficient funding. The School Committee nevertheless rejected any suggestion of racial segregation, whether de facto or by design. The NAACP, in turn, demanded more black administrators and teachers, acknowledgment of racially concentrated schools, and curriculum changes to help poor children. The School Committee rebutted, "We have no inferior education in our schools. What we have been getting is an inferior type of student."[8]

Bill and Rose watched the School Committee dismiss the concerns of black parents and insult black children as culturally inferior. They obviously understood injustice beyond the Jim Crow of the South, witnessing larger political, economic, and cultural inequalities rooted in race.[9]

On June 18, 1963, the NAACP organized a "Stay Out for Freedom Day," a one-day boycott of Boston schools. More than eight thousand students missed school, and about three thousand black children gathered at ten "freedom schools," singing civil rights anthems and learning African American history. Russell captivated the students. He toured freedom schools, advising children to embrace not only education but also black pride. "Wear your color as a badge," he urged.[10]

In 1964, Russell secured a $90,000 loan from the Small Business Administration to buy a barbecue restaurant on Tremont Street called Slade's. A black institution since the 1930s, it added live music in the 1950s. Russell's celebrity made Slade's even more popular. Though situated in a black district, it now attracted whites, too. As sales bulged, Russell plugged into the rhythms of black Boston. His lessons in urban power grew more advanced. City inspectors wanted bribes, police officers wanted free meals, and gangsters wanted to provide protection. He resisted these entreaties, but life as a restaurateur involved new stresses and new sources of cynicism.[11]

Boston's clannish, racist culture already disillusioned Russell. A policeman once demanded his license and registration while he idled in a parking lot, just because he was a black man driving a fancy convertible. "Hey, nigger, how many crap games did it take you to win that car?" he heard. Some reporters sprinkled "nigger" into their conversations, and Boston Garden's second gallery was nicknamed "Nigger Heaven." Few blacks came to Boston Garden, Fenway Park, or other civic institutions. WASP "Brahmins" ruled Boston's financial institutions and high society, and ethnic whites dominated city politics and culture. Their sports heroes reflected their "whiteness." "I'll never be another Ted Williams or a Bob Cousy," said Russell. "Not in this town."[12]

Soon after integrating the Boston Red Sox in 1959, Elijah "Pumpsie" Green listened while Russell toured the city, pouring out his tortured soul. Russell explained where a black man was welcome or unwelcome. They rolled down Washington Street, home to great jazz clubs such as Connolly's and the Hi-Hat. When they drove through South Boston or Charlestown, Russell darkened. Crouched behind the wheel, bubbling with fury, he warned about the "brick-throwing racists" in such Irish Catholic enclaves.[13]

Russell continued to resent the Boston media. "He considered some of us fools," recalled Bud Collins of the *Herald* and then *Globe*, "and he didn't suffer us so gladly." Few reporters understood his public aloofness, or what it meant to be black in Boston. Tim Horgan of the *Traveler* considered him difficult to understand. "One day, you'd talk to him and he'd tell you things that came from the deepest corners of his soul," explained Leigh Montville of the *Globe*. Russell could expound on basketball, politics, and everything in between for forty-five minutes. "The next day, he'd see you and look at you as if you were a fly who just landed on his breakfast." He kept reporters uncomfortable, on the defensive.[14]

Once, while sharing a cab with George Sullivan of the *Traveler*, Russell called Boston the most racist city in America. Sullivan asked if that was on the record. "Your paper hasn't got the guts to run that story!" Russell replied. He believed that white Bostonians had a self-imposed blindness about racism. They condemned Jim Crow in the South, but not racial inequality in the North. Sullivan wrote the article, but his managing editor killed the story, claiming that it would ratchet up racial tension. Sullivan entered the locker room the next day to find a cackling Russell, holding the *Traveler*. "I've been reading this back and forth," he said. "I can't find the story."[15]

Russell's celebrity magnified his antagonisms. Whites sometimes remarked how distinct he seemed from other blacks, as if most were lazy, craven, or stupid. One week after "Stay Out for Freedom Day," Russell arrived late for a Red Sox game, wearing a bright yellow shirt. Fans stood and applauded, and the cheers spread through Fenway Park. He received those same types of cheers in Boston Garden. But in his mind, such gestures clouded a deeper racial hatred. His family once returned from a weekend vacation to find their home robbed, their pool table ripped up, beer cans emptied, and trophies smashed. "NIGGA" had been spray-painted on the wall. Under the bed covers, he found human feces.[16]

Boston's black athletes all faced bigotry. The Red Sox ignored that Pumpsie Green and Earl Wilson endured segregation during spring training in Florida, and they felt little support from the organization or its fans. K. C. Jones had a cross burned on his lawn. Back Bay landlords and Kenmore Square nightclubs turned away Satch Sanders, who settled in Roxbury. Furthermore, the Celtics still played second fiddle to the pitiful Bruins, and many blamed the growing black influence on basketball. One reporter in the Boston Garden press box called the sport "African handball."[17]

Yet only Russell became a lightning rod for the city's racial friction. While Jones, Sanders, or Green might share Russell's frustrations, they more easily shrugged off Boston's biases. If someone insulted K. C. Jones, Russell thought, "he would just turn around and walk away from him. He wouldn't dignify him with an answer." Similar insults drove Russell into fits of frustrated fury. The most famous African American in Boston, he was becoming Boston's most visible critic.[18]

The civil rights struggle stoked his political fire. Hours after a televised presidential address endorsing civil rights legislation, NAACP field secretary Medgar Evers was assassinated in Jackson, Mississippi. Operating in a state with brutal race relations and trenchant poverty, Evers had been documenting racial injustices, registering voters, and organizing mass meetings for nearly a decade. On June 19, just one day after the Boston school boycott, Russell attended Evers's funeral at Arlington National Cemetery.[19]

In late August, Russell returned to the nation's capital for the March on Washington. The evening before the march, he met Martin Luther King Jr. in their hotel lobby. After they spoke, an organizer invited Russell onto the dais for the speeches. Russell admired Dr. King's dedication to the universality of humanity, his faith in nonviolence. But he declined the invitation. Appearing on stage, he believed, would only inflate his ego. Instead, after marching toward the Lincoln Memorial with 250,000 others, he sat in the second row. King's iconic "I Have a Dream" speech climaxed the generous, hopeful spirit of the demonstration.[20]

Other NBA players at the March on Washington included Wilt Chamberlain, Elgin Baylor, and Walt Bellamy. Most black athletes maintained faith in integration. "We still thought the best way to narrow the gap between the races was to demonstrate how blacks and whites could work together to achieve a common goal," recalled Wayne Embry, the burly center of the Cincinnati Royals. "Sports provided that opportunity." But Russell's optimism disintegrated. His festering disillusion oozed into public, and he became basketball's pariah—articulating anger at racist double standards, forging a distinctive identity, and sacrificing adoration for his principles.[21]

. . .

Russell's critiques stemmed from individual sensitivity and political upheaval. They found expression due to transformations in American sports writing. By the 1960s, television could relay scores and summaries as well as newspapers. Perceptive writers moved beyond mundane narratives and puff pieces. They explored personalities, conveyed scenes and telling details, and included social and political analysis. The civil rights movement compelled a few writers' interest in race. The Boston beat writers lacked this outlook, but during the 1963–64 season, Gilbert Rogin of *Sports Illustrated* and Edward Linn of the *Saturday Evening Post* profiled Russell, revealing his rage, quirks, and political ideology.[22]

In the *Sports Illustrated* article, called "We Are Grown Men Playing a Child's Game," Russell relayed anxiety about the value of sports. He expressed frustration with preconceptions about him. He criticized the NBA for bad officiating and weak promotion. He cherished his experiences in Africa. Where once he sought to refute black stereotypes, now he abandoned image politics: if he wanted to drive a flashy convertible or eat a watermelon, he did so. His beard reflected that desire for self-definition. He had regrown his goatee after his first championship. In the clean-shaven sports world, that was subversive. "I've always fought so hard to be different," he said. "Maybe it's just my own little revolution."[23]

Like no athlete before him, Russell also challenged the black political orthodoxy. Though he appreciated the March on Washington, he questioned nonviolent tactics. "If Martin Luther King is wrong," he said, "he has failed as a leader." Had Russel endured violence, he would have fought back—otherwise, he would have been untrue to himself. Nonviolence depended on man's essential morality, and he lacked that faith.[24]

Russell further appreciated the Nation of Islam and Malcolm X, whom so many white Americans feared and reviled. With a razor-sharp mind and astonishing charisma, Malcolm X orated about the necessity of violent revolution, the value of black self-determination, and whites' intransigent racism. Russell rejected any blanket characterization of the white man as a devil. Yet he said, "I dislike most white people because they are people. I like most black people because I am black." Like many other African Americans, he identified with elements of black nationalism: racial pride, self-defense, economic autonomy, political liberation, black unity.[25]

In the *Saturday Evening Post* article, called "I Owe the Public Nothing," Russell again supported the Nation of Islam. "I don't think any thinking Negro can completely reject them," he said. The civil rights movement had lifted African Americans' self-regard, an essential steppingstone to equality. But neither the Constitution nor liberal consciences nor admiration for Bill Russell could deliver justice. "We have got to make the white population uncomfortable and keep it uncomfortable," he said, "because that is the only way to get their attention."[26]

Russell thus contradicted expectations of celebrity behavior. Fans wanted athletes who expressed gratitude, acceded to requests, and embraced responsibility as role models. But pandering to fans, Russell believed, would be a personal misrepresentation. "I refuse to smile and be nice to the kiddies," he said. "I don't think it's incumbent upon me to set a good example to anybody's kids but my own." He expected nothing from the public, and the public should expect nothing back. He despised signing autographs. He considered it a dehumanizing experience, an asinine demonstration of celebrity worship. Autograph seekers approached him as a commodity, not a person, and he detected racial overtones in the supposition that the public "owned" him in any respect.[27]

At USF, Russell once accompanied his signature with the note "You honor me." Sometimes he still signed for a gaggle of fans. Other times he scribbled his name with detachment and defiance. Still other times he ignored the other person's existence. In the winter of 1964, he stopped signing autographs altogether. He quit them just as he had quit his fifteen-year smoking habit: with abrupt self-discipline. He rebuffed requests not just from boors and profiteers, but even from innocent children or longtime friends. He considered it a matter of principle.[28]

Reactions to Russell revealed cleavages in how Americans viewed race and sport. Some readers of *Sports Illustrated* and the *Saturday Evening Post* wrote letters praising Russell's character, contributions, and insights that "take on a stature and importance worthy of a Martin Luther King." One woman wrote, "I deeply admire Mr. Russell for refusing to accept the deference often accorded to a Negro celebrity in exchange for the respect he is entitled to as a human being." A fifteen year old from Long Island named Tony Kornheiser added that "too many of us regard athletes merely as tools for man's entertainment, and it is refreshing to hear an intelligent, articulate sportsman destroy this myth. Bill Russell, a man obviously in a state of rebellion, gave me a view of sports I had never been exposed to before."[29]

But others deemed Russell a threat to racial peace. "If I were a white person, I would not take kindly to Mr. Russell's remarks. As a Negro I am surprised at his apparent bitterness in the Lap-of-Plenty," remarked a major in the Marines. Some thought that his declarations of pan-black brotherhood implied a reverse bigotry. Others emphasized that Russell could achieve progress by thriving at basketball, not by complaining about problems. "Mr. Russell doesn't want equality," wrote an Iowa woman. "He wants to get even."[30]

Russell disaffected some past admirers. Joe Looney of the *Boston Herald* thought him hypocritical for claiming, "I owe the public nothing," since Russell had just appealed to Boston Garden fans for contributions to a cancer fund. Jerry Nason of the *Boston Globe* wrote that "I felt betrayed by a man I had admired openly, typographically, from the day of his first Celtics' press conference, for what I suspected was his enormous dignity, intelligence and manly qualities." Nason realized American's racial division. He once considered Russell part of the solution. But Russell's comments made liberal whites feel that racism was intractable, that their goodwill meant nothing. Now Nason considered Russell part of the problem: "The answers Bill offered seemed to lead nowhere but deeper into that wasteland."[31]

Russell received about five thousand letters. Many contained unimaginably venal, racist insults. He had offended those who expected black athletes to exude deference, modesty, or happy-go-lucky cheer. The FBI's file on Russell called him "an arrogant Negro who won't sign autographs for white children." Reporters disparaged him as "Felton X." He should "count his blessings once in a while," one wrote. Tim Horgan of the *Boston Traveler* believed that "Russell could help the situation he deplores if he would simply smile at the public." His angry demeanor increased resistance to integration. "Russell strikes me as the type who's going to keep this race trouble alive and festering much longer than necessary."[32]

Russell especially raised hackles by accusing the NBA of a racial quota system. "In order to reach the top of my field, I don't have to be *as* good, I have to be better," he said. "Because whether they'll admit it or not, I'm of the opinion that most teams in this league have a quota." White owners, players, and reporters grumbled and howled. Few American institutions were more racially progressive than the

NBA. The accusation stung Boston owner Walter Brown, who responded that he wanted the best player available, "whether he's Eskimo or Chinese."[33]

But Russell had a point. Every team had four or five black players—no more, no fewer. Though most superstars were black, the end of the bench seemed reserved for whites. In fact, Maurice Podoloff had suggested a formal racial quota at a board of governors meeting in the early 1960s. The proposal stayed out of the minutes, but the owners shared an implicit understanding that a black majority might disaffect white fans. After Russell's charge, open-minded sportswriters started noting this delicate racial balance. Black players already realized it. When they gathered for pregame meals or postgame drinks, they inevitably discussed the quota. Satch Sanders, for instance, knew NBA-level talents who played for Eastern League teams, the Globetrotters, or playground teams. Bob Boozer of the Knicks publicly supported Russell, adding that only whites got to prolong their careers as role players.[34]

The black press lauded Russell's courage. That summer, a long article in *Sepia* dismissed Mal Whitfield's call for a boycott of the 1964 Olympics, upholding the traditional role of the black athlete as a democratic hero. Yet "when a Negro athlete feels that he should participate in militant actions, then he should." Like Jackie Robinson, Russell possessed sensitivity and intelligence. His anger had riled feathers, but "by its very nature, it set people to thinking."[35]

Russell nevertheless shocked many whites, including his teammates. He had concealed his rage under his gregarious personality or cool persona. Gene Conley left the Celtics in 1961 harboring no sense of Russell's bitterness, calling his Boston stint "an innocent time." Bob Cousy saw little resemblance between this angry public figure and his old teammate. Cousy fancied himself a supporter of civil rights, but he believed that "a Negro celebrity has a responsibility. He is a spokesman for his people. And if he genuinely wants to help his race, I don't think he accomplishes it through caustic, overly critical statements and articles that alienate whites sympathetic to their cause."[36]

After reading the "I dislike most white people" quote, Frank Ramsey asked if Russell hated him. Russell said that he was misquoted. They dropped the matter, since both men cherished team harmony. Russell later insisted that he appreciated many whites, especially mentors such as George Powles and Ross Giudice. But after the quota accusations, even teammates kept their distance, fearing the stigma of black radicalism before signing their next contract.[37]

Blacks in the NBA wrestled with complicated tensions, a push-and-pull between pride and fear. "One minute I was an All-American basketball player as full of myself as a powerful young man could be," recalled Chet Walker of the Philadelphia 76ers. "But the next minute, I was reduced to the nigger in the doorway." Despite wealth and fame, they were outsiders. When Lenny Wilkens joined the St. Louis Hawks, restaurants refused him service, friends warned him against white women, and neighbors poisoned his dog. Black players constantly discussed such affronts amongst themselves, but few aired racial grievances in public.[38]

Russell thus helped clear a new path for black athletes. The retired Jackie Robinson challenged his fellow athletes to become politically involved. Jim Brown organized his black teammates on the Cleveland Browns; his 1964 memoir *Off My Chest* criticized legendary coach Paul Brown, exposed racism, and demanded recognition as a man. In February 1964, the brash, handsome, poetry-spouting Cassius Clay beat Sonny Liston for the heavyweight boxing title and then announced his conversion to the Nation of Islam. Russell, Robinson, Brown, and Clay demonstrated new political possibilities: where average athletes might avoid controversy to preserve their jobs, and where black musicians and actors catered to the white mainstream, these sports idols had the status and freedom to challenge the racial order.[39]

Russell had met Clay in April 1962 in Los Angeles during the NBA Finals, during Clay's preparations for fighting George Logan. Almost two years later, before his Liston bout, Clay attended a sports banquet in Boston. Russell then took him to various nightclubs. They talked for hours. Russell suspected the impending religious conversion, because Clay never drank—he wanted only ice cream. That summer, the new heavyweight champion visited Russell in Reading. They embraced with affection, joked about each other's weight, and talked politics. In an interview with *Muhammad Speaks,* Russell supported many principles of the Nation of Islam.[40]

The columnist Milton Gross saw the athletes in disparate terms. The white liberal had long admired black athletes, and he believed that sports promoted democracy. He despised Clay, "whose poetry was a short of childish, amiable nonsense until he started to sound off in the syllables of hate." Though he mourned Russell's accusations, he admired "a man of sincere convictions. Nobody puts words into Russell's mouth or ideas into his head."[41]

In different ways, Russell and Clay snapped the political shackles on black athletes. Both rejected sport's myths of racial justice, and both faced a backlash. But Clay, soon known as Muhammad Ali, was neither well educated nor politically sophisticated. He thrived on attention, communicated in sound bites, and exuded charisma. Injecting messages of black pride into the American consciousness, he created an alternative icon to the humble, Joe Louis-style hero.[42]

Russell, by contrast, essentially demanded to express his personality and principles, devoid of any artifice. "A man should always say what he thinks to be right," he said. "I received no money for those stories. They were not written to be sensational. They were simply my answers to questions of my time. I answered them as truthfully as I could. That, to me, is the only way a man should live his life— saying what he thinks is so, not catering to what is called the 'model' of being a public figure. Many public figures say one thing and feel another. I just say what I think is right."[43]

That insistent honesty placed Russell within a broader political tradition. Al- though most black leaders and celebrities preached nonviolence and appealed to white liberals, Russell's questioning of that strategy echoed the political vanguard: grassroots organizers such as Medgar Evers, Ella Baker, and the young activists of the Student Nonviolent Coordinating Committee (SNCC), or advocates of armed self-defense such as Robert F. Williams or the Deacons for Defense and Justice. Es- pecially in the rural South, black people defended themselves. Russell had learned those lessons from the Old Man and Mister Charlie. He also thought that the old black leadership had failed the South. "Teachers and preachers were selling Ne- groes down the river," he said, recalling his childhood. So the codes of self-respect and self-defense resonated with him.[44]

Russell had inconsistencies: he wanted love and emitted hate, he wanted peace and proclaimed anger, he wanted respect and projected arrogance. But that was the point. He was a human being, not a symbol. His ideas sprung from different sources, and his personality embodied different elements. He would not craft an image to garner goodwill. "Bill Russell, or any other black man like him, does not want the white man's sympathy, or, indeed, his friendship," wrote Gil Rogin. "What he wants is recognition of himself as an individual, a black individual, who can meet the world on equal terms and fare unequally, according to his merit." Russell il- lustrated the distinction between black images and black people.[45]

. . .

Meanwhile, the ghost of Bob Cousy haunted the Celtics. "You'd better hustle now that you don't have Cousy to carry you," sneered one fan to Russell. That remark only inflamed Russell's annoyance with the media's constant invocation of the re- tired point guard: "He's not here. He's not going to be. He no longer exists as a bas- ketball player so far as we're concerned. He's almost an opponent now, kind of a shadow we're playing against."[46]

Russell cherished the opportunity to erase the final, lingering questions about his central importance to the Celtics. He and Frank Ramsey were the new captains. Russell had worried about the responsibility, lest he upset the fragile balance of egos by criticizing a teammate. During a press luncheon, however, he announced that John Havlicek "is going to need some coaching" and that an out-of-shape Tom Heinsohn "should be played until he falls down, have Red Auerbach pour water over him and then play some more." Russell soon learned to avoid such impolitic remarks, as he was becoming the face of the franchise.[47]

Cousy's retirement initiated a shift in the team's racial composition. After the 1963–64 season, three other white mainstays would retire: Jim Loscutoff, Clyde Lovellette, and Frank Ramsey. "The day of the 6'4" basketball forward is about over," explained Ramsey. Yet the sublime "Sixth Man" remained a versatile, intelligent weapon with a bag of cheeky tricks for drawing fouls, as he outlined that season in a *Sports Illustrated* article entitled "Smart Moves by a Master of Deception." The article backfired, earning Ramsey an angry meeting with the league president. When opponents hacked him in ensuing games, the referees swallowed their whistles.[48]

The Celtics also added Willie Naulls in 1963. After seven losing seasons in New York and San Francisco, Naulls was overweight and unhappy. He reenrolled at UCLA to prepare for dental school. Then Russell recruited him to the Celtics "as a personal favor." It rejuvenated Naulls. "Willie the Whale" dropped twenty pounds during training camp. He collapsed during his first practice, but he embraced Boston's team-first approach. For years, he had ignored defense. Now, he said, "I'm loaded with hustle scars." The five-time All-Star joined Ramsey, Loscutoff, and Havlicek on a deep bench. Naulls backed up Heinsohn, the only white starter. When Auerbach played Naulls with Russell, Sanders, Sam Jones, and K. C. Jones, it put five blacks on the court at once. That NBA milestone came so naturally to the Celtics, however, that Sanders never noticed until after the game.[49]

The ascension of K. C. Jones to starting point guard indicated a philosophical as well as racial adjustment. Jones lacked Cousy's flash, but no one played more tenacious defense. Whereas Cousy dribbled with aplomb, now the team passed faster. With his jackrabbit reflexes and studied approach, Jones operated a smooth fast break. He even developed some confidence in his shot, flipping an occasional one-hander from the top of the key. The Celtics defined themselves on speed, defense, and defiance of their post-Cousy doubters. They opened the season 15–1. "I never saw Boston better," said Cincinnati coach Charley Wolf.[50]

On January 14, 1964, Boston Garden hosted the All-Star Game. Now, just as Russell attacked the racial status quo, the players challenged the NBA's paternalistic labor system. Their frustrations dated to 1957, during Boston's last All-Star Game, when Cousy, head of the newly formed National Basketball Players Association (NBPA), met with the AFL-CIO to discuss an affiliation. His threat jolted Maurice Podoloff and the owners, who finally agreed to minor concessions on expenses, fines, exhibition games, and play-off bonuses.[51]

But Podoloff deflected any future labor agitation. The players complained about no health insurance, second-class hotels, no trainers on road trips, no preseason pay, and a frantic schedule. New NBPA head Tom Heinsohn proposed a pension. He hired Harvard-educated lawyer Larry Fleischer, and the NBPA proposed that players and owners each contribute $500 a year, funding a thirty-year life-insurance policy with a modest annuity. "In reply," said Russell, "we received the swerve and the stall and the screws."[52]

In 1963 Walter Kennedy replaced Podoloff. For years, Podoloff had wrung compromises out of squabbling owners, shepherding a continuing stability. That summer two franchise relocations placed every team in a major market with a big arena: the failing Chicago Zephyrs became the Baltimore Bullets, and the Syracuse Nationals became the Philadelphia 76ers. But "Poodles" lost a national television contract, and he earned little respect. Kennedy was hired to elevate the league's image. The public relations director for the original BAA and former mayor of Stamford, Connecticut, detailed expansion plans, secured continuing antitrust legislation, and negotiated for twelve nationally televised contests, including the 1964 All-Star Game.[53]

At the All-Star Game, Kennedy inherited a crisis resulting from Podoloff's equivocations with the NBPA. Kennedy envisioned a "big league" showcase, a springboard to a network television contract. The players wanted a pension plan. The day before the game, a blizzard crushed the northeast. Most players endured twenty-four-hour ordeals of airport hotels, early-morning flights, and train rides to reach Boston Garden before the 9:00 tip-off. That day, Heinsohn and three others met with Detroit owner Fred Zollner, who promised that owners would consider a pension. But Fleischer wanted a specific signed commitment, and Kennedy did not return his calls. So at 5:40, Heinsohn and Bob Pettit knocked on Kennedy's hotel door. Ten minutes later they held an emergency meeting with Fleischer, Lenny Wilkens, and Russell. Without a pension agreement signed by the owners, the All-Stars threatened to boycott the game.[54]

Kennedy tracked down the owners, who refused to sign anything. They resented the players' defiance. So at 8:25, Kennedy gathered all twenty All-Stars in the Celtics' cramped locker room. Promising a commitment to the pension, he urged the players to consider the public relations disaster of a nationally televised labor demonstration. Then he left, and the players debated. Russell supported a boycott. He had tired of empty promises. As game time approached, the players talked and talked, turning back nervous visits from league officials. Red Auerbach raged outside the room. A security guard relayed a threat from Los Angeles owner Bob Short to Jerry West and Elgin Baylor. "You tell Bob Short to fuck himself," relayed back Baylor.[55]

Initially, only Wilt Chamberlain favored playing. He thought that the NBA might not survive the blow. But on the first ballot, eleven elected to play, with nine dissents. On the second ballot, two more voted to play. Heinsohn voiced trust for Kennedy, but many "yes" votes came out of fear. Russell remembered one player crouched over, sitting on his hands to prevent their shaking. After a fifteen-minute delay, the game began. Oscar Robertson, who won MVP, remained glum after the game, disappointed by the slow labor progress. Only Russell, who sat next to Robertson cracking jokes, seemed unaffected by the day's twists and turns. He had already sacrificed popularity for principles.[56]

The NBA averted a boycott, but it had irrevocably changed: the players no longer considered the owners benevolent patriarchs. Walter Brown thundered, "Tom Heinsohn is the No. 1 heel in my long association with sports. If I had a team in Honolulu, I'd ship him there." In general, public opinion sided against the players. In a satirical column mocking any association between professional athletes and the working class, Bud Collins linked Russell with a broader challenge to sport's traditional order. "Personally I favored a strike," said his fictional player-author. "We didn't owe the public nothing."[57]

. . .

No season had ever offered such trials and rewards. As his controversial statements reached print, Russell's body wore down. He was ten pounds overweight. He had a pulled right thigh muscle and arthritis in both knees. In early January, the Celtics and Lakers went into overtime on Saturday night, and in the Sunday afternoon re-match, Russell walked up the court, scoring zero field goals. Later that month, Wilt Chamberlain dominated him in consecutive games. Russell called the season his "worst in eight years."[58]

Yet while averaging career highs in rebounds and assists, Russell won new lev-els of respect. "Every game is like a war," said Guy Rodgers. "He seems to want to prove something." Walt Bellamy and Sihugo Green judged his defense even more devastating. "Russell is better than ever," reported Los Angeles coach Fred Schaus. The Boston press, moreover, started explaining Russell's centrality to Boston's title hopes. "Without him," wrote Jerry Nason, "the C's have as much chance as a snow-ball in a Turkish bath."[59]

Boston finished 59–21, one win shy of its own record. Auerbach listed the hur-dled barriers: doubts about Cousy's absence, backlash to Ramsey's shenanigans, resentment of Heinsohn's labor leadership, and anger at Russell's magazine arti-cles. (Auerbach also wasted his first draft choice, Billy Green of Colorado State, who refused to board airplanes.) The team had exhibited exceptional character, defended with passion, and balanced the scoring burden.[60]

Before the 1964 play-offs, however, Russell revealed that he might retire. "I'm tired," he said. "I don't see how I can go through another season like this." He slept only two hours a night. He worried about dying in a plane crash. His knees throbbed. He needed surgery for a growth on his eyelid. He resented questions about Cousy, and he obsessed about proving the skeptics wrong. He was "severely depressed." He read all his hate mail, even responding to those who left return ad-dresses. He fretted that anyone considered him the white man's enemy. Yet even though friends advised him to avoid controversy, his conscience compelled him to decry racial inequality.[61]

After three consecutive MVP awards, Russell lost the 1964 honor to Oscar Robertson. While averaging 31.4 points, 9.9 rebounds, and 11 assists, Robertson willed Cincinnati into genuine challengers for Boston's crown, taking seven of their twelve regular-season matchups. Russell finished a distant third in the MVP vot-ing, and Wilt Chamberlain took his first-team spot on the NBA All-Stars. "The silent voice of protest may be speaking out against him," suspected Jerry Nason, inti-mating that other players resented Russell's accusations of a racial quota.[62]

But Robertson, too, suspected racial motivations in a midseason trade that shipped away Bob Boozer, a longtime starter for Cincinnati. In 1963 the Royals added Ohio State superstar Jerry Lucas. With Jack Twyman and Tom Hawkins also playing forward, Cincinnati exchanged Boozer for the mediocre, white Larry Staverman. "A lot of good Negro ballplayers should be in the league but only generally four or five spots are open on a team," said Robertson, supporting Russell's claims. "We had five until Bob Boozer was traded. Whether this had anything to do with Boozer being traded, I don't know."[63]

Various experts favored the Royals in the Eastern Division play-offs. Robertson's penetrations into the lane challenged Russell, and Wayne Embry's outside shooting pulled Russell away from rebounds. But the Celtics knew play-off pressure. They got extra rest, avoided gimmick plays, and remembered the emotional and financial rewards of victory. Russell, moreover, still possessed that all-encompassing need to win. Indeed, he recalled feeling trapped, pained, "on the verge of a nervous breakdown." Then, "I woke one morning and the play-offs were beginning and suddenly, it was all right again and I was whole again. I was Bill Russell again."[64]

Russell crushed the Royals. He demoralized Lucas, holding him to single-digit rebounds and four field goals in the first two games at Boston Garden, which the Celtics won 103–87 and 101–90. He pulled down rebounds "like a giant octopus," and in a 102–92 victory at Cincinnati Gardens, he led Boston with 22 points, including a breathtaking dunk "from the second balcony." The Royals had averaged 114 points a game, and now they could barely crack 90. "He blocks everything. He's got everybody bothered," admitted Robertson. Cincinnati took Game Four 102–93, but Russell notched 20 points and 35 rebounds in Game Five's 109–95 series clincher, squelching the last doubts about his mental health. "Nobody in hoopla is entitled to a breakdown," quipped Harold Kaese, "except those who have to play against him."[65]

Now the Boozer trade looked especially foolish. Russell felt validated. He reflected that "as despicable as the quota system was, it won a title for the Celtics. The Royals could have beaten us, but in my opinion they virtually gave Bob Boozer away to get down to their black quota, and that gave us the championship in the bargain."[66]

. . .

The 1964 Finals revived the Russell-Chamberlain rivalry on the league's biggest stage. New San Francisco coach Alex Hannum molded his center in Russell's image: shooting less, passing more, attacking the basket, rebounding better, and concentrating on defense. Hannum engaged in a full-scale psychological campaign of cajoling Chamberlain, praising his open-mindedness, and even threatening a fight. While his assist totals surged, Chamberlain's scoring average dipped to "only" 36.9 points. "I still think I should be shooting more," said Chamberlain. "But Hannum's a helluva coach. And how can you argue with what's happening?" The media trumped a "New Wilt Chamberlain," and the Warriors finished first in the

West. They reached the Finals with a fourth-quarter, Game Seven comeback over St. Louis.[67]

"It burns Wilt inside, the rap that he can't win," said Hannum. "He'll do anything to get a title—and to wipe out those comparisons to Bill Russell." But Boston routed San Francisco in the opening two home games, 108–96 and 124–101, which featured all the Celtic trademarks: zealous defense, sparkplugs off the bench, and Russell checking Chamberlain. The only dramatic moment arrived in the fourth quarter of Game Two, when Auerbach was yapping at Chamberlain. Russell sensed trouble. To Auerbach's later gratification, Russell warned, "Get back, Red. You're about six inches too close." Russell had his hand on Chamberlain's arm. Like the rest of the NBA fraternity, Russell was grateful that Chamberlain's anger almost never exploded; the goliath possessed freakish strength. This time, however, Chamberlain tossed Russell back with the flick of his arm.

Clyde Lovellette entered the fray. The merry fan favorite had spent the season as a human victory cigar, entering blowouts to chants of "We Want Clyde! We Want Clyde!" He saw more time against San Francisco, however, because Chamberlain teamed with 6'11" rookie Nate Thurmond, and the Celtics needed frontline beef. Lovellette and Chamberlain already despised each other, and Lovellette annoyed Chamberlain with shoves, pinches, and pulls. Now, as the loudmouthed Lovellette put his dukes up, Chamberlain reared back and popped him, dropping him to the floor.[68]

That punch captured the Warriors' frustrations, and it energized them. Hannum promised rough, physical defense for Game Three. Professional basketball seemed to have finally arrived in San Francisco. The Cow Palace had an official capacity of 13,852, but 14,862 crammed into every corner of the old, cold barn to watch the Warriors crush the uncharacteristically listless Celtics, 115–91.[69]

Before Game Four, Boston adjusted. During the off-day practice, Russell stayed in street clothes, but he spent about thirty-five minutes on the court in individual consultations with Ramsey, K. C. Jones, Sanders, and Heinsohn, fine-tuning different situations. Auerbach also decided to cover Thurmond with Ramsey. The Boston forward gave up seven inches, but if Thurmond ventured into the post, he clogged Chamberlain's space and faced a potential Russell block. When Thurmond took a longer shot, Ramsey sprinted away, looking for an outlet pass. The adjustment sparked Boston's fast break and planted hesitation in Thurmond's mind. In Game Four, Boston edged San Francisco, 98–95. The difference, many Celtics thought, was Ramsey's defense of Thurmond.[70]

Russell arrived for Game Five dressed in black. "It's my funeral suit," he explained, suitable for burying the Warriors. Throughout the play-offs, the Boston Garden crowd had given him standing ovations. "They have done this," explained Bill McSweeny of the Boston Record-American, "because they recognize his exceptional value, both as a player and a person." The cheers connoted a deep appreciation of his dominance, encouraged him to eschew early retirement, and even communicated respect for his principled stands. They heightened his paradoxical status—athlete and intellectual, entertainer and provocateur, hero and outlaw.[71]

With ten seconds left, Boston led only 101–99, and Heinsohn missed a hook shot. A mass of bodies vied for the critical rebound. Russell soared above them all. In one powerful motion, he rebounded with two hands and slammed the ball, reaching through the rim down to his elbows. Seconds later the frenzied crowd was storming the court, carrying off Russell on its shoulders.[72]

With their sixth straight championship, the Celtics surpassed a record once shared with baseball's New York Yankees and hockey's Montreal Canadiens. They had dispelled their doubters. "This has been a particularly trying season for me," Russell admitted amidst the locker-room showers of beer and orange juice. He had grown weary of the questions about Cousy's absence, persevered through personal angst and political iconoclasm, and captained Boston's consistent dominance. No title had ever meant more.[73]

11

Russellphobia

On Labor Day of 1964, while vacationing on Cape Cod, Walter Brown died of a heart attack. The funeral procession stretched a mile long. Despite founding the Celtics to fill empty arena dates, Brown had shepherded sport's greatest dynasty. "The Celtics—the very name implies basketball supremacy around the globe—stand as the most towering monument to a man who thought he had devoted his life to hockey," wrote Jerry Nason. Arthur Siegel lauded Brown's support of Russell's battles against Jim Crow, adding that "his Celtics are living exponents of the theory that all men are created equal."[1]

Brown's passing reflected the NBA's ongoing drift from its petty entrepreneurial past. After his widow Marjorie and minority owner Lou Pieri rewarded Red Auerbach with 10 percent of the franchise, they placed the team for sale. The Celtics represented a good investment. True, regular season attendance remained weak, due to some combination of New England's historic indifference to basketball, the team's routine dominance, a lack of off-season promotion, and the increasingly black roster. But the annual play-off run earned an extra $100,000 to $200,000. Moreover, Walter Kennedy sold a package of Sunday afternoon telecasts to ABC, restoring the NBA to national television. During the 1964–65 season, Pieri rejected bids of $2 million or more, including one from a consortium headed by entertainer Bob Hope.[2]

The Celtics dedicated the 1964–65 season to Brown's memory, a pledge spearheaded by Russell. "We'll win this one for Walter," he promised Auerbach. The tragedy unearthed the sincere compassion underneath his stoic demeanor. Winning another title would not only honor Brown but also restore Russell's focus from the ravages of individual, racial, and cultural turmoil. Two trips in the summer of

1964 had just stirred those demons. The journeys demonstrated different political applications of his celebrity. Together, they illustrated his evolving pursuit of personal clarity and social justice.[3]

. . .

In May and June, Russell joined an All-Star tour to Eastern Europe and the Middle East. Basketball remained an American game: the United States again won gold at the 1964 Olympics in Tokyo. But the sport had grown popular on both sides of the Iron Curtain. Europeans revered NBA stars much more than Mickey Mantle or Jim Brown. When Jerry Lucas met a Soviet team in 1962, they quizzed him on the relative merits of Bill Russell and Wilt Chamberlain.[4]

Auerbach had long fumed that the AAU let inferior players from industrial teams represent the country. At the 1963 World Championships, the United States finished fourth. Foreign nations, he believed, respected only American force. So when the State Department asked him to lead a goodwill tour, Auerbach recruited Russell, Bob Cousy, Tom Heinsohn, K. C. Jones, Oscar Robertson, Jerry Lucas, Tom Gola, and Bob Pettit. The Soviet Union, fearing a propaganda disaster, declined to host the Americans. Instead, after a personal briefing by Secretary of State Dean Rusk and a meet-and-greet with President Lyndon Johnson, they left for Poland, Romania, Yugoslavia, and Egypt.[5]

The athletes proved popular ambassadors. On the streets of Krakow, a happy mob of students tossed Auerbach, Cousy, and Pettit into the air. In Polish nightclubs, Gola recalled, "guys would consider it a dishonor if you didn't have a vodka and dance with their wife." Romanians crowded their bus, asking for autographs, pins, and chewing gum. European players imitated Cousy's no-look passes or Robertson's powerful drives, and their officials filmed all the Americans' games, practices, and clinics. Those films circulated through Communist bloc sporting bureaucracies, globalizing the Celtic style: Robertson, Gola, Lucas, and Pettit knew Boston's seven basic plays, so they ran Auerbach's offense.[6]

Like Russell's previous trips to Latin America and Africa, this State Department junket advertised African American sports heroes. Heinsohn believed that their interracial teamwork counteracted communist propaganda about the turbulence of American race relations. The black players faced many questions about race, and they encountered some romanticized stereotypes. Fans gave them flowers, gifts, and toys. After sympathizing with the black plight, Bulgarian students in Poland asked Russell to sing or dance. They suggested "Go Down Moses."[7]

The team also visited the former Nazi concentration camp at Auschwitz. They toured barracks piled high with the victims' clothes, hair, and eyeglasses, as well as the gas chambers and mass incinerators. Auschwitz touched Russell, especially in light of his recent gloom. He considered the complicity of ordinary citizens in the horrors of the Nazi regime. "A man who believes in saying what he thinks, popular or not, can learn a lesson about the value of standing up for a cause from what happened there," he thought.[8]

The sobering excursion failed to stop them, however, from yelling "Deutsch! Deutsch!" and pointing at their Teutonic teammate, Tom Heinsohn. Germans were not exactly popular in postwar Poland. In Krakow, Auerbach and Cousy convinced two locals to dress in trench coats, pose as policemen, knock on Heinsohn's door, demand his passport, march him through the hotel lobby, and deposit him at a café with brusque instructions to sit still. Heinsohn burned through cigarette after cigarette—at least until he saw Auerbach, Cousy, and trainer Buddy LeRoux on the street, laughing hysterically.[9]

The oppressed people within the Soviet bloc embraced the American superstars; the Yugoslavians felt otherwise. In Marshal Tito's nonaligned communist regime, animosity flowed both east and west. Yugoslavia, moreover, had beaten the United States at the 1963 World Championships. Their officials ignored Auerbach's diatribes on the distinctions between AAU and NBA players. During some exhibitions, fans jeered and tossed debris, and players kicked, elbowed, and punched Americans without penalty. After one cheap shot too many, Russell led a post move with his elbow. His defender got carried off the court.[10]

Radivoj Korac starred for OKK Belgrade. The left-handed, undersized center was a national hero. That year he scored ninety-nine points in one European Champions Cup game. But Russell swatted away all of his attempts. Korac grew so frustrated after six consecutive blocks that he fired a thirty-foot line drive off the backboard, just to avoid another block. The next time he shot, Russell smacked it straight down, off Korac's head. Korac concluded his subsequent tantrum by punting the ball into the stands.[11]

The trip heightened Russell's international outlook. In Egypt he bent through tiny passageways into the inner chambers of the Pyramids, and he and Robertson toured a Cairo marketplace in traditional headdresses and long, flowing robes of red and white. But Russell also sank into a trademark gloomy spell. His team won all twenty-two games by at least twenty points, so he earned no satisfaction from competition. Nor did he embrace the tour's mission. He snored through State Department briefings, begged out of games with cramps, and complained about homesickness. He also proclaimed independence from authority. When Auerbach criticized his brooding attitude, he yelled back. Later, when Russell emitted a squeaky cackle and Auerbach barked for silence, Russell cussed at him. "Don't say anything to me," he warned. "Not ever." Removed from professional obligation, his pride surfaced in these bursts of sullen aggravation.[12]

His next trip offered a stiffer challenge. In early July, Russell received a call from Charles Evers in Jackson, Mississippi. After years in Chicago's black underworld, the independent-minded, sharp-tongued Charles had replaced his brother Medgar atop the Mississippi NAACP. He proceeded to irritate local activists, national headquarters, and other civil rights organizations by pursuing his own agenda. Though his oratory and courage inspired people, he promoted himself at the expense of grassroots movements, and he made his decisions unilaterally.[13]

At Medgar's funeral, Russell had offered any possible help. Charles cashed in, asking Russell to conduct integrated basketball clinics in Jackson, Canton, Meridian, and Clarksdale. The visit would boost black Mississippians' flagging morale, along with Evers's own standing. Rose pleaded that Bill decline. Friends advised him of potential dangers. Russell was scared. But he would teach basketball and even march in demonstrations, he said, "because a man has to do what he thinks is right."[14]

Upon landing in Jackson on July 9, Russell stepped onto the front lines of a racial revolution. It was "Freedom Summer," when hundreds of young volunteers—men and women, black and white, rural locals and elite students—converged in Mississippi. They conducted voter-registration campaigns, established community centers, and launched Freedom Schools. Without much police protection, they faced a resurgent Ku Klux Klan. The first volunteers had arrived a few weeks earlier. By then, civil rights workers James Chaney, Andrew Goodman, and Michael Schwerner had disappeared after investigating a church arson. (Authorities later found their corpses in an earthen dam.) It was a time of heightened black hopes, surging media attention, and escalating white violence.[15]

Russell acted edgy throughout his three-day visit. He learned that Evers cradled a pistol in his sleep. The NAACP scrapped his travel outside Jackson—the Klan was liable to notice a 6'9" goateed black man. Four armed guards accompanied him in public. He heard constant streams of racist invective. A Jackson restaurant refused to serve him. He and Marvin Gilmore, chairman of the Boston NAACP, stayed at the Heidelberg Hotel, which had just hosted its first black customer. Mysterious sounds emanated from the alley. Their doorknob rattled. White customers surrounded their dining-room table, brandishing guns. Yet Russell experienced firsthand how blacks resisted their oppressors. When cars of drunken whites followed them at night, his escorts brandished guns, and the hoodlums pulled back.[16]

Within this repressive environment, Russell expressed the best of human nature. At the Negro YMCA, he regaled twenty awe-struck kids with childhood tales as a jayvee benchwarmer. He asked them to embrace hard work, and he discussed his own responsibilities. "I guess they call people like me 'outside agitators,'" he added, "but no American is an outside agitator anywhere in America. What happens in Mississippi concerns people in Massachusetts and vice versa." The next day he conducted an integrated clinic at Jackson Auditorium, the first of its kind. This barrier-breaking act did not threaten larger racial patterns, as even the Jackson mayor endorsed white children learning basketball from an NBA star. But Russell had entered the heart of the black freedom struggle. That night, he spoke at a mass meeting at New Jerusalem Baptist Church.[17]

The first star athlete to participate firsthand in the Southern civil rights movement, Russell had put himself on the line. Evers recalled no other celebrity with such courage. "Russell inspired the hell out of us," he said. "I'll never forget that." Attorney William Kunstler remembered Russell bowing into a sweaty diner on North Farish Street. Activists, lawyers, and kids gaped, incredulous that a star athlete had stepped into this bubbling cauldron. "Thank God you're here," said Kunstler. "I wouldn't have missed it," replied Russell.[18]

After returning to Massachusetts, Russell publicized Evers's claims that twelve black Mississippians had disappeared in the past year. The FBI had focused only on a single case, since Goodman and Schwerner were white. "This is a time of crisis and we're closer to the crossroads," said Russell. Black activists were abandoning the tactic of nonviolence, chafing at intransigent racism, and growing disillusioned with white liberals. If it furthered African American rights, he would even quit basketball. He considered his contributions miniscule compared to the daily struggles of Southern blacks. At the least, he prodded sports fans to consider political injustice. He compared the United States to apartheid South Africa. It saddened him that he had aroused a white backlash, but he refused to compromise his principles. "I'm a man," he said. "If I have to be a boy to be popular, then I don't want popularity."[19]

. . .

Russell's team, too, crumbled the old racial codes. In December 1964, Tom Heinsohn injured his foot. John Havlicek had led Boston in scoring the previous year, but with Frank Ramsey retired, Auerbach wanted Havlicek to remain the Sixth Man. So Willie Naulls started alongside Russell, Sanders, K. C. Jones, and Sam Jones. No NBA team had started five blacks before. After smashing the taboo, the Celtics rattled off sixteen consecutive wins.[20]

The streak fell one short of the NBA record. They had earlier won eleven straight, and by late January they stood 41–8, seven and a half games ahead of Cincinnati. *Sports Illustrated* had titled its preseason preview "The Pack Closes on Boston," but Boston again sprinted away from the pack. "The Jones Boys" had matured into the league's best backcourt. Russell called K. C. Jones "our most valuable player" because his defense tormented such stars as Oscar Robertson and Jerry West. Sam Jones emerged as a bona fide superstar. Lightning-fast with a catalog of lethal bank and jump shots, he asserted himself as a go-to scorer, becoming the first Celtic to surpass two thousand points in one season. He finished fourth in MVP balloting.[21]

After a one-year hiatus, Russell reclaimed first place in that MVP vote. The Celtics finished a record-breaking 62–18, and Russell's significance again transcended statistics. "When Bill feels like it, there's little that can stop us," said Sam Jones. "The players know before the game when Russ is really ready. They can feel it and it perks all of us up." No team in basketball history defended like these Celtics, who drew their cue from their center and captain.[22]

Frayed by his dual role as coach and general manager, Auerbach leaned more on Russell. Their spats in Europe aside, they remained partners in pursuit of victory. They developed a standard patter: Russell asked to speak with the general manager, and Auerbach cautioned him for going over the coach's head. Russell also coached whenever Auerbach got ejected. In March, Auerbach left to scout college players, and for two games Russell acted as player-coach. Auerbach won his first Coach of the Year award in 1965. Nothing shaped his success more than his alliance with Russell.[23]

On occasion, Russell failed to summon competitive fires. Now thirty-one, he still logged massive minutes. In November 1964 he checked into a hospital. He was suffering from exhaustion. He then started taking iron pills for anemia. Yet Celtics trainer Buddy LeRoux called him "the most perfectly coordinated athlete I have ever seen—in any pro sport." Russell's troubles remained more psychological than physical, as he juggled commitments to the Celtics, politics, Slade's, a Roxbury auto dealership, and his Liberian plantation. He nevertheless dismissed rumors of impending retirement: basketball rewarded him, both psychically and financially.[24]

"He is Bill Russell and he owns the game of basketball as no one ever has before and as no one ever will again," wrote Jim Murray. Neither Babe Ruth nor Jack Dempsey nor Bill Tilden had revolutionized their sport like Russell, waxed Murray. Even Boston reporters began considering him a civic institution. "What Can City Give to Russell?" asked one column. "Russell Rates with Ruth as Boston's Best," proclaimed another. Russell belonged in Boston's sports pantheon with such icons as John L. Sullivan, Eddie Shore, and Ted Williams.[25]

John Thompson idolized Russell. The center from Providence College had a comparable intellectual curiosity, offered similar contributions of defense and rebounding, and was undergoing an analogous journey of self-definition. After joining the Celtics in 1964, he marveled at Russell's competitive focus, adherence to principles, and generosity to friends. He admired that Russell did not *ask* for respect—he *expected* it. Russell called himself "black" before it was fashionable. His pride communicated a broader message about overcoming fear, even to a 6'10" man built like a bear. "Russell made me feel safe," said Thompson. "Somehow I knew it was going to be all right so long as I was with him."[26]

Opponents shared that appreciation of Russell's smoldering coolness. Every All-Star Game, recalled Auerbach, an Eastern Division teammate revealed anxiety that he might disappoint Russell. Willis Reed first met Russell at the 1965 All-Star Game, where he absorbed lessons on how to exploit individual opponents' proclivities, mind-sets, and weaknesses. Nate Thurmond thought that Russell walked in Jackie Robinson's footsteps, clearing a path for fellow black athletes with pride, talent, and intelligence. "He wasn't meek," said Thurmond. "He was a man." Jerry West realized that during the national anthem, his eyes gravitated toward Russell, who stood quiet and graceful, like a Greek statue. "Some people have an aura about them," West said. "He's just got it."[27]

That constant sense of Russell's presence only intensified when the game started. Reed had grown up in Louisiana emulating and admiring his fellow left-handed center. "He was the greatest," said Reed. "He was my boyhood idol." He eagerly anticipated his first game against the Celtics. When Russell blocked his first shot, it surprised him. When Russell blocked his second shot, it discouraged him. When Russell blocked his third shot, he accepted the inevitability.[28]

Russell applied psychological intimidation better than anyone in NBA history. Especially as he got older, he wanted young opponents to think of him as a "legendary hero." He sauntered to the tip-off with a regal nonchalance—his arms crossed, his chin raised, his strut unhurried, his manner haughty. He then inspired paroxysms of panic and paranoia, which Tom Hawkins of Cincinnati called "Russellphobia." Though he could not block every shot, the opposition constantly worried that he might. When he squelched an attempt, he smiled like he could do it every time. When rookies attacked the basket, he feigned fury. "Don't you know who I am?" he hissed at Chicago rookie Bob Love. "Don't ever dunk on me. Don't even dream of dunking on me." His cackles, needles, scowls, and growls nudged shooters out of their comfort zones. He even catalogued his methods in a *Sports Illustrated* article called "The Psych . . . and My Other Tricks."[29]

Tom Meschery of the San Francisco Warriors lyrically captured Russell's impact. The child of Russian exiles, Meschery spent World War Two in a Japanese concentration camp. The young immigrant found an American identity through sports. He brought a dogged, sweaty passion to the court, but he also wore tweed jackets, smoked pipes, and wrote poetry, expressing a romantic appreciation for the game's spirit and personalities. In his ode "To Bill Russell," he likened the Celtic to "an eagle with a beard," a mythical creature out of Hindu tradition. "You will return," he wrote, "and beat your wings/violently/over my grave"—offering one more blocked shot, one last intimidation, one final torment from a demon defender.[30]

· · ·

Russell's rivalry with Wilt Chamberlain still lent the NBA its premier plotline. It also offered sports fans a choice with fascinating racial implications. "You've got the two best players in the league," said Russell, "and you had to take sides, and you couldn't take the side of a white guy because"—he stopped to cackle—"*there wasn't one!*"[31]

Russell's gruff demeanor and racial anger may have repelled many whites, but compared to Chamberlain, he was the "good guy." He not only led integrated championship teams but also withstood the invasion of Goliath. "If it weren't for W. F.

Russell," wrote Jim Murray, "the game would right now be being slowly digested by Wilton Chamberlain." Chamberlain appeared the dark giant, the tortured monster from a horror flick. He got booed throughout the league. Fans called him a lazy, selfish loser. He earned the public's awe, but it was slathered in derision.[32]

Ironically, Chamberlain sought an image that comforted the white mainstream. Unlike Russell, he talked to fans, participated in league publicity, and signed autographs. He also avoided politics—if he stood on a political limb, he might fall and injure his marketability. "The best way to help integration is to live a good, clean life," he proclaimed. He declined to campaign for John F. Kennedy during the 1960 presidential election. He opposed the 1964 All-Star boycott. He even shrugged off the NBA's racial quotas, reasoning that owners looked out for themselves. Instead of sensing collective injustice, he roiled with individual grievances: complaining that fans and reporters belittled him, bellyaching at his critics, bemoaning his image as a cartoon ogre. "One thing I wish is that people didn't always cast me as the villain," he said. "Just once, I wish somebody would root for me."[33]

Chamberlain's grumbles, quirks, and bursts of ego prompted as much interest as his scoring. Seemingly afraid of his own strength, he whined about physical defense rather than responding in kind. He took difficult fall-away jump shots, just to prove that he was no clumsy leviathan. Despite his extraordinary grace, however, he converted just over half his foul shots. He sank them in practice, but in games he treated them like trips to the dentist's office, flipping hurried line drives with one twitchy hand. Russell shot free throws no better, but he built his reputation on defense, rebounding, and titles.[34]

Chamberlain hated that Russell won eminence at his expense. "I have made Russell what he is today because they've used me as a steppingstone," he cried. He cited his myriad scoring and rebounding titles. But that only heightened his frustrating paradox: If he was so great, why did he never win championships? So he developed twisted rationalizations, celebrating second-tier achievements such as making the NCAA Final or winning the division championship. "In a way, I like it better when we lose," he added. "It's over, and I can look forward to the next game. If we win, it builds up the tension, and I start worrying about the next game." He could not define victory as his ultimate ambition, because then he was a failure.[35]

Early in the 1964–65 season, Chamberlain's reputation plummeted. In September and October, an irregular heartbeat and pancreatic inflammation hospitalized him. In December, he broke his nose and wore a grotesque face mask. By early January, the Warriors had lost more games than in the previous season. Fans sneered that Chamberlain had reverted to his low-post, shoot-first mentality. Cow Palace crowds dwindled.[36]

San Francisco owner Franklin Mieuli had trouble justifying a $70,000 salary for his troubled luminary, especially since young, popular Nate Thurmond could play center. The advertising and television tycoon also resented Chamberlain. After Chamberlain visited his personal physician in Philadelphia, Mieuli greeted him at the airport with a custom-made diamond stickpin. "What's this piece of shit?" said Chamberlain. So when the Warriors faltered, he put Chamberlain on the trading block. Remarkably, the greatest offensive force in basketball history fetched a low price. Los Angeles needed a center to counteract Russell, but the Lakers brass, in consultation with Elgin Baylor and Jerry West, refused to relinquish Dick Barnett. Los Angeles thus rebuffed a roster featuring three superstars in their prime.[37]

The Philadelphia 76ers became Chamberlain's primary suitor. The franchise had drawn weak crowds since moving from Syracuse—old Warriors fans failed to summon enthusiasm for the rival Nationals. But Philadelphians declared ambivalence about their hometown hero. Some considered Chamberlain's style boring, and others worried about team chemistry. The 76ers had sweet-shooting guard Hal Greer, smart and unselfish forward Chet Walker, and explosive big man Lucious Jackson. Presumably, San Francisco would demand at least two of this young, talented core.[38]

Instead, Philadelphia gave up a pittance. At the All-Star Game, the 76ers acquired Chamberlain for Paul Neumann, Connie Dierking, Lee Shaffer, and $300,000. Neumann and Dierking were average players, and Shaffer never again played in the NBA. The trade wounded Chamberlain's pride, and he announced that Philadelphia had made a "bad deal." He planned to retire after the season, his frequent ploy to milk more money. The media mocked him. "The petulant moods of Wilt the Stilt are getting to be a bore," sniffed Frank Deford.[39]

Chamberlain remained ill tempered after joining Philadelphia. As a Syracuse National, Dolph Schayes had lambasted Chamberlain for his retirement threats and hideous free-throw shooting. "I don't think he ever forgave me," recalled Schayes. He now coached the 76ers, and they kept clashing. Chamberlain got enraged when Schayes substituted him out. During a late-season slump, Chamberlain complained that he was a scapegoat. He returned to the hospital with stomach pains. The team finished with forty wins and forty losses.[40]

Yet Chamberlain injected the 76ers into Philadelphia's sports culture. The local press rejoiced at his return. "Wilt Chamberlain was its favorite subject, larger than life, homegrown," recalled Walker. Reporters had constant copy on "the prodigal son who had returned with his superhuman feats, his constant commentary on the league, his ailments, his battles with coaches." Also, Chamberlain, Greer, Walker, Jackson, and Larry Costello composed a potent starting five. Chamberlain shined in duels against Russell, and he averaged almost thirty-five points a game. He played good defense, set screens, and passed to open shooters throughout an opening play-off series against Cincinnati. The lopsided trade had tipped the NBA's balance of power.[41]

. . .

The 1965 play-offs featured Chamberlain's signature feats and foibles, and they established Philadelphia as Boston's premier rival. Auerbach, however, carped, "They don't even deserve to be playing us." He accused Philadelphia of coasting through the regular season. In response, Chamberlain declared an immense longing to "shut up Mr. Auerbach just once."[42]

Each franchise painted the other as shoddy and petty. The Celtics won the Boston Garden opener 108–98 behind a suffocating full-court press, but Philadelphia officials whined that the official scorer credited too many rebounds to Russell (he got thirty-two, Chamberlain thirty-one). The series turned to Convention Hall, which Auerbach called a "snake pit" in a "bush town." Eggs, drinks, and insults rained upon the visitors. While fans grabbed and pushed them, the police looked the other way. One fan swung at Auerbach, and the stressed-out coach—already suffering from insomnia, severe congestion, and choking coughs—fought back. Philadelphia won 109–103, evening the series.[43]

Chamberlain was peaking. "That's the best I've ever seen him play," said Auerbach after Game One. Game Two, Russell contended, was "the finest performance he has ever had against me." Chamberlain seemed energized, focused, resolved. He talked in terms of "we" instead of "I." Still, the comparison to Russell irked him. "I've beaten Russell a lot more than he's beaten me," he insisted. "The difference is that Boston has beaten the teams I've played for a lot more than we have beaten them." Whatever his accomplishments, his ego imprisoned him.[44]

Chamberlain then displayed his self-absorption—as well as his outrageous talent for self-sabotage—in a *Sports Illustrated* cover feature. "I'm Punchy from Basketball, Baby, and Tired of Being a Villain," ran the article's headline. Written with Bob Ottum and told in Chamberlain's voice, it contained multitudes of grievances. He whined about reporters, fans, stomach pains, and substandard facilities. "Defeat and victory all smell exactly the same in a pro basketball dressing room after a while," he wrote. He characterized coach Dolph Schayes as an amiable dolt. The cover title was the NBA's worst nightmare: "My Life in a Bush League."[45]

"It's a good article," said teammate Johnny Kerr, "if you like science fiction." Schayes now deflected questions about a rift with his star. Owner Ike Richman restricted press access to the players. Walter Kennedy fined Chamberlain $750. Philadelphia fans felt betrayed. Most correspondents to *Sports Illustrated* judged Chamberlain an egocentric loser. "Fortunately," wrote one man, "intelligent, dignified men with keen competitive pride, like Bill Russell, are more characteristic of the league than pompous, self-centered 'bushers' like Wilt Chamberlain."[46]

Chamberlain lent the controversy a surreal twist by considering suing *Sports Illustrated* for libel, even though his byline accompanied the article. He never agreed to the title "My Life in a Bush League," which subjected him "to uncalled for embarrassment and humiliation." (He nevertheless used "bush" eight times, as well as "bush league" and "bushville.") Compounding the absurdity, the next *Sports Illustrated* carried part two of "My Life in a Bush League," in which Chamberlain chronicled the pressures of high school and college, his lack of a "killer instinct," and his reputation as a loser.[47]

Only one man defended Chamberlain: Bill Russell. Before Game Three, he heard reporters talking to Auerbach, and he interjected. "Everybody's entitled to his opinion," he said, remembering his own controversial articles. "Big men like us live in a different world," he elaborated a few days later. "Nobody seems to understand that we are human beings and not freaks. It sometimes takes two or three years for even my friends to realize that." Russell and Chamberlain directed their energies in different directions, but both were tall, black athletes transcending the constraints of the sports world.[48]

Chamberlain's foibles lent an entertaining subplot to Game Three, as Russell held Chamberlain to three field goals in the first three periods. Boston's full-court press elicited myriad turnovers, and the Celtics won 112–94. Yet Chamberlain mustered tenacity for the rematch at Convention Hall, tabbing thirty-four points and thirty-four rebounds in a rousing, rollicking game. Boston led 117–115 with one second left. Philadelphia inbounded at midcourt. Hal Greer caught the ball, pivoted toward the basket, and sank a thirty-five-foot desperation heave that tied the game. Auerbach ranted and raved that time had expired, but the basket stood. Philadelphia won in overtime, 134–131.[49]

Chamberlain again pushed Russell to the brink. The Celtics center popped sleeping pills to conquer his Goliath-induced insomnia. "I'm an old man," he said. "I can no longer bounce back the way I used to." In Game Five, he got his fifth personal foul with ten minutes left, but he avoided fouling out until one second remained, helping preserve a 114–108 victory. Even though Chamberlain got thirty points and twenty-one rebounds, Russell took pride in his effort. His stoic glare cracked as he walked to the bench, because Boston Garden was rumbling with a two-minute ovation in his honor.[50]

Yet Philadelphia scrambled back in Game Six, winning 112–106 in sweaty, packed-beyond-capacity Convention Hall. After the exciting game, the Wilt Chamberlain sideshow hopped back on center stage. Ike Richman burst into the locker room, demanding that reporters desist questioning his star. The tirade insulted Chamberlain, who jawed back at his owner. The exchange added another layer of intrigue for Game Seven. The 76ers had momentum, but they had lost ten straight in Boston Garden, stirring all sorts of hairy associations: the clanking plumbing of the roach-infested locker room, 13,909 fans tossing rotten eggs and toilet paper, the frenetic defense and preternatural poise of the Celtics. Schayes feared that the 76ers had a "mental block."[51]

The Celtics, too, suffered under extraordinary stress. "This was the first game in my life that I went into scared, really scared," said Russell. "I honestly was afraid of Philadelphia and what they might do to us." Auerbach washed down pills with Cokes, Sanders agonized about Chet Walker, and Heinsohn bewailed a terrible Game Six. Sam Jones never felt such pressure. He took one consolation: "Of course, the weight now is on Mr. Russell's shoulders in this seventh game. It's always on Mr. Russell's shoulders in big games. It's all up to Mr. Russell."[52]

So Boston hosted another Game Seven classic, another iconic chapter in the Russell-Chamberlain rivalry and the embellishment of the Celtic mystique. The momentum kept shifting: Boston opened an eighteen-point lead; in the second quarter, Philadelphia pitched ahead 66–61; Boston regained the lead by the fourth quarter. Russell emptied his bag of tricks, constantly switching his defensive position on Chamberlain, who nevertheless finished with thirty points and thirty-two rebounds. Boston led 110–103 with 1:45 left. Chamberlain then tipped in a rebound, hit two free throws, and dunked over Russell. With five seconds on the clock, Boston led by one.[53]

Before that clock ticked to zero, Boston Garden witnessed its signature drama, with the arena's peculiarities in a key supporting role. To steady the basket, guy wires strung from the backboard to the balcony. When the court lengthened ten feet in 1963, those wires moved closer to the baseline. If an inbounds pass struck a wire, the defending team gained possession. Before the series, Auerbach and Russell actually discussed removing the wires, but decided against it. Then, after Philadelphia lost the ball on such a play in Game One, Dolph Schayes suggested that the inbounding team keep possession in this circumstance. Auerbach scotched the suggestion.[54]

Now, in the closing seconds of Game Seven, Russell inbounded from under the Boston basket. Chet Walker jumped with arms outstretched, bouncing ever closer to Russell, even crossing the baseline, pushing Russell further back. Russell threw the ball. It hit the wire. He collapsed to one knee, slamming his fist into the ground. "Oh my God!" he screamed. Philadelphia had the ball.[55]

The ensuing time-out illustrated the difference between a champion's pride and a contender's anxiety. "Somebody bail me out," said Russell. "I blew it." That moment burned into the memory of trainer Buddy LeRoux, who admired Russell's character and accountability. Russell then steeled himself, figuring that the 76ers might feed Chamberlain. Meanwhile, the Philadelphia huddle embodied chaos. The Boston crowd chanted "Defense! Defense!" and all the 76ers shouted ideas. Finally, they quieted. Without much conviction, Schayes instructed to "get the ball to Wilt." No, said Chamberlain. He feared getting fouled and missing his free throws. So Schayes decided that Greer would inbound to Walker, Kerr would set a screen, and Walker would pass back to Greer. Schayes later regretted the decision: the complicated plan was difficult to execute in such pressurized circumstances.[56]

Greer had five seconds to inbound. One thousand one, counted John Havlicek. One thousand two, he counted while shadowing Walker through picks, cuts, grabs, and pushes. One thousand three, he counted as Walker broke away. One thousand four, he counted as Greer lobbed the ball over the defense. Havlicek knew that Greer must have passed, so he peeked over his shoulder. He saw the ball. He jumped. Colliding with Walker, he tipped the ball toward Sam Jones, who dribbled away the waning seconds. "HAVLICEK STOLE THE BALL!" rasped an overstimulated Johnny Most. "IT'S ALL OVER! JOHNNY HAVLICEK IS BEING MOBBED BY THE FANS. IT'S ALL OVER! JOHNNY HAVLICEK STOLE THE BALL!"[57]

The moment immediately entered Boston sports lore. The next day, television and radio kept replaying Most's call, a shorthand celebration of the Celtic mystique. When fans saw Most or Havlicek, they yelled, "Havlicek stole the ball!" The steal made no one happier than Bill Russell. When Boston won, he rushed over and lifted Havlicek into the air. The steal saved his winning reputation, and it rewarded his faith in his teammates.[58]

The steal further enshrined Chamberlain as a giant loser. Russell lauded him as the ultimate competitor, and Auerbach admitted that "he was absolutely great in this series." But Chamberlain declined the last shot, and his team again faltered by a tantalizingly close margin. "I guess I'm snake bit," he mourned, recounting past miseries. "I'm not looking forward to another chance next year," he added, eschewing that cliché in favor of continued retirement threats. As Schayes considered resigning and Richman considered firing him, Chamberlain reentered the hospital with stomach pain. His prodigious talent had again burnished Russell's myth, and it embittered him. "I find it ironic that no one remembers that Russell almost blew the game for Boston," he said, decades later. "Was it a choke, or just a bad play? No one needed to answer that question because Havlicek stole the ball."[59]

. . .

After the steal, Russell had watched frenzied fans shred Havlicek's jersey and grab his shorts. Russell then caught Chamberlain's eye, and through all the jostling and trampling, he absorbed his rival's blank stare. Instead of relief, Russell now felt emptiness, a nebulous despair. He invested so much in victory, and still he wondered if sport served any social good. Basketball both inspired and unsettled him.[60]

The anticlimactic NBA Finals heightened these contradictions. The Celtics faced the Los Angeles Lakers, but minus Elgin Baylor. The manic-mouthed, sharp-dressed forward set the Lakers' personality, and his blend of power and grace made him the NBA's most exciting player. Russell considered him a close friend—a partner not only for movies and dinners but also for the smooth moves and countermoves that transformed sport into art. But calcium deposits in his knees had slowed Baylor, and in the first game of the 1965 play-offs, he shattered his kneecap. Russell missed his challenge.[61]

The first game, wrote Jim Murray, "was as one sided as a firing squad." Jerry West had averaged a Herculean forty-six points a game during the six-game series against Baltimore, but amidst the nipping and bumping from K. C. Jones, he managed only twenty-six points. Boston won 142–110, breaking the Finals scoring record. West scored forty-five in the next day's rematch, but five Celtics scored at least twenty points, and Boston won again, 129–123. Laker coach Fred Schaus delivered the annual refrain that these Celtics were the best team ever.[62]

The Celtics hit a bump in Los Angeles, as West scored forty-three more points, the Lakers won 126–105, and the celebrity-studded Sports Arena mocked Auerbach by tossing cigars at him. West finally wore down in Game Four, making only six of twenty-seven shots as the Celtics won, 112–99. The lean, nerve-wracked West Virginian had nevertheless elevated himself into the highest echelon of NBA idols.[63]

Tom Heinsohn, by contrast, was in crisis. After getting ejected in Game Three, he almost attacked the referee. He had already watched the Celtics win sixteen straight during his injury. An eye condition spurred painful headaches. He was the villain on the road, the clown at home. On a team of stoic, defense-minded, and disciplined athletes, Heinsohn bared his scowls and grunts, flipped unconscionable hooks and jumpers, and indulged in cigarettes and second helpings. He delayed an official decision on a lucrative full-time job offer in the insurance industry, since he was only thirty years old. But he was playing below snuff and planning to retire.[64]

Heinsohn sulked from the bench as Boston clinched its seventh straight title. Already leading 87–71, the Celtics scored twenty straight points to begin the fourth quarter, and Auerbach rode the red-hot shooting of Willie Naulls. The crowd chanted "We want Heinsohn!" but Auerbach worried that a late insertion would further insult him.[65]

As Heinsohn moped, Boston Garden roared. The Celtics kept shooting and rebounding and stealing and running and scoring and scoring and scoring. "We were not just beating this team," Russell recalled. "We were destroying it. The people were screaming. They were yelling for blood. It was like the Colosseum of Rome." Auerbach lit his victory cigar with 8:15 left. He tossed handfuls of cigars into the crowd. He removed his starters one by one, starting with Russell, whose stony shell crumbled. He bear-hugged his coach, lifting him off the ground. Boston won 129–96, the biggest margin in NBA Finals history. "I've never felt anything like it," said Russell. "When I hugged Red as I came out, that had to be my biggest moment since our first win, I'd say."[66]

While leaving the court, Russell had looked to the rafters, spied the "Celtic 1" banner commemorating Walter Brown, and pointed in tribute. Minutes later Red Auerbach pulled out the St. Christopher's medal that Brown had held during games. Marjorie Brown had given it to him, and he had carried it all season. The Celtics upheld their pledge, honoring the patron saint of Boston sports.[67]

Now they reaped the fruits sown by Brown. "When I first came here I never thought anyone would appreciate me," Russell wrote in the last installment of a diary for the *Boston Herald-American*. He thanked the fans for their booming tributes. "I think that at last the people of Boston have come to appreciate the Celtics and basketball. The sport has finally become big league." Once the bastard child of Boston sports, the Celtics now inspired enthusiastic fans, awestruck reporters, and adoring politicians such as Governor John Volpe and Mayor John Collins. Two days after the 1965 title, thousands of Bostonians braved inclement weather to cheer a celebratory motorcade from City Hall to Boston Garden.[68]

Russell missed that parade, as well as the ensuing breakup banquet. Jerry West had accidentally poked his eye during the last game, and he was recovering in bed. The satisfaction of another victory started eroding. The more he thought about that fourth quarter, the more it chilled him. The fans, he ruminated, "were egging us on to destroy, to kill, to reduce an opponent to nothing." Worse, "we were responding. We were, in a basketball sense, killing them, leaving them shattered among the ashes of their pride." Basketball had provided individual self-worth, collective devotion, spiritual transcendence. It had also exposed a zest for annihilation. The 1965 title was a career highlight. But that final frame's bloodlust, he reflected, "was my worst moment in sports."[69]

12

The Hidden Fear

After 1965, Russell never again won MVP, and his Celtics never again won the Eastern Division. Yet they remained the NBA's benchmark throughout the decade. Early in his career, Russell had complemented a cast of scorers. Then, his defensive domination established a new team identity. Now, his Celtics upheld their standing through institutional memory—the guile, grit, and poise to grind out championships. Absent overwhelming talent, they won titles by painting beautiful details.

Victory enhanced Russell's status, as did his continuing contrast to Wilt Chamberlain. During the summer of 1965, Chamberlain mulled an offer to become a professional boxer. He possessed the athletic ability: he could have been a world-class decathlete, and he attracted serious interest from the Kansas City Chiefs of the American Football League. Boxing, moreover, offered leverage with the 76ers. So he skipped rope, punched the bag, and discussed million-dollar paydays. Of course, Chamberlain returned to the NBA, signing a three-year, six-figure deal that the 76ers called "the largest contract in organized sports."[1]

Reports of Chamberlain's annual salary ranged from $100,000 to $105,000 to $110,000 to $125,000. Philadelphia officials insisted that the quoted figures were low, and Chamberlain later claimed that owner Ike Richman promised him 25 percent of the franchise. Russell took the $100,000 figure into his own negotiations. He signed a three-year deal for $300,003—one dollar more per year than Chamberlain. The money mattered less than the principle: the acknowledgment of his superior contribution, the headline "Russell Beats Wilt Again." It was just one dollar, but it was a beautiful detail.[2]

. . .

When Russell accused the NBA of racial quotas, his critics complained that he cultivated bitterness among young blacks. But on Harlem's pickup basketball courts, that bitterness already existed. Everyone knew someone that belonged in the NBA. But, they believed, "the pros aren't looking for blacks who are going to fill their bench. If you can start, fine. Otherwise, go home."[3]

By the 1960s, playgrounds and gymnasiums in black, urban neighborhoods such as Harlem featured players of surpassing talent and ambition. An African American aesthetic had suffused the sport. Black basketball showcased individual abilities, flamboyant styles, graceful improvisations, and complex rhythms—behind-the-back dribbles, shake-and-shimmy moves, no-look passes, trash talk, and high-flying, rim-rattling dunks. The Rucker League, a two-month extravaganza at 130th Street and Seventh Avenue, brought together playground legends, college talents, and NBA stars. The games spawned spectacular feats and oral legends, such as when Chamberlain muscled in ten straight dunks, avenging a hook-dunk from Connie Hawkins and a backboard-pinning block by "Jumping" Jackie Jackson. Like dance or music, basketball had become a black cultural hallmark.[4]

By mid-decade, African Americans composed about half of NBA players, two-thirds of starting lineups, three-fourths of the All-Stars, and nearly all of the highest paid stars. Pro scouts drafted Willis Reed, Dick Barnett, Zelmo Beaty, and Bob Love from historically black colleges and universities. Poor blacks envisioned basketball as a path out of the ghetto. In 1966, Texas Western College inherited the path-breaking tradition of Russell's USF teams. Starting five blacks, the Miners defeated all-white University of Kentucky in the NCAA championship game.[5]

In January 1966, Chamberlain told Howard Cosell, "We are overpopulated with first-class and star Negro players," crippling the league's marketability. *Sport* analyzed this claim in an article entitled "Pro Basketball's Hidden Fear." During the black surge into the NBA, attendance had risen, the league had signed a national television contract, and Southern cities had applied for expansion teams. Dynamic, highly paid black stars had elevated the game's appeal and prestige, infusing it with speed, flair, and grace. Yet white fans identified with white players, a fact that concerned white owners. *Sport* implied that more white stars could boost gate revenues, television ratings, and expansion prospects.[6]

The Celtics both spurred and mediated anxiety about the black influx. With Tom Heinsohn's retirement, Auerbach started five blacks throughout the 1965–66 season. Yet neither Sam Jones nor Willie Naulls displayed a particular flamboyance, and Russell, K. C. Jones, and Satch Sanders specialized on defense. While admiring the grace of black basketball, Jeremy Larner mourned that the Celtics "still employ the sort of hacking, hawking defense that can turn a game into a bloody shambles." Instead of creating art, "they go on playing with the raw-edged foul humor of men who are out to take everything they can get." Larner suggested despite five black starters, the Celtics stifled black expression.[7]

The Boston bench, moreover, featured four important whites. John Havlicek continued as the consummate Sixth Man. Larry Siegfried, a hard-nosed backup guard, had joined the Celtics after riding the bench in the ABL, teaching school, playing in an independent league, and getting cut from St. Louis. Forward Don Nelson thrived upon coming to Boston five games into the 1965–66 season, after the Lakers sold him for only $1,000. Mel Counts proved a good backup center after surviving a disastrous experimental conversion to forward. Though other teams had racial cliques, the Celtics exhibited cooperation and character. "The club offers a lesson in human relations," admired the *Boston Herald*. "They serve a vital community function demonstrating integration in action."[8]

Russell still embodied that interracial team spirit. He hosted teammates in Reading, and they visited Slade's for barbecue or sweet potato pie. While a callow rookie, Counts was surprised when Russell offered a ride home in his Lamborghini—a small gesture that built an easy camaraderie. Russell also made grander offerings. After practice on Christmas Eve of 1965, he learned that Nelson was spending Christmas alone. Russell invited him to Reading. Nelson demurred, not wishing to intrude. But Russell insisted. The next day, the Russells had wrapped him presents, and Nelson had a great time. "I'll never forget that," he said. "No one can ever say anything bad about Bill Russell to me."[9]

Russell further honed his leadership skills. In frequent media sessions, he discussed his championship ambitions, analyzed the NBA, and extolled his teammates. In mid-December, the Celtics were in first place, but they worried about drifting from their self-imposed standards. With Russell's support, K. C. Jones and Nelson called a players-only meeting. They hashed out who needed to shoot more, run harder, talk more on defense, and signal plays better. Behind closed doors, Russell said that they relied too much on his shotblocking, letting players drive the lane. But at a press luncheon at Slade's, he shifted the burden. "I'm having my worst year. I've had too many ordinary games," he said. He promised to work harder, get in better shape, and concentrate more.[10]

Boston, Philadelphia, and Cincinnati each had eight-game winning streaks between Christmas and Valentine's Day, and none could control the Eastern Division. "It gets tougher to win every year," lamented Auerbach. "The other teams keep getting stronger and smarter and we keep getting last pick in the draft." Boston's starting five, moreover, averaged thirty years old, while Cincinnati's averaged twenty-seven and Philadelphia's twenty-six. Sanders hurt his leg and back, Havlicek his groin and thigh, Naulls his back and hamstring, Counts his wrist. Sam Jones had strep throat, and assorted viruses circulated through the locker room.[11]

Russell had a tender right hamstring. After missing three straight games, he played only five minutes against the Lakers in early December. With the score tied at 102, he asked to enter. He fed Sam Jones for a cutting layup, blocked Jerry West, forced a turnover, dished to K. C. Jones for a basket, and blocked Rudy LaRusso.

In two minutes and twenty-one seconds, he sealed the game. After the victory, Russell admitted to soreness. Then he noticed the huddling reporters, and he resisted puffing himself up at his teammates' expense. "It ain't no big deal," he scoffed. "Hell, we're pros."[12]

. . .

Russell obsessed about death. "Sure I think about death," he said. "It doesn't scare me. Sometimes I think, '*I'm going to die.*'" He had premonitions that he would die in a plane crash. This dark outlook helped rationalize time away from home with the Celtics, in Liberia, at Slade's, or with friends and girlfriends. He figured that he could die tomorrow, so he should find fulfillment and provide for his family. Once, while brooding about hurting a friend's feelings, he said, "I'll be glad when I die and then I'll be alone and I won't hurt anyone again."[13]

Indeed, Russell could be unpredictably cruel. While he arranged a business trip, Rose asked if he realized the date. "Yeah, it's December 9 and I'll be married nine years. Don't rub it in," he laughed, not realizing his wife's pain. Journalist Fred Katz sat in Russell's kitchen, a scene of domestic delight: Rose doted on him, Buddha did homework in his Cub Scout uniform, and Jacob and Karen drew pictures of trucks. But throughout their relaxed conversation, Russell kept turning away and reading the newspaper, as if Katz periodically ceased to exist. Rose explained her husband's behavior through his enduring loneliness, stemming from childhood insecurities. His meanness or moodiness kept people at bay.[14]

"I'm not a basketball player," Russell once explained. "I'm a man who plays basketball." He bristled when told that children admire him. He wanted consideration as an individual, not a celebrity. One manifestation of this desire was an increasingly eccentric wardrobe: custom-tailored suits with monogrammed cuffs, winklepicker boots dotted with fabric, lace-front shirts, opera capes, berets, derby hats. His sartorial flourishes later included Nehru jackets, love beads, African-inspired caftans, five-button Edwardian whipcord suits with foot-long back vents and hip-hugging bell-bottoms, and Persian lamb cavalier coats with detachable capes of Alaskan seal.[15]

Nothing sharpened Russell's provocative profile more than his autobiography, *Go Up for Glory*. In the winter of 1964, during the uproar over the *Saturday Evening Post* and *Sports Illustrated* articles, Russell was playing cards in a Cincinnati hotel room with Bill McSweeny of the *Boston Record-American*. McSweeny possessed the outgoing confidence of a good reporter. He also had uncommon maturity and intelligence, with interests beyond sports. His friendship with Russell informed some perceptive columns about the Celtics superstar.[16]

Russell told McSweeny that he wanted to convey the draining alienation of professional sports. He wanted to expose hypocrisy and racism, to explore his intellectual journey and personal frailties. Over more late-night card games in more anonymous hotel rooms, they talked. In 1965, Russell returned from Liberia with some notes. "The words he put on the paper were bare, barren, straight out," recalled McSweeny. "Every sentence, every thought, every memory burned out of the paper, etched deep." They signed with publisher Coward-McCann.[17]

Russell and McSweeny forged a genuine collaboration. McSweeny tried taping interviews, but Russell kept playing new records from Africa, drowning out their words. Instead McSweeny took notes during postmidnight conversations. Russell slashed through drafts with a red pencil, insisting on the right message. "Truth, truth," he said, "I want it to be the absolute truth." When McSweeny painted a heroic portrait, Russell demanded a rewrite. "It makes me look too good," he objected. "Make me look like me."[18]

Yet Russell also rejected the humble conventions of sports autobiographies, angering McSweeny. For one month, they stopped talking. They reconciled, however, and the night before the publisher's deadline, they broke out champagne to celebrate their typed final draft. Then they started discussing their dissatisfactions. Before dawn, they rewrote the foreword, introduction, epilogue, and various other sections. Though infuriated by Russell's ego and obstinacy, McSweeny told Rose that he considered Bill among the most special, compassionate men in the world.[19]

Typical sports books muted athletes' personal, professional, and political conflicts. For instance, Al Hirshberg's *Bill Russell of the Boston Celtics,* published in 1963, painted a gangly, insecure teenager transforming into an eager, self-effacing hero filled with race pride. Russell called it "tacky."[20]

Go Up for Glory, by contrast, unearthed a mound of buried gripes. In a clipped, rat-a-tat style, Russell exposed the stain of childhood prejudice, the casual "nigger" out of racists' mouths, the brutality of the Oakland police. He ridiculed the exploitative paternalism of Abe Saperstein and the Harlem Globetrotters. He smirked at the sanctimonious amateurism of the AAU and Olympic Committee. He recalled racist slurs on enemy courts, segregation on road trips, bigoted reporters in Boston, prejudiced neighbors in Reading. "If all this sounds like sour grapes, let me say that I have grown tired of sports biographies in which everyone is a do-gooder and everything is sugar and spice," he wrote. "Either you tell the truth as you see it, just as you play your guts out, or you shouldn't be in it."[21]

So Russell disemboweled sport's sacred cows. He characterized Phil Woolpert as aloof with praise, insensitive to the psychology of African Americans. That depiction stung Woolpert, who considered Russell his friend. Red Auerbach, moreover, beefed at a story from their 1964 State Department tour, when Russell challenged his authority. "As far as Auerbach's attitude towards Negroes," Russell also wrote, "I feel in all honesty that he can be characterized as a middle-of-the-roader," an advocate of racial justice only if it benefited the Celtics. Russell appreciated his coach and teammates, but he eschewed glossy clichés.[22]

Russell also staked new intellectual ground. He described his connection to

Africa, journey to Mississippi, and political opinions. On the one hand, he tempered his previous anger. He found acceptance in Boston, trust in white people, faith in the American Dream. "The concept of the United States is probably the most beautiful one ever conceived by man," he wrote. On the other hand, he expressed disillusion with the black freedom movement. He wrote one chapter alone, titling it "Human Rights" rather than "Civil Rights," addressing injustice beyond legal inequities. He judged most black leaders too willing to compromise. He decried job discrimination, police brutality, divisions between poor whites and blacks, and educational disparities. He now believed that the March on Washington should have excluded whites, showcasing a united black voice crying out in anger. Once again mixing integrationist and nationalist philosophies, Russell commanded ownership of his destiny. "It is a thing you want to scream," he wrote. "I MUST HAVE MY MANHOOD."[23]

Upon the book's publication in February 1966, detractors called Russell a selfish rabble-rouser. They found him too angry, too political, too acid. But others acclaimed the book's fearless honesty, its linkage of sports with racial and personal travails, its "preoccupation with dignity, pride, manhood and respect." The black press beamed. A syndicated Negro Press International review called it "a source of enlightenment for those seeking insight and understanding into the racial enigma that is America." One reviewer juxtaposed a shallow, baseball-centric autobiography by Willie Mays with Russell's introspective analysis.[24]

Go Up for Glory wove sport into the larger fabric of racial revolt. By eroding the myth that sport promoted black uplift, it became The Autobiography of Malcolm X for the sports world. Excerpts soon appeared in multiple anthologies of African American letters, alongside selections from Booker T. Washington and W. E. B. Du Bois, Richard Wright and James Baldwin, Martin Luther King and Malcolm X.[25]

Harry Edwards had grown up poor in East St. Louis. His father, who considered sports a means of black progress, worshipped Joe Louis and Jesse Owens. But the ghost of Bill Russell stalked the younger Edwards, reminding him of sport's inequalities. He remembered the St. Louis Hawks trading away Russell's draft rights. When playing basketball at San Jose State in the early 1960s, he felt Russell's historic presence during trips to USF. During his own intellectual awakening, he read Russell's incendiary quotes in national magazine articles. He entered graduate school at Cornell University, and while developing his ideas on the sociology of sport, he devoured Russell's memoir. Go Up for Glory, he realized, was the whistle blast of an onrushing train—the first warning "that a revolt by black athletes was imminent."[26]

· · ·

During halftime of a February home game, Russell gave Red Auerbach a copy of Go Up for Glory. Governor John Volpe, Mayor John Collins, Marjorie Brown, and

Bob Cousy also bore gifts. One month earlier, after coaching his tenth straight All-Star Game and winning his thousandth game, Auerbach had confirmed his impending retirement from coaching. His bathroom mirror revealed a haggard man, frayed from travel, competition, and responsibilities as executive vice president and general manager. He considered retiring in 1965 but stayed another season, lending his enemies "one last crack at me."[27]

Russell also gave Auerbach an engraved gold lighter. By now, the coach's cigars exemplified the Celtic Mystique. Rival fans lit cigars upon beating Boston. A Philadelphia man flung a burning cigar at Auerbach's forehead, and a Cincinnati woman blew smoke in his face—until he grabbed the foot-long roll and flicked ashes at her. Looming retirement failed to mellow him. He needed police protection in Philadelphia, where fans whipped beer cans at his head. He got ejected for foul language five minutes into one game. He complained about another ejection by calling Commissioner Walter Kennedy at home at 7:30 a.m.[28]

Russell tried giving Auerbach one last gift: a win. When he reaggravated his hamstring injury in the third quarter, he demanded to numb his leg with freeze spray. "I want this game, Red," he said. He led a furious comeback, but the Celtics succumbed. He grabbed one last rebound as the buzzer sounded, and as others emptied the court, he stood alone, staring at the ball with disgust. Finally, he flipped it away and trudged off the floor.[29]

Every loss stung, because Philadelphia kept stalking Boston for first place. Rookie Billy Cunningham and sophomore Wally Jones added athleticism to an already potent lineup, featuring an entire season of Wilt Chamberlain. The 76ers drew inspiration, moreover, from the sudden death of Ike Richman in December 1965. The jovial, bespectacled co-owner collapsed from a heart attack while in the front row at Boston Garden. His death shook Chamberlain, a close friend and financial associate.[30]

Chamberlain remained the quintessential scoring machine, breaking the all-time scoring mark in February, despite playing four fewer seasons than previous record-holder Bob Pettit. He netted sixty-five points in one game, sixty-two in another. But he also set more screens, dished more outlet passes, blocked more shots, and drove to the basket more. He and Russell both won unanimous election to the All-Star team, but the players voted Chamberlain MVP, and Russell finished fourth. "Wilt owns Russell now," claimed one coach.[31]

Dolph Schayes won Coach of the Year. He promoted Chamberlain to the press, despite his star's persistent proclivity for disrupting team chemistry. Chamberlain missed the first day of training camp and assorted practices. His teammates resented his private, contract-guaranteed hotel suite on road trips. He complained when Schayes pulled him from games. He cried about getting fouled. He kept moaning about comparisons to Russell, bad breaks in past play-offs, and critics who wanted him to shoot free throws underhanded, shoot free throws one-handed, shoot less, or shoot more. After one game against Detroit, he carped that his teammates cost him ten assists. "If these guys keep missing like they have been, I'm not going to play this way much longer," he huffed. "I'll just try to do it all myself."[32]

Still, Chamberlain deserved his end-of-season honors. In early March, the 76ers swept a weekend home-and-home series, leapfrogging the Celtics for first place. Boston won its final six games, but Philadelphia won its last seven, prying off Boston's nine-year stranglehold on the Eastern Division. As always, Russell recognized his great rival's talents, conceding Chamberlain's superior value to his team.[33]

Had Russell lost his edge? "I don't want to comment on that," snapped Auerbach. Then he paused. He got quiet. "A guy like Chamberlain, he's got ambition. His ambition is to beat Russell. What ambition can Russell have now? Beat Chamberlain?" He harrumphed. "He has beaten Chamberlain," he barked, getting louder and louder. "Year after year, he has beaten him." Auerbach was puffing on a figurative victory cigar, blowing smoke in his enemy's face. Then, again, his voice dropped. "But if it happens—if it happens this year, remember that it didn't happen until Russell was over 30." The soliloquy conveyed pride and fear, faith and doubt, defiance and resignation—a stew of emotions about his great warrior, his own legacy, and the potential eclipse of sport's greatest dynasty.[34]

. . .

As the 1966 play-offs began, the dynasty seemed dead. Stuck in the unfamiliar position of the best-of-five Eastern Division semifinals, Boston faced Cincinnati. The Royals had two superstars in Oscar Robertson and Jerry Lucas, but race exacerbated an internal rivalry. Robertson remained the game's most complete player, but he seethed with discontent. He believed that management promoted Lucas at his expense, and that prejudice cost him money and respect. Cincinnati had equal talent to Boston or Philadelphia, but less winning spirit. They lost seven of their final eight games.[35]

It thus shocked the Celtics to drop the opener, 107–103, which the *Cincinnati Enquirer* judged "one of the most damaging defeats in Boston history." Although the Celtics rallied to win a Saturday game at Cincinnati Gardens, 132–125, they dropped Sunday's rematch at Boston Garden, 113–107, squandering a six-point lead with seven minutes left. Superb performances from Robertson, Lucas, and a dynamic supporting cast stoked anticipation that Cincinnati would finish Boston. Havlicek admitted a "terrible pressure." K. C. Jones wept. Russell acted like a funeral mourner. "We're not dead yet," grumbled Auerbach."[36]

Boston won the series for four reasons. First, Lucas tore a ligament in his left knee, and a heavy brace weighed him down. Second, Auerbach switched Havlicek to starting forward, accelerating the Boston attack. Third, Boston had experience in tight situations, and as the *Enquirer* reported after the 120–103 landslide win in Game

Four, "the Celtics had a hero every time they needed one." Sanders, Havlicek, Siegfried, and Sam Jones each carried the offensive load for stretches. Fourth, Boston had Russell. In the deciding Game Five, he sucked up thirty-one rebounds and keyed the fast break. The Celtics surged ahead by thirteen in the fourth quarter, and the Royals' comeback fizzled when Russell blocked a "sure basket" by Tom Hawkins. Boston won, 112–103, and Mayor John Collins ceremoniously lit Auerbach's cigar.[37]

The deposed Royals, like most observers, figured the 76ers would beat the Celtics. But Philadelphia, idle for almost two weeks, lost its emotional momentum from winning the Eastern Division. Then six 76ers caught the flu, including Chamberlain. Finally, the Ringling Brothers' circus overtook Convention Hall during Game One; Philadelphia Arena had fewer seats, a less intimidating atmosphere, and a shorter court—perfect for the Celtics' full-court press. Boston forced nineteen turnovers, and Philadelphia shot just 36 percent during the Celtics' 115–96 runaway upset.[38]

Suddenly Philadelphia's optimism seemed dead, not Boston's dynasty. During Game Two at Boston Garden, the Celtics dominated end-to-end, winning 114–93. In the fourth quarter, annoyed by chippy defense, Billy Cunningham swung at Larry Siegfried. The benches emptied, the crowd spilled toward the floor, and Russell and Chamberlain came face-to-face, glaring and screaming. Earlier that season, Russell had warned Chamberlain against holding an opponent during dust-ups, which allowed other 76ers to pummel the rival. When Chamberlain entered this fracas, Russell grew so enraged that their mutual friend Woody Sauldsberry intervened. "Look out Wilt," he warned. "He'll kill you. He's mad."[39]

Chamberlain was still playing the angst-ridden, egotistical villain. He annoyed teammates by constantly glaring at referees and players. Before the second half he ignored the team huddle, grabbed a stat sheet from the scorer's table, and studied it with friends. Russell, meanwhile, had adopted the role of grizzled captain, leading his bandage-swathed mates into battle. This time Governor John Volpe lit Auerbach's victory cigar, but when Volpe bounded into the locker room, he found Russell and the Celtics acting solemn, already steeling themselves for the next night in Philadelphia.[40]

The circus left Convention Hall before Game Three, but the animals stuck around. Governor Volpe got hit with an egg. Others tossed cigars and toilet paper. One fan threatened Siegfried that "they'll carry you out of here in a box tonight!" As the 76ers roared ahead 53–29, the crowd yelled "kill, kill!" The Celtics showed resilience, rattling off the next nineteen points. Three times, they trailed by only one point. But Philadelphia held on, winning 111–105. Chamberlain got thirty-one points and twenty-seven rebounds. Russell blamed the loss on his own slow start.[41]

After the game, Schayes announced practice at 1:00 the next afternoon. "I'm awful tired, Dolph," moaned Chamberlain. "I don't want to practice tomorrow."

Schayes pleaded that it was a light shootaround; Chamberlain said no. Schayes asked him to just practice free throws; Chamberlain said no. The press corps watched the coach's face redden with embarrassment. "Could you picture Bill Russell and Red Auerbach playing a scene like that in the Celtic locker room?" asked the *Philadelphia Bulletin*.[42]

While Chamberlain complained, Russell worried. His insomnia returned. The night before Game Four, he watched the late movie on television, read a book, woke up Rose for conversation, listened to records on his front porch, and then waited for Rose to wake up again and make breakfast. The next afternoon, he held Chamberlain to only fifteen points. With the score tied at one hundred, he blocked Lucious Jackson's potential game-winner. Boston pulled away in overtime, winning 114–108. "I just can't believe it," said Chamberlain, his season and reputation once again in tatters.[43]

Some Philadelphians booed Chamberlain before Game Five. He had skipped practice the previous day. Schayes claimed that he excused his center, but the players grumbled. Boston won, 120–112. Chamberlain scored forty-six points and grabbed thirty-four rebounds, but he also missed seventeen of twenty-five free throws. When a reporter asked if he should have practiced more foul shots, the Goliath raged. He swung at the reporter, got restrained by bystanders, kicked over his half-gallon milk container, and pushed another reporter into a locker. While reinforcing the NBA's "bush league" reputation, he made a monkey of Schayes, who soon got fired.[44]

In the other locker room, Russell was touched by the improbable 4–1 series victory. "It may sound like the same old crock," he said, "but I'm for the green uniforms." During a recent Boston newspaper strike, he had been reading out-of-town reports, and he resented assumptions that the Celtics were finished. "It's not me against Wilt. It's a team. It's all I've known my whole adult life." Auerbach excused him from the next practice, but amidst Chamberlain's controversy, Russell vowed to run the session himself. He had written another chapter in basketball's best story, and a headline captured the key plotline: "Wilt Unable to Match Russell's Spirit and Desire."[45]

· · ·

While listening to radio broadcasts of the Western Division play-offs, Auerbach kept hearing, "Baylor, twisting . . . Baylor, jumping . . . Baylor, driving." Just months ago, it seemed impossible. After the top third of Elgin Baylor's left patella had cracked during the 1965 play-offs, he wore a hip-to-ankle cast for six weeks. He lost his speed, explosiveness, and swagger. He also missed a month with calcium deposits in his right knee. He averaged fewer than seventeen points and ten rebounds. Reporters suggested that he was tarnishing his sterling legacy. But in February 1966, his doctor implored him to bury anxieties about his knee. The strategy worked. Baylor became the leaping, driving, battling, yapping superstar of years past, and the Lakers returned to the NBA Finals.[46]

In Game One, Baylor scored thirty-six points and Jerry West notched forty-one more as the Lakers won in overtime, 133–129. The Lakers overcame an eighteen-point first-quarter deficit, dictated the high-scoring pace, and negated Boston's home court advantage. In sixteen of nineteen championship series, the Game One winner took the series. Had Los Angeles healed the scars of past play-offs? Auerbach spun the game to erode that confidence. He complained about discrepancies in foul calls. He maintained that Boston would have won, but Mendy Rudolph made a bogus goaltending call. And he dropped a bombshell. The next day, he would formally announce the next coach of the Boston Celtics: Bill Russell.[47]

All season, Auerbach had been canvassing Celtic alumni for his successor. Bob Cousy saw little advantage in piloting a sinking ship, and he still liked coaching Boston College. Frank Ramsey had business interests, three young children, and a sick father in Kentucky. Bob Brannum kept coaching Norwich University. Tom Heinsohn cited his new foothold in the insurance business. Besides, he said, "I couldn't handle Russell." He suggested hiring Russell as player-coach. As early as January 1966, the Boston newspapers had broached that same idea. Dave DeBusschere of the Detroit Pistons and Richie Guerin of the St. Louis Hawks had both done it, but Auerbach argued that double duty compromised both the player and coach.[48]

Still, could any bench coach better elicit commitment from Sam Jones, K. C. Jones, John Havlicek—or Bill Russell? During a March road trip, Auerbach gauged his captain's interest in the job. Russell thought that Auerbach was joking. He had declined various offers from college teams, and coaching involved many aggravations. But he mulled the suggestion. In the meantime, Boston lost the regular season title to Philadelphia and trailed Cincinnati in the play-offs. At that point Auerbach called old nemesis Alex Hannum, arranging to talk more after Boston's elimination. But as the Celtics prolonged their run, Russell decided that he wanted the job.[49]

Why? First, Russell had heard black players throughout the league complain about coaches with latent racial prejudices. Second, Russell wanted Auerbach's successor from within the Celtics family. Third, Russell possessed an opportunity to become the first black coach in any major professional team sport. Embracing the challenge, he shook hands with Auerbach on a salary bump to $125,001, one dollar more than Willie Mays's contract with the San Francisco Giants, the richest pact in professional sports. Before Sunday's Game One, Auerbach mentioned a press conference the next day, presumably to announce the new coach. But when he revealed his successor immediately after the game, the headlines instead concentrated on the history-making hire.[50]

"I consider this one of the most personal challenges I've had in the past 10 years," said Russell. He acknowledged the toppling racial barrier, though he insisted that

skin color affected neither his hiring nor his performance. He was no Jackie Robinson, who cracked into an all-white league. "But this is part of the thing Robinson
did," he added. "It is part of the same story. Now maybe there will be some more
Negro coaches and managers in sports."[51]

African Americans cheered the landmark in sports history. Robinson himself
called the hire "a tremendous inspiration to a lot of young kids." The black press
ran multiple features on Russell. Sam Lacy of the *Baltimore Afro-American* lauded
Boston's leadership in the integration of professional sports. Doc Young rejoiced
that "once more the world of sports assumed the lead in the human relations league"
and displayed "the natural drive toward total democracy that no other profession,
not even modern jazz, can match." *Muhammad Speaks* ascribed Russell's rise to
the sensational quality and quantity of black athletes.[52]

Time and *Newsweek* now analyzed Russell's compelling personality, controversial statements, and political consciousness. *Sport* positioned Russell at the forefront of racial progress, publishing a long interview with him and Robinson called
"Where the Negro Goes from Here in Sports." Columnists admired Russell's leadership. The *Boston Globe* celebrated the American Dream: "For the first time in the
history of our democracy—in one of the major professional sports which are a product of our economic success—a descendant of slaves will have complete charge of
a team." The *New York Times* reported the news on the front page, appreciated his
principles in a feature article, celebrated his partnership with Auerbach in Arthur
Daley's column, and applauded his hire on the editorial page.[53]

Yet some sounded discordant notes. This glowering, goateed man in an opera
cape satisfied no stereotype of an integrationist barrier-breaker. Russell rejected
suggestions that he might use "prejudice in reverse" against white players. Various
columnists hoped that coaching would dull his sharpest edges. Melvin Durslag
construed the hiring as faith that Russell had overcome his "foibles," "goofy conclusions," and orations "on subjects which he should have left to others of greater
depth and understanding." Clif Keane proclaimed that Russell could no longer
act like "a glum, morose, moody character" who refused autographs and glared
at fans. Jim Murray joked that Russell was now a "functioning member of the Establishment" who would join the Republican Party and trash his Thelonius Monk
records.[54]

Fan reaction, reported the *Boston Globe*, "was a combination of delight, disbelief and disgust"—the wide emotional scope compelled by Russell throughout his
Boston tenure. "Bush league," grunted one fan. Most had expected the Celtics to
hire Hannum, and Russell had denied interest in coaching. Some questioned the
effectiveness of any player-coach. But others cheered the signpost of racial progress.
As one South Boston man said, "It's a good choice. Russell is lot like Auerbach in
that he can inspire a club. He can become a real fine coach." Before Game Two, an

ovation rumbled through Boston Garden even before Russell began his regal saunter to center court.[55]

The series momentum shifted. Boston crushed Los Angeles 129–109, holding West and Baylor to a combined thirty-one points. When the series moved west, Boston again won, 120–106. Game Four offered considerably more drama, as the teams raced neck-and-neck to the finish. West scored forty-five points, Havlicek got thirty-two, and according to Fred Schaus, the athletic shooters were battling like "the cobra and the mongoose." Boston clinched the 122–117 win on Russell's clutch free throws in the final minute. Despite the ailments and pressures, Russell relished the play-offs. "The Bearded Wonder," marveled the *Los Angeles Times*, "was cavorting like a rookie getting ready for his first game."[56]

Excited Boston fans anticipated another title clincher, commemorated by Governor Volpe again lighting Auerbach's cigar. They screamed themselves hoarse as the Celtics, down by seventeen in the second quarter, heaved ahead by nine in the third quarter. Yet the Lakers responded, with Baylor juking, bulling, and flipping his way to forty-one points. West hit a seventeen-foot baseline jumper to break a last-minute deadlock. Boston missed three chances to tie, and Los Angeles won 119–115. The Lakers then prevailed at the Sports Arena, 123–115. Russell sat on a stool, hunched over. His long finger tapped the stat sheet, pointing to twenty-eight points by Gail Goodrich and twenty by Rudy LaRusso. He expected spectacular shooting from West and Baylor, who combined for fifty-seven points, but Boston could not allow such scoring from supporting players.[57]

The topsy-turvy series featured wild, unpredictable scoring swings. Both teams used small lineups, encouraged fast breaks, and relied on outside shots, which often ran hot-and-cold. During the regular season, Boston averaged 111 points, and Los Angeles 110. In this series, Boston averaged 122 points, and Los Angeles 118. Without a center to offset Russell, Fred Schaus used a quick, three-guard lineup. Meanwhile, as Boston played seventeen full-court-press, fast-break games in thirty-five days, Auerbach shortened his bench to only Siegfried and Nelson—even though the five starters wore a combined eight leg wraps, including a full-leg contraption on K. C. Jones. Russell also had broken a bone in his foot, which he kept secret.[58]

For the ninth time in ten years, the Celtics played a winner-take-all elimination game. In his final pregame talk, Auerbach was characteristically blunt. Ignoring the past two losses, he eschewed inspiring rhetoric in favor of "defense and dollars"—the path to victory, and its material rewards. "Arnold Auerbach is a man with genius," Bud Collins had written. "The genius wears No. 6 and is named W. Felton Russell." Indeed, Russell gave another virtuoso performance, finishing with twenty-five points and thirty-two rebounds, often straining with physical pain and mental exhaustion. In a scrappy and sloppy match, Boston led 10–0 after four minutes, went up by sixteen in the third quarter, and still held a ten-point advantage with forty-five seconds left, when Russell swatted away a Baylor shot. At that point Jerry West congratulated Havlicek for yet another Boston title.[59]

The fans surged to the edges of the court, even piling onto the basket supports. West remembered them "screaming for our blood." Programs, paper cups, and hats flew through the air. Volpe lit Auerbach's cigar, stirring an ever-greater frenzy. But K. C. Jones got called for an offensive foul. The Lakers scored. Then, while squeezing between shoving fans, Sam Jones threw away an inbounds pass. The Lakers scored again. Havlicek and Sam Jones each lost possession while slipping on orange drink, which had spattered onto the parquet floor. The Lakers scored twice more. Boston's lead shrunk to 95–93! Auerbach looked like he might choke on his cigar. Finally, with three seconds left, K. C. Jones passed to Havlicek, who ran out the clock. The feral fans overran the court, ripped the jersey off Sanders, and bowled over Russell.[60]

In the relative peace of the locker room, the Celtics dumped Auerbach in the shower, and Russell called this team the "shortest on ability and longest on heart." In the stands, his wife gushed with tears, her head in her hands. In the other locker room, the Lakers rued another missed opportunity, another exhibit of vintage Bill Russell. He had led the Celtics to their eighth consecutive championship. "He's one in a million," said West. "Nobody dominates a game like Russell."[61]

. . .

Amidst the jubilance, a photographer asked Russell to kiss Auerbach. Russell declined. "It would have been a great picture for the Mississippi readers," sighed the *Boston Globe*. Instead, at the annual breakup dinner at the Lenox Hotel, Russell extolled Auerbach in the same thoughtful, touching terms with which he once paid tribute to Bob Cousy. He spoke for almost an hour. He had sometimes loved and sometimes hated Auerbach, but he had always appreciated him. Auerbach hired him not out of liberal goodwill, but out of personal respect. "The most important thing is that he's always treated me like a man and I treated him like one." Now, he even liked Auerbach. "We'll be friends until one of us dies."

"I've said before that I don't owe anyone anything," Russell added. "But to the Celtics, I owe something." During the players-only meeting in December, he had revealed a hidden fear that their title run had halted. "I was depressed. I didn't think we were going to make it." K. C. Jones had held his hands while he sobbed. His teammates had again sustained him, again compelled him to new heights. But Russell had not only feared losing. He had feared winning. Each championship added to his mystique, to the notion that victory defined him. Yes, he was a winner, but he was imperfect . . . a father, a husband, a friend, a businessman . . . a man trying to measure up to Mister Charlie and the Old Man . . . a geeky mascot who got cut from adolescent sports teams . . . a bookworm inspired by Henri Christophe and Leonardo Da Vinci . . . a lonely boy who missed his dead mother.[62]

Go Up for Glory, his promotion to coaching, and the improbable continuation of championships shone a light on Russell's personal journey. He had emerged a stronger person, grounded in a solid foundation. "I've known fear, but I'm not afraid now," he said. "I've always had the fear of being alone. I've had the fear of failure, but no longer." He had worried that sports lent him a psychological crutch. He had pondered his self-worth independent of basketball. Finally, he surmounted his misgivings. "The hardest person to convince I was a man," he said, "was myself."[63]

13

Boston Is Dead

Through sport, Russell embodied the triumphs of the civil rights era. His leadership of the Celtics, his heroic image vis-à-vis Wilt Chamberlain, his rewarding relationships with teammates, and his ascension to player-coach represented the pinnacle of basketball achievement. Yet Russell also established an intellectual independence. He had questioned nonviolence, assailed white liberals, and condemned prejudice in a northern city. As black nationalists now sensationalized that critique, Russell possessed a distinctive political voice, both liberal and radical, magnified by his stardom and refined by his intelligence.

On June 1 and 2, 1966, Russell joined twenty-four hundred delegates at "To Fulfill These Rights," a civil rights conference hosted by the White House. Representatives included government officials, industry magnates, grassroots activists, entertainers, and such black giants as A. Philip Randolph, Roy Wilkins, Thurgood Marshall, and Martin Luther King Jr. Although President Lyndon Johnson had shepherded the 1964 Civil Rights Act and 1965 Voting Rights Act, SNCC and the Deacons for Defense boycotted the conference. Other militants yelled "Go home, Uncle Tom" at black delegates. CORE sponsored a resolution calling for American withdrawal from Vietnam, which moderate delegates voted down, sparing LBJ a political embarrassment.[1]

Russell eschewed the radical posturing of the picketers, but he also expressed aggravation with the status quo. On a panel examining the poor condition of city schools as a symptom of urban poverty, Russell asked why the committee excluded business leaders. "Why are there not representatives of General Motors, Ford and Chrysler here? What good is education without jobs?" An awkward silence ensued. As columnist Carl Rowan noted, the White House conference had indicated the necessity of "powerful, costly remedies" to overturn centuries of racism, but it "neither produced nor identified those remedies. Indeed, it was a basketball player, Bill Russell of Boston, who made the sage observation that not all the ingredients necessary for the curing potion were on hand."[2]

Russell returned to the White House days later for a reception honoring 121 Presidential Scholars. He chafed that neighborhoods such as Roxbury produced no such scholars—"not because the students aren't intelligent enough, but because the schools in Roxbury stunt their intellectual growth." Indeed, in August 1965, in response to an NAACP school discrimination suit, Massachusetts had passed the Racial Imbalance Act, outlawing de facto segregation in education. Yet the all-white Boston School Committee stalled racial integration, enraging black activists.[3]

On June 16, 1966, that anger exploded during the graduation ceremony at the Patrick T. Campbell Junior High School in Roxbury. School Committee chair Louise Day Hicks, the most outspoken opponent of integration, sat on the stage, offending many Boston blacks. Local Southern Christian Leadership Conference chairman Virgil Wood launched a demonstration, described the *Boston Herald,* "with the precision and shocking suddenness of a commando raid." As supporters blocked off police, Wood rallied the crowd into chanting, "Go home, Mrs. Hicks." Students tossed wastebaskets at intervening officers, delivered Wood to the stage, and cheered as he called Hicks "the Hitler of Boston."[4]

The *Bay State Banner,* Roxbury's new community newspaper, described the next development in a huge front-page headline: "BILL RUSSELL JOINS THE FIGHT." The Celtics star would speak at an alternate "Freedom Graduation." A street rally and press conference also solicited funds for the Meredith March Against Fear, then moving through Mississippi. That civil rights crusade dramatized the movement's competing tensions, as young militants eschewed nonviolence and white liberals. As this school graduation inflamed black Boston, Stokely Carmichael of SNCC emerged from jail in Greenwood, Mississippi, and roused a crowd with a new slogan: Black Power.[5]

Russell voiced that fury at the Freedom Graduation. "A poisoned atmosphere hangs over this city," he charged. "It is an atmosphere of hate, distrust and ignorance." He spoke to seven hundred emotional people in the basement auditorium of a Catholic church, since the School Committee had denied the use of school grounds. He lamented "every dilapidated, antiquated, rat-infested fire trap of a school in Roxbury." He remembered how France and Britain had ignored the warnings of Ethiopia's Haile Selassie, and how the fire of fascism then swept Europe. "There's a fire here in Roxbury and nobody is listening, and the fire that consumes Roxbury will also consume Boston," he said. "The fire will spread." The students cheered and stomped their feet. Russell signed their citations, and each graduate got a copy of *Go Up for Glory.*[6]

Yet Russell remained a critical contact to Boston's white power structure. After

skewed media coverage of the original graduation (Hicks herself narrated one television report), black leaders complained to media outlets through a telegram
signed by Russell. Two days after the Freedom Graduation, Russell hosted forty
news editors and executives at Slade's. A panel proposed more black reporters and
staff, balanced coverage of black communities, and a liaison committee to foster
communication. With support from the editor of the *Boston Globe,* they established
the Boston Community Media Committee. Blacks soon appeared before and behind the cameras of local television stations. Activist Mel King credited Russell's
leadership and notoriety for effecting this progress.[7]

That fall, Massachusetts elected Edward W. Brooke, the first African American
senator since the nineteenth century. A *Boston Globe* column suggested that black
athletes, by demonstrating talent and spirit, had smoothed this path. Russell resisted such thinking—it rendered him a symbol, diminishing him as a man. But he
had applied his celebrity to political change, through both the government and the
grass roots. Now he straddled the widening rift in black politics from his historic
new position: coach.[8]

. . .

For the first practice of training camp, Russell walked out in socks. "You sons of
bitches are going to pay for the SOB who hid my sneakers!" he yelled. For the next
two and a half hours, the Celtics did sprints, laps, and calisthenics, all in ostensi-
ble revenge for a prank. Russell had actually found the hidden sneakers, but he
locked them away. Throughout his career, he had both shirked practices and invested in personal relationships with teammates. This demonstration articulated
his new responsibility and authority.[9]

Russell maintained continuity from the Auerbach era. He kept the same plays,
the same routines, the same professional standards. During the customarily grueling exhibition tour, he most fretted about paring the roster from sixteen to
twelve, as his memory of getting cut in high school still burned. Yet he also staked
out authority. During a preseason tour in Puerto Rico, Auerbach carped that Russell had a suite, while he had a regular room. When Russell matter-of-factly reminded him that the coach gets the suite, Auerbach accepted this shift in power
relations.[10]

The integrationist milestone created unique pressures. "You're compelled to
pull for Bill because a head coaching job for a Negro in major league pro sports
was so long coming," wrote Doc Young in the *Chicago Defender,* addressing black
sports fans nationwide. "You know that Bill is virtually compelled to win—because
of his race."[11]

The Boston dynasty, moreover, stared at a closing window. Russell turned thirty-
three that February. K. C. Jones was thirty-four, Sam Jones thirty-three. The Celtics
always picked last in the draft, and since selecting John Havlicek in 1962, the or-

ganization had developed no stars. Only seven-foot Mel Counts seemed a legitimate prospect. Now Auerbach exploited that commodity, trading Counts to Baltimore for thirty-year-old Bailey Howell. The new starting forward was a twenty-point scorer, ferocious offensive rebounder, and five-time All-Star. One reporter called it "the steal of the century."[12]

The Celtics also got Wayne Embry to back up Russell. Another thirty-year-old veteran, the Royals' behemoth had tired of the NBA life. But as Russell once lured Willie Naulls, now he coaxed Embry. He floated the idea over a round of golf at Kutsher's Resort. Then he sweet-talked Embry's wife Terri, who resisted leaving Cincinnati. Auerbach acquired Embry for draft picks and cash. "Wayne the Wall" never regretted his decision, even after sweating off twenty-five pounds during training camp. He marveled at his new team's lack of ego, abundance of character, appreciation of role players, and interracial friendships.[13]

As coach, Russell fostered this spirit. He talked more to rookies, and he at least paid lip service to enthusiasm for practice. On road trips, he ate meals with different teammates, not just his best friends. "Don't think that doesn't help the over-all cooperation of the guys, on and off the court," said Embry. "It's one reason why Boston has been so tough to defeat over the years." Once, Russell hitched a ride from the airport with Howell's family. The black players had wondered if Howell—a white Southerner—would assimilate with the Celtics, but he earned everyone's affection and respect. As Russell folded into the backseat, one of Howell's young daughters asked, "Do I have to sit on the black man's lap?" Howell blanched, but Russell cackled, defusing any possible tension.[14]

Russell's idiosyncratic humor balanced his roles as authority and colleague. After one half-hearted effort, he burst into the locker room, threatening physical harm to each individual—until he reached the massive Embry and quipped, "Everyone but you." On road trips, he made rookies carry his uniform in a tattered, smelly gym bag nicknamed "Old Yella." Once, while scolding a player for breaking curfew, he asked, "Did you get laid?" The confused player asked why. "If you did not get laid, I figure you were up all night trying and did not get any sleep," Russell responded. "That's why I asked, and that's why I would have to fine you."[15]

Larry Siegfried thought that Boston no longer needed a traditional coach. Russell, he said, "didn't have to tell Havlicek to be in a certain spot at a certain time. He didn't have to tell Sam Jones where to be on the fast break. He didn't have to tell Satch Sanders how to play defense." The players made adjustments on the floor, suggested ideas at halftime, and diagrammed situations in the huddle. Russell trusted that in practice, Siegfried could better demonstrate how to break a full-court press, since he played guard. That collective sense of responsibility allowed Russell to concentrate on his best player: himself. Siegfried considered him a player first, a coach second.[16]

Russell did establish professional distance. Some teammates jokingly referred to him as "The Lord," yet they accepted his constructive criticism because Russell held himself to the same standards. He upbraided mistakes with unflinching honesty. He called his turnover-prone team "the dumbest I've ever seen in a long time," punishing them with laps. He had believed that Auerbach needled Nelson and Sanders too much, but now he realized that certain players needed that jockeying. So he adapted Auerbach's psychological tactics to his own circumstances and personality. To one reporter, he threatened to trade Sanders. To another, he said, "Trading one of these fellows is like trading my brother."[17]

Coaching layered additional burdens on Russell. He ached when players ignored instructions, referees favored opponents, or friends created off-court distractions such as ticket requests. Long responsible for just himself, he now considered each individual's ego, vulnerability, and incentive. A moody eccentric like Siegfried drove him to distraction. He liked Howell, but they never developed a close bond. Each veteran had a strong sense of self.[18]

The players got frustrated with Russell's blunders. In a season-opening victory over San Francisco, he forgot to substitute for K. C. Jones, who slumped with exhaustion after playing all forty-eight minutes. In a close game against New York, he left out Havlicek and Sam Jones in the fourth quarter. After playing uneven minutes in a January loss to Philadelphia, Sam Jones bared his angst. A reporter asked if he would ever player-coach, and he said no, taking an obvious swipe at Russell. "You can't do both jobs. When you've got to play Wilt Chamberlain you've got to have your mind on playing him and nothing else."[19]

Russell now signed the occasional autograph as a concession to his position, but he often reverted to his gruff old ways. He skipped press luncheons, ignored telephone messages, and spurned interviews. His coaching debut attracted the first opening-game sellout in Boston Garden history, and the crowd gave him a thirty-second standing ovation. Still, Russell ambled stiffly to center court, where he folded his arms, kicked at nothing, and impassively stared at the parquet floor. "I been going to the Celtics for 10 years, but I never seen that man smile yet," grumbled a Boston cabdriver.[20]

That indifference to public relations stirred criticisms of Russell's coaching, as well as his outside business and political interests. A midseason minislump, when the Celtics dropped four of eight games, left them at 30–12. The record beat last season's pace, but they lacked defensive effort and offensive explosiveness. Siegfried and Embry wanted more playing time. Sam Jones wanted more shots. Some thought Havlicek should play forty minutes a game, not thirty. The *Boston Traveler* suggested that players resented Russell's lackadaisical practice habits. He once called an extra practice and never showed up. While his teammates sweated through workouts, Russell often read the newspaper, ate doughnuts, and sipped coffee.[21]

Yet the Celtics carried their cooperative ethic into a new era. In January, Russell appointed Havlicek as captain, providing much-needed help with substitutions and time-outs. Havlicek saw no reason to act as a "go-between" for disgruntled teammates. "The great thing about our team always has been the rapport among the players," he said. "We've still got it." Even the newcomer Howell reflected, "We loved each other, respected each other, rooted for each other, played for each other."[22]

Russell also benefited from Auerbach's support. The general manager never usurped the coach's authority. Although they discussed Auerbach coaching the play-offs, Auerbach pooh-poohed that possibility to the press. He also pilloried Russell's detractors, including Wilt Chamberlain, who opined that "the stupidest thing he ever did was coach. He ought to quit and go back to playing only." In his new and belligerently frank memoir, *Red Auerbach: Winning the Hard Way*, one chapter detailed Russell's superiority to Chamberlain.[23]

Throughout the season, angry letters reminded Russell that he was not Red Auerbach. To outside observers, he carried the world on his shoulders—a sweat-soaked, gimpy-kneed giant running up and down the hardwood while juggling substitutions, instructions, referees, and Wilt Chamberlain. But Russell stayed confident. No one could better lead this particular group. His teammates accepted his authority. Moreover, he loved the challenge. He was sleeping more, vomiting less. He had new motivation. He needed this job, surface indications to the contrary. "You can't know me," he said. "No man can."[24]

. . .

Every so often, the sporting press proclaimed a "New Wilt Chamberlain." This character harnessed his bottomless talents to team ends. He shot less, passed more, and defended better. He cared about winning championships, not scoring titles. During the 1966–67 season, Chamberlain finally realized that potential. As a high-post hub for looping and cutting teammates, he dished to weapons such as Hal Greer, Chet Walker, and Billy Cunningham. He attacked the basket, eschewing his fadeaway jumper. He made an otherworldly 68 percent of his shots, including a record thirty-five in a row.[25]

Russell pined for the Old Wilt Chamberlain. "Before, the only question was which shot Wilt would take," he said. "Now, you have to worry about—number one, will he shoot?—number two, if he does, what will he shoot?—and number three, will he pass off?" Chamberlain averaged a mere twenty-four points per game, but his stylistic transformation sparked team chemistry, on and off the court. New coach Alex Hannum, who had already earned Chamberlain's respect in San Francisco, stood up to his star, yet he also solicited Chamberlain's advice on personnel and strategy, and he praised Chamberlain's winning spirit. The 76ers jumped to a 39–3 record, the fastest start in league history.[26]

Most of the NBA offered little resistance. The expansion Chicago Bulls had thinned the overall talent, and seven of ten teams finished under .500. Only Boston slowed Philadelphia, because Russell and K. C. Jones could handle Chamberlain and Greer, respectively. Each contest had a play-off-like atmosphere. The 76ers massacred the Celtics on Halloween, 138–96; the Celtics stopped two long 76er winning streaks; Philadelphia won the next two face-offs, establishing a 9½ game lead in the standings; Boston snapped Philadelphia's thirty-six-game home winning streak; Hannum protested a one-point loss because the Celtics played a short stretch with six men; Philadelphia beat the Celtics, clinched the division, and broke their record of sixty-two regular season wins. The 76ers finished 68–13. But when Russell hit a fifteen-foot jump shot with two seconds left to win their final game, the Celtics took the regular season series, five to four.[27]

Boston finished 60–21, a winning percentage topped by only two of Auerbach's teams. If coaching inexperience cost a few games, Russell compensated with renewed energy and leadership. The Celtics raised his salary for the next year. He had validated his promotion. At first, wrote Doc Young, "the lingering bigots were wondering aloud whether or not a Negro could handle the job." Now, "Bill handles the job, and nobody blames any of his losses on race or the color of his skin."[28]

Philadelphia owned the best team and record, but only a fool dismissed the Celtics in the play-offs—not after Boston's sixty wins, classic battles against the 76ers, and eight consecutive titles. Any play-off prediction, however, assumed that the NBA was staging a play-off. A player strike loomed.

· · ·

The Celtics reflected basketball's arrival into modern professional sports. In 1965 Marjorie Brown, Lou Pieri, and Auerbach sold their interests to the Ruppert Knickerbocker Brewery. Then a holding company called National Equities paid $3 million for the team. By the early 1970s, the franchise's ownership had bounced from P. Ballantine and Sons Brewery to Trans-National Communication to Investors Funding Corporation.[29]

National Equities chairman Marvin Kratter often had the franchise on the market, seeking his next big profit. The real estate magnate traveled in his own Lockheed Jet, got a daily shave in his personal barber chair at his New York office, and meddled with Auerbach despite no basketball background. Once, Kratter urged the team to rub a polished stone for luck. Russell refused. The Celtics won nine titles without rubbing any stones, he explained. Furthermore, he kicked Kratter out of the locker room. Kratter huffed away. He had substantial wealth and a matching ego, but none of the trust or affection once accorded Walter Brown.[30]

A business journal touted "The Coming Boom in Pro Basketball." After buying the Lakers in 1959 for $200,000, Bob Short sold them in 1965 for over $5 million. Club owners claimed players as depreciating assets, creating huge tax shelters. Attendance had risen by 20 percent. The play-off pool doubled in four years. The San

Francisco Warriors had stabilized, the Philadelphia 76ers were moving into a modern new arena, and the Chicago Bulls entered a major market. Walter Kennedy announced ambitious expansion plans, starting with Seattle and San Diego in 1967. New franchises' entry fees made existing owners even wealthier.[31]

Television fueled the business of basketball. ABC had picked up sixteen games only to counter taped programming on CBS, but visionary producer Roone Arledge soon saw possibilities in the NBA. The "Roone Revolution" in televised sports included not only technical innovations, such as close-ups and split screens, but also an impulse to capture a dramatic atmosphere, building identification between a sport and its fans. Television had already fostered growth in the NFL and rival American Football League. Basketball offered the same speed and grace, and viewers could see the players' faces, free of helmets or caps. Indoor courts confined seminaked athletes into a small, intense space.[32]

Arledge spotted cameras throughout the arena. He shot from multiple angles, with close-ups on players, coaches, and fans. He produced sixty-second mini-biographies, personalizing the stars. And he spotlighted Bill Russell and Wilt Chamberlain. Long the league's chief marketing device, the rivalry now became a Sunday afternoon staple, beamed into living rooms from sea to sea. As ABC's ratings climbed, the NBA finally enjoyed the trappings of a genuine "big league."[33]

In February 1967, that big league got some competition with the formation of the American Basketball Association. The legendary George Mikan acted as commissioner. Inspired by the 1966 AFL-NFL merger, the ABA sought to lure prime talent and force a lucrative merger. Even before the league's initial press conference, reports surfaced that Wilt Chamberlain would join the ABA. As he flirted with ABA officials about possible part-ownership in Oakland or New York, the Indianapolis franchise inquired about Oscar Robertson, and New Orleans tried enticing Bailey Howell.[34]

Now NBA players demanded a bigger slice of the pie. Their talents had elevated the league's profile, yet they had little negotiating power. The reserve clause shackled their rights to one franchise. As profits surged, they claimed an average salary of only $9,500 (Walter Kennedy insisted it was $17,000). They traveled tourist class, got measly meal money, and stayed in dingy hotels throughout a long season. They had no medical plan. Professional baseball, football, and hockey players had superior pension plans.[35]

It was no accident that an African American led the NBA's labor struggle. Many black players had grown up poor. While experiencing lifetimes of injustice, they matured during the civil rights era. Whites tended to trust coaches and owners; blacks tended to suspect ulterior motives in white paternalism. Oscar Robertson, new president of the National Basketball Players Association (NBPA), transmitted not only a fierce intelligence but also a racial bitterness over how Cincinnati had rebuffed his demands, constructed the roster, and marketed the team. Working with attorney Larry Fleisher, he adhered to "one basic core understanding: When owners dealt with players, whatever they attempted was against our interests."[36]

In June 1966, Robertson and player representatives demanded a better pension, a medical plan, a schedule without back-to-back Saturday night/Sunday afternoon games, an All-Star Game break, and a ten-game limit on the exhibition season. The owners only pledged to study the issue. In January 1967, the NBPA again outlined its grievances. Throughout February, Fleisher met with Walter Kennedy, who relayed counterproposals. Fleisher then convened player representatives at Leone's Restaurant in New York City. After antipasto and veal scaloppini, they rejected the owners' offer. The NBPA filed for certification with the National Labor Relations Board. Unless the owners improved the pension plan, they would boycott the play-offs.[37]

Since the 1964 All-Star Game, the NBPA had learned how to generate coverage, and its claims won media sympathy. The players wanted only a $600 monthly pension for ten-year veterans, about half that of baseball players. The owners hollowly argued that basketball players' college educations cut the need for large pensions, and they failed to even convene until March 9. Just before the March 14 deadline, the two sides reached consensus. The players claimed victory for the agreement in "principle" on a "satisfactory" pension plan by June. The ABA had given them some pull. The play-offs proceeded, but the NBA had stepped toward a system of modern labor relations, with open antagonism between employers and employees.[38]

Russell had not voted on the proposed strike. As a coach, he kept his distance from the struggle. "I know I get a lot more for playing than for coaching," he allowed, "but that's all I'm going to say." The restored play-offs nevertheless satisfied him. Without play-offs, after all, nobody won. And without winning, basketball meant nothing.[39]

. . .

Vestiges of a "bush league" still dogged the NBA. The play-offs expanded to eight teams, so the eighty-one-game regular season eliminated only two cellar-dwellers. The Celtics first drew the 36–45 New York Knicks, who last made the postseason in 1959. Boston had beaten them nineteen consecutive times. The Knicks last won in Boston Garden on December 22, 1962. New York did possess a young and promising core led by Willis Reed, but Boston peaked in the play-offs. "The great and bearded one shall lead us as always," predicted Satch Sanders.[40]

The great and bearded Russell looked like a spring chicken in the opener, snaring twenty-three rebounds and keying a frenetic fast break. Sam Jones, John Havlicek, and Bailey Howell hit thirty-nine of fifty-one shots, and Boston blasted New York, 140–110. The Knicks led by eleven in the next game at Madison Square Garden, but the poised Celtics prevailed again, 115–108. Then, finally, the Knicks snapped their various streaks of futility, winning 132–112 at Boston Garden. The loss provoked the fears and frustrations of Boston fans: the Celtics had aged, they lacked their old fire, Bill Russell was no Red Auerbach. The crowd actually booed Russell, an abominable act of ingratitude for the all-time leader in play-off games, play-off rebounds, and NBA championships. Boston nevertheless closed out New York, 118–109, behind fifty-one points from Sam Jones, a franchise play-off record.[41]

Oddsmakers favored Philadelphia to beat Boston. After a shocking opening loss, Philadelphia had regained its impeccable form, sweeping the next three games from Cincinnati. The 76ers combined frontline power with a Celtic-style commitment to defense and passing. In one game, Chamberlain tied Bob Cousy's play-off record of nineteen assists. Alex Hannum had his team humming, respectful of the Celtics yet confident in themselves.[42]

In the first period of the opener, a driving Chet Walker floored Russell with his shoulder. By the time Russell caught his wind, the 76ers had opened a fourteen-point lead, and they sailed to an easy 127–113 win. Chamberlain submitted the impressive line of twenty-four points, fourteen assists, and thirty-two rebounds. "It's like Wilt's got venom," said K. C. Jones. "He smells something. He wants to win real bad and he's playing both ends."[43]

Could Philadelphia surmount Boston? Could Chamberlain overcome Russell? ABC televised the critical Game Two at Boston Garden. But just as labor trouble had threatened the play-offs, now it endangered the broadcast. The American Federation of Radio and Television Artists was on strike, so Chris Schenkel and Jack Twyman refused to narrate the game. Other craft unions declined to cross the picket line. Instead of showcasing the NBA's premier rivalry, ABC broadcast with a single camera in black-and-white. Producer Chet Forte manned the microphone.[44]

As the league's reputation suffered, so did Boston. The Celtics blew an eleven-point lead, falling behind by fourteen in the fourth quarter. Russell staged a comeback behind a small lineup of K. C. Jones, Larry Siegfried, John Havlicek, and rookie Jim Barnett to cut the margin to one point. But Philadelphia prevailed, 107–102. Never before in the Russell era had the Celtics trailed by two games in the play-offs. Well afterward, the Celtics remained in uniform, shell-shocked. Wayne Embry fought back sobs. Don Nelson stared through a stat sheet. K. C. Jones sprawled on the floor. Red Auerbach buried his face in his hands. The mass of reporters surrounded Bill Russell, who pulled at his tape, scratched his goatee, sipped his soda, and whispered justifications for a contest gone awry.[45]

The fans had again booed Russell. This time, the press piled on. Sam Jones and Bailey Howell sat in the closing minutes, when Boston needed their shooting. Wayne Embry sat the entire game, though Russell needed a breather during Philadelphia's third-quarter run. Russell never broke Philadelphia's momentum by calling time-out, despite the urgings of the Boston bench. "Celtics Learn, Sadly, That Russell Is No Auerbach," read one headline. "The Celtics do not deserve to win the play-offs for the ninth year in succession because in cold-blooded pre-meditation they handicapped themselves by making Russell, their meal ticket, handle two big jobs," wrote Harold Kaese. Clif Keane believed that Russell needed to concentrate on playing—that is, "if there is any life left in his game."[46]

"BOSTON IS DEAD! BOSTON IS DEAD! BOSTON IS DEAD!" screamed the 13,007 fans at Game Three in Convention Hall, the largest indoor sports crowd in Philadelphia history. From the pregame introductions, when Wilt Chamberlain got a deafening ovation, through a dramatic fourth quarter, when Philadelphia overcame a last-ditch Boston challenge, the fans lifted the 76ers. They also taunted Red Auerbach, who churlishly moaned that the 76ers faked injuries for extra time-outs. Russell got twenty-nine rebounds, nine assists, and ten points, but Chamberlain overwhelmed him on a few dunks, and he notched twenty points, forty-one rebounds, and nine assists—many from full-court baseball passes for layups. The next day, even Auerbach admitted that Boston was dead.[47]

Yet back in Boston, "the corpse wiggled its toe." Now accepting the Celtics' inevitable decline, the fans offered unflinching support. "Thank You, Celtics. You Are Always No. 1 With Us," proclaimed one banner. Only Boston had ever swept a best-of-seven play-off series, in 1959 against Minneapolis. These Celtics sidestepped a similar fate. They rediscovered their shooting touch, and their gritty defense withheld myriad onslaughts. Despite suffering from severe leg cramps, Russell sank two clinching free throws with fourteen seconds left. Boston won 121–117—a final, defiant gasp of Celtic pride.[48]

The Boston title streak ended with the next game. The Celtics opened a sixteen-point lead midway through the second quarter, but in the last thirty minutes, the 76ers outscored the Celtics 97–57, winning 140–116. Chamberlain, Hal Greer, Chet Walker, Wally Jones, and Billy Cunningham each scored at least twenty points. Chamberlain added thirty-six rebounds and thirteen assists. Leonard Koppett described Convention Hall as "a cross between a Roman arena and a garbage dump," wobbling on the brink of chaos. Public address announcer Dave Zinkoff whipped fans to a frenzy. They mocked Auerbach by lighting cigars. Eggs, potatoes, and coins littered the court. As Koppett wrote, the spectacle explained "why professional basketball languished so long as a dance-hall and bush-league enterprise."[49]

"BOSTON IS DEAD! BOSTON IS DEAD! BOSTON IS DEAD!" Again the chant shook the building. A sign with that slogan paraded through the aisles. Indeed, Russell had lacked Auerbach's coaching acumen, Sam Jones and John Havlicek had been streaky, Satch Sanders and Don Nelson had been ineffective, and the aging Celtics had withered in the fourth quarter. The 76ers seemed the next great dynasty. They had exorcised their demons: Boston's winning knack, Chamberlain's losing reputation. They would beat the San Francisco Warriors, four games to two, to capture their first NBA title.[50]

Chamberlain deserved all his accolades. No one had ever blended so many talents so well. Yet as he watched the final seconds tick on the ultimate triumph over Boston, he retained his cool aloofness, sipping from a paper cup and ignoring the tumult. As his teammates doused each other in champagne, he sat alone in a side room, expressionless. "No," wrote Jeremy Larner, "he won't let go of his image." Chamberlain already insisted that he was the greatest player ever, so he found no validation in beating the Celtics. Nor could he soak in the cheers. The boos would someday return. "He is stuck inside himself," concluded Larner, "a standout, with no place to hide and nothing to do year in and year out but to assert and reassert his simple sterile pride in his own existence."[51]

In those same final seconds, Russell felt no rage, no bitterness—just disappointment. He had no regrets. "We dressed quietly and went on our way," recalled Wayne Embry. "No finger-pointing at each other or blaming the officials. If you lose with dignity, then you don't become a loser." They congratulated the victors in the Philadelphia locker room, and at the breakup banquet, Russell had kind words and silly jokes for every individual. While leaving the court, however, he had searched out K. C. Jones.[52]

In 1965, Jones accepted the head-coaching job of Brandeis University, starting in 1966. Then Auerbach convinced him to play another season. During this final campaign, Russell hosted a farewell party in Reading, and he expressed noble admiration during a Boston Garden tribute. "I have known him longer than I know my wife," he reflected. They had such different personalities, but he admired his humble, gracious friend. "He's always been a man. Of all the men I know in life, K. C. is the one I would like one of my sons to be like."[53]

Jones had first inspired Russell in the possibilities of team basketball. Together they won two NCAA titles, an Olympic gold medal, and eight NBA championships. Jones, moreover, saw the best in people. It was Jones who mentored the poor, awkward freshman at USF; it was Jones who once bought his needy friend a pair of shoes. Now, as chants of "Boston Is Dead" echoed through Convention Hall, rabid Philadelphians climbed the basket supports, and tomatoes and eggs rained upon the Celtics streaming into the tunnel, it struck Russell that their extraordinary partnership was over. While their teammates covered their heads with sweatshirts, Russell and Jones walked off the court together, their arms around each other's shoulders.[54]

. . .

The civil rights movement created new possibilities for blacks. "It's the first time in history that the American Negro can create his own history," Russell wrote in *Go Up for Glory*.[55]

In January 1967, Russell helped found a national sports committee for the

NAACP Legal Defense and Educational Fund. He cochaired the committee with football's Gale Sayers and baseball's Bill White. Eighteen athletes pledged to raise $100,000 for the organization, which advocated equal opportunities in housing, jobs, and education. At Russell's urging, the committee also studied the dearth of endorsements for black stars. He recounted how white teammates had received more money for similar speaking engagements. One advertising executive offered him union scale to endorse a national drug company, justifying that it advanced integration. A City College study reinforced Russell's claims: blacks appeared in few commercials during sports-related television programming. By publicizing such inequities, the committee broadened understanding of discrimination, exposing its more subtle forms.[56]

Russell also joined the Negro Industrial and Economic Union (NIEU), an organization headed by Jim Brown. The football superstar had retired from the Cleveland Browns in 1966 to launch an acting career. Brown shared Russell's political outspokenness. The smart, proud, accomplished athletes had developed a friendship, and when Brown started the NIEU (later renamed the Black Economic Union), Russell became a founding officer. Athletes such as John Wooten and Mudcat Grant took administrative roles, future Cleveland mayor Carl Stokes served as attorney, and black MBAs lent their talents. They raised money through membership dues, fund-raising contributions, and grants from the Ford Foundation and Department of Commerce.[57]

The NIEU considered both racial integration and black pride desirable, but it focused on economic autonomy. The organization financed and trained young black entrepreneurs. It also taught economic self-sufficiency to black youth. Within a few years, the NIEU birthed success stories in Cleveland, Oakland, Kansas City, and elsewhere. Before civil rights groups launched economic development programs or the federal government sponsored minority business initiatives, this alliance of athletes helped establish numerous black-owned businesses.[58]

Through the NIEU, Russell also engaged the national debate ignited by Muhammad Ali. The heavyweight champion had refused induction into the Vietnam War, and the Department of Justice rejected his claimed exemption as a conscientious objector. He refused compromise proposals, labeling the war imperialist and racist. Old-guard sportswriters were aghast. "He has reached the boundaries of fanaticism," wrote Milton Gross. Red Smith called him a "slacker" and "draft-dodger." Ali got stripped of his title, and a federal grand jury indicted him. Yet if he embodied rebellion to those that cherished order and loyalty, he inspired others—especially the masses of black Americans—with his spirit, charisma, and principles. This stand fortified his icon of black pride.[59]

In early June 1967, Brown held a "draft summit" at NIEU headquarters in Cleveland, bringing together ten black athletes including Ali, Russell, UCLA All-American Lew Alcindor, and NFL players John Wooten, Willie Davis, and Bobby Mitchell.

Newspapers reported that they would urge Ali to enter the army. As one columnist wrote, "It is the successful, adjusted Negro American athlete who holds the deepest regret and the most shame for him"—implying that Ali had diminished the achievements of Brown and Russell. Yet the athletes came to Cleveland to listen to Ali, not pressure him. In any case, Ali welcomed the gesture. "He worships Jim Brown and Bill Russell," revealed a girlfriend.[60]

They had a long, fervid discussion. Outside lurked a curious press corps and residents from the black neighborhood of Hough, who chanted, "Hell no, we won't go!" Inside they peppered Ali with questions. Did he understand his sacrifices? Had he considered alternatives? Was he acting from principle? Ali held his ground. He preached the glories of the Nation of Islam, spinning such eloquent rhapsodies that heads started nodding, grunts started affirming him. Russell broke up the room by announcing that if Elijah Muhammad would relax the prohibition on pork, he would sign up. After five hours, they emerged. "He is completely sincere," said Brown. "His position is completely in accord with his religious beliefs."[61]

The summit fostered respect for Ali's decision, especially since more Americans questioned the Vietnam War by 1967. Dick Edwards of the *New York Amsterdam News* accepted their viewpoint, since "all of the men who tried to reason with Ali are college men and they used all of their experience, both real and book learned." But the meeting inspired little consensus, even among the black press. "Black Athletes Backed the Champ!" exclaimed *Muhammad Speaks* over a photograph of Ali flanked by Russell and Alcindor. "Athletes Fail to Talk Ali into the Army," stated the *Chicago Defender,* maintaining the earlier rationale for the summit. Even Brown considered Ali under the spell of religious zealotry.[62]

But Russell painted Ali as earnest, contented, and thoughtful. He authored a *Sports Illustrated* article called "I Am Not Worried About Ali." No one should doubt the champion's conviction, he wrote. Ali could spend five years in prison for draft evasion. He surrendered popularity, wealth, his title, and even his wife for his religion. Russell envied such faith.[63]

While decrying how racism tarred Ali's reputation, Russell denounced an entire culture of "guilt by association." He condemned all sorts of ignorance. He rejected communism, but only after educating himself on its tenets. He criticized Ronald Reagan's race baiting in the campaign for California governor. He condemned the Vietnam War because "too many issues are being decided on the basis of hate and violence." And he lamented any label as a black spokesman; he considered himself a voice for simple justice. "The hysterical and sometimes fanatical criticism of Ali is, it seems to me, a symptom of the deeper sickness of our times."[64]

Russell admired Ali's moral charisma. The boxer's soul was free, and his conviction shone like a beacon. Ali had a spiritual destiny. "I never aspired to be anything like that," Russell later said. "I was just a guy trying to get through life." But through his own journey for self-understanding and self-pride, Russell had established a unique position. As a barrier-breaking champion, he related to readers of a mass-circulation sports magazine. As a figure of fearless honesty, he possessed credibility among blacks of all political stripes. As a man of deep intelligence, he sifted through obfuscating labels, emotions, and hyperbole in pursuit of integrity. The temper of black revolt had started rocking the sports world. Russell stood as not only a touchstone of progress, but also a chronicler of the nation's ills.[65]

14

The Lighthouse

Three generations of Russells convened in the fall of 1967 for an exhibition against the St. Louis Hawks in Alexandria, Louisiana. Mister Charlie drove from Oakland, stopped in Monroe, and rode one hundred miles south with his father. Although the Old Man had never seen a basketball game, he seemed more interested in the corroding color line. He looked without success for a colored section, a colored restroom. Mister Charlie tried explaining basketball's subtleties, but the Old Man asked only one question: "Do them white boys really have to do what William tells them to do?"

After the game, they visited the locker room. The eldest Russell wandered off, past jabbering reporters and half-naked athletes. Then he started crying. Bill panicked. What was wrong? Was it a heart attack? The Old Man stared into the shower, where Sam Jones and John Havlicek lathered and chatted. "I never thought I'd live to see the day when the water would run off a white man onto a black man, and the water would run off a black man onto a white man," he explained with deliberation. "I've been to church all of my days, but I never thought I'd see anything like this."

An insistent self-determination flowed through the Russell blood. The Old Man established autonomy within a harsh, segregated world. Mister Charlie kept his foundry job despite his son's riches. Bill carved his own independence—whether winning championships, accepting the challenge of coaching, engaging in politics, or refusing autographs. Yet this moment illustrated their generational differences, the shifting consciousness of African American life. The Old Man cried tears of joy at Jim Crow's death; Mister Charlie nurtured his son's accomplishments and his father's pleasure. Bill expected that light of freedom, but saw bigots in the shadows.[1]

. . .

During that same preseason, while in Puerto Rico, Russell called together Boston's veterans. They represented a century of experience, he said. While establishing authority as coach, he had spread himself thin. Now, he would rely on them. "He was man enough to put away some of his stubbornness and pride after his first year, and then ask for help," recalled Wayne Embry. Russell also invited criticism. He had a tendency to rest after grabbing a rebound and starting the fast break. But if prodded to hustle, he skipped to attention and pushed himself down the court.[2]

Russell carried 230 pounds, 15 more than usual. Age slowed him down. "I'm not the player I was five years ago," he said. "I'm not quite as quick as I was, I don't go out as far from the basket as I did, and I can't do the little things I used to do." He gave Embry more minutes. While averaging career lows for points and rebounds, he complained about feeling like a "300-year-old center." Cortisone shots dulled his aching knees. He likened himself to a gunfighter: a generation had grown up watching, studying, and yearning to face the old sheriff. "They keep coming," he said, "and sometimes I wonder if I still have to prove myself."[3]

The Celtics mirrored Russell's apparent decline. Russell, Sam Jones, Bailey Howell, and Satch Sanders had moved another year past thirty. Their age showed especially on the second leg of back-to-back games, when they went only 17–16. They also lost four consecutive games for the first time since January 1962, when Russell had been injured. In February 1968 the Lakers thrashed them, 141–104, the worst home loss in Celtics history.[4]

Both in person and through the press, Red Auerbach tongue-lashed the Celtics for lacking aggressiveness, losing concentration, and pacing themselves. He blamed Russell. He chastised Russell, moreover, for missing a November 1967 game during a surprise blizzard. Howell walked along frozen train tracks, and John Havlicek trudged two miles across the Mystic River Bridge to reach Boston Garden on time. Russell hiked through snow and hitched a ride with a police car, but he arrived when the game ended. By then Auerbach had coached a victory over San Francisco. In the locker room, before rookies and veterans alike, the general manager upbraided the player-coach about his responsibilities.[5]

The 76ers further provoked Boston's anxieties. One preseason assessment tabbed Philadelphia a budding "minidynasty," and following recent tradition, their games featured physical clashes and play-off-style passion, with each team dominating its home contests. After trading first place back and forth through the season's early months, the 76ers opened a lead. When Philadelphia finally won at Boston Garden on March 3, it essentially locked Boston in second place, which some fans commemorated by dumping garbage on the parquet floor.[6]

The Celtics finished 54–28, their lowest winning percentage since Russell's rookie year. Philadelphia had eclipsed Boston, and Wilt Chamberlain had transcended

Russell. Boston's aging warrior still garnered respect: his teammates believed in him, reporters admired him, and referees cut him slack. But Chamberlain thought his rival lacked consistency. "Russell is slowing up, but don't put that in the papers," he said. "Oh, go ahead. He knows he's slowing up."[7]

Philadelphia's success only highlighted Chamberlain's boasts, flourishes, exploits, and contradictions. "He is the most conspicuous athlete in the world, and one of the most conspicuous human beings, and he appears to have come to the decision to make his conspicuousness worth watching," wrote Albert Hano. Chamberlain drove lavender Bentleys and custom Maseratis, kept a lush apartment on Central Park West, and wore full-length white leather coats and diamond-studded cuff links. He renewed negotiations to fight Muhammad Ali. He also attracted throngs of women, many of whom considered him a paradox: an egomaniac, yet gentle and attentive. "The prima-donna act he puts on is a big façade," said one girlfriend. She thought that he resented childhood teasing, celebrity pressures, and the notion that he owed his success to his size. "I don't think he's capable of loving. Just himself."[8]

After a prolonged holdout, Chamberlain had signed a one-year, $250,000 contract. Yet the highest-paid athlete in history lacked gusto for another campaign. "I'd broken my own records year after year," he recalled. "I'd even been on a championship team. What else could I do?" Defending the NBA title did not qualify as a goal. He still defined excellence in individual terms.[9]

So Chamberlain motivated himself with another individual, statistical goal: leading the NBA in assists. He stopped attacking the basket, favored passes to quick shooters like Chet Walker and Billy Cunningham, and passed up easy shots. In one game, he failed to take a single shot. He remained capable of fifty-two and sixty-eight point outbursts, but he got obsessed with assists. Once he even searched out the scorekeeper in an emptying arena to dispute his tally. He led the NBA with 8.6 assists a game—a remarkable feat for a center. He also won his third straight MVP, surpassed twenty-five thousand career points, and put his team eight games ahead of Boston. Yet, somehow, Chamberlain had made unselfishness selfish.[10]

The 76ers, moreover, failed to maintain their previous chemistry. Chamberlain occupied the center of the storm. Reporters scrutinized his reluctance to shoot. His foul shot foibles—hasty overhand stabs, experimental fadeaways, pathetic underhanders—inspired meditations on his psychological state. He sometimes ignored instructions, and he expected a superstar's considerations. Once, after losing to Boston, Alex Hannum lectured about victory. Chamberlain interrupted. "I think there are more important things than winning," he said. "I think you have to learn how to lose, too."[11]

Philadelphia beat New York to open the 1968 play-offs, but injuries slowed Luke Jackson and Wally Jones, and a broken arm shelved Sixth Man Billy Cunningham. The players' condition mirrored that of the Spectrum, the new arena described as "a big tuna fish can" and "an architectural abortion." In early March, strong gusts ripped fiberboard and tarpaper off the roof, so the 76ers moved to Convention Hall until the Eastern Division finals. They still remained title favorites. "Who knows how far they may go?" cracked one wag. "With no roof over their heads, the sky's the limit."[12]

Boston opened against the Detroit Pistons, starring the NBA's leading scorer, second-year guard Dave Bing. Born and raised in Washington, DC, Bing had known Auerbach since he was twelve, and he had admired the Celtics. During a series of preseason exhibitions the previous year, he had hoped Russell would "at least acknowledge that I existed." Russell ignored him. But once Bing established himself, Russell made a connection. Like other young blacks, Bing went to Russell for historical perspective, a sense of the sport's changing texture.[13]

Meanwhile, Russell fretted like a frustrated mechanic under an old luxury car. While decked in mod civilian clothes and resting a sore hamstring during the last three regular season games, he had grumbled at sloppy play. Before the play-offs, he canceled practice and held a long meeting, with every player airing suggestions and grievances. Even after leading Boston to an opening 123–116 win, he criticized his team's defensive energy. His play-off insomnia returned. Before the next day's game at Cobo Hall, he listened to television on a fuzzy screen until 4:00 a.m., read every printed word in his hotel room, and finally nodded off for an hour and a half.[14]

Russell spent the next game in foul trouble, and Detroit won, 126–116. His teammates allowed the Piston guards to penetrate, overrelying on Russell's shotblocking and rebounding. When the series returned to Boston, Bing ignited a third-quarter rally, and Detroit won again, 109–98. The shell-shocked Celtics trailed the series, two games to one.[15]

Russell now made the key repairs to his sputtering squad. In the midst of Game Four at Cobo Hall, he warned the Detroit guards to stay out of the lane. "He really got into your mind as a player," recalled Bing, who started pulling up for jumpers. Russell also started John Havlicek at guard. Only Havlicek could play forty-eight minutes at top speed. The erstwhile Sixth Man had evolved into a star, doggedly polishing every facet of his game. At Cobo Hall, he kept driving to the rim. He got thirty-five points, nine rebounds, and nine assists. Riding a second-half run, Boston routed Detroit 135–110.[16]

"We're in the groove now—the winning groove that should take us all the way to the title," proclaimed Don Nelson. They had recovered their tough, hustling style. Indeed, another late spurt propelled Boston to a 110–96 victory in Game Five. Havlicek played another forty-eight minutes, and Russell dominated on defense, despite a freak accident on the plane ride home, when he tore the skin and nail off his right middle finger. Boston clinched the series the next day, withstanding Bing's forty-four points to prevail 111–103.[17]

Basketball's giants steeled for yet another collision. "For years," wrote Frank De-ford, "everything else has been peripheral to the personal duel between Bill Rus-sell and Wilt Chamberlain. It is a long-running act, second in endurance in the sport only to the Harlem Globetrotters, but it is still box-office, and it is still the very best." The 1968 play-offs accentuated this extraordinary rivalry—which now tossed in a swirling storm of black anger, sporting revolt, and national tragedy.[18]

. . .

The Black Power movement affirmed African American pride and independence. Organizations such as SNCC, CORE, and the Black Panthers assailed white liber-als, rejected nonviolence, and stoked white fears of black rage. But Black Power also asserted self-determination by celebrating black culture, which encompassed such expressions as soul music, natural hairstyles, and a black aesthetic in arts and literature. In sport, this movement built upon the foundation laid by Jackie Robin-son, Muhammad Ali, Jim Brown, and Bill Russell. The "Revolt of the Black Athlete" argued that sport reinforced stereotypes and inequality. It gained momentum un-der a twenty-six-year-old sociology professor at San Jose State University, Harry Edwards.[19]

Goateed and 6'8", Edwards oozed radical chic. He styled a black beret, black sun-glasses, and black jacket while lauding revolutionaries such as Stokely Carmichael and H. Rap Brown. He also decried how universities exploited black athletes: iso-lating them on campus, pressuring them to ignore academics, exposing them to racist taunting, establishing implicit racial quotas. San Jose State boasted a track-and-field dynasty known as "Speed City." During the 1967 University Games in Tokyo, Speed City sprinter Tommie Smith first mentioned the possibility of boy-cotting the 1968 Olympic Games in Mexico City—an idea soon backed by the Na-tional Conference of Black Power.[20]

Edwards formed the Olympic Project for Human Rights (OPHR) in October 1967. Martin Luther King Jr., as well as younger radicals, supported the OPHR's platform, which included the restoration of Muhammad Ali's title, the removal of International Olympic Committee (IOC) chairman Avery Brundage, the restric-tion of apartheid South Africa from the Olympics, the appointment of black coaches and administrators by the U.S. Olympic Committee, and the desegrega-tion of the New York Athletic Club (NYAC). In February 1968, many black ath-letes boycotted the NYAC's nationally televised track meet, while nearly two thou-sand demonstrators protested outside Madison Square Garden.[21]

The proposed Olympic boycott divided the sports world. A six-part series in the *Los Angeles Times* engaged debates over blacks' "natural" athleticism, and a long feature in *Life* chronicled the grievances of black athletes. Tommie Smith and Ralph Boston debated the boycott in *Sport*. In the *Saturday Evening Post*, Edwards explained "Why Negroes Should Boycott Whitey's Olympics." An *Ebony* poll revealed that most athletes wanted to go to Mexico City. The venerated Jesse Owens blasted the OPHR, reinforcing the traditional stance that sport fostered black progress.[22]

Edwards enticed a backlash. Hate mail denounced him. Vandals ransacked his apartment and murdered his two dogs. Reports surfaced that the OPHR threatened picket line crossers at the NYAC meet. Columnists also questioned the boycott's premise: "Athletics is one field in which discrimination hardly exists," declared a *Chicago Tribune* editorial. It ridiculed the notion of the exploited athlete. "Is Wilt Chamberlain exploited, or Bill Russell?" it asked. "Their salary checks would tell a different story."[23]

Yet Russell had already attacked sport's structural inequities and discriminatory attitudes. Edwards described the Revolt of the Black Athlete as the "things that Jackie Robinson wanted to say in 1947 but couldn't; that Bill Russell tried to say in 1957 but was not heard; and that Jesse Owens should have said in 1967, but didn't."[24]

Russell was the first professional athlete to support Edwards. "He called *me*," marveled Edwards. "He was like an African prince. There was a regality about Russell that demanded a kind of deference." Money and fame may have dulled other stars, but Russell's moral and intellectual clarity evoked the legendary athlete, actor, singer, and activist Paul Robeson. Russell offered strategic advice. As Edwards said, "He was the person that I looked to, to understand not just the principle, but the price."[25]

Russell attended OPHR meetings, where he described attitudes toward black athletes as exchangeable commodities. He defended boycotters to the press, insisting that "a man should do what he feels is right." He supported the NYAC demonstration because the organization should not profit from discriminated athletes. He also labeled critics such as Jesse Owens and Ralph Boston "do-nothings who wait until something happens, then say the people involved are wrong."[26]

That stance earned the vitriol of Doc Young, a longtime champion of sport's benefits to race relations. Disparaging the "log-sized chip" on Russell's shoulder, the *Chicago Defender* columnist burst with indignation. "You hear this Bill Russell stuff and you wonder: What, specifically, has BILL RUSSELL done that is so great—except play basketball?" Yet Russell eschewed the radical theater of Black Power advocates. Edwards dressed like a Black Panther, smeared his black opponents as "Uncle Toms," and sprinkled "honkies," "pigs," and "crackers" into his public vocabulary. Russell, by contrast, offered thoughtful respect for individual opinions. He stood behind the OPHR, but his coaching position and winning reputation placed him at the center of the black sports world.[27]

On Thursday, April 4, the evening before the Eastern Division finals, Martin Luther King Jr. was assassinated in Memphis, Tennessee. King's evolving vision of social justice had transformed the racial landscape, and his assassination stirred grief, despair, and rage within Black America.[28]

The seven African Americans on the Celtics and the six on the 76ers struggled for an appropriate response. Walter Kennedy let the owners decide upon a possible postponement, despite the NBA's black majority and black superstars. "If the players are upset let them tell the management," shrugged a league official. "It would be different if this were the president." Before flying to Philadelphia, the Celtics called a meeting. Together, they chose to play. The 76ers, by contrast, drifted into the Spectrum as confused, distraught individuals.[29]

"I was in a state of shock all day," said Russell on Friday. "I just sat around for five hours before I could think of anything else." He had not slept. In the late afternoon he called Chamberlain. Both preferred to postpone the game, but they worried that a late cancellation might stir unrest among arriving fans. They called the squads together. Racial wounds burned. "What was his title? Why should we call off the game for him?" asked Bailey Howell, angering those who believed that Dr. King transcended any official title. Then the 76ers held their own closed-door meeting. Seven men voted to play. Chamberlain and Wally Jones voted not to play. Chet Walker abstained—the league had disrespected its black players, general manager Jack Ramsay had crassly invoked contractual obligations, and the late hour made postponement impossible. No one had taken initiative, and this vote was a "dreary charade."[30]

Basketball's greatest rivalry thus resumed under clouds of grief and doubt. The Celtics filed out first, their silence broken by a single bouncing ball. Chamberlain shut his eyes and shook his head before walking through the tunnel. An eerie feeling hung over the contest. The Spectrum had sold out all season, but not tonight. The 76ers never recovered focus. The Celtics divorced national tragedy from professional obligation. Havlicek, Jones, and Howell combined for eighty-seven points, and Boston took a surprise 127–118 victory.[31]

The NBA did postpone the next game, which was scheduled for the national day of mourning on Sunday. That Tuesday, Russell and Chamberlain attended King's funeral in Atlanta. Russell also planned to walk Boston's black districts, part of a NIEU program to prevent urban violence. In recent years, riots had plagued black ghettoes, as poor residents destroyed white-owned property, looted stores, and fought the police. After King's death, these riots started anew—violent, futile cries against persistent poverty, inferior housing, police harassment, and segregated schools.[32]

Once again, Russell balanced liberal and radical impulses. He had wanted the NBA to postpone the first game, but he recognized the dangers of a last-minute decision. He condemned the late postponement of the second game, but he understood that the NBA was the most integrated professional sports league. He considered basketball trivial in such circumstances, but he delivered his utmost effort. And he pointed to the Celtics as a racial metaphor. Satch Sanders and Tom Thacker, he said, had opposite personalities; they nevertheless got lumped together based on skin color. No one, moreover, asked Havlicek about race. "This isn't black and white," Russell insisted. "It's an American problem."[33]

According to Russell, blacks already knew the findings of the Kerner Commission, which implicated the entire nation for urban riots. "Nobody loves the country like the black people do," he said. "It's like the black people are trying to save this country." The government launched space programs and fought wars, but it ignored economic and educational inequities. "Where is the perspective or sense of values?" he cried. "The average black man then figures that going to the moon and Vietnam is more important than me living here. I have to think people are the most valuable resource."

Martin Luther King Jr. had been the "the last buffer" between hope and rage. "Stuff that I said 10 years ago, that everybody dismissed as an angry Negro talking, is coming out today," said Russell. Now everyone realized the depths of black despair, but it was too late. "We are on a collision course," he predicted, a desperate assessment in a desperate time.[34]

. . .

When the series resumed on Wednesday, the Celtics looked overmatched. Philadelphia's bench supplied uncharacteristic point production in a grubby, discombobulated 115–106 win at Boston Garden. The next night at the Spectrum, Hal Greer scored twenty-one points in the fourth quarter, and Philadelphia won again, 122–114. Chamberlain dominated, despite calf and hamstring injuries. Boston got little bench scoring, allowed third-quarter runs, and failed to mount fourth-quarter comebacks.[35]

In the final quarter of the critical fourth game at Boston Garden, Russell assigned Wayne Embry to cover Chamberlain. Russell planned to sag on Luke Jackson and help contain Greer. Jackson promptly sank three straight outside shots. Russell played forty-eight determined minutes, getting twenty-four points and twenty-four rebounds, but after his strategy backfired, Philadelphia never looked back, prevailing 110–105.[36]

"Clean up the place," wrote Clif Keane. "The Celtics have seen the Garden for the last time until October." No team in NBA history had recovered from a 3–1 series deficit. The Celtics defined themselves on defense and poise, but in three losses they allowed 347 points and committed seventy-eight turnovers. Larry Siegfried and Satch Sanders had painful injuries. Talking to Frank Deford before Game Five, Red Auerbach kept referring to Russell in the past tense: "I don't want you to forget, Frank, how good he was."[37]

Russell delivered no pep talks. He reviewed such fundamentals as moving your feet on defense, running offensive plays at full speed, and maintaining concentration. He joked that Don Nelson dreaded leaving Boston for his sleepy hometown of Moline, Illinois. "Just go out there and play the best you can," he concluded. Each veteran had a quiet, determined confidence rooted in past triumphs. Each focused on the immediate circumstances, not the myriad obstacles. And each delivered a complete, gutsy effort in Boston's finest defensive performance of the year. Philadelphia converted only two of twenty shots in one fourth-quarter stretch, and Boston won 122–104. "If there's a team which now may be doubting itself, it's not the Celtics," chortled radio voice Johnny Most.[38]

Boston's democratic culture drove its resurgence. Their mutual trust stanched any leaking confidence. As Russell had urged in preseason, they sought solutions together. Chamberlain hated defending pick-and-rolls, which pulled him away from rebounds. So the next night at Boston Garden, the Celtics kept running their #2 play; Russell set picks on the high post, and Chamberlain hesitated before switching onto the shooter. Harried by this strategy and a spat with the pesky Siegfried, Chamberlain made only six of twenty-one shots, and he accumulated five fouls by the fourth quarter. Now Havlicek urged Russell to attack the basket; Chamberlain compromised his defense out of bizarre pride in never fouling out of a game. Boston triumphed 114–106, tying the series at three.[39]

In two nights, the momentum had flip-flopped. The younger 76ers looked tired. Besides Hal Greer, they shot poorly. They missed Billy Cunningham's energy, and Chamberlain had injuries. If they lost, said Wally Jones, "it'll be a long, hot summer." Meanwhile, the older Celtics defended with frantic enthusiasm. They erased a fifteen-point deficit in five minutes during Game Six. Moreover, Boston had won eight previous Game Sevens—though always in Boston Garden, not before the 15,202 rabid Philadelphians brandishing angry signs: "Boston's old men meet their end tonight!"; "Boston ex-world chumps"; "Boston is dead."[40]

Philadelphia's shooters stayed stone-cold throughout a tight, tense match. In the final minute the 76ers trailed by two. Chet Walker's off-balance flip bounced off the rim—once, twice, three times—before Russell grabbed it. Chamberlain fouled him with thirty-four seconds left. When the exhausted player-coach missed his first free throw, Sam Jones approached him. Observers figured that, during this high-stress circumstance, Jones was inspiring or reassuring Russell. Not exactly. "Flex your knees, Bill," he said. Russell hit the shot, blocked Walker's attempt, and snagged a Greer miss in the closing seconds. Boston won 100–96. Now some plucky Bostonians hoisted their own signs: "Celtics No. 1"; "Celtics Rule Again."[41]

The extraordinary, historic comeback cemented the Russell-Chamberlain dynamic for a new era. Had Philadelphia won, Chamberlain would have been the centerpiece of a new superpower. But his 76ers collapsed in the clutch. He grew frustrated with Wayne Embry's shoving, and he got aggravated at Hannum's pleas to switch while defending pick-and-rolls. Most remarkably, in the second half of Game Seven, Chamberlain took only two shots. True, injuries limited his mobility, and Hannum's strategy dictated that he dish from the perimeter. But at this critical juncture, the greatest scorer in basketball history failed to impose his will.[42]

Meanwhile, Russell's reputation soared into the stratosphere. His scintillating defense drove the comeback. In Game Seven, he blocked ten shots and altered many more. His teammates lauded his shrewd substitutions, poised leadership, and extraordinary character. Columnists admired his play-off record and coaching maturity. He had outplayed Chamberlain and outcoached Hannum. "Supposedly a tired old man near the end of his trail, who has known defeat like other mortals, he had managed to bring his own new team of hustlers and scramblers and even castoffs to the brink of one final great success," wrote Frank Deford. Russell himself called it "my most satisfying victory."[43]

Al Hirshberg of the *Boston Herald-Traveler* had grown disillusioned with Russell's contempt for autographs, fans, and reporters. "I am not a Russell fan—as a man," he wrote. He had not believed that anyone could thrive as player-coach. Nor could someone "be a racist and still handle those of his own and other races effectively." Now, Hirshberg offered an apology. He still mourned Russell's arrogance, but he admired "the heart and the ability and the savvy and the will." Hirshberg compared him to Ted Williams, who had also lived as an individual, unconcerned with public relations.[44]

Boston never worshipped Russell like it did the graceful, humble, and white Bobby Orr of the Bruins. Russell remained the outsider, aloof and haughty. If he refused to lionize athletes, he also refused his own lionization. If people prickled at his political frankness, he paid no mind. "Most players care about projecting the image of the typical athlete," he said. He cared more about living by his convictions.[45]

. . .

On late Saturday night, admirers congratulated Russell as he walked down a corridor in the Spectrum with a tired smile, his arm slumped over his teary-eyed wife. On early Sunday afternoon, a still-exhausted Russell sat on a stool in Boston Garden, preparing for the opener against the Los Angeles Lakers.[46]

The Celtics may have tortured no man like Wilt Chamberlain, but they tormented no team like Los Angeles. In five play-offs, Boston won five times. Yet new coach Butch Van Breda Kolff had replaced a freewheeling style with discipline, fundamentals, and a fluid motion offense. The brash, beer-swilling ex-Marine also infused his team with enthusiasm and camaraderie. Since January 17, the Lakers had gone 38–9, including a play-off sweep of San Francisco. Confident and determined, they cheered for Boston to beat Philadelphia.[47]

The series shifted like a series of fast breaks. The Celtics overcame fatigue and a fifteen-point deficit to win Game One, 107–101. But in Game Two, Jerry West and Elgin Baylor led a third-quarter surge, and Los Angeles won 123–113.[48]

The undulations continued before record crowds of more than seventeen thousand in the brand-new Fabulous Forum. Boston took an eighteen-point lead in

Game Three and then staved off a Baylor hot streak. Russell combined phenomenal defense with twenty-five points, and Boston won, 127–119. The next game was
sloppier. "This is a lousy game," said Auerbach in his new gig as a television com-
mentator. "Both teams are playing lousy." The Celtics stopped running, the Lakers looked off, and Van Breda Kolff got ejected. West and Baylor lent the difference, combining for sixty-eight points to prevail, 118–105.[49]

Back in Boston Garden, the seesawing style spawned a classic match. The Celtics
led by fourteen after one quarter. The Lakers pulled within two by halftime. The
Celtics again surged ahead, crashing for offensive rebounds and improbably riding Don Nelson, who scored a career-high twenty-six points. Boston led by fourteen entering the fourth quarter. Again, Los Angeles fought back. West, despite a
severely sprained ankle, finished with thirty-five points, including a layup that tied
the score at 108 with twelve seconds left. Russell got called for traveling, giving the
Lakers the last shot—but Baylor's corner jump shot caromed away. After trading
baskets through an incredible overtime period, Boston led by two with twenty-four
seconds left. Baylor powered past Nelson. Russell left his man, reached over Nelson's shoulder, and slapped the ball away. One clinching free throw later, Boston
won Game Five, 120–117.[50]

The dramatic victory broke the Lakers' spirit. Two nights later, the Celtics opened
a twenty-point lead and never relented. Even in the final minutes, Russell was making spectacular blocks, and Siegfried was crashing after loose balls. Boston won the
game 124–109, securing its tenth title in twelve years. The triumph reflected John
Havlicek's climb onto the NBA's top rung—the tireless swingman had crested in
the clutch, scoring forty points in the decisive Game Six. It gratified Sam Jones, the
thirty-five-year-old scorer who again peaked for the play-offs. It rewarded Bailey
Howell and Wayne Embry, veterans seeking their first championship. It validated
Larry Siegfried and Don Nelson, scrappy exiles from lesser squads. But it most celebrated Bill Russell: the architect of key strategies and adjustments, the first player-
coach to win a major professional sports title since 1948, and a successful black
leader in an uncertain time. "Suddenly," described one writer, "people were talking about the greatness of Bill Russell again."[51]

Jerry West wore his anguish on his bony face. He pulled off his sweat-soaked
uniform and stood under the shower, trying to wash off the failure. Then he
slouched alone in a corner, his eyes welling with tears. He took each loss personally. He also realized the importance of Russell. If he could pick any player, he said,
he would pick Russell. Wilt Chamberlain had more notoriety, more power, more
talent. But professionals understood, in ways that average fans might not, that Russell willed his team to victory. "Russell has one big thing that Chamberlain doesn't
have," he said. "A winner's pride."[52]

Instead of champagne-soaked pandemonium, a quiet satisfaction imbued the
visitors' locker room. Russell ejected reporters, photographers, friends, and televi-

sion cameramen, ignoring their protests about contracts and deadlines. Then he asked Bailey Howell to lead a prayer. "You pray?" asked his good friend Sam Jones. "Yeah, Sam," he responded. Russell had never before bared any spirituality. But the gesture acknowledged Howell, with whom Russell shared nothing but a common commitment to the Celtics. For the next few minutes, as the outside world waited, the team prayed together.[53]

What else could Russell achieve? "Well, I don't know, because I never had a goal," he explained as reporters spilled back in. "To tell you the truth, it's been a long time since I tried to prove anything to anybody." He quieted for a moment. "*I* know who I am."[54]

. . .

That October at the Mexico City Olympics, Tommie Smith and John Carlos made themselves icons. They accepted gold and bronze medals for the 200-meter dash clad in black socks. Each wore one black glove. During the Star Spangled Banner, they raised their fists in a Black Power salute—signifying, irrevocably and vividly, the Revolt of the Black Athlete.[55]

Few athletes boycotted the Olympics; they had trained for this ultimate event, and most eschewed radical protest. But UCLA stars Lew Alcindor, Mike Warren, and Lucius Allen had declined invitations from the Olympic basketball team. The International Olympic Committee, moreover, had withdrawn South Africa's invitation, bowing to pressure from African nations, the OPHR, and such high-profile athletes as Jackie Robinson, K. C. Jones, Wilt Chamberlain, Arthur Ashe, and Bob Gibson. The new consciousness spread widest on college campuses. At thirty-five different institutions, reported a long *Newsweek* feature, "Negro athletes have stunned coaches and administrators with sweeping demands for change. They want black coaches, black trainers, black cheerleaders—and new black dignity."[56]

In July 1968, *Sports Illustrated* published "The Black Athlete—A Shameful Story." Jack Olsen's five-part series examined this new political awareness. Texas Western College (since renamed University of Texas at El Paso) had won the 1966 NCAA title with an all-black starting five, but those players had not graduated; Olsen reported their lack of academic preparation, resentment of implicit racial codes, and sense of exploitation. Racial divisions had destroyed the St. Louis Cardinals of the NFL. Blacks surged into professional sports, but they lacked leadership positions, on and off the field.[57]

Olsen posited the Celtics as an exception to the rule—"a small squad led by a dynamic, militant black under conditions that hardly would permit internal racism." Russell revealed how sports promoted a level playing field, yet his "anti-white remarks" and "six-figure check" inflamed white racism.[58]

So Russell refracted both optimism and pessimism. In a *New York Times Magazine* article called "Are You Guilty of Murdering Martin Luther King?" Michael

Halberstam wondered if liberals should take pride in Russell's achievements, just as they took shame in racial injustice. In the seven-part CBS special "Of Black America," one episode explained that Russell was the only black coach in professional sports. "His presence in that job has not been a source of comfort to the black community," narrated Harry Reasoner. "He stands out like a lighthouse, signaling tokenism."[59]

Yet Russell never defined himself through liberal satisfaction or radical bluster. While lending unqualified support to the OPHR in lectures and interviews, he warned against black separatism: "As long as you've got black people referring to white people as 'them' and white people referring to black people as 'them,' you've got a problem." He criticized those who chose vengeful harangues over concrete initiatives. He distinguished himself from "the Negro," an obsolete archetype that kowtowed to white standards, but also from "the Superblack," a preening mouthpiece of ignorance and hatred. He defined himself as "a Black"—"a man who is proud of being black and who sees people as they are no matter what their color."[60]

Throughout the tumult of 1968, moreover, Russell participated in distinct strands of political activity. When Boston activists established a "Tent City" in a South End parking lot to protest a lack of affordable public housing, Russell fed them soul food from Slade's. He explored distribution to Africa for New Breed, a black-owned fashion company sponsored by the NIEU. He campaigned for Robert F. Kennedy until the tragic assassination that June. Then he toured Latin America for the Middle American Sports Foundation, which staged goodwill clinics in a traditional cold-war framework. Yet he condemned cold-war struggles in Vietnam, Czechoslovakia, and Nigeria, and he defended the student protests sweeping the world. When USF's Black Student Union invited him to campus, he called for racial understanding. "If we don't, I'll hate you for being condescending, and you'll hate me for being unappreciative." He moved many students to tears.[61]

"Russell is one of the most interesting and significant of all athletes," mused sportswriter Stan Isaacs. "He has become a symbol of black militancy to the black youth, yet he has maintained standing in the white community as something more than a popoff. He has credentials." In one emblematic instance, Russell attended the Olympic track-and-field trials in Los Angeles. Doc Young sneered that despite the warm temperatures, "Bill was wearing some sort of African cape." He sat with Harry Edwards in the cheap seats, which Edwards celebrated as "the poor people's section." During the National Anthem, Edwards sat down. Russell stood up.[62]

Russell's political stature, like his basketball reputation, had its foil in Wilt Chamberlain. The 1968 presidential election deepened the cleavages opened by Vietnam, Black Power, and white backlash. Chamberlain campaigned for Richard Nixon. Chamberlain believed in the Republican's "black capitalism" initiatives, and he identified with Nixon, who also owned a "loser" stigma. Almost all other African Americans had shifted to the Democrats, and many interpreted Nixon's "law-and-order" initiatives as veiled racism. They criticized Chamberlain. "He's made his own pile," said Edwards. "Now he's forgetting the ones who haven't made theirs." Nixon won, but Chamberlain looked like a selfish contrarian.[63]

Russell, by contrast, earned the admiration of the rising generation, both black and white. Tony Kornheiser, the Long Island teenager who had praised Russell in a 1964 letter to *Sports Illustrated,* now marveled at Russell from his dormitory lounge at Binghamton University. Young white intellectuals saw in Russell "an antidote to racial stereotypes." He emitted intelligence, pride, and social consciousness. "Russell was the coolest cat on earth," thought Kornheiser. "The way he handled Chamberlain, it was like he was laughing at him."[64]

For African Americans, Russell was something out of folk legend, both hero and antihero, flouting convention, dismissing white judgments while excelling in the white world. After Nelson George attended a 1968 doubleheader at Madison Square Garden, all the young black man remembered was the determined intensity, cool grace, and champion's pride of Boston's player-coach. "Russell," he thought, "was all a man could hope to be."[65]

15

Grand Old Man

By 1968 George Plimpton had boxed Archie Moore, pitched against the National League All-Stars, and quarterbacked the Detroit Lions. Now *Sports Illustrated* sent him to training camp with the Boston Celtics for another experiment in "participatory journalism." The patrician writer had never played much basketball. When finally allowed into an exhibition against the Atlanta Hawks, he recalled "a certain amount of feckless charging about, usually with my back to the ball in the hope no one would ever throw it to me."[1]

Plimpton never polished his basketball skills, but from the first practice, he glimpsed the austere, straightforward existence of Bill Russell's Celtics. They carried their gear in kit bags to Tobin Gymnasium in Roxbury, looking "like refugees from a rag-pickers convention." They had only one sorry basketball until Russell arrived thirty minutes late, wearing street clothes. Russell looked bored while leading basic drills. He reviewed the same plays from the past two decades. Whenever he seemed unsure what to do, they ran laps. "The Great Bearded One" seemed a distant icon—the essence of basketball, and yet somehow above it.[2]

Instead of publishing this stab at training camp, *Sports Illustrated* ran another Plimpton story. Plimpton described Russell fussing around his house, analyzing his own competitiveness, and teasing his friend Willie Mays. Plimpton also interspersed reminisces from Russell's teammates, painting a man treasured beyond the realm of sports. The story accompanied the magazine's bestowal of its highest honor: "Sportsman of the Year."[3]

"At a time when the host of superb Negro athletes commands esteem for performance," it explained, "Russell has proven his ability to lead athletes of both races—and leadership has been an area of sport inaccessible to black men." *Sports*

Illustrated had been wrestling with race throughout 1968. Although it had run Jack Olsen's groundbreaking series, it remained a magazine with white writers for a white audience. The choice of Russell addressed the nation's racial temper, but it resonated with sports fans. Russell thrived within a racially integrated framework. Unlike Muhammad Ali, he never totally alienated the white mainstream. Yet he expressed black anger and frustration, and as Plimpton's profile reinforced, he forced a public consideration of his intelligence, introspection, and idiosyncrasies.[4]

The honor touched Russell. His basement was full of trophies, but this one, he said, "was my kind of thing." At a Harvard Club reception attended by family, teammates, Red Auerbach, Jim Brown, and Governor John Volpe, Russell explained that most awards recognize athletic accomplishments. This prize meant something more: "You've been a man. We respect you." He spent his career in search of that respect.[5]

· · ·

As Russell won public reverence, his private life contained selfish ambivalence. He had spent the summer in Los Angeles. While he hobnobbed with celebrities at posh nightclubs, his family stayed in Reading. Absent any passion for Rose, his extramarital partners multiplied. By the late 1960s, he recalled, "women seemed to be going by me in a blur." Despite this escape from the NBA's all-consuming male competition, neither sexual affairs nor domestic life satisfied him—even his children seemed like strangers. Though he yearned to trust another with his deepest insecurities, his protective shell hardened. He spent more time in his hotel room. He acted rude to strangers. He mocked reporters' questions. In life, as in basketball, Russell focused on defense.[6]

Russell had gone to Hollywood with an eye on his future. He emulated his friend Jim Brown, who had transitioned from athlete to actor. Russell had already acted on the short-lived ABC series *Cowboy in Africa,* starring Chuck Connors as a rodeo champion working on a Kenyan ranch. In one episode, Russell plays an amiable Kikuyu mechanic. That summer he filmed sundry bit parts. He appeared on the NBC series *I Spy,* which introduced Bill Cosby in a groundbreaking role as an intelligent, resourceful black man. Russell was still learning the ropes: while getting tied up by the villain, his "unconscious" character helpfully moves his legs together. "You weren't supposed to notice that," he chuckled to his teasing teammates.[7]

In July 1968 Russell appeared on the premiere of Hugh Hefner's *Playboy After Dark,* a bizarre mixture of hedonism and social consciousness. Supposedly staged in the Playboy Mansion, the variety show was actually filmed in a Los Angeles studio. "This is a hip, hip pad. This is out of sight," says Russell, clad in a long, electric-blue, velour coat. After listening to Johnny Mathis sing "Feeling Groovy" and Mort Sahl riff on women, Hefner pulls Russell into a book-lined den, where the tone gets serious. They discuss sport and racism. "Athletes are beginning to realize they can't live in two different worlds," Russell intones. Then Mathis ushers them onto a dance floor dotted with women in miniskirts and go-go boots.[8]

After returning to Boston, Russell signed a two-year, $400,000 contract. "It ain't no big thing," he shrugged during a press conference at the Hotel Lenox, while wearing a black mohair suit with three-quarter sleeves, a turtleneck, flared pants, and a gold peace medallion. His straightforward acceptance of such riches reflected the NBA's journey since December 1956, when he joined the all-white Celtics. Now an African American coached the world champions, blacks dominated the league, and Russell even helped make Ken Hudson the first black referee in NBA history.[9]

The league's economic structure had also upended. Phoenix and Milwaukee joined the NBA in 1968. The league now had fourteen teams, with planned expansion to eighteen or twenty teams. New franchises paid $2 million expansion fees. Metropolitan population and television markets dictated financial growth, as evidenced by the migration of the St. Louis Hawks to Atlanta.[10]

The ABA added eleven more franchises to the professional sports landscape. It had sparse crowds, no television contract, and only a few stars (such as the breathtaking Connie Hawkins, whom the NBA had blacklisted after the 1961 gambling scandal). The ABA nevertheless established its own personality with a red-white-and-blue ball, three-point line, and free-flowing playground style of basketball. It also lured Rick Barry, who jumped from the San Francisco Warriors. A court ruling forced the cocksure, high-scoring forward to sit out one season, but when he joined the Oakland Oaks in 1968, the ABA scored a coup.[11]

The ABA also competed for collegians, including underclassmen. It allowed rookies to choose their franchise, enticing them with long-term annuities. NBA players won leverage. The older league moved up its college draft, and even stalwarts like Red Auerbach considered negotiating with agents. Salaries boomed and conditions improved. Superstars such as Oscar Robertson, Nate Thurmond, and Elgin Baylor made more than $100,000 a year, as did hyped youngsters such as Cazzie Russell, Jimmy Walker, and Bill Bradley. In time, players gained severance pay, pension benefits, minimum salaries, and medical insurance.[12]

No player better understood his market value than Wilt Chamberlain. While parlaying his influence, he again altered the NBA's power balance. Alex Hannum had resigned as 76ers coach. Chamberlain grumbled when Frank McGuire, his preferred replacement, declined a return to the Philadelphia bench. So he mused about becoming player-coach, demanded part-ownership of the franchise, and negotiated with the Los Angeles Stars of the ABA. The 76ers allowed Chamberlain to explore trade options. Few Philadelphians objected. Various season-ticket holders considered him lazy, conceited, and arrogant. "He single-handedly lost the championship," said one. "He was too big for the team."[13]

Jack Kent Cooke appreciated big. The forceful, whip-smart mogul got started selling encyclopedias door-to-door in his native Canada. He made a fortune in the radio and magazine industries, acquired a minor league baseball team, moved to the United States, expanded his radio and television holdings, bought the NHL's Los Angeles Kings, and purchased 25 percent of the NFL's Washington Redskins. In 1965 he paid $5.175 million in cash for the Los Angeles Lakers. He then built the Fabulous Forum, an ultramodern arena in the classical tradition. He micromanaged day-to-day operations, fed his gargantuan ego through professional sports, and mass-marketed a product for national consumption.[14]

In July 1968, the modern NBA star and modern NBA owner joined forces. Cooke traded Darrall Imhoff, Archie Clark, and Jerry Chambers for Chamberlain. An elaborate press conference at the Fabulous Forum announced his new five-year, million-dollar contract. Chamberlain had considered an offer from the Seattle Supersonics, but the Lakers offered Hollywood's glittering star power, not to mention Elgin Baylor and Jerry West. Analysts predicted a championship cakewalk. Cooke thought they might go 82–0. "We'll simply have the best team in basketball history," said Chamberlain.[15]

Blending three superstars, however, proved a tricky recipe. The Lakers offense sputtered and grinded. Only sometimes did Chamberlain deign to attack the basket—he scored two points in one game, sixty and sixty-six in two others. He also clogged the lane, hampering Baylor's drives. Egos clashed. Baylor's chatty, teasing personality had long defined the Los Angeles locker room, but now attention gravitated to the sulking, imperious Chamberlain, who still groaned about being a scapegoat. West took neither side. Tension stayed at a high simmer.[16]

The relationship between Chamberlain and Butch Van Breda Kolff was particularly poisonous. The Lakers coach resented that Chamberlain disrupted his free-flowing offense; Chamberlain hated Van Breda Kolff's rabble-rousing style of leadership. Van Breda Kolff wanted Chamberlain passing from the high post; Chamberlain planted in the low post. Van Breda Kolff complained to the *Times;* Chamberlain responded in the *Herald-Examiner.* After one February game, they almost traded blows. This mutual hatred dated to their first meeting, when Van Breda Kolff had urged Chamberlain to block more shots. Chamberlain objected that he blocked more than anyone. "But," said the coach, "I want you to do it like *Russell.*"[17]

Back in Boston, Russell kept the Celtics on an even keel. His coaching had matured. While experimenting more with substitutions, he admitted mistakes. He welcomed Auerbach's help during practice sessions. He rarely screamed or threatened his players, but his strength filtered throughout the team. "If he stays healthy we can win it again," said John Havlicek. "He has so much pride and discipline within himself to be the winner he always has been."[18]

With expansion's dilution of the talent pool, the elite teams had elite centers. Before Russell, no one combined size with such agility. "Once upon a time," mused the *Sporting News,* "before Bill Russell came to Boston fresh from the Olympics, a center who could block shots, clog the middle and race around the court like a deer was unheard of. Centers grabbed some rebounds, threw in some hook shots from the pivot, handed off from the high post and lumbered down court. Unheard of also was a Negro coach in the major leagues. Russell changed everything."[19]

Now there was Chamberlain, Nate Thurmond, and Willis Reed. Wes Unseld transformed the hapless Baltimore Bullets into Eastern Division champions, and fellow rookie Elvin Hayes averaged twenty-eight points and seventeen rebounds for the San Diego Rockets. Russell was the grand old man; Hayes had obsessed about facing Russell since his childhood in Rayville, Louisiana. Russell now weighed too much, balanced coaching responsibilities, and appeared constantly fatigued. Chamberlain had won the past three MVP awards, and Unseld won the next one. Still, an anonymous poll of coaches ranked Russell the best. For one game, especially, coaches valued him above all others.[20]

Over eighty-two games, though, age caught up with Russell's Celtics. Their top eight players averaged thirty-one years. Despite an 11–3 start, they fell behind in a four-way race with Baltimore, Philadelphia, and New York. They lacked a genuine playmaker, and backup center Wayne Embry left in the expansion draft. Sam Jones missed six weeks with a groin pull, forcing Russell to start Havlicek. The erstwhile Sixth Man also endured a shooting slump. The players professed confidence, but they kept losing ground.[21]

On February 2, 1969, Russell suffered his worst injury ever. In the closing seconds of their third game in three days, the Celtics trailed the Knicks by three. Russell converted an alley-oop dunk, but he lost his balance while rolling on the back of Willis Reed, who had turned to avoid fouling. Russell landed on his right knee. He writhed on the floor. The trainer wrapped his knee in cold towels, and Russell left on a stretcher. As he lay on a training table, he entered a state of shock. He fought off tears, and he refused to let people touch him. Finally some medication calmed him down. On the drive to University Hospital, he buried his face in his hands, wincing with pain and shivering under blankets.[22]

Russell had not just hurt his knee. He was absolutely exhausted. For weeks he had suffered a heavy cold, and his two jobs had worn his nerves. The team doctor banned telephones from his hospital room. Russell slept and slept, long and deep. Despite initial fears of a career-ending injury, his acute ligament sprain needed only about ten days of rest. Unfortunately, the Celtics dropped four games in his absence, entrenching them in fourth place. Boston reversed the losing streak only upon Russell's return. Russell, dragging his braced knee, extended a game against Philadelphia to overtime on the same alley-oop play that had caused his injury. Thirteen years after his professional debut, basketball still offered extraordinary trials and rewards.[23]

Yet basketball no longer inspired Russell with wonder, possibility, and magic. One month after his return, in the final seconds of a tie game against Baltimore, Boston stole the ball and called time-out. Russell burst into the huddle, pumped with adrenaline. Then he started laughing. He chuckled. He chortled. He all-out cackled. The players gaped while Russell wiped his eyes. He was a grown man of thirty-five years, clad in a tank top and tiny shorts, and everyone in the arena was screaming for blood, including him. All of a sudden, it seemed ridiculous. His team-mates failed to appreciate his insight. In fact, Boston threw away the ball, and Baltimore won. "If I couldn't be serious at a time like that," Russell thought, "it was time to quit."[24]

. . .

Sam Jones had already announced his retirement. The league's oldest player had achieved fifteen thousand points and nine titles without recognition as a superstar. Unlike top guns such as Jerry West or Oscar Robertson, Jones never wanted the pressure of dominating every game. Instead, the straight-faced, sweet-tempered guard reserved something extra for big moments, especially in the play-offs. "Sam never had a bad clutch game," contended Russell. The Celtics gave him a moving tribute at season's end. Russell vowed that Jones would depart with one last championship.[25]

Their friendship had survived Russell's vault into coaching. Russell gave Jones freedom. Once, he asked Jones to call the plays; "I don't have the authority," Jones insisted. Russell gave him that very authority, but out of respect and trust, he accepted such quirks. Jones, in turn, gave Russell unconditional esteem. When Jones hurt his groin and Boston slumped, Russell never pushed him to return, even though the injury became more psychological than physical. Then, thirty minutes before one January game, Russell instructed him to get dressed. "I didn't say no more," Jones recalled. "He's the coach. I do what he tells me." Jones scored twenty points, including the game-winner, and the Celtics salvaged a critical weapon.[26]

As Jones recovered form, Russell made adjustments. John Havlicek bumped Satch Sanders as starting forward, allowing Havlicek to race past bigger defenders for easy baskets. Russell also started Emmette Bryant over Larry Siegfried, whose hustle and sharpshooting made him an ideal Sixth Man. Bryant supplied scrambling, ball-hawking defense. The high school dropout from Chicago had served in the air force, attended DePaul, and spent four seasons with the New York Knicks. He planned to retire when Phoenix picked him in the expansion draft. Then, Red Auerbach traded for him. Like Willie Naulls or Wayne Embry before him, Bryant valued Boston's unselfish, competitive ethic. He also found a patron in Russell: both liked flashy clothes, and they shared political sympathies as members of the Black Economic Union.[27]

But Bryant's late-season injection as point guard occurred with the team locked into fourth place in the Eastern Division. "Celtic Reign Now History," announced one headline. "Mighty Celtics Yielding to Old Father Time," declared another. After a mid-March 108–73 thrashing at home against Los Angeles, Boston lost twenty-one of thirty-seven games. Russell ripped his team in a frustrated, furious, closed-door session. The embarrassing rout finally spurred some crisp passes, sturdy screens, good shots, and tough defense. The Celtics averaged 121 points a game in their final four contests, all victories, but they finished 48–34, the lowest winning percentage of the Russell era.[28]

Few believed that the Celtics could win three series as underdogs. They opened against second-place Philadelphia, which had flourished in Wilt Chamberlain's absence. Jack Ramsay's fluid offense of cuts, screens, and drives opened one-on-one opportunities for Chet Walker and Billy Cunningham. Hal Greer remained a great shooting guard, and Darrell Imhoff had thrived in the pivot. The 76ers won seven more games than the Celtics, and they again owned home-court advantage.[29]

But in the play-offs, some cagey professionals summoned the ghosts of Celtics Past. Spurred by feverish defense and dedicated rebounding, Boston's fast break clicked throughout the 114–100 opening victory. Boston then won at home, 134–103, and held off a late rally to win on the road, 125–118. Russell embodied the team's new focus. In the first game he recorded twelve blocks, fifteen rebounds, and eight assists. He controlled the boards, whipped outlet passes, and sprinted up court. After coasting through the last few months, Russell was embracing one final challenge. "It was obvious he wasn't capable of playing as consistently outstanding ball as he had in the past," reflected Havlicek. "He might have been thinking that this was his last chance."[30]

Although the 76ers sidestepped a sweep by winning the fourth game, 119–116, the defending champions closed out the series with a third triumph at the Spectrum, 93–90. Defense charged the upset. Greer averaged only fifteen points on 32 percent shooting, and Boston's offense thrived in transition. "Philly is dead!" yelped Bryant. "Cool it," advised Havlicek. Bigger challenges loomed.[31]

The New York Knicks had swept the first-place Baltimore Bullets in the other semifinal, stirring hope in basketball's Mecca. After decades of apathetic management, the franchise had reversed its fortunes. They had become entertaining, charismatic media darlings. A modern new Madison Square Garden opened in February 1968. Coach Red Holzman installed a new discipline, as well as a trapping defense and patterned offense. In December 1968, the Knicks traded Walt Bellamy for tough, versatile forward Dave DeBusschere. Willis Reed now occupied his natural position at center. The spectacular Walt Frazier teamed in the backcourt with sharpshooter Dick Barnett. The skilled forward Bill Bradley glued these talents together into a cohesive whole.[32]

Bradley had entered the NBA in 1967, a "great white hope" after a celebrated career at Princeton and a stint at Oxford. Upon meeting Bradley, Russell interrogated him on the "black history" of Cecil Rhodes. "I knew what he was saying," recalled Bradley. "He was talking about taking a Rhodes scholarship from a racist diamond miner." Despite entering professional basketball from disparate circumstances, Russell and Bradley were the game's two great intellects. Bradley grew fascinated with Russell's defensive artistry, psychological tricks, and compulsion to validate himself through victory.[33]

The Knicks won six of their seven regular season contests, but like the 76ers, they learned that that the Celtics recharged for the play-offs. The Celtics won the opener, 108–100. By refusing to collapse on Frazier's dribble drives, the defense limited Bradley and DeBusschere, and Havlicek and Jones kept countering the Knicks' surges. Then, at Boston Garden, the Celtics denied a single basket for six and a half minutes and never looked back, winning 112–97. "Russell emasculated the Knicks," wrote Stan Isaacs. While surprising Reed with offensive aggressiveness, Russell flustered all the New York shooters into high-arcing, off-target stabs.[34]

Once in awe of the Celtics, the Knicks had since grown overconfident. They finally found their bearings in Madison Square Garden, gaining a taut 101–91 win. Back at Boston Garden, they had a tight, hard-hitting, back-and-forth contest. Russell maintained his energetic renaissance, Reed battled in the pivot, Frazier juked his way into the lane, Havlicek motored at top speed, DeBusschere wrestled down rebounds, Bryant flourished as a floor leader, and Nelson and Siegfried lent X-factors off the bench. In the closing seconds Boston led by a point, and Frazier challenged Havlicek one-on-one. Havlicek held his ground through fakes and cuts and spins, forcing a dish to Reed, who got blocked by Russell. After a scrum, Boston gained possession and won 97–96.[35]

That victory proved critical, because once the Knicks recovered form, they looked unstoppable before the massive, screaming crowds in New York. Boston never stood a chance in the fifth game, falling behind by twenty-four before losing 112–104. Dreading a return to Madison Square Garden, the Celtics needed a win in Boston.[36]

They won with trademark poise, as well as a fat dollop of luck. Sam Jones had struggled, averaging 11.6 points on 32 percent shooting. But at the end of Game Five, Walt Frazier hurt his groin. So Russell turned to his great old friend for Game Six, instructing Jones to attack the limping Frazier, often using Russell's high-post picks. Jones led all Celtics with twenty-nine points. It was Havlicek, though, who sealed the game. With Boston clinging to a two-point lead with thirty-nine seconds left and the shot clock expiring, he dribbled away from the basket, left of the free throw line, and heaved an awkward shot, hoping only for a rebound. It rattled in. After a quick Reed basket, Havlicek again controlled the ball. He milked the shot clock before driving to the left baseline and popping in the clinching hoop. Boston won the game, 106–105, and the series, four games to two.[37]

New York's glittering young talent looked forward; Boston's veterans hearkened their glorious past. The memory of old triumphs shaped the Celtics' passion, concentration, and execution. One last series would be haunted by history. Six times, Russell had vanquished Wilt Chamberlain in the play-offs. Six times, the Celtics had conquered the Los Angeles Lakers for the NBA championship. The 1969 finals reunited all these ghosts. Russell had extended his career to an improbable, stirring coda.[38]

. . .

If the past buttressed Russell, it weighed heavy on Chamberlain. "Except for this break or that, I could be a member of six or seven world championship teams," lamented the Lakers' star. He still rejected the notion of a personal rivalry with Russell. He cited his statistical superiority, and he ascribed Boston's ten titles to overall talent and lucky twists. But Los Angeles entered these finals as 9–5 favorites. Chamberlain had thrived in play-off triumphs against San Francisco and Atlanta, and the Lakers finally owned a center to negate Russell. "If we don't beat the Celtics this time," said Jerry West, "it will be a crime for the game of basketball."[39]

West had become basketball's tragic hero. The spare, skinny guard had overcome countless broken noses, twisted ankles, and pulled hamstrings to make himself the sport's greatest shooter, yet Russell's Celtics always snatched his most coveted prize. Instead of rationalizing failures, he bared his agony. Reporters admired his relentless passion, clutch performances, and soft-spoken confidence. Part of his "boy-next-door" image stemmed from his white skin, but West's drive, toughness, and talent commanded universal respect.[40]

In the first two games, the Lakers strode toward redemption. First came a high-speed, quick-shooting scramble with fourteen ties and twenty-seven lead changes; West scored fifty-three points, including seventeen in the nip-and-tuck final quarter, and the Lakers won 120–118. West scored forty-one more in another Lakers triumph, 118–112. Injuries had hampered Baylor throughout a mediocre play-off campaign, but he clinched the second game by scoring the Lakers' last twelve points. Chamberlain, meanwhile, occupied Russell's attention, freeing space for his teammates. Record crowds packed the Fabulous Forum, and the Los Angeles locker room was finally loose and jovial. "Things haven't been that bad at all lately," said Van Breda Kolff.[41]

The Celtics had never lost the first two games of the final series, yet no one moped or raged. After the second defeat, Russell gathered them together. Though he neutralized Chamberlain, his team defense suffered. He now accepted a heavier burden. He insisted, moreover, that they would prevail. "He had a kind of courage and toughness that filtered down across the team almost by osmosis," said Havlicek. "He was a winner himself and he didn't want anything to do with other people who weren't the same way." If Russell had confidence in them, they had confidence in themselves.[42]

Returning to Boston Garden, the Celtics denied the Lakers a single field goal for the first 3:39. Boston led 57–40 by halftime. The Lakers staged a furious third-quarter rally, tying the score at seventy-eight, but it exhausted them. The Celtics recovered defensive intensity and revived their running game. Russell's picks freed Havlicek and Siegfried for midrange jumpers, and the Ohio State alumni combined for sixty-two points. Hamstring, hip pointer, and elbow injuries had almost prevented Siegfried from playing, but his accurate shooting and scrappy defense boosted Boston in a necessary, 111–105 triumph.[43]

Boston then evened the series, thanks once again to poise, luck, and mutual trust. The game itself was an aesthetic calamity: despite an up-and-down pace, the point total was the lowest in a play-off since 1958. Boston shot 31 percent. The teams combined for fifty turnovers. West scored forty of the Lakers' eighty-eight points. With fifteen seconds left, Los Angeles had the ball and a one-point advantage. Neither team had scored in the last 4:05. A simple inbounds would send the Lakers home with a 3–1 lead. But a double team swarmed Johnny Egan, and Emmette Bryant knocked the ball to Sam Jones. He missed a jump shot, but Chamberlain could not hold the rebound. Baylor stepped out of bounds with the ball, restoring possession to Boston with seven seconds left.[44]

Weeks earlier, during the New York series, the Celtics had installed a last-second play. Neither Auerbach nor Russell had ever employed one, but that season they lost seventeen games by three or fewer points. So while Russell was late for practice, Havlicek introduced an elaborate triple-screen from his Ohio State days. Using this play, he and Siegfried had each scored buzzer-beaters in college. Russell accepted this modification of tradition, but not before drilling the play for hours, shaving seconds off its execution.[45]

Now that practice bore fruit. Each Celtic had mastered his role. Bryant inbounded to Havlicek and sprinted left of the key. Don Nelson and Bailey Howell rushed to either side of Bryant. Havlicek passed to Jones, who cut right, past this wall of teammates. His defender bounced into Howell, but Jones slipped while catching the pass. Leaning off-balance on his left foot, he lofted a parabola over Chamberlain's outstretched fingertips. "I thought to shoot it with high arc and plenty of backspin," he said afterward, "so if it didn't go in Russell would have a chance for the rebound." Only then did Jones learn that Russell had taken himself out. After inserting Nelson as an extra shooter, Russell cursed the shot from the sideline. It looked short.[46]

It hit the front rim. It hit the back rim. It bounced in.

While Jones looked stunned, the other Celtics exulted, and fans rushed the court. The referees restored order because one second remained on the clock, but when West aimed a long lob for Chamberlain, Satch Sanders tipped it away, and Boston triumphed 89–88. The remarkable finish devastated the Lakers. Chamberlain had grimaced and slammed the basket support after Jones scored, and after the final horn he paced the court, silently shaking his head. Twenty minutes later, all he could mutter was "unbelievable, unbelievable." West uncharacteristically sprayed profanity and moaned that "we must have a bunch of losers on this team."

Other Lakers cursed that Egan got fouled, that Baylor stayed inbounds, that the Celtics were lucky.[47]

Yes, the Celtics were lucky. How might basketball history have looked if Bob Pettit converted that full-court, off-the-backboard pass in double overtime of the deciding game of the 1957 finals? What if Frank Selvy hit that last-second shot in 1962? How about in 1965, when "Havlicek stole the ball"? What if the Lakers completed their comeback in 1966, or the 76ers exploited their 3–1 series advantage in 1968? The Celtics were lucky, but they created their luck. Their relentless effort forced the opposition's mistakes, and their tradition fostered composure in tight situations. On the Celtics, ruminated Howell, "you expect things to happen that make it possible for you to win."[48]

Boston squandered momentum, however, in its return to the Fabulous Forum. "Russell had one of the worst games of his career and just couldn't contend with Chamberlain," reported Will McDonough. Russell looked listless, allowing open shots and getting in foul trouble. Chamberlain outrebounded him, 31–13. West scored thirty-nine points, and Los Angeles won 117–104—but at a cost. With 2:20 left, West pulled his left hamstring. He limped off the floor.[49]

West hobbled on a bandaged leg through Game Six at Boston Garden. Though he managed twenty-six points, his teammates made few adjustments. Baylor's aching knees sapped his old explosiveness, and Chamberlain scored only eight points. "We got the ball into him at times," complained Van Breda Kolff about his center, "but he didn't do anything with it." Behind twenty-five points from old Lakers castoff Don Nelson, the Celtics held onto a 99–90 win. Before the game, the crowd had showered Sam Jones with an eighty-five-second ovation, and as his eyes got moist, he stared at the ten championship banners hanging from the rafters. "Please," he thought, "can't we just have one more?" Thanks to the Lakers' irresolution and the Celtics' tenacity, that dream stayed alive.[50]

Now basketball's titans each confronted questions. Could Chamberlain pick up the scoring slack for West? Chamberlain had dominated Russell in Los Angeles, but his passivity cost a potential clincher in Boston. Van Breda Kolff announced that in Game Seven, the Lakers would feed Chamberlain. Could Russell once more negate his colossal rival? He had offered only silence after his ineffectual Game Five, but he looked spry in Game Six, powering the team defense. Afterward, someone repeated an opinion from Chamberlain. "Who cares what Wilt says?" Russell snapped. "That's all I've heard over and over through the years—'Wilt this and Wilt that.' I don't give a damn what Wilt has to say." After a decade of praising Chamberlain, Russell steeled himself for one final collision.[51]

Boston had never lost a Game Seven, but the home team had won every game in this series. Los Angeles was a three-point favorite for the Fabulous Forum finale. It was the one hundredth game of the year. Larry Siegfried sat in a whirlpool, trying to loosen his injury-ravaged body while talking to Russell. "He said that this was it, that he just didn't think he could get up for the big games anymore," recalled Siegfried.[52]

Sam Jones entered the locker room holding a memo circulated by Jack Kent Cooke, detailing the Lakers' championship celebration: first the University of Southern California marching band would play "Happy Days Are Here Again," then balloons would fall from the rafters, and then Chick Hearn would interview Baylor, Chamberlain, and West. Russell read the memo to his team. He also offered his typical matter-of-fact reminders to keep grinding on defense and running on offense. "I don't care what happens," he added, his sentiment stirred by swirling emotions, "I wouldn't trade you guys for any guys in the world."[53]

The Celtics then delivered the type of unselfish, scrambling, opportunistic basketball that had characterized the Russell era. Boston opened an early lead by forcing a quick pace. Russell acted as the offense's hub, setting picks and dishing passes, while Havlicek, Jones, and Bryant shot with accuracy. When Russell got his third foul early in the second quarter, the Lakers started fighting back. West and Chamberlain combined for thirty-five first-half points. Los Angeles finally tied the score, 60–60, two minutes into the third quarter. At that point, Don Nelson got hot, scoring thirteen third-quarter points. Meanwhile, the Lakers got collectively cold, misfiring fifteen straight times. Heading into the fourth quarter, the Celtics opened a 91–76 lead.[54]

Los Angeles chipped away in the fourth quarter. Russell picked up his fifth foul. Sam Jones fouled out with 7:05 left, claiming twenty-four points in his swan song. Los Angeles again turned to the brilliant West, who gutted through his injury by scoring on jumpers, drives, and free throws. Now the Celtics got cold. Boston still led 101–94, however, when Chamberlain leaped for a rebound and banged his knee. The clock stopped at 5:32. Chamberlain stood by his basket, rubbing the injury. He limped off the court, and the trainer sprayed local anesthetic on his knee. After a minute, Chamberlain signaled that he could return.[55]

Van Breda Kolff ignored him. Substitute Mel Counts stayed out of the low post, freeing space for perimeter scorers, further driving the Los Angeles comeback. West hit two free throws. The Celtics missed. West scored a basket. The Celtics missed. West hit two more free throws. He had forty-two points, and Boston led only 103–100. "Suddenly we couldn't make a shot and we couldn't stop them on defense," said Nelson. "The clock was taking an eternity." When Counts sank a foul-line jumper, Boston's lead dwindled to one point. The Fabulous Forum echoed with roars.[56]

Again, Chamberlain relayed that he was ready. "We don't need you," said Van Breda Kolff. The fiery, bullheaded coach operated on his own terms, consequences be damned. Chamberlain tossed his hands in the air and stalked away. West kept peeking at the sideline, wondering when Chamberlain would return. Jack Kent Cooke stormed down to the bench, demanding his star center's insertion; Van Breda

Kolff cussed him out. The score was stuck at 103–102, but the Lakers had momentum, and the Celtics were fumbling through a succession of missed shots, offensive fouls, and shoddy passes. With fewer than ninety seconds left, Havlicek tried a fumbling drive into the lane, but Keith Erickson tipped it away. Instead of racing back downcourt, however, the Celtics caught another lucky break. The ball caromed to Don Nelson. With the shot clock winding down, he pushed a hasty line drive off the heel of his hand.[57]

It hit the back rim. It popped up. It swished in.

"What can I say?" laughed Nelson. "It was a lucky shot—the luckiest shot of my life." The auspicious bounce stanched the Lakers' comeback. With forty-six seconds left, the ball swung to Counts, who drove past Russell, under the basket. But his nervous shot fell short. For two years Counts had backed up Russell on the Celtics, and for another three he had faced Russell. As he later realized, he missed not because Russell would have blocked his shot, but because he *feared* that Russell would block it. Russell snatched the ball, and Siegfried and Havlicek iced the game with free throws. After some meaningless points by Los Angeles, the horn sounded on Boston's 108–106 victory.[58]

Twelve years earlier, when the Celtics won their first championship, the rookie Russell had jumped for joy, landing in the arms of a friend. Eleven titles later, he walked off the floor with a satisfied half-smile, a regal grace—a champion's pride.[59]

. . .

"What are they gonna do with all those balloons now?" crowed Auerbach. The Lakers could hear the celebration in the adjacent locker room, but they could barely believe it. Five cases of champagne sat unopened. Baylor judged it the most painful loss ever, given the home crowd and expectations. West looked like a ghost. Tom Hawkins blamed the accommodation of three superstars, which had marginalized the role players: "We had the talent, but not the team. We had a few players who didn't think they could win."[60]

Chamberlain's reputation sank to its nadir. In the second half of the final game, he failed to exploit Russell's foul trouble. He missed forty-one of sixty-five free throws in the series, including nine of thirteen in Game Seven. Worst of all, his rift with Van Breda Kolff had spilled onto the floor of the Fabulous Forum. Now Chamberlain roasted his coach in the newspapers. Van Breda Kolff left the Lakers for the Detroit Pistons. Following the previous year's collapse and this year's fiasco, Chamberlain got stuck with all his old tags: coach-killer, villain, loser. At a press conference for winning the play-off MVP, West had to stand up for Chamberlain. "Bill Russell's teammates defend world championships," snickered one writer. "Wilt Chamberlain's teammates defend Wilt Chamberlain."[61]

The Russell-Chamberlain contrast had never glared so brightly. Even West admitted the paradox: Chamberlain was better at scoring, rebounding, and blocking shots, but for one game West would choose Russell. "I can't think of any guy in any sport at any time that has dominated the game the way that Russell has," he said. "I think the players in the league respect him the most of any player." While Chamberlain followed a joyless quest for recognition of individual greatness, Russell enshrined his mythology as the intellectual athlete, savvy leader, and clutch winner. In his 1,182 NBA games, the Celtics won 824 times. In fourteen winner-take-all championship games in college, the Olympics, and the NBA, Russell's team won every time.[62]

The indispensable element of this dynasty had showed character, courage, and humanity. Jerry Nason of the *Boston Globe* described the Celtic mystique: "All it is, and ever has been, is white guys and black guys harmonizing, sharing a common pride." When Russell accepted the coaching position, he assumed a historic burden. His success broadened Boston's legacy. "Suddenly," Nason wrote, "the Celtics story is bigger than the sports page."[63]

If the press resorted to cliché, the *Baltimore Afro-American* maintained that Russell "made the hated cliché permissible," waxing that "basketball has never seen his equal in the past, and may not ever in the future." The *New York Times* celebrated Boston's embodiment of "the true athletic virtues—determination, unflagging effort and alertness, absolutely unselfish teamwork, applied intelligence, mechanical skill and poise maintained under the greatest emotional pressure." Boston columnists sentimentally reflected on Walter Brown's legacy, the Celtics' winning tradition, and Russell's leadership. An enthusiastic crowd welcomed the team home at Logan Airport, and Mayor Kevin White announced a celebratory parade.[64]

Russell skipped the motorcade through downtown Boston and the ceremony at City Hall. Most Bostonians ignored the Celtics until every spring, when yet another title ignited civic pride and political pomp. Russell had long resisted the trappings of hero worship. He instead drew strength from victory, respect, and the safety of the team unit. "We see each other as men," he wrote in the final installment of a play-off diary for the *Boston Globe*. "We judge a guy by his character." Through his courageous iconoclasm, he had demanded the same of the public.[65]

After Game Seven, in a mostly empty locker room, Leigh Montville had approached Russell. Fellow *Boston Globe* reporter Will McDonough suspected that Russell had played his last game, but Russell hated McDonough—the conspiratorial, opinionated Irishman from Southie personified Russell's resentments about Boston. So McDonough sent his twenty-five-year-old colleague, the self-described "red-headed kid with freckles, the whitest guy in America." Russell was getting congratulated by Jim Brown, another of sport's most accomplished and intimidating black men. Montville stuttered out a question about possible retirement. "Retire!" bellowed Brown. "The man just won the world championship! What are you talking about, retire?" Russell said nothing substantial. Montville slinked away.[66]

Russell pulled on a lavender shirt and tan suit. He had a beat-up suitcase in one hand, a bottle of champagne in the other. He said goodbye to trainer Joe DeLauri, who was picking up the last stray towels and sweat socks. Russell started to leave, then paused and wheeled back. He shook DeLauri's hand. "Joe," he said. "I've just played my last game." DeLauri told no one, and no one else heard. Russell left. As he walked up the stairs, an usher stepped in front of him. She pushed a pencil and paper in his face. "You've refused all these years," she said. "How about signing this now, just this once?"

Russell kept walking.[67]

16

Color Man

Soon after the 1969 title, Russell walked into Auerbach's office. "Red, I've had enough," he said. "I'm going to hang 'em up." Hoping that his star might reconsider, Auerbach convinced Russell to postpone any decision. So Russell drove to Los Angeles with his official status in limbo. He stayed with Jim Brown, visited the *Mike Douglas Show,* and stayed mum on his future. On June 13, the *Boston Herald-Traveler* reported that Russell was abandoning basketball for Hollywood, citing an anonymous friend from a late-night card game. Auerbach denied it. Russell had promised that if he retired, he would first inform the Celtics, by telephone and in writing.[1]

Six weeks later, Russell announced his retirement in *Sports Illustrated.* "There are professionals and there are mercenaries in sports," he wrote. "The difference between them is that the professional is involved." And as the article's title stated, "I'm Not Involved Anymore." He loved the challenges, the championships, and the cooperative culture of the Celtics. But he no longer poured his soul into basketball—the endless shots, screens, and rebounds now elicited déjà vu. Nor could he just coach. He identified with players, not coaches. So he bid goodbye to the NBA.[2]

Russell retired in print because he hated the pomp of a press conference, and he appreciated an unfiltered explanation of his motives. Plus, *Sports Illustrated* paid him $25,000. "Now you can make another $25,000 by writing, 'Why I Changed My Mind,'" implored Auerbach. Even after acquiring center Henry Finkel and hiring Tom Heinsohn to coach, Auerbach welcomed Russell's return. "As far as I'm concerned, Bill Russell will be retired only if he does not show up on the first day of training camp," he said.[3]

Russell had at least 200,000 reasons to play. His contract cushioned various financial blows. Always careless with money, he burned bridges in Boston over business deals and debts. In 1967 the IRS threatened to imprison him for owed taxes. He had mismanaged Slade's; he pulled spending money out of the cash register, and his employees followed suit. He lost $60,000 upon selling the restaurant in 1968, and the Small Business Administration later pursued an unpaid portion of his $90,000 loan. He had also invested more than $250,000 in his failing plantation in Liberia. His trees, planted in 1960, needed about seven years to yield natural liquid rubber. Since then, the industry had perfected the process for synthetic rubber. In 1973 the IRS placed a lien on Russell's home in Reading, claiming $34,430 in back taxes.[4]

Russell nevertheless discarded his lucrative contract. "I don't care about money," he shrugged. "It's the easiest thing in the world to make money." That phlegmatic proclamation captured his unique image upon retirement. He rendered himself distinct from the crassness, banality, and overindulgence creeping into commercialized sports, yet he dove into the maw of American celebrity culture, reaping its rewards.[5]

. . .

When Russell left Boston, he sought freedom. He packed one suitcase into his Lamborghini. He rented a small, furnished apartment on Wilshire Boulevard. He wore sneakers or sandals, jeans or shorts, ratty shirts and dark glasses. He walked down the street, and no one asked for autographs. He dabbled with vegetarianism, though his self-discipline occasionally cracked and he gobbled down four steaks. Other athletes considered retirement a type of death, but not Russell. He defined himself beyond sports, and the NBA involved fetters of competition, contracts, and public expectations. After the 1969 title, he never again played a proper, five-on-five game of basketball.[6]

This personal liberty, however, entailed leaving his children in Reading. His justification was self-serving: "I consider it the best thing I can do to let them grow up without interference from me. It is very difficult to be the children of a famous person." Yet his separation compelled a better sense of parental responsibility. In 1970, he started spending summers with thirteen-year-old Buddha, eleven-year-old Jacob, and eight-year-old Karen Kenyatta. They took long road trips to the Grand Canyon, the Pacific Northwest, and Canada. In 1972 they went to the Olympics in Munich, Germany. Answering their questions, negotiating their disputes, and cultivating their identities posed new challenges for a man accustomed to following his own path.[7]

His marriage's last flimsy threads disintegrated. Rose filed for divorce in December 1972, citing "cruel and abusive treatment" in their September 1973 settlement. Bill now had more substantial affairs. His NBA schedule meant that previous mistresses neither received nor expected commitment. In Los Angeles, new complications arose. Different women pulled at his heartstrings, and sometimes his affections went unrequited. He dreaded breaking up with women—in the past, he had just escaped. He loved one woman named Mary, but his self-absorbed insistence on personal liberty thwarted any lasting bond. His children, resenting any replacement for Rose, undermined various other girlfriends.[8]

Arriving in Hollywood amidst a sexual revolution, Russell pushed his own boundaries. Unlike Wilt Chamberlain or Jim Brown, he never possessed a "stud" reputation. But Los Angeles contained exclusive nightclubs, aspiring actresses, and hedonistic adventurers. Once he walked into Brown's house and saw writer James Toback having sex with an actress on the couch. Russell's eyes bugged out. Then Brown regaled him with his own tales of multiple sex partners. Russell was shocked, yet intrigued. A while later he called Brown, hesitating to reveal his news. "Jim," he finally said, "I did it. I had two girls with me. I like it!"[9]

Russell considered Brown among his few genuine friends. Russell believed that friendship involved prodigious attention and responsibility, to be conferred only alongside unconditional trust. Whether discussing politics, movies, or women, they valued each other's opinions. They rode motorcycles together. They sampled Hollywood nightlife and considered Hollywood projects. Mostly, they played golf. After Brown beat him with just one club, Russell got obsessed, playing every day. Brown still spotted him strokes, but golf fed their competitive streaks. Toback marveled at their mutual "devotion to success in games and struggle," their "religious identity of good with it." Without such "single-minded ferocity," he presumed, neither would have influenced sport and society.[10]

While driving Russell home in August 1969, Brown had a minor traffic accident. Four days later, he got arrested. He had a history with the Los Angeles police department—in June 1968, his girlfriend either fell or got tossed off a twenty-foot balcony. Prosecutors dropped charges then, but now, a man named Arthur Brush accused Brown of banging his car and tossing him off a hood. Police declined to interview Russell (the sole witness) and never examined any evidence. To the press, Russell condemned this abuse of authority. In fact, the combative Brush had initiated the accident and jumped onto Brown's hood. A jury threw out the criminal case. Remembering his own run-ins with gratuitously suspicious policemen, Russell despised the authorities' resentment of proud, outspoken black men in the limelight.[11]

In response to the botched frame-up, a coalition of athletes and actors arranged a golf tournament honoring Brown, with proceeds benefiting the Black Economic Union. In other ways, too, Russell applied his celebrity to social gain: appearing at charity sporting events, speaking at the National Youth Development Conference, serving on a committee to designate a national holiday for Martin Luther King Jr. In 1971 Russell returned to Mississippi, again at the behest of Charles Evers. During Freedom Summer, Russell had witnessed harrowing racial intimidation. Now

Evers was mayor of Fayette and running for governor, representing both black and poor white voters. As Russell's visit generated press, a *Jackson Daily News* columnist moaned that Evers "is receiving more enduring free campaign propaganda than any white candidate could dream to obtain."[12]

Russell also supported Jesse Jackson and Operation PUSH (People United to Save Humanity). Russell attended the founding meeting in 1971, after Jackson's break with SCLC. PUSH employed direct-action tactics to foster economic opportunity in various realms, including sports; a 1973 conference in Chicago examined racial disparities in pay, media coverage, and front-office positions. By then Russell was a vice chairman of the board of operation, replacing Jackie Robinson, who died of a heart attack in 1972.[13]

Russell served as a pallbearer at Robinson's funeral, the only one besides former Brooklyn Dodgers. They had long admired each other's intelligence and courage. Robinson's widow Rachel told him that he had been Jackie's favorite athlete. Russell was an heir, of sorts. The baseball legend had once proclaimed that sports needed "men of integrity" like Russell, men "who are involved in the area of civil rights and who are not willing to sit back and let Mr. Charlie dictate their needs and wants for them or spread the message for them."[14]

Like Robinson, Russell had stretched the boundaries on black athletes. Now young African Americans infiltrated big-time sports and protested injustice. Bastions of sporting segregation, such as Bear Bryant's University of Alabama football program, integrated their squads by the early 1970s. At universities such as Detroit, Oklahoma State, Wyoming, Cornell, Indiana, and Hartford, basketball and football players boycotted autocratic coaches and prejudiced administrations. Curt Flood challenged baseball's reserve clause, maintaining that "a well-paid slave is nevertheless a slave." Tennis player Arthur Ashe defied apartheid after gaining a visa to South Africa. Even the Harlem Globetrotters boycotted games to protest shoddy travel conditions.[15]

Russell lent particular perspective on sport's racial upheavals. Basketball projected black culture to wider audiences. African Americans dictated the game's texture. Russell had introduced an athleticism and attitude that now manifested in the high-flying Connie Hawkins, the flashy Earl Monroe, or the stylish Walt Frazier. In the foreword to Frazier's *Rockin' Steady,* Russell defined this cool: "Easy going, yet intense. Relaxed, cautious. But always knowing who he is and where he's at." To like basketball was to appreciate an African American aesthetic.[16]

Yet the cultural intertwining of basketball and blackness had ironic consequences. Some athletes complained that coaches cramped the individualistic, flamboyant style of the playgrounds. Some white traditionalists got offended; one Philadelphian stopped attending 76ers games because "in basketball you sit right on the playing floor and the men are almost undressed and their blackness hits you right in the face." But even white aficionados fetishized black basketball: by extolling the style as more emotional, more instinctual, or more inherently physical, they implied that it was less civilized.[17]

From his elevated perch, Russell attacked any implication of inherent racial difference. He skewered exclusions of black sportswriters, bigoted baseball managers, and fishy selection procedures for Olympic basketball. When a *Sports Illustrated* article examined blacks' "natural" athletic ability, Russell fumed that it ignored their ambition and intelligence. In 1970 Russell wrote another article for *Sports Illustrated,* crafted during a week's visit from Frank Deford. When Deford started covering the NBA in 1964, Russell emitted prickliness, testing the fresh-faced Yale graduate. Over the years, his trust grew. The article, "Success Is a Journey," looked both backward and forward, explaining personal and social triumphs. Mostly, it skewered the hypocrisies in big-time sports. Everyone obsessed over college athletes' eligibility, but no one cared about education. Sports brought people together but also gathered their hatreds. Once society valued humble black athletes who absorbed untold abuse; now it sought white hopes.[18]

Russell also appeared on an extraordinary episode of the public television program *Black Journal* with Jackie Robinson, Arthur Ashe, Johnny Sample, and Harry Edwards. The athlete-activists praised the spirit of the Olympic boycott movement, calling for more demonstrations through sports. Russell decried the pampering and puffing of athletes: "Nobody really cares what you think. It's like you gradually become a product, and not a person." To uphold black superstars as exemplars of equal opportunity, he added, made rules out of exceptions. They remained commodities, outside the halls of power.[19]

At least fifty times a year, Russell shared his opinions with college students. Campus lecture tours kept him moving, and each gig paid between $1,000 and $2,500. After delivering funny, rambling talks for about an hour, he fielded questions. Sometimes he performed a skit called "label and dismiss," pretending to choke a student volunteer. Russell explained that his victim was a Nazi. When Russell released his grip, the student could only defend himself against the accusation, not engage in genuine debate. Russell employed this metaphor to explain how mass media pigeonhole people and manipulate politics.[20]

Russell went to state universities and private schools, military academies and drama schools, historically black schools and historically white ones. He had students drive him from the airport, eat with him in the cafeteria, or chat with him in the student union. In his lectures, he criticized the government's misplaced priority on international credibility, rather than the welfare of its citizens. He carped about the new hysteria over drugs, since drugs had long infiltrated black communities. While affirming pride in blackness, he called for interracial connections. He especially liked the question-and-answer period. Sportswriters confined their questions to basketball, but students asked about everything from the Black Panthers to Vatican II.[21]

Of course, they also asked about basketball. In May 1969, at the University of Wisconsin, a student claimed that Wilt Chamberlain deserved greater acclamation, but had inferior teammates and lousy luck. Russell boiled. For a decade, he had bathed Chamberlain in acclaim. But as the media inflated their rivalry, it tested their friendship. Russell grumbled when Chamberlain contended that bad breaks blocked him from multiple championships. He particularly resented that Chamberlain missed the final minutes of their final game. The moment had meant so much to Russell. "Wilt's leaving," he reminisced, "was like finding a misspelled word at the end of a cherished book."[22]

In Wisconsin, Russell's emotions spilled out. Chamberlain "copped out" of their final duel, Russell claimed. "Any injury short of a broken leg or a broken back isn't good enough." Chamberlain had talent, "but basketball is a team game. I go by the number of championships. I play to bring out the best in my teammates." Chamberlain never elevated those around him, though he played with Paul Arizin, Tom Gola, and Guy Rodgers on the Warriors; Hal Greer, Chet Walker, and Billy Cunningham on the 76ers; Elgin Baylor and Jerry West on the Lakers. Given his "human frailties," Chamberlain deserved his critics. "He talks a lot about what he's going to do. What it's all about is winning and losing, and he's done a lot of losing. He thinks he's a genius. He isn't."[23]

This belittling became national news. Chamberlain felt betrayed. He had considered Russell his friend, and he refused to comment. But Russell never apologized. In fact, he scattered jibes at Chamberlain over the coming years, and they stopped speaking to each other. In time, Chamberlain wondered if Russell had grown jealous of his talent, celebrity, and lifestyle. Russell ascribed their gulf to each man's stubborn pride. His championships spoke for themselves, but his competitiveness continued into retirement. With this cruel verbal jab, he painted the final detail on their rivalry's public portrait.[24]

. . .

Ironically, Chamberlain's Bunyanesque icon broadened Russell's post-basketball possibilities. Chamberlain always had a touch of Hollywood, an awareness of his own theatricality. He built a palatial sex pad in Bel Air, again flirted with boxing Muhammad Ali, appeared all over television, publicized women's track and volleyball, prompted a security crisis in the Philadelphia airport after jokingly threatening to shoot someone, and endorsed an energy drink called "Wilt's," as well as a children's laxative. His 1973 bestseller—*Wilt: Just Like Any Other 7-foot Black Millionaire Who Lives Next Door*—contained a litany of athletic and sexual boasts, self-defenses and self-justifications, sympathetic appeals and unsolicited potshots. While launching basketball into the realm of celebrity, he hoisted along Russell.[25]

After moving to Los Angeles, Russell started reading scripts for Western films. "How many parts are there for a black man 6'10"?" griped Auerbach. Yet Russell considered a movie career feasible. Hollywood had begun casting more African Americans, and with a Black Power backlash against the stardom of the mannered, too-perfect Sidney Poitier, studios sought sexually charged black action heroes. Sports provided ready-made icons: Jim Brown and Fred Williamson busted villains and bedded women in various B movies.[26]

But Russell lacked the hammy heroics or sexual charisma for such parts. He lost a role as a chuckwagon cook in John Wayne's *The Cowboys* to Roscoe Lee Browne. When he asked for advance pay on a Spanish film, the producers hired someone else. He landed no movie roles. "I was assured by my first agent that I had star possibilities," he joked. "My next four agents told me the same thing."[27]

Russell fared better in television. Though he appeared on Robert Wagner's action-adventure series *It Takes a Thief,* his personality was better suited for light comedy. He guest-starred on *The Bill Cosby Show* and acted in *Love, American Style,* which featured rotating casts in funny, romantic stories. He proved a natural on variety shows, joining multiple episodes of *Rowan and Martin's Laugh In* and *The Flip Wilson Show.* In one skit for Wilson's program, he films a mock commercial for a nighttime sleep-aid. First, he reads the cue cards (including stage instructions) in a monotone. He keeps screwing up, but on each take he drinks more "Doze Off"—by the end, he dozes off. Of course, he talks in his sleep, and he delivers the lines perfectly.[28]

Russell's wit best suited the talk-show circuit. He chatted with Johnny Carson, Merv Griffin, Mike Douglas, Steve Allen, Virginia Graham, Art Linkletter, and Dick Cavett. Russell twice guest-hosted for Cavett, proving adept at it. One columnist wrote that Russell "has the popularity and brains to become a first-rate politician." He instead started his own syndicated television program. *The Bill Russell Show* first aired in January 1972, appearing in about twenty markets. Russell interviewed such disparate figures as George Wallace, Rod Steiger, Johnny Mathis, Ted Kennedy, Edward Teller, and Lester Maddox. Howard Cosell and Muhammad Ali appeared on the pilot, and Cosell returned for another episode with Joe Namath. To Russell's disappointment, it proved too expensive for its middling ratings, ceasing production after twelve episodes.[29]

A version of *The Bill Russell Show* moved to radio. Starting in November 1972, Monday through Friday, 5:00 to 7:00 p.m., Russell offered candid opinions and bantered with callers on Los Angeles station KABC. On one typical day, he discussed the barriers to a college football play-off, the integrity of the martyred Roberto Clemente, the blackballing of NFL labor organizer John Mackey, and the glory days of the old NHL. Russell also interviewed friends such as Elgin Baylor, Howard Cosell, Jim Murray, and Larry Brown. The night before his fight with Bob Foster, Muhammad Ali gave Russell some banter, boasts, and poetry. Yet Russell also discussed social issues. Women called about problems with children and husbands, and a group of housewives even organized a Bill Russell Fan Club. KABC moved from fifteenth to second in the afternoon drive-time slot.[30]

As an athlete, Russell could be aloof because he got paid for basketball. As an entertainer, the formerly brooding outsider exposed his sociable, funny dimensions beyond his inner circle. Further, the public embraced him. In an era of Black Power and counterculture radicals, Russell no longer seemed dangerous. More people now appreciated his thoughtful individualism. Cosell called him "the *authentic* athlete of the Sixties."[31]

Advertisers determined that Russell' frank, genuine personality elicited consumers' trust. In a 1973 national television commercial for AT&T, Russell sat behind a large desk, pitching long-distance service. At the end, according to script, he spins on his swivel chair, takes a shot at a faraway basket, and continues, "I can miss, but you can't miss if you use long distance." But on the first take, Russell swished the shot and improvised, "I can't miss, and you can't miss either, by using long distance." After hours of filming, the director used this original take. The commercial grew so popular that Carol Burnett and *Saturday Night Live* spoofed it.[32]

Russell filmed another AT&T commercial in 1975, and it became a phenomenon. The advertisement shows Russell chatting with a Washington, DC, executive named Ron Watts. A white southerner nine years his junior, Watts appeared in twenty-nine games with the Celtics between 1965 and 1967. Despite their differences, said Watts, "we hit it off immediately. We had the same sort of sense of humor. We shared the same philosophy." But their conviviality seemed at odds with stubborn perceptions of the imperious black center; AT&T received thousands of letters wondering if Watts was real. Russell and Watts heard the same questions. As news spread of their genuine friendship, it further softened Russell's image.[33]

By the early 1970s, sports reflected battling visions of America's soul. A coach like Vince Lombardi—or a football fanatic like Richard Nixon—embodied a traditional vision of sport as building character, sacrifice, and manliness. A star like Joe Namath or Wilt Chamberlain threw sex and celebrity into this mix. But a generation of rebellious journalists, academics, and athletes indicted the entire culture of sports; this "Athletic Revolution" condemned the corruption of the NCAA, autocracy of coaches, compliance of most sportswriters, and inhumane exploitation of athletes. Russell bridged all these divides: his Celtics illustrated sport's highest character, his celebrity magnified, and his critiques foreshadowed this generation of protest. So he seemed more palatable, more trustworthy, more real.[34]

"He's a strange guy," said an AT&T executive. "He doesn't do anything unless he believes in it."[35]

. . .

In March 1972, the Celtics arranged a ceremony to retire Russell's number. He resisted. This ritual, he thought, celebrated the athlete but ignored the human. Nor could he accept public gratitude: discrimination had inflamed his sensitivities, and his principles had molded his stoicism. "From my very first year I thought of myself as playing for the Celtics, not for Boston," he explained. "The fans could do and think whatever they wanted. If they liked what they saw, fine; if not, the hell with it."[36]

But Red Auerbach pressed on, forcing a compromise. Ten minutes before the first customers entered Boston Garden, Russell and Auerbach met at center court with John Havlicek, Satch Sanders, Tom Heinsohn, Don Nelson, and Don Chaney. Together they raised a green flag bearing the number six to the rafters, joshing together in an atmosphere devoid of pomp. About twenty-five people watched. The lights were low. A few ushers applauded. Hours later, during the game, the public address announcer explained the number retirement. For the next two minutes, the crowd stood, roared, and hailed Russell in waves of claps and huzzahs. "Please stand up and take a bow, Bill," implored the announcer. Russell stared straight ahead, motionless, his face blank—ignoring the cheers, maybe remembering the boos.[37]

Russell had been obligated to attend the game, because in 1971, he had started announcing NBA games on ABC. He had not missed basketball: he rejected a $300,000 offer to rejoin the Celtics in 1970, and in two years he watched a handful of games. (The number retirement marked his first return to Boston Garden.) As a player-coach, moreover, he had resented television time-outs and intrusive cameras. But Russell agreed to work with Chris Schenkel and then Keith Jackson on the NBA *Game of the Week,* as well as some college games and the Munich Olympics. "I did it for two reasons," he explained. "One, a vulgar thing called money. Two, I was able to convince ABC that my job on the air should be to entertain."[38]

Russell entertained by subverting television clichés. Most announcers engaged in relentless hyperbole, but Russell refused to call average players "great" or great players "the greatest." If someone dogged it, he said so. He tempered that honesty with humor, bringing an irreverent appreciation to the game. "Have you EVER seen a more INCREDIBLE game played with more INTENSITY than THIS one?" his partner might plead. Russell would pause, smile, and deadpan: "Yes."[39]

Sports announcing demanded adjustments. He had to speak in sound bites. He heard producers and directors through his earpiece, and he learned to incorporate their suggestions. Because he tended to turn away from microphones, he wore a headset with an attached mouthpiece. He also fluctuated between mumbles and guffaws, so producers fine-tuned the settings to catch his tonal range. At times he contradicted himself, stumbled over words, or sounded haughty. Yet Russell invigorated the ABC broadcast, and he became a critical darling. Unlike most ex-jocks, his interests stretched far beyond basketball, so his perspective seemed fresh and funny. *Newsweek* called him "simply the wisest, wittiest and most forthright basketball analyst in broadcasting—if not the best 'color man' (a phrase rarely used to his face) in sport."[40]

As basketball's greatest hero, Russell had unparalleled authority. The Associated Press named him the best basketball player of the 1960s, and the *Sporting News* christened him "Athlete of the Decade." His stature magnified in light of his former team's troubles. During the 1969–70 season, Boston finished 34–48, missing its first play-offs in two decades. The defense allowed layups, the fast break faltered, and the half-court offense missed Russell's passing. The histrionic Heinsohn got little respect, and poor Henry Finkel became the fans' scapegoat. Exacerbating the chaos, parent company Trans-National Communications had such financial trouble that its chairman proposed moving to Long Island's Nassau Coliseum.[41]

The NBA's signature franchises now resided elsewhere. The New York Knicks won the 1970 championship, igniting frenzy in the nation's media capital. Basketball's new glamour boys triumphed over the star-crossed Lakers, with Knicks center Willis Reed grabbing the mantle of hero. When Reed missed the sixth game with a serious leg injury, Chamberlain got forty-five points and twenty-seven rebounds, but afterward he launched into a bizarre polemic that American culture overemphasizes winning—an apparent psychological preparation for yet another failure. In Game Seven, Reed hobbled onto the court, and Madison Square Garden went nuts. It energized the Knicks and rattled Chamberlain.[42]

Despite this setback, however, Chamberlain no longer inspired much vitriol. First Russell retired, delivering that nasty parting shot. Then Chamberlain ruptured tendons and tore ligaments in his knee; he elicited much-appreciated sympathy during an arduous rehabilitation through most of the 1969–70 season. Most important, a new bogeyman emerged: a nimble skyscraper named Lew Alcindor.[43]

"Can Basketball Survive Lew Alcindor?" asked the *Saturday Evening Post* in 1967, echoing its decade-old question about Chamberlain. The 7'2" star from New York City led UCLA to an 88–2 record and three NCAA titles. With the potential for both Chamberlain's offense and Russell's defense, he provoked similar anxieties among sport's traditionalists. The NCAA banned dunking after his first season; some resuscitated proposals for a twelve-foot basket.[44]

Alcindor revered Russell. While in high school, he studied Russell during games at Madison Square Garden. He admired how Russell understood a game's dynamic, altering it at the appropriate moment with a block or pass. He further respected Russell's erudite candor. When he was a sophomore, the Celtics practiced at his school's gymnasium. His coach took him to meet the Celtics. Russell ignored him. "I'm not standing up for no kid," he said. Rather than take offense, Alcindor identified with Russell's intelligence, pride, and outsider mentality.[45]

Like Russell, Alcindor ruffled feathers. Shy and introspective, he emitted the cool, sullen style of his favorite jazz artists. Stirred by *The Autobiography of Malcolm X* and the Qu'ran, he converted to Islam. He embraced the Revolt of the Black Athlete. He volunteered with HARYOU-ACT rather than participate in the Mexico City Olympics. "I live here," he explained, "but it's not really my country."[46]

In 1969, after spurning the Globetrotters and the ABA, Alcindor joined the Milwaukee Bucks. No rookie had engendered such hysteria since Chamberlain. Alcindor dominated with graceful consistency, winning Rookie of the Year in 1970 . and MVP in 1971. After Oscar Robertson engineered a trade to Milwaukee, they captured the 1971 NBA title. Yet Alcindor lacked either Chamberlain's swagger or Russell's passion. He seemed alienated and aloof, a self-described "minority of one." In 1971 he formally adopted his new name, Kareem Abdul-Jabbar.[47]

Abdul-Jabbar and Chamberlain lent basketball its new rivalry. Thousands watched their first duel at the Catskills benefit for Maurice Stokes, and reporters hyped their clashes, which got coated in a personal frostiness. Chamberlain had once taken the teenage Alcindor under his wing, introducing him to NBA stars and New York nightlife. Yet as Abdul-Jabbar matured, their priorities and personalities forked apart, and the media widened that wedge. Jealous pride spoiled their friendship. On court, they barely acknowledged each other.[48]

Now Chamberlain was the "good guy." Abdul-Jabbar threatened to rule the NBA. Abdul-Jabbar represented a new generation of black anger. Abdul-Jabbar practiced a religion mysterious to many Americans. Chamberlain no longer seemed such a menace. As soul music, blaxploitation films, afros, street slang, and other representations of black urban culture infiltrated mainstream American life, Chamberlain possessed a particular cool: when he started donning sweatbands, it sparked a fashion trend. Young black men, especially, recognized him as the ultimate sports celebrity, the consummate individualist, the conspicuous consumer of cars, clothes, and women.[49]

Chamberlain won more admirers during the 1971–72 season, when Celtic Pride got imported to Hollywood. New Lakers coach Bill Sharman imposed fastidious routines, attention to detail, and fast-break basketball. He hired assistant coach K. C. Jones. He left self-driven Jerry West to his own demons. He compelled broken-down Elgin Baylor to retire in midseason. Most remarkably, he turned Chamberlain into a lane-clogging defender who whipped quick outlet passes. He solicited Chamberlain's opinions, praised Chamberlain's self-sacrifice, and appointed Chamberlain captain. It worked to perfection. The Lakers went 69–13, had a record thirty-three-game winning streak, and captured the NBA title. In the clincher, Chamberlain got twenty-four points, twenty-nine rebounds, and ten blocks with a sprained, numbed, heavily bandaged right wrist. He had displayed a winner's pride, the virtue long associated with Bill Russell.[50]

Yet Chamberlain never escaped his own talent. When the Lakers lost to the Knicks in the 1973 NBA Finals, critics complained that he concentrated *too much* on rebounds and defense. Could he ever win? The greatest scorer in basketball history had sacrificed his gift under the weight of public pressure, and his burden just grew heavier.[51]

Chamberlain congratulated the Knicks in their locker room. As he left, dipping his head under the doorway, he encountered Russell. Chamberlain carried a sweat-soaked terry-cloth headband, and perspiration dripped off his beard. Russell wore a gold blazer with an ABC crest, preparing to interview the victors. In that Fabulous Forum hallway, with the Knicks' muffled joy as background noise, Russell and Chamberlain made one second of eye contact. Torn by a public rivalry, each man's eyes broke off, and they glided past without acknowledgment—two dark and giant ships, passing in the night.[52]

. . .

The next day, the Seattle Supersonics announced "one of the major deals in sports history": Bill Russell was their new head coach and general manager. The Sonics and their supporters gushed over the hire. "His name lends dignity to the sport, and should do the same for this team, and this city," intoned an editorial in the *Seattle Post-Intelligencer*.[53]

From the beginning, Russell acted on his own terms. Seattle owner Sam Schulman announced the pact with Russell's attorney. Russell stayed in Los Angeles, refusing press requests. On his radio show that evening, he joked that in his first order of business, "the guys should be introduced to each other and make sure they all have on the same uniforms." Reporters deciphered his plans from a recent question-and-answer session at a Seattle college. Russell did consent to one telephone interview. He communicated his desire to instill discipline, build chemistry, and move star forward Spencer Haywood to center. Then he hopped on his motorcycle for a week's vacation, with no specific destination in mind.[54]

Russell called his return to coaching an "accident." He enjoyed living in Los Angeles and bouncing among television, radio, and college lecture gigs. That spring, he had rebuffed Schulman's entreaties. Schulman had a reputation as a meddling owner. "Besides," Russell added, "it would cost too much." That barb only spurred a mogul accustomed to paying top dollar. Russell, in turn, got intrigued with molding a franchise in his image. He had listened to multiple offers, but he preferred the West Coast. Russell signed a five-year, $625,000 contract that included stock options and other incentives.[55]

His new team revealed the complexities of the professional basketball boom. The city of Seattle—like San Diego, Milwaukee, Houston, and Portland—had "big league" aspirations, and professional sports lent an imprimatur for downtown revitalization and national relevance. The Sonics started in 1967. Baseball's Seattle Pilots followed in 1969, but left for Milwaukee after one season, trailing a wake of losses, lawsuits, and liquidations. The NFL's Seattle Seahawks would arrive in 1976, and the Mariners would restore baseball in 1977.[56]

Expansion fed the NBA's growth, and television money washed it down. Starting with Seattle and San Diego, the NBA grew from ten to seventeen teams in three years, with the newest franchises paying expansion fees of $3.7 million. In 1973, Jack Kent Cooke spearheaded a jump to CBS, which paid $27 million for three years, promising Saturday afternoon games. ABC had nurtured the NBA for the previous nine years, so a betrayed Roone Arledge drove the NBA off Saturdays by saturating the airwaves with college football promotions. ABC doubled CBS's basketball ratings with a Sunday version of *Wide World of Sports.* Like expansion, the CBS contract reflected short-term greed over long-term growth. Basketball nevertheless ranked as the third most popular spectator sport behind baseball and football.[57]

The NBA still dueled with the ABA. Despite rampant instability and ramshackle organization, the ABA lured young stars such as Artis Gilmore, George McGinnis, and the dazzling, swooping, hook-dunking Virginia Squires forward, Julius Erving. ABA teams fared well in preseason games against NBA squads, and the two players' associations staged a nationally televised All-Star exhibition in 1972. Players negotiated between leagues, and their salaries skyrocketed. Connie Hawkins sued the NBA to join the Phoenix Suns in 1969, and Rick Barry jumped back to the Golden State Warriors in 1972. Kareem Abdul-Jabbar made $400,000 a year, Walt Frazier $350,000, Jerry West $300,000.[58]

As early as April 1970, the two leagues neared a merger. That move would enrich ABA owners, restore superstars to the NBA, and undercut the players' leverage. Then the National Basketball Players Association filed a class-action suit, claiming that consolidation violated antitrust law. This "Oscar Robertson suit" blocked the merger. In 1972 the Senate Subcommittee on Antitrust and Monopoly maintained the antimerger injunction until settlement of the NBPA lawsuit. The players ultimately destroyed the reserve clause, signed a collective-bargaining agreement, and obtained a pension plan. The NBA and ABA still pursued a merger, but as the rival leagues battled over players and contracts, the key stories occurred in legal courts as well as on basketball courts.[59]

"There is a disease in sports now," wrote Tom Meschery. Basketball's warrior-poet quit coaching the ABA's Carolina Cougars in 1972, lamenting that agents bribed clients, players jumped leagues, and owners treated players as investments. Meschery referenced Pete Maravich as a symptom of the sickness. The Atlanta guard hogged the ball and alienated teammates, but he justified his $1.8 million contract with trick passes, flashy dribbles, and outrageous shots, as well as his doe eyes, floppy hair, and floppy socks—wrapping black style in a cute, white package. Meschery missed the old values. What happened to pride, loyalty, and honor? Where were the mythic figures, the venerable heroes? Where was Bill Russell, the Eagle with a Beard?[60]

. . .

Sam Schulman embodied sport's culture of greed. By the time he hired Russell, his Sonics had accumulated fourteen lawsuits, with costs and fees totaling $1.4 million. Schulman grew up in Brooklyn, got his MBA from Harvard, and built a business fortune in Los Angeles; after revitalizing a bankrupt book publisher, he di-

rected various car leasing, insurance, publishing, and savings and loan corporations. Like many of his colleagues, he owned everything but public adoration. He
wanted glory, and he paid for it.[61]

During the 1970–71 season Schulman stole ABA Rookie of the Year and MVP
Spencer Haywood with a six-year, $1.5 million offer. Haywood had left the Uni-
versity of Detroit early to join the Denver Rockets, so his college class had yet to
graduate. The NBA thus rejected the signing; it undermined the free farm system
of the NCAA. But Haywood's legal challenge on antitrust grounds reached the
Supreme Court. The NBA settled, and the next season Haywood averaged twenty-
six points and thirteen rebounds while leading the Sonics to a 47–35 record, just
missing the play-offs. Seattle ranked third in NBA attendance.[62]

The Sonics' fortunes then plummeted. Emboldened by his coup of Haywood,
Schulman gave Jim McDaniels a seven-year, $1,870,000 contract. The seven-footer
had been selected in a clandestine midseason draft by the Utah Stars, somehow
extricated himself to join the Carolina Cougars (while still playing for Western Kentucky University), and then abandoned his team in midseason, demanding a better contract. After luring McDaniels, Schulman sought John Brisker, a 6'5" intim-
idator with marginal defensive skills. Brisker had been pouring in points for the
Pittsburgh Pipers, so Schulman paid him $1,020,000 over six years. Compound-
ing this foolishness, Schulman forced player-coach Lenny Wilkens to choose between playing and coaching. Since 1969, Wilkens had lifted the Sonics from mediocrity to respectability, and the fans adored him. In 1972, after he chose to keep
playing, Seattle traded him.[63]

The Sonics went 26–56 in 1973. Average attendance dropped by almost two
thousand. Shareholders of the parent corporation sued the franchise. The players
allegedly "dumped" a game to hasten the firing of new coach Tom Nissalke. Fans
grew disenchanted. In six years, Schulman had jettisoned four coaches and three
general managers. *Sports Illustrated* described the Sonics as "a team of malcontents
and prima donnas."[64]

When Russell arrived in Seattle, he represented not only a proven winner but
also an antidote to the ills of modern sports—an oasis of integrity in a sea of greed
and grievances. As team vice president Zollie Volchok stated, "We didn't just buy
a coach, we bought a voice, a style, an image." Russell's honesty won a distinctive
admiration. While building the sport's historical foundation, his Celtics embodied pride and unity. To deliver that image to Seattle, he had demanded complete
authority. A desperate Schulman had to concede that power.

"Let's face it," said a Sonics official, "Bill Russell *is* the Seattle basketball franchise."[65]

17

Seattle's New Dictator

In Russell, Seattleites foresaw more than a basketball coach. Their city had undergone traumas: massive layoffs at Boeing, demonstrations at the University of Washington, unrest in the predominantly black Central District. They craved a unifying figure, an icon of importance. Russell heralded a surge in civic spirit, racial harmony, and national relevance. They watched reruns of his television show, laughed at his telephone commercials, and gobbled up t-shirts, books, and posters produced through Russell's Kenyatta Corporation. They loved that he conducted practices in local high schools. They appreciated his admiration of their tolerant spirit, his promise "to be a citizen of Seattle."[1]

They envisioned Russell cleaning up the Sonics' mess, instilling his values, and captivating the city. "Seattle's New Dictator," proclaimed billboards with Russell's picture. In training camp he brandished a baseball bat, along with his trademark wit. "Most of the guys can run. The ones that can't will walk to the unemployment line," he quipped. On defense, he added, "we'll pick up some teams at the airport." The Sonics had great talent, Russell insisted, but they needed discipline and cohesiveness.[2]

The force of Russell's personality—his celebrity, his charisma, his cackle—rebuilt the faith of Seattle fans. Rebuilding the Sonics proved a bigger challenge.

. . .

To reach training camp in Port Angeles, the Sonics took a bus from downtown Seattle. Slick Watts, an undrafted free agent from Xavier University in Louisiana, waited with the other rookies. The veterans arrived late, clad in leather suits, accompanied by gorgeous women. John Brisker emerged from an ivory cream Mercedes, Spencer

252

Haywood from a huge green Cadillac. "So this is how the pros do it," thought Watts, looking through the window. Then Russell arrived, all by himself, reminding every-one who was in charge.[3]

Russell confronted a new basketball generation. His NBA peers had college ed-ucations and started with middle-class incomes. The African Americans integrated the league amidst the sacrifices of the civil rights movement. Now professional basketball had more players raised in poverty, puffed and dazzled by multiple bid-ders for their services, laden with sudden wealth, molded by Black Power. The rich-est had no-cut contracts, so coaches had minimal clout. As the ABA watered down talent, it inflated salaries and egos. Russell thought that this generation lacked "mental toughness." Drug use increased. Money inflated every petty jealousy, every sensitivity.[4]

"Sensitive is a right you earn," Russell insisted. Many players had selfish instincts, surly attitudes, and deficient court sense. In one exhibition, someone launched a twenty-foot jump shot, while his wide-open teammate stood under the basket, call-ing for a pass. "Don't start messing with me while I'm shooting!" scolded the shooter. Disgusted by this antithesis of Celtic Pride, Russell attacked their sense of entitlement. He employed ironclad discipline. Absent any sense of collective iden-tity, he built a powerful cult of personality.[5]

The NBA's standard late fine was one dollar per minute; Russell charged $100. He made everyone wear black sneakers, just like the Celtics. On road trips, he as-signed roommates. He banished radios, musical instruments, and tape recorders. Anyone who missed a plane paid his own way, along with a hefty fine. Most of all, Russell intimidated players: staring them down, doling out laps, abruptly shifting from loquacious to standoffish. He chastised them for shooting too much, even after good shots. He sliced their egos. Well aware of its degrading racial ramifications, he called them "boy."[6]

Russell also imposed the Celtics' principles by preaching conditioning, defense, fast breaks, and teamwork. Assistant coach Emmette Bryant led rigorous calis-thenics. They drilled basic fundamentals, over and over. When one man made a mistake, everyone ran laps.[7]

The Sonics started with Spencer Haywood at center, Jim McDaniels and John Brisker at forward, and Dick Snyder and Fred Brown at guard. But Russell kept juggling the lineup as the team started 5–14. He threatened a lap for every point conceded in a loss. He described one game as "an awful and disgraceful exhibition of basketball." He complained that no other teams wanted his players or their fat, long-term contracts. By December, his optimism dissipated. "I've seen enough," he said. "In all candor, we are a very bad defensive team. There are going to be some changes, I can promise you that."[8]

Before the New Year, Russell released Jim McDaniels. When McDaniels signed his enormous contract, Seattle fans had expected a star. But after posting gaudy statistics in the ABA, he lacked the physical or mental fortitude for the NBA. He averaged six points and five rebounds with Seattle. Russell tried converting the seven-footer to forward, but McDaniels never progressed. Russell benched him, then belittled him. McDaniels had trouble executing basics such as a drop step. Finally, Russell gave up.[9]

"Worst Flop in History?" asked one headline. Schulman still had to pay McDaniels's contract, so Russell's decision shocked the basketball world. As Merv Harris wrote, "Russell emerged as that much greater a force for integrity, so strongly dedicated a coach that he was able to convince a title-hungry owner to pay more than $150,000 per year for an ill-starred adventure rather than attempt to compound a mistake with further false hope."[10]

Weeks later, Russell exiled John Brisker to the Eastern League. When Russell arrived, recalled Brisker, "we were elated. It could have been very good all the way around—from business, to basketball, to a personal level of consciousness." He even threw Russell a welcome party. Brisker owned a tough-guy reputation, thanks to his hardscrabble upbringing in Detroit's ghettoes, his menacing demeanor, and frequent fisticuffs in the ABA. He also possessed shooting range and athleticism. Just before the demotion, he dropped forty-seven points on the Kansas City Kings.[11]

Yet Russell had alienated Brisker since training camp. Joby Wright, a 6'8" mountain from Indiana University, was hacking Brisker. They jawed at each other. "This is where we separate the men from the boys," said Russell. "Let 'em play." He was provoking Brisker by pitting him against a hardworking banger scrapping for a roster spot. Brisker could not back down. The play got rougher, the pushes got harder, the tempers got hotter. Then Brisker threw a punch. Wright thudded onto the floor. His teeth scattered across the court. Everyone hushed. Brisker wanted to cry, but he resisted losing face. Goaded into attacking his teammate, his rage spilled out in a wild scream, delivered right in Russell's face. From then on, Brisker sat in Russell's doghouse.[12]

Officially, Russell sent Brisker to a weekend minor league to work on defense. Really, it was a public humiliation. "The Eastern League is as much an atmosphere for defense as a brothel is for Bible reading," cracked one writer. In three weeks, Brisker averaged fifty-four points. His rift with Russell continued. He thought that Russell considered him a threat, because players congregated at his house. When he returned to Seattle, Russell benched him. They had angry conversations, locker-room staredowns. The next season, Brisker played in only twenty-one games. After he had foot surgery without the Sonics' consent, the team declared a breach of contract, and Brisker never again played professional basketball.[13]

Fans assumed that Russell held a grudge against Brisker, whom they liked for his shooting. Russell denied any personal beef. He maintained only that other players contributed more. When crowds chanted "We Want Brisker!," he scowled into the stands. By disgracing a tough and headstrong player, Russell fortified his own authority.[14]

His iron hand nudged the Sonics toward unselfish offense and aggressive defense. On December 11, they stood 10–23. After that, they went 26–23. In the last two-thirds of the season, they went a respectable 13–14 against winning teams and 11–13 on the road. Spencer Haywood thrived on returning to forward, and Slick Watts delivered infectious hustle. Russell had altered the team's culture. "It's a vibration that you get from him, a glow that he has about himself," explained Fred Brown. "That glow has been pushed onto us." Seattle finished 36–46, stirring hope for the future.[15]

Russell was the face of the Supersonics. In a weekly *Seattle Times* column called "Take a Shot!," he answered questions about players, lineups, strategies, rules, personal experiences, and politics. He did a Saturday morning call-in show on KTW Radio. He announced ticket-price increases, discussed television contracts, and selected the cheerleaders. He also inspired continued enthusiasm from fans. Seattle finished third in attendance, behind only New York and Los Angeles. That summer, *Time* listed Russell among "200 Faces for the Future," leaders under age forty-five from all realms of American life.[16]

For the 1974–75 season, Russell revamped the roster. He traded Dick Snyder and Seattle's first draft pick to Cleveland to obtain Tom Burleson, a seven-footer from national champion North Carolina State. Russell craved a genuine shot-blocker and rebounder, and he outbid the ABA for Burleson's services. Burleson and five other rookies—Rod Derline, Leonard Gray, Wardell Jackson, Talvin Skinner, and Dean Tolson—contributed to the Sonics. Russell also traded for Archie Clark and hired a new assistant coach: his own cousin, Bob Hopkins.[17]

Russell and Hopkins met as children in Louisiana, during weeklong family reunions and religious revivals. When Russell was at USF, Hopkins starred at Grambling. They grew close in the NBA. After four seasons with the Syracuse Nationals, Hopkins coached at Alcorn State and Xavier University. During Russell's first year, Hopkins recommended Slick Watts, part of his network of unheralded players from historically black institutions. "Hoppy" proved perfect for the Sonics, focusing on scouting and technical details while Russell painted the big picture.[18]

These new Sonics displayed spirit, potential, and maddening inconsistency. They opened 8–4, unveiling a new resolve on defense. Rival coaches lauded their potential. "A year ago, Bill Russell faced an almost impossible situation," wrote Gil Lyons of the *Seattle Times*. "He had a team with almost no hope. By midseason, Russell had cleared away some of his dead wood and now has a young, promising group of players who seem to have a good future." Yet as late as February 9, the Sonics stood 25–30. They had endured losing skeins of five, four, and four games. They also had a five-game winning streak with star Spencer Haywood sidelined by viral pneumonia. Russell alternated between play-off hopes and gloomy postmortems.[19]

Seattle put together a late-season charge as Haywood returned to the lineup, Slick Watts hit a panoply of game-winners, Fred Brown sank devastating outside shots, Leonard Gray offered toughness, Archie Clark brought experience, and Tom Burleson continued his professional maturation. The Sonics clinched their first playoff spot in franchise history on March 30, 1975. Watts danced a jig. The scoreboard flashed "PLAYOFF PLAYOFF PLAYOFF." Russell hugged Haywood and Schulman. With his ego on the line, he had snapped the roots of mediocrity.[20]

The Sonics won their last seven games to finish 43–39, tying the club record. They finished second in the Pacific Division, fourth in the Western Conference. Under a new play-off format, they faced fifth-place Detroit in a best-of-three series. In the crucial opening contest, Burleson neutralized 6'11", 275-pound center Bob Lanier. Hopkins designed a sagging defense to prevent the Pistons from penetrating, and Seattle won 90–77. "That was the best defense we've played all year," said a grinning Russell. Although the Pistons triumphed at Cobo Hall, 122–106, the Sonics won the rubber match, 100–93, fending off a late Detroit comeback before a frantic Seattle crowd.[21]

In the Western Conference semifinal, Seattle faced Golden State, featuring the superlative Rick Barry. "The prototype of an ideal forward" was also the NBA's resident villain—an inveterate league-jumper, chirpy whiner, and cocksure gunner. Barry got thirty-nine points, eleven assists, and eight steals in the opener, leading a fast-breaking, slam-dunking thrashing, 123–96. But the Sonics stole home-court advantage by winning the next game, 100–99. The renewed competition, screaming crowd, and play-off stakes then ignited a frenzied contest in the Seattle Coliseum. It included multiple fracases, beginning when Barry elbowed Watts. The referees took the rare measure of stopping play, calling the coaches to midcourt, and warning against future shenanigans. In the end, Golden State won, 105–96. "I just spoiled 14,000 people's evening," snickered Barry.[22]

Two days later, when Barry fouled out of Seattle's series-tying 111–94 win, fans waved handkerchiefs and held "Crybaby, Barry" signs. But Golden State advanced past Seattle. In Game Five, the Warriors won 124–100, while Brown broke a finger on his shooting hand. In Game Six, Seattle fell again, 105–96. At the end some rowdies jostled Barry, dousing him with beer and bonking him with a purse.[23]

The Sonics looked forward. "We established that we are a winning team," said Russell. With the addition of one or two key players, he believed, the Sonics would contend for championships. Under the headline "Civic Pride Rekindled," a *Seattle Post-Intelligencer* editorial celebrated the season: "We can only be optimistic about the future of one of the youngest, most aggressive teams in major league sports." The Sonics had brought them excitement, honor, and spirit. With professional football and baseball on the horizon, Bill Russell was pulling Seattle into the big leagues.[24]

. . .

The 1975 NBA Finals included a little-noted milestone: both coaches—Al Attles of the Warriors, K. C. Jones of the Washington Bullets—were black. Basketball remained at the forefront of sports' integration. Ray Scott coached Detroit, and Lenny Wilkens led Portland. Before coaching the Bullets, Jones had piloted the ABA's San Diego Conquistadors (replacing Wilt Chamberlain, who had halfheartedly coached one season after squabbling with the Lakers, signing with San Diego, losing an arbitrators' hearing, and then retiring). In 1972 Wayne Embry became general manager of the Milwaukee Bucks, and in 1974 Simon Gourdine started as the NBA's deputy commissioner. Russell was the first African American with primary control of a professional sports franchise.[25]

Basketball had more liberal owners, less history of racial exclusion, and a generation of extraordinary, college-educated African Americans. Basketball also had Russell, a touchstone of black leadership. "Russell was such a mental giant," said Jones. "With his back-to-back championships, it chipped away at the idea that black coaches were a step below." Embry credited Russell for absorbing him in a winning culture, fostering his later opportunities in management.[26]

When Frank Robinson lobbied to break baseball's managerial color line, he pointed to his McClymonds High School teammate: "I think the fans are ready," he said in 1969. "Bill Russell proved that with the Boston Celtics. The world is ready now. It'll judge an individual by the job he does." Robinson would not manage the Cleveland Indians until 1975. The NFL had no black head coaches until 1989. By contrast, when the Knicks hired Willis Reed in 1977, Russell appreciated that "nobody said anything about his being black. When I was first appointed they made all this fuss about my being the first black coach and I said then that the time it would become important was when nobody mentioned it anymore."[27]

Yet if Russell reflected historic progress, he still stirred political pots. During his first press conference in Seattle, he called life in Boston "a very traumatic experience." He attacked the implicit, separate "code of conduct" for black athletes. After eleven titles, "all I could hear was that there were too many black guys on the team." Boston, he added, "is probably the most rigidly segregated city in the country." These incendiary comments made national news, riling the Boston media. "I am not a racist sports writer," responded Larry Claflin of the Boston Herald-American, citing his advocacy of black athletes. "I suspect Russell is the racist."[28]

But race always mattered in Boston sports, as evidenced by the newly popular Celtics. When Red Auerbach rebuilt a championship team, it included such black talents as Jo Jo White, Don Chaney, and Paul Silas. But it had two white superstars: John Havlicek and Dave Cowens. The ageless, tireless Havlicek retired in 1978 as Boston's all-time leading scorer, and Russell himself had recommended Cowens, an undersized center with dogged passion and all-around skills. While winning NBA titles in 1974 and 1976, this incarnation of the Celtics inspired a newfound fervor. During Russell's last campaign, Boston Garden's average attendance was 8,948. By the 1974–75 season, it was 13,307.[29]

Sport's erstwhile embodiments of racial integration now resonated with working-class whites in Boston's tribal pockets. These same neighborhoods contained a powder keg of economic and cultural frustrations. In 1974, a controversial court order mandated busing to desegregate Boston schools, surfacing a crude racism. Mobs spewing racist slurs greeted buses of black children. Violence plagued the city. Like Birmingham or Selma a decade earlier, South Boston and Charlestown showcased graphic images of white brutality. "I expected what's happening in Boston," said Russell. He had decried its ethnic segregation, its petty politics, its underlying bigotry. He had been called a troublemaker. Now he seemed a prophet.[30]

In Seattle, Russell said, "I am going to try to erase the scars." He appreciated the city's embrace of blacks such as Lenny Wilkens and Walt Hazzard. Seattle had experienced less virulent racism, and civil rights activists had accelerated its integration of schools, workplaces, and neighborhoods. Russell bought a home overlooking Lake Washington, on a hillside covered in tall fir trees, in the well-heeled suburb of Mercer Island. In 1964 a realtor showed houses there to a black family, and she almost got fired. By the 1970s, a voluntary program and an open-housing law had eroded such resistance. Five or six black families lived near Russell.[31]

Yet police cars still followed blacks on Mercer Island, and African Americans experienced isolation amidst affluence—including Russell's children. During the divorce, Rose learned that she had cancer, so the children moved to Seattle. After her successful recuperation, middle son Jacob joined her in a small town in California, where she practiced Buddhism. Buddha and Karen stayed with their father. Buddha graduated from Mercer Island High School and attended Bellevue Community College. Karen started the sixth grade as her school's only black child. Her father doted on her. She was precociously intelligent and exceptionally mature, and he called her "the woman in my life, the only one."[32]

In his initial Seattle years, Russell had no lasting romances. "I'm impossible to live with, and I realize that now," he said in 1975. People snickered about his relationship with personal assistant Anita Dias, but Russell insisted that they were good friends—best friends, in fact. She reminded him of his mother. Still, genuine love required stripping one's defenses, accepting pain along with pleasure. "I'd like to think that someday soon I'll be able to do that. But so far in my life, I haven't depended on anyone but myself."[33]

Russell remained wary in public. He still avoided autographs and sidestepped most appearances, and in interviews he eschewed introspection or personal details. With a few exceptions—hosting a fund-raiser for Mayor Wes Uhlman, sponsoring an exhibition by artist Phoebe Beasley—he declined opportunities for civic engagement. He once charged $2,500 to attend a luncheon of minority contractors and then sued when their check bounced. Seattle wanted a public hero; instead it got a celebrity who guarded his privacy, jealously and zealously.[34]

In February 1975, Russell rejected induction into the Basketball Hall of Fame. "For my own personal reasons, which I don't want to discuss, I don't want to be a part of it," he said. Once again, Russell launched sport's traditionalists into states of apoplexy. Executive Director Lee Williams expressed befuddlement. He left messages with the Sonics, unsure how to proceed, challenging Russell to explain himself. Russell stayed quiet. He had chosen his path with deliberation and confidence. Reporters barraged him with questions, but he refused to elaborate.[35]

The Hall of Fame inducted Russell anyway, installing a stained-glass portrait in its "Court of Honor." Russell avoided the ceremony. Speculation endured about his motives. Did he consider the Hall of Fame racist? Did he decry basketball's old-boy network? Was Russell enjoying this nose-tweaking of sporting bigwigs? Was he acting from principle?[36]

Yes, yes, yes, and yes. Russell declined association with inductees such as Adolph Rupp, who maintained an all-white University of Kentucky team until 1969, or Abe Saperstein, whose Harlem Globetrotters fettered legitimate black basketball. He disdained any institution that enshrined Bill Mokray, a Celtics statistician who insulted Russell, both in person and in print. He scorned those who bowed before corrupt institutions. Mostly, he regarded the Hall of Fame like autographs or retirement ceremonies. "I took fairly consistent stands on all three," he reflected. "In each case, my intention was to separate myself from the star's idea about fans and fans' ideas about stars." For Russell, hero worship spoiled an authentic awareness of oneself and others.[37]

Russell revealed these motivations years later. At the time, his stubborn silence inflamed basketball's guardians of order. "Why anyone would refuse defies understanding. I say if he doesn't want to be enshrined, forget about it," thundered Rupp. Hall of Fame trustee Edwin Steitz added, "Bill Russell, in my opinion, owes a lot to basketball. Basketball doesn't owe Bill Russell a thing." Ray Fitzgerald of the Boston Globe remembered Russell's refusal to accept a number-retirement ceremony: "People cheered you for a dozen years in Boston and you kicked them in the teeth when they wanted to honor you. You labeled them racists, 13,909 racists who merely wanted to let you know they loved the way you played basketball." Spurning the Hall of Fame represented more ingratitude. Russell got volumes of hate mail—some haughty and insulted, some vulgar and racist.[38]

The controversy nevertheless buttressed respect for Russell. James Michener realized how sports had educated him about the black experience. Once appalled by the Black Power salute of John Carlos and Tommie Smith, the writer now applauded Russell. Black athletes hurdled high barriers, and Russell demanded justice with pride and dignity. "When a man does that," wrote Michener, "he builds his own

Hall of Fame." Russell also bolstered African American pride. From Russell's side of the racial divide, few questioned his rejection of a hypocritical institution. "Your history makes a man who has pride in his race idiosyncratic," wrote a black correspondent to the *New York Times*. "My history makes that man a giant."[39]

. . .

Bill Russell represented the heights of basketball's black revolution; Bob Presley signified its depths. Presley grew up in Detroit, poor and troubled and shiftless. A discreet network of sports entrepreneurs funded the seven-footer's transition to California, where he finished high school and junior college. At the University of California at Berkeley, he got enmeshed in sport's racial revolt. Presley accused coach Rene Herrerias of suspending him for his "natural" haircut. Yet Presley had also cut practice and called Herrerias incompetent. Then the administration reinstated Presley. White players protested, black athletes issued grievances, and Herrerias and athletic director Pete Newell resigned. Presley's game still lacked consistency, concentration, or resolve.[40]

Basketball fed Presley's dreams, but it lent no path to maturity. Despite his prodigious talent, he got cut by two ABA teams, drifted through the Western Basketball Association and a league in the Philippines, worked odd jobs, and tried petty scams. In March 1975 he attended a Sonics game, trying to coax Russell into a tryout. At halftime, Russell brushed him off. After the game, he somehow wandered into Seattle's locker room, muttering about a fair shake. He even put on Tommy Burleson's sneakers. Presley was deranged, clad in rags, his fingers swollen from drug use. After getting escorted away, he took a bus to Portland and killed himself by jumping off a bridge.[41]

Spencer Haywood arose from similarly desperate circumstances. One of ten siblings in Silver Spring, Mississippi, Haywood picked cotton, sometimes subsisting on government handouts. As a teenager he migrated to Chicago and then Detroit. Street life enmeshed him, but basketball saved him. He was 6'8", 215 pounds, a powerful leaper with long arms and huge hands. He led Pershing High School to a state title. After failing the entrance examination at the University of Tennessee, he attended Trinidad Junior College in Colorado, where he read Malcolm X and Stokely Carmichael, grew an afro, and joined the Black Athletes Association.[42]

Ironically, the eighteen-year-old Haywood proved the savior of the 1968 Olympic basketball team, starring for the undermanned, gold-medal-winning Americans. After dominating for one year at the University of Detroit, earning MVP with the ABA's Denver Rockets, winning his legal challenge to enter the NBA, and starring for the Sonics, Haywood established himself among basketball's elite. By age twenty-three, he had earned more than $500,000.[43]

Yet if Haywood embodied the promise of modern black athletes, he also exuded disillusion. Contract battles and court cases had embittered him. Poverty and racism scarred him, and Black Power sculpted him. He found solace in jazz and beautiful women. He also grew paranoid of exploitation. A young prima donna on a turbulent team, he craved recognition, and he needed a strong father figure.[44]

A teenage Haywood once watched Russell stride out of a Cobo Hall locker room, wearing a black overcoat, a black cape, and a scowl. Haywood stared, saying nothing. He revered Russell's unapologetic pride and smooth confidence. "I wanted to be just like him," he thought. He sought his own identity as he got older, richer, and more cynical, but Russell remained his measure of manhood.[45]

When Russell arrived in Seattle, Haywood bubbled with optimism. "We regarded him as an absolute god," he recalled. "We wanted him to inspire us and teach us, elevate us to a higher human condition." Russell treated Haywood like a son. They drove to games together and shared dinners. Russell regaled him with old basketball tales. Russell taught his hook shot, defensive tricks, and life philosophies. Russell also rebuffed frequent questions about trading Haywood, his most valuable asset. If directing an adaptation of the Celtics dynasty, then he cast Haywood in the role of Bill Russell.[46]

Yet over time, their relationship disintegrated. Teammates teased that Haywood was the coach's pet; Haywood wanted to be his own man. During practice, when Russell ambled over and placed an arm over his shoulder, Haywood squirmed. He resented how Russell embarrassed players. He wanted credit for sacrificing statistics or overcoming injuries. He started complaining during practice. Russell, in turn, stopped mentoring or lauding his superstar. In March 1975, he benched Haywood for the final 19:34 of a loss to Milwaukee. Both men had big egos and thin skins. "We were once so close," remembered Haywood. "It was like being rejected by your father."[47]

During training camp in 1975, Russell informed Haywood about a possible trade with the New York Knicks. Haywood endorsed it. On October 22, the Sonics exchanged Haywood for $2 million and rookie forward Eugene Short. Russell faced little backlash: Haywood never totally committed to moving the ball, running the floor, or locking up scorers. Still, Russell insisted that he opposed the trade. He claimed to accede to Haywood's demands, implying that a disaffected star might poison team chemistry.[48]

Haywood denounced Russell as a paternalistic overlord. He said that Russell banished strong-willed black men like John Brisker, and that whites like Tom Burleson got more chances than blacks like Jim McDaniels. Russell attacked his confidence by shuffling him on and off the court. Russell prohibited him from a lucrative appearance on ABC's *Superstars* competition. Russell, moreover, had initiated trade talks. "Russell could not have me around anymore. I'm a man and he's a man, but he wants boys around men. There's no superstar allowed in Seattle—only Russell."[49]

Haywood did himself no favors by also ripping players, reporters, and fans. Some Sonics "don't come to play every night. Let them take the load." He felt unappreciated. "Basketball is the only pro sport in Seattle, and I put the city on the map. But nobody remembers that." The media scapegoated him, and rival teams considered Seattle crowds "bush." Fans never embraced him, as he explained it, "because I wasn't the kind of nigger they wanted. They couldn't call me 'boy' and kiss me on the head." He contrasted himself with Slick Watts, who "doesn't have the pride a black man has to have. He lets people slap his hands and his head and does the Globetrotter thing."[50]

Watts won all the affection that Haywood craved. People loved his nickname, tilted headband, shaved head, high-wattage smile, and spectacular hustle. They related to Watts, only 6'1" and 175 pounds, who in three seasons went from undrafted free agent to team leader. He patrolled passing lanes to ignite fast breaks, and his dribble penetrations created opportunities in Seattle's free-flowing offense. "Here's one guy who's worth every cent he gets," said assistant general manager Bob Walsh. "If Washington were ready for a bald black governor from Mississippi, Slick would be the guy." Despite his self-confidence, Watts retained an "aw shucks" humility, making constant appearances at hospitals, schools, and charity functions. He won the NBA's Citizenship Award and the *Seattle Post-Intelligencer*'s "Man of the Year." He reversed the overpaid, oversensitive, underachiever image personified by Haywood.[51]

"The chemistry on this team is excellent, like the old Celtics," said Russell. "Slick is the guy that does most to keep it that way." During the 1975–76 season, Watts led the league in both steals and assists, and his enthusiasm proved contagious. The Sonics pressed and sprinted and gambled and scrambled. The Coliseum filled to average 95 percent capacity. Russell had dumped all his high-priced superstars and acquired a collection of castoffs that included Zaid Abdul-Aziz, Herm Gilliam, Bruce Seals, and Willie Norwood. Second-year forward Leonard Gray, a tough and athletic scorer, co-captained with Watts. Fred Brown became an All-Star, a twenty-three-point scorer with a stone-smooth jump shot.[52]

The NBA's youngest team had an emotional, hustling style that fed off raucous home crowds. After the Knicks visited a sold-out Coliseum on January 7, 1976 (Haywood got booed throughout a Seattle victory), the Sonics stood 20–18, a surprising second place in the Pacific Division. After losing eleven of fourteen and falling to fourth place, they ripped off eight straight wins to regain second. "They've got momentum and confidence," admired Lakers coach Bill Sharman. "They're playing the best I've seen them play." They won their last sixteen home games and finished 43–39, second in the Western Division, with home-court advantage in a best-of-seven series against the Phoenix Suns.[53]

Seattle's merry ride derailed in the 1976 play-offs. After an opening 102–99 win in which Burleson controlled the lane and Brown scored thirty-four points, the Sonics finally lost at home in Game Two, 116–111. In Phoenix, the Suns twice crushed the Sonics, 103–91 and 130–114. Their balanced offense, led by Paul Westphal and

Alvan Adams, adjusted to Seattle's pressure. Their frontline outmuscled the Sonics. Seattle fans now accepted the inevitable: Russell had installed the Celtics' attitude, but he lacked the Celtics' talent. Yet when some Sonics made a public appearance before Game Five, three thousand supporters greeted them. Another sellout crowd then watched Seattle extend the series, 114–108, with its trademark attacking style.[54]

The season ended after a 123–112 loss in Phoenix, concluding a measured success. The franchise had cemented its well-being, and the team had exhibited cohesion, energy, and charisma. But the Era of Good Feelings was fading. In between losses in Phoenix, even the typically unflappable Russell blinked during a heated, closed-door airing of frustrations. Then, after the season, the players withheld conventional dispersals of play-off bonuses to the assistant coach, trainer, and support staff. Their greed shocked Russell. He thought that he was installing values of self-motivation and unselfishness. "It hit me then that not only was my program for the team failing," he recalled, "but that I didn't like most of the players or want to be around them."[55]

. . .

The next season exposed the lingering troubles from Russell's entire tenure: his roster's limited talent, his indifference for teaching, his disdain for public relations, and his cynicism with the NBA's next generation.

In the 1976 offseason, the NBA and ABA finally consummated a merger. The New York Nets, San Antonio Spurs, Indiana Pacers, and Denver Nuggets entered the NBA, bringing the total to twenty-two teams. The affair left all the principals reeking with greed: New York and Denver betrayed other ABA franchises by independently applying to join the NBA in 1975, NBA owners extracted punitive concessions from the entering ABA teams, and players stalled the merger to keep their salaries rising.[56]

After the merger, six teams from each conference qualified for the play-offs. Seattle depended on the same young core of Slick Watts, Fred Brown, Tom Burleson, and Leonard Gray. Also, Russell drafted Bobby Wilkerson and Dennis Johnson, two big guards with great potential. The continued reliance on youth and enthusiasm helped explain a remarkable early pattern: Seattle lost its first ten on the road and won its first thirteen at home.[57]

The season crashed in December. Russell offered Burleson, Gray, and $2 million for high-scoring, ball-dominating Buffalo Braves forward Bob McAdoo. The potential deal imploded when Schulman insisted on negotiating a contract extension. The New York Knicks got McAdoo instead, as his agent leveraged Seattle's offer for a better deal. The bungled trade signaled a departure from Russell's team-first philosophy.[58]

Schulman still urged Russell to unload Burleson, whose development had stalled. Instead, Russell sent Leonard Gray to Washington for Nick Weatherspoon. Russell and Gray disliked each other. When Russell berated him, Gray responded with cold stares. Then, during the McAdoo negotiations, Gray arrived late for practice. Russell threatened a fine and Gray shrugged, "Bill me." Russell made him run laps; Gray muttered insults under his breath. After that, Gray stopped coming to practices. Rather than discipline him, Russell traded him. A subsequent six-game losing streak dropped Seattle into the Pacific Division cellar.[59]

Popular opinion turned against Russell. The fans' expectations had risen. They had also grown frustrated by continual player turnover. They liked Gray, who had better statistics than Weatherspoon. Correspondents to "Take a Shot!" accused Russell of pettiness and arrogance. Signs at Seattle Coliseum mocked him as "Herr Dictator" and "Der Fuhrer." Another read: "Only One Thing Wrong With Sonics: Trade Russell."[60]

Russell still ran the Sonics in body, but no longer in spirit. "I was withdrawn, not giving the players what I knew, not being as good a coach as I could have been and should have been," he reflected. Bob Hopkins controlled practices and Bob Walsh handled most general manager duties. Sometimes players learned the starting lineup from the public address announcer. Russell haphazardly yanked them in and out of games. Discipline lagged. Although the trading continued—after Mike Bantom left in January 1977, only five remained from the 1976 play-offs—Russell never drilled a patterned, ball-movement system with any commitment.[61]

Russell had always afforded a haughty contempt for public relations, but as the Sonics waned, he exposed himself to disparagement. His sarcastic quips in "Take a Shot!" now elicited frustration. He courted few allies in the media, exhibiting particularly icy disdain for sportscaster Wayne Cody. When Ralph Barbieri of *Sport* researched a profile on Slick Watts, Russell treated the writer like dirt. After witnessing Watts sign autographs, win friends, draw crowds, and cause a traffic jam over autographs, Barbieri juxtaposed their popularity in an article called, "Slick Watts Towers over Bill Russell."[62]

Open dissension now poisoned the Sonics. In February 1977, banner headlines announced that Watts demanded either a trade or a long-term, no-cut deal commensurate with his stardom. That same winter, Bobby Wilkerson and Frank Oleynick aired grievances over playing time, and Fred Brown complained about incessant roster manipulations, suggesting his own trade. Others grumbled that Russell offered little constructive instruction. He never scouted or watched game footage. He taught little during practice, and he said nothing during time-outs. Instead, he degraded them. "You're all assholes," he berated after one loss. He turned around and bent over. "Kiss my ass."[63]

As Russell's grip weakened, Sam Schulman assured himself a lame-duck coach. During a radio interview, Schulman stated that Russell cost too much to retain as both coach and general manager. Russell's contract concluded after the 1977–78 season. At that point, Schulman wanted Russell to just coach. That comment sparked speculation of Russell's demise. Seattle dropped to fifth in NBA attendance. A dissatisfied Schulman knew that his proud, sensitive leader would reject any cut in pay or status. Indeed, Russell chafed that Schulman called him "too expensive."[64]

Hope drained by early March, after seven losses in nine games. Russell looked dejected. The players' gripes smacked of selfishness. They had stopped listening, stopped executing. Seattle finished 40–42, four games behind Detroit and Chicago for the last play-off spot. After the final game, a loss to the Lakers before a quiet and emptying Coliseum, Russell talked about acquiring one or two players and improving the team's concentration. His plans seemed vague, empty, rote. He had checked out, descending into cold disengagement. For four days in late March, amidst their final play-off push, Russell had failed to hold a single practice.[65]

The Sonics did practice before their last away game. After Slick Watts converted a twisting scoop shot, Russell, dressed in flared jeans and sneakers, walked onto the floor of Oakland Coliseum and said, "If you ever brought that shit in on me, I'd make you eat it." Watts accepted the challenge. Watts drove and flipped a shot. Russell swatted it away. Watts tried again; Russell blocked it. "Anyone else?" asked Russell. Dennis Johnson drove, stopped, faked, pivoted, and pushed a five-footer. Russell turned in midair and pinned the ball to the backboard. Finally, Nick Weatherspoon bobbed and weaved, moved right, and tried a fifteen-foot fallaway. Russell swallowed it.

Did Russell know that they had grumbled about his alleged greatness, figuring him for an antique? Was he proving something? Why was he wearing sneakers, anyway? Russell took the ball and dunked it, cackling his way off the court. He had enough, he said.[66]

. . .

Blaine Johnson, beat writer for the *Seattle Post-Intelligencer*, wrote perceptive columns about the Sonics. He explored personalities, explained histories, relayed tensions and joys. Young, hip, white, and fascinated with black athletes, he built complicated friendships with players, balancing personal and professional responsibilities. In 1978 Johnson published *What's Happenin'?: A Revealing Journey Through the World of Professional Basketball*, a behind-the-scenes chronicle of Seattle's 1976–77 season. Russell lords over the story. Johnson obsesses over the Russell paradox: How could one man be so charming yet so cold, so sensitive yet so cruel, so freethinking yet so despotic, so articulate yet so aloof?[67]

Johnson had already spilled some frustrations in a late-season article called "Why Russell Won't Return." He admired "a man of deep pride, apparent honesty and an unwavering code," but he criticized Russell's work ethic. "The team has hit the rocks," Johnson wrote, and Russell's tenure had run its course. Most others shared that opinion. Neither Schulman nor Russell said anything definitive, though Russell termed all the speculation "kind of funny." He deserved responsibility for the team's shortcomings, but "it's not important to the world whether I coach or not. Inflation is important."[68]

On May 4, 1977, Schulman announced the end of the Bill Russell era. The termination surprised no one: Schulman was pursuing Jerry Tarkanian, Bob Walsh had already been fired, and anonymous sources had confirmed Russell's settlement. "He didn't give 150 percent effort," said Schulman, who regretted ceding so much authority. Schulman thought that he had hired a dynamic public personality; after four years, he learned that Russell was private, sensitive, stubborn, and inscrutable.[69]

Aptly, Russell skipped the farewell press conference. After backpacking in Western Canada during the buyout negotiations, he issued a statement praising Schulman as "civic-minded," conveying "mixed emotions about leaving the Sonics," and relaying a desire "to pursue other activities." He returned to Seattle the next week, proclaiming peace of mind. He made mistakes, but he rid Seattle of burdensome contracts and disgruntled underachievers, twice made the play-offs, restored an enthusiastic fan base, reaped profits for Schulman, and stockpiled young, inexpensive players and future draft picks. As he said, "I took a franchise that was in a shambles, and it's not in a shambles now."[70]

But the Sonics reached the Promised Land under Lenny Wilkens, not Russell. In 1977 Wilkens returned to Seattle as director of player personnel. New head coach Bob Hopkins proved too intense a disciplinarian, and the players associated him with Russell; Hopkins got fired after a 5–17 start. Wilkens became coach, and the dark cloud lifted. Seattle finished the regular season 42–18 and reached the 1978 Finals, falling in seven games to the Washington Bullets. In 1979 Seattle won the NBA title, dispatching Washington in five games.[71]

On that championship team, only Fred Brown and Dennis Johnson remained from Russell's regime. After Russell's final disastrous campaign, Wilkens rebuilt the roster with draft picks and trades, acquiring Jack Sikma, Paul Silas, and Gus Williams. He even dealt away civic institution Slick Watts. As coach, he urged that basketball could be fun, and he coolly won his players' respect.[72]

Russell's legacy was slippery. "We were so young, trying to understand this complicated man," recalled Brown. When Russell arrived, he inspired awe. When he left, he bred cynicism. Ultimately, neither the players nor their leader bridged their gulf. However Russell shrugged off sport, he always considered basketball a crucible of character. The Sonics had different values, so he froze them out. "He has no regrets," reported Hopkins, who golfed with Russell every day. "He just didn't believe there wasn't more pride in the league."[73]

18

Russell Redux

"My life is the best it's ever been right now," insisted Russell after his dismissal from the Sonics. He planned to stay in Seattle. Karen attended an excellent public school, and he cherished her stability. He golfed whenever possible, though he never took lessons and seldom went to driving ranges. More than competition, golf delivered recreation and comradeship. He had invested sport with everything and dismissed it as nothing, but he now understood sport as an institution like politics, religion, or art—capable of noble truth and base hypocrisy, awesome beauty and crude hatred. Teammates and competition had rewarded him, but he finally felt comfortable with himself, which made genuine happiness possible.[1]

Since 1970, Russell had known Dorothy "Didi" Anstett, the 1968 Miss USA and fourth runner-up for Miss Universe. After these successes, she earned a master's degree in educational psychology. At first, Russell called her on the telephone, acting on a friend's behalf. After some awkward conversations, they met, became good friends, and fell in love. They got married in a small ceremony on Mercer Island on June 8, 1977.[2]

Russell's marriage to a white beauty queen surprised many people, given his association with black pride. Yet, Russell figured, both professional athletes and attractive women get pampered, considered products more than people, and discarded after their prime. As celebrities, Russell and Anstett shared that "skewered view of reality." Both were also intelligent, unpredictable, and private, with similar philosophies on marriage. "We don't expect marriage to work wonders or change all our glooms into joy," he reasoned. "It just makes life better."[3]

Russell also found fulfillment in new professional challenges. From 1977 to 1981, he wrote a Sunday column for the *Seattle Times*. His old "Take a Shot!" column involved quick answers to readers' questions. This new endeavor—an eight-hundred-word column, conceived and written himself—demanded more discipline. Sometimes he cranked it out. Other times he procrastinated all week, rejecting ideas and fretting about deadlines. But he enjoyed expressing political opinions and personal values.[4]

Russell's columns offered a liberal, if idiosyncratic, voice. He criticized homophobia, religious hypocrisy, and rampant militarism. He supported the legalization of marijuana. He decried an inconsistent criminal justice system. He investigated relationships in the age of women's liberation. He asked children about "forced busing," Vietnam veterans about their hardships, Native Americans about Thanksgiving. He interviewed mayoral candidates. He attacked the United States' policies toward African nations. Some of his final pieces analyzed the departing Jimmy Carter and arriving Ronald Reagan. Russell was no wordsmith, but his columns revealed curiosity, empathy, and an intellectual bent beyond sports.[5]

Russell whetted this reputation with the 1979 publication of *Second Wind: Memoirs of an Opinionated Man*. Conceived as "more philosophy than anything else," Russell pulled ideas from private musings, rap sessions, and college lectures. He collaborated with political journalist Taylor Branch, who collected the bulk of raw material in tape-recorded conversations while riding golf carts or heading to golf courses. "At least three times we woke up in Seattle and decided to drive to a golf course in San Francisco," recalled Branch. "Once, we drove from Seattle to Los Angeles and back." Together they crafted a classic sports memoir.[6]

Where *Go Up for Glory* spit bitterness with tight and snappish sentences, *Second Wind* enlightens with lush and lyrical language. It digs up Russell's roots and polishes them, admiring the Old Man and Mister Charlie and his sweet, strong mother. It extols the art of imagination, a voyage of self-discovery with books and basketballs. It carves open Russell's contradictions: the gregarious hero and sullen recluse, the ultimate winner and brittle egoist. It investigates the intricate recipe for championship teams. It celebrates sport's magic, and it reviles sport's hypocrisies. It frankly explores his romantic foibles, marriage to Rose, and affairs. "He insists upon being taken as a man," reviewed Larry McMurtry. Mel Watkins praised Russell's "folk wit" and "capacity for self-criticism." Roy Blount called *Second Wind* "a rich mixture of wonderment and control."[7]

The book's final pages describe an ascent up Mount Rainier. As Russell's group reached the halfway camp, he experienced extraordinary fatigue. His lungs burned with every breath of icy, thin air. Didi turned back at 10,000 feet. Russell pushed on, roped to team members, his crampons crunching fresh snow with each methodical step, the pain surpassing any of Red Auerbach's training camps. At 12,200 feet, 2,210 from the summit, Russell turned back, too. He realized that victory meant not reaching the summit, but achieving self-awareness. He had expanded his personal barriers, and the experience had awed him.[8]

But if Russell no longer felt a constant compulsion to prove himself, could he remain a central figure of American popular culture? Ironically, as the private Russell found peace, the public Russell lost salience.

. . .

Russell and Anstett divorced in 1981. If he divulged little about their union, he offered less about their separation. He remained, fundamentally, a loner. He loved long, solitary road trips. "I still think he's a shy, mother's son," said his daughter Karen. In the 1980s she went to Georgetown University and then Harvard Law School, leaving his nest empty. Sometimes, after stocking his kitchen and setting his burglar alarm, he watched television, read books, and napped on couches without leaving home for an entire week.[9]

Russell still disdained awards, though his buried need for appreciation occasionally surfaced. In 1980, while attending a luncheon honoring the All-Time NBA team, he gave a speech and got emotional, nearly breaking down. He also offered an enthusiastic reminiscence at a 1985 event reinstating USF basketball after a three-year suspension for NCAA violations. The event inflamed his sensitivities, though. When the chancellor offered him twelve credits to finish his degree in exchange for some guest lectures and a paper about his NBA experiences, Russell got insulted. He eliminated contact with USF.[10]

Russell also dabbled in the occasional acting gig. In November 1979, he hosted *Saturday Night Live.* By its fifth season, the sketch show had achieved commercial clout and celebrity chic, reinventing comedy with bold energy. Russell was nervous. How could he compare to Steve Martin, who hosted the season opener? Then he remembered that Ralph Nader once hosted. He knew that he was funnier than Ralph Nader. Indeed, the first athlete to ever host *Saturday Night Live* acquitted himself without embarrassment.[11]

In 1981, Russell made his movie debut in *On the Right Track,* a 20th Century Fox Production exploiting the popularity of Gary Coleman, the impish star of television's *Diff'rent Strokes.* Russell played a locker-room attendant who befriends Coleman, a homeless shoeshine boy with a gift for picking racehorses. "It isn't exactly Shakespeare," said Russell. After this forgettable drama, he never returned to the big screen, though he popped up on television in a 1981 cameo on *The White Shadow* and in a 1986 turn as a corrupt judge on *Miami Vice.*[12]

Russell also took a surprising turn in the legitimate theater. In 1985 he joined a one-act, two-character play by Irving Horowitz, *The Former One-on-One Basketball Champion.* Staged at the Seattle Children's Theater, the play offered miniscule pay and minimal exposure, but Russell enjoyed the challenge. He took tips from his fourteen-year-old co-star, Jonas Bascom. In the play, Bascom's Irving Katz comes across Russell's Irving Allen, a washed-up and depressed basketball star, and challenges him to a game. The audience learns that Allen's son once killed Katz's father. These survivors confront those demons. Despite crippling stage fright, Russell did fine. "Russell is clearly no stage star, but then no one expected him to be," reviewed *Variety*. "He carries off the part with no muffed lines and his expertise on the court (even a fake one) is good entertainment."[13]

Russell foresaw greater impact as a television personality. In 1978 he signed with ABC, giving producers substantial leeway for his assignments. He expressed interest in interviewing Supreme Court justices, investigating the plight of small farmers, and revealing Antarctic marine life. If assigned to sports, he favored football and baseball. ABC President of News and Sports Roone Arledge admired Russell's intelligence and integrity, and he considered using Russell on news features. As an experiment, Russell worked for KABC-TV in Los Angeles, filming two midweek reports while commuting from Seattle. He covered not only sports but also local, national, and international issues.[14]

For the national network, however, Russell never fulfilled his vision. Instead of reports for ABC News, his assignments included hosting *Superstars*, a made-for-television "trash sport" that pitted athletes in various competitions. So in 1980 Russell signed with CBS as an NBA analyst, relenting in his quest for a television identity beyond basketball.[15]

CBS needed Russell. In fact, the entire NBA needed a boost. Since facilitating the ABA merger, Commissioner Larry O'Brien had lacked vision or energy. Ratings declined. The major markets had weak teams. The league lacked defining rivalries. Television dictated stretched-out, watered-down play-offs. According to one report, somewhere between 40 to 75 percent of professionals used cocaine, and a significant minority freebased it.[16]

Negative racial connotations infected the NBA's image. When black Kermit Washington nearly killed white Rudy Tomjonavich with one shocking punch in December 1977, it confirmed a stereotype of a violent, haphazard league. Almost 75 percent of the players were black, and 75 percent of the fans were white. "People see them dissipating their money, playing without discipline," complained one executive. "How can you sell a black sport to a white public?"[17]

Russell promised celebrity, irreverence, and legitimacy that crossed the color line. At the same time, he added a black face to an all-white broadcast team. (Rick Barry lost his announcing job in 1981 after commenting that Russell had a "watermelon smile.") Russell first worked with Brent Musberger and Hot Rod Hundley, and he later paired with Dick Stockton. He still delivered particular frankness. Only Russell would say, "The Trailblazers have a terrible combination of players out there. There is no way they can play good team defense or team offense with those people."[18]

But instead of highlighting his distinctiveness, Russell's return to broadcasting exposed his shortcomings. Confined by the sound-bite structure, he related few technical aspects. He tried reaching common viewers by commenting on momentum rather than strategy, but it fell flat. He cackled without explanation. Sometimes he mumbled, sometimes he rambled. If the game was boring, he got bored. As basketball and television grew more complex, Russell appeared unprepared. "Sadly, the game seems to have passed him by," mourned *Sports Illustrated*. In 1983 CBS replaced him with Tom Heinsohn. Russell resurfaced the next year on cable superstation WTBS, but his commentary projected the same apathy.[19]

Meanwhile, the NBA began its Golden Age. As counsel to O'Brien, David Stern had negotiated landmark pacts instituting drug testing and a salary cap. These advances structured an era of astounding growth—cleaning the league's image, stabilizing costs, and distributing revenues. Soon after becoming commissioner in 1984, Stern applied new institutions of consumer culture such as Nike and ESPN to promote charismatic personalities, amazing athletes, and a sport tailor-made for global television audiences. Salaries mushroomed and owners prospered. In 1987 expansion franchises in Minneapolis, Charlotte, Miami, and Orlando paid $32.5 million each in entry fees. In 1990 NBC bid $600 million to broadcast the NBA for four years.[20]

The resurgence of a historic rivalry drove this commercial explosion. Between 1980 and 1988, the Los Angeles Lakers won five NBA titles, and the Boston Celtics won three. Their contrasting styles had a racial subtext: Earvin "Magic" Johnson, an African American from inner-city Lansing, Michigan, fueled the Lakers' fast break with ebullient creativity, while Larry Bird, the pale-white product of rural French Lick, Indiana, led the Celtics with stoic resolve. Actually, Johnson and Bird shared gifts of court vision, unselfishness, work ethic, competitiveness, and leadership. But in the public mind, Johnson exuded cool showmanship, and Bird was the blue-collar hero, an emblem of a mythic past, the Great White Hope.[21]

The most racially progressive major league franchise in sports history had flip-flopped its image. In the mid-1980s, the Celtics had eight whites and four blacks, a reverse of the typical NBA roster. Bob Ryan noted that whites adored Larry Bird and Kevin McHale not only for their ability but also for trumping black athletes. By contrast, few African Americans supported the Celtics, even in Boston. "The whole Irish trip, the Celtic green, even the organ music," explained one black community activist. "You get the sense it's not your party, it's their party." Black professionals, moreover, perceived Boston as inhospitable, a reputation enforced in 1990, when police in suburban Wellesley mistakenly identified rookie Celtic Dee Brown as a robbery suspect, forcing him to the pavement at gunpoint.[22]

Yet if the Celtics benefited from marketing white players, their multiple championships evidenced Red Auerbach's tradition of colorblind excellence. And as the NBA boomed, the Celtics became living history, a tangible link to a rich past. Boston Garden anchored in tradition. The trains from North Station still squealed, the parquet floor still created odd bounces, the locker rooms were still too hot or too cold, the Celtics still wore black sneakers, the rafters still bore championship banners.

Howie McHugh still did publicity. Johnny Most still rasped from high above court-side. Havlicek still stole the ball—at least on television clips, accompanied by Most's frantic call. Auerbach retired numbers for stars and role players alike, reveling in his old gang.[23]

But the old resentments between Russell and Boston festered. His rejection of autographs, ceremonies, and racial palliatives continued to defy convention. In a 1980 promotional election for the best in Celtics history, Russell finished behind Havlicek and Cousy. "To let stand such outrageous voting is to countenance either a) racism or b) abysmal ignorance," thundered Bob Ryan. "Russell remains one of this town's favorite whipping boys," wrote Joe Fitzgerald in 1984, who criticized this "misplaced sense of outrage." Added Charles Pierce in 1988, "We've got no right to feel betrayed because Bill Russell doesn't want to be who we think he should be." Athletes, he wrote, "are not custodians of our desires."[24]

Outside his broadcasting obligations, Russell kept his distance from Boston Garden. But in January 1985, he returned for a weekend celebration of Red Auerbach. He coached against Auerbach in an old-timers game (Auerbach barked at the referees) and helped hoist Auerbach's number two to the rafters (Walter Brown was number one). To the tune of *With a Little Help from My Friends,* Celtics legends strode out, decade by decade, capped by each era's marquee hero: Cousy, Russell, Havlicek, Bird. Russell pulled Auerbach into a bear hug, lifting him off the ground. It was a touching and warmhearted gesture.

That same weekend, during a buffet luncheon, Russell said, "Red, I just want to tell you one thing." Emotion flecked his voice, prepping a sentimental moment. "I'm already sick of this!" He cackled, loud and long.[25]

· · ·

In April 1987 the Sacramento Kings announced that Russell had signed a seven-year contract. After coaching for two to four years, he would move to general manager and president, with options for part ownership. A decade removed from the Sonics, Russell would again try resuscitating a moribund franchise.

The Sacramento Kings began as the Rochester Royals, a BAA franchise since 1948. In 1957, the Royals moved to Cincinnati, where they descended from championship contenders to also-rans. In 1972, they became the Kansas City-Omaha Kings. In 1975, they settled in Kansas City. In 1985, real estate developer Gregg Lukenbill shipped the debt-ridden franchise to Sacramento. Dodging political resistance, he built a temporary Arco Arena in the small capital city, and fans embraced the Kings, cheering an overachieving 37–45 team. The next season, however, the Kings crashed to 29–53. They had traded for overrated Derek Smith, who feuded with resident star Reggie Theus. Coach Phil Johnson got fired after losing to Los Angeles on February 2, 1987. After one quarter, Sacramento had trailed 40–4.[26]

A few weeks later, Russell called longtime friend and Kings general manager Joe Axelson, asking advice about a management position in the Eastern Conference. Axelson warned him against it. Three days later, Axelson called back with a proposition: Would Russell coach the Kings? When Axelson retired, Russell could assume his front-office job. They soon met for a four-hour lunch in Sacramento. The job intrigued Russell: he preferred the West Coast, and Sacramento's ownership and fan base indicated growth potential. From Lukenbill's perspective, this plan furthered Sacramento's bid for credibility. The thirty-three-year-old owner aspired to lure a major league baseball franchise, and he envisioned Russell as a stepping-stone to the big leagues. Upon the official announcement, players, reporters, and fans expressed optimistic joy about Russell's return to the NBA.[27]

"Winning can be taught," said Russell at his introductory press conference. "And I know about winning." As with Seattle, he had a young team that needed to learn defense. He dismissed past accusations of his lazy work habits as racist ignorance, but he adhered to his coaching philosophy, letting assistants Willis Reed and Jerry Reynolds run practices and intervening only for specific instructions. During time-outs, he preferred individual conversations. He mellowed his approach, choosing humor over scorn.[28]

Russell elevated expectations, even though the Kings landed sixth in the NBA draft lottery, dashing dreams of picking center David Robinson. They drafted Kenny Smith, a good point guard from North Carolina, and moved Reggie Theus to shooting guard. They also traded sharpshooter Eddie Johnson for banger Ed Pinckney, despite the presence of power forward Otis Thorpe. At center was the adequate trio of LaSalle Thompson, Joe Kleine, and Jawann Oldham. The Kings aspired to respectability.[29]

Instead, the 1987–88 season devolved into an epic disaster. Russell kept rotating his centers, eroding their confidence. During games he exhibited little patience, yanking players for mistakes. The defense lacked cohesion—for months, Russell failed to even introduce a full-court press. By December, out-of-town reporters were ripping Russell's apathy. He once refused to call time-out while Los Angeles outscored Sacramento, 17–1. Another time, Russell put his arm on Joe Kleine's shoulder after substituting him out, and Kleine pushed it away, precipitating a brief shoving match. At the New Year the Kings stood 7–21.[30]

"You have the sense of a pilot at the controls of a plunging airliner, his hands limp upon the controls," sighed the *Sacramento Bee*. Russell alienated everyone around the Kings. He took a girlfriend to the All-Star Game with tickets slated for the team's well-liked publicist. He ignored interview requests and declined public appearances. He angered the media by closing practices. Reporters contrasted the down-home exuberance of the previous, interim coach Jerry Reynolds with Russell's imperial standoffishness.[31]

By midseason, players grumbled about practices full of long-winded instruction. Russell seemed unapproachable. The mood turned grim. Discipline fell apart. Russell set a poor example: "He was late for buses, seemed inattentive at practices, picked odd times to wax philosophical, and became the lowest common denominator for road-trip dress code," wrote one observer. He also avoided direct confrontation. During a postgame speech, Jawann Oldham got up and started showering. His teammates just laughed. They sometimes sat together in bars, mocking Russell with bawdy, drunken songs.[32]

Derek Smith called Russell "a total contradiction." Though Sacramento's scapegoat, his career undone by bad knees and personality clashes, Smith joined Russell for long conversations about everything except basketball. While others lambasted Russell, Smith insisted on his goodness. He also noticed how Russell took a color-blind approach to evaluating players. Yet he also described how Russell demanded that white guard Joe Arlauckas fetch him coffee. "Boy, I want my coffee today, not tomorrow," he said, bullying Arlauckas into a jog. Russell then turned to two blacks and said, "If you could, wouldn't you?" The scene disgusted Smith.[33]

As late as February 27, Russell professed, "I'm enjoying coaching again. I intend to stay in coaching for two or three years." But fan support eroded amidst an eight-game losing streak. On March 7, Sacramento was 17–41. Lukenbill announced a shakeup. Russell moved upstairs to vice president of basketball operations, where his primary duties involved scouting, drafting, and trading. Willis Reed had left to coach New Jersey, so Jerry Reynolds reassumed coaching duties. Two-thirds through the season, Russell's coaching stint crashed.[34]

Russell's spell in management proved just as catastrophic. Lukenbill established an office in Arco Arena, overseeing a four-headed management team plagued by rivalry and jealousy. Russell kept colleagues in the dark about personnel moves. After the Kings limped to a 24–58 finish, Russell traded franchise star Reggie Theus and drafted Ricky Berry. As a rookie Berry showed great potential. The next summer, he committed suicide.[35]

The Kings started the 1988–89 season with seven consecutive losses, accelerating a wholesale makeover. By February 1989, Russell had dealt away Otis Thorpe, LaSalle Thompson, Ed Pinckney, and Joe Kleine. He also waived Derek Smith. The Sacramento media complained—not because of diminished talent, but because Russell operated without patience or planning. The Kings finished the season with six guards and zero centers. It made sense to acquire youth, but veterans such as Danny Ainge and Rodney McCray offered no long-term solutions. Most frustrating, Russell offered no explanations—he maintained a complete public silence.[36]

Fortunately, Sacramento won the 1989 draft lottery. Unfortunately, the 1989 class had no clear-cut top pick. When Russell chose Pervis Ellison, thirty-five hundred fans at the team's draft party booed. After leading Louisville to a national championship as a freshman, Ellison had plateaued. "Never Nervous Pervis" possessed a well-rounded game, but he stood only 6'9", had no outstanding skills, and looked lethargic. Bone spurs and tendonitis delayed his NBA debut until February 1990. Russell also traded for another injury-prone disappointment—the 7'4" Ralph Sampson, a veteran of three knee operations. Sampson played in only twenty-six games that season.[37]

On December 19, 1989, Lukenbill fired Russell. The Kings were 6–15, so few in Sacramento mourned his departure. Despite an eye for talent, he demonstrated no capacity for constructing a team. He took bad risks and overpaid his starters, leaving low-paid, low-skilled men on his bench. His lack of patience stalled player development, and his penchant for privacy sealed his fate. "Ultimately," wrote Jack McCallum, "he was ineffective because he treated people like dirt and because he had lost touch with a league that had become ten times more sophisticated than when he was last involved."[38]

Russell acted with such regal confidence that he seemed immune to self-doubt, impossible to hurt. When Lukenbill fired him, he issued no statements. He gathered his things and drove home. He holed up for three weeks, leaving only for supplies and golf, neither watching television nor reading newspapers. "To this day, I don't know what they said about me," he recalled.[39]

Was he above the criticism, or did it hurt too much? Right after his dismissal, just before he left his office, he had paused for a moment. He stooped over his desk. He looked devastated.[40]

• • •

In 1980, sportswriters named Russell the best player in the thirty-five-year history of the NBA. Wilt Chamberlain scoffed. "If you want to go by individual records, I own 'em all. If you want to go by who is the most prominent, I was, there's no doubt about that." Throughout the ensuing decade, Chamberlain defended his legacy opposite Russell's. He scored more, adapted his style to suit various teams, and faced multiple defenders. With Russell's teammates, he might own all those championship rings. Russell must have been jealous of his fame, endorsements, financial success, and sexual freedom.[41]

Modern fans drew fascination from Chamberlain's statistical accomplishments. *One hundred points in one game?* The New York Knicks, Chicago Bulls, Cleveland Cavaliers, and Philadelphia 76ers all tried luring Chamberlain out of retirement, testifying to his extraordinary physical condition. The press never stopped gravitating to the gregarious celebrity.[42]

Alas, Chamberlain poisoned himself with his own pen. In his 1991 memoir *A View from Above*, he claimed to have bedded twenty thousand women. "Yes, that's correct, *twenty thousand ladies.* At my age, that equals out to having sex with 1.2 women a day, every day since I was fifteen years old." He became a national punch line, inspiring disbelief and derision. "I felt more pity than sorrow for Wilt as his macho accounting backfired on him," wrote tennis legend Arthur Ashe. "This admission (or exaggeration?) will probably haunt him the rest of his life." While reinforcing the stereotype of black male hypersexuality—in the age of AIDS, no less—Chamberlain again demonstrated colossal ego and crippling insecurity.[43]

Meanwhile, Russell clouded the memory of his own greatness. His reclusiveness, patchy television commentary, and mismanagement in Sacramento tarnished his legacy. "Do the people who write history remember the rebuff better than the rebound?" asked Leigh Montville. Russell returned to Mercer Island, to marathons of golf and books and *Star Trek*. He took protracted road trips listening to National Public Radio, soul, country, old-fashioned pop standards, and complete silence. Seattle writer David Shields described seeing Russell in his green Rolls Royce, license plate KELTIC6, and getting enchanted by "the way he swerved into the left-hand-turn lane and scooted through the yellow light: the rhythm, the pace, the left-handed *lurchingness"* that reminded him of Russell's jump hook. Even in Seattle, Russell seemed more a fleeting specter than a sporting celebrity.[44]

"I've tried to keep my life as small as possible," said Russell. "I have some good friends, and I have fun." Those friends included a new companion. He had known Marilyn Nault since 1973, when he entered the jewelry store where she worked. They stayed friends as Russell got married and divorced, bounced among broadcasting jobs, and worked in Sacramento. In 1995 Russell's secretary died, and she offered to help him. They soon realized their mutual love. She moved into his home. She rode along on road trips, indulged his habit of watching late-night Golf Channel, and laughed at his jokes. More than ever, he seemed content.[45]

Russell also started earning money in the most ironic way possible: signing autographs. Exploiting a burgeoning sports memorabilia market, his seven-year, $2 million agreement had him sign jerseys ($995), basketballs ($495), sneakers ($495), and glossy photographs ($295). "In all the world, the four toughest autographs to get are Mikhail Gorbachev, Fidel Castro, Pope John Paul II, and Bill Russell. And not necessarily in that order," claimed his firm. Only Russell did card shows, however. In June 1994, he signed autographs at Boston College High School—no interviews, no photographs—for $295 a pop. Some reveled in the rare brush with a legend. Others saw the signature as a commodity—the same reason Russell had long resisted autographs.[46]

In January 1995 Russell returned to Boston for another card show. This time he brought Chamberlain. Their rapprochement had begun two years earlier, when filming a Reebok commercial with Kareem Abdul-Jabbar and Bill Walton. They still enjoyed each other's company. Soon they resumed long, rambling, late-night telephone conversations about everything under the stars. They called each other by their middle names, Felton and Norman. "Age has mellowed everything," said Chamberlain. Now, they "chat on the phone like old ladies."[47]

At the Boston card show, they sat in adjacent booths, separated by a yellow curtain. While Russell refused interviews, Chamberlain celebrated Russell's mag-nificence, publicized his charity work, and discussed his recent celibacy. "That is the final paradox of the Russell-Chamberlain rivalry," wrote Michael Gee. "The man who met mostly boos in the arena is secure in the limelight. The man who flourished as a public figure craves privacy." The media-driven contrast contin-ued. Russell signed five hundred autographs for $120,000; Chamberlain signed one thousand for $40,000. Reporters chuckled that Russell once again trumped Chamberlain.[48]

But Russell and Chamberlain found assurance in each other. In October 1996, during an NBA celebration of its top fifty players, Chamberlain acknowledged Russell as a great champion, and Russell called Chamberlain's "loser" label unfair. They accepted that their egos, skills, and teams demanded different contributions, dismissing comparisons between them. When Bob Costas interviewed them to-gether at the 1997 All-Star Game, Russell brought up his comment, twenty-eight years earlier, that Chamberlain "copped out" of his final game. "I said something I shouldn't have said. I was wrong." Russell refused to elaborate on television, but he had apologized in private, and he wanted the record settled.[49]

On October 12, 1999, Chamberlain died of heart failure. "I feel unspeakably injured," Russell mourned in a statement. "Many have called our competition the greatest rivalry in sports. We didn't have a rivalry; we had a genuinely fierce com-petition that was based on friendship and respect." They had elevated each other. As they grew older, their legacies intertwined. At the funeral in Los Angeles, Rus-sell delivered a eulogy. He recalled how Chamberlain "put me through hell so many nights," and he savored their mutual appreciation.

"As far as I'm concerned, he and I will be friends through eternity."[50]

. . .

"Grandpa, were you as good as Michael Jordan?" It was Christmastime, the year 2000, and the Russell family was laughing. The patriarch was guffawing loudest. The child looked confused. "You've got the question backwards!" Russell told his grandson.[51]

However one posed it, Michael Jordan represents Russell's most legitimate ri-val as the greatest player ever. With an ineffable blend of explosiveness, grace, confi-dence, and charm, Jordan led the Chicago Bulls to six NBA championships, won five MVP awards, and averaged more than thirty points a game. He also embod-ies the NBA's rise as a platform of global capitalism. Perhaps the world's most fa-mous figure, he made $33 million in salary one season, and he dwarfed that figure in endorsements. His partnership with Nike transformed sports marketing. He sold McDonald's, Gatorade, and Hanes. He had his own cologne and clothing line. He even starred in children's movies. The Jordan icon was an advertiser's dream, a blank slate, all things to all people: cool artist and hot-blooded competitor, familiar friend and handsome sex symbol, black culture hero and postracial corporate logo.[52]

Jordan further illustrates the ambiguities of the black revolution in basketball. On the one hand, sport remains an expression of black power. African Americans have become central to a multibillion dollar endeavor with fans of all colors, creeds, and nationalities. Blacks have assumed more leadership positions, and black basketball stars symbolize the United States to the world, whether as Olympic stars or global icons.[53]

On the other hand, critics see basketball as crippling racial progress, both from within and without. They argue that poor, young, black males fixate on sport, substituting basketball fantasies for education, self-esteem, and positive interpersonal relationships. They see the NBA harnessing, manipulating, and fetishizing black bodies, marketing a "safe" association with "dangerous" black masculinity. And they condemn modern black athletes for abandoning politics. Most famously, Michael Jordan declined to endorse African American Democrat Harvey Gantt, who sought to unseat North Carolina Senator Jesse Helms. "Republicans buy sneakers, too," said Jordan.[54]

With the potential of NBA riches, few dared tread in Russell's controversial footsteps. Yet Russell himself dismissed the historical comparisons. "Whether or not guys will take a stand or not take a stand likely depends on how they got to this place," he said. "All of us can't have the same view. All I tried to do was live my life as responsibly as possible."[55]

As the millennium closed, Russell considered his place in history. In 1998, his business adviser Alan Hilburg and daughter Karen reminded him that retrospectives would soon judge the century's greatest athletes. As his grandson's question reinforced, his privacy masked his greatness. Now age sixty-four, Russell agreed. Hilburg met with Frank Deford in New York. The *Sports Illustrated* correspondent embraced the opportunity to analyze Russell's legacy. "The Ring Leader," published in May 1999, won a National Magazine Award. It connected Russell's modern contentment with his historic accomplishments. Deford also worked at HBO, and Russell cooperated on a documentary released in 2000, *Bill Russell: My Life, My Way.*[56]

The article and documentary ignited a marketing campaign that the *New York Times* dubbed "Russell Redux." It created opportunities that celebrated and enriched Russell. It obscured his complicated personality, his grievances with racism and celebrity, and his incendiary historic persona. Instead it emphasized his credentials as the greatest team player in history, a message that resonated with corporate America. The most unique, iconoclastic figure in American sports history became a brand.[57]

Russell returned to the lecture circuit—no longer for college students seeking authenticity in uncertain times, but for executives who paid $25,000 a speech. "My message is team effort," he explained. "What you have to find out in a team is what are your strengths and how to use them effectively." With Hilburg and David Falkner, Russell also wrote *Russell Rules: 11 Lessons on Leadership from the Twen-*

tieth Century's Greatest Winner. Published in 2001, it possesses neither the gritty candor of *Go Up for Glory* nor the artistic reflection of *Second Wind*. Instead it repackages his stories into obvious lessons for business success, complemented by bullet-point lists. Russell got a $400,000 advance.[58]

Corporations also marketed Russell's reputation. He endorsed Coors, which associated with "revolutionary or groundbreaking" images. Invesco filmed a commercial of Russell discussing his on-court psychology to promote its slogan, "You Should Know What Invesco Knows." To support his media relations company, Russell offered that "Virgil Scudder is to me in this era of my life what Red Auerbach was during my playing days with the Celtics."[59]

In turn, Russell rediscovered comfort with public life. He campaigned for Bill Bradley in the 2000 presidential election. He raised money for charities and spent time with sick children. He delivered the commencement address at Suffolk University and received an honorary degree from Harvard. He accepted induction into the National Collegiate Basketball Hall of Fame and the FIBA Hall of Fame. He wrote a *Boston Globe* editorial about the value of African American history. He started a celebrity basketball camp. He golfed with Samuel L. Jackson on *Iconoclasts*, a Sundance Channel show that paired celebrities in conversation. And in 2009 he published *Red and Me*, a slim memoir about his friendship with Auerbach, who died in 2006. Written with Alan Steinberg, it touchingly recounts their mutual respect and commitment to winning, the basis for a unique friendship.[60]

Russell also counseled young NBA stars, urging them "to honor yourself and your family." He even fostered a truce between feuding stars Shaquille O'Neal and Kobe Bryant. Before a game on Martin Luther King Jr. Day in 2006, O'Neal hugged his former teammate and current rival because, as he explained, "I had orders from the great Bill Russell."[61]

"The great Bill Russell" still acted on his own terms, still refused autographs, still guarded himself from strangers. But he found peace with himself, and he confronted his demons—Chamberlain, relationships, celebrity, even the city of Boston.

. . .

During the construction of Boston's "Big Dig," various citizens and editorialists proposed naming a soaring, cable-stayed bridge after Bill Russell—an appropriate bookend to the Ted Williams Tunnel. It would honor another athlete with an independent spirit, and it would symbolically bridge a racial chasm. The suggestion never gained ground. Many perceived a racial double standard. "Look," said Tom Heinsohn, "all I know is, the guy won two NCAA championships, 50-some college games in a row, the Olympics, then he came to Boston and won 11 championships in 13 years, and they named a fucking tunnel after Ted Williams."[62]

Russell had his own sticky aversions to Boston. In *Second Wind,* he wrote that "if Paul Revere were riding today, it would be for racism: 'The niggers are coming!

The niggers are coming!' he'd yell as he galloped through town to warn neighborhoods of busing and black homeowners." While coaching the Kings, he joked, "I
would rather be in jail in Sacramento than be the mayor of Boston." He visited
Boston Garden only as a broadcaster, coach, or favor to Auerbach. At Auerbach's
retirement in 1985 or a farewell to Boston Garden in 1995, Russell offered few comments, ignored ovations, and slipped away.[63]

But Russell's return on May 26, 1999, signified a new beginning. Coinciding with
his public resurgence, the Fleet Center hosted a gala, produced by Alan Hilburg
and Karen Russell, with proceeds benefiting the National Mentoring Foundation
and the Mass Mentoring Partnership. Thousands sat in the stands, and sixty-five
tables dotted the parquet floor. Bill Cosby and Bryant Gumbel emceed. Aretha
Franklin sang the national anthem. Tom Brokaw spoke. Bill Clinton, Bill Bradley,
Magic Johnson, and Michael Jordan delivered videotaped tributes. "Thank you for
gracing our game," said David Stern, who gave Russell a championship ring that
commemorated the other eleven.

Old friend Johnny Mathis crooned a tune. George Plimpton and Frank Deford
lent insights into the Russell mystique. Jim Brown extolled his partner in altering
the politics of black sport. John Thompson, once Russell's back-up center and then
an iconic coach at Georgetown, discussed the National Mentoring Partnership. Old
rivals such as Willis Reed, Bob Pettit, and Dolph Schayes attended. So did Hal De-
Julio, the scout who brought Russell to USF. Larry Bird, Bill Walton, Dave Cowens,
and Kareem Abdul-Jabbar took the stage together. Walton remembered when his
mother, a librarian, brought home *Go Up for Glory*: "Bill became my hero for life."

Bob Cousy, Bill Sharman, K. C. Jones, Arnie Risen, Tom Heinsohn, Frank Ramsey, Jim Loscutoff, and John Havlicek were there. So was Wilt Chamberlain. Just
months before his death, Chamberlain battled ill health to attend the tribute. He
remembered an old conversation. "You got 11 rings and only 10 fingers; how about
giving me one?" he had asked Russell. "Here, I'll give you a finger to put it on."
Chamberlain stuck out his middle finger.

Finally, Auerbach and Russell hoisted the number six to the rafters. Remembering the overwrought celebrations for Bob Cousy, Russell had long vowed to avoid
sentimental hero worship. But he submitted to this ceremony. It unearthed his appreciation of validation. When he first arrived, the crowd had cheered for five minutes, bringing him to tears. After the number re-retirement, Russell took the microphone. In an echo of Bob Cousy Day from March 1963, a fan bellowed, "We
love you, Bill." Russell looked into the stands. As if closing a book on his misgivings, he responded, "I love you, too."[64]

It was a time to heal wounds. Before the gala, Cousy lamented his failure to help
Russell deal with Boston's racism. "I was the one who should have stepped forward
more," he told the *Boston Herald*. "I wasn't demonstrative enough when things were

happening to him away from the court." Cousy expressed the same regret on an *ESPN Sportscentury* feature about Russell, this time blubbering with tears. But Russell believed that Cousy had done everything possible—the Celtics had respected his humanity, which was all he wanted. Russell and Cousy met soon after the television special. "For the first time, we had an intimate conversation," said Cousy. United by mutual admiration, divided by submerged egos, they finally arrived at a deeper understanding.[65]

Russell now visited Boston to accept an award from Northeastern University's Center for the Study of Sports and Society, join the Greater Boston Chamber of Commerce Hall of Fame, speak about the value of mentoring at Charlestown High School, throw out the first ball on opening day at Fenway Park, and inspire the New England Patriots. He may not have christened a Bill Russell Bridge, but he dedicated basketball courts in Dorchester.[66]

Russell also returned to the Boston Celtics as a team consultant. He periodically visited practices, tutored centers and forwards, delivered motivational talks, and mentored star young forward Antoine Walker. "He's the most insightful person I've been around," said coach Rick Pitino. "He is Celtic Pride." Unfortunately, by the time Russell and the Celtics ended their professional relationship in 2005, Pitino had long since resigned, his incompetence further crippling a franchise that had fluctuated between mediocre and abysmal since the early 1990s.[67]

Then, in 2008, the Celtics won their 17th championship. The circumstances illustrated the distance from Russell's era: Boston reconstructed its team the previous offseason, acquiring multimillionaire veterans through blockbuster trades. In one year, the record reversed from 24–58 to 66–16—hardly the steady Celtics dynasty of the 1960s. Yet the title run showcased the legacies of Russell's basketball revolution. Doc Rivers, one of thirteen black head coaches in the NBA, coached a fifteen-man roster with thirteen black players. He preached a Bantu word for togetherness, *ubuntu*—a new and old take on Celtic Pride, sublimating superstars' egos for the common good. Like their Celtic ancestors, they made defense their hallmark. The ghosts of history smiled upon them: in the finals they beat their ancient rivals, the Los Angeles Lakers.[68]

This new chapter had an engaging subplot. Russell treated Boston's prize new acquisition, Kevin Garnett, like an adopted son. Skilled and quick, the seven-footer shared Russell's lean body, zeal for defense, unselfish ethic, and all-consuming intensity. When the Celtics won, Garnett embraced Russell. "I got my own," Garnett said. "I hope we made you proud." There, on the crowded parquet floor, amidst the joyous celebration so familiar to Russell, basketball's past embraced its present.[69]

During the play-offs, Russell had urged Garnett to keep playing the right way. He offered one of his championship rings, in case the Celtics fell short on their quest. And he told Garnett about his personal happiness. He always knew that his parents loved him, and he tried passing that love to his children. Buried in this lesson was Russell's lifelong quest for meaning, a journey through sport and race and women and fame, a journey past childhood scars, past triumphs, past bitterness, past ego, past fears and frailties.[70]

He once wrote in *Go Up for Glory:* "In the end, I live with the hopes that when I die, it will be inscribed for me: Bill Russell. He was a man." By now, he knew that he deserved the epitaph.[71]

NOTES

INTRODUCTION

1. *Boston Herald*, 23 December 1956.
2. *Boston Herald*, 23 December 1956; J. Fitzgerald, *That Championship Feeling*, 52.
3. *Boston Herald*, 23 December 1956; Carey, *High Above Courtside*, 101; D. Halberstam, *Fifties*, 696. See also Gowdy, *Seasons to Remember*, 120–21.
4. Koppett, "Does Pro Basketball Have a Future?" 81–84; Cousy, "Pro Basketball Needs a Bill of Rights," 12–13, 68–69; Linn, "Is the N.B.A. Big League?" 10–11, 82–85.
5. For statistics on NBA's integration, see R. Thomas, *They Cleared the Lane*, 251–55.
6. On integrationist black icons in sport, see W. Baker, *Jesse Owens*; Hietala, *Fight of the Century*, 148–322; McRae, *Heroes Without a Country*; Rampersad, *Jackie Robinson*; Tygiel, *Baseball's Great Experiment*.
7. On the Fabulous Forum, see Lazenby, *Lakers*, 164–65. On NBA's structural transformations, see Koppett, *24 Seconds to Shoot*, 134–219; Rader, *In Its Own Image*, 90–91, 125–26; T. Murray, "Coming Boom in Pro Basketball," 52–53, 115–19.
8. Koppett, *Essence of the Game*, 66–71.
9. On Russell's last season, see Whalen, *Dynasty's End*. On Russell and Chamberlain, see J. Taylor, *Rivalry*.
10. On Celtics dynasty, see J. Fitzgerald, *That Championship Feeling*; Greenfield, *World's Greatest Team*; Johnson and Johnson, *Celtics in Black and White*; Ryan, *Boston Celtics*; Freedman, *Dynasty*; Shaughnessy, *Ever Green*; G. Sullivan, *Picture History*.
11. On black style and basketball, see Andersen and Millman, *Pickup Artists*, 28–29, 61–64; Axthelm, *City Game*, 3–17, 125–56; Boyd, "Day the Niggaz Took Over," 134–37; George, *Elevating the Game*, 57–199; Novak, *Joy of Sports*, 98–114.
12. Russell touches on these issues in four memoirs of his life and career: B. Russell, *Go Up for Glory*; Russell and Branch, *Second Wind*; B. Russell, *Russell Rules*; B. Russell, *Red and Me*. The only biographies of Russell are intended primarily for juvenile audiences: Hirshberg,

Bill Russell of the Boston Celtics; Nelson, *Bill Russell;* Shapiro, *Bill Russell.* See also Goudsouzian, "Bill Russell and the Basketball Revolution"; Maureen Smith, "Bill Russell," 223–40.

13. On boxers in the black outlaw image, see Gorn, *Muhammad Ali;* Remnick, *King of the World;* Hauser, *Muhammad Ali;* Hietala, *Fight of the Century,* 13–147; L. Levine, *Black Culture and Black Consciousness,* 429–33; R. Roberts, *Papa Jack;* G. Ward, *Unforgivable Blackness;* Wiggins, *Glory Bound,* 152–74; Zang, *SportsWars,* 96–118.

14. On "Revolt of the Black Athlete," see Bass, *Not the Triumph;* Edwards, *Revolt of the Black Athlete;* Hartmann, *Race, Culture;* Olsen, *Black Athlete.* Sport historians have not yet fully examined an athlete such as Russell, who simultaneously embodied a range of political strategies.

15. Recent historians of the African American freedom struggle have demonstrated how liberal and radical impulses often sprang from similar sources. In this vein, an examination of Russell reveals how one athlete could melt the barriers imposed on black icons of the civil rights era. See Ransby, *Ella Baker;* Singh, *Black Is a Country;* Tyson, *Radio Free Dixie.*

16. W. Russell, "Success Is a Journey," 81–93.

1. RUSSELL MOVES

1. See Litwack, *Trouble in Mind,* 3–51.

2. Russell and Branch, *Second Wind,* 19–23.

3. "Monroe and Ouachita Parish History," 9 May 1936, in "Monroe History—1900–1959 #2" File, Special Collections, Ouachita Parish Public Library; *Monroe News-Star,* Bicentennial Edition, 10 March 1983; Heberle, *Labor Force in Louisiana,* 28–29, 44.

4. Magdalene Young, telephone interview with author, 9 March 2006; Ron Downey, telephone interview with author, 10 March 2006; Reverend John Russell, interview with author, 10 March 2006; *Ouachita Citizen,* 21 May 1961; Fairclough, *Race and Democracy,* 9, 29–30.

5. *Papers of the NAACP,* Part 12: Selected Branch Files, 1913–1939, Series A: The South, Reels 13–14; Heberle, *Labor Force in Louisiana,* 81–101; Fairclough, *Race and Democracy,* 47; *The Sepia Socialite presents The Negro in Louisiana,* special edition dated April 1942, 54–63, Special Collections, Ouachita Parish Public Library; "Local History Makers," booklet in "Black Contributions #2" File, Special Collections, Ouachita Parish Public Library; Linn, "Bill Russell's Private World," 64.

6. Litwack, *Trouble in Mind,* 52–61; Russell and Branch, *Second Wind,* 28–31; Fairclough, *Race and Democracy,* 35–36.

7. Magdalene Young interview; Russell and Branch, *Second Wind,* 3–8; John Russell interview; Hirshberg, *Bill Russell,* 19; Deford, "Bill Russell—Center," 219; B. Russell, *Red and Me,* 2–9.

8. Russell and Branch, *Second Wind,* 8–15, 30–31; B. Russell, *Red and Me,* 9; *Bill Russell: My Life, My Way;* J. Jones, *Labor of Love,* 79–109, 196–231. According to Russell, Katie gave him the middle name Felton after Felton Clark, the president of Southern University. But Clark became president in 1938, four years after Bill's birth. On Felton Clark, see Fairclough, *Race and Democracy,* 266–71.

9. *Seattle Times,* 23 April 1978; Russell and Branch, *Second Wind,* 15–16; "Along Came Bill," 36–37.

10. Russell and Branch, *Second Wind,* 16–20; *Seattle Post-Intelligencer,* 28 November 1976.

11. F. Katz, "Unknown Side," 80.

12. Russell and Branch, *Second Wind,* 26–27; B. Russell, *Go Up for Glory,* 12–13.

13. Russell and Branch, *Second Wind,* 24–26; B. Russell, *Go Up for Glory,* 10–13.

14. Lemann, *Promised Land,* 6–7; Russell and Branch, *Second Wind,* 26–27; B. Russell, *Red and Me,* 10–11; B. Russell, *Go Up for Glory,* 14.

15. Rhomberg, *No There There,* 97–98.

16. Self, *American Babylon,* 4–6, 50–54. On wartime transformations in the Bay Area, see also Crowe, *Prophets of Rage,* 15–95; Starr, *Embattled Dreams,* 73–85.

17. *Oakland Observer,* 11 March 1944, quoted in Keown, *Skyline,* 161–62.

18. M. Johnson, *Second Gold Rush,* 51–59, 93–96, 105–7, 167–71; Self, *American Babylon,* 46–58; B. Russell, *Go Up for Glory,* 13.

19. B. Russell, *Go Up for Glory,* 13–14; B. Russell, *Russell Rules,* 171–72.

20. Deford, "Ring Leader," 102; Russell and Branch, *Second Wind,* 10, 31; B. Russell, *Red and Me,* 9–10.

21. Self, *American Babylon,* 82–83; B. Russell, *Russell Rules,* 28; B. Russell, *Red and Me,* 12–13.

22. Russell and Branch, *Second Wind,* 31; B. Russell, *Go Up for Glory,* 16; Deford, "Ring Leader," 104.

23. Russell and Branch, *Second Wind,* 31–32.

24. See Gutman, *Black Family.*

25. Russell and Branch, *Second Wind,* 33–34, 40.

26. Russell and Branch, *Second Wind,* 34–36; Greene, "Bill Russell Is Better Than Ever," 26; *Oakland Tribune,* 28 February 1965.

27. Greene, "Bill Russell Is Better Than Ever," 26; *San Francisco Chronicle,* 10 February 1955; *Boston Traveler,* 17 December 1956; B. Russell, *Go Up for Glory,* 17–19; *Seattle Times,* 3 September 1978; M. Shapiro, *Bill Russell,* 31.

28. Russell and Branch, *Second Wind,* 35–36, 40–41; B. Russell, *Russell Rules,* 146–48; Deford, "Ring Leader," 102.

29. Russell and Branch, *Second Wind,* 36–40; B. Russell, *Go Up for Glory,* 15–16, 20; Halliburton, *Complete Book of Marvels,* 117–24. In *Go Up for Glory* Russell calls the book *Seven Marvels of the World,* and in *Second Wind* he calls it *Complete Marvels of the World.* On Haitian revolution, see Langley, *Americas in the Age of Revolution,* 87–144.

30. *Sacramento Bee,* 28 April 1987; Deford, "Ring Leader," 108; Linn, "Bill Russell's Private World," 64; Rhomberg, *No There There,* 120–22; B. Russell, *Go Up for Glory,* 14–15; Russell and Branch, *Second Wind,* 189–90. For African American population statistics, see W. Brown, "Class Aspects," 74, 76, 141.

31. France, *Some Aspects,* 103; B. Russell, *Go Up for Glory,* 18–19; Russell and Branch, *Second Wind,* 52–54.

32. Russell and Branch, *Second Wind,* 51–60; B. Russell, *Go Up for Glory,* 16.

33. Flood, *Way It Is,* 26–31; Belth, *Stepping Up,* 12–15; Snyder, *Well-Paid Slave,* 34–35; F. Robinson, *My Life Is Baseball,* 30–31.

34. B. Russell, *Go Up for Glory,* 18–21; J. Johnson, *Dandy Dons,* 4.

35. J. Johnson, *Dandy Dons*, 4–5; San *Francisco Chronicle*, 16 January 2006; Rogin, "We Are Grown Men Playing a Child's Game," 87.

36. *New York Times*, 28 December 1955; Linn, "Bill Russell's Private World," 64; B. Russell, "Psych," 34; *Boston Traveler*, 17 December 1956.

37. Hirshberg, *Bill Russell*, 34; B. Russell, "I Was a 6'9" Babe in the Woods," 68. McClymond's High School produced an extraordinary number of athletes. Russell's basketball teammates included Frank Robinson. Other professional athletes who attended McClymond's include professional baseball's Vada Pinson and Charlie Beamon Sr., the NBA's Paul Silas and Joe Ellis, and the NFL's Wendell Hayes. Sam "Touchdown" Brown was an All-American football player at UCLA. See *Los Angeles Sentinel*, 25 October 1956, 28 January 1971.

38. Deford, "Ring Leader," 109–10; Transcript of Interview with Phil Donahue, Bill Russell File, Basketball Hall of Fame; Russell, "I Was a 6'9" Babe in the Woods," 68; Linn, "Bill Russell's Private World," 64; Wooden and Sharman, *Wooden-Sharman Method*, 108; Undated *Boston Herald* article, Mokray Scrapbook, September 1961–January 1962.

39. B. Russell, *Go Up for Glory*, 22; *Oakland Tribune*, 22 December 1951, 13 January 1952; Russell and Branch, *Second Wind*, 61–62.

40. Bee and Norton, *Science of Coaching*, 11; Russell interview with Phil Donahue. Among those who played in Saturday and Sunday morning pickup games with Russell was John Henry Johnson, a Hall of Fame running back with the Pittsburgh Steelers. *Pittsburgh Courier*, 22 September 1973.

41. Naismith, *Basketball*, 32–56, 181–83; Cole, *Loose Game*, 16–21; Applin, "From Muscular Christianity," 18–50; W. Baker, *Playing with God*, 55–63, 111–12; Myerscough, "Game with No Name"; Horger, "Play by the Rules," 3–4, 16–27. On Naismith, see also Webb, *Basketball Man*; Cosentino, *Almonte's Brothers of the Wind*.

42. Naismith, *Basketball*, 77, 117–27; Horger, "Play by the Rules," 98–209; Applin, "From Muscular Christianity," 55–225; Peterson, *Cages to Jump Shots*, 22–68. Allen Guttmann sees basketball's continual movement away from Naismith's vision through organizations such as the YMCA, AAU, and NCAA. See Guttmann, *Whole New Ball Game*, 71–74.

43. Allen, *Better Basketball*, 191–93, 297–305; Holman, *Holman on Basketball*, 15–39; Bee and Norton, *Science of Coaching*, 14–16; Rupp, *Rupp's Championship Basketball*, 15–16.

44. Koppett, *Essence of the Game*, 94–110; Christgau, *Origins of the Jump Shot*; Woodcock, "One Hand Behind His Back," 97–98; *Sporting News*, 14 March 1962; Hobson, *Scientific Basketball*, vii, 186–89, 196–99. On rules changes, see also McConnell, "Chronology of Changes."

45. Horger, "Play by the Rules," 19; M. Nelson, *Originals*, 13–19, 125–37; Dickey, *History of Professional Basketball Since 1896*, 11–17; Baker, W. *Playing with God*, 184–87; P. Levine, *Ellis Island to Ebbets Field*, 3–73; Riess, "Introduction," in *Sports and the American Jew*, 1–28.

46. Riess, *City Games*, 93, 113–16; S. Fox, *Big Leagues*, 323–26; Ruck, *Sandlot Seasons*, 125–28; Chalk, *Black College Sport*, 70–117; Kuska, *Hot Potato*, 1–119; Ashe, *Hard Road to Glory*, 1:104–8, 2:55–58; Gems, "Blocked Shot," 135–48; Thompson, "History of the National Basketball Tournaments"; George, *Elevating the Game*, 15–33.

47. Rayl, "New York Renaissance Professional Black Basketball Team"; Kuska, *Hot Potato*, 120–85.

48. B. Green, *Spinning the Globe*, 52–152; Wilker, *Harlem Globetrotters*, 35–51.

49. Anderson and Millman, *Pickup Artists*, 28–29, 61–64; Russell and Branch, *Second Wind*, 64–65.

50. Cherry, *Wilt*, 8–11; Robertson, *Big O*, 9–11, 20–21; Cope, "Life with Elgin Baylor," 62.

51. Rowell, "Interview with John Edgar Wideman," 53; Majors, "Cool Pose," 109–14; Messner, *Power at Play*, 30–34. See also Wideman, *Hoop Roots*, 6–7, 13–14.

52. Russell and Branch, *Second Wind*, 62–63; J. Johnson, *Dandy Dons*, 9.

53. B. Russell, *Russell Rules*, 20–22, 184–86; Russell and Branch, *Second Wind*, 65–70.

54. Russell and Branch, *Second Wind*, 69–74.

55. Caponi-Tabery, "Jump for Joy," 39–74; Caponi-Tabery, *Jump for Joy*, 68–112. See also Pope, "Decentering 'Race,'" 147–77.

56. *San Jose Mercury News*, 31 March 2005; J. Johnson, *Dandy Dons*, 7–8; *Austin American-Statesman*, 1 April 2005; Ross Giudice, telephone interview with author, 12 April 2007.

57. *St. Louis Post-Dispatch*, 6 February 2005; Lee, "Unstoppable San Francisco," 39; Russell and Branch, *Second Wind*, 74–76.

58. Nelson, *Bill Russell*, 24; Russell and Branch, *Second Wind*, 76; W. Johnson, "Triumph in Obscurity," 74.

59. Linn, "Bill Russell's Private World," 64–65.

2. BIG MAN ON CAMPUS

1. *Foghorn*, 19 September 1952; *The Don*, 1953. For overviews of Russell's college years, see Goudsouzian, "'House That Russell Built'"; J. Johnson, *Dandy Dons*.

2. Ross Giudice, telephone interview with author, 12 April 2007; W. Johnson, "Triumph in Obscurity," 74.

3. *Foghorn*, 24 October 1952, 31 October 1952; Milton Gross column dated 15 January 1959, Mokray Scrapbook, 1959–60 Season; Linn, "Bill Russell's Private World," 65; B. Russell, *Russell Rules*, 57–58; B. Russell, *Red and Me*, 24.

4. *Foghorn*, 3 December 1954, 17 October 1955; *The Don*, 1954; Mike Farmer, interview with author, 9 March 2005; Griffin, "Hoops and Hurdles," 4–5. For photographs, see Schermeister, *University of San Francisco*, 96–111.

5. J. Connolly, *University of San Francisco*; B. Russell, *Red and Me*, 127; B. Russell, *Russell Rules*, 68–69.

6. B. Russell, *Red and Me*, 23–24; *Bill Russell: My Life, My Way*; J. Johnson, *Dandy Dons*, 43–44, 54; *Seattle Times*, 27 August 1978.

7. W. Johnson, "Triumph in Obscurity," 74; *Foghorn*, 24 October 1952, 31 October 1952; Milton Gross column dated 15 January 1959, Mokray Scrapbook, 1959–60 Season; Linn, "Bill Russell's Private World," 65; Russell and Branch, *Second Wind*, 81–82.

8. *Contra Costa Times*, 12 June 2006; Ross Giudice interview; B. Russell, *Russell Rules*, 115–19; *Sporting News*, 1 March 1999.

9. B. Johnson, *What's Happenin'?* 54.

10. *San Francisco Chronicle*, 11 March 1956; *Los Angeles Times*, 18 January 1973; *USF Alumnus*, winter 1972; *Foghorn*, 6 March 1956; Hal Perry, telephone interview with author, 22 May 2007.

11. K. C. Jones, *Rebound*, 41–52; Tom Nelson, telephone interview with author, 11 July 2006; Mike Preaseau, telephone interview with author, 11 July 2006; Stan Buchanan, telephone interview with author, 28 January 2008.

12. B. Russell, *Go Up for Glory*, 24–26; *Seattle Post-Intelligencer*, 1 November 1990. Russell writes that Jones was his roommate during freshman year, but Perry insists that he and Russell roomed together as freshmen, and Jones lived with Russell the next year.

13. Russell and Branch, *Second Wind*, 82–85; *Contra Costa Times*, 12 June 2006.

14. *The Don*, 1953; *Foghorn*, 31 October 1952, 6 March 1953, 13 March 1953, 17 April 1953; J. Johnson, *Dandy Dons*, 54. After winning myriad awards and championships in college and professional basketball, Russell called the trophy for "Most Promising Player" his favorite, perhaps reflecting his pride in his early athletic development. Plimpton, "Reflections," 41.

15. Linn, "Bill Russell's Private World," 65; *Foghorn*, 20 March 1953.

16. *Seattle Times*, 16 September 1979; Auerbach and Sann, *Red Auerbach*, 131.

17. Hirshberg, *Bill Russell*, 60–61; *Boston Herald*, 15 July 1998; *Foghorn*, 23 April 1954, 7 May 1954, 21 May 1954; Linn, "Bill Russell's Private World," 65; Terrell, "Tournaments," 40.

18. *San Francisco Chronicle*, 1 December 1953, 2 December 1953; *Los Angeles Sentinel*, 10 December 1953; *Atlanta World*, 10 December 1953; Lee, "Unstoppable San Francisco," 39; Isaacs, *All the Moves*, 192; Bill Bush, telephone interview with author, 28 January 2008.

19. Lee, "Unstoppable San Francisco," 39; K. C. Jones, *Rebound*, 53–54; *San Francisco Chronicle*, 8 December 1953, 14 January 1954, 15 January 1954, 16 January 1954; *Foghorn*, 11 December 1953, 8 January 1954; *The Don*, 1954, 1955.

20. Hal Perry, telephone interview with author, 22 May 2007; B. Russell, *Russell Rules*, 41–43, 57–58.

21. W. Johnson, "Triumph in Obscurity," 74; Bill Bush interview; B. Russell, *Red and Me*, 26.

22. K. Anderson, "In Their Own Style," 100; Russell and Branch, *Second Wind*, 119–21; B. Russell, *Red and Me*, 24–27; *Contra Costa Times*, 12 June 2006.

23. *San Francisco Chronicle*, 15 January 1954; *Foghorn*, 5 March 1954; *The Don*, 1954; *Los Angeles Times*, 15 December 1954.

24. B. Russell, "I Was a 6'9" Babe in the Woods," 68; *Boston Herald-American*, 16 September 1973.

25. B. Russell, *Russell Rules*, 119; B. Russell, "I Was a 6'9" Babe in the Woods," 68; Russell and Branch, *Second Wind*, 230.

26. K. C. Jones, *Rebound*, 53–54; *Boston Globe*, 13 June 1982; Russell and Branch, *Second Wind*, 114.

27. Davies, *America's Obsession*, 18–27; Maraniss, *When Pride Still Mattered*, 90; Clark, *Undefeated, Untied, and Uninvited*; *San Francisco Chronicle*, 31 May 2006.

28. Jay, *More than Just a Game*, 36–37; R. Kahn, "Success and Ned Irish," 39–46; Isaacs, *All the Moves*, 78–80; Weyand, *Cavalcade of Basketball*, 111–12; Bjarkman, *Biographical History*, 180–82.

29. *Foghorn*, 11 March 1949, 25 March 1949, 3 December 1954, 7 January 1955, 18 March 1956; 1949 NIT Program, "Basketball Programs" Folder, USF Archives; "Basketball at its Best," *Life*, 29 January 1951, 86.

30. "Basketball at its Best," 86; Rice, "Annals of Crime," 44; "Young Businessmen," 80–82; Charles Rosen, *Scandals of '51*, 28; Hobson, "How to Stop Those Basketball Scandals," 65; S. Cohen, *Game They Played*, 59–67, 77; Gross, "Gambling," 68–73.

31. "Young Businessmen," 80–82; Sperber, *Onward to Victory*, 294–302; Shecter, *Jocks*, 234–37; Rice, "Annals of Crime," 38; Hobson, "How to Stop Those Basketball Scandals," 26–27, 65–67; S. Cohen, *Game They Played*, 79–85, 122–25.

32. P. Levine, *Ellis Island to Ebbets Field*, 74–86; Figone, "Gambling and College Basketball," 44–61; Rice, "Annals of Crime," 38–66; S. Cohen, *Game They Played*, 105, 225; Sperber, *Onward to Victory*, 327–42; Fitzpatrick, *And the Walls Came Tumbling Down*, 99–101.

33. See Crawford, "Consensus All-American," 114–48; Riesman, *Lonely Crowd*, 28–38; Susman, "Did Success Spoil the United States?" 19–37; *Post* quote in Charles Rosen, *Scandals of '51*, 133–34; *Herald-American* quote in Weyand, *Cavalcade of Basketball*, 159; *Herald Tribune* quote in Hobson, "How to Stop Those Basketball Scandals," 26.

34. "Basketball Bounces Back," 66; Sperber, *Onward to Victory*, 302–42; Lawrence, *Unsportsmanlike Conduct*, 50–63; Byers, *Unsportsmanlike Conduct*, 5, 54–57; Dunnavant, *Fifty-Year Seduction*, 17–28; Yaeger, *Undue Process*, 7–27; S. Cohen, *Game They Played*, 214.

35. W. Johnson, "Triumph in Obscurity," 68–71; *Foghorn*, 3 December 1954, 2 December 1955; Mike Farmer interview; Woolpert, "Scene Behind the Scene on Dons," 12; Tom Nelson interview; Lee, "Unstoppable San Francisco," 38–39. On Woolpert, see also J. Johnson, *Dandy Dons*, 71–81.

36. W. Johnson, "Triumph in Obscurity," 71–72; Isaacs, *All the Moves*, 191–92; O. Harris, "African American Predominance in Sport," 40; Chalk, *Black College Sport*, 130–33; *San Francisco Chronicle*, 15 March 1979. See also Graham and Graham Cody, *Getting Open*, 89–190.

37. *San Francisco Call-Bulletin*, 26 November 1954; *Los Angeles Times*, 21 December 1954; *San Francisco Chronicle*, 6 December 1954, 15 December 1954; *Foghorn*, 24 September 1954, 29 October 1954, 3 December 1954, 10 December 1954; *Los Angeles Daily News*, 15 December 1954.

38. *San Francisco Chronicle*, 30 November 1954, 13 January 1955; *Foghorn*, 3 December 1954; *Hayward Review*, 22 March 1955; R. Kahn, "Preview," 20–21. West Coast teams had achieved prominence before. Besides USF's NIT championship in 1949, Oregon won the NCAA title in 1939 and Stanford won it in 1942.

39. Isaacs, *All the Moves*, 192–93; *Foghorn*, 2 December 1955; *San Francisco Chronicle*, 12 December 1954; undated *Boston Traveler* article, Bill Russell File, Basketball Hall of Fame; *New York Times*, 13 December 1956; *Los Angeles Daily News*, 15 December 1954.

40. *USF Alumnus*, Souvenir Edition, April 1955; *Austin American-Statesman*, 1 April 2005; Hal Perry, telephone interview with author, 22 May 2007; Bill Bush interview; Stan Buchanan interview.

41. M. Harris, *Lonely Heroes*, 21–22; *San Francisco Chronicle*, 19 December 1954.

42. Broussard, *Black San Francisco*, 1–7, 131–220; Tang, "Pushing at the Golden Gate," 1–10, 117–43, 252–53. On *Brown* decision and 1950s aftermath, see J. Patterson, *Brown v. Board of Education*, 1–117; Wilkinson, *From Brown to Bakke*, 3–95.

43. *Sporting News*, 15 January 1996; *St. Louis Post-Dispatch*, 6 February 2005.

44. *San Jose Mercury News*, 31 March 2005; *San Francisco Chronicle*, 15 March 1979; *Seattle Times*, 7 May 1987.

45. Steve Balchios, telephone interview with author, 12 July 2006; Warren Baxter, telephone interview with author, 12 July 2006; Tom Nelson interview; Stan Buchanan interview; Lee, "Unstoppable San Francisco," 85.

46. *Austin American-Statesman*, 1 April 2005; Stan Buchanan interview.

47. *St. Louis Post-Dispatch*, 7 February 2005; K. C. Jones, *Rebound*, 55–56; *Seattle Times*, 30 March 1986; *San Jose Mercury News*, 31 March 2005.

48. Isaacs, *All the Moves*, 193; *Seattle Times*, 30 March 1986; *San Francisco Examiner*, 24 December 1954; uncited article in USF Scrapbook, University of San Francisco Archives; *San Francisco Chronicle*, 22 December 1954, 23 December 1954, 4 January 1955.

49. *San Francisco Chronicle*, 4 January 1955, 6 January 1955; *The Don*, 1956; *USF Alumnus*, Souvenir Edition, April 1955; Lee, "Unstoppable San Francisco," 85.

50. *Foghorn*, 7 January 1955; *San Francisco Chronicle*, 30 December 1954, 5 January 1955, 6 January 1955, 11 January 1955, 13 January 1955, 15 January 1955; *San Francisco Examiner*, 5 January 1955; Isaacs, *All the Moves*, 193.

51. Ron Tomsic, telephone interview with author, 29 October 2008; *San Francisco Chronicle*, 17 January 1955, 18 January 1955, 25 January 1955, 26 January 1955, 30 January 1955, 1 February 1955; *San Francisco Examiner*, 29 January 1955, 31 January 1955; *Foghorn*, 2 December 1955; *Oakland Tribune*, 1 February 1955; *Sacramento Bee*, 1 February 1955. On Cow Palace, see *Sporting News*, 16 March 1960, 25 January 1964.

52. *San Francisco Chronicle*, 19 December 1954, 13 January 1955, 1 February 1955; *Bakersfield Californian*, 31 January 1955.

53. Holman, *Holman on Basketball*, 76–77; *San Francisco Chronicle*, 3 February 1955, 28 February 1955.

54. *San Francisco Examiner*, 31 January 1955; *San Francisco Chronicle*, 3 February 1955; *Sporting News*, 19 January 1955.

55. *San Francisco Chronicle*, 7 February 1955, 8 February 1955, 10 February 1955, 15 February 1955, 24 February 1955, 3 March 1955, 8 March 1955; *The Don*, 1955.

56. *Los Angeles Sentinel*, 13 January 1955; *Pittsburgh Courier*, 5 February 1955, 12 March 1955; *Chicago Defender*, 12 March 1955; *Atlanta Daily World*, 5 March 1955, 15 March 1955. After USF had won the NCAA title, Russell won tournament MVP, Maurice Stokes won MVP of the NIT, all-black Crispus Attucks High School won the Indiana state tournament, and black athletes achieved various successes at the Golden Gloves boxing tournament and the Pan-American Games in Mexico City, Russ J. Cowans of the *Chicago Defender* called March 1955 "the greatest month of achievements in the history of Negro athletes." *Chicago Defender*, 2 April 1955.

57. *San Francisco Chronicle*, 28 February 1955, 1 March 1955, 3 March 1955, 11 March 1955; *Los Angeles Times*, 1 March 1955, 3 March 1955, 11 March 1955; Russell, *Go Up for Glory*, 32–33; W. Johnson, "Triumph in Obscurity," 74. In his most recent memoir, Russell denies giving the speech. See B. Russell, *Red and Me*, 27–28.

58. *San Francisco Chronicle*, 19 February 1955, 21 February 1955, 7 March 1955, 9 March 1955; Rappoport, *Classic*, 102; *USF Alumnus*, Souvenir Edition, April 1955; *Foghorn*, 2 December 1955.

59. *San Francisco Chronicle*, 11 March 1955, 12 March 1955; *USF Alumnus*, Souvenir Edition, April 1955.

60. *San Francisco Chronicle,* 12 March 1955; Rappoport, *Classic,* 102; W. Johnson, "Triumph in Obscurity," 77; Lee, "Unstoppable San Francisco," 85–86.

61. *San Francisco Chronicle,* 12 March 1955, 14 March 1955; J. Johnson, *Dandy Dons,* 107–8; *Los Angeles Times,* 22 February 1955; *USF Alumnus,* Souvenir Edition, April 1955; John Cunningham, telephone interview with author, 30 January 2008; Rappoport, *Classic,* 103.

62. *San Francisco Chronicle,* 13 March 1955, 14 March 1955; *Los Angeles Times,* 14 March 1955; K. Anderson, "In Their Own Style," 98; Lee, "Unstoppable San Francisco," 86; Rappoport, *Classic,* 103–4.

63. *Pittsburgh Courier,* 9 April 1955.

64. Christgau, *Origins of the Jump Shot,* 154; Rappoport, *Classic,* 104.

65. Burdette Haldorson, telephone interview with the author, 30 October 2008; 1955 NCAA Final Program, 1955–56 Dons Basketball Folder, USF Archives; Lee, "Unstoppable San Francisco," 86; *San Francisco Chronicle,* 15 March 1955, 17 March 1955, 18 March 1955, 20 March 1955; *USF Alumnus,* Souvenir Edition, April 1955; *Foghorn,* 25 March 1955.

66. Gross, "In Philadelphia Nearly Everybody Likes Gola," 30, 62–63; Glickman, "All-America Basketball Preview," 12–15, 91; *Sporting News,* 2 February 1955; *Philadelphia Inquirer,* 29 December 1954, 1 February 1955, 2 February 1955; Bjarkman, *Biographical History of Basketball,* 24–25, 135–38.

67. *Kansas City Star,* 19 March 1955; Lee, "Unstoppable San Francisco," 86.

68. Rappoport, *Classic,* 98, 104.

69. *San Francisco Chronicle,* 20 March 1955, 21 March 1955, 22 March 1955; *Los Angeles Times,* 22 March 1955.

70. Lee, "Unstoppable San Francisco," 86; *San Francisco Examiner,* 21 March 1955.

71. *Los Angeles Times,* 20 March 1955; *Chicago Tribune,* 21 March 1955; *Seattle Times,* 30 March 1986; *San Francisco Chronicle,* 23 March 1955, 7 April 1955.

3. RUSSELL RULES

1. Mike Farmer, interview with author, 9 March 2005; *San Francisco Examiner,* 22 March 1955; *San Francisco Chronicle,* 22 March 1955; *Foghorn,* 25 March 1955; *The Don,* 1955.

2. *Sporting News,* 18 January 1956; *Foghorn,* 25 March 1955; Brachman quoted in *The Don,* 1955.

3. *San Francisco Chronicle,* 23 March 1955; *Foghorn,* 25 March 1955; *New York Times,* 23 March 1955.

4. *San Francisco Chronicle,* 23 March 1955; *San Diego Union,* 23 March 1955.

5. "Dons on Defense," 50–51; "Big Surprise of 1955," 17–19; *Richmond Independent,* 2 February 1955; *San Francisco Chronicle,* 10 February 1955; *Chicago Defender,* 12 March 1955; *Pittsburgh Courier,* 5 March 1955, 2 April 1955.

6. Russell and Branch, *Second Wind,* 42–43; B. Russell, *Go Up for Glory,* 37–38.

7. "Dons on Defense," 51; "Big Surprise of 1955," 19; Deford, "Ring Leader," 110.

8. K. Anderson, "In Their Own Style," 98–100.

9. *San Francisco Examiner,* 22 March 1955; Allen, *Better Basketball,* 23–26, 77–83.

10. Peterson, *Cages to Jump Shots,* 9–10, 142–45. On Allen, see also Kerkhoff, *Phog Allen.*

11. "Giants of Schoolboy Basketball," 59–62; "Those Big Galoots," 22; *New York Times,* 28 December 1956; Hobson, *Scientific Basketball,* 103–21; "Letters to the Editor," *Saturday Evening Post,* 23 January 1954, 4; Povich, "Basketball Is for the Birds," 24–27; Berkow, *Red,* 70, 156–57.

12. *San Francisco Chronicle,* 22 March 1955; *New York Times,* 18 March 1955, 22 March 1955. On debates over basketball style and rules changes, see *Philadelphia Inquirer,* 7 December 1954, 25 January 1955, 8 February 1955; Luisetti, "Racehorse Basketball Stinks!" 10–11, 84–85; *Sporting News,* 26 January 1955, 7 December 1955, 14 December 1955; *San Francisco Chronicle,* 12 February 1955, 20 March 1955, 22 March 1955, 25 March 1955, 28 January 1956; T. Sullivan, "History of the National Association of Basketball Coaches," 120–22; *Foghorn,* 30 September 1955, 9 December 1955. For a comprehensive chronicle of earlier rules modifications, see McConnell, "Chronology of Changes in Basketball Rules."

13. *Sporting News,* 18 January 1956; *Los Angeles Times,* 1 December 1955; *Sporting News,* 7 December 1955, 14 December 1955; *Foghorn,* 14 April 1955, 2 December 1955, 13 January 1956; Glickman, "All-America Basketball Preview," 12–13, 64–65. On Boldt, see *San Francisco Chronicle,* 12 March 1956. On Farmer, see *San Francisco Chronicle,* 13 March 1956. Hal Perry later said that the Dons had an "all-minority" starting five, since Farmer was Cherokee Indian and Boldt had spent part of his childhood in a black foster home. Boldt countered that Perry was the only "nonminority" because only he grew up surrounded by white people. J. Johnson, *Dandy Dons,* 130–31.

14. *San Francisco Chronicle,* 2 December 1955, 4 December 1955, 7 December 1955; *Sporting News,* 14 December 1955; *Foghorn,* 9 December 1955; Terrell, "Basketball Bounces In," 24; Terrell, "Basketball" (19 December 1955), 44.

15. *New York Daily News,* 3 November 1996; *Seattle Times,* 23 November 1975.

16. "Basketball's All-Time All-America," 20–23; Mikan, *Mr. Basketball,* 1–40; Mikan and Oberle, *Unstoppable,* 25–66; Schumacher, *Mr. Basketball,* 1–60.

17. Koppett, *24 Seconds to Shoot,* 67–80; Mikan, *Unstoppable,* 67–175; Schumacher, *Mr. Basketball,* ix–xiv, 61–237.

18. *San Francisco Chronicle,* 17 December 1955, 18 December 1955; *Washington Post and Times Herald,* 20 December 1955; *Chicago Tribune,* 31 January 1967.

19. M. Harris, *Lonely Heroes,* 23.

20. *San Francisco Chronicle,* 21 December 1955.

21. Eugene Brown, telephone interview with author, 28 January 2008; Warren Baxter, telephone interview with author, 12 July 2006; Tom Nelson, telephone interview with author, 11 July 2006.

22. *Los Angeles Sentinel,* 22 December 1955; C. Martin, "Integrating New Year's Day," 175–99; C. Martin, "Jim Crow in the Gymnasium," 233–39; Grundman, "Image of Intercollegiate Sports"; Jay, *More than Just a Game,* 74. The Supreme Court ruled Louisiana's law unconstitutional in 1959, but the Sugar Bowl did not include another black player until 1965. For overview of blacks in college athletics, see Spivey, "Black Athlete in Big-Time Intercollegiate Sports."

23. *New York Times,* 26 November 1954; *San Francisco Chronicle,* 21 December 1955, 23 December 1955; *New York Post,* 21 December 1956; *Chicago Defender,* 31 December 1955; Warren Baxter interview.

24. Eugene Brown interview; *Bill Russell: My Life, My Way*. Russell, Jones, and Perry some-times played in springtime interfraternity tournaments against black Greek-letter organiza-tions across California. See *Los Angeles Sentinel*, 28 May 1953, 28 April 1955.

25. *Sacramento Bee*, 20 March 2006; Eugene Brown interview; *San Francisco Chronicle*, 21 December 1955, 3 April 2005; B. Russell, *Go Up for Glory*, 163; *Seattle Times*, 30 March 1986.

26. W. Johnson, "Triumph in Obscurity," 74.

27. *San Francisco Chronicle*, 23 December 1955, 24 December 1955, 4 April 2005; W. Johnson, "Triumph in Obscurity," 74; Tom Nelson interview; Mike Farmer interview; *Atlanta Daily World*, 28 December 1955; *Pittsburgh Courier*, 31 December 1955.

28. Jim Murray, *Jim Murray*, 106–7; Terrell, "Tournaments and the Man Who," 38; Charles Rosen, *God, Man and Basketball Jones*, 62.

29. *New York Post*, 12 December 1955; *New York World-Telegram and Sun*, 22 Decem-ber 1955; *San Francisco Chronicle*, 24 December 1955, 26 December 1955; *New York Times*, 29 December 1956.

30. *New York Times*, 25 December 1955; *San Francisco Chronicle*, 8 January 1956; Hirsh-berg, *Bill Russell*, 68; Terrell, "Tournaments and the Man Who," 40; *Foghorn*, 13 January 1956.

31. Terrell, "Tournaments and the Man Who," 40; *San Francisco Chronicle*, 27 Decem-ber 1955, 28 December 1955, 8 January 1956; *New York Times*, 28 December 1955.

32. Pluto, *Tall Tales*, 120; *New York Journal-American* quoted in *Foghorn*, 13 January 1956; *New York Post*, 27 December 1955; *San Francisco Chronicle*, 4 January 1956.

33. *San Francisco Chronicle*, 4 January 1956; *New York Post*, 28 December 1955, 29 De-cember 1955; *New York Times*, 29 December 1955. See also "Talent, Inc.," 42; Heinsohn, *Hein-sohn, Don't You Ever Smile?* 76–77.

34. Heinsohn and Fitzgerald, *Give 'Em the Hook*, 26–29; B. Russell, *Russell Rules*, 78–79; Bill Bush, telephone interview with author, 28 January 2008; *Los Angeles Times*, 29 Decem-ber 1955; *San Francisco Chronicle*, 29 December 1955; *Foghorn*, 13 January 1956; *New York Post*, 29 December 1955.

35. *Los Angeles Sentinel*, 13 January 1955; B. Russell, "Psych," 34.

36. *San Francisco Chronicle*, 31 December 1955; *New York Times*, 31 December 1955; Wooden and Sharman, *Wooden-Sharman Method*, 116–17; *Foghorn*, 13 January 1956.

37. *Chicago American*, 31 December 1955. On Lapchick, see also J. Lapchick, *50 Years of Basketball*, 3–32; Alfieri, *Lapchick*, 15–175.

38. *San Francisco Chronicle*, 7 January 1956, 11 January 1956, 14 January 1956; *New York Times*, 14 January 1956; *Los Angeles Times*, 6 December 1955, 4 January 1956, 18 January 1973; *San Francisco Progress*, 18–19 January 1956; B. Russell, *Go Up for Glory*, 28–29.

39. "Best Big Man on View," 12–14; "Bill Russell—The Antenna with Arms," 66–68; "Bas-ketball's Leaning Tower," 50–51; "Along Came Bill," 36–37; *New York Times*, 28 December 1956; *Chicago Tribune*, 21 March 1956; *Los Angeles Times*, 18 January 1973; *Chicago Defender*, 7 January 1956, 14 January 1956, 29 February 1956, 3 March 1956, 26 March 1956, 31 March 1956, 7 April 1956; *Pittsburgh Courier*, 26 March 1955, 4 February 1956, 3 March 1956, 10 March 1956; *Atlanta Daily World*, 29 November 1955; *Los Angeles Sentinel*, 9 February 1956; *New York Amsterdam News*, 31 December 1955, 10 March 1956; *San Francisco Chronicle*, 6 February 1956, 17 March 1956; uncited article in USF Scrapbook; Lee, "Unstoppable San Fran-cisco," 86.

40. Mike Preaseau, telephone interview with author, 11 July 2006; *Boston Herald,* 26 May 1999; Hal Perry, telephone interview with author, 22 May 2007. Tom Nelson interview; Bill Bush interview; Mike Farmer interview; *Los Angeles Times,* 18 January 1973.

41. *San Francisco Chronicle,* 9 March 1956; Tom Nelson interview; Steve Balchios, telephone interview with author, 12 July 2006; Mike Preaseau interview; John Cunningham, telephone interview with author, 30 January 2008; Michelson, "Eagles and Priests," 10; Warren Baxter interview.

42. *Los Angeles Times,* 18 January 1973; *Foghorn,* 6 March 1956.

43. Tom Nelson interview; Steve Balchios interview; Mike Preasaeu interview; *Oroville Mercury-Register,* 2 April 2007; *Los Angeles Times,* 18 January 1973.

44. W. Johnson, "Triumph in Obscurity," 68, 77; Lee, "Unstoppable San Francisco," 86.

45. *San Francisco Chronicle,* 12 January 1956, 16 January 1956, 23 January 1956, 25 January 1956, 27 January 1956, 28 January 1956.

46. *New York Times,* 29 January 1956; Rappoport, *Classic,* 105–6; J. Johnson, *Dandy Dons,* 152–53; Eugene Brown interview; *San Francisco Chronicle,* 29 January 1956.

47. *San Francisco Chronicle,* 29 January 1956, 30 January 1956, 31 January 1956, 1 February 1956.

48. *San Francisco Chronicle,* 1 February 1956, 3 February 1956, 4 February 1956, 7 February 1956, 8 February 1956, 11 February 1956, 15 February 1956, 18 February 1956, 25 February 1956, 3 March 1956, 30 March 1956; B. Russell, "Psych," 34; K. Anderson, "In Their Own Style," 98; *New York Times,* 7 March 1956; Terrell, "Black Saturday," 54–55.

49. *San Francisco Chronicle,* 13 February 1956, 11 March 1956, 28 March 1956.

50. *USF Alumnus,* Souvenir Edition, April 1955; *The Don,* 1956; *San Francisco Chronicle,* 8 February 1956, 2 March 1956, 7 March 1956, 8 March 1956, 9 March 1956, 16 March 1956; *Foghorn,* 17 February 1956; *New York Times,* 7 March 1956.

51. *Foghorn,* 4 November 1955, 13 January 1955; *San Francisco Chronicle,* 12 January 1956, 17 February 1956; Terrell, "Basketball," (23 January 1956), 45; Terrell, "It's Dayton and the Dons," 21.

52. *San Francisco Chronicle,* 7 February 1956, 24 February 1956, 2 March 1956, 6 March 1956, 7 March 1956, 8 March 1956; Mike Farmer interview; *Foghorn,* 6 March 1956, 9 March 1956; Lee, "Unstopppable San Francisco," 86; Bernie Schneider, "USF Basketball '55–'56: The Repeat," in "USF Basketball—Schneider" Folder, USF Archives. See also *Seattle Post-Intelligencer,* 14 October 1973.

53. *San Francisco Chronicle,* 14 March 1956, 16 March 1956; Terrell, "Dayton and the Dons," 46; *The Don,* 1956; *Foghorn,* 9 March 1956, 20 March 1956.

54. *San Francisco Chronicle,* 17 March 1956; *Foghorn,* 20 March 1956.

55. *San Francisco Chronicle,* 18 March 1956; *Foghorn,* 20 March 1956; Terrell, "NCAA Semifinals," 47.

56. *San Francisco Chronicle,* 19 March 1956, 20 March 1956, 23 March 1956; *New York Times,* 19 March 1956; *San Francisco Examiner,* 23 March 1956; *Los Angeles Times,* 23 March 1956; Terrell, "Victory No. 55," 42.

57. "Easy Does It," 93–94; *San Francisco Chronicle,* 24 March 1956; Lee, "Unstoppable San Francisco," 87.

58. *San Francisco Chronicle,* 24 March 1956; Lee, "Unstoppable San Francisco," 87; Terrell, "Victory No. 55," 42. On Carl Cain, see *Des Moines Register,* 6 April 1980.

59. Eugene Brown interview; Warren Baxter interview; *Los Angeles Times,* 24 March 1956; *New York Times,* 24 March 1956; *San Francisco Chronicle,* 24 March 1956; Terrell, "Victory No. 55," 43. A video recording of the 1956 NCAA Final is available in Special Collections at the University of San Francisco.

60. *Los Angeles Times,* 24 March 1956, 25 March 1956; *New York Times,* 26 March 1956; "Wilt the Stilt," 61–62.

61. B. Russell, *Go Up for Glory,* 34; *Los Angeles Times,* 24 March 1956; Lee, "Unstoppable San Francisco," 87; *San Francisco Chronicle,* 25 March 1956, 26 March 1956; *New York Times,* 30 March 1956.

62. *San Francisco Chronicle,* 27 March 1956, 28 March 1956; *New York Times,* 27 March 1956, 1 April 1956; *Chicago Defender,* 7 January 1956; *Atlanta Daily World,* 6 March 1956; *Pittsburgh Courier,* 10 March 1956, 31 March 1956, 7 April 1956.

63. *San Francisco Chronicle,* 26 March 1956, 28 March 1956; *New York Times,* 27 March 1956; *San Francisco Call-Bulletin,* 9 April 1956; "After Five Years"; C. Martin, "Jim Crow in the Gymnasium," 237.

64. UP Photograph dated 5 April 1956 in "1955–56 Dons Basketball" Folder, USF Archives; *San Francisco Examiner,* 3 March 1955; *USF Alumnus,* April 1955; *Foghorn,* 24 February 1956; *San Francisco Chronicle,* 3 March 1956, 4 March 1956, 22 March 1956, 23 March 1956, 13 January 1956, 6 December 1956.

4. THE AMATEUR

1. Domer, "Sport in Cold War America," 107–10; *Washington Post and Times Herald,* 12 July 1955; B. Russell, "I Was a 6'9" Babe in the Woods," 68. On Eisenhower and sport, see also Watterson, *Games Presidents Play,* 185–200. On sport, mass culture, and the cold war, see also Crawford, "Consensus All-American."

2. "Russell Promises President He Will Play in the Olympics," 52–54; *Boston Globe,* 7 December 2000; *Boston Traveler,* 19 December 1956.

3. B. Russell, *Go Up for Glory,* 36–37.

4. Russell and Branch, *Second Wind,* 106.

5. Horger, "Play by the Rules," 46–49; Applin, "From Muscular Christianity to the Market Place," 182–92, 272–83; Tuttle, "High-Test Hoops," 34–90; Cunningham, "American Hoops," 130–34; Cunningham, "Russell Model," 62–64; Grundman, *The Golden Age of Amateur Basketball,* 55–157. On Kurland, see Bjarkman, *Biographical History of Basketball,* 145–48; *New York Times,* 28 March 1995.

6. Terrell, "Tournaments," 43; B. Russell, *Go Up for Glory,* 44; *Chicago Defender,* 27 March 1956; *San Francisco Chronicle,* 17 February 1956, 23 March 1956, 24 March 1956; *Washington Post and Times Herald,* 29 February 1956, 11 March 1956, 25 March 1956; *Los Angeles Times,* 2 April 1956. On the AAU's expanding jurisdiction and involvement in international sport, see also Karsgaard, "History of the Amateur Athletic Union," 147–205.

7. *Washington Post and Times Herald,* 2 April 1956; *Chicago Defender,* 3 April 1956;

Chicago Tribune, 3 April 1956, 5 April 1956; *Atlanta Daily World,* 5 April 1956; *Los Angeles Times,* 4 April 1956, 6 April 1956; *New York Times,* 6 April 1956; B. Russell, *Go Up for Glory,* 44–45. See also Grundman, *Golden Age of Amateur Basketball,* 172–75. The exclusion of high-scoring African American Willie Naulls surprised some observers, who judged him the tournament's second-best player behind Russell. *Chicago Defender,* 9 April 1956.

8. B. Russell, *Go Up for Glory,* 35–36; "Along Came Bill," 36; Griffin, "Hoops and Hurdles," 20–22, 27; *Los Angeles Times,* 21 December 1955, 1 May 1956, 9 May 1956, 1 June 1956, 12 June 1956; *USF Alumnus,* June 1956. University of Kansas coach Phog Allen was a particularly vociferous critic of the AAU's shortsightedness and ignorance. He called the organization "a bunch of quadrennial, transoceanic hitchhikers who don't own a hurdle." Falkenstein, *Max and the Jayhawks,* 57.

9. *Seattle Times,* 27 October 1974, 16 September 1979; Griffin, "Hoops and Hurdles," 14–26; Plimpton, "Reflections in a Diary," 42.

10. *Los Angeles Times,* 10 May 1956; *Chicago Tribune,* 11 May 1956; *Chicago Defender,* 15 May 1956.

11. D. Thomas, "'Good Negroes,'" 1–224; Dudziak, *Cold War Civil Rights,* 3–114; Von Eschen, *Satchmo Blows Up the World,* 91; *Chicago Defender,* 3 July 1956, 7 July 1956; Owens, *Blackthink,* 129; Domer, "Sport in Cold War America," 118–19. On Emmett Till, see Whitfield, *Death in the Delta.* On King and Montgomery, see Branch, *Parting the Waters,* 1–205.

12. *Los Angeles Times,* 12 June 1956, 11 July 1956, 7 August 1956; *Pittsburgh Courier,* 23 June 1956; *Chicago Defender,* 23 June 1956, 6 August 1956, 11 August 1956; *Washington Post and Times Herald,* 25 June 1956; *New York Times,* 12 July 1956, 21 July 1956, 31 July 1956, 13 December 1956; *Seattle Times,* 18 September 1977; Jones, *Rebound,* 57–58; *USF Alumnus,* June 1956.

13. D. Thomas, "'Good Negroes,'" 195–200; Domer, "Sport in Cold War America," 120–21, 143–44.

14. *Baltimore Afro-American,* 25 September 1956; *Chicago Defender,* 16 October 1956; *Washington Post and Times Herald,* 21–25 October 1956, 5 November 1956; *Los Angeles Times,* 23 October 1956, 25 October 1956, 30 October 1956, 8 November 1956, 10 November 1956; *Pittsburgh Courier,* 22 December 1956.

15. Ron Tomsic, telephone interview with author, 29 October 2008; Burdette Haldorson, telephone interview with author, 30 October 2008; B. Russell, *Go Up for Glory,* 45.

16. Roberts and Olson, *Winning Is the Only Thing,* 2–14; Guttmann, *Games Must Go On,* 1–160; Koppett, *Sports Illusion, Sports Reality,* 179–86; Guttmann, *Olympics,* 85–102; *Chicago Defender,* 6 August 1956.

17. *Chicago Tribune,* 3 August 1956; *Chicago Defender,* 6 August 1956; *Los Angeles Times,* 2 September 1956; *Boston Traveler,* 19 December 1956; *New York Times,* 20 December 1956.

18. Dyreson, *Making the American Team,* 1–6; Tait, "Politicization of the Modern Olympic Games," 6–10; Pope, *Patriotic Games,* 37–58.

19. Guttmann, *Olympics,* 86–102; Tait, "Politicization of the Modern Olympic Games," 93–99, 183–86; Senn, *Power, Politics, and the Olympic Games,* 105–8; "War Threats Mess Up Olympics," 55–56; "Olympic War," 65; "It's Get Set and Go," 86; *New York Times,* 10 November 1956, 11 November 1956, 12 November 1956, 13 November 1956.

20. *Sporting News*, 19 December 1956; "Parting in Melbourne," 27; Laguerre, "World's Eye on Sport," 13–14; "Hungary's Heroes," 22–23; Domer, "Sport in Cold War America," 157; "End of the Affair," 80; " 'Score' at Melbourne," 67–68; "Our Flag on Wings," 98; *Boston Globe*, 27 November 1956; *San Francisco Chronicle*, 29 November 1956; *New York Times*, 19 December 1956, 26 November 1956.

21. Chalk, *Black College Sport*, 341–65; Wiggins, *Glory Bound*, 61–79; W. Baker, *Jesse Owens*, 89–128; McRae, *Heroes Without a Country*, 131–76; Hartmann, *Race, Culture, and the Revolt of the Black Athlete*, 15–17; Page, *Black Olympian Medalists*, 162; *Chicago Defender*, 14 April 1956, 15 December 1956.

22. J. Jones, *Rebound*, 66–67.

23. *Boston Globe*, 7 December 2000; *San Francisco Chronicle*, 8 December 1956; Guttmann, *Games Must Go On*, 159–61; Lardner, "Letter From the Olympics," 137–44; *New York Times*, 23 December 1956; W. Baker, *Sports in the Western World*, 268–69. On ceremony, see also R. Johnson, *Best that I Can Be*, 97–98.

24. Carlson and Fogarty, *Tales of Gold*, 261–63; Cunningham, "Russell Model," 74; B. Russell, *Go Up for Glory*, 47; *Boston Globe*, 7 December 2000; *Sporting News*, 26 December 1956; B. Russell, "I Was a 6'9" Babe in the Woods," 68.

25. Guttmann, *Games and Empires*, 101–10; *New York Amsterdam News*, 10 November 1956; *New York Times*, 24 November 1956, 25 November 1956; *Los Angeles Times*, 24 November 1956, 25 November 1956, 26 November 1956; *Baltimore Afro-American*, 27 November 1956; B. Russell, "I Was a 6'9" Babe in the Woods," 68; *Washington Post and Times Herald*, 25 November 1956.

26. *Pittsburgh Courier*, 22 December 1956; Ron Tomsic interview; Burdette Haldorson interview; undated article from *Springfield Union*, Bill Russell File, Basketball Hall of Fame; Rudolph, *Wilma*, 88; *San Francisco Chronicle*, 27 November 1956; *New York Times*, 3 December 1956. Only much later did Russell reveal any dissatisfaction with his Olympic coaches. They never engaged him in conversation and disrespected his talents by bringing him off the bench. See B. Russell, *Red and Me*, 28–29.

27. Burdette Haldorson interview; Ron Tomsic interview; *Los Angeles Times*, 27 November 1956; *New York Times*, 27 November 1956

28. *San Francisco Chronicle*, 29 November 1956; Edelman, *Serious Fun*, 125–28; W. Baker, *Sports in the Western World*, 264–68.

29. Edelman, *Serious Fun*, 144–45; Brokhin, *Big Red Machine*, 135–41; *Foghorn*, 6 March 1956; *Los Angeles Times*, 19 November 1956; *New York Times*, 23 May 1956, 18 November 1956, 25 November 1956.

30. Burdette Haldorson interview; *New York Times*, 29 November 1956; *Sporting News*, 26 December 1956. Olympic basketball proved quite popular in Melbourne; 73,400 spectators attended the eighteen games. Yet the only television coverage in the United States was through nightly thirty-minute newsreels aired on independent stations. See Weyand, *Cavalcade of Basketball*, 229; Battema, "Going for the Gold," 32–41.

31. *Sporting News*, 16 January 1957; *Washington Post and Times Herald*, 1 December 1956; Grundy, *Learning to Win*, 202–3; *Pittsburgh Courier*, 22 December 1956; *San Francisco Chronicle*, 29 November 1956.

32. *Washington Post and Times Herald*, 1 December 1956; *New York Times*, 1 Decem-

ber 1956, 3 December 1956; Laguerre, "World's Eye on Sport," 14; *Sporting News*, 26 December 1956.

33. *New York Times*, 2 December 1956, 3 December 1956; *Los Angeles Times*, 2 December 1956. Fourteen African Americans in total won gold medals during the Olympics. *Los Angeles Sentinel*, 13 December 1956.

34. Cunningham, "Russell Model," 81; Cunningham, "American Hoops," 167–69; *New York Times*, 29 January 1959, 31 January 1959, 3 February 1959, 24 November 1959, 27 November 1959, 30 November 1959, 3 December 1959, 12 December 1959; "Oh, Those Russian Gals!" 20; *Chicago Defender*, 28 April 1958.

35. "Who Won the Olympics?" 13; "Melbourne Concluded," 96; Lardner, "We Hung in the Stretch," 98; "Faster, Higher, Farther," 58–59; *Boston Globe*, 8 December 1956; *New York Times*, 8 December 1956, 9 December 1956, 23 December 1956; Guttmann, *Olympics*, 101– 102; Carlson and Fogarty, *Tales of Gold*, 265–84; Fitokova Connolly, "Love Made Me an American," 15–17, 52–54. On fallacies of medal counts, see Mandell, *Sport*, 235–36. See also Moretti, "Cold War and the Olympics," 209–16.

36. Russell and Branch, *Second Wind*, 216.

37. B. Russell, *Go Up for Glory*, 47–49; *New York Times*, 22 November 1956, 2 December 1956, 25 January 1957; *Boston Globe*, 7 April 1960. In Melbourne, Brundage suspended American hammer thrower Cliff Blair for "violating the amateur code" by writing for the *Boston Globe*, even though sports editor Jerry Nason denied that Blair received any pay. See *New York Times*, 23 November 1956.

38. *San Francisco Chronicle*, 8 December 1956; *New York Times*, 9 December 1956; *Chicago Tribune*, 10 December 1956; *Los Angeles Times*, 10 December 1956; *Boston Traveler*, 4 December 1956, 7 December 1956. By then, Russell had already stood up at Perry's wedding. Perry was a law student at Lincoln University at San Francisco. He would practice law in Oakland for thirty years, most notably defending the Black Panthers. Perry credits his basketball experience at USF for helping shape his support of the Panthers, as he admired "leadership, direction, determination." Hal Perry, telephone interview with author, 17 May 2007.

39. *San Francisco Chronicle*, 8 December 1956.

40. B. Green, *Spinning the Globe*, 1–252; Kline, *Never Lose*, 61, 91–92; Christgau, *Tricksters in the Madhouse*; Young, *Negro Firsts in Sports*, 230–33; Zinkoff, *Around the World*, 146– 50; "Americans Abroad," 85–86.

41. Marshall Smith, "Basketball's Court Jester," 91–99; Orr, "Magicians of the Basketball Midway," 28–31, 68–71; Lemon, *Meadowlark*, 152–54; Lombardo, "Harlem Globetrotters," 60–63; George, *Elevating the Game*, 45–56; Roberts and Olson, *Winning Is the Only Thing*, 30–31. On black stereotypes, see Bogle, *Toms, Coons, Mulattoes, Mammies, and Bucks*; Boskin, *Sambo*.

42. B. Green, *Spinning the Globe*, 272; B. Russell, *Go Up for Glory*, 40. Russell recalled an offer of $50,000. But that winter, upon hearing rumors that other teams had offered Russell that sum, his assistant Harry Hannin said, "I am wondering where they are going to get that kind of money. If they can come up with it, they are welcome to him." See *Chicago Defender*, 7 March 1956.

43. B. Green, *Spinning the Globe*, 288–89; *New York Post*, 17 January 1966; B. Russell, *Go Up for Glory*, 40–41; *San Francisco Chronicle*, 4 December 1956; B. Russell, "I Was a 6'9" Babe in the Woods," 68.

44. Linn, "Bill Russell's Private World," 65–66; B. Russell, *Go Up for Glory*, 41; *San Francisco Chronicle*, 25 January 1956. In *Go Up for Glory*, Russell misidentifies Harry Hannin as "Harry Hanna."

45. *San Francisco Chronicle*, 5 March 1956; Wilker, *Harlem Globetrotters*, 89–90; "Harlem Magicians," 51–52; *Los Angeles Sentinel*, 26 April 1956; *Chicago Defender*, 7 March 1956, 24 April 1956.

46. *Boston Globe*, 13 December 1963; *New York Post*, 17 January 1966; Lazenby, *Lakers*, 96–98. Auerbach later denied the trade's near-inevitability, but Hartman claimed to possess the paperwork from the NBA commissioner's office. According to Hartman, play-by-play announcer Dick Enroth loved Mikkelson and dreaded announcing games for a last-place team, so he convinced owner Ben Berger to nix the trade. See Hartman, *Sid!* 76–77.

47. Donald Fisher, "Rochester Royals"; Cook, "Rochester Royals"; Pluto, *Tall Tales*, 120–21; *New York Post*, 17 January 1966; Russell, *Go Up for Glory*, 42–43.

48. Isaacs, *Vintage NBA*, 80; Pluto, *Tall Tales*, 120–21, 307–10.

49. Auerbach and Sann, *Red Auerbach*, 8–15; Auerbach and Fitzgerald, *Red Auerbach*, 21–39; Auerbach, *On and Off the Court*, 1–11; Shaughnessy, *Seeing Red*, 27–40; Auerbach and Feinstein, *Let Me Tell You a Story*, 18–28.

50. Auerbach and Fitzgerald, *Red Auerbach*, 40–53; Auerbach with Fitzgerald, *On and Off the Court*, 11–14; Shaughnessy, *Seeing Red*, 40–55; Auerbach and Feinstein, *Let Me Tell You a Story*, 40–46. On Armed Forces basketball during World War Two, see also Aamidor, *Chuck Taylor*, 84–94.

51. Auerbach and Sann, *Red Auerbach*, 24–34; Auerbach and Feinstein, *Let Me Tell You a Story*, 45–58; Shaughnessy, *Seeing Red*, 40–66; Charley Rosen, *First Tip-Off*, 195–210, 217–22. In between professional jobs, Auerbach spent a brief stint as assistant basketball coach at Duke University. On the NBL, BAA, and formation of the NBA, see Dickey, *History of Professional Basketball Since 1896*, 25–42; Koppett, *24 Seconds to Shoot*, 13–56; Charley Rosen, *First Tip-Off*, 11–35.

52. Auerbach and Fitzgerald, *Red Auerbach*, 81–87; *Sporting News*, 26 January 1956, 21 January 1959; *Boston Globe*, 8 February 1954; Auerbach, "Every All-American Doesn't Make a Pro," 34–35, 76–77; Auerbach, *Basketball for the Player, the Fan, and the Coach*, 186–90.

53. Auerbach and Sann, *Red Auerbach*, 90; Auerbach and Fitzgerald, *Red Auerbach*, 97–118.

54. Auerbach and Sann, *Red Auerbach*, 85–89; Auerbach, *Basketball For the Player, the Fan, and the Coach*, 142; *Boston Traveler*, 18 December 1956; *Boston Globe*, 11 December 1956. In his 1966 memoir with Paul Sann, Auerbach claims Reinhart lauded Russell when he was a 6'7" sophomore. In fact, USF played George Washington in December 1954, during Russell's junior year, just as Russell emerged on the national sporting scene.

55. R. Thomas, *They Cleared the Lane*, 109–31; *Boston Traveler*, 18 December 1956; Pluto, *Tall Tales*, 121.

56. Shaughnessy, *Seeing Red*, 108–11; Pluto, *Tall Tales*, 120–25.

57. Ed Macauley, telephone interview with author, 2 April 2007; *New York Amsterdam News,* 23 April 1955; *Boston Globe,* 14 April 2005; Salzberg, *From Set Shot to Slam Dunk,* 93–101; G. Sullivan, *Picture History,* 144–47.

58. Maurice Podoloff Testimony before Senate Committee on the Judiciary, 31 August 1958, S1292–3, 564–65; *Christian Science Monitor,* 17 November 1959; *Sporting News,* 15 January 1958, 8 February 1961; Goodman, "Never A Dull Moment," 32–35, 85–87; Rogin, "You're Looking at Success," 48–49; Marecek, *Full Court,* 1–6, 34–35; Pluto, *Tall Tales,* 122; Cliff Hagan, telephone interview with author, 28 August 2007.

59. *Boston Globe,* 6 March 1960; Auerbach and Sann, *Red Auerbach,* 89–90.

60. *New York Times,* 1 May 1956. NBA teams drafted twelve African Americans in total during the 1956 draft. St. Louis, despite trading Russell, did draft three other black players: Willie Naulls, Morrie Taft, Julius McCoy, and Wally Choice. *Chicago Defender,* 12 May 1956. On territorial draft, see also *Sporting News,* 18 January 1956; Maurice Podoloff Testimony before House of Representatives Committee on the Judiciary, 7 August 1957, H1634–3, 2857–2860.

61. *Boston Traveler,* 7 December 1956.

62. R. Johnson, *Century of Boston Sports,* 121–22; Greenfield, *World's Greatest Team,* 20–21; Johnson and Codagnone, *Boston Garden,* 45–62.

63. Bjarkman, *Boston Celtics Encyclopedia,* 177–81; Charley Rosen, *First Tip-Off,* 17–20; Greenfield, *World's Greatest Team,* 21–24; Shaughnessy, *Ever Green,* 51–52; Dickey, *History of Professional Basketball Since 1896,* 29–30.

64. *Boston Globe,* 6 January 1953, 29 December 1953, 12 January 1955, 28 March 1955, 20 April 1965; Charley Rosen, *First Tip-Off,* 37–63; Gowdy, *Seasons to Remember,* 110.

65. Greene, "Bill Russell Is Better Than Ever," 26; *Washington Post and Times Herald,* 23 October 1956; Auerbach and Feinstein, *Let Me Tell You a Story,* 77–78; Auerbach and Sann, *Red Auerbach,* 92–94.

66. *Bridgeport Post,* 14 March 1973; Linn, "Bill Russell's Private World," 66; B. Russell, *Go Up for Glory,* 46. As late as 1958, Brown and Auerbach—unwilling to publicly contradict the amateur ideal—maintained that they never approached Russell before the Olympics. See Goodman, "Cousy, Sharman, Russell & Co.," 58.

67. B. Russell, *Go Up for Glory,* 46; *San Francisco Chronicle,* 4 December 1956; *Los Angeles Times,* 4 December 1956; *New York Amsterdam News,* 15 December 1956; *Baltimore Afro-American,* 11 December 1956; *Boston Traveler,* 4 December 1956.

68. *San Francisco Chronicle,* 9 December 1956; *Chicago Tribune,* 9 December 1956; *Pittsburgh Courier,* 15 December 1956. The *Courier* reported his reply as "Thanks for the offer, but no soap."

69. *Chicago Tribune,* 13 December 1956, 15 December 1956, 16 December 1956; *Chicago Defender,* 12 December 1956, 15 December 1956, 22 December 1956; *Boston Record,* 17 December 1956; *New York Times,* 18 December 1956. The Dons nevertheless made it back to the NCAA tournament in 1957, losing to Wilt Chamberlain and the University of Kansas in the national semifinals.

70. *Chicago Tribune,* 17 December 1956; *San Francisco Chronicle,* 17 December 1956; *Chicago Defender,* 18 December 1956; *Boston Globe,* 19 December 1956; *New York Times,* 18 December 1956, 20 December 1956; "Events and Discoveries," 37.

71. *Los Angeles Times,* 11 December 1956, 12 April 1957; *Memphis Commercial Appeal,* 17 January 2006; Bill Russell, Martin Luther King Day Symposium, FedEx Forum, Memphis, Tennessee, 16 January 2006. Bill Margolis, another publicity man for the Globetrotters, told the press in January 1957 that Saperstein was relieved that Russell turned him down, as he was not sure Russell was worth the money. One black newspaper labeled that reaction "sour grapes." *Los Angeles Sentinel,* 17 January 1957.

5. BIG LEAGUE, BUSH LEAGUE

1. *New York Post,* 19 December 1956.

2. *New York Post,* 30 December 1955, 19 December 1956. See also Gross, "Pros Tell Their Favorite Bill Russell Stories," 45.

3. *New York Post,* 19 December 1956; *Chicago Tribune,* 24 November 1957.

4. *New York Times,* 19 December 1956.

5. Isaacs, *Vintage NBA,* 229-32; Charley Rosen, *First Tip-Off,* 21-24.

6. *Sporting News,* 15 January 1958; Koppett, *24 Seconds to Shoot,* 34-66, 159; Salzberg, *From Set Shot to Slam Dunk,* 189. See also Danielson, *Home Team,* 23-25; Nelson, *National Basketball League.*

7. Maurice Podoloff testimony before Senate Committee on the Judiciary, 31 August 1958, S1292-3, 565-567, 571-572; Maurice Podoloff testimony before House of Representatives Committee on the Judiciary, 7 August 1957, H1634-3, 2864-2869; Riess, *City Games,* 232-33; *Sporting News,* 19 December 1956; *Boston Globe,* 14 November 1957; Tax, "Blessed Event," 37-38.

8. Podoloff testimony before Senate Committee, 574-75; Podoloff testimony before House of Representatives Committee, 2871-2872; *Sporting News,* 2 February 1955; Cousy, "Pro Basketball Needs a Bill of Rights," 12-13, 68-69; Cousy, *Basketball Is My Life,* 125-43.

9. On All-Star Game, see Glickman, "Night Stars Came Out for the NBA," 69-74; *Sporting News,* 9 January 1957, 15 January 1958, 18 January 1961. On effects of college scandals, see *Sporting News,* 25 January 1956; Koppett, *Championship NBA,* 15-22; Cole, *Loose Game,* 50-52; Charles Rosen, *Scandals of '51,* 192-93; Charley Rosen, *Wizard of Odds,* 101-54.

10. Podoloff testimony before Senate Committee, 569-70; Rader, *In Its Own Image,* 32-35; Isaacs, *Vintage NBA,* 234; Salzberg, *From Set Shot to Slam Dunk,* 201; *Sporting News,* 1 February 1956, 23 January 1957, 12 February 1958.

11. Pluto, *Tall Tales,* 23-27; *Boston Globe,* 26 February 1954.

12. *Sporting News,* 18 January 1956, 15 January 1958; *Boston Globe,* 15 January 1957; Associated Press, 10 August 2004, found at http://msnbc.msn.com/id/5652455; Fox, *Big Leagues,* 298-99.

13. Palmer, "Six Best Shots in Basketball," 44-47, 89; Rupp, *Rupp's Championship Basketball,* 44-45; Sharman, *Sharman on Basketball Shooting,* 55; Linn, "Is the N.B.A. Big League?" 10-11, 82-85; *Boston Globe,* 10 February 1955, 17 January 1956; *New York Times,* 27 December 1957; *Sporting News,* 5 February 1958, 7 January 1959; Astor, "Halfway Point in Pro Basketball," 46-49.

14. Linn, "Is the N.B.A. Big League?"; "NBA Is Big League—Almost," 98; Nucatola, "Trouble with Pro Basketball," 30-31, 66-69; Koppett, "Does Pro Basketball Have a Future?" 36,

302 NOTES TO PAGES 74–77

81–84; J. Lapchick, "Toughest Big League of Them All," 91–94; Pluto, *Tall Tales*, 32–43; *Sporting News*, 21 December 1955, 18 January 1956, 19 December 1956, 23 January 1957, 30 January 1957, 18 December 1957, 14 January 1959; undated *Boston Globe* article, Mokray Scrapbook, 1958–59 Season. The 1955 NBA Finals revealed this "bush league" reputation. They featured Syracuse and Fort Wayne, the league's two smallest markets. The Pistons held home games at the Indiana State Fairgrounds in Indianapolis because the Allen County Memorial Coliseum had been overtaken by a bowling tournament. See Gould, *Pioneers of the Hardwood*, 216–23.

15. *Boston Globe*, 17 December 1956, 19 December 1956; *Boston Herald*, 19 December 1956.

16. *Boston Globe*, 6 December 1956, 13 December 1956, 15 December 1956; Holzman, *View from the Bench*, 27–28; *Boston Traveler*, 19 December 1956; *Boston Herald*, 20 December 1956; Cousy and Ryan, *Cousy on the Celtic Mystique*, 32–33; *Chicago Tribune*, 24 November 1957.

17. *Los Angeles Times*, 23 August 1956; *Boston Globe*, 6 December 1956, 25 March 1965; *New York Times*, 20 December 1956; *Chicago Defender*, 5 January 1957; *San Francisco Chronicle*, 7 January 1957.

18. *Boston Globe*, 2 December 1956, 12 December 1956, 19 December 1956, 28 March 1957; *Boston Herald*, 13 December 1956; Tax, "Family Affair," 40–42; Arnie Risen, telephone interview with author, 15 June 2007; *Boston Traveler*, 15 December 1956, 21 December 1956.

19. *Boston Globe*, 23 December 1956; *Chicago Tribune*, 23 December 1956; *Los Angeles Times*, 23 December 1956; *Boston Herald*, 23 December 1956.

20. *Los Angeles Times*, 24 December 1956; *Boston Globe*, 22 January 1957, 20 January 1960; Linn, "Bill Russell's Private World," 66; uncited article dated 10 February 1957, Mokray Scrapbook, 1956–57 Season; *Boston Herald*, 22 January 1957.

21. Newcombe, "Clumsy Sharpshooter," 18–19, 74–75; "Three in One" 16–19; Cousy and Ryan, *Cousy on the Celtic Mystique*, 33–35.

22. *Boston Traveler*, 26 December 1956; *Boston Globe*, 26 December 1956, 27 December 1956; *Boston Herald*, 27 December 1956; B. Russell, "Psych," 39.

23. *New York Times*, 2 January 1957; *San Francisco Chronicle*, 3 January 1957, 4 January 1957; *New York Post*, 4 January 1957; *Boston Globe*, 4 January 1957, 12 February 1957; *Boston Herald*, 4 January 1957, 12 February 1957; uncited article dated 8 January 1957, Mokray Scrapbook, 1956–57 Season; *Sporting News*, 16 January 1957; Tax, "All in the Mind," 48–49. On January 12, the Celtics lost to the Hawks 100–98. On a late and crucial possession, Russell was called for a goaltending violation; some reporters suspected that the call stemmed from Gottlieb's earlier protestations. See *Boston Globe*, 13 January 1957; uncited article in Mokray Scrapbook, 1956–57 Season.

24. Daley, "Education of a Basketball Rookie," 53–56; *New York Amsterdam News*, 7 April 1956; *Sporting News*, 6 February 1957; Auerbach, *Red Auerbach*, 124. On the misuse of statistics, see Koppett, *Essence of the Game*, 218–25.

25. Goodman, "Royal Rookie," 37–38; B. Russell, "I Was a 6'9" Babe in the Woods," 25, 66–68; *Boston Globe*, 14 January 1957.

26. *Sporting News*, 16 January 1957; *New York Times*, 9 January 1957; *Boston Globe*, 9 January 1957, 20 January 1957, 21 January 1957; Daley, "Education of a Basketball Rookie"; B. Russell, "I Was a 6'9" Babe in the Woods," 66–68.

27. Auerbach, *On and Off the Court*, 45–46; Linn, "Bill Russell's Private World," 66; *Boston Globe*, 21 January 1957.

28. B. Russell, *Go Up for Glory*, 102–3; Auerbach, "How I Handle the Boston Celtics," 94; *Boston Globe*, 1 March 1957; *Pittsburgh Courier*, 9 March 1957.

29. *Boston Globe*, 22 January 1957; B. Russell, "I Was a 6'9" Babe in the Woods," 68; *Sporting News*, 30 January 1957.

30. *Pittsburgh Courier*, 5 January 1957, 19 January 1957; *Boston Globe*, 26 December 1956, 7 January 1957; *Boston Herald*, 22 January 1957; *Los Angeles Times*, 26 April 1957.

31. *Boston Globe*, 24 December 1956; Earl Lloyd, telephone interview with author, 16 March 2007; Ed Macauley, telephone interview with author, 2 April 2007; Cliff Hagan, telephone interview with author, 28 August 2007; J. Fitzgerald, *That Championship Feeling*, 53. See also Pettit, *Bob Pettit*, 79–80.

32. B. Russell, *Go Up for Glory*, 94.

33. Russell and Branch, *Second Wind*, 188; Heinsohn, *Heinsohn, Don't You Ever Smile?* 81.

34. Arnie Risen interview; *Boston Herald*, 25 May 1999; *Boston Traveler*, 17 December 1956; *Boston Herald*, 17 December 1956; *Boston Globe*, 22 December 1956; Shaughnessy, *Ever Green*, 79; Tax, "Man Who Must Be Different," 31; B. Russell, *Go Up for Glory*, 121.

35. *Boston Globe*, 27 November 1956, 20 March 1957, 28 March 1957; *Sporting News*, 30 January 1957, 22 February 1961; *New York Times*, 11 January 1965; *Boston Herald*, 16 March 1960.

36. Heinsohn, *Heinsohn, Don't You Ever Smile?* 43–47, 115; Heinsohn and Fitzgerald, *Give 'Em the Hook*, 69, 79–80; Cousy, *Last Loud Roar*, 126.

37. Heinsohn and Fitzgerald, *Give 'Em the Hook*, 28–29, 179.

38. B. Russell, *Russell Rules*, 45–47; *Chicago Defender*, 5 January 1957; Heinsohn and Fitzgerald, *Give 'Em the Hook*, 62–65.

39. *Boston Herald*, 1 January 1957, 25 January 1957, 4 March 1957; "Shorties of the Court," 86–87; *St. Louis Post-Dispatch*, 3 April 1957; *Boston Globe*, 26 December 1956, 1 January 1957, 23 January 1957, 24 January 1957, 30 January 1957, 4 February 1957, 28 February 1957. Auerbach had finagled the drafting of Ramsey, Cliff Hagan, and Lou Tsioropoulos in 1953—all three had starred at the University of Kentucky, but Adolph Rupp redshirted them during the school's one-year ban from tournament play in the wake of the point-shaving scandals. Auerbach convinced the league that since their original graduating class was 1953, they could be drafted. See Auerbach and Fitzgerald, *Red Auerbach*, 112–13.

40. Hirshberg, "Boston Gets a Winner," 36, 113–14; *Boston Globe*, 4 March 1957, 26 March 1957; B. Russell, *Russell Rules*, 29–30, 119–22.

41. *Boston Globe*, 15 April 1957; *Boston Herald*, 15 April 1957; Heinsohn, *Heinsohn, Don't You Ever Smile?* 91–92; Heinsohn and Fitzgerald, *Give 'Em the Hook*, 68–69.

42. *Boston Globe*, 2 March 1957, 11 March 1957, 12 March 1957, 19 March 1957, 21 March 1957, March 1957; *Boston Herald*, 18 March 1957, 21 March 1957. After one late-season game,

Syracuse coach Paul Seymour stirred Boston's anger by accusing Auerbach of ordering Jim Loscutoff and Jack Nichols to batter his star forward Dolph Schayes.

43. *Boston Globe,* 22 March 1957; *Boston Herald,* 22 March 1957, 23 March 1957.

44. *Boston Globe,* 31 December 1956, 6 January 1956, 21 March 1957, 24 March 1957, 25 March 1957, 29 March 1957; *Boston Herald,* 5 January 1957, 25 March 1957.

45. United Press Report dated 10 December 1956 and Associated Press report dated 21 January 1957, both from Mokray Scrapbook, 1956–57 Season; *Boston Globe,* 13 January 1957; *Sporting News,* 15 January 1958; Hannum, "I've Barely Begun to Fight," 34–35; Hannum, "Old Days and Changed Ways," 40; Marecek, *Full Court,* 48–51; Pluto, *Tall Tales,* 129–30. For an oral history with Slater Martin, see Salzberg, *From Set Shot to Slam Dunk,* 65–84.

46. Koppett, *24 Seconds to Shoot,* 113–14; *Boston Globe,* 24 March 1957, 27 March 1957; *Boston Herald,* 27 March 1957, 2 April 1957. The new excitement even prompted the Celtics to consider rearranging the court to seat more fans, a laughable notion in earlier years.

47. *Boston Globe,* 30 March 1957, 1 April 1957; *Boston Herald,* 30 March 1957, 1 April 1957; *St. Louis Post-Dispatch,* 1 April 1957.

48. *Boston Globe,* 6 April 1957, 9 April 1957, 10 April 1957; *St. Louis Post-Dispatch,* 6 April 1957; *Boston Herald,* 6 April 1957, 9 April 1957.

49. Bob Cousy, telephone interview with author, 23 April 2007; Cliff Hagan interview; Marecek, *Full Court,* 44–45; Pluto, *Tall Tales,* 130–31, 138; *Boston Herald,* 4 April 1957.

50. *Boston Globe,* 7 April 1957; Pluto, *Tall Tales,* 138–39; Auerbach and Sann, *Red Auerbach,* 182–84; *New York Times,* 7 April 1957; *Boston Herald,* 7 April 1957.

51. *St. Louis Post-Dispatch,* 7 April 1957; *Boston Globe,* 7 April 1957, 9 April 1957; *Boston Herald,* 7 April 1957, 9 April 1957.

52. *Boston Globe,* 31 March 1957, 8 April 1957; *Boston Herald,* 8 April 1957.

53. *Boston Globe,* 9 April 1957, 10 April 1957, 11 April 1957; *Boston Herald,* 10 April 1957, 11 April 1957.

54. *Boston Globe,* 12 April 1957; *Boston Herald,* 12 April 1957.

55. *Boston Globe,* 12 April 1957, 13 April 1957; *Boston Herald,* 13 April 1957; *St. Louis Post-Dispatch,* 10 April 1957, 13 April 1957.

56. *Boston Globe,* 13 April 1957; Koppett, *24 Seconds to Shoot,* 114.

57. B. Russell, *Go Up for Glory,* 129; Wind, "Hubbub in the Hub," 17–19; Hirshberg, *Bill Russell of the Boston Celtics,* 10–12.

58. *Boston Record-American,* 14 April 1957; *Boston Herald,* 14 April 1957; *New York Times,* 14 April 1957; *Boston Globe,* 14 April 1957.

59. *Boston Herald,* 14 April 1957; *New York Times,* 14 April 1957; *Boston Globe,* 14 April 1957, 15 April 1957.

60. Heinsohn and Fitzgerald, *Give 'Em the Hook,* 70–71; Heinsohn, *Heinsohn, Don't You Ever Smile?* 61–63, 70–71; *Boston Herald,* 14 April 1957.

61. B. Russell, *Go Up for Glory,* 129; Schwartz, "Me and Red See It Through," 57.

62. *Boston Globe,* 14 April 1957; Cousy, *Basketball Is My Life,* 175.

63. *Boston Globe,* 14 April 1957; *Boston Herald,* 14 April 1957.

64. Pluto, *Tall Tales,* 131–32.

65. Auerbach and Sann, *Red Auerbach,* 5; *Sporting News,* 30 November 1955, 27 Janu-

ary 1960; Pluto, *Tall Tales,* 98–102; Silverman, "Bob Pettit," 24, 84–86; Burnes, "Bob Pettit and the Hawks," 24–25, 89; Stump, "Bob Pettit," 70–76; Hannum, "Old Days and Changed Ways," 39; Wind, "Hubbub in the Hub," 19.

66. Carey, *Voice of the Celtics,* 30 (see also accompanying CD); *Boston Globe,* 14 April 1957; *Boston Herald,* 14 April 1957; *Boston Record-American,* 14 April 1957.

67. *Boston Globe,* 14 April 1957; *Boston Herald,* 14 April 1957; *Boston Record-American,* 14 April 1957.

68. W. Russell, "Success Is a Journey," 92; Rogin, "We Are Grown Men," 77.

6. THE MAN WHO MUST BE DIFFERENT

1. Two uncited articles in Mokray Scrapbook, 1956–57 Season; Cousy, *Basketball Is My Life,* 138; *Los Angeles Sentinel,* 7 February 1957; *Los Angeles Times,* 28 April 1957. Per the players' contracts, the exhibition tour needed the approval of the NBA. The board of governors allowed the tour despite Maurice Podoloff's consternation that a plane crash could wipe out a group of NBA stars. *Boston Globe,* 21 February 1957; uncited article dated 26 February 1957, Mokray Scrapbook, 1956–57 Season.

2. B. Russell, *Go Up for Glory,* 50; *Los Angeles Times,* 2 April 2007; John LoSchiavo, telephone interview with author, 13 April 2007; Goodman, "Cousy, Sharman, Russell & Co.," 60; B. Russell, "I Was a 6'9" Babe in the Woods," 68. Other Celtics had full-time off-season jobs: Bob Cousy ran a summer camp, Tommy Heinsohn sold insurance, Bill Sharman was a golf pro. Russell had originally intended on taking courses at Boston College to finish his degree, but the Celtics consumed his energies. See uncited article dated 16 December 1957, Mokray Scrapbook, 1956–57 Season. Charlie Russell also attended Santa Rosa Junior College. In 1959, he joined the Baltimore Bullets of the Eastern League, a lesser professional basketball league. See *Oakland Tribune,* 28 February 1965; *Baltimore Afro-American,* 17 October 1959. Russell and his teammates all received vanity license plates with their jersey numbers as gifts, presented by Mark Furcolo, son of Massachusetts governor Foster Furcolo. Freedman, *Dynasty,* 66.

3. Nelson, *Bill Russell,* 46–47; Tax, "Man Who Must Be Different," 32; *Reading Chronicle,* 23 May 1963. On African Americans and postwar consumer culture, see L. Cohen, *Consumers' Republic,* 166–91.

4. B. Russell, "I Was a 6'9" Babe in the Woods," 68; B. Russell, *Go Up for Glory,* 13.

5. *Washington Post and Times Herald,* 1 September 1957; Goodman, "Cousy, Sharman, Russell & Co.," 53; *Boston Globe,* 7 April 1957; Tax, "This Vintage Year," 38. On Fort Wayne's move to Detroit, see Gould, *Pioneers of the Hardwood,* 225–29.

6. *Boston Herald,* 18 April 1957; Auerbach and Sann, *Red Auerbach,* 242–43; B. Russell, *Go Up for Glory,* 88. Jones almost chose a high-school teaching career in North Carolina over a Celtics tryout. The defending champions returned a full slate of guards, and few blacks had slots on NBA teams. Had Second Ward High School in Charlotte offered $500 more, Jones never would have auditioned for the Celtics. See undated articles from *Christian Science Monitor, Boston Globe,* and *Boston Herald,* Sam Jones File, Basketball Hall of Fame; Hirshberg, "Celtics' Cinderella Star," 70.

7. Hirshberg, "Celtics' Cinderella Star," 70; uncited article dated 26 October 1957,

Mokray Scrapbook, 1957–58 Season; Carey, *High Above Courtside,* 110–12; G. Sullivan, *Picture History,* 163; Plimpton, "Reflections in a Diary," 42.

8. Undated *Boston Globe* article from 1968, Sam Jones file, Basketball Hall of Fame; Koppett, "Celtics Look Better than Ever," 42–45, 70–71; Tax, "This Vintage Year," 39; "Better than the Best?" 88; *Boston Globe,* 27 November 1957, 29 November 1957, 4 December 1957, 10 December 1957, 15 December 1957, 22 December 1957, 27 December 1957, 1 February 1958; *Sporting News,* 25 December 1957; *Boston Herald,* 1 February 1958; *Chicago Defender,* 15 March 1958. Ramsey deserved to join Cousy, Sharman, and Russell at the All-Star Game, but the NBA restricted each team to a maximum three representatives.

9. *Chicago Defender,* 20 November 1957; *Boston Herald,* 17 November 1957; *Boston Globe,* 17–19 November 1957, 28 December 1957; *New York Times,* 17 November 1957; *Los Angeles Times,* 17 November 1957; *San Francisco Chronicle,* 17 November 1957; *Washington Post and Times Herald,* 19 November 1957, 20 February 1958.

10. *Chicago Tribune,* 30 December 1957; *Boston Globe,* 31 December 1957; *Sporting News,* 29 January 1958. That season Walter Brown also scolded Maurice Podoloff for ignoring Ben Kerner's violation of league policy. During a winning streak, Kerner had been promising the Hawks gifts for every win: first sports jackets, then shirts, then slacks, then shoes, and so on. "We here in Boston try to sell basketball," sniffed Brown, "and not cheapen the league by such actions." See Goodman, "Never a Dull Moment," 34.

11. Ed Macauley, telephone interview with author, 2 April 2007; *Boston Herald,* 14 March 1958, 1 April 1958; *New York Times,* 19 February 1958; *Chicago Defender,* 28 December 1957; *Boston Globe,* 6 December 1957, 17 January 1958, 19 January 1958, 19 February 1958, 22 February 1958.

12. *Boston Herald,* 1 April 1958; Hirshberg, *Bill Russell of the Boston Celtics,* 124–25.

13. *Boston Globe,* 13 December 1961; Russell and Branch, *Second Wind,* 201.

14. McRae, *Heroes Without a Country,* 99–100.

15. Hietala, *Fight of the Century,* 148–322; W. Baker, *Jesse Owens,* 89–128; Erenberg, *Greatest Fight of Our Generation;* Margolick, *Beyond Glory;* Myler, *Ring of Hate;* J. Schaap, *Triumph.*

16. Tygiel, *Baseball's Great Experiment,* 99–208; Rampersad, *Jackie Robinson,* 158–218; Eig, *Opening Day.* See also Crawford, "Consensus All-American," 193–241.

17. Branch, *Parting the Waters,* 206–71; Bogle, *Primetime Blues,* 9–59; Jay, *More than Just a Game,* 104–7. Sports could upset racial convention enough that many newspapers in the Deep South refused to publish photographs of black athletes. Mandell, *Sport,* 224.

18. See Wiggins, *Glory Bound,* 200–20; Zirin, *What's My Name, Fool?* 37–52; Miller, "Muscular Assimilationism," 146–82; Fuse, "Jazzing the Basepaths," 119–40; Kaliss, "Everyone's All-Americans," 1–159.

19. Kamp, "Only the Ball Was Brown," 284–89, 343–47; Ashe, *Hard Road to Glory,* 3:40–41. No blacks from the NBL or BAA joined the newly formed NBA in 1949.

20. Schumacher, *Mr. Basketball,* 174; Gould, *Pioneers of the Hardwood,* 175–77.

21. R. Thomas, *They Cleared the Lane,* 26–31, 49–70, 109–31; Pluto, *Tall Tales,* 59–62. For oral histories with Cooper, see Rust and Rust, *Art Rust's Illustrated History,* 312–14; G. Sullivan, *Picture History,* 137–40. The Boston Celtics drafted Bill Garrett in 1951. When the army honorably discharged the Indiana University star in 1953, he chose the Celtics over the

Globetrotters. But the Celtics released him—perhaps because they already reached their black "quota" with Cooper and Barksdale, or perhaps to avoid further alienating Saperstein. See Graham and Cody, *Getting Open,* 164–68.

22. R. Thomas, *They Cleared the Lane,* 98–108; Earl Lloyd, telephone interview with author, 16 March 2007; Bob Hopkins, telephone interview with author, 13 October 2008. Saperstein had promised Clifton to split his sale price. Clifton later learned that Saperstein pocketed $22,500 and he received $2,500. Wilker, *Harlem Globetrotters,* 72–73.

23. For oral history with Clifton, see Salzberg, *From Set Shot to Slam Dunk,* 129–41.

24. Goodman, "Royal Rookie," 36–39, 69–71; E. Lawson, "Tragedy of Maurice Stokes," 18–19, 88–89; Pluto, *Tall Tales,* 80–87. On Stokes, see also Wideman, *Hoop Roots,* 200–208.

25. *Los Angeles Sentinel,* 27 December 1956, 14 February 1957, 4 April 1957, 2 May 1957; *Atlanta Daily World,* 5 January 1957; *Chicago Defender,* 2 January 1957, 10 January 1957; *New York Amsterdam News,* 15 February 1958.

26. *Sporting News,* 8 January 1958; Goodman, "Cousy, Sharman, Russell & Co.," 54. On Russell's practice habits, see Cousy and Ryan, *Cousy on the Celtic Mystique,* 42; *Sporting News,* 25 December 1957. Some drawings depict black athletes as whites with burr haircuts, as if denying the racial integration of sports in the 1950s. On the back of high-school teammate Frank Robinson's 1959 baseball card, Russell looks like a tall white person. Hoose, *Necessities,* xxvi.

27. Gross, "Pros Tell Their Favorite Bill Russell Stories," 46; B. Russell, "I Was a 6'9" Babe in the Woods," 25, 66–68; *Boston Globe,* 16 December 1958, 11 April 1959; *New York Post,* 15 January 1959; Goodman, "Cousy, Sharman, Russell & Co.," 58.

28. Frank Deford, telephone interview with author, 22 September 2008; MacCambridge, *Franchise,* 4–5, 38, 55–56; "Letter from the Publisher," 6.

29. Tax, "Man Who Must Be Different," 29–32.

30. *Boston Globe,* 14 March 1958, 17 March 1958, 19 March 1958, 23 March 1958, 24 March 1958, 27 March 1958, 28 March 1958; *Boston Herald,* 20 March 1958, 23 March 1958, 24 March 1958, 28 March 1958.

31. *Boston Herald,* 30 March 1958, 31 March 1958, 3 April 1958; *Boston Globe,* 30 March 1958, 31 March 1958, 3 April 1958, 7 April 1958.

32. *Boston Globe,* 3–6 April 1958; *Boston Herald,* 3–6 April 1958.

33. *Boston Globe,* 7–12 April 1958; *Boston Herald,* 9–12 April 1958; *Los Angeles Times,* 8 April 1958; Russell, *Go Up for Glory,* 170–71.

34. *Boston Globe,* 13 April 1958; *Boston Herald,* 13 April 1958; Tax, "Bob Pettit," 31; Pluto, *Tall Tales,* 144; Stump, "Bob Pettit," 75; Ed Macauley interview.

35. Marecek, *Full Court,* 80; Goodman, "Never a Dull Moment," 35; *Boston Globe,* 30 March 1958, 14 April 1958.

36. *New York Times,* 6 April 1958; *Chicago Defender,* 21 April 1958.

37. Harold Furash, telephone interview with author, 19 March 2007; *Boston Globe,* 15 January 1988; Peggy White, telephone interview with author, 15 March 2007; Peggy White correspondence, in author's possession; B. Russell, *Go Up for Glory,* 171–73.

38. Montville, *Ted Williams,* 67–72; Bryant, *Shut Out,* 1–12, 31–36, 43–48; Stout, "Tryout and Fallout," 11–37.

39. *Boston Herald,* 28 January 1958, 11 February 1959, 1 March 1959, 2 March 1962,

24 March 1969; *Boston Globe,* 29 January 1958, 10 March 1958, 19 March 1958, 22 March 1958, 18 December 1959, 20 January 1960, 7 March 1960, 24 February 1961, 26 February 1962. For average attendance figures, see Bjarkman, *Boston Celtics Encyclopedia,* 117. The Bruins actually integrated their team before the Red Sox, calling up Willie O'Ree from the minors for two games in 1958. O'Ree played two games with the Bruins that year and played forty-one more games in 1961. See O'Ree, *Autobiography of Willie O'Ree,* 53–80; C. Harris, *Breaking the Ice,* 75–76.

40. Hardy, "Long Before Orr," 267–72; Isaacs, *Checking Back,* 73–77, 114–22. Murry Nelson, "Professional Basketball in New England in the Early 20th Century," article manuscript in author's possession; Ryan and Pluto, *Forty-Eight Minutes,* 68–70; R. Johnson, *Century of Boston Sports,* 53, 91–92; B. Reynolds, *Our Game,* 29–39.

41. Carey, *High Above Courtside,* 49–54, 386–87, 402; Auerbach and Fitzgerald, *Red Auerbach,* 106–8; Auerbach and Feinstein, *Let Me Tell You a Story,* 283–84; *Boston Globe,* 6 March 1957, 10 March 1957, 4 February 1958, 4 December 1958, 7 December 1958, 21 December 1961, 12 December 1964, 10 December 1965. One interesting illustration of basketball's tenuous tradition and emerging place in New England was Arthur Sampson's short, near-daily column on the history and principles of the sport, titled "Basketball for Everybody." See *Boston Herald* from 4 February 1961 to 11 March 1961.

42. Auerbach and Fitzgerald, *Red Auerbach,* 63–66, 201–3.

43. Auerbach and Fitzgerald, *Red Auerbach,* 67–69; Cousy, *Basketball Is My Life,* 102–25; *Philadelphia Inquirer,* 30 December 1953.

44. Cousy, *Basketball Is My Life,* 1–85, 144–47; Reynolds, *Cousy,* 3–65; Cousy, *Last Loud Roar,* 54–55; Cousy, *Killer Instinct,* 3–4, 96–98.

45. *Boston Globe,* 2 January 1953, 30 March 1954, 30 January 1958, 7 February 1960; "The Cousy Circus," *Newsweek,* 21 January 1952, 80–81; Hirshberg, "Cousy Shoots Like Crazy," 28–31, 82–83; "Basketball's Little Big Shot," 37; Frank, "Basketball's Amazing Showboat," 25, 58–59; Hirshberg, "Roommate," 48–56; Wind, "Bob Cousy," 42–58; Wind, "Bob Cousy: The Man," 28–32, 56–58; "Celtics Climb on Cousy's Clever Coups," 77–80; Hirshberg, "Visit With Bob Cousy," 30, 91–92; Linn, "Wonderful Wizard of Boston," 52–60; *Sporting News,* 25 November 1959; *New York Times,* 10 July 1960.

46. Hirshberg, "Sharman at the Crossroads," 22–24, 89–90; Linn, "Bill Sharman Story," 52–61; G. Sullivan, *Picture History,* 147–49; Salzberg, *From Set Shot to Slam Dunk,* 145–55; Kaplan, "Bill Sharman," 78–81; Tax, "Perfect Free Throw," 44–45; *Sporting News,* 19 December 1956, 19 March 1958. See also Sharman, *Sharman on Basketball Shooting;* Wooden and Sharman, *Wooden-Sharman Method.* The Brooklyn Dodgers called up Sharman in 1951, promising to play him as soon as they clinched the pennant. The New York Giants promptly whittled away Brooklyn's 13½ game lead; Sharman watched Bobby Thomson's "Shot Heard 'Round the World" from the dugout, and he never played in the major leagues. By then Auerbach had obtained him and Bob Harris from the Fort Wayne Pistons—in a trade for Charlie Share, Auerbach's draft pick over Cousy.

47. *Boston Globe,* 6 March 1957, 23 December 1960; *Sporting News,* 7 January 1959, 14 January 1959; *New York Post,* 15 January 1959; *Chicago Defender,* 10 January 1960, 5 November 1962; Hirshberg, "A Visit With Bob Cousy," 91.

48. On the makings of sports heroes, see Teitelbaum, *Sports Heroes,* 1–7.

49. Bob Cousy, telephone interview with author, 23 April 2007; B. Russell, *Go Up for Glory*, 73; B. Russell, *Russell Rules*, 69; Auerbach and Sann, *Red Auerbach*, 204–5.

50. Tax, "Roundball Bounces Back," 31, 58–61; "Negroes in Pro Basketball," 55–58; J. Fisher, "Elgin Baylor," 177–88.

51. Cope, "Life with Elgin Baylor," 63–65; *Sporting News*, 12 February 1958; Watson, "Elgin Baylor," 55–64; Olderman, "Elgin Baylor," 24–26, 80–81; Tax, "Bunyan Strides Again," 18–19; uncited article dated 23 January 1959 in Mokray Scrapbook, 1958–59 Season; "Dollars in His Legs," 64. Baylor could enter the NBA after his junior year in 1958 because his original graduating class had started school four years earlier. On Baylor's beginnings with Minneapolis, see also *New York Post*, 15 November 1965; Lazenby, *Lakers*, 120–31; Lazenby, *Show*, 58–61.

52. *Los Angeles Times*, 10 April 1958; *Chicago Defender*, 22 April 1958; *Boston Globe*, 15 April 1958, 24 December 1958, 9 December 1959, 20 December 1996; *Boston Traveler*, 23 October 1963; K. C. Jones, *Rebound*, 64–65, 75–76, 86; Auerbach and Sann, *Red Auerbach*, 244–45. On 1958 exhibition tour, see also Embry, *Inside Game*, 98–101. K. C. Jones had been drafted to the Rams by Pete Rozelle, the former sports information director at USF.

53. *Boston Herald*, 23 April 1958; *Boston Globe*, 27 May 1958; "Hidden Fear that Is Not Our Fear," 104; W. Russell, "Success Is a Journey," 86; B. Russell, *Go Up for Glory*, 93–95, 117–19. Traveling college basketball teams offered similar clashes of racial practices. Between 1956 and 1959, Harvard, Cincinnati, Colorado State, and Duquesne canceled games against southern teams after Louisiana's law banning interracial athletics. The Mississippi state college board forced all-black Jackson State to withdraw from the 1957 NCAA small college tournament rather than play integrated teams, and Mississippi State withdrew from the 1959 NCAA tournament rather than face integrated competition. See *New York Times*, 5 October 1956, 6 October 1956, 26 October 1956, 6 March 1957, 13 December 1957, 1 March 1959, 22 December 1959. On black press and the segregation of traveling athletes, see Lacy, *Fighting for Fairness*, 95–97.

54. *Chicago Defender*, 27 November 1958, 2 December 1958, 6 December 1958; *Boston Globe*, 26 November 1958, 18 January 1959; B. Russell, *Go Up for Glory*, 113–14.

55. *New York Times*, 17–19 January 1959, 23 January 1959; uncited article dated 18 January 1959, Mokray Scrapbook, 1958–59 Season; *Boston Globe*, 17 January 1959, 18 January 1959; *Chicago Defender*, 21 January 1959; *Sporting News*, 18 February 1959.

56. *Boston Herald*, 25 March 1958; *New York Times*, 27 February 1959; *Chicago Defender*, 14 March 1960; M. Harris, *Lonely Heroes*, 15, 21–22; Charles Rosen, *God, Man and Basketball Jones*, 116, 122. Koppett, *Essence of the Game*, 66–71; *Boston Globe*, 10 April 1959. On more general respect for defensive basketball by the turn of the decade, see Iba, "Defense Decides the Big Ones," 36, 71–73; Cave, "Long-Neglected Art," 48–49. For opinions from those who still ranked Mikan's teams superior, see *Boston Globe*, 24 January 1957; *Sporting News*, 22 January 1958.

57. *Boston Globe*, 22 November 1958, 26 December 1958, 30 December 1958, 6 January 1959, 13 January 1959, 28 February 1959, 1 March 1959, 2 March 1959, 9 March 1959; *New York Times*, 28 March 1959; *Sporting News*, 12 February 1958, 11 March 1959; *Boston Herald*, 28 February 1959, 1 March 1959.

58. Gene Conley, telephone interview with author, 10 April 2007; Conley, *One of a Kind*,

118–217; McKenney, "Conley's on the High Road," 42–45, 62–63; Tax, "Now Pitching for Boston," 60–62; *Boston Herald,* 25 October 1958, 8 February 1959, 16 February 1959; uncited articles dated 23 October 1958 in Mokray Scrapbook, 1958–59 Season; *Boston Globe,* 1 November 1958, 21 February 1959, 11 March 1959; *Sporting News,* 27 January 1960. Upon Conley's refusal to report to spring training, the Milwaukee Braves traded him to the Philadelphia Phillies.

59. *Boston Globe,* 17 March 1959, 1 April 1959; Earl Lloyd interview.

60. Frank, "Basketball's Toughest War Horse," 61–62; Rosenthal, "Schayes Is a Hustler," 40–41, 71–73; "Events and Discoveries," 25–26; *Sporting News,* 17 February 1960, 18 January 1961; Simons, "Interview with Adolph Schayes," 287–307; Salzberg, *From Set Shot to Slam Dunk,* 109–28.

61. Gross, "Basketball's Unhappy Gunner," 30, 53–55; *Sporting News,* 5 February 1958, 11 March 1959; Dolph Schayes, telephone interview with author, 13 April 2007. On New York series, see *Boston Herald,* 16 March 1959, 17 March 1959.

62. *Boston Globe,* 30 December 1958, 20 February 1959, 19 March 1959, 20 March 1959; *Boston Herald,* 20 February 1959, 21 March 1959; Araton and Bondy, *Selling of the Green,* 26–34; Hannum, "Old Days and Changed Ways," 37; Cousy, *Last Loud Roar,* 49; Carey, *High Above Courtside,* 74–77; Salzberg, *From Set Shot to Slam Dunk,* 118–19; Dolph Schayes interview.

63. *Boston Globe,* 22–30 March 1959; *Boston Herald,* 22–30 March 1959.

64. *Boston Globe,* 2 April 1959, 3 April 1959; *Boston Herald,* 2 April 1959, 3 April 1959. Togo Palazzi, a backup forward for Syracuse, resented Boston and Red Auerbach for cutting him in 1956. He never got to play in Game Seven, which occurred the day his son was born. Palazzi told Schayes that if he had played and Syracuse had won, he would have named his child "Victor." Dolph Schayes interview.

65. *Boston Globe,* 4 January 1959, 19 January 1959, 21 January 1959, 27–30 January 1959, 5 February 1959, 7 February 1959, 30 March 1959; *Boston Herald,* 3 January 1959, 4 January 1959, 19–21 January 1959, 27 January 1959, 29 January 1959, 2 March 1959, 3 March 1959.

66. *Boston Globe,* 5–11 April 1959; *Boston Herald,* 5–12 April 1959; AP Report dated 8 April 1959, Mokray Scrapbook, 1958–59 Season; Tax, "Short, Sweet Series," 66–68.

67. *Boston Herald,* 11 April 1959; Conley, *One of a Kind,* 216–17.

7. GOLIATH'S SHADOW

1. *Boston Globe,* 12 November 1958.

2. *San Francisco News,* 16 March 1957; "Events and Discoveries," 37; *Chicago Defender,* 11 December 1956; *University Daily Kansan,* 28 March 1956; *New York Times,* 14 January 1957; *San Francisco Chronicle,* 17 December 1956; Bob Billings, "My Friend, Wilt Chamberlain," Wilt Chamberlain Morgue File, 1959 Folder, Spencer Research Library, University of Kansas.

3. *Lawrence Journal-World,* 28 December 1956, 19 March 1957, 23 March 1957; *New York Amsterdam News,* 8 December 1956; *Pittsburgh Courier,* 15 December 1956; *Philadelphia Bulletin,* 16 December 1956, 13 December 1957; *Boston Globe,* 13 December 1957. Abe Saper-

stein actually gave Russell a slight edge, but that was in December 1956, when the Globetrotters were still trying to sign the Olympian.

4. *Los Angeles Times*, 23 December 1956.

5. Cherry, *Wilt*, 3–11; Libby, *Goliath*, 15–18; Chamberlain and Shaw, *Wilt*, 6–17.

6. Chamberlain and Shaw, *Wilt*, 36; *Philadelphia Inquirer*, 11 March 1955; *Philadelphia Daily News*, 2 February 1960. For clippings of Chamberlain's exploits, especially from high school and his professional stints in Philadelphia, see the Wilt Chamberlain file at the Urban Archives at Temple University.

7. "Giants of Schoolboy Basketball," 59–62; "Wilton the Wonder," *Senior Scholastic*, 15 September 1954, 30; Staff of the Philadelphia Daily News, *Philly Hoops*, 99–101; Auerbach and Fitzgerald, *Red Auerbach*, 272–73, 277–78; Auerbach and Sann, *Red Auerbach*, 77–82; Chamberlain, "I'm Punchy from Basketball," 40. On basketball in the Catskills, see Anderson and Millman, *Pickup Artists*, 46–51; Cousy, *Basketball Is My Life*, 44–48; Charles Rosen, *Scandals of '51*, 41–43; S. Cohen, *Game They Played*, 97–99.

8. Goodman, "High-School Kid," 30–33, 58–59; *Philadelphia Bulletin*, 31 July 1955; "What It Took to Get Wilt," 113–17; Goodman, "I Remember Basketball," 104–5; Breslin, "Can Basketball Survive Chamberlain?" 106; Goudsouzian, "'Can Basketball Survive Chamberlain?'" 152–54.

9. *New York Times*, 27 October 1960; *Boston Globe*, 18 February 1957, 19 February 1957; *Boston Herald*, 19 February 1957. Former Kansas coach Phog Allen responded to Brown with trademark buttery verbosity: "Walter Brown, a silk-stocking boy with a fabulous inheritance, wouldn't know what real struggle means. Wilton Chamberlain does." Considering the historic abolitionist ties between Boston and Kansas, "it is ironical that another Boston personality would try to fetter a fine Negro citizen." *Pittsburgh Courier*, 2 March 1957; *Chicago Defender*, 9 March 1957. In 1960, the NCAA placed the University of Kansas on probation for illegal payments to Chamberlain. See "Athletic Office (NCAA)" Folder, 1960–61, Chancellor Wescoe Correspondence, Spencer Research Library; *New York Times*, 27 October 1960.

10. Breslin, "Can Basketball Survive Chamberlain?" 104–8; "Seven-Foot Freshman," 11; "Wilt the Stilt," 61–62; "7-Foot Man," 96; Deford, "Team that Was Blessed," 58–75; Chamberlain, "Why I Am Quitting College," 91–101; Kaliss, "Everyone's All-Americans," 160–240; Goudsouzian, "'Can Basketball Survive Chamberlain?'" 167–73. In another early intersection of Russell's and Chamberlain's fates, a *Look* reporter first established contact with Chamberlain in St. Louis, during the 1958 NBA Finals between the Celtics and the Hawks. See G. Sullivan, *Wilt Chamberlain*, 51–52.

11. B. Green, *Spinning the Globe*, 283–301; Chamberlain, "Pro Basketball Has Ganged Up on Me," 55–58; *Philadelphia Bulletin*, 12 September 1958; Chamberlain and Shaw, *Wilt*, 79–100. While on tour in the Soviet Union, Chamberlain met Nikita Khruschev. The Soviet premier popped out of the lead car in a motorcade near the Kremlin. He exclaimed "Ah, basketball!" shook hands, and posed for pictures.

12. Goodman, "Wilt vs. the NBA," 21.

13. Deford, "Eddie Is the Mogul," 42–45; Rosin, *Philly Hoops*, 1–20; P. Levine, *Ellis Island to Ebbets Field*, 62–65; Charley Rosen, *First Tip-Off*, 25–29, 179–93; *Boston Globe*, 28 October 1959.

14. *Philadelphia Bulletin,* 19 February 1959, 23 April 1959, 24 April 1959, 12–14 May 1959, 17 May 1959, 4 February 1960; Goodman, "Wilt vs. the NBA," 86. On other Warriors, see Goodman, "Arizin," 40–41, 70–73; "Wonderful Warriors," 48–51; *Sporting News,* 24 December 1958, 18 February 1959; Olderman, "Tom Gola Mystery," 48, 72–73. Gottlieb and Saperstein were longtime friends, and Saperstain owned stock in the Warriors. But when Saperstein tried signing Chamberlain for a second year, the men feuded. Gottlieb sold his stake in the Warriors. B. Green, *Spinning the Globe,* 309.

15. *Philadelphia Bulletin,* 19 August 1959, 20 August 1959, 20 October 1959; undated article from *Boston Globe,* Mokray Scrapbook, 1958–59 Season; *Philadelphia Inquirer,* 17 October 1959, 4 December 1959; *New York Times,* 14 October 1959; *Los Angeles Times,* 15 October 1959; *Washington Post,* 17 October 1959.

16. *New York Post,* 7 November 1959; Tax, "Here Comes the Big Fellow at Last," 16.

17. Gottehrer, "When Wilt and Russell Meet," 40.

18. Gottehrer, "When Wilt and Russell Meet," 40–41; Cosell, "Wilt vs. Russell, No. 1," 78; *New York Post,* 7 November 1959.

19. Goodman, "Big Collision," 16–17, 76–77; *Christian Science Monitor,* 9 November 1959; Tax, "Tall Ones in Boston," 28; *Philadelphia Inquirer,* 8 November 1959; *New York Times,* 8 November 1959. See also Taylor, *Rivalry,* 3–10.

20. Tax, "Wilt Knocks 'Em Dead"; *Boston Globe,* 25 November 1959, 26 November 1959, 7 January 1960, 16 January 1960, 18 January 1960, 6 February 1960, 25 February 1960, 2 March 1960, 3 March 1960, 11 March 1960, 15 January 1961; *Philadelphia Inquirer,* 26 November 1959, 27 November 1959, 16 January 1960, 18 January 1960, 3 February 1960; *Sporting News,* 9 March 1960; *New York Times,* 10 March 1960; "Basketball's Best," 52–53; *Boston Herald,* 10 March 1960.

21. *Boston Globe,* 18 November 1959, 6 January 1960, 16 January 1960; *New York Post,* 13 January 1960; *Philadelphia Bulletin,* 26 October 1959, 23 January 1960, 10 February 1960, 13 March 1960; *Philadelphia Inquirer,* 20 October 1959, 16 November 1959; *Kansas City Star,* 10 February 1960; *Lawrence Journal-World,* 27 October 1959; *Chicago Defender,* 23 January 1960; *Sporting News,* 9 March 1960; *New York Times,* 16 March 1960.

22. D. Schaap, "Real Wilt Chamberlain," 54–57; *New York Post,* 13 January 1960; *Philadelphia Bulletin,* 11 January 1960, 27 January 1960, 4 February 1960; *Sporting News,* 18 November 1959, 3 February 1960; "Leap that No One Can Stop," 57; "Little Man, What Now?" 73; *Boston Globe,* 28 March 1960; *Philadelphia Daily News,* 1 February 1960. The B-Side was called "That's Easy to Say." Few copies of the record have survived, and it has become quite a collector's item. See *Lawrence Journal-World,* 21 March 2001, 23 March 2001.

23. Chamberlain, *Who's Running the Asylum?* 93–94; *Philadelphia Bulletin,* 15 November 1959; *Philadelphia Daily News,* 5 February 1960; Chamberlain and Shaw, *Wilt,* 116–17; Taylor, *Rivalry,* 123.

24. *Philadelphia Bulletin,* 25 August 1959, 27 September 1959, 5 May 1972; *Philadelphia Inquirer,* 25 October 1959, 26 October 1959; Rosin, *Philly Hoops,* 43; Libby, *Goliath,* 91; *Christian Science Monitor,* 9 November 1959; *Philadelphia Daily News,* 5 February 1960, 26 April 1979.

25. *Philadelphia Bulletin,* 11 November 1959, 17 November 1959, 16 February 1960; *Philadelphia Inquirer,* 10 January 1960; *New York Times,* 10 January 1960; Chamberlain,

"Pro Basketball Has Ganged Up on Me," 51–55; *Sporting News,* 24 February 1960; *Boston Globe,* 2 December 1959; *Boston Herald,* 16 February 1960; *Chicago Defender,* 16 February 1960; *Philadelphia Daily News,* 1–5 February 1960.

26. *Philadelphia Daily News,* 1 February 1960.

27. Greene, "Bill Russell Is Better than Ever," 25–26.

28. Uncited article dated 8 November 1959, Mokray Scrapbook, 1959–60 Season; *Philadelphia Inquirer,* 22 November 1959; Gottehrer, "When Wilt and Russell Meet," 41; *New York Times,* 10 January 1960; *Boston Globe,* 2 December 1959, 16 March 1960; *Kansas City Star,* 10 January 1960.

29. *Pittsburgh Courier,* 19 December 1959; *Philadelphia Bulletin,* 15 March 1960; *Philadelphia Inquirer,* 15–17 March 1960; *Boston Globe,* 15–17 March 1960.

30. *Philadelphia Inquirer,* 19 March 1960; *Boston Globe,* 19 March 1960; *Boston Herald,* 19 March 1960; Heinsohn, *Heinsohn, Don't You Ever Smile?* 9–13; Heinsohn and Fitzgerald, *Give 'Em the Hook,* 90–91; Rosin, *Philly Hoops,* 40-41.

31. *Philadelphia Inquirer,* 20 March 1960; *Boston Globe,* 20 March 1960; Heinsohn, *Heinsohn, Don't You Ever Smile?* 13–14; Heinsohn and Fitzgerald, *Give 'Em the Hook,* 91–92; *Boston Herald,* 20 March 1960.

32. *Philadelphia Inquirer,* 22 March 1960, 25 March 1960; *Boston Herald,* 23–25 March 1960; *Boston Globe,* 22–25 March 1960.

33. Goodman, "Never a Dull Moment," 86; Marecek, *Full Court,* 87–88, 114–15; Rogin, "You're Looking at Success," 48–49; *Boston Herald,* 26 March 1960, 28 March 1960; *New York Times,* 26 March 1960.

34. *Boston Herald,* 28–30 March 1960; *Boston Globe,* 28–30 March 1960.

35. *Boston Herald,* 3–4 April 1960; *Boston Globe,* 3–5 April 1960; *Los Angeles Times,* 5 April 1960.

36. *Boston Herald,* 6 April 1960; *Boston Globe,* 5 April 1960, 7 April 1960, 8 April 1960.

37. *Boston Herald,* 9 April 1960; *Boston Globe,* 9 April 1960.

38. Auerbach, *MBA Management by Auerbach,* 98.

39. Leggett, "'Cooz' and the Celtics," 62–63; *New York Times,* 10 April 1960; *Boston Herald,* 10 April 1960; *Boston Globe,* 10 April 1960.

40. *Boston Globe,* 10 April 1960.

41. *Philadelphia Bulletin,* 7 February 1960, 23 March 1960, 25 March 1960, 26 March 1960; *Boston Globe,* 24 February 1960, 25 March 1960; *Philadelphia Inquirer,* 2 February 1960, 25 February 1960, 26 March 1960.

42. *New York Times,* 26 March 1960; *Boston Globe,* 26 March 1960; *Boston Herald,* 26 March 1960.

43. *Philadelphia Inquirer,* 25 March 1960, 27–29 March 1960, 4 April 1960; *Philadelphia Bulletin,* 27 March 1960, 30 March 1960, 31 March 1960, 3 April 1960, 11 April 1960; *New York Times,* 28 March 1960, 31 March 1960, 3 April 1960, 8 April 1960; Tax, "Chamberlain's Big Mistake," 58–59.

44. *New York Times,* 27 March 1960, 10 July 1960; *Boston Herald,* 26 March 1960; "Off Again, On Again Chamberlain," 8; *Boston Globe,* 25 March 1960, 27 March 1960.

45. Schayes, "Wilt Chamberlain," 19, 66–68.

46. *Philadelphia Bulletin,* 29 March 1960, 5 May 1960, 22 June 1960, 1 August 1960,

10 August 1960, 11 August 1960; *New York Times,* 11 August 1960; *Kansas City Star,* 10 August 1960.

47. *Sporting News,* 18 January 1961; *New York Post,* 19 January 1961; R. Thomas, *They Cleared the Lane,* 205–10. See also Berkow, *To the Hoop,* 162–63.

48. R. Roberts, *"But They Can't Beat Us";* R. Pierce, "More than a Game," 3–23; Goudsouzian, "'Ba-ad, Ba-a-ad Tigers,'" 5–43; Paino, "Hoosiers in a Different Light," 63–80; Hoose, *Hoosiers,* 143–93; Robertson, *Big O,* 42–71.

49. *Sporting News,* 22 January 1958, 10 February 1960, 2 March 1960; Gross, "Basketball's Moody Marvel," 19, 60–62; Tax, "What Price Glory for Oscar?"; *Chicago Defender,* 17 February 1959; Berkow, *Oscar Robertson,* 137–39; Robertson, *Big O,* 72–129.

50. Robertson, *Big O,* 130–48; "Graceful Giants," 54–61; *Sporting News,* 25 January 1961.

51. Leggett, "New Kid on the Block," 24–25; *Boston Globe,* 18 October 1960, 6 November 1960, 5 February 1961; *Los Angeles Times,* 22 October 1960; "Scouting Reports," 50–53; *Philadelphia Inquirer,* 9 December 1960.

52. *Philadelphia Inquirer,* 30 October 1960, 5 November 1960, 20 November 1960, 8 January 1961, 15 January 1961, 17 January 1961; *Sporting News,* 25 January 1961; *Philadelphia Bulletin,* 8 November 1960, 6 January 1961, 13 January 1961, 8 February 1961.

53. *Philadelphia Inquirer,* 25 November 1960, 9 December 1960, 11 December 1960, 14 December 1960, 27 December 1960, 8 January 1961, 15 January 1961, 27 January 1961, 30 January 1961, 12 February 1961; *Boston Globe,* 4 January 1960, 14 January 1961, 30 January 1961, 4 February 1961, 12 February 1961, 13 February 1961, 2 March 1961, 13 March 1961; *New York Post,* 2 December 1960; undated Milton Gross column in *New York Post,* Mokray Scrapbook, 1960–61 Season; Libby, *Goliath,* 96. In the preseason, Chamberlain also refused to leave an exhibition game, indicating his disrespect for Johnston and his teammates. Pluto, *Tall Tales,* 327–28.

54. *New York Times,* 15 March 1961; *Boston Globe,* 13 November 1960; Gross, "Pros Tell Their Favorite Bill Russell Stories," 46; *Los Angeles Times,* 18 November 1960; *Baltimore Afro-American,* 22 November 1960.

55. *Boston Globe,* 30 November 1960; *New York Times,* 8 March 1961.

56. *Boston Globe,* 25 November 1959, 21 February 1961, 12 March 1961.

57. *Boston Globe,* 14 March 1961; Greene, "Bill Russell Is Better than Ever," 25–27, 78–79.

58. *Boston Globe,* 7 March 1961, 12 March 1961; *Philadelphia Bulletin,* 15 January 1961, 20 March 1961, 25 March 1961; Dolson, "Fiasco at the Foul Line," 76; *Philadelphia Inquirer,* 24 November 1960, 27 November 1960.

59. *Philadelphia Bulletin,* 10 January 1961, 22 January 1961, 7 February 1961; *Philadelphia Inquirer,* 10 January 1961; *Los Angeles Times,* 22 January 1961; *Washington Post,* 10 January 1961; *Sporting News,* 8 February 1961, 1 March 1961; *Boston Globe,* 18 January 1960, 18 March 1960.

60. *Boston Globe,* 14 February 1961, 24 March 1961, 25 March 1961, 13 December 1961; *Boston Herald,* 24 March 1961, 26 March 1961; two uncited articles in Mokray Scrapbook, 1960–61 Season; D. Anderson, "Trials of the Tall Men," 4–7, 94.

61. Heinsohn, *Heinsohn, Don't You Ever Smile?* 166–67; B. Russell, *Russell Rules,* 47–51,

106–7, 187–89, 205; W. Russell, "Success Is a Journey," 86; B. Russell, "Tale of Two Very Big Men," 60.

62. *Los Angeles Times,* 22 August 2006; *Boston Globe,* 26 May 1999; Pluto, *Tall Tales,* 348; Russell and Branch, *Second Wind,* 158–61. Frank McGuire, Chamberlain's coach during the 1961–62 season, claimed that "Russell's most valuable skill against Chamberlain is their close friendship." Chamberlain resisted overpowering his friend. "He simply will not get mad, and put Russell in the basket." *Pittsburgh Courier,* 1 September 1962.

63. Gottehrer, "When Wilt and Russell Meet," 39; *Chicago Defender,* 19 December 1959; Goodman, "Big Collision," 16–17; Tax, "Two Big Men," 46–49; *Sporting News,* 20 January 1960; *Boston Globe,* 29 December 1959, 13 February 1962; *Los Angeles Sentinel,* 3 March 1960; "Bill vs. Wilt," 51–55.

64. *Philadelphia Inquirer,* 20 March 1961; *Boston Herald,* 24 March 1961; *Philadelphia Bulletin,* 30 March 1961.

65. *Washington Post,* 20 March 1961; *Boston Globe,* 20–27 March 1961; *Boston Herald,* 20–23 March 1961; Auerbach and Sann, *Red Auerbach,* 194–96.

66. *Boston Record-American,* 29 December 1960; uncited articles dated 29 December 1960 and 19 January 1961, Mokray Scrapbook, 1960–61 Season; *Boston Herald,* 10 April 1961.

67. *Boston Herald,* 3 April 1961, 6 April 1961, 9 April 1961, 10 April 1961, 12 April 1961; *Boston Globe,* 5–12 April 1961; "Scorecard," 13. See also Dexter, "Fabulous Predictions," 25.

68. *Boston Herald,* 12 April 1961; *Boston Globe,* 12 April 1961; uncited article dated 12 April 1961, Mokray Scrapbook, 1960–61 Season.

8. THE MYSTIQUE

1. Russell and Branch, *Second Wind,* 93–118, 155–57; Plimpton, *X Factor,* 99–100. See also Guttmann, *From Ritual to Record,* 137–61. On sport's spiritual and political dimensions, see also Novak, *Joy of Sports,* 1–55, 98–114; Mandelbaum, *Meaning of Sports,* 1–39; Boyd, "Day the Niggaz Took Over," 134–37; Lipsky, *How We Play the Game,* 5–45; Eitzen, *Fair and Foul;* Sydnor, "Sport, Celebrity and Liminality," 221–37; Burstyn, *Rites of Men,* 131–36; Guttmann, *Sports Spectators,* 176–85; Higgs, *God in the Stadium,* 1–21; Cooper, *Playing in the Zone,* 1–19, 76–150.

2. For Murray quote, see *Los Angeles Times,* 5 February 1962. On references to "pride" by players and reporters, see *Boston Globe,* 16 February 1960, 21 February 1961, 24 March 1963, 27 December 1963; *Boston Herald,* 17 March 1964; *Los Angeles Times,* 4 January 1963.

3. Robertson, *Big O,* 142.

4. Auerbach and Fitzgerald, *Red Auerbach,* 218–21; Frank Ramsey, interview with author, 8 May 2006; Bob Cousy, telephone interview with author, 23 April 2007.

5. Goodman, "Hothead," 28–29, 88–92; Goodman, "Winning Ways," 69–76; Auerbach and Sann, *Red Auerbach,* 137–217; *Sporting News,* 21 February 1962, 24 November 1962, 19 March 1966; *Los Angeles Times,* 4 January 1963, 10 January 1967; *Boston Globe,* 25 January 1963, 28 April 1964; R. Powers, *Overtime!* 54–55.

6. On coaches, see Wilkens, *Unguarded,* 72; Pluto, *Tall Tales,* 378–79. On Auerbach's personal life, see Shaughnessy, *Seeing Red,* 8–23, 77–79. Auerbach claimed that his family

lived in Washington because his daughter Nancy had asthma and found it easier to breathe there. That rationale deserves skepticism.

7. *Washington Post*, 19 January 1964; *Sporting News*, 19 January 1963, 16 January 1965, 22 March 1969; *Boston Globe*, 24 January 1961; Auerbach and Sann, *Red Auerbach*, 260–61; Frank Ramsey interview.

8. Larry Siegfried, telephone interview with author, 25 January 2008; *Sporting News*, 9 March 1968; Auerbach, *On and Off the Court*, 61–62, 146–51; Auerbach, "How I Handle the Boston Celtics," 92–95; Auerbach and Fitzgerald, *Red Auerbach*, 234–40; Auerbach, *MBA Management by Auerbach*, 96–98.

9. *Sporting News*, 18 December 1957; *Boston Globe*, 3 March 1958, 24 March 1964; Ryan, *Pro Game*, 124–25; Frank Ramsey interview. Russell's talents made it possible for the undersized Ramsey to play forward. Ramsey concentrated on just boxing out his man and letting Russell rebound.

10. Larry Siegfried interview; Heinsohn, "Of Charley Horses and Little Old Ladies," 40; Sharman, *Sharman on Basketball Shooting*, 122; Cousy, *Last Loud Roar*, 90–92, 168–70, 216–19.

11. *Boston Globe*, 5 February 1960, 21 March 1962; *Boston Record-American*, 28 January 1964; *Christian Science Monitor*, 9 February 1964; "Basketball's Best," 52–53; Berger, "*Sport* Interview," 24; Auerbach and Fitzgerald, *Red Auerbach*, 228–33; B. Russell, *Russell Rules*, 64–66.

12. Walsh, "Jones & Jones at Court," 49–52; *Sporting News*, 15 March 1961; Gowdy, *Seasons to Remember*, 122–23. On Sam Jones, see Hirshberg, "Celtics' Cinderella Star," 52, 70–71; *Chicago Defender*, 7 May 1962; *Sporting News*, 8 February 1964; *Boston Globe*, 23 December 1959, 24 December 1963, 25 March 1964; Ryan, *Boston Celtics*, 44. On K. C. Jones, see *Boston Globe*, 29 March 1959; *Boston Herald*, 29 March 1959; Wooden and Sharman, *Wooden-Sharman Method*, 91.

13. *Boston Globe*, 12 April 1960, 28 March 1961, 9 April 1961; *Boston Herald*, 28 March 1961; *Chicago Defender*, 9 April 1966; Grenier, *Don't They Ever Stop Running?* 134–36.

14. Tom "Satch" Sanders, telephone interview with the author, 25 August 2008; Shaughnessy, *Seeing Red*, 116–17; Bob Cousy, telephone interview with author, 23 April 2007; *New York Post*, 18 December 1961; *Boston Traveler*, 27 December 1961; *Boston Globe*, 11 February 1961.

15. C. Pierce, "Red Auerbach," 114–15; Montville, "Blowin' Smoke," 54–59; Shaughnessy, *Seeing Red*, 114; G. Sullivan, *Picture History*, 135, 159; *Christian Science Monitor*, 9 February 1964; *Philadelphia Inquirer*, 28 March 1962; Rogin, "They All Boo When He Sits Down," 111; *Boston Globe*, 9 March 1965.

16. *USA Today*, 9 June 2004; B. Russell, *Red and Me*, 104–6; Auerbach and Sann, *Red Auerbach*, 228–29; Auerbach and Fitzgerald, *On and Off the Court*, 48–50; Cope, "Last Cigar for a Last Hurrah?" 112.

17. B. Russell, *Red and Me*, 37–52.

18. Cousy and Ryan, *Cousy on the Celtic Mystique*, 19; B. Russell, *Go Up for Glory*, 113–14; B. Russell, *Red and Me*, 74–79. The exchange between Russell and Auerbach in Charlotte illustrated a classic tension in black-Jewish relations, as the groups so often shared progressive political inclinations and Jewish Americans occupied economic positions close to

African Americans, including entrepreneurial positions in entertainment and sports. Yet the relative power of Jewish Americans, which included access to "whiteness," created black resentment, particularly by the 1960s. See Greenberg, *Troubling the Waters*.

19. Frank Ramsey interview; Bob Cousy interview.

20. On Celtics' burgeoning status, see Koppett, *Championship NBA*, 61; "Pro Basketball's Dynasty," 64–66; *Boston Globe*, 28 October 1962; Ed Macauley, telephone interview with author, 2 April 2007; Ryan, *Pro Game*, 19–20. On debates over historical greatness, see *Sporting News*, 15 March 1961; *Boston Globe*, 24 December 1959, 2 March 1961, 12 April 1961, 31 March 1963, 26 April 1963, 18 November 1963, 27 March 1963, 12 January 1964; *Boston Herald*, 7 March 1961, 13 April 1961, 13 February 1962, 13 March 1962, 6 January 1963, 17 March 1963. On comparisons to New York Yankees, see *Boston Globe*, 18 December 1959, 29 March 1960, 24 November 1960, 25 April 1963, 1 March 1965; *Atlanta Daily World*, 2 May 1962; *Chicago Defender*, 21 November 1962, 30 April 1964, 28 April 1965, 30 November 1965.

21. *Sporting News*, 26 January 1963, 11 January 1964; Carey, *High Above Courtside*, 44–54; *Boston Herald*, 12 March 1962; G. Sullivan, *Boston Celtics*, 30.

22. Ryan and Pluto, *Forty-Eight Minutes*, 51; *Boston Herald*, 3 February 1963, 6 January 1966; *New York Times*, 16 April 1995; Havlicek and Ryan, *Hondo*, 101–2; Heinsohn and Fitzgerald, *Give 'Em the Hook*, 57.

23. *New York Times*, 22 April 1995; Mike Farmer, interview with author, 9 March 2005. On loyal Boston fans, see *Boston Globe*, 11 April 1963, 26 February 1963, 22 November 1964, 12 April 1966. Johnny Most admitted that visitors' complaints about the hot-and-cold locker room were legitimate, but not the work of Auerbach. Boston's cantankerous equipment manager Walter Randall opened and closed windows to maximize the level of discomfort, and he sometimes shut off the hot or cold valves to the shower. Carey, *High Above Courtside*, 141.

24. Uncited AP article dated 1 April 1961, 1960–61 Season, Mokray Scrapbook; *Boston Record-American*, 27 March 1962; *Boston Herald*, 28 March 1961, 26 April 1963; *Boston Globe*, 8 March 1961, 21 March 1963, 11 November 1964.

25. Frank Ramsey interview; J. Fitzgerald, *That Championship Feeling*, 128–33; Heinsohn, *Heinsohn, Don't You Ever Smile?* 93–96; *New York Post*, 29 March 1965; *Boston Herald* article from March 1961, Mokray Scrapbook, January 1961–March 1961; Carey, *High Above Courtside*, 121–23.

26. *Sporting News*, 8 January 1958; Frank Ramsey interview; Cliff Hagan, telephone interview with author, 28 August 2007; Koppett, *Essence of the Game*, 178–80, 191–93; Wilkens, *Unguarded*, 81, 100–101; Hundley, *Hot Rod Hundley*, 38–45. See also Bradley, *Life on the Run*, 31, 41–42, 93–94, 201–3. Teams lost home dates when the league staged doubleheaders, and most teams also placed some home contests in other cities. Also, late-night and early morning travel could be dangerous: in January 1960, a DC-3 carrying the Minneapolis Lakers made an emergency landing in a snow-covered field in Carroll, Iowa. See Lazenby, *Show*, 62–67; Ostler and Springer, *Winnin' Times*, 37–39.

27. Russell and Branch, *Second Wind*, 126–27; Frank Ramsey interview; Sharman, *Sharman on Basketball Strategy*, 162; Heinsohn, "Of Charley Horses and Little Old Ladies," 43.

28. Messner, *Power at Play*, 7–23, 30–34, 44, 91–92, 102–4; Burstyn, *Rites of Men*, 101–31; G. Sullivan, *Picture History*, 160–61. See also McLaughlin, "'Man to Man,'" 169–91.

29. *Boston Traveler,* 18 April 1961; uncited article dated 20 April 1961, Mokray Scrapbook, 1960–61 Season; Auerbach and Sann, *Red Auerbach,* 56–58; *Boston Globe,* 20 January 1959, 5 January 1961, 18 January 1961, 19 January 1961, 22 January 1961, 3 March 1961, 21 March 1961, 13 April 1961.

30. Four uncited articles from October and November 1961, Mokray Scrapbook, September 1961–January 1962; *Boston Globe,* 13 October 1961, 29 October 1961, 9 November 1961, 9 January 1962, 23 December 1965.

31. B. Green, *Spinning the Globe,* 308–9; Koppett, *24 Seconds to Shoot,* 146–48; *Sporting News,* 1 February 1961; *New York Times,* 6 June 1961. The ABL's coaches included Phil Woolpert in San Francisco and John McClendon, the first African American coach of an integrated professional basketball team, in Cleveland. McClendon resigned in midseason and was replaced by Bill Sharman, whose Los Angeles Jets had just folded. M. Katz, *Breaking Through,* 134–47; *Boston Globe,* 19 January 1962; *New York Times,* 31 January 1962.

32. On 1961 scandal, see Charles Rosen, *Scandals of '51,* 234; S. Cohen, *Game They Played,* 226–33; Tax, "Facts About the Fixes," 18–19. On Hawkins and ABA, see Wolf, *Foul!* 92–165; Breslin, "Untold Facts," 16–19, 78–80; *Sporting News,* 7 February 1962.

33. Charley Rosen, *Wizard of Odds,* 244–85; *Boston Globe,* 11 January 1961, 5 February 1963; B. Russell, *Go Up for Glory,* 121–22; uncited article in Mokray Scrapbook, March 1962–August 1962; *New York Times,* 8 September 1961; Underwood, "True Moral Crisis," 16–19, 83; Koppett, *24 Seconds to Shoot,* 140–42. In 1967 *Life* revealed Bob Cousy's associations with known gamblers and those with ties to organized crime, forcing Cousy to call a tearful press conference denying any type of wrongdoing. See "Are Some of Our Best Friends Gamblers?" 8; Cousy, *Killer Instinct,* 61–64. On gambling in sport, see also Guttmann, *Whole New Ball Game,* 78–79.

34. On ABL instability, see *Boston Globe,* 23 December 1961; *Sporting News,* 14 February 1962; *New York Times,* 13 April 1962. On Sharman, see uncited articles dated 17 July 1962 and 19 July 1962, Mokray Scrapbook, March 1962–August 1962. On NBA, see *New York Times,* 3 November 1959; *Christian Science Monitor,* 20 December 1960; *Sporting News,* 10 February 1960; *Boston Globe,* 22 January 1960, 18 March 1964; uncited articles dated 10 January 1962 and 17 January 1962, Mokray Scrapbook, September 1961–January 1962; Leggett, "Growing to Greatness," 41. See also "Bob Cousy Examines Pro Basketball's Problems and Progress," 24–27, 95.

35. On Chicago, see *Sporting News,* 4 January 1959, 11 January 1961, 24 January 1962, 31 January 1962; *Chicago Tribune,* 31 December 1961. On New York, see R. Kahn, "Success and Ned Irish," 39–46; *Boston Globe,* 25 November 1958, 8 February 1961; *Boston Herald,* 7 February 1961; *New York Post,* 7 February 1961.

36. Uncited article dated 14 November 1957, Mokray Scrapbook, 1957–58 Season; *Los Angeles Times,* 12 February 1957; *New York Times,* 28 April 1960, 16 November 1960; *Sporting News,* 7 January 1959, 21 January 1959, 25 January 1961, 2 February 1963, 14 March 1964; Danielson, *Home Team,* 26–28; James Murray, "Trip for Ten Tall Men," 52–59; Jim Murray, *Jim Murray,* 102–5; Lazenby, *Lakers,* 118–29; Heisler, *Madmen's Ball,* 1–11; Lazenby, *Show,* 68–83. Had the Lakers beat St. Louis in the 1961 play-offs, they would have faced the Celtics in the finals. Until fixing a scheduling conflict at the Sports Arena, Lakers officials considered staging games at the Los Angeles Coliseum, a huge outdoor stadium. See *Boston*

Globe, 29 March 1961; *Boston Herald,* 30 March 1961; uncited article dated 30 March 1961, Mokray Scrapbook, January 1961–March 1961.

37. West, *Mr. Clutch,* 1–68; Cope, "Unpredictable All-American," 28, 54–55; "Jerry West," 96–98; Pluto, *Tall Tales,* 184–88.

38. On West, see Williams, "Long Leap Forward," 82; *Sporting News,* 13 December 1961, 24 January 1962, 21 February 1962, 28 February 1962; Hano, "Jerry West's Burden," 22–23, 72–73; Underwood, "Eye of an Eagle," 14–17; Libby, "Jerry West," 24–27, 101–3. On Baylor's military duty, see *Philadelphia Inquirer,* 19 November 1961; *Los Angeles Times,* 10 January 1962; *Boston Globe,* 19 November 1961, 27 December 1961, 12 March 1962. On rise of Lakers, see Lazenby, *Lakers,* 134–35; Leggett, "Growing to Greatness," 40–43.

39. Uncited article dated 11 April 1964, Mokray Scrapbook, January 1961–March 1961; *Boston Herald,* 3 April 1961; Danielson, *Home Team,* 98–100; Bellamy, "Professional Sports Organizations," 127–28; McChesney, "Media Made Sport," 60–63; Fortunato, "Ultimate Assist," 83–99, 128–29; Isaacs, *Vintage NBA,* 17; Rader, *In Its Own Image,* 145–47; *Christian Science Monitor,* 4 December 1962; *Patriot Ledger,* 8 January 1963; *Boston Globe,* 1 April 1963.

40. *Philadelphia Inquirer,* 4 January 1960, 14 January 1960, 8 December 1961; *Sporting News,* 9 January 1957, 11 January 1957, 5 February 1958, 26 February 1958, 15 March 1961, 28 March 1959; Koppett, *24 Seconds to Shoot,* 159–60; Charles Rosen, *God, Man and Basketball Jones,* 24–31; Pluto, *Tall Tales,* 291–302. On Sid Borgia, see also *Sporting News,* 22 January 1958, 21 February 1962, 16 February 1963; *Boston Herald,* 24 February 1963. On a referee's myriad in-game responsibilities, see Ryan, *Pro Game,* 58–66.

41. *Boston Traveler,* 14 November 1961; uncited articles dated 13 November 1961 and 17 November 1961, Mokray Scrapbook, September 1961–January 1962; *Boston Globe,* 10 November 1961, 12 November 1961, 15 November 1961, 18 November 1961, 20 December 1961; *Boston Herald,* 13 November 1961, 26 February 1962, 14 March 1962; *New York Times,* 14 March 1962. On Carl Braun, see *New York Post,* 16 May 1961, 20 April 1962.

42. *Boston Globe,* 25 January 1962, 29 January 1962, 31 January 1962, 1 February 1962; *Boston Herald,* 25 January 1962, 29 January 1962, 1 February 1962; *Los Angeles Times.* 30 January 1962; Hirshberg, *Bill Russell of the Boston Celtics,* 165–70; *New York Post,* 3 January 1962.

43. *Boston Herald,* 11 March 1962; *Los Angeles Times,* 13 March 1962; *Sporting News,* 14 March 1962.

44. Gross, "Elgin Baylor," 29, 94–96; Cousy, "High Scoring Has Become Ho-Hum," 53–56; *Sporting News,* 25 February 1961, 15 March 1961, 28 February 1962, 2 March 1963, 9 January 1965; *Chicago Defender,* 23 January 1960; *Boston Globe,* 20 January 1988; "Toughest Job in Basketball," 39; Newell, "It's Time to Raise the Baskets," 79–84.

45. *Pittsburgh Courier,* 25 March 1961, 24 March 1962.

46. Chamberlain and Shaw, *Wilt,* 128–32; Libby, *Goliath,* 98–102; G. Sullivan, *Wilt Chamberlain,* 103–5; Cherry, *Wilt,* 105–7; J. Taylor, *Rivalry,* 144–47; Pluto, *Tall Tales,* 224–30; *New York Post,* 24 November 1961, 9 February 1962; *New York Times,* 9 December 1961, 14 January 1962, 15 March 1962, 17 March 1962; *Philadelphia Inquirer,* 14 January 1962, 15 March 1962; *Philadelphia Bulletin,* 9 December 1961, 16 January 1962, 30 January 1962, 2 March 1962, 14 March 1962, 15 March 1962, 29 March 1962; *Sporting News,* 13 December 1961; *Boston Globe,* 16 November 1962. See also "Ubiquitous Hands," 28–35.

47. Pomerantz, *Wilt, 1962*. For contemporary press coverage, see *New York Times*, 3 March 1962, 4 March 1962; *Philadelphia Inquirer*, 3 March 1962. See also Chamberlain and Shaw, *Wilt*, 135–37; Libby, *Goliath*, 100–106; G. Sullivan, *Wilt Chamberlain*, 107–11; Cherry, *Wilt*, 108–15; J. Taylor, *Rivalry*, 151–56; Pluto, *Tall Tales*, 217–24.

48. *Boston Globe*, 4 March 1962; *Sporting News*, 14 March 1962; *Philadelphia Bulletin*, 10 December 1961; "Unstoppable," 81.

49. *New York Post*, 22 December 1961; *New York Times*, 7 January 1962; *Philadelphia Inquirer*, 21 December 1961, 18 January 1962; *Philadelphia Bulletin*, 15 March 1961; *Boston Traveler*, 19 January 1962; *Boston Globe*, 5 March 1962.

50. Rader, *In Its Own Image*, 175–85; "How Do You Stop Him?" 40–41; uncited article entitled "ABL Saints Go After Wilt," Mokray Scrapbook, March 1962–August 1962; *Philadelphia Bulletin*, 4 September 1959, 27 January 1960, 14 May 1961, 2 May 1962, 23 May 1962, 3 July 1962, 19 May 1964, 25 August 1964, 6 November 1965, 29 January 1967; *Philadelphia Inquirer*, 30 April 1960, 3 May 1962; "Café Society Rediscovers Harlem," 35–36; L. Robinson, "Big Man, Big Business," 57–64; Pomerantz, *Wilt, 1962*, 16–19. For television appearances, see http://www.tvtome.com/tvtome.servlet/PersonDetail/personid-68914.

51. Undated *New York Post* column by Milton Gross, Mokray Scrapbook, September 1961–January 1962; *New York Post*, 9 February 1962; *Washington Post*, 18 March 1962; Grady, "Master Plan," 16–17, 67–69; Holtzman, "Sound Off!" 26–28, 82–84.

52. *Washington Post*, 18 March 1962; *New York Times*, 21 February 1960, 14 January 1963; *Chicago Defender*, 14 March 1960, 10 December 1962; *Boston Globe*, 25 December 1961, 5 March 1962; *Boston Herald*, 26 March 1960; *Philadelphia Inquirer*, 23 November 1961; uncited article dated 20 September 1962, Mokray Scrapbook, August 1962–September 1963.

53. Gross, "Who Is the Best of Basketball's Superstars?" 24–27, 93–95; *Baltimore Afro-American*, 16 April 1963; Rosin, *Philly Hoops*, 44–45; *New York Post*, 2 November 1961; Pluto, *Tall Tales*, 341–49; West, *Mr. Clutch*, 133, 141, 180. See also Cousy, *Last Loud Roar*, 94–98; Auerbach and Sann, *Red Auerbach*, 96–107. Walt Bellamy won Rookie of the Year in 1961, averaging more than thirty points a game. "When he started, Walt was scared to death of Chamberlain and Russell," said Auerbach. "Now he's only scared of Russell." Furlong, "Walt Bellamy vs. the NBA," 35–37, 68–69.

54. D. O'Connor, "Wilt Versus Russell," 116–128; Koppett, *Essence of the Game*, 50–63.

55. *Philadelphia Inquirer*, 16 March 1962–24 March 1962.

56. *Philadelphia Inquirer*, 25 March 1962–28 March 1962; *Boston Herald*, 25 March 1962, 26 March 1962; *Boston Globe*, 25 March 1962, 28 March 1962.

57. *Philadelphia Inquirer*, 30 March 1962, 1 April 1962; *Boston Herald*, 29 March 1962, 30 March 1962; *Boston Globe*, 29 March 1962–1 April 1962. "I'm not going to take it next time," Chamberlain announced upon Loscutoff's continued physical play. The Celtics forward responded: "Tell him to bring his lunch."

58. *Philadelphia Inquirer*, 2 April 1962; *Philadelphia Bulletin*, 2 April 1962; *Boston Herald*, 2 April 1962; *Boston Globe*, 2 April 1962; Heinsohn, *Heinsohn, Don't You Ever Smile?* 140–41.

59. G. Sullivan, *Wilt Chamberlain*, 115; *Philadelphia Inquirer*, 3 April 1962; *Boston Herald*, 3 April 1962; *Boston Globe*, 3 April 1962.

60. *Boston Globe*, 30 March 1962, 4–6 April 1962; undated *Boston Globe* article by Arthur Siegel, Mokray Scrapbook, March–August 1962; *Philadelphia Inquirer*, 3 April 1962.

61. *Philadelphia Inquirer*, 5 April 1962, 6 April 1962; *Boston Herald*, 6 April 1962; *Boston Globe*, 6 April 1962.

62. *Boston Herald*, 7 April 1962, 8 April 1962; *Boston Globe*, 6–9 April 1962.

63. *Boston Herald*, 9 April 1962, 10 April 1962; West, *Mr. Clutch*, 113; *Boston Globe*, 9–11 April 1962, 13 April 1962. Celtic fans howled that no one could steal the ball, sprint down-court, and score in three seconds. Days later, Boston's Channel 5 ran the tape on the news, proving that West had done it.

64. *Boston Globe*, 12 April 1962; Lazenby, *Show*, 86.

65. *Boston Herald*, 13–15 April 1962, 20 April 1962; *Boston Globe*, 13–15 April 1962; *Los Angeles Times*, 16 April 1962.

66. *Boston Herald*, 13 April 1962; *Boston Globe*, 14 April 1962, 16 April 1962, 17 April 1962; *Los Angeles Times*, 17 April 1962.

67. *Boston Herald*, 18 April 1962; *Boston Globe*, 17 April 1962, 8 April 1962.

68. *Boston Globe*, 8 April 1962, 17 April 1962, 30 March 1963; Bjarkman, *Boston Celtics Encyclopedia*, 117.

69. *Boston Traveler*, 19 April 1962; *Los Angeles Times*, 19 April 1962; *Boston Globe*, 19 April 1962.

70. Hundley, *Hot Rod Hundley*, 18–19; *Los Angeles Times*, 28 September 1970; Lazenby, *Show*, 88–89.

71. *Sporting News*, 14 February 1962; *New York Post*, 19 February 1962; Nadel, *Night Wilt Scored 100*, 98–111.

72. *Boston Herald*, 19 April 1962; Schardt, "Too Much To Beat This Year," 16; West, *Mr. Clutch*, 115; *Boston Record-American*, 19 April 1962. While Selvy's shot bounced above the rim, Elgin Baylor leaped for a tip-in but never touched the ball. Baylor later claimed that Sam Jones had pushed him in midair. Referee Richie Powers believes that Baylor pulled his hands away because Baylor did not want to repeat an incident from earlier that season, when he had tipped in a ball after the buzzer sounded, nullifying the basket. Lazenby, *Show*, 89; R. Powers, *Overtime!* 47.

73. Gene Guarilia, telephone interview with author, 14 January 2008; *Boston Herald*, 19 April 1962; *Boston Traveler*, 29 April 1962; *New York Times*, 19 April 1962; *Boston Record-American*, 19 April 1962

74. *Boston Herald*, 19 April 1962; Hearn and Springer, *Chick*, 9–10.

75. Schardt, "Too Much To Beat This Year," 16; Gene Guarilia interview; *Boston Globe*, 19 April 1962.

9. FAMILY MAN

1. B. Russell, *Go Up for Glory*, 174–75.

2. Russell and Branch, *Second Wind*, 44–45, 49–50; Reverend John Russell, interview with author, 10 March 2006.

3. *Boston Globe*, 13 December 1962; *San Francisco Chronicle*, 1 January 1963.

4. *Boston Globe*, 18 January 1963; *Boston Herald*, 5 February 1963; *Chicago Defender*,

9 February 1963; *Christian Science Monitor,* 5 February 1963, 26 October 1963; *Los Angeles Times,* 21 April 1963; *Sporting News,* 16 February 1963; Linn, "Bill Russell's Private World," 61.

5. Maraniss, *Rome 1960,* 100–106, 261–66, 283–84, 300–307; "Negro in American Sport," 28–35; Guttmann, *From Ritual to Record,* 15–55; Young, *Negro Firsts in Sports,* 1–14. See also Bontemps, *Famous Negro Athletes;* Lacy, *Fighting for Fairness,* 49–50.

6. On baseball, see Tygiel, *Baseball's Great Experiment,* 285–344; J. Robinson, *Baseball Has Done It,* 97–209; D. Halberstam, *October 1964,* 53–63. On Patterson, see F. Patterson, *Victory over Myself;* Maureen Smith, "Identity and Citizenship," 105–31; On Jim Brown and the NFL, see Ross, *Outside the Lines.* 81–158; MacCambridge, *America's Game,* 164–66; Freeman, *Jim Brown,* 29–128; Jable, "Jim Brown," 241–62; Jimmy Brown, *Off My Chest,* 159–73; Thomas Smith, "Civil Rights on the Gridiron," 251–67. On Gibson, see Gibson, *I Always Wanted to Be Somebody;* Gray and Lamb, *Born to Win,* 61–130; Schoenfeld, *Match,* 57–65, 79–87, 241–57; Festle, "'Jackie Robinson Without the Charm,'" 187–205. On Rudolph, see Maraniss, *Rome 1960,* 225–27, 272–76, 336–40; Rudolph, *Wilma,* 113–53; Wilson, "Wilma Rudolph," 207–22; Goudsouzian, "Wilma Rudolph," 305–32.

7. R. Thomas, *They Cleared the Lane,* 180–82, 253; "Professional Basketball's Dream Team," 54–56; *Chicago Defender,* 7 January 1964; *Sporting News,* 24 February 1960; *Philadelphia Inquirer,* 25 December 1961, 2 February 1962; *Boston Globe,* 12 January 1966; Pluto, *Tall Tales,* 83–87; Tax, "Brave Man and a Good Friend," 10–15. In another example of crumbling racial barriers through basketball, Mississippi State University accepted an invitation to the 1963 NCAA tournament, where it faced teams with black players, defying an unwritten law in a bastion of segregation. See Henderson, "The 1963 Mississippi State University Basketball Controversy and the Repeal of the Unwritten Law"; *New York Times,* 4 March 1963, 11 March 1963.

8. Jay, *More than Just A Game,* 115–45; Pluto, *Tall Tales,* 339; B. Johnson, *What's Happenin'?* 115.

9. *Boston Traveler,* 6 April 1963; Bob Cousy, telephone interview with author, 23 April 2007; *Boston Globe,* 8 March 1961, 13 April 1961.

10. Heinsohn, *Heinsohn, Don't You Ever Smile?* 82–83.

11. B. Russell, *Go Up for Glory,* 115; R. Fitzgerald, *Champions Remembered,* 66–67.

12. Three uncited articles dated 18 October 1961, Mokray Scrapbook, September 1961–January 1962; *New York Times,* 18 October 1961; *Boston Globe,* 1 February 1981; Auerbach and Sann, *Red Auerbach,* 121–23; B. Russell, *Red and Me,* 79–84; *Atlanta Daily World,* 19 October 1961. The manager told the press that the Phoenix Hotel had previously served college teams with black players without incident, and that he unsuccessfully sought the black Celtics, so that he could "offer them a free dinner on the house." *Chicago Defender,* 19 October 1961.

13. *St. Louis Post-Dispatch,* 18 October 1961; uncited article, Mokray Scrapbook, September 1961–January 1962. Boston rookie Al Butler boycotted the game, as well, but he did not fly to Boston that night because his fellow black Celtics could not locate him. Sihugo Green of the Hawks did not go to Lexington due to an injury.

14. Pluto, *Tall Tales,* 71; two uncited articles dated 18 October 1961, Mokray Scrapbook, September 1961–January 1962; Frank Ramsey, interview with author, 8 May 2006; Cousy, *Last Loud Roar,* 99.

15. *Christian Science Monitor,* 28 February 1961, 4 March 1963; *Sporting News,* 15 March 1961, 7 February 1961; *Boston Record-American,* 23 January 1962; *Boston Herald,* 28 February 1961, 12 March 1961, 23 January 1962, 5 March 1963; *Boston Globe,* 28 February 1961, 23 January 1962, 5 March 1963; *Sporting News,* 27 January 1968; Heinsohn, *Heinsohn, Don't You Ever Smile?* 193–94. K. C. Jones's wife Beverly was the sister of Carl Cain, who had played against Russell and Jones in the 1956 NCAA Final and then joined them on the Olympic team.

16. Auerbach and Fitzgerald, *Red Auerbach,* 234–35.

17. Bob Cousy interview; Cousy, *Killer Instinct,* 147–48; Tom "Satch" Sanders, telephone interview with author, 25 August 2008; *Boston Herald,* 24 May 1999; Linn, "Bill Russell's Private World," 62. Only once did racial tension directly threaten team harmony. Before a play-off game in St. Louis, Gene Guarilia called Sam Jones "Sambo." Guarilia meant it as a friendly sign of affection, but in the anxious circumstances, Jones detonated, interpreting the nickname as a racial insult. Teammates stepped between them until Jones accepted Guarilia's innocence, cooling the air. Heinsohn, *Heinsohn, Don't You Ever Smile,* 83–84. On history of Sambo stereotype, see Boskin, *Sambo,* 3–197.

18. *New York Times,* 1 February 1963; *Sporting News,* 16 February 1963; Shaughnessy, *Seeing Red,* 156–57; undated *Boston Globe* article, Mokray Scrapbook, September 1964-December 1964; Frank Ramsey interview. On Kennedy and sports, see Watterson, *Games Presidents Play,* 201–15.

19. *Boston Herald,* 17 February 1963; Frank Ramsey interview.

20. B. Russell, *Go Up for Glory,* 176; Russell and Branch, *Second Wind,* 182; *Rocky Mountain News,* 25 February 1975.

21. Meriwether, *Proudly We Can Be Africans,* 150–207; Gaines, *American Africans in Ghana,* 77–91; Von Eschen, *Satchmo Blows up the World,* 27–91; *New York Times,* 24 May 1959; B. Russell, *Go Up for Glory,* 192–94; Russell and Branch, *Second Wind,* 177–79.

22. B. Russell, *Russell Rules,* 31–33; Russell and Branch, *Second Wind,* 88–91; Rogin, "We Are Grown Men Playing a Child's Game," 85.

23. Linn, "Bill Russell's Private World," 67; Pham, *Liberia,* 37–41; Harold Furash, telephone interview with author, 19 March 2007; *Sporting News,* 10 April 1965.

24. S. Ellis, *Mask of Anarchy,* 43–50; Pham, *Liberia,* 43–46, 51–59. See also "Ol' Massa Russell?" 211. By 1965, Russell still employed about one hundred workers, paying them fifty cents a day. *Sporting News,* 6 February 1965.

25. *Sporting News,* 14 December 1960, 14 March 1962, 10 April 1965; *Washington Post,* 21 January 1962; *Chicago Defender,* 14 January 1961, 29 November 1962, 23 October 1962, 10 December 1962; uncited clipping from 1962, Bill Russell File, Basketball Hall of Fame; *Baltimore Afro-American,* 23 March 1962; *Pittsburgh Courier,* 12 May 1962.

26. See Chafe, *Civilities and Civil Rights,* 42–101; Weisbrot, *Freedom Bound,* 19–63; Arsenault, *Freedom Riders,* 1–10, 93–476.

27. Linn, "Bill Russell's Private World," *Sport,* 67.

28. See Estes, *I Am a Man!* 1–86.

29. Hirshberg, *Bill Russell of the Boston Celtics,* 123, 137; *Washington Post,* 21 January 1962; *New York Amsterdam News,* 10 June 1967; F. Katz, "Unknown Side," 80. For Russell's esteem of Jomo Kenyatta, see *Seattle Times,* 27 August 1978.

30. B. Reynolds, *Our Game,* 48; L. Shapiro, *Big Man on Campus,* 37–38; *Los Angeles Times,*

18 January 1966. The Celtics selected Hadnot in third round of the 1962 draft, but Auerbach cut him before the season. *Boston Globe*, 27 March 1962. Another example of Russell's paternal role was that while a college student in the early 1960s, Clarence Holder's son Edwin was listed as a legal resident of Russell's Reading home. Reading residential listings from 1964, correspondence by Peggy White in author's possession.

31. Rogin, "We Are Grown Men Playing a Child's Game," 90; K. Russell, "Growing Up," 27; John Hollingsworth, telephone interview with author, 10 October 2007; Harold Furash, telephone interview with author, 19 March 2007; F. Katz, "Unknown Side of Bill Russell," 76; Linn, "I Owe the Public Nothing," 61–63; Hirshberg, *Bill Russell of the Boston Celtics*, 155–56; *Christian Science Monitor*, 12 February 1975; *Boston Globe*, 26 April 1963; *Christian Science Monitor*, 15 March 1966; *Sporting News*, 6 April 1968.

32. Transcript of Interview with Phil Donahue, Bill Russell File, Basketball Hall of Fame; *Christian Science Monitor*, 12 February 1975; Russell and Branch, *Second Wind*, 216–18.

33. Jim Brown, *Out of Bounds*, 272–73; Heinsohn and Fitzgerald, *Give 'Em the Hook*, 216–18; Russell and Branch, *Second Wind*, 218.

34. Russell and Branch, *Second Wind*, 218–26.

35. Russell and Branch, *Second Wind*, 226–32.

36. Russell and Branch, *Second Wind*, 178–80, 229–30.

37. Russell and Branch, *Second Wind*, 232, 241; *New York Amsterdam News*, 24 June 1961; Charles Rosen, *God, Man and Basketball Jones*, 151. On athletes and women, see also S. Fox, *Big Leagues*, 143–55.

38. Plimpton, "Reflections in a Diary," 43; F. Katz, "Unknown Side," 24, 76, 79–80.

39. Earl Lloyd, telephone interview with author, 16 March 2007; Embry, *Inside Game*, 108; Al Attles, telephone interview with author, 5 August 2008; Salzberg, *From Set Shot to Slam Dunk*, 235–36; Walsh, "Jones & Jones at Court," 50–52; Furlong, "Walt Bellamy vs. the NBA," 68.

40. Russell and Branch, *Second Wind*, 233; Al Attles interview; Chamberlain, "I Love the Game, Baby," 39, 118; Walker, *Long Time Coming*, 166–67; B. Russell, *Russell Rules*, 48.

41. Tom "Satch" Sanders, telephone interview with the author, 25 August 2008; K. C. Jones, *Rebound*, 79–86. In 1963 Jones, Jones, and Sanders tried to follow in Wilt Chamberlain's footsteps by cutting a record called "Basketball Twist"; the flip side was "Side by Side." Two years later, K. C. Jones and Sanders teamed with an East Boston man named Paul Ippolitano to cut "Dance Little Girl" and "Funny Feeling". Neither record was successful. Uncited article dated 16 April 1963, Mokray Scrapbook, March–September 1963; *Boston Record-American*, 30 March 1965; *Boston Globe*, 25 April 1965.

42. Gene Conley, telephone interview with author, 10 April 2007; Bob Cousy, telephone interview with author, 23 April 2007; Frank Ramsey interview; Gene Guarilia, telephone interview with author, 14 January 2008; Mel Counts, telephone interview with author, 10 January 2008; *Boston Globe*, 15 January 1988; Deford, "Ring Leader," 100; K. C. Jones, *Rebound*, 85–86; *Boston Herald-American*, 9 February 1975; Carey and McClellan, *Boston Celtics*, 68–69; *Boston Herald*, 20 May 1999, 24–26 May 1999, 12 May 2005.

43. Harold Furash interview; Harold Furash Interview at www.celtic-nation.com; *Boston Globe*, 25 February 1980; John Hollingsworth interview. On Furash and Horwitz, see also L. Shapiro, *Big Man on Campus*, 41–42, 57.

44. Bob Cousy interview; Carey, *High Above Courtside*, 94–95; J. Fitzgerald, *That Championship Feeling*, 96.

45. *Christian Science Monitor*, 12 February 1975; Harold Furash interview; Carey, *High Above Courtside*, 96–98, 387–88.

46. Bob Cousy interview; B. Russell, *Russell Rules*, 45, 108; J. Fitzgerald, *That Championship Feeling*, 96; Russell and Branch, *Second Wind*, 236; K. Russell, "Growing Up," 28.

47. *Boston Herald*, 20 May 1999.

48. Undated *Newsday* article in Bill Russell File, Basketball Hall of Fame; Bob Cousy interview.

49. *Philadelphia Inquirer*, 28 January 1962, 3 February 1962, 4 March 1962, 3 May 1962–5 May 1962, 24 May 1962; *Boston Herald*, 6 March 1962; *Los Angeles Times*, 16 April 1962; *New York Times*, 5 May 1962, 24 May 1962, 8 June 1962; *Philadelphia Bulletin*, 13 April 1962, 24 May 1962, 2 June 1962, 4 June 1962, 5 June 1962, 7 June 1962, 17 November 1962; *San Francisco Chronicle*, 17–20 October 1962; *Sporting News*, 23 February 1963. See also Dickey, *History of Professional Basketball*, 114–17. Before taking the San Francisco job, Gottlieb had first tried importing another team from Syracuse, Detroit, or Chicago.

50. Chamberlain and Shaw, *Wilt*, 148–53; *San Francisco Chronicle*, 6 November 1962, 6 December 1962, 10 December 1962, 12 December 1962, 27 December 1962, 1 January 1963, 3 January 1963, 23 January 1963, 9 February 1963, 22 February 1963, 27 February 1963, 28 February 1963, 6 March 1963, 12 March 1963; *Philadelphia Inquirer*, 25 March 1962, 6 November 1962, 1 March 1963, 3 March 1963; *New York Times*, 20 March 1963; *Philadelphia Bulletin*, 2 January 1963, 23 January 1963, 19 March 1963; *New York Post*, 10 March 1963; *Boston Globe*, 18 November 1962, 26 December 1962, 28 December 1962, 3 January 1963, 9 January 1963, 31 January 1963, 10 February 1963, 27 February 1963; *Boston Herald*, 26 December 1962; West, *Mr. Clutch*, 118. Despite San Francisco's liberal reputation on race relations, Chamberlain encountered some difficulty purchasing a home in an otherwise all-white development overlooking the Pacific Ocean. *Philadelphia Inquirer*, 29 April 1963.

51. *Boston Traveler*, 17 October 1962, 27 November 1962; Cliff Hagan, telephone interview with author, 28 August 2007; Goodman, "Second Chance for Lovellette," 26–27, 66; *Boston Globe*, 21 March 1963. See also Lovellette, "Pro Basketball Is Not for Me," 30–31, 84.

52. Havlicek and Ryan, *Hondo*, 31–78; *Sporting News*, 21 February 1962; Devaney, "What Makes Havlicek Run," 64–71.

53. On drafting of Havlicek, see *Boston Globe*, 26 March 1962, 27 March 1962; Charles Rosen, *God, Man and Basketball Jones*, 91–94; *Boston Herald*, 23 August 1962. On Cleveland's failed merger, see uncited articles dated 11 July 1962, 15 July 1962, 31 July 1962, 29 August 1962, 30 August 1962 in Mokray Scrapbook, March 1962–August 1962; *New York Times*, 16 May 1962, 5 July 1962, 11 July 1962, 12 July 1962, 26 July 1962. On ABL disbanding, see two uncited articles dated 31 December 1962, Mokray Scrapbook, August 1962–January 1963; *San Francisco Chronicle*, 1 January 1963; *New York Times*, 2 January 1963; *Boston Globe*, 2 January 1963; *Sporting News*, 2 April 1966.

54. Havlicek, "What Lucas Will Have to Learn," 28, 76–77; *Boston Globe*, 5 November 1962, 19 December 1962, 12 January 1963, 20 February 1963, 26 March 1963; uncited article dated 5 February 1963, Mokray Scrapbook, January–March 1963; G. Sullivan, *Picture History*, 170–72; *Sporting News*, 2 February 1963, 7 December 1963; Havlicek and Ryan,

Hondo, 79–86; *Seattle Times,* 16 April 1978. Another rookie, Jack "The Shot" Foley, was Boston's second pick in the 1962 draft. The local hero hailed from Worcester and starred at Holy Cross. Though obviously an excellent shooter, the bony forward lasted only half a season before getting sold to the New York Knicks. *Boston Globe,* 27 March 1962, 18 December 1962, 23 January 1963, 27 January 1963; *Boston Herald,* 22 January 1963, 23 January 1963.

55. *Boston Globe,* 27 November 1962, 1 December 1962, 26 December 1962, 28 December 1962, 1 January 1963, 10 January 1963; Boston Herald, 1 January 1963.

56. *Boston Globe,* 20 October 1962, 7 December 1962, 21 January 1963, 5 February 1963, 13 February 1963, 11 March 1963; *Boston Herald,* 20 October 1962; *Christian Science Monitor,* 7 January 1963, 13 February 1963, 26 February 1963; uncited article dated 24 February 1963, Mokray Scrapbook, January–March 1963; *Boston Traveler,* 4 March 1963; "Stars Are Ready," 44–46; Leggett, "Basketball at its Toughest," 12–16.

57. *San Francisco Chronicle,* 1 January 1963, 3 January 1963, 10 February 1963; Auerbach and Fitzgerald, *Red Auerbach,* 224; *Boston Herald,* 22 March 1963, 24 March 1963; *Boston Globe,* 17 January 1963, 18 January 1963, 4 February 1963; *Washington Post,* 10 March 1963, 24 March 1963. Russell also won MVP of the All-Star Game, leading an upset win over the alleged "greatest basketball team ever assembled," a West team starring Chamberlain, Bob Pettit, Walt Bellamy, Jerry West, and Elgin Baylor. During that same All-Star break, Maurice Podoloff elicited more ridicule when he declared, "Nobody gets into the NBA if he owns a bar," as it exposed players to gamblers and other undesirables. But Wilt Chamberlain and others already owned interest in bars and nightclubs, and Podoloff quickly backtracked: "Bars can be a legitimate business. What I object to is the habitué of a bar and the mingling of objectionable characters." *Sporting News,* 19 January 1963, 26 January 1963; *Philadelphia Bulletin,* 15 January 1963; *San Francisco Chronicle,* 15 January 1963, 16 January 1963; *Boston Herald,* 16 January 1963; *Boston Globe,* 16 January 1963.

58. *Boston Globe,* 23 February 1961, 30 November 1962, 20 December 1962, 4 March 1963, 8 March 1963, 10 March 1963, 14 March 1963, 17 March 1963; *Boston Traveler,* 16 February 1962; *Boston Herald,* 6 February 1962, 16 February 1962, 21 February 1962, 17 March 1962, 21 March 1962, 22 March 1962, 26 March 1962; *New York Times,* 7 April 1962; Cousy, *Last Loud Roar,* 52, 176–79; Cousy, *Basketball Is My Life,* 177–79; Hirshberg, "Farewell to Bob Cousy," 20–21, 75–76; *Sporting News,* 23 February 1963; Wind, "Sporting Scene," 146–66.

59. *Boston Globe,* 17–20 March 1963; *Boston Herald,* 17–18 March 1963; *Sporting News,* 30 March 1963; Cousy, *Basketball Is My Life,* 180–83; Dolph Schayes, telephone interview with author, 13 April 2007.

60. *Boston Globe,* 28 March–1 April 1963; *Boston Herald,* 26–31 March 1963. On Robertson, see also *Boston Globe,* 22 December 1962, *Sporting News,* 2 March 1963. Cousy even got booed by Royals fans—Cincinnati coach Charley Wolf had baselessly accused the aging superstar of dirty defense. *Boston Globe,* 7 February 1963; *Boston Herald,* 7 February 1963, 10 February 1963.

61. Uncited article dated 31 March 1963, Mokray Scrapbook, January-March 1963; *Boston Globe,* 2–6 April 1963; *Boston Herald,* 2–6 April 1963; *Boston Traveler,* 3 April 1963;

Robertson, *Big O*, 167. "We are the only sports league in the business that doesn't have first call on the buildings we play in," complained Walter Brown after the Cincinnati circus fiasco. *Boston Globe*, 9 April 1963.

62. Uncited article dated 30 October 1962, Mokray Scrapbook, August 1962–January 1963; *Boston Globe*, 8 January 1963, 11 January 1963, 20 February 1963, 7–9 April 1963; *Boston Herald*, 2–6 April 1963, 9 April 1963; uncited articles dated 8 April 1963, and 14 April 1963, Mokray Scrapbook, March–September 1963; *Boston Traveler*, 22 April 1963; Underwood, "Last Fling for a Wizard," 16–17, 58–60. In his autobiography, Robertson claimed that the circus forced the Royals' home games to Xavier for "the duration of the playoffs," but Game Six took place at Cincinnati Gardens. Robertson, *Big O*, 167–68.

63. *Boston Traveler*, 10 April 1963; *Boston Herald*, 10 April 1963; *Boston Globe*, 10 April 1963, 11 April 1963; Underwood, "Last Fling for a Wizard," 58.

64. Underwood, "Last Fling for a Wizard," 58–60; *Boston Globe*, 11 April 1963, 12 April 1963; *Boston Herald*, 11 April 1963, 12 April 1963; Robertson, *Big O*, 168–69.

65. Cousy, *Last Loud Roar*, 35–36, 60–63, 105–10; *Boston Globe*, 13 April 1963, 14 April 1963; *Boston Herald*, 12 April 1963, 14 April 1963; "Better to Die than Lose," 85. On arguments for Baylor's supremacy, see *Boston Globe*, 10 December 1961; *Chicago Defender*, 21 January 1961; *Los Angeles Times*, 31 January 1961, 14 November 1961.

66. *Boston Globe*, 15–17 April 1963; *Boston Herald*, 15–17 April 1963; undated article by Bob Cousy in *Boston Record-American*, Mokray Scrapbook, March–September 1963; *New York Times*, 16 April 1963; *Los Angeles Times*, 16 April 1963. A sampling of Russell's witticisms regarding the elbow at the end of Game One: "Even my goatee couldn't cushion the fall. People keep asking me why I have one. Now I'm starting to wonder myself"; "My chin must be really fragile. I guess you can compare it to that china—Wedgewood—that my wife likes so much"; "Now I know how the fighters feel. I wanted to move, but my legs didn't. I guess there's more glass in my chin than the U.N. building."

67. *Boston Globe*, 20–21 April 1963; *Los Angeles Times*, 20 April 1963. In his first autobiography Russell recounts the fateful charge call against Baylor. But he erringly recalls it occurring during Game Six. B. Russell, *Go Up for Glory*, 180–81.

68. Undated article by Bob Cousy in *Boston Record-American*, Mokray Scrapbook, March–September 1963; *Boston Globe*, 22–24 April 1963; *Boston Herald*, 21–23 April 1963.

69. *Boston Herald*, 24 April 1963; *Boston Globe*, 24 April 1963; Leggett, "Up to Their Old Tricks," 54–55; Cousy, *Last Loud Roar*, 16, 78–84.

70. *New York Times*, 25 April 1963, 26 April 1963; Cousy, *Basketball Is My Life*, 185–86; Cousy, *Last Loud Roar*, 230–35.

71. *Boston Herald*, 25 April 1963; *Boston Globe*, 25 April 1963; "Better to Die than Lose," 85–86; Leggett, "Up to Their Old Tricks," 55–56; Cousy, *Last Loud Roar*, 16, 236–63.

72. *Boston Herald*, 25 April 1963; *Boston Globe*, 25 April 1963, 26 April 1963; *Boston Record-American*, 26 April 1963; Leggett, "Up to Their Old Tricks," 56; Cousy, *Last Loud Roar*, 16, 267–68.

73. B. Russell, *Go Up for Glory*, 180.

74. *Boston Record-American*, 26 April 1963; *Boston Globe*, 26 April 1963; *Boston Herald*, 26 April 1963; *Chicago Defender*, 9 May 1963.

10. HIS OWN LITTLE REVOLUTION

1. *Reading Chronicle,* 16 May 1963, 23 May 1963; Heinsohn, *Heinsohn, Don't You Ever Smile?* 86; Harold Furash, telephone interview with author, 19 March 2007.

2. F. Katz, "Unknown Side," 79; Peggy White correspondence, in author's possession; John Hollingsworth, telephone interview with author, 10 October 2007; Heinsohn, *Heinsohn, Don't You Ever Smile?* 86–87.

3. Peggy White correspondence; Plimpton, "Reflections in a Diary," 41–42; *Boston Herald,* 25 April 1965.

4. K. Russell, "Growing Up," 26; F. Katz, "Unknown Side," 79.

5. Du Bois, *Souls of Black Folk,* 1–5.

6. *Harvard Crimson,* 9 May 1963; *Chicago Defender,* 13 May 1963; M. King, *Chain of Change,* 27. On Birmingham demonstrations, see Branch, *Parting the Waters,* 703–802; Branch, *Pillar of Fire,* 41–49, 75–78; McWhorter, *Carry Me Home,* 303–422; Roberts and Klibanoff, *Race Beat,* 305–6, 311–24.

7. Lukas, *Common Ground,* 58–61; Lupo, *Liberty's Chosen Home,* 85–88, 133–36; T. O'Connor, *Building a New Boston,* 58–62, 225–26; Bluestone and Stevenson, *Boston Renaissance,* 25–26, 40, 87; Clay, *Emerging Black Community in Boston,* 117–19; Thernstrom, *Other Bostonians,* 178–83, 197–219; Formisano, *Boston Against Busing,* 25–27.

8. Mel King, telephone interview with author, 25 January 2008; Linn, "I Owe the Public Nothing," 61; Theoharis, "'They Told Us Our Kids Were Stupid,'" 17–44; *Papers of the NAACP,* Part 3: The Campaign for Educational Equality, Series D: Central Office Records, Reel 12; Hillson, *Battle of Boston,* 52–54; J. Smith, "Boston," 56–58.

9. Linn, "I Owe the Public Nothing," 61; Theoharis, "'I'd Rather Go to School in the South,'" 125–51.

10. *Boston Globe,* 18 June 1963, 19 June 1963; *Boston Herald,* 18 June 1963, 19 June 1963; *New York Times,* 18 June 1963, 19 June 1963; *Chicago Defender,* 19 June 1963. In the 1963–64 academic year the Boston NAACP continued to maintain this political pressure by staging a sit-in at the offices of the School Committee and School Superintendant, organizing another one-day boycott, and launching a lawsuit to desegregate Boston schools. See *Papers of the NAACP,* Part 3: The Campaign for Educational Equality, Series D: Central Office Records, Reel 5.

11. *New York Post,* 19 August 1964; *Washington Post,* 9 June 1973; Lukas, *Common Ground,* 60; www.sladesbar.com; Harold Furash interview; "Where the Negro Goes from Here in Sports," 58; Russell and Branch, *Second Wind,* 205–7; *Sporting News,* 5 March 1966. To manage Slade's, Russell hired "ex-Harlem barmaid" Stacy Jones, whom the *New York Amsterdam News* had suggested was linked romantically to Russell in 1961. *New York Amsterdam News,* 24 June 1961, 27 March 1965.

12. Russell and Branch, *Second Wind,* 193–94; Whalen, *Dynasty's End,* 52–53; J. Powers, *Short Season,* 4; O'Brien, " 'We Want a Pennant, Not a White Team,' " 176–81; *Boston Record-American,* 28 March 1964.

13. Elijah "Pumpsie" Green, telephone interview with author, 28 August 2007; Bryant, *Shut Out,* 58–59, 112.

14. Tim Horgan, telephone interview with author, 21 February 2008; Bud Collins, tele-

phone interview with author, 20 February 2008; Pluto, *Tall Tales,* 372; Leigh Montville, telephone interview with author, 5 August 2008.

15. R. Thomas, *They Cleared the Lane,* 177.

16. Bryant, *Shut Out,* 58; *Washington Post,* 26 June 1963; K. Russell, "Growing Up," 26.

17. *Boston Globe,* 25 February 1980, 23 February 1997; Bryant, *Shut Out,* 8–12, 52–62, 76–80; Araton and Bondy, *Selling of the Green,* 56; *Boston Herald,* 24 September 1996; Whalen, *Dynasty's End,* 64.

18. Elijah Green interview; Bryant, *Shut Out,* 55–59, 81–86; "Where the Negro Goes From Here in Sports," 59.

19. Weisbrot, *Freedom Bound,* 75–76, 92–95; Payne, *I've Got the Light of Freedom,* 47–56, 285–89; *New York Times,* 20 June 1963; M. Shapiro, *Bill Russell,* 78.

20. Branch, *Parting the Waters,* 872–83; *Chicago Sun-Times,* 16 January 2006; *USA Today,* 16 January 2006; *Boston Globe,* 8 April 1968; *Seattle Times,* 18 January 1981; *Memphis Commercial Appeal,* 17 January 2006; Martin Luther King Day Symposium, FedEx Forum, Memphis, Tennessee, 16 January 2006.

21. *Baltimore Afro-American,* 31 December 1963; Embry, *Inside Game,* 125–26.

22. Deford, *World's Tallest Midget,* 9–12; D. Halberstam, *October 1964,* 174–81.

23. Rogin, "We Are Grown Men Playing a Child's Game," 74–90. Russell claimed that in 1959 the board of governors considered a ban on facial hair. The measure never passed, and Russell kept his beard. Russell and Branch, *Second Wind,* 201.

24. Rogin, "We Are Grown Men Playing a Child's Game," 82.

25. Rogin, "We Are Grown Men Playing a Child's Game," 82. On Russell's views on the Nation of Islam, see also *Muhammad Speaks,* 14 August 1964; B. Russell, *Go Up for Glory,* 197–98. On Nation of Islam ideology, see Malcolm X, *Autobiography of Malcolm X,* 175–365; Ogbar, *Black Power,* 11–67.

26. Linn, "I Owe the Public Nothing," 60–63.

27. Izenberg, "Unpopular Star," 44–47, 81–82; Linn, "I Owe the Public Nothing," 61; *New York Post,* 19 August 1964; *Washington Post,* 25 April 1972; *Boston Globe,* 16 November 1988; *New York Amsterdam News,* 13 April 2000.

28. Uncited article from 1992, Bill Russell File, Basketball Hall of Fame; B. Russell, *Go Up for Glory,* 140–42; Russell and Branch, *Second Wind,* 196–200.

29. "Letters," 4; "19th Hole," 2 December 1963, 94.

30. "Letters," 4; "19th Hole," 2 December 1963, 94.

31. *Boston Herald,* 15 January 1964; *Boston Globe,* 24 March 1964.

32. *Boston Record-American,* 28 March 1964; B. Russell, *Go Up for Glory,* 197; K. Russell, "Growing Up," 26; *Boston Traveler,* 14 January 1964. See also Ozersky, "Felton X," 13–15.

33. Linn, "I Owe the Public Nothing," 60; *New York Post,* 21 January 1964; *Boston Globe,* 6 December 1963.

34. *New York Post,* 21 January 1964; *Providence Journal,* 16 January 1964; D'Agostino, *Garden Glory,* 52–53; Embry, *Inside Game,* 122; Auerbach and Sann, *Red Auerbach,* 133–34; Al Attles, telephone interview with author, 5 August 2008; Tom "Satch" Sanders, telephone interview with author, 25 August 2008.

35. *Baltimore Afro-American,* 12 January 1963; *Chicago Defender,* 23 April 1962, 29 April 1963, 13 November 1963, 13 January 1964; B. Russell, "I Don't Have to Prove a Thing," 12–

21 (adapted from Rogin, "We Are Grown Men Playing a Child's Game"); *Atlanta Daily World*, 2 June 1963; *Chicago Defender*, 29 April 1963, 13 January 1964; *Los Angeles Sentinel*, 23 January 1964; "Negro Athletes and Civil Rights," 35–39.

36. Gene Conley, telephone interview with author, 10 April 2007; Bob Cousy, telephone interview with author, 23 April 2007; *Boston Traveler*, 18 August 1965.

37. Deford, "Ring Leader," 107–8; *San Francisco Chronicle*, 20 April 1964; W. Russell, "Success Is a Journey," 85.

38. Walker, *Long Time Coming*, 82, 161; Wilkens, *Lenny Wilkens Story*, 4–10; Wilkens, *Unguarded*, 69–71, 93–94; Pluto, *Tall Tales*, 75–79; Embry, *Inside Game*, 137.

39. On Robinson, see Rampersad, *Jackie Robinson*, 349–92; J. Robinson, *I Never Had It Made*, 162–82. On Brown, see Freeman, *Jim Brown*, 132–53; Jimmy Brown, *Off My Chest*, 159–73. On Ali, see Remnick, *King of the World*, 183–218; Gorn, *Muhammad Ali*. On black entertainers and politics, see B. Ward, *Just My Soul Responding*, 123–216; Goudsouzian, *Sidney Poitier*, 145–227. Bobby Mitchell of the Washington Redskins recalled that "during the years that Bill was playing, he was one of the few Black athletes that those of us in the sport really looked up to. . . . We held onto the future just merely by watching and listening to the Bill Russells and Jim Browns and those people who were outspoken." *New York Amsterdam News*, 13 April 2000. For another example of the shifting black mood in sports, see Maureen Smith, "New Orleans, New Football League, and New Attitudes," 3–22. For an uneven parallel in baseball, Dick "Richie" Allen, a young slugger for the Phillies, embodied the "Angry Negro." Many white Philadelphians resented him, perceiving him as too willing to confront racism, too unwilling to show gratitude, and too hot-tempered. See Jacobson, "'Richie' Allen, Whitey's Ways, and Me," 19–46; Kashatus, *September Swoon*, 147–77.

40. B. Russell, "I Am not Worried About Ali," 21; *Muhammad Speaks*, 14 August 1964. See also K. Russell, "Growing Up," 26.

41. *Boston Globe*, 29 January 1964.

42. Kindred, *Sound and Fury*, 32–60; Rose and Friedman, "Television Sports as Mas(s)culine Cult of Distinction," 1–15; Van Deburg, *Black Camelot*, 84–126; Early, *Tuxedo Junction*, 119, 168.

43. Undated article in *Boston Herald-American*, Mokray Scrapbook, March–August 1964.

44. Tyson, *Radio Free Dixie*, 189–308; Ransby, *Ella Baker and the Black Freedom Movement*, 273–329; Carson, *In Struggle*, 45–129; Hill, *Deacons for Defense*, 1–51; F. Katz, "Unknown Side," 26.

45. Rogin, "We Are Grown Men Playing a Child's Game," 78. See also T. Green, "Ali, Forman, Mailer, and Me," 158–59.

46. *New York Post*, 14 November 1963. On Celtics without Cousy, see also *New York Times*, 15 November 1963; *Washington Post*, 1 February 1964.

47. F. Katz, "Unknown Side," 78; *Boston Record-American*, 2 December 1963; *Boston Globe*, 2 December 1963; *Boston Traveler*, 3 December 1963; *Christian Science Monitor*, 6 December 1963.

48. On Loscutoff, see *Boston Globe*, 21 January 1964; *Sporting News*, 21 March 1964. On Ramsey, see *Boston Globe*, 22 November 1963, 10 December 1963, 11 December 1963, 24 March 1964; Ramsey, "Smart Moves," 57–63; *New York Post*, 10 December 1963, 11 De-

cember 1963; *Los Angeles Times*, 12 December 1963; *Sporting News*, 4 April 1964; Ballard, "Frank Ramsey," 14; Strom, *Calling the Shots*, 64–65. Auerbach constantly clashed with Lovellette about his propensity for outside shots. Auerbach wanted him to stay under the basketball and rebound. "Clyde wouldn't buy it, so I had to let him go." Auerbach and Sann, *Red Auerbach*, 231.

49. *Christian Science Monitor*, 11 November 1963; "Scouting Reports," 28 October 1963, 38; *Boston Record-American*, 3 April 1964; *Boston Herald*, 27 November 1963; *Boston Globe*, 27 November 1963, 5 April 1964; *Sporting News*, 11 December 1965; Hoose, *Necessities*, 146.

50. *Boston Record-American*, 21 November 1963; Bill Russell Chat Transcript at www .celtics.com, 18 September 2007; *Boston Traveler*, 17 October 1963; *Boston Herald*, 11 February 1964; "And Still Champions," 92–93; *Boston Globe*, 26 April 1963, 7 November 1963, 28 January 1964, 9 March 1965.

51. *Boston Globe*, 12 January 1957; *Boston Herald*, 14 January 1957, 16 January 1957, 2 March 1961; *New York Times*, 13 January 1957, 15 January 1957; *Sporting News*, 30 January 1957, 15 January 1958; Maurice Podoloff testimony before House of Representatives Committee on the Judiciary, 7 August 1957, H1634–3, 2875–2881.

52. Robertson, *Big O*, 179–81; Jerry West, telephone interview with author, 16 March 2007; *Boston Traveler*, 17 January 1964; Berkow, *Oscar Robertson*, 148.

53. *New York Times*, 23 May 1963, 5 August 1963, 22 August 1963, 17 December 1963; *Sporting News*, 5 December 1964; Koppett, *24 Seconds to Shoot*, 157–58; undated article from *Christian Science Monitor*, Mokray Scrapbook, May 1963–January 1964; *Boston Globe*, 9 October 1963; *Boston Record-American*, 22 October 1963; Terry Smith, "Basketball's Irish Czar," 54–55; Walter Kennedy Testimony before the Senate Committee on the Judiciary, 31 January 1964, S1630–1, 53–61; Paxton, "Walter Kennedy Answers the NBA's Critics," 40–41, 89–91; uncited article dated 22 August 1963, Mokray Scrapbook, May 1963–January 1964. Kennedy also fined Red Auerbach an unprecedented $500 for failing to leave the court after getting ejected.

54. *New York Post*, 16 January 1964; *Boston Herald*, 15 January 1964; *New York Times*, 15 January 1964; Wilkens, *Lenny Wilkens Story*, 168–69; *Boston Globe*, 21 January 1964; Pettit, *Bob Pettit*, 159–60.

55. Robertson, *Big O*, 184–85; *New York Post*, 16 January 1964; *Boston Record-American*, 17 January 1964; W. Russell, "Success Is a Journey," 85; Jerry West interview; Heinsohn and Fitzgerald, *Give 'Em the Hook*, 225–26. For a good narrative of the 1964 All-Star controversy, see J. Taylor, *Rivalry*, 198–205.

56. Walker, *Long Time Coming*, 155; Embry, *Inside Game*, 127–28; Heinsohn, *Heinsohn, Don't You Ever Smile?* 123–24; B. Russell, *Go Up for Glory*, 84–85; *New York Post*, 16 January 1964; *Sporting News*, 25 January 1964; *Boston Globe*, 15 January 1964.

57. *Sporting News*, 7 March 1964; *Boston Herald*, 17 January 1964, 18 January 1964; *Boston Globe*, 15–17 January 1964, 5 January 1965; *New York Times*, 23 January 1964.

58. *Rocky Mountain News*, 25 February 1975; *San Francisco Chronicle*, 20 April 1964; *Christian Science Monitor*, 6 December 1963; *Boston Traveler*, 19 January 1964, 20 January 1964; *Los Angeles Times*, 6 January 1964, 21 January 1964; *Boston Globe*, 20 December 1963, 7 January 1964, 9 January 1964, 20 January 1964, 30 January 1964, 1 February 1964, 28 March 1964.

59. *San Francisco Chronicle*, 6 January 1964; *Los Angeles Times*, 3 January 1964; *Boston Traveler*, 5 February 1964; uncited article dated 28 January 1964, Mokray Scrapbook, January–March 1964; *Boston Globe*, 12 November 1963, 15 November 1963, 17 February 1964, 16 March 1964, 24 March 1964. Harold Kaese figured that only Sandy Koufax of the Brooklyn Dodgers similarly dominated a team sport, and Koufax pitched every fifth game.

60. *Boston Herald*, 10 March 1964; *Christian Science Monitor*, 12 March 1964; *Boston Globe*, 12 March 1964. On Billy Green blunder, see Auerbach, *MBA Management by Auerbach*, 188–89.

61. *Boston Record-American*, 28 March 1964; *Boston Herald*, 28 March 1964, 29 March 1964; *Boston Globe*, 28 March 1964, 29 March 1964; *Pittsburgh Courier*, 4 April 1964; *San Francisco Chronicle*, 28 March 1964; *Washington Post*, 28 March 1964; *Los Angeles Times*, 28 March 1964; *Boston Traveler*, 25 April 1964.

62. Linn, "Oscar Robertson," 57–63; *Boston Globe*, 28 December 1963, 2 January 1964, 10 January 1964, 20 February 1964, 24 February 1964, 6 March 1964, 24 March 1964; *Boston Traveler*, 30 March 1964; *Boston Herald*, 31 March 1964.

63. Robertson, *Big O*, 172–78; Berkow, *Oscar Robertson*, 132–36; Linn, "Oscar Robertson," 63. Cincinnati general manager Tom Grace tried defending the trade by labeling Boozer a malcontent, and then later claiming that Boozer asked for a trade. Boozer rejected both rationales.

64. *Boston Globe*, 20 February 1964, 9 March 1964, 13 March 1964, 25 March 1964, 29–31 March 1964, 4 April 1964, 5 April 1964, 7 April 1964, 11 April 1964; Linn, "Oscar Robertson," 58; undated article from *Christian Science Monitor*, Mokray Scrapbook, January–March 1964; B. Russell, *Go Up for Glory*, 185–86.

65. *Boston Globe*, 1–10 April 1964; *Boston Herald*, 1–3 April 1964, 7 April 1964; Deford, "How K. C. Won an Oscar in the NBA."

66. Robertson, *Big O*, 188–89; W. Russell, "Success Is a Journey," 88.

67. *Philadelphia Bulletin*, 11 August 1963, 9 October 1963, 6 November 1963, 13 November 1963, 14 November 1963, 4 February 1964; *Christian Science Monitor*, 29 November 1963; *Philadelphia Inquirer*, 4 March 1964; *Sporting News*, 23 November 1963, 14 March 1964, 21 March 1964; Chamberlain and Shaw, *Wilt*, 153–55; Libby, *Goliath*, 118–22; Hano, "Fight to Remodel," 24–26, 84–86; Brody, "Meet the New Wilt Chamberlain," 24–25.

68. *Philadelphia Bulletin*, 20 April 1964, 21 April 1964; *Boston Globe*, 12 April 1964, 18–21 April 1964; *Boston Herald*, 18–20 April 1964; *San Francisco Chronicle*, 19 April 1964, 21 April 1964; undated article in *Boston Traveler*, Mokray Scrapbook, January–March 1964; *Boston Traveler*, 22 April 1964; *New York Post*, 22 April 1964; B. Russell, *Red and Me*, 124–25; B. Russell, *Go Up for Glory*, 134–35; Strom, *Calling the Shots*, 85–86. Chamberlain claimed that Russell later told him that Lovellette was a dirty player and "had it coming a long time." Chamberlain and Shaw, *Wilt*, 158.

69. *Boston Globe*, 22 April 1964, 23 April 1964; *Boston Herald*, 22–24 April 1964; *Boston Traveler*, 27 April 1964; *San Francisco Chronicle*, 22–25 April 1964, 27 April 1964, 28 April 1964.

70. *Boston Globe*, 22 April 1964, 24 April 1964, 25 April 1964; *Boston Herald*, 25 April 1964, 26 April 1964; *New York Times*, 27 May 1986; Russell and Branch, *Second Wind*, 137–38; Auerbach and Sann, *Red Auerbach*, 257–58.

71. "How to Make Contact," 58; undated article in *Boston Record-American*, Mokray Scrapbook, March–August 1964.

72. *Boston Record-American*, 27 April 1964; *Boston Globe*, 27 April 1964; "How to Make Contact," 58.

73. Deford, "Follow the Bouncing Ball," 81–84; *Boston Herald*, 10 April 1964; *Boston Globe*, 27 April 1964; *New York Times*, 27 April 1964; *New York Amsterdam News*, 2 May 1964; undated articles in *Boston Record-American* and *Christian Science Monitor*, Mokray Scrapbook, March–August 1964.

11. RUSSELLPHOBIA

1. *Boston Globe*, 8 September 1964. On Brown's generosity and status, see *New York Post*, 28 January 1960; *Boston Globe*, 11 April 1962, 9 September 1964, 11 September 1964, 13 September 1964; Bob Cousy, telephone interview with author, 23 April 2007. At the 1964 championship banquet, Brown's ire at Heinsohn for the 1964 All-Star Game finally dissipated. He made a point of lauding Heinsohn's contributions, swaddling Heinsohn back into the family fold. See Heinsohn, *Heinsohn, Don't You Ever Smile?* 120–29; *Boston Herald*, 28 April 1964.

2. *Providence Journal*, 22 September 1964; *Boston Herald*, 27 March 1964, 8 November 1964, 16 February 1965, 17 February 1965, 14 March 1965; *Boston Globe*, 9 September 1964; *Sporting News*, 7 November 1964, 27 February 1965; *Boston Globe*, 20 April 1964, 11 February 1965, 12 February 1965, 23 March 1965; *Boston Record-American*, 23 March 1965; Rader, *In Its Own Image*, 147; Fortunato, "Ultimate Assist," 129; *New York Post*, 24 March 1965. Other potential buyers included Billy Sullivan, owner of the American Football League's Boston Patriots.

3. *Boston Record-American*, 24 September 1964.

4. Brody, "Who Says You Can't Win 'Em All," 104–5; Guttmann, *Sports Spectators*, 107–10; *Washington Post*, 28 May 1965; Creamer, "Rough Night," 76–77.

5. *Washington Post*, 15 December 1961, 10 April 1964, 9 June 1964; Auerbach and Fitzgerald, *Red Auerbach*, 292–95; Auerbach and Sann, *Red Auerbach*, 274–76; *New York Times*, 10 April 1964, 2 May 1964. In February 1965, Auerbach received a medal from Boston mayor John Collins. He also lectured at Tufts University's Fletcher School of Diplomacy, where he called the American ambassador to Egypt "stupid" for not finding time to greet his players. *Washington Post*, 7 February 1965; *Boston Herald*, 24 February 1965.

6. *Boston Globe*, 31 May 1964, 1 June 1964, 9 June 1964; *New York Post*, 24 May 1964, 2 June 1964; *Boston Herald-American*, 9 June 1964; Pettit, *Bob Pettit*, 104. The next season, nine basketball coaches from foreign countries came to observe American methods. A Romanian coach who followed the Celtics for ten days marveled not only at Russell's defense but also at the players' motivation, even without supervision. *Washington Post*, 30 January 1965.

7. Undated article in *Boston Globe*, Mokray Scrapbook, March–August 1964; B. Russell, *Go Up for Glory*, 110–11.

8. Pettit, *Bob Pettit*, 100; B. Russell, *Red and Me*, 98–99; B. Russell, *Go Up for Glory*, 111.

9. *Boston Globe*, 31 May 1964; Heinsohn, *Heinsohn, Don't You Ever Smile?* 98–102.

10. Campbell, *Tito's Separate Road,* 1–9, 48–66, 130–70; Pettit, *Bob Pettit,* 102–4; Auerbach and Sann, *Red Auerbach,* 281–82. Auerbach got his dander up during one exhibition because a huge display of flags did not include the stars and stripes. He refused to play until someone found and hoisted an American flag.

11. Auerbach and Fitzgerald, *Red Auerbach,* 295–97. On Korac, see www.eurobasket .com/srb/HallOfFame.asp. In his final book, Auerbach refers to Korac as "Belov," evidently confusing him with Sergei Belov, a Soviet basketball star of the 1960s. See Auerbach and Feinstein, *Let Me Tell You a Story,* 121–22.

12. Russell and Branch, *Second Wind,* 171–72; Gross, "Pros Tell Their Favorite Bill Russell Stories," 88; Pettit, *Bob Pettit,* 99; *New York Post,* 2 June 1964; Auerbach and Sann, *Red Auerbach,* 280–81; B. Russell, *Go Up for Glory,* 111.

13. Crosby, "'God's Appointed Savior,'" 165–92; Crosby, *Little Taste of Freedom,* 86–90, 125–28, 139–40; Dittmer, *Local People,* 177–78. See also Evers, *Evers,* 102–17.

14. *Boston Globe,* 9 July 1964; *Washington Post,* 9 July 1964; B. Russell, *Go Up for Glory,* 211–12; *Baltimore Afro-American,* 9 July 1964; *New York Post,* 19 August 1964.

15. McAdam, *Freedom Summer,* 66–115; Dittmer, *Local People,* 225–65.

16. Evers and Szanton, *Have No Fear,* 135; *Boston Herald,* 18 July 1964; *New York Post,* 19 August 1964; *Seattle Post-Intelligencer,* 22 April 1974; *Chicago Defender,* 15 July 1964; *Boston Globe,* 10 July 1964; B. Russell, *Go Up for Glory,* 212–13.

17. *Boston Globe,* 10 July 1964; Correspondence dated 9 July 1964, Mississippi Sovereignty Commission Records, SCR ID# 9-31-2-2-1-1-1; Evers and Szanton, *Have No Fear,* 135.

18. Charles Evers, telephone interview with author, 10 January 2008; Kunstler, "Bill Russell," 39. "When I went down to Mississippi," Russell later recalled, "I was asked to try to get other Negro ballplayers to go down there." He declined. He insisted that African Americans had different political viewpoints, and he refused to pressure others to follow his footsteps. "Where the Negro Goes From Here in Sports," 59.

19. *Chicago Defender,* 15 July 1964, 16 July 1964, 20 July 1964; *Boston Globe,* 10 July 1964; McAdam, *Freedom Summer,* 116–60; *New York Post,* 19 August 1964; *Boston Herald,* 18 July 1964.

20. *Boston Globe,* 21 January 1965, 11 February 1965; Cope, "Last Cigar for a Last Hurrah?" 112.

21. On winning streaks and success, see *Boston Globe,* 13 November 1964, 17 November 1964, 8 January 1965, 24 January 1965; "Can't Anybody Here Beat These Guys?" 60; "Pack Closes on Boston," 50–56. On K. C. Jones, see *Boston Globe,* 10 November 1964; *San Francisco Chronicle,* 4 April 1964; *Los Angeles Times,* 26 February 1965; West, *Mr. Clutch,* 94. On Sam Jones, see *Pittsburgh Courier,* 6 February 1965; *Boston Globe,* 26 January 1965, 28 January 1965, 25 February 1965, 15 March 1965, 16 March 1965, 29 March 1965; 4 April 1965; *Sporting News,* 13 February 1965. When someone proposed that the Celtics should scrimmage the Harlem Globetrotters, columnist Jim Murray offered contrary advice: "When they come to you to play Bill Russell, don't. You may never feel like being funny again." The justifiable ridicule reflected black basketball's upheaval in the decade since Russell spurned Abe Saperstein. The Globetrotters now represented sport's version of vaudeville, and the

NBA was the only viable stage for elite black talent. *Chicago Defender,* 6 January 1965; *Los Angeles Times,* 29 January 1965.

22. On end-of-season awards and Celtics' record, see *New York Times,* 4 March 1965, 7 March 1965, 15 March 1965, 22 March 1965, 25 March 1965. On Jones's quote, see *Boston Globe,* 1 December 1964. The impact of centers was supposed to be lessened by the 1964 adoption of a widened sixteen-foot lane, but it seemed to have little effect on stars such as Russell and Chamberlain. *Los Angeles Times,* 5 August 1964.

23. On Russell as player-coach and confidante see *Boston Globe,* 4 November 1964, 9 January 1965, 11 March 1965, 13 March 1965; *Boston Herald,* 9 March 1965. On Auerbach's double-duty and award, see *Boston Traveler,* 22 September 1964, *Boston Globe,* 20 September 1964, 23 March 1965, 28 March 1965. In late January, when huge New York coach Harry Gallatin was at near-blows with Auerbach, Russell stepped in and said, "Harry, you've been a coward all your life. Why change now?" See *Boston Herald,* 1 February 1965, 3 February 1965, 4 February 1965; *Boston Globe,* 1 February 1965, 2 February 1965; *Sporting News,* 19 February 1965; Auerbach and Sann, *Red Auerbach,* 269–71.

24. Undated *New York Post* article, Mokray Scrapbook, September–December 1964; *Washington Post,* 19 January 1965; *Sporting News,* 6 February 1965, 20 February 1965; *Boston Globe,* 2 February 1965; *Boston Herald,* 2 February 1965, 12 February 1965; *Los Angeles Times,* 17 November 1964, 10 December 1964. A reporter asked Auerbach about Russell's possible departure to concentrate on his Liberian holdings. "Have you ever eaten rubber?" he snapped back. *Los Angeles Times,* 8 December 1964.

25. *Boston Globe,* 17 January 1965, 25 February 1965, 27 April 1965.

26. L. Shapiro, *Big Man on Campus,* 18–31, 36–37, 51–54, 57–59; *Washington Post,* 17 January 1965, 21 March 1965; *New York Amsterdam News,* 13 April 2000; Kornheiser, "Bill Russell," 184–89; Deford, "Ring Leader," 107.

27. *Sporting News,* 27 January 1973; Reed, *View from the Rim,* 28, 52–54; Nate Thurmond, telephone interview with the author, 10 January 2008; Jerry West, telephone interview with the author, 16 March 2007; Deford, "Ring Leader," 104.

28. *Los Angeles Times,* 21 September 1974; Gross, "Pros Tell Their Favorite Bill Russell Stories," 46–47.

29. Dave Bing, telephone interview with author, 19 August 2008; Ottum, "Panic Is on Again," 18–19, 60–61; Russell and Branch, *Second Wind,* 148, 166–67; B. Russell, *Go Up for Glory,* 161–62; B. Russell, *Red and Me,* 120–21; Love, *Bob Love Story,* 74; Gross, "Pros Tell Their Favorite Bill Russell Stories," 46–47; B. Russell, "Psych," 32–34, 39. Love did once squeeze a dunk past Russell, who snapped, "Didn't I tell you not to even dream about dunking on me?" Love responded, "Yes, Mr. Russell. But dreams do come true." *Boston Globe,* 3 October 1990.

30. Pluto, *Tall Tales,* 162–67; Meschery, *Over the Rim,* 42.

31. Kamp, "Only the Ball Was Brown," 347.

32. *Boston Globe,* 6 May 1966; uncited Jim Murray column dated 10 February 1963, Mokray Scrapbook, January–March 1963; Jim Murray, "Wilt Chamberlain," 49, 136; Rosenblatt, "Way We Look at Giants," 142.

33. *Philadelphia Journal,* 3 May 1979; Pluto, *Tall Tales,* 331, 347; "How Do You Stop

Him?" 40–41; D. Schaap, "Real Wilt Chamberlain," 59; Chamberlain and Shaw, *Wilt*, 157; Ostler and Springer, *Winnin' Times*, 46; *Chicago Defender*, 19 March 1963; *San Francisco Chronicle*, 2 April 1964; *Philadelphia Bulletin*, 16 May 1965; *New York Post*, 18 May 1965; Hano, "Fight to Remodel Wilt Chamberlain," 85; *Sporting News*, 21 March 1964.

34. Pluto, *Tall Tales*, 231–35; Charles Rosen, *God, Man and Basketball Jones*, 124–25; Chamberlain, *View from Above*, 50–53.

35. *Philadelphia Bulletin*, 15 January 1965; *New York Post*, 15 January 1965; Bradley, *Life on the Run*, 157–60; Hano, "Fight to Remodel Wilt Chamberlain," 86.

36. *Philadelphia Bulletin*, 23 September 1964, 2 October 1964, 6 October 1964, 13–15 October 1964, 19 October 1964, 20 October 1964, 22 October 1964, 26 November 1964, 5 December 1964, 18 February 1965, 26 April 1965; *San Francisco Chronicle*, 23 October 1964, 4 January 1965; *Boston Globe*, 3 December 1964, 7 December 1964; *New York Amsterdam News*, 23 January 1965. In 1972 Alex Hannum told reporters that Chamberlain had suffered a heart attack in 1964, but Chamberlain contended that he had only been diagnosed by an irregular heartbeat. His pancreas caused him much more discomfort. *Washington Post*, 30 April 1972; *Los Angeles Times*, 30 April 1972, 1 May 1972; Chamberlain and Shaw, *Wilt*, 159–61.

37. On Mieuli, see *San Francisco Chronicle*, 8 April 1964; *Sporting News*, 4 December 1965; Barry, *Confessions of a Basketball Gypsy*, 86–90. On Thurmond, see Libby, "Nate Thurmond," 72–75, 107–8; Hano, "Nate Thurmond at the Summit," 54–62; M. Harris, *Lonely Heroes*, 56–76. For the stickpin story, see Hannum, "I've Barely Begun to Fight," 40. On potential trade with Los Angeles, see Lazenby, *Show*, 92–94; *Philadelphia Bulletin*, 17 December 1964, 24 December 1964; *Boston Globe*, 25 December 1964, 26 December 1964; *Boston Traveler*, 23 April 1965.

38. On the 76ers, see *Christian Science Monitor*, 21 November 1963; *Philadelphia Bulletin*, 31 December 1964, 7 January 1965; Walker, *Long Time Coming*, 148–51, 155–57; *Boston Globe*, 11 December 1964; *Sporting News*, 22 February 1964, 22 February 1964, 14 March 1964; 6 February 1965; T. Fox, "Hal Greer," 32–33, 103–4; Devaney, "Chet Walker's Tug O'War," 34–35, 84–86. On trade talks, see *Philadelphia Bulletin*, 27 December 1964, 8 January 1965, 11 January 1965; *San Francisco Chronicle*, 6 January 1965, 9 January 1965, 12 January 1965; *Boston Globe*, 13 January 1965.

39. *Philadelphia Bulletin*, 14 January 1965; *Philadelphia Inquirer*, 15 January 1965; *San Francisco Chronicle*, 14 January 1965, 15 January 1965; Dickey, *History of Professional Basketball*, 117–19; *Sporting News*, 30 January 1965; *Los Angeles Times*, 15 January 1965; Deford, "Another Big Bluff," 18.

40. Dolph Schayes, telephone interview with author, 13 April 2007; *Philadelphia Bulletin*, 3 March 1965, 6 March 1965, 15 March 1965, 22 March 1965.

41. *Philadelphia Bulletin*, 21 January 1965, 25 January 1965, 28–30 January 1965; *Philadelphia Inquirer*, 21 January 1965, 24 January 1965, 26 January 1965, 30 January 1965; *Boston Globe*, 3 February 1965; uncited article dated 8 February 1965, Wilt Chamberlain File, Basketball Hall of Fame; Walker, *Long Time Coming*, 159–60, 210.

42. *Boston Traveler*, 1 April 1965; *Philadelphia Daily News*, 2 April 1965; *Boston Herald*, 30 March 1965, 2 April 1965; *Boston Globe*, 28 March 1965, 2 April 1965, 3 April 1965; *Philadelphia Inquirer*, 1–4 April 1965.

43. *Boston Record-American,* 4 April 1965; *Boston Globe,* 4–8 April 1965, 25 April 1980; *Boston Herald,* 5–8 April 1965, 24 April 1965; *Washington Post,* 8 April 1965; *Philadelphia Inquirer,* 5–7 April 1965; *Philadelphia Bulletin,* 7 April 1965; *Boston Traveler,* 13 April 1965.

44. *Boston Globe,* 4–8 April 1965; *Christian Science Monitor,* 6 April 1965; *Boston Record-American,* 5 April 1965, 6 April 1965.

45. Chamberlain, "I'm Punchy from Basketball," 32–43.

46. *Philadelphia Bulletin,* 9 April 1965, 10 April 1965, 14 April 1965, 14 June 1965; *Philadelphia Inquirer,* 16 March 1965; *Boston Traveler,* 9 April 1965; *Boston Globe,* 10 April 1965; *Boston Herald,* 10 April 1965; *Boston Record-American,* 10 April 1965, 14 April 1965; "19th Hole," 26 April 1963, 118.

47. *Philadelphia Inquirer,* 10 March 1965, 23 June 1965; three uncited articles in Mokray Scrapbook, March–May 1965; *Philadelphia Bulletin,* 25 June 1965; Shecter, *Jocks,* 114–16; Chamberlain, "I Love the Game," 39–41, 116–18.

48. *Philadelphia Bulletin,* 9 April 1965; *New York Post,* 12 April 1965.

49. *Boston Globe,* 8–11 April 1965; *Boston Herald,* 9 April 1965, 11 April 1965; *Philadelphia Inquirer,* 9–11 April 1965. A later study of the videotape vindicated the referees' decision to allow the basket.

50. *Boston Traveler,* 12 April 1965; uncited article dated 13 April 1965, Mokray Scrapbook, March–May 1965; *Boston Globe,* 12 April 1965, 13 April 1965, 15 April 1965; *Boston Herald,* 12 April 1965, 13 April 1965; *Philadelphia Inquirer,* 13 April 1965.

51. *Boston Globe,* 14 April 1965; *Boston Herald,* 14 April 1965; *Philadelphia Inquirer,* 14 April 1965, 15 April 1965; *Philadelphia Bulletin,* 14 April 1965; Walker, *Long Time Coming,* 162–63; uncited article dated 14 April 1965, Mokray Scrapbook, March–May 1965.

52. Strom, *Calling the Shots,* 83; *Boston Herald,* 15 April 1965; *Boston Globe,* 14–16 April 1965.

53. *Boston Globe,* 16 April 1965; *Philadelphia Inquirer,* 16 April 1965; undated article by Bill Russell in *Boston Record-American,* Mokray Scrapbook, March–May 1965.

54. *Boston Globe,* 19 April 1965; *Boston Herald,* 17 April 1965, 15 April 1995; *Boston Traveler,* 16 April 1965; Carey and McClellan, *Boston Celtics,* 21.

55. Undated article by Bill Russell in *Boston Record-American,* Mokray Scrapbook, March–May 1965; B. Russell, *Go Up for Glory,* 145–47.

56. J. Fitzgerald, *That Championship Feeling,* 148; Pluto, *Tall Tales,* 260–61; B. Russell, *Go Up for Glory,* 147–48; Walker, *Long Time Coming,* 164–65; Salzberg, *From Set Shot to Slam Dunk,* 213; Lynch, *Season of the 76ers,* 120–21; *Boston Herald,* 9 April 1995; Dolph Schayes interview. Walker, Schayes, Dave Gambee, and Johnny Kerr all contradict what Chamberlain later told Terry Pluto: "There never was a time when I didn't want the ball, and I wanted it at the end of the game." Pluto, *Tall Tales,* 262.

57. Pluto, *Tall Tales,* 261–62; *Boston Record-American,* 16 April 1965; *Boston Globe,* 16 April 1965, 14 April 1985, 9 April 1995; "Play that Won the Title," 26–27.

58. Havlicek and Ryan, *Hondo,* 129–30; *Boston Globe,* 16 April 1965, 14 April 1985, 9 April 1995; Carey, *High Above Courtside,* 153–57; Carey, *Voice of the Celtics,* 45–47. On the 1965 Eastern Conference play-offs, see also R. Roberts, "Battle of the Beards," 293–315. Fleetwood Records titled a 1966 album of Most's broadcasts *Havlicek Stole the Ball.*

59. *Boston Globe,* 16 April 1965; *Boston Record-American,* 16 April 1965; undated arti-

cle in *Boston Traveler*, Mokray Scrapbook, March–May 1965; uncited article dated 15 April 1965, Mokray Scrapbook, March–May 1965; *Philadelphia Bulletin*, 16 April 1965; *Philadelphia Inquirer*, 17 April 1965; *New York Post*, 19 April 1965; Pluto, *Tall Tales*, 261–62.

60. B. Russell, *Go Up for Glory*, 148–49.

61. Cope, "Life with Elgin Baylor," 58–65; "Elgin Baylor Comes Back," 35–37; Deford, "Tiger Who Can Beat Anything," 45–47; West, *Mr. Clutch*, 128–30, 174–76; Russell and Branch, *Second Wind*, 161–62; *Minneapolis Tribune*, 11 December 1963; *San Francisco Chronicle*, 29 January 1964; *Los Angeles Times*, 4 February 1964, 18 April 1965; *Boston Globe*, 19 April 1965.

62. *Philadelphia Bulletin*, 17 April 1965; *Boston Globe*, 18–20 April 1965; *Boston Herald*, 19 April 1965, 20 April 1965; *Boston Record-American*, 21 April 1965.

63. *Boston Globe*, 21–24 April 1965; *Boston Herald*, 21 April 1965, 22 April 1965; *Boston Traveler*, 22 April 1965; *Boston Record-American*, 23 April 1965; Deford, "Playoff Was Child's Play," 28. On West, see *Philadelphia Inquirer*, 19 April 1965.

64. On Heinsohn, see *New York Post*, 21 November 1962; *Boston Globe*, 22 April 1965, 23 April 1965, 27 April 1965, 28 April 1965; *Sporting News*, 29 January 1966; Cousy, *Last Loud Roar*, 24–25, 37–38; Greenfield, *World's Greatest Team*, 76–80.

65. Heinsohn, *Heinsohn, Don't You Ever Smile?* 143–45. Heinsohn officially retired in September 1965. *Boston Globe*, 13 September 1965; *Boston Herald*, 13 September 1965.

66. B. Russell, *Go Up for Glory*, 150–52; *Boston Herald*, 26 April 1965; *Los Angeles Herald-Examiner*, 26 April 1965; *New York Times*, 26 April 1965; *Boston Globe*, 26 April 1965.

67. *Los Angeles Times*, 26 April 1965; J. Fitzgerald, *That Championship Feeling*, 151.

68. *Boston Traveler*, 5 April 1965; *Boston Herald*, 9 April 1965, 28 April 1965; *Boston Globe*, 16 April 1965, 25 April 1965, 26 April 1965, 1 May 1966; *Los Angeles Times*, 28 April 1965; undated article in *Christian Science Monitor*, undated article in *Boston Herald*, and four undated articles in *Boston Record-American*, Mokray Scrapbook, March–May 1965.

69. *Los Angeles Times*, 26 April 1965, 28 April 1965; *New York Post*, 27 April 1965; *Boston Globe*, 26–27 April 1965; *Boston Herald*, 27 April 1965; B. Russell, *Go Up for Glory*, 150–51.

12. THE HIDDEN FEAR

1. *Philadelphia Inquirer*, 16 April 1965; *Philadelphia Bulletin*, 22 June 1964, 23 June 1964, 26 June 1964, 9 July 1964, 24 February 1965, 30 June 1965, 1 July 1965, 4 July 1965, 11 July 1965, 20 July 1965, 21 July 1965, 27 July 1965, 1 August 1965, 14 August 1965, 16–18 August 1965; *New York Post*, 19 August 1965.

2. *New York Times*, 18 August 1965; *Washington Post*, 26 August 1965; *Los Angeles Times*, 18 September 1986; *Boston Globe*, 26 August 1965, 24 February 1966; *Chicago Defender*, 28 August 1965; *Boston Herald*, 23 August 1965. Dolph Schayes remembers watching Russell and Chamberlain hug at center court before their first exhibition game that season; he assumed that Russell was thanking Chamberlain for the salary boost. Dolph Schayes, telephone interview with author, 13 April 2007.

3. Axthelm, *City Game*, 127.

4. George, *Elevating the Game*, xv–xx, 10–16, 61–62; Wideman, *Hoop Roots*, 48–50; Caponi, "Introduction," 2–41; Cochran, "Folk Elements," 398–403; Greenfield, "Black and

White Truth," 170–71; *New York Times,* 2 August 1970; Kirkpatrick, "Place in the Big-City Sun," 20–23; Mallozzi, *Asphalt Gods,* 37–38, 65–70, 80–91; Andersen and Millman, *Pickup Artists,* 65–68, 82–86, 98–99; Wolf, *Foul!* 131–33; Axthelm, *City Game,* 5–8. Different versions exist of the Hawkins, Jackson, and Chamberlain story. Axthelm's account describes only Hawkins and Chamberlain. Mallozzi's account has Jackson dunking and Hawkins blocking. On Philadelphia's Baker League, see P. Ellis, "Tall Boys of Summer," 139–44. On playground basketball, see also Telander, *Heaven Is A Playground.*

5. Devaney, "Pro Basketball's Hidden Fear," 32; "Pro Basketball Roundup," 71–72; *Baltimore Afro-American,* 21 September 1965; Love, *Bob Love Story,* 62–63, 76–77; Riess, *City Games,* 116–17; Koppett, *Essence of the Game,* 131–38; Fitzpatrick, *And the Walls Came Tumbling Down.* On HBCUs and basketball, see also *Black Magic;* M. Katz, *Breaking Through,* 25–57, 75–110, 149–58. Another sign of basketball's growing black influence arrived in the 1967 state basketball tournaments, when three all-black teams won their class state titles in Georgia and Tennessee. "Scorecard," 27 March 1967, 8.

6. *Boston Globe,* 27 January 1966; Devaney, "Pro Basketball's Hidden Fear," 32–33, 89–91; "Hidden Fear that Is Not Our Fear," 104. On blacks in NBA by mid-1960s, see also D. Halberstam, *Breaks of the Game,* 35–36, 180–81, 186–87.

7. Auerbach and Sann, *Red Auerbach,* 135; Berger, "Pro Basketball's Best Defenders," 30–35; McGinniss, "One Celtic's Formula," 46–47, 73–74; Larner, "Basketball," 30–38. On Larner's article, see also *Los Angeles Times,* 11 February 1966.

8. On Siegfried, see Hirshberg, "It's Larry Siegfried," 50–51, 86–87; *Boston Globe,* 13 February 1966; *Sporting News,* 23 April 1966; Larry Siegfried Interview at www.celtic-nation .com. On Nelson, see *Boston Record-American,* 27 September 1965; *Sporting News,* 4 December 1965; J. Jones, *Rebound,* 76. On Counts, see *Chicago Defender,* 1 February 1966; undated article from *Boston Record-American,* Mokray Scrapbook, December 1965–February 1966; *Boston Herald,* 15 December 1965; *Sporting News,* 14 November 1964, 5 December 1964, 15 January 1966; *Boston Globe,* 15 December 1965, 10 February 1966, 24 February 1966; Carey and McClellan, *Boston Celtics,* 18–22. On racial cliques, see Hannum, "Old Days and Changed Ways," 37. On Celtics' interracial spirit, see *Boston Herald,* 12 September 1965. Siegfried got the last roster spot in his first year, 1963. Auerbach chose him over a fine shooting guard from South Boston High School and Providence College named Ray Flynn, who overcame the setback by becoming mayor of Boston in 1984. Auerbach, *MBA Management by Auerbach,* 54–55.

9. Mel Counts, telephone interview with author, 10 January 2008; Freedman, *Dynasty,* 174; *Boston Globe,* 30 May 1999.

10. *Los Angeles Times,* 5 January 1966; *Boston Record-American,* 22 December 1965; 15 February 1966; undated article from *Boston Record-American,* Mokray Scrapbook, February–April 1966; Auerbach and Sann, *Red Auerbach,* 318–25; *Boston Globe,* 2 November 1965, 9 November 1965, 1 December 1965, 21 December 1965; *Boston Herald,* 14 September 1965, 9 November 1965, 21 December 1965.

11. *Boston Globe,* 2 November 1965, 11 November 1965, 12 November 1965, 1 February 1966; *Boston Traveler,* 23 February 1966; *Boston Herald,* 27 January 1966, 4 February 1966, 16 February 1966; *New York Post,* 14 October 1965; *Los Angeles Times,* 18 January 1966; *Sporting News,* 30 October 1965; *Chicago Defender,* 2 February 1966; *Philadelphia In-*

quirer, 22 March 1966; uncited article dated 7 February 1966, Mokray Scrapbook, February–April 1966; "Lame and the Fat," 83; Jares, "Celtics Isn't Dead Yet," 32–35; *Boston Record-American*, 8 December 1965, 4 February 1966.

12. *Boston Record-American*, 8 December 1965; M. Harris, *Lonely Heroes*, 12–14.

13. F. Katz, "Unknown Side," *Sport*, March 1966, 76, 79.

14. F. Katz, "Unknown Side," 24–26, 76–80; B. Russell, *Go Up for Glory*, 215.

15. Deford, "Bill Russell—Center," 220; Plimpton, "Gods," 228; *Boston Globe*, 21 April 1966, 21 February 1968; Plimpton, "Reflections in a Diary," 42; *Chicago Defender*, 19 February 1969.

16. Bud Collins, telephone interview with author, 20 February 2008; Tim Horgan, telephone interview with author, 21 February 2008; undated article in *Boston Record-American*, Mokray Scrapbook, March–August 1964.

17. *Boston Record-American*, 15 February 1966.

18. *Boston Globe*, 15 February 1966; *Boston Record-American*, 15 February 1966.

19. *Boston Globe*, 15 February 1966; *Boston Record-American*, 15 February 1966.

20. Hirshberg, *Bill Russell of the Boston Celtics; Seattle Times*, 22 December 1974.

21. B. Russell, *Go Up for Glory*, 11–119, 153–73. As the book approached its launch date, he claimed that lawyers forced him to exclude other, potentially libelous material. *New York Post*, 17 January 1966.

22. *San Francisco Chronicle*, 25 February 1966; B. Russell, *Go Up for Glory*, 41–44, 113–18; *Boston Globe*, 15 February 1966.

23. *Boston Globe*, 15 February 1966; undated article from *Boston Record-American*, Mokray Scrapbook, February–April 1966; B. Russell, *Go Up for Glory*, 174, 199–210. On the language and implications of civil rights versus human rights, see C. Anderson, *Eyes Off the Prize*, 1–7, 271–76.

24. *Philadelphia Inquirer*, 7 March 1966; *Boston Globe*, 15 February 1966, 22 February 1966; *Boston Herald*, 15 February 1966; *New York Times Book Review*, 20 March 1966; *Chicago Tribune*, 20 March 1966; uncited article by Bob Cousy, Mokray Scrapbook, February–April 1966; *Publishers Weekly*, 17 October 1966; *New York Post*, 23 February 1966; *Muhammad Speaks*, 15 April 1966; Gelman, "View from the Locker Room," 4.

25. R. Lapchick, *Broken Promises*, 139–41; Weisbrot, *Freedom Bound*, 196–234; David, *Growing Up Black*, 185–93; Adoff, *Black on Black*, 124–34.

26. Harry Edwards, telephone interview with author, 23 May 2007; Edwards, *Struggle that Must Be*, 1–149; Edwards, *Revolt of the Black Athlete*, 139–40.

27. Auerbach and Sann, *Red Auerbach*, 286–87; *Boston Record-American*, 5 August 1965, 7 August 1965, 13 February 1966; *Boston Globe*, 13 January 1966, 17 January 1966, 14 February 1966; *Boston Herald*, 10 January 1966, 14 February 1966; *New York Times*, 13 March 1966, 30 April 1966; *Sporting News*, 29 January 1966; G. Sullivan, *Picture History*, 71.

28. Rogin, "They All Boo When Red Sits Down," 101–2; Cope, "Last Cigar for a Last Hurrah?" 107–8; *Philadelphia Inquirer*, 14 January 1966; *Boston Globe*, 16 January 1966, 20 January 1966, 9 February 1966. On Auerbach and last season, see also *Los Angeles Times*, 22 April 1966; *New York Times*, 2 May 1966.

29. *Boston Record-American*, 13 February 1966.

30. *Sporting News*, 26 March 1966, 9 April 1966; *Boston Globe*, 4 December 1965; *Philadelphia Inquirer*, 4–6 December 1965

31. *Sporting News*, 26 February 1966; *Boston Record-American*, 3 November 1965; *New York Post*, 15 November 1965; *Philadelphia Inquirer*, 2 December 1965, 10 January 1966, 15 January 1966, 8 February 1966, 21 March 1966; *Chicago Defender*, 26 March 1966; *Philadelphia Bulletin*, 3 January 1966, 15 January 1966, 8 February 1966, 15 February 1966, 4 March 1966, 24 March 1966; *Boston Traveler*, 1 December 1965; *Los Angeles Times*, 4 January 1966; *New York Times*, 15 February 1966, 14 March 1966, 10 April 1966; *Boston Herald*, 10 January 1966, 11 January 1966; "Wilt Talks Back," 76; "Making the Giant Jolly," 64–65. Jerry West and Oscar Robertson finished second and third, respectively, in the MVP voting.

32. *Philadelphia Inquirer*, 14 December 1965, 1 April 1966; *Sporting News*, 26 February 1966, 9 April 1966; *New York Times*, 15 November 1965; *New York Post*, 21 March 1966; Shecter, "Startling Change in Wilt Chamberlain," 79; *Boston Globe*, 6 February 1966, 6 March 1966; *Boston Traveler*, 16 February 1966; 25 February 1966; *Los Angeles Times*, 9 February 1966, 15 February 1966; Walker, *Long Time Coming*, 176–77; *Philadelphia Bulletin*, 17 September 1965, 2 December 1965, 15 December 1965, 19 January 1966, 23 February 1966, 9 March 1966, 16 March 1966, 29 March 1966.

33. *Christian Science Monitor*, 6 March 1966, 15 March 1966; *Boston Herald*, 6 March 1966; *Philadelphia Inquirer*, 6–8 March 1966, 10 March 1966, 14 March 1966, 18 March 1966, 20 March 1966, 21 March 1966; *Philadelphia Bulletin*, 21 March 1966; *Boston Traveler*, 10 January 1966; *Sporting News*, 26 February 1966.

34. *Philadelphia Inquirer*, 1 February 1966.

35. Embry, *Inside Game*, 130–34; Vecsey, "Behind Oscar Robertson's Discontent," 36–39, 71; Linn, "There's No Telling How High He Can Go," 62–64; *Cincinnati Enquirer*, 21 March 1966. On Robertson, see also *Sporting News*, 13 January 1968, 14 December 1968, 15 March 1969.

36. *Cincinnati Enquirer*, 24–28 March 1966; uncited articles dated 28 March 1966 and 29 March 1966, Mokray Scrapbook, February–April 1966; Kirkpatrick, "Celtics Stretch an Era," 30–31.

37. *Cincinnati Enquirer*, 30–3 April 1966; Kirkpatrick, "Celtics Stretch an Era," 31; *Boston Herald*, 10 April 1966; *Boston Globe*, 14 April 1966.

38. Koppett, *Championship NBA*, 85–87; *Cincinnati Enquirer*, 3 April 1966; *Philadelphia Inquirer*, 3–6 April 1966.

39. *Philadelphia Inquirer*, 7 April 1966; *Philadelphia Bulletin*, 8 April 1966; uncited article dated 8 April 1966, Mokray Scrapbook, February–April 1966; *Boston Globe*, 8 April 1966. Sauldsberry had signed with Boston in November 1965. Commissioner Walter Kennedy refused to accept the contract, fearing that Sauldsberry would get arrested at an NBA arena due to existing court orders for failure to pay child support. After suing that the league had conspired to keep him from professional basketball, Sauldsberry played in thirty-nine games for the Celtics. *Boston Herald*, 23 November 1965, 25 November 1965; *New York Times*, 23 November 1965, 14 December 1965; *Boston Globe*, 24 December 1965, 25 November 1965, 1 December 1965, 25 January 1966.

40. *Philadelphia Bulletin,* 10 April 1966; *Boston Globe,* 8 April 1966, 9 April 1966, 11 April 1966; uncited article dated 8 April 1966, Mokray Scrapbook, February–April 1966.

41. *Philadelphia Inquirer,* 8 April 1966, 12 April 1966; *Philadelphia Bulletin,* 10 April 1966; *Christian Science Monitor,* 8 April 1966; *Boston Globe,* 8 April 1966; *Boston Traveler,* 8 April 1966, 9 April 1966.

42. *Philadelphia Bulletin,* 10 April 1966; "Old Math," 66.

43. *Philadelphia Inquirer,* 11 April 1966; *Boston Globe,* 11 April 1966; *New York Times,* 11 April 1966; *Boston Herald,* 11 April 1966; *Boston Traveler,* 11 April 1966.

44. *Philadelphia Bulletin,* 12–15 April 1966; *Philadelphia Inquirer,* 13 April 1966, 14 April 1966, 19 April 1966.

45. *Boston Herald,* 12–14 April 1966; *Boston Globe,* 8 April 1966, 12–14 April 1966. The thirty-three-day newspaper strike ended April 8, 1966.

46. *Boston Globe,* 17 April 1966, 28 April 1966; *Sporting News,* 25 December 1965, 15 April 1967, 25 March 1967; undated *Boston Herald* article, Mokray Scrapbook, December 1965–February 1966; *New York Post,* 10 January 1966; Deford, "Tiger Who Can Beat Anything," 45–47; Libby, "Elgin Baylor Miracle," 34–36, 82.

47. *Boston Globe,* 18 April 1966; *Boston Herald,* 17–18 April 1966.

48. *Boston Globe,* 20 June 1965, 4 January 1966, 18 January 1966, 3 February 1966, 17 February 1966, 6 January 1967; *Boston Herald,* 18 January 1966, 19 April 1966; Cousy, *Killer Instinct,* 50; Frank Ramsey, telephone interview with author, 8 May 2006; uncited article, Mokray Scrapbook, February–April 1966; Heinsohn, *Heinsohn, Don't You Ever Smile?* 153; uncited article, Mokray Scrapbook, September 1961–January 1962; *New York Post,* 8 December 1965, 2 February 1966.

49. *Boston Globe,* 19 January 1966, 19 April 1966; *Los Angeles Times,* 19 April 1966; *Chicago Tribune,* 19 April 1966; *Washington Post,* 19 April 1966; *Boston Herald,* 10 April 1966, 19 April 1966; Hannum, "I've Barely Begun to Fight," 36.

50. B. Russell, *Red and Me,* 146–47; *Washington Post,* 19 April 1966; *Boston Globe,* 18 April 1966, 1 May 1966; *Los Angeles Times,* 19 April 1966; *Chicago Tribune,* 19 April 1966; *San Francisco Chronicle,* 19 April 1966; *Philadelphia Inquirer,* 19 April 1966; Auerbach and Sann, *Red Auerbach,* 351–53. Preceding Russell, John McClendon coached the Cleveland Pipers of the short-lived ABL in 1961. M. Katz, *Breaking Through,* 134–47.

51. *Boston Globe,* 19 April 1966.

52. "Where the Negro Goes from Here in Sports," 56; *Los Angeles Sentinel,* 21 April 1966, 28 April 1966; *New York Amsterdam News,* 23 April, 1966; *Chicago Defender,* 19 April 1966, 20 April 1966, 25 April 1966, 2 May 1966, 14 May 1966, 19 May 1966, 31 December 1966; *Baltimore Afro-American,* 26 April 1966, 3 May 1966, 27 August 1966; *Muhammad Speaks,* 29 April 1966.

53. "All the Credentials," 104–6; "Coach Russell," 72–73; *Sporting News,* 30 April 1966; "Where the Negro Goes from Here in Sports," 56–59, 87–88; *Boston Herald,* 19 April 1966; *Boston Globe,* 19 April 1966, 22 April 1966; *Los Angeles Times,* 19 April 1966; *Washington Post,* 3 May 1966; *New York Times,* 19 April 1966, 20 April 1966. Bud Collins cheekily opened his column: "Bill Russell made history Monday. He became the first bearded man ever to coach or manage a major league team." *Boston Globe,* 19 April 1966.

54. *Los Angeles Times,* 22 April 1966; *Boston Herald,* 19 April 1966; *Boston Globe,* 19 April 1966, 22 April 1966. "Why does a guy like you grow a goatee and wear caped clothes," an acquaintance asked Russell. He responded, "What do you want me to do—look like just any other seven-foot guy?" *Boston Globe,* 24 January 1967.

55. *Boston Globe,* 18 April 1966; *Boston Herald,* 20 April 1966.

56. *Boston Globe,* 20–23 April 1966; *Boston Herald,* 20–23 April 1966; *Sporting News,* 22 October 1966; *Los Angeles Times,* 22 April 1966.

57. *Boston Globe,* 25–27 April 1966; *Boston Herald,* 25–28 April 1966.

58. *Boston Globe,* 25 April 1966, 27 April 1966, 28 April 1966; Deford, "Some Old Pros Refuse to Die," 32. With Havlicek starting and playing forty-eight minutes in close games, Willie Naulls was barely getting on the court, and he planned retirement at season's end. Mel Counts was only getting spot duty behind Russell. *Boston Globe,* 16 April 1966.

59. Auerbach and Sann, *Red Auerbach,* 358–59; *Boston Herald,* 29 April 1966; *Boston Globe,* 17 April 1966, 29 April 1966; "One Last Smoke"; *Sporting News,* 14 May 1966.

60. Carey, *High Above Courtside,* 162–63; West, *Mr. Clutch,* 183; "One Last Smoke," 54; Deford, "Some Old Pros Refuse to Die," 32; *Boston Herald,* 29 April 1966; *Boston Globe,* 29 April 1966.

61. *Boston Herald,* 29 April 1966; *Boston Globe,* 29 April 1966.

62. *Boston Globe,* 29 April 1966, 30 April 1966; *Sporting News,* 11 March 1967; *Boston Herald,* 29 April 1966.

63. *Boston Globe,* 19 April 1966.

13. BOSTON IS DEAD

1. *Washington Post,* 1–3 June 1966; *New York Times,* 2 June 1966, 3 June 1966; Branch, *At Canaan's Edge,* 470–73. Floyd McKissick of CORE called the discussion-only format "rigged," prompting an abrupt change to allow voting and the drafting of resolutions.

2. *Baltimore Afro-American,* 4 June 1966; *Los Angeles Sentinel,* 9 June 1966; *Chicago Defender,* 18 June 1966; Lantz, "Righteous Anger Need Not Be Silenced," 18–19; *Chicago Daily News,* 7 June 1977.

3. *Bay State Banner,* 2 July 1966; J. Smith, "Boston," 63–66; Formisano, *Boston Against Busing,* 40–47.

4. *Boston Herald,* 17 June 1966, 19 June 1966; *Boston Globe,* 17 June 1966; *Bay State Banner,* 25 June 1966.

5. *Bay State Banner,* 2 July 1966; *Boston Herald,* 18–21 June 1966; *Boston Globe,* 18–21 June 1966. On Meredith March, see Branch, *At Canaan's Edge,* 475–95; Joseph, *Waiting 'Til the Midnight Hour,* 132–47.

6. *Boston Globe,* 22 June 1966, 23 June 1966; *Bay State Banner,* 2 July 1966.

7. *Los Angeles Times,* 29 July 1966; *Bay State Banner,* 2 July 1966; Lukas, *Common Ground,* 496–97; Mel King, telephone interview with author, 25 January 2008. Russell also explored business interests such as a middle-income housing development in the South End. *Boston Globe,* 19 April 1966.

8. *Boston Globe,* 10 November 1966.

344   NOTES TO PAGES 196-199

9. Embry, *Inside Game*, 147–48; B. Russell, *Russell Rules*, 75–76.

10. "Scouting Reports," 24 October 1966, 51; *Sporting News*, 22 October 1966; *Chicago Defender*, 22 October 1966, Embry, *Inside Game*, 149–50.

11. *Chicago Defender*, 23 January 1967. Young also criticized a John Peterson article in the *National Observer* that kept referencing Russell's race. See *National Observer*, 7 November 1966; *Chicago Defender*, 10 November 1966.

12. Bailey Howell interview at www.celtic-nation.com/; *Chicago Defender*, 13 September 1966; *Boston Globe*, 4 November 1966; *Sporting News*, 26 March 1966, 18 March 1967; Zanger, "Better-Late-Than-Never Celtic," 56–59, 81–83; Bailey Howell, telephone interview with author, 25 January 2008.

13. *National Observer*, 7 November 1966; Embry, *Inside Game*, 138–42; *Los Angeles Times*, 16 September 1966, 12 October 1966; *Boston Globe*, 8 May 1992; *Chicago Defender*, 28 October 1967; Wayne Embry Interview at www.celtic-nation.com/.

14. *Boston Globe*, 29 November 1966; Embry, *Inside Game*, 144–45.

15. *Los Angeles Times*, 15 December 1974; Carey and McClellan, *Boston Celtics*, 100–101; Embry, *Inside Game*, 143–44.

16. Larry Siegfried, telephone interview with the author, 25 January 2008; Larry Siegfried Interview at www.celtic-nation.com/; Tom "Satch" Sanders, telephone interview with author, 25 August 2008; Leigh Montville, telephone interview with author, 5 August 2008; *Washington Post*, 13 September 1966; *National Observer*, 7 November 1966; "New Role for Bill Russell," 60.

17. *Boston Globe*, 1 November 1966, 1 December 1966; Embry, *Inside Game*, 141; Shaughnessy, *Seeing Red*, 174–75.

18. *Chicago Tribune*, 20 January 1967; Russell and Branch, *Second Wind*, 203–5; *Sporting News*, 17 December 1966; Bailey Howell interview.

19. Undated article from *Boston Record-American*, Mokray Scrapbook, 1966–67 Season; Vecsey, "Bill Russell's Most Trying Season," 40–41; "For All the Marbles"; *Boston Traveler*, 16 January 1967; *Boston Globe*, 16 January 1967, 26 January 1967. Jones echoed those comments in a television interview after the season. *Washington Post*, 27 May 1967; *Springfield Union*, 31 May 1967.

20. *Bay State Banner*, 22 October 1966; *National Observer*, 7 November 1966.

21. *Boston Herald*, 12 January 1967; *Boston Globe*, 10 November 1966, 2 December 1966, 20 December 1966, 9 January 1967, 25 January 1967, 5 February 1967, 21 February 1967, 26 February 1967, 23 March 1967, 26 November 1967; *Boston Traveler*, 15 January 1967, 18 January 1967; *Philadelphia Inquirer*, 15 January 1967; *Philadelphia Bulletin*, 25 January 1967; *Sporting News*, 17 December 1966; Embry, *Inside Game*, 145–46, 153.

22. *Boston Herald*, 17 January 1967; *Boston Globe*, 17 January 1967, 22 January 1967; Bailey Howell interview.

23. G. Sullivan, *Picture History*, 74; *Baltimore Afro-American*, 18 October 1966; *Chicago Defender*, 19 November 1966, 25 January 1967; *New York Post*, 28 December 1966, 4 January 1967; *Boston Record-American*, 10 January 1967, 12 January 1967; *Boston Traveler*, 10 January 1967; *Boston Herald*, 8–11 January 1967, 24 January 1967; *Boston Globe*, 5 January 1967, 11 January 1967, 23 January 1967, 24 January 1967; Undated article from *Boston Globe*, Mokray Scrapbook, 1966–67 Season; *Philadelphia Bulletin*, 11 January 1967, 12 January 1967.

On Auerbach's memoir, see Auerbach and Sann, *Red Auerbach;* five uncited articles in Mokray Scrapbook, 1966–67 Season; *Boston Herald,* 10 January 1967; *Boston Globe,* 11 January 1967, 18 January 1967; *Sporting News,* 14 January 1967. Dolph Schayes had coached the team with the best record in the East during the 1965–66 season, earning him the right to coach the 1967 All-Star Game. But Schayes got fired, and the league asked Auerbach to coach. Chamberlain complained that Philadelphia deserved to pick the All-Star coach, and he intimated that he might rest his sore Achilles' tendon anyway. Chamberlain did finally consent to playing for Auerbach in the All-Star Game. For old times' sake, Auerbach got ejected.

24. *Boston Globe,* 26 January 1967; undated article in *Boston Record-American,* Mokray Scrapbook, 1966–67 Season; Vecsey, "Bill Russell's Most Trying Season," 38–39.

25. Shecter, "Startling Change in Wilt Chamberlain," 74–80; *Los Angeles Times,* 17 March 1967; *Philadelphia Bulletin,* 30 October 1966, 5 November 1966, 28 January 1967, 1 March 1967; *Boston Globe,* 11 December 1966.

26. *Philadelphia Bulletin,* 12 October 1966, 13 December 1966; Chamberlain and Shaw, *Wilt,* 176–79; Deford, "Sarge Takes Philly to the Top," 8–13; *New York Times,* 23 September 1966; "Nose to Chin Whiskers"; "Spirited 76ers," 88; Pluto, *Tall Tales,* 319–23. Hannum fined Chamberlain $1,050 for a seven-day preseason holdout. He also challenged Chamberlain during a heated locker-room argument.

27. *Sporting News,* 24 December 1966; *Philadelphia Bulletin,* 28 December 1966; *Philadelphia Inquirer,* 30 October 1966, 6 November 1966, 12 December 1966, 21 December 1966, 29 December 1966, 16 January 1967, 25 January 1967, 13 February 1967, 14 February 1967, 9 March 1967, 12 March 1967, 19 March 1967; *Boston Herald,* 16 January 1967, 25 January 1967, 13 February 1967, 9 March 1967; *Boston Globe,* 30 October 1966, 6 November 1966, 18 November 1966, 19 November 1966, 12 December 1966, 29 December 1966, 16 January 1967, 25 January 1967, 14 February 1967, 9 March 1967, 12 March 1967. For an in-depth portrait of Philadelphia's season, see Lynch, *Season of the 76ers.*

28. *Sporting News,* 8 April 1967; *Boston Globe,* 3 February 1967, 28 February 1967, 8 March 1967, 30 March 1967; *Boston Herald,* 23 March 1967; *Los Angeles Times,* 17 February 1967; *New York Times,* 23 March 1967, 30 March 1967; *Chicago Defender,* 21 March 1967, 20 November 1967.

29. *New York Times,* 25 June 1965, 17 August 1968, 13 August 1969; *Boston Record-American,* 28 June 1965; *Boston Globe,* 4 July 1965; J. Fitzgerald, *That Championship Feeling,* 168–69.

30. *Boston Record-American,* 30 December 1965; *Boston Globe,* 17 April 1965; *Wall Street Journal,* 29 March 1966; *Sporting News,* 29 January 1966, 6 May 1967; *Philadelphia Inquirer,* 21 April 1967; Auerbach and Fitzgerald, *Red Auerbach,* 308–10; Embry, *Inside Game,* 152.

31. T. Murray, "Coming Boom in Pro Basketball," 52–53, 115–19; *New York Times,* 28 January 1966, 22 November 1966, 21 December 1966; *Christian Science Monitor,* 8 March 1966, 10 January 1967; *Boston Herald,* 17 February 1967; *Sporting News,* 27 November 1965, 12 February 1966, 26 March 1966, 3 December 1966.

32. Sugar, " Thrill of Victory," 122–23; Roberts and Olson, *Winning Is the Only Thing,* 113–20; Rader, *In Its Own Image,* 83–99, 125–26; D. Halberstam, *Breaks of the Game,* 240–45; Jay, *More than Just A Game,* 81, 91–93; Chandler, *Television and National Sport,* 1–23, 110–11; Fortunato, "Ultimate Assist," 12–70, 73.

33. Arledge, *Roone*, 82–83; Kornheiser, "Bill Russell," 179–80; Sugar, *"Thrill of Victory,"* 122.

34. Pluto, *Loose Balls*, 39–44; uncited article dated 2 February 1967, Mokray Scrapbook, 1966–67 Season; *Philadelphia Inquirer*, 2 February 1967, 9 February 1967; *Philadelphia Bulletin*, 18 January 1967, 2 February 1967, 8 February 1967, 9 May 1967, 18 June 1967; *Philadelphia Inquirer*, 9 February 1967; *Boston Herald*, 22 February 1967, 13 April 1967; *Boston Globe*, 5 April 1967; *Sporting News*, 4 March 1967, 15 April 1967, 20 May 1967. On Mikan as NBA commissioner, see Schumacher, *Mr. Basketball*, 252–59. On AFL and NFL merger, see Mac-Cambridge, *America's Game*, 193–94, 200–201, 216–30. The ABA also held its college draft one month before the NBA. The Detroit Pistons and Baltimore Bullets had to sign top picks Jimmy Walker and Earl Monroe one day before the NBA's official draft.

35. *Boston Herald*, 23 January 1967, 27 January 1967, 28 January 1967; *Boston Globe*, 11 January 1967, 2 March 1967; undated article in *Patriot Ledger*, Mokray Scrapbook, February–April 1966; DeBusschere, *Open Man*, 83, 104–5. Los Angeles forward Rudy LaRusso got suspended after rejecting a January 1967 trade to Detroit, citing "the personal dignity of the athlete."

36. Koppett, *Essence of the Game*, 152–60; Bradley, *Life on the Run*, 142–48; D. Halberstam, *Breaks of the Game*, 344–47; Robertson, *Big O*, 191–214.

37. *Sporting News*, 11 March 1967, 25 March 1967; *Boston Herald*, 11 January 1967, 1 March 1967; *Boston Globe*, 1 March 1967; *New York Times*, 1 March 1967.

38. *Boston Herald*, 2 March 1967, 4 March 1967, 5 March 1967, 14 March 1967; *Boston Globe*, 2 March 1967, 4 March 1967, 8 March 1967, 11 March 1967, 13 March 1967, 15 March 1967; *Philadelphia Inquirer*, 11 March 1967, 14 March 1967, 15 March 1967, 17 March 1967; *New York Times*, 11 March 1967, 14 March 1967, 15 March 1967.

39. *Boston Herald*, 2 March 1967, 15 March 1967; *Boston Globe*, 15 March 1967.

40. *Philadelphia Inquirer*, 22 January 1967, 25 January 1967; *Boston Globe*, 22 February 1967, 12 March 1967, 21 March 1967; *Boston Herald*, 21 March 1967, 23 March 1967, 24 March 1967.

41. *Boston Globe*, 22 March 1967, 26–29 March 1967; *Boston Herald*, 22 March 1967, 26–29 March 1967; J. Fitzgerald, *That Championship Feeling*, 174–75.

42. *Boston Herald*, 30–31 March 1967; *Boston Globe*, 30 March 1967, 31 March 1967; *Philadelphia Bulletin*, 25 March 1967; *Philadelphia Inquirer*, 22–27 March 1967, 31 March 1967.

43. *Boston Herald*, 1 April 1967; *Boston Globe*, 1 April 1967, 4 April 1967; *Philadelphia Inquirer*, 1 April 1967.

44. *Boston Globe*, 2 April 1967; *Philadelphia Inquirer*, 2 April 1967; *Philadelphia Bulletin*, 3 April 1967; Lynch, *Season of the 76ers*, 130–31.

45. *Boston Herald*, 3 April 1967, 4 April 1967; *Boston Globe*, 4 April 1967; *Philadelphia Inquirer*, 3 April 1967; *Philadelphia Bulletin*, 3 April 1967.

46. *Philadelphia Inquirer*, 3 April 1967; *Boston Globe*, 3 April 1967; Deford, "New Spirit of the 76ers," 31.

47. *Boston Globe*, 6 April 1967; *Philadelphia Inquirer*, 6 April 1967, 7 April 1967; *Philadelphia Bulletin*, 6 April 1967, 9 April 1967; *Boston Herald*, 6 April 1967, 7 April 1967.

48. *Philadelphia Inquirer,* 10 April 1967, 11 April 1967; *Boston Globe,* 9 April 1967, 10 April 1967; *Boston Herald,* 10 April 1967. A broadcast of this game is available for public viewing at the Museum of Television and Radio, New York City.

49. *Boston Globe,* 12 April 1967; *Boston Herald,* 11 April 1967, 12 April 1967; *Philadelphia Inquirer,* 12 April 1967; *Philadelphia Bulletin,* 12 April 1967; Deford, "Fans Get the Booby Prize," 28–31; *New York Times,* 13 April 1967.

50. *New York Times,* 13 April 1967; Lynch, *Season of the 76ers,* 136–41. On 1967 NBA titles, see Deford, "Waiting Made It Sweeter," 54–56. *Philadelphia Inquirer,* 17–26 April 1967; *Philadelphia Bulletin,* 17–26 April 1967.

51. *Sporting News,* 8 January 1968; *Boston Globe,* 9 April 1967; Larner, "Just Too Much Giant," 82–88. See also Chamberlain and Shaw, *Wilt,* 182–84.

52. W. Russell, "Success Is a Journey," 85; Pluto, *Tall Tales,* 290; *Los Angeles Times,* 12 April 1967; *Boston Globe,* 13 April 1967; *Boston Herald,* 13 April 1967.

53. K. C. Jones, *Rebound,* 101–2; *Boston Record-American,* 6 December 1965; *Sporting News,* 11 March 1967; Heinsohn, *Heinsohn, Don't You Ever Smile?* 151; *Boston Herald,* 28 April 1965, 5 March 1967, 6 March 1967; *Boston Globe,* 7 December 1965, 6 March 1967.

54. Deford, "Fans Get the Booby Prize."

55. "Where the Negro Goes From Here in Sports," 88; B. Russell, *Go Up for Glory,* 199–200.

56. *New York Times,* 24 January 1967, 24 August 1967; *Chicago Tribune,* 24 January 1967; *Baltimore Afro-American,* 28 January 1967; *New York Amsterdam News,* 28 January 1967; *Bay State Banner,* 5 October 1967. See also Russell and Branch, *Second Wind,* 191–92.

57. Maule, "Curtain Falls on a Long Run," 18–24; *Chicago Defender,* 16 February 1967, 12 June 1968; Freeman, *Jim Brown,* 144–45, 175; Jim Brown, *Out of Bounds,* 96–99; John Wooten, telephone interview with author, 20 February 2008.

58. John Wooten interview; *Los Angeles Sentinel,* 9 February 1967, 29 May 1969; *New York Amsterdam News,* 24 June 1967, 14 December 1968; *Chicago Defender,* 3 August 1966, 4 February 1967, 28 February 1970. See also Toback, *Jim,* 18–23, 51–57.

59. Hauser, *Muhammad Ali,* 165–77; Wiggins, "Victory for Allah," 93–102; Maureen Smith, "Identity and Citizenship," 157–90. On Ali's ambiguities and contradictions, see also Olsen, *Black Is Best;* Zang, *Sportswars,* 96–118. On athletes and Islam, see also Baker, *Playing with God,* 218–39.

60. *Chicago Tribune,* 3 June 1967; *Washington Post,* 3 June 1967; *Los Angeles Times,* 26 April 1967; *New York Times,* 13 June 1967; John Wooten interview; *Los Angeles Sentinel,* 15 June 1967. Herbert Muhammad, the son of Nation of Islam leader Elijah Muhammad, did ask Brown for help. Herbert wanted Ali to accept a noncombat role and retain his title, but he wanted Brown to float the compromise proposal. When Brown ate dinner with Ali the night before the other athletes arrived, he realized the futility of that approach. Jim Brown, *Out of Bounds,* 291–92; Hauser, *Muhammad Ali,* 177–78.

61. *Chicago Tribune,* 5 June 1967; *Washington Post,* 5 June 1967; *Los Angeles Times,* 5 June 1967; John Wooten interview; Jim Brown, *Out of Bounds,* 292–93; *Chicago Defender,* 5 June 1967; *New York Amsterdam News,* 10 June 1967.

62. *New York Amsterdam News*, 10 June 1967, 24 June 1967; *Muhammad Speaks*, 16 June 1967; *Chicago Defender*, 5 June 1967, 26 June 1967.

63. B. Russell, "I Am Not Worried About Ali," 18–20. See also B. Russell, *Russell Rules*, 143; *Philadelphia Inquirer*, 8 March 1968.

64. B. Russell, "I Am Not Worried About Ali," 20–21.

65. Hauser, *Muhammad Ali*, 178–79.

14. THE LIGHTHOUSE

1. Russell and Branch, *Second Wind*, 46–48.

2. Plimpton, "Reflections in a Diary," 44; Pluto, *Tall Tales*, 362; *Boston Globe*, 7 April 1968.

3. *Boston Globe*, 12 December 1967, 23 December 1967, 21 February 1968; *Chicago Tribune*, 12 December 1967; *Los Angeles Times*, 12 December 1967; *Sporting News*, 30 December 1967; Plimpton, "Reflections in a Diary," 42–43. Auerbach hoped to draft a replacement for Russell. "He's got to quit sometime," said the general manager. "When it'll be is entirely up to him. Personally, I think he'll play next year, but circumstances might be such at the end of this season that he'll quit then. I just don't know." *Boston Herald Traveler*, 3 March 1968.

4. *Chicago Defender*, 28 February 1968; *Boston Herald Traveler*, 4 January 1968, 6 January 1968, 12 February 1968; *Boston Globe*, 29 January 1968, 11 February 1968. During one frustrating stretch, Russell even fined trainer Joe DeLauri $30 for arriving late at practice. *Washington Post*, 17 December 1967.

5. *Boston Globe*, 14 November 1967, 16 November 1967, 1 December 1967, 13 February 1968, 20 February 1968; *Boston Herald Traveler*, 13 February 1968, 20 February 1968; *Chicago Tribune*, 16 November 1967, 28 November 1967; Bailey Howell Interview at www.celtic-nation.com/; Auerbach, *MBA Management by Auerbach*, 68.

6. *Sporting News*, 21 October 1967; *Philadelphia Inquirer*, 19 November 1967, 15 December 1967, 30 December 1967, 4 March 1968, 9 March 1968; *Boston Herald Traveler*, 29 January 1968, 30 January 1968, 6 February 1968; *Philadelphia Bulletin*, 31 January 1968; *Boston Globe*, 20 November 1967, 15 December 1967, 30 December 1967, 2 January 1968, 8 January 1968, 20 January 1968, 28 January 1968, 30 January 1968, 31 January 1968, 3 March 1968, 4 March 1968.

7. *Boston Herald Traveler*, 3 January 1968, 11 March 1968, 20 March 1968; *Boston Globe*, 9 January 1968, 5 March 1968, 18 March 1968, 20 March 1968; DeBusschere, *Open Man*, 58, 87; *Sporting News*, 30 March 1968; *Philadelphia Bulletin*, 31 January 1968.

8. Hano, "On the Road with Wilt and the 76ers," 73; Shecter, "Startling Change," 78; *Boston Globe*, 14 February 1967; *Philadelphia Bulletin*, 3 April 1966, 6 January 1967, 14 February 1967, 15 February 1967, 14 March 1967, 28 June 1967, 12 September 1967, 19 October 1967, 8 January 1968, 21 April 1968; *Washington Post*, 21 July 1968; *Los Angeles Times*, 12 January 1967; *Philadelphia Inquirer*, 15 March 1968; "People," *Sports Illustrated*, 17 June 1968, 57; Chamberlain and Shaw, *Wilt*, 158, 172, 240–47, 255–66; Michelson, "Confessions of a Basketball Groupie," 165–66, 318–20. Chamberlain defied many of the taboos on black men dating white women. His girlfriends included the blonde actress Kim Novak, whom

he dated while living in San Francisco. See Meschery, *Caught in the Pivot,* 39; Jim Brown, *Out of Bounds,* 188–89, 273–74.

9. *Philadelphia Bulletin,* 14 June 1967, 11 July 1967, 4 August 1967, 28 August 1967, 14 September 1967, 22 September 1967, 12 October 1967; *Philadelphia Inquirer,* 6 August 1967, 11 October 1967, 12 October 1967; Chamberlain and Shaw, *Wilt,* 184–87. Chamberlain held out after getting frustrated by owner Irv Kosloff's refusal to uphold his handshake deal with the deceased Ike Richman for part-ownership. Chamberlain also believed that his deal with Kosloff, despite a contract that included the NBA's standard reserve clause, freed him from contractual obligation the following season, allowing him to join the ABA or the Globetrotters.

10. "Chamberlain and Shaw, *Wilt,* 187; "Shoot, Wilt,"45; *Los Angeles Times,* 8 November 1967; *Philadelphia Inquirer,* 5 November 1967, 2 December 1967, 17 December 1967; *Philadelphia Bulletin,* 8 November 1967, 2 December 1967, 6 December 1967; Staff of the Philadelphia Daily News, *Philly Hoops,* 34–35; *New York Times,* 27 March 1968. Chamberlain also registered the first-ever "triple-double-double" with twenty-two points, twenty-five rebounds, and twenty-one assists in February against Detroit.

11. *Philadelphia Inquirer,* 24 January 1968; *Sporting News,* 6 January 1968, 24 February 1968; Hano, "On the Road with Wilt and the 76ers," 71–73; *Philadelphia Bulletin,* 24 November 1967, 1 December 1967, 14 March 1968, 20 March 1968, 7 April 1968, 30 April 1968.

12. *Philadelphia Inquirer,* 17 October 1967, 7 December 1967, 2 March 1968, 3 March 1968, 11 March 1968, 19 March 1968, 24 March 1968, 28–31 March 1968.

13. Dave Bing, telephone interview with author, 19 August 2008.

14. *Boston Globe,* 21–24 March 1968, 27 March 1968; *Boston Herald Traveler,* 22–26 March 1968.

15. *Boston Globe,* 26 March 1968, 28 March 1968; *Boston Herald Traveler,* 26 March 1968, 28 March 1968.

16. Dave Bing interview; *Boston Globe,* 29 March 1968; *Boston Herald Traveler,* 29 March 1968; Devaney, "What Makes Havlicek Run," 64–71; Grenier, *Don't They Ever Stop Running?* 141–44; *Sporting News,* 27 April 1968.

17. *Boston Globe,* 31 March–2 April 1968, 27 March 1968; *Boston Herald,* 30 March–2 April 1968.

18. Deford, "Push Comes to Shove," 34.

19. See Van DeBurg, "Villains, Demons, and Social Bandits," 197–210; Martin, *No Coward Soldiers;* Van DeBurg, *New Day in Babylon;* Ogbar, *Black Power;* Joseph, *Waiting 'Til the Midnight Hour.* In his classic *Soul on Ice,* Eldridge Cleaver lumps athletes and entertainers with a too-compliant black leadership as "puppets and lackeys of the white power structure." He interprets Muhammad Ali as a challenge to this tradition, calling the boxer "the first 'free' black champion ever to confront white America." Cleaver, *Soul on Ice,* 84–96.

20. Hano, "Black Rebel Who 'Whitelists' the Olympics," 32–33, 39–50; Edwards, *Struggle that Must Be,* 150–73; Edwards, *Revolt of the Black Athlete,* 1–29. See also Lomax, "Bedazzle Them with Brilliance," 55–89. For a case study on the complexities of the black revolt and college basketball, see the example of Charlie Scott at the University of North Carolina in Kaliss, "Un-Civil Discourse"; Kaliss, "Everyone's All-American," 295–366.

21. Edwards, *Revolt of the Black Athlete,* 38–65; Bass, *Not the Triumph but the Struggle,* 80–99, 145–57; Hartmann, *Race, Culture, and the Revolt of the Black Athlete,* 29–132. Re-

garding Brundage's racial attitudes, the IOC chairman proclaimed, "I think there should be a qualified Negro on the USOC Board. I think Jesse Owens is a fine boy." Owens was fifty-seven at the time. "Should Negroes Boycott the Olympics?" 112.

22. *Los Angeles Times*, 24–29 March 1968; "Olympic Jolt," 20–27; "Should Negroes Boycott the Olympics?" 110–16; Tommie Smith, "Why Negroes Should Boycott," 40–41, 68; Boston, "Why They Should Not," 42–43, 68–69; Edwards, "Why Negroes Should Boycott Whitey's Olympics," 6–10; "Should Negroes Boycott the Olympics?" 110–16. See also Owens, *Blackthink*, 75–78; R. Johnson, *Best that I Can Be*, 188–90; *Sporting News*, 1 November 1969.

23. Edwards, *Struggle that Must Be*, 176–79; *Boston Globe*, 29 November 1967; *Philadelphia Inquirer*, 18 February 1968; *Chicago Tribune*, 25 November 1967

24. *Chicago Tribune*, 25 November 1967; Edwards, *Revolt of the Black Athlete*, 119–20. See *Chicago Tribune*, 30 November 1967, for a letter to the editor in response to the *Tribune* editorial.

25. Harry Edwards, telephone interview with author, 23 May 2007.

26. Edwards, *Revolt of the Black Athlete*, 72; *Los Angeles Times*, 1 December 1967; *New York Amsterdam News*, 3 February 1968; *New York Post*, 16 February 1968; *Chicago Defender*, 2 December 1967. When high jumper John Thomas considered participating in the NYAC meet, Russell called him "naïve, terribly naïve." *New York Post*, 16 February 1968. Tommie Smith had announced that Russell and Chamberlain would attend an initial organizing meeting during Thanksgiving in 1967, but they had an NBA game that day. *Washington Post*, 10 November 1967.

27. *Chicago Defender*, 6 December 1967; Hano, "Black Rebel Who 'Whitelists' The Olympics," 32, 39.

28. See Branch, *At Canaan's Edge*, 683–766; Honey, *Going Down Jericho Road*, 335–482.

29. *Boston Globe*, 6 April 1968; *Philadelphia Inquirer*, 7 April 1968, 11 April 1968; Walker, *Long Time Coming*, 196–98.

30. *Boston Herald Traveler*, 6 April 1968; *Boston Globe*, 6 April 1968; *Philadelphia Inquirer*, 6 April 1968, 7 April 1968; Walker, *Long Time Coming*, 198–99.

31. *Philadelphia Inquirer*, 6 April 1968, 7 April 1968, 11 April 1968; *Boston Globe*, 6 April 1968; *Boston Herald-Traveler*, 6 April 1968.

32. *Boston Herald-Traveler*, 7 April 1968; *Boston Globe*, 10 April 1968; *Philadelphia Bulletin*, 8 April 1968; *Philadelphia Inquirer*, 9 April 1968, 10 April 1968; *New York Times*, 9 April 1968; *Los Angeles Sentinel*, 11 April 1968; Joseph, *Waiting 'Til the Midnight Hour*, 174–91, 226–28.

33. *Philadelphia Inquirer*, 7 April 1968; *Boston Globe*, 8 April 1968.

34. *Report of the National Advisory Commission on Civil Disorders*; *Philadelphia Inquirer*, 6 April 1968; *Boston Globe*, 8 April 1968.

35. *Boston Globe*, 11–14 April 1968; *Philadelphia Inquirer*, 11–14 April 1968; *Boston Herald Traveler*, 11 April 1968, 13 April 1968.

36. *Boston Globe*, 15 April 1968; *Philadelphia Inquirer*, 15 April 1968; *Boston Herald Traveler*, 15 April 1968. Adding insult to injury, Russell left Boston Garden after the loss and found his license plate stolen.

37. *Boston Garden*, 15 April 1968; *Sporting News*, 4 May 1968; *NBA Dynasty Series—The Boston Celtics*.

38. Bailey Howell, telephone interview with author, 25 January 2008; Havlicek and Ryan, *Hondo*, 104; Havlicek, "Behind the Celtics' Startling Comeback," 64; *Philadelphia Inquirer*, 16 April 1968, 17 April 1968; *Boston Globe*, 16 April 1968, 19 April 1968; *Boston Herald*, 16 April 1968; Carey, *High Above Courtside*, 165.

39. Carey, *High Above Courtside*, 165–66; G. Sullivan, *Picture History*, 78; *Boston Herald Traveler*, 18 April 1968; *Philadelphia Inquirer*, 18 April 1968; Havlicek, "Behind the Celtics' Startling Comeback," 64.

40. Deford, "Two Seconds Stretch for First," 25–26; *Philadelphia Inquirer*, 19 April 1968, 21 April 1968; *Boston Herald Traveler*, 19 April 1968. Reflecting Boston's confidence, just before the Celtics ran out to begin warm-ups, Bailey Howell broke the nervous energy by turning around and asking, "This may be out of line, Russ, but can I guard Baylor in L.A.?" J. Fitzgerald, *That Championship Feeling*, 184.

41. *Philadelphia Inquirer*, 20 April 1968, 21 April 1968; *Sporting News*, 11 May 1968; *Boston Herald Traveler*, 19 April 1968, 20 April 1968, 24 April 1968; B. Russell, *Russell Rules*, 191–92.

42. *Boston Herald Traveler*, 21 April 1968, 26 April 1968; Embry, *Inside Game*, 161–62; *Philadelphia Inquirer*, 20 April 1968, 7 May 1968; *Philadelphia Bulletin*, 25 April 1968; Chamberlain, *Who's Running the Asylum?* 155–56.

43. *Philadelphia Inquirer*, 20 April 1968, 21 April 1968; *Chicago Defender*, 30 April 1968; *Los Angeles Times*, 22 April 1968; *Washington Post*, 28 April 1968; Deford, "Two Seconds Stretch for First," 27; *Boston Globe*, 20 April 1968, 24 April 1968.

44. *Boston Herald Traveler*, 24 April 1968. During that January's All-Star Game, Russell caused a stir by refusing to sign a game ball for the Basketball Hall of Fame, unlike the other twenty-three players. He later relented to signing the All-Star Game ball after Auerbach's pleading. *Boston Herald Traveler*, 18 February 1968; *Boston Globe*, 21 February 1968.

45. *Philadelphia Inquirer*, 8 March 1968; *Boston Globe*, 21 April 1968, 3 November 1968, 7 November 1968. On Bobby Orr, see R. Roberts, "Number 4 Is the One," 273–92; R. Johnson, *Century of Boston Sports*, 178–80, 190–91. Though Russell remained an outsider in Boston's sports culture, he remained the center of a black sports fraternity. During the 1967 World Series, for instance, he invited visiting black stars from the St. Louis Cardinals such as Bob Gibson and Lou Brock to his home in Reading. John Hollingsworth, telephone interview with the author, 10 October 2007.

46. *Boston Globe*, 21 April 1968.

47. Jares, "Tiger in the House of Ivy," 20–23; Olsen, "Hedonist Prophet of the Spartan Game," 28–38, 58–61; *Sporting News*, 13 March 1967, 23 March 1968; West, *Mr. Clutch*, 187–91.

48. Deford, "Two Seconds Stretch for First," 26–27; *Boston Globe*, 22–26 April 1968; *Boston Herald-Traveler*, 22 April 1968, 23 April 1968, 25 April 1968.

49. *Los Angeles Times*, 27 April 1968; *Boston Herald Traveler*, 27 April 1968, 29 April 1968, 30 April 1968; *Bay State Banner*, 2 May 1968; *Boston Globe*, 27–30 April 1968.

50. *Boston Globe*, 1 May 1968, 2 May 1968; *Boston Herald Traveler*, 1 May 1968, 2 May 1968; West, *Mr. Clutch*, 197–98; Havlicek, "Behind the Celtics' Startling Comeback," 64.

51. *Boston Globe*, 3 May 1968, 4 May 1968; *Boston Herald Traveler*, 3 May 1968; *New York Times*, 3 May 1968; *Bay State Banner*, 9 May 1968; *Los Angeles Sentinel*, 25 April 1968;

Chicago Defender, 12 April 1969; *Sporting News,* 18 May 1968. In 1948, Lou Boudreau player-managed the Cleveland Indians to a World Series victory, and Buddy Jeannette player-coached the Baltimore Bullets to the BAA title.

52. West, *Mr. Clutch,* 198–200; Heisler, *Madmen's Ball,* 15–16; "Effortless Age," 59; *Boston Globe,* 23 May 1968

53. *Boston Globe,* 5 May 1968; Embry, *Inside Game,* 164; Plimpton, "Reflections in a Diary," 44.

54. Deford, "This One Was Worth Shouting About," 34.

55. *Sporting News,* 2 November 1968; Hartmann, *Race, Culture, and the Revolt of the Black Athlete,* 3–26, 150–66; Bass, *Not the Triumph but the Struggle,* 227–89; Maureen Smith, "Identity and Citizenship," 233–59; Tommie Smith, *Silent Gesture,* 20–41; Carlos, *Why?* 171–212.

56. Wiggins, *Glory Bound,* 216–17; Maureen Smith, "Identity and Citizenship," 192–232; Edwards, *Revolt of the Black Athlete,* 104–14; *New York Times,* 9 February 1968, 12 April 1968; "Angry Black Athlete," 56–60. On impact of boycott movement, see also H. Lawson, "Physical Education and Sport in the Black Community," 187–89; Izenberg, *How Many Miles to Camelot?* 15–21; Koppett, *Sports Illusion, Sports Reality,* 197–206.

57. Olsen, "Cruel Deception," 12–27; Olsen, "Pride and Prejudice," 18–31; Olsen, "In an Alien World," 28–43; Olsen, "In the Back of the Bus," 28–41; Olsen, "Anguish of a Team Divided," 20–35. These articles were the basis for Olsen, *The Black Athlete.* See also readers' responses: "19th Hole," 15 July 1968, 94; "19th Hole," 22 July 1968, 71–72; "19th Hole," 29 July 1968, 62–64.

58. Olsen, "In the Back of the Bus," 40; Olsen, "Cruel Deception," 15.

59. M. Halberstam, "Are You Guilty of Murdering Martin Luther King?" 27–29, 54–66. *Of Black America* aired over the summer of 1968. It is available for viewing at Museum of Television and Radio, New York City.

60. *Baltimore Afro-American,* 21 May 1968; *Chicago Defender,* 8 June 1968, 31 August 1968; *Philadelphia Inquirer,* 8 March 1968; *Newsday,* 20 January 1969.

61. *Boston Globe,* 7 November 1968, 21 February 1969, 2 May 1998; *New York Amsterdam News,* 18 May 1968, 8 June 1968, 22 June 1968; *New York Times,* 8 June 1968, 3 July 1968; *Los Angeles Sentinel,* 13 June 1968, 27 June 1968; *Chicago Defender,* 29 June 1968; *Chicago Tribune,* 21 February 1969. Russell also played in a charity game to raise money for Martin Luther King's SCLC. *New York Amsterdam News,* 10 August 1968, 17 August 1968.

62. *Newsday,* 20 January 1969; *Chicago Defender,* 8 July 1968; *New York Amsterdam News,* 3 August 1968; Underwood, "Non-Trial Trials," 11–13.

63. *Philadelphia Bulletin,* 8 April 1968, 9 April 1968, 16 June 1968, 17 July 1968; *New York Times,* 29 June 1968, 30 June 1968, 5 August 1968; 8 August 1968; *Los Angeles Times,* 6 August 1968, 5 November 1968; Chamberlain and Shaw, *Wilt,* 200–207; Axthelm, "Wilt Chamberlain," 42–47. See also Lipsyte, *Sportsworld,* 11–15; Kotlowski, *Nixon's Civil Rights,* 16–21, 127–33.

64. Kornheiser, "Bill Russell," 179–86.

65. George, *Elevating the Game,* 105. On heroes and antiheroes, see also Vande Berg, "Sports Hero Meets Mediated Celebrityhood," 134–53; L. Levine, *Black Culture and Black Consciousness,* 407–20; Van Deburg, *Hoodlums,* 108–24.

15. GRAND OLD MAN

1. Plimpton, "My Team," 17–20. On Plimpton's previous exercises in participatory journalism, see Plimpton, *Out of My League;* Plimpton, *Paper Lion;* Plimpton, *Bogey Man;* Plimpton, *Shadow Box.*

2. Plimpton, "My Team," 17–20; *Boston Globe,* 24 September 1968.

3. Plimpton, "Reflections in a Diary," 40–44.

4. *Washington Post,* 18 December 1968; MacCambridge, *Franchise,* 158–68. Russell was the second African American to win the magazine's Sportsman of the Year. Rafer Johnson won in 1958. *New York Amsterdam News,* 4 January 1969.

5. *Boston Globe,* 19 December 1968; *Baltimore Afro-American,* 24 December 1968; *Bay State Banner,* 26 December 1968; *Los Angeles Times,* 16 January 1969.

6. *Los Angeles Times,* 14 September 1967; Russell and Branch, *Second Wind,* 234–36, 246.

7. *Chicago Defender,* 7 May 1968, 31 August 1968; *New York Amsterdam News,* 30 September 1967; *Los Angeles Sentinel,* 9 June 1968, 29 August 1968; *New York Times,* 18 February 1968; *TV Guide,* 19 February 1972; *Boston Herald Traveler,* 10 September 1968; Embry, *Inside Game,* 163. On *I Spy,* see Bogle, *Primetime Blues,* 115–25. Russell drew a fine from the NBA because of his Hollywood commitments. He skipped a meeting in upstate New York with all the league's coaches and officials. "Throughout the meetings the guys kept asking about Russ," relayed Dolph Schayes, now the supervisor of officials. "They wanted to know why he didn't show up." *Boston Herald Traveler,* 22 August 1968.

8. *Seattle Times,* 26 June 1992. The episode of *Playboy After Dark* is available for viewing at the Museum of Television and Radio, New York City.

9. *Boston Globe,* 24 September 1968; *Springfield Union,* 24 September 1968; *Washington Post,* 24 September 1968; *Boston Herald Traveler,* 5 May 1968; *Chicago Defender,* 8 May 1968, 31 August 1968, 28 September 1968; *Baltimore Afro-American,* 20 August 1968; George, *Elevating the Game,* 154–61.

10. *New York Times,* 23 January 1968; *Philadelphia Inquirer,* 25 January 1968; *Sporting News,* 3 February 1968, 18 May 1968; *Boston Herald Traveler,* 14 January 1968; Deford, "Changing Game," 22–25.

11. Pluto, *Loose Balls,* 44–118; Wolf, *Foul!* 208–96; *Sporting News,* 27 January 1968, 2 March 1968; Devaney, "Four Stars the NBA Wouldn't Touch," 54–57, 84–85; "ABA," 46–47. On Rick Barry, see Arnold Hano, "Rick Barry's Drive to Greatness," 66–71; Deford, "Razor-Cut Idol of San Francisco," 32–35; "Scorecard," 12 June 1967, 17; *Sporting News,* 26 October 1968, 23 November 1968, 1 February 1969; Barry, *Confessions of a Basketball Gypsy.*

12. Pluto, *Loose Balls,* 177–86; Love, *Bob Love Story,* 91–92; *Philadelphia Inquirer,* 2 April 1968; *Boston Herald Traveler,* 14 March 1968; "Basketball," 64–70; DeBusschere, *Open Man,* 104–5.

13. *Philadelphia Bulletin,* 25 April 1968, 29 April–3 May 1968, 9 June 1968, 21–23 June 1968, 5 July 1968, 9 July 1968, 10 July 1968, 19 July 1968; *Philadelphia Inquirer,* 9 May 1968, 12 June 1968, 15 June 1968, 24 June 1968; *Los Angeles Times,* 4 July 1968, 12 July 1968.

14. Havill, *Last Mogul,* 23–161; Lazenby, *Lakers,* 141–42, 159–65; Lazenby, *Show,* 99–111; Ostler and Springer, *Winnin' Times,* 56–62; Heisler, *Madmen's Ball,* 13; Hearn and Springer, *Chick,* 35–36, 87, 136.

15. *Los Angeles Times,* 10 July 1968, 12 July 1968; Chamberlain and Shaw, *Wilt,* 193–200; *Sporting News,* 19 October 1968; "Romp in the NBA West," 30–31; "Go West, Tall Man," 48–49.

16. *Los Angeles Times,* 1 November 1968, 18 December 1968, 27 January 1969, 10 February 1969, 23 February 1969, 8 March 1969, 2 June 1985; *Sporting News,* 23 November 1968, 15 March 1969; *New York Times,* 28 November 1968; Chamberlain, *Wilt,* 208–12; West, *Mr. Clutch,* 204–7; Pluto, *Tall Tales,* 354–56; Jares, "Beard Moves into a New and Ticklish Pad," 76–77; Deford, "On Top—But In Trouble," 10–13; Hano, "Wilt, West, and Baylor," 62–69.

17. Lewin, "Wilt Chamberlain Controversy," 16–19, 84; *Los Angeles Times,* 27 October 1968, 10 December 1968, 11 December 1968, 13 December 1968; *Sporting News,* 21 December 1968; "Tilting With Wilt," 48; Lazenby, *Show,* 116–19; Hundley, *Hot Rod Hundley,* 58–59; Nack, "I've Made My Own Bed," 69.

18. *Los Angeles Times,* 10 July 1968, 19 November 1968; B. Russell, *Red and Me,* 158–60; *Boston Globe,* 7 November 1968, 17 December 1968.

19. *Sporting News,* 26 April 1969.

20. *Los Angeles Times,* 11 November 1967; *USA Today,* 17 January 2003; Vecsey, "Unseld Makes the Difference," 66–69, 81–83; Hano, "Elvin Hayes vs. Wilt," 18–20, 86–88; Vecsey, "Unseld Makes the Difference," 66–69, 81–83; Olsen, "Cruel Deception," 20–23; Hayes, *They Call Me the Big E,* 1–71, 130–31; Zanger, "NBA Coaches Rate the Players," 34–37, 94–96.

21. Jares, "Four for the Bundle," 14–19; *Boston Herald,* 7 May 1968; *Boston Globe,* 5 November 1968, 3 December 1968, 17 December 1968, 19 December 1968, 7 January 1969, 27 January 1969; *Sporting News,* 15 February 1969; *Chicago Defender,* 3 December 1968, 3 February 1969. Auerbach had tried trading Larry Siegfried for Lenny Wilkens, but Siegfried refused to sign a contract until Wilkens got traded elsewhere. Carey, *High Above Courtside,* 166–67.

22. *Boston Globe,* 3 February 1969; Holzman, *View from the Bench,* 46–47; *Chicago Defender,* 3 February 1969, 4 February 1969.

23. *Chicago Defender,* 5 February 1969; *Boston Globe,* 3 February 1969, 4 February 1969, 6 February 1969, 8 February 1969, 10 February 1969.

24. Russell and Branch, *Second Wind,* 167–68; *Los Angeles Times,* 15 January 1970. While eating dinner after a game against Milwaukee, Russell intimated to former teammate Wayne Embry that he might retire. After his last game against Cincinnati, Russell also thanked Oscar Robertson for their battles over the years. Pluto, *Tall Tales,* 373; Russell and Branch, *Second Wind,* 169–70.

25. W. Russell, "Success Is a Journey," 88; *Boston Herald Traveler,* 10 March 1969; *Baltimore Afro-American,* 6 May 1969; *Boston Globe,* 14 January 1969, 9 March 1969, 10 March 1969, 12 March 1969. In the mid-1960s Jones had mentored Jimmy Walker, the Roxbury teenager who then starred for Providence College and the Detroit Pistons.

26. Russell and Branch, *Second Wind,* 149–51; *Sporting News,* 15 February 1969, *Chicago Defender,* 1 March 1969; *Boston Globe,* 11 January 1969.

27. *Boston Globe,* 3 January 1969, 20 February 1969, 3 March 1969; *Sporting News,* 26 April 1969; *Bay State Banner,* 21 November 1968; *Boston Herald Traveler,* 30 March 1969; *Chicago Defender,* 12 April 1969.

28. *Sporting News,* 1 March 1969, 22 March 1969; *Boston Herald Traveler,* 13 March 1969, 15 March 1969, 17–19 March 1969, 23 March 1969; *Los Angeles Times,* 17 March 1969; *Boston Globe,* 11 March 1969, 17 March 1969, 24 March 1969. For a detailed account of Boston's entire season, see Whalen, *Dynasty's End,* 67–181.

29. *Sporting News,* 22 February 1969; *Boston Herald Traveler,* 26 March 1969; *Boston Globe,* 25 March 1969, 26 March 1969.

30. *Boston Herald Traveler,* 27 March–1 April 1969; *Boston Globe,* 27 March–1 April 1969; *Sporting* News, 10 May 1969; Havlicek and Ryan, *Hondo,* 108–9.

31. *Boston Herald Traveler,* 2–5 April 1969; *Boston Globe,* 2–5 April 1969; Deford, "Comebacks All Over," 28–31.

32. *Sporting News,* 18 January 1969, 22 March 1969, 19 April 1969; *Boston Herald Traveler,* 1 April 1969; *Pittsburgh Courier,* 22 March 1969; Deford, "New York Gets a Top Team," 28–32; Baumbach, "Aesthetics of Basketball," 140–46; Spitz, *Shoot Out the Lights,* 25–37; Holzman and Frommer, *Red on Red,* 63–67; Frazier and Jares, *Clyde,* 88–90; Frazier, *Walt Frazier,* 88–92, 166–67; Jackson, *Maverick,* 56–58, 65–66, 75, 81, 104–5; Bradley, *Life on the Run,* 11–12, 16–17, 34–36, 60–64, 74–77, 86.

33. *Boston Globe,* 28 February 2000; *Seattle Post-Intelligencer,* 20 March 1977; Bradley, *Life on the Run,* 182–85. On Bradley's college years, see McPhee, *Sense of Where You Are.*

34. *Boston Herald Traveler,* 7 April 1969, 10 April 1969; *Boston Globe,* 7 April 1969, 10 April 1969; Frazier and Jares, *Clyde,* 114; Deford, "At the End," 66–71; *Newsday,* 10 April 1969.

35. D'Agostino, *Garden Glory,* 85; *Boston Herald Traveler,* 11 April 1969, 14 April 1969; *Boston Globe,* 11 April 1969, 14 April 1969; *Sporting News,* 14 April 1969; *Sporting News,* 26 April 1969.

36. *Boston Herald Traveler,* 15 April 1969; *Boston Globe,* 15 April 1969, 17 April 1969

37. *New York Times,* 18–20 April 1969; *Boston Herald Traveler,* 16 April 1969, 17 April 1969, 19 April 1969; *Boston Globe,* 19 April 1969; Frazier and Jares, *Clyde,* 115; Deford, "And that Old Celtics Wheel," 24–25.

38. *Boston Herald Traveler,* 22 April 1969.

39. *Los Angeles Times,* 21 April 1969, 23 April 1969; *Boston Herald Traveler,* 23 April 1969; *Boston Globe,* 23 April 1969; *Sporting News,* 3 May 1969; Maule, "Rescued from Disaster," 32–33.

40. Underwood, "Eye of an Eagle," 14–17; Libby, "Jerry West," 24–27, 101–3; Hano, "I Was Wrong," 64–69; Libby, "Courage and Splendor," 26–29, 64–65; Burnes, "Long Way with West," 46–50; Deford, "Teddy Bear's Picnic," 46–56; *Sporting News,* 30 April 1966, 18 May 1968, 29 April 1972.

41. *Boston Herald Traveler,* 24–26 April 1969; *Boston Globe,* 24–26 April 1969; *New York Times,* 25–27 April 1969; *Philadelphia Bulletin,* 28 April 1969.

42. *Los Angeles Times,* 26 April 1969; *Boston Globe,* 27 April 1969; Larry Siegfried Interview at www.celtic-nation.com/; Toback, "What the NBA Playoffs Can Do," 24.

43. "Elgin Baylor's Playoff Diary," 36–37; *Los Angeles Times,* 28 April 1969; *Boston Globe,* 28 April 1969; *Boston Herald Traveler,* 28 April 1969.

44. Deford, "Last Drop," 23; *Los Angeles Times,* 30 April 1969; *Boston Globe,* 30 April 1969; *Boston Herald Traveler,* 30 April 1969.

45. Havlicek and Ryan, *Hondo,* 111; B. Russell, *Russell Rules,* 202–4. Russell claims that he initiated the plan for the last-second shot; Havlicek's earlier memoir is probably more accurate.

46. Deford, "Last Drop," 24; *Boston Herald Traveler,* 30 April 1969.

47. Deford, "Last Drop," 24; West, *Mr. Clutch,* 211; *Philadelphia Bulletin,* 30 April 1969; *Boston Globe,* 30 April 1969; *Los Angeles Times,* 30 April 1969, 1 May 1969.

48. *Boston Globe,* 1 May 1969; Bailey Howell interview.

49. *Boston Globe,* 2 May 1969, 3 May 1969; *Los Angeles Times,* 2 May 1969, 3 May 1969; *Boston Herald Traveler,* 2 May 1969.

50. *Los Angeles Times,* 4 May 1969; *Boston Globe,* 4 May 1969.

51. *Boston Globe,* 5 May 1969, 7 May 1969; *Boston Herald Traveler,* 5 May 1969; *Los Angeles Times,* 5 May 1969.

52. *New York Times,* 5 May 1969; Larry Siegfried Interview at www.celtic-nation.com/.

53. *NBA Dynasty Series—Boston Celtics;* B. Russell, *Russell Rules,* 190; *Boston Globe,* 6 May 1969.

54. *New York Times,* 6 May 1969; *Boston Globe,* 6 May 1969; *Boston Herald Traveler,* 6 May 1969.

55. *Boston Globe,* 6 May 1969; *Boston Herald Traveler,* 6 May 1969; Chamberlain and Shaw, *Wilt,* 218. Footage of the entire fourth quarter is available on *NBA Dynasty Series— Boston Celtics.*

56. *Boston Globe,* 6 May 1969; Pluto, *Tall Tales,* 368.

57. Chamberlain and Shaw, *Wilt,* 218; *Los Angeles Times,* 9 May 1969; Pluto, *Tall Tales,* 368–70; *Wilt Chamberlain: Larger Than Life; NBA Dynasty Series—Los Angeles Lakers.*

58. *Boston Globe,* 6 May 1969; Mel Counts, telephone interview with author, 10 January 2008.

59. On the 1969 play-offs, see also Whalen, *Dynasty's End,* 187–243; J. Taylor, *Rivalry,* 334–53.

60. *Los Angeles Times,* 6 April 1969, 9 April 1969; "Elgin Baylor's Playoff Diary," 86; *Boston Globe,* 6 May 1969;

61. *Los Angeles Times,* 6 May 1969, 7 May 1969, 9 May 1969, 11 May 1969, 13 May 1969, 19 May 1969, 20 May 1969; *Boston Globe,* 7 May 1969, 8 May 1969; *Boston Herald Traveler,* 8 May 1969, 10 May 1969; *Sporting News,* 17 May 1969, 7 June 1969; *New York Times,* 20 May 1969; *Philadelphia Bulletin,* 8 May 1969, 9 May 1969, 25 May 1969.

62. *Philadelphia Bulletin,* 9 May 1969; *New York Times,* 28 April 1969, 9 May 1969; *Los Angeles Times,* 8 May 1969; Deford, *Sports People,* 26–28; *Chicago Defender,* 13 May 1969; Deford, "Ring Leader," 98.

63. *Boston Globe,* 6 May 1969, 7 May 1969.

64. *Baltimore Afro-American,* 10 May 1969; *New York Times,* 6 May 1969, 7 May 1969; *Boston Globe,* 6 May 1969, 7 May 1969; *Boston Herald-American,* 7 May 1969. See also "Boston's Old, Old Pros," 77; *New York Amsterdam News,* 10 May 1969; *Chicago Defender,* 13 May 1969; *Sporting News,* 31 May 1969, 14 March 1970; *Boston Globe,* 21 December 1969.

65. *Boston Herald-American,* 9 May 1969; *Boston Globe,* 6 May 1969, 9 May 1969; *Los Angeles Times,* 8 May 1969.

66. Leigh Montville, telephone interview with author, 5 August 2008; Pluto, *Tall Tales*, 372–73.

67. J. Fitzgerald, *That Championship Feeling*, 194–95; *Los Angeles Times*, 6 May 1969.

16. COLOR MAN

1. Auerbach and Fitzgerald, *Red Auerbach*, 149–50; *Boston Herald-Traveler*, 7 May 1969, 13 June 1969; *Chicago Defender*, 13 May 1969, 5 June 1969, 16 June 1969; *Baltimore Afro-American*, 21 June 1969; *Los Angeles Sentinel*, 19 June 1969; *New York Amsterdam News*, 28 June 1969; *Pittsburgh Courier*, 28 June 1969; *Los Angeles Times*, 13 June 1969, 14 June 1969.

2. W. Russell, "I'm Not Involved Anymore," 18–19. See also B. Russell, *Russell Rules*, 207–9. On the reaction of black press, see *Baltimore Afro-American*, 2 August 1969; *Chicago Defender*, 31 July 1969, 2 August 1969, 6 August 1969; *Los Angeles Sentinel*, 7 August 1969.

3. *Los Angeles Times*, 31 July 1969, 13 August 1969; *New York Times*, 31 July 1969, 16 September 1969; "Letter from the Publisher," 6; *Boston Herald*, 7 October 1993; *Chicago Defender*, 9 August 1969, 25 August 1969, 11 September 1969; *Washington Post*, 23 August 1969, 27 August 1969, 4 September 1969; Heinsohn, *Heinsohn, Don't You Ever Smile?* 171–72. After announcing Russell's retirement, the *Boston Herald Traveler* reported that Frank Ramsey would succeed Russell as coach. *Boston Herald-Traveler*, 14 June 1969.

4. Harold Furash, telephone interview with author, 19 March 2007; Leigh Montville, telephone interview with author, 5 August 2008; *Chicago Defender*, 17 December 1969; Shaughnessy, *Seeing Red*, 176; *Sporting News*, 1 March 1969; *Boston Herald Traveler*, 13 June 1969; Russell and Branch, *Second Wind*, 205–6; *Christian Science Monitor*, 12 February 1975; *Washington Post*, 9 June 1973; *Springfield Union*, 9 June 1973; *New York Amsterdam News*, 23 June 1973.

5. Libby, "Bill Russell, Laughing," 19.

6. Russell and Branch, *Second Wind*, 215, 236–38; *Los Angeles Times*, 17 July 1973; *Seattle Times*, 29 January 1978, 30 July 1978; Libby, "Bill Russell, Laughing," 19–20; B. Russell, *Russell Rules*, 3. On athletes and retirement, see Pipkin, *Sporting Lives*, 97–126. On Russell's earlier desires to leave sports behind after retirement, see *Sporting News*, 30 January 1965.

7. Libby, "Bill Russell, Laughing," 22; Russell and Branch, *Second Wind*, 246–48; *Los Angeles Times*, 17 July 1973; *Seattle Times*, 20 August 1978. In other family news, Russell's brother Charlie had become an accomplished playwright within the nascent Black Arts Movement. His play *Five on the Black Hand Side* used comedy but examined the generational and political conflicts within a Harlem family. It debuted in December 1969 at the American Place Theatre in New York City. See C. Russell, *Five on the Black Hand Side*.

8. *Boston Herald Traveler and Record American*, 5 December 1972; *Boston Herald-American*, 16 September 1973; *New York Times*, 16 September 1973; Russell and Branch, *Second Wind*, 241, 247, 249–54.

9. Jim Brown, *Out of Bounds*, 200–201.

10. Libby, "Bill Russell, Laughing," 22; Jim Brown, *Out of Bounds*, 272–73; *Los Angeles Sentinel*, 4 November 1971; Russell and Branch, *Second Wind*, 238–40; Toback, *Jim*, 90–97

(quotation on 93). "When I was growing up my mother wouldn't allow me near a golf course. She didn't think the people were very nice," said Russell. "Now I play every day, and you know what? She was right." "They Said It," 12.

11. *Chicago Defender*, 11 August 1969, 4 September 1969; *Los Angeles Sentinel*, 14 August 1969, 28 August 1969, 15 September 1983; Freeman, *Jim Brown*, 204–10; Toback, *Jim*, 103–23.

12. *Los Angeles Sentinel*, 14 August 1969, 5 March 1970, 12 March 1970, 9 April 1970, 7 April 1971; *Chicago Defender*, 14 February 1970; *New York Amsterdam News*, 28 February 1970; *Washington Post*, 7 May 1971; *Pittsburgh Courier*, 2 January 1971, 22 July 1972, 12 August 1972; *Memphis Commercial Appeal*, 8 October 1971; *New Orleans Times Picayune*, 25 September 1971; *Jackson Clarion Ledger*, 24 September 1971, 26 September 1971; *Jackson Daily News*, 24 September 1971, 27 September 1971. On Evers's rise in prominence, see Crosby, *Little Taste*, 176–85, 189–99, 207–23, 255–57. On failed 1971 gubernatorial campaign, see Berry, *Amazing Grace*.

13. *Los Angeles Sentinel*, 23 December 1971; *Chicago Defender*, 4 September 1971, 11 March 1972, 3 April 1973; *Chicago Tribune*, 20 January 1973, 30 March 1973; *Atlanta Daily World*, 27 March 1973; *Pittsburgh Courier*, 15 September 1973; Frady, *Jesse*, 253–80.

14. *New York Times*, 28 October 1972; *New York Amsterdam News*, 4 November 1972; *Boston Globe*, 13 April 2007; Maureen Smith, "Identity and Citizenship," 301.

15. Paul, McGhee, and Fant, "Arrival and Ascendance of Black Athletes"; Yaeger, *Turning of the Tide*; Kaliss, "Everyone's All-Americans," 295–366; Jacobs, *Across the Line*; *Chicago Defender*, 23 December 1969; *Pittsburgh Courier*, 28 April 1973; *New York Times*, 6 November 1970, 18 November 1970, 17 November 1971, 18 November 1971, 27 November 1971, 10–14 December 1971, 19 December 1971, 27 December 1972, 24 October 1974; Snyder, *Well-Paid Slave*, 1–15, 82–312; Ashe and Rampersad, *Days of Grace*, 103–6.

16. "Big, Big Men Cash In," 164–73; Banks, "Take the Money and Run," 99–104; *Los Angeles Times*, 6 February 1973; Frazier and Berkow, *Rockin' Steady*, 6–7. See also Guzzie, "Courtside," 221–36.

17. Charles Rosen, *God, Man and Basketball Jones*, 58; Michener, *Sports in America*, 171; Lipsyte, *SportsWorld*, 167–68; Tate, "Nigs R Us," 1–14; Cole, *Loose Game*, 94–122.

18. *Chicago Defender*, 25 July 1970, 18 June 1975; *Los Angeles Times*, 26 May 1971, 18 April 1974; *New York Post*, 11 June 1976; *New York Amsterdam News*, 13 June 1970; Kane, "Assessment," 72–83; Russell and Branch, *Second Wind*, 174–75; Frank Deford, telephone interview with author, 22 September 2008; W. Russell, "Success Is a Journey," 80–93. On the debate over blacks and natural athleticism, see also Sailes, "Myth of Black Sports Supremacy"; Miller, "Anatomy of Scientific Racism," 327–44; Entine, *Taboo*; Hoberman, *Darwin's Athletes*, 143–242; Edwards, *Sociology of Sport*, 193–202; Gladwell, "Sports Taboo," 50–55. On media stereotypes in sport, see Davis and Harris, "Race and Ethnicity," 155–69.

19. *Chicago Defender*, 25 July 1970; Bass, *Not the Triumph but the Struggle*, 281–85. A recording of this program is available for viewing at the Museum of Radio and Television.

20. *Washington Post*, 25 April 1972; Durslag, "Man Who Gave Up $200,000 a Year Tells Why," 13–14; *Los Angeles Sentinel*, 26 March 1970; *New York Times*, 5 October 1972; Russell and Branch, *Second Wind*, 175–77.

21. *Washington Post*, 17 May 1969, 11 March 1970, 25 April 1972; *Los Angeles Times*,

15 January 1970; *Los Angeles Sentinel*, 26 March 1970; *New York Times*, 5 October 1972; *Chicago Defender*, 21 October 1972; *Seattle Times*, 27 October 1978; *Memphis Commercial Appeal*, 22 January 2006; Russell and Branch, *Second Wind*, 242.

22. Russell and Branch, *Second Wind*, 169–70, 242–44; *Boston Herald Traveler*, 6 May 1969.

23. *New York Times*, 22 May 1969.

24. *Washington Post*, 22 May 1969; *Los Angeles Times*, 22 May 1969, 23 May 1969, 11 April 1970; *Philadelphia Bulletin*, 22 May 1969; *Chicago Tribune*, 23 May 1969; "Parting Shots," 67; *New York Times*, 12 November 1969; *Los Angeles Sentinel*, 17 July 1969; B. Russell, "Success Is a Journey," 86; "People"; *Gazette-Telegraph* (Colorado Springs, CO), 20 May 1979; Chamberlain and Shaw, *Wilt*, 219–23; Russell and Branch, *Second Wind*, 245.

25. *Los Angeles Times*, 31 January 1971. On Chamberlain's home, see "Womb with a View," 55; "House that Wilt Built," 60–63; *New York Times*, 15 March 1972; *Sporting News*, 15 April 1972. On near-fight against Ali, see *Los Angeles Times*, 23 April 1971; *New York Times*, 23 April 1971, 24 April 1971, 28 June 1971; *Chicago Tribune*, 24 April 1971. On television roles, see *Washington Post*, 2 September 1969; *Los Angeles Times*, 16 August 1969, 2 July 1970, 9 October 1973, 20 October 1973. On track and volleyball, see Huey, *Running Start*, 213–28, 236–37; *Philadelphia Bulletin*, 17 July 1970, 25 May 1972; *Los Angeles Times*, 27 August 1971; *New York Times*, 15 August 1971, 3 June 1973. On the Philadelphia airport incident, see *Philadelphia Bulletin*, 14 December 1972; *Los Angeles Times*, 14 December 1972; *New York Times*, 14 December 1972; Mravic, "Fed Up," 30. On advertisements, see *Los Angeles Times*, 18 June 1970; *New York Times*, 28 December 1972. On memoir, see Chamberlain and Shaw, *Wilt*; *Philadelphia Bulletin*, 30 September 1973, 14 October 1973; *Publisher's Weekly*, 21 May 1973; *Los Angeles Times*, 29 August 1973, 7 October 1973, 27 November 1973; L. Robinson, "High Price," 94–101.

26. *Los Angeles Times*, 15 January 1970; *Sporting News*, 21 February 1970; *Boston Herald-American*, 17 May 1973. On Black Hollywood in this era, see Bogle, *Toms, Coons*, 215–45; Leab, *From Sambo to Superspade*, 233–63; Goudsouzian, *Sidney Poitier*, 315–36.

27. Durslag, "Man Who Gave Up $200,000 a Year Tells Why," 14.

28. *Atlanta Daily World*, 5 October 1972; www.imdb.com; *Los Angeles Sentinel*, 21 September 1972. An episode of *The Flip Wilson Show* guest starring Russell is available for viewing at the Museum of Television and Radio, New York City. On *The Flip Wilson Show*, see also Bogle, *Prime Time Blues*, 175–83.

29. *Atlanta Daily World*, 5 October 1972, 5 May 1972; Durslag, "Man Who Gave Up $200,000 a Year Tells Why," 14; *New York Amsterdam News*, 21 May 1970; *Los Angeles Sentinel*, 2 November 1972, 22 February 1973; Cosell, *Cosell*, 382; *Seattle Times*, 14 June 1973. Russell also appeared on *Goin' Back to Indiana*, a 1971 special celebrating the Jackson 5, and in a 1972 episode of *Soul Train*.

30. *Los Angeles Times*, 22 November 1972, 9 January 1973, 19 October 1973; *Seattle Post-Intelligencer*, 2 November 1973.

31. *Chicago Defender*, 2 July 1970; Cosell, *Cosell*, 381.

32. M. Roberts, *Fans!* 89; *Los Angeles Times*, 23 March 1973; *New York Times*, 25 June 2000.

33. *New York Times*, 16 August 1974, 10 June 1975; *Seattle Times*, 12 January 1975,

19 February 1975; 14 December 1975; *Binghamton Press*, 5 March 1975. For Watts's admiration of Russell during his playing career, see Vecsey, "Bill Russell's Most Trying Season," 40.

34. For sport's growing cultural rifts, see Zang, *SportsWars*. For traditional views of sport, see Maraniss, *When Pride Still Mattered*, 429–504; MacCambridge, *America's Game*, 231–33, 262–64, 299–301. For celebrity, see Kriegel, *Namath*, 282–87; Goudsouzian, "'My Impact Will Be Everlasting,'" 244–45. For Athletic Revolution, see Scott, *Athletic Revolution*; Edwards, *Sociology of Sport*, 87–92, 103–30, 176–86; Shecter, *Jocks*; Gemme, *New Breed*; Lipsyte, *SportsWorld*; Dickey, *Jock Empire*; Izenberg, *How Many Miles to Camelot?*; Hoch, *Rip Off the Big Game*; Shaw, *Meat on the Hoof*; Meggysey, *Out of Their League*.

35. M. Roberts, *Fans!* 89.

36. *Boston Herald Traveler*, 12 February 1972; Russell and Branch, *Second Wind*, 202–3.

37. *New York Times*, 13 March 1972; *Springfield Union*, 10 February 1975; *Boston Globe*, 13 March 1972; *Boston Herald Traveler*, 13 February 1972.

38. *New York Times*, 18 August 1970, 12 October 1971, 9 August 1972; *Pittsburgh Courier*, 18 August 1970; Shecter, *Jocks*, 75; *Los Angeles Sentinel*, 7 January 1971, 17 August 1972; *Atlanta Daily World*, 14 December 1973; *Seattle Times*, 24 January 1974; *Los Angeles Times*, 17 July 1973; Durslag, "Man Who Gave Up $200,000 a Year Tells Why," 13.

39. Dickey, *Jock Empire*, 101–3; *Chicago Defender*, 4 December 1971; *Los Angeles Sentinel*, 22 February 1973; *Los Angeles Times*, 8 May 1972; *Washington Post*, 26 April 1972; *Chicago Tribune*, 15 February 1980

40. *New York Times*, 20 December 2002; *Seattle Times*, 10 December 1978; *Phoenix Gazette*, 20 February 1975; *Sporting News*, 1 April 1972; Cyclops, "Eagle and Stork," 8; Cosell, *Like It Is*, 217–19; "Can't Miss," 61.

41. On Russell's honors, see *Chicago Defender*, 14 March 1970, 19 December 1970; *New York Times*, 5 February 1970; *Los Angeles Times*, 11 February 1970; *Sporting News*, 14 March 1970. On Celtics during 1969–70 season, see Ryan, *Celtics Pride*, 10–21; Deford, "Two Guys," 22–25; *Sporting News*, 10 January 1970, 21 February 1970, 28 March 1970; *New York Times*, 12 March 1970; *Boston Globe*, 26 January 1970, 23 March 1970; DeBusschere, *Open Man*, 39, 43–44, 143, 184; Greenfield, *World's Greatest Team*, 195–203; M. Connolly, *Rebound!* 79–81. On financial troubles, see Auerbach, *MBA Management by Auerbach*, 192; *Sporting News*, 9 May 1970.

42. Shainberg, "Fan's Notes," 28–48; "Dazzling Knicks," 64–69; Kirshenbaum, "Overdue Winner," 16–21; *New York Times*, 9 May 1970, 10 May 1970; "You Gotta Have Heart," 93–94; Deford, "In for Two Plus the Title," 14–17; Axthelm, *City Game*, 3–122, 159–210; Berger, *Miracle on 33rd Street*; D'Agostino, *Garden Glory*, 113–22; Holzman, *Knicks*, 156, 205; Holzman and Frommer, *Red on Red*, 104; Reed, *View from the Rim*, 194–201; Jackson, *Maverick*, 102; Kalinsky and Jackson, *Take It All!*; DeBusschere, *Open Man*, 248–64; Frazier, *Walt Frazier*, 235; Frazier and Jares, *Clyde*, 267–68; *Philadelphia Inquirer*, 11 May 1970.

43. *Los Angeles Times*, 8 November 1969; *Sporting News*, 14 February 1970; Wright, "For the Lakers," 42–47; Chamberlain and Shaw, *Wilt*, 224–32.

44. R. Lardner, "Can Basketball Survive Lew Alcindor?" 70–73; L. Fox, "Presenting Lew Alcindor," 72–73; "Making of a Legend," 59–62; Deford, "Terror in the Air," 16–21; Hano,

"Heart of Lew Alcindor," 73–78; Pepe, "Lew Alcindor Sounds Off!" 34–37, 91–92; Alcindor, "My Story," 82–88; Alcindor, "UCLA Was a Mistake," 34–40, 45; Hyman, "Case for the 12-foot Basket," 78–83.

45. Gross, "Pros Tell Their Favorite Bill Russell Stories," 46; Abdul-Jabbar, *Kareem*, 30–32.

46. Abdul-Jabbar and Knobler, *Giant Steps*, 1–194; Abdul-Jabbar, *Kareem*, 239–45; Abdul-Jabbar, *On the Shoulders of Giants*, 239–50; Pepe, *Stand Tall*, 94, 108–17; *New York Times*, 23 July 1968.

47. Alcindor, "Year of Turmoil and Decision," 35–46; Klein, *Rookie*, 8–51; R. Kahn, "Lew Alcindor's Life as a Pro," 58–65; Maule, "Lew Turns Small Change to Big Bucks"; Furlong, "Bob Cousy vs. Oscar Robertson," 22–24, 81–83; Axthelm, "Sports," 76"; Carry, "Hey Look, Ma! Only One Hand," 26–31; *Sporting News*, 15 April 1972; Abdul-Jabbar, *Kareem*, 83–84. See also D. Halberstam, *Breaks of the Game*, 191–95.

48. *Los Angeles Times*, 24 October 1969, 25 October 1969, 28 April 1971, 16 April 1972; *New York Times*, 20 August 1969, 7 February 1981; DeBusschere, *Open Man*, 6–7; *Chicago Defender*, 7 November 1981; "Eyeball to Eyeball," 58–59; "It's Still a Big Man's Game," 83–91; Markus, "Who's the Greatest?" 32–36, 38–41; Abdul-Jabbar, *Giant Steps*, 76–90; Garth Williams, "The Truth Behind the Chamberlain-Jabbar Feud," uncited article in Wilt Chamberlain File, Basketball Hall of Fame.

49. *Los Angeles Times*, 15 March 1972; B. Ward, *Just My Soul Responding*, 339–415; Van Deburg, *New Day in Babylon*, 192–247; George, *Elevating the Game*, 164–65; Wolf, *Foul!* 461–63, 469. In 1973, Nation of Islam henchmen murdered seven followers of Abdul-Jabbar's spiritual mentor, in a Washington, DC, townhouse purchased by Abdul-Jabbar. See Carry, "Center in a Storm," 16–19; Abdul-Jabbar, *Giant Steps*, 223–35, 257–66.

50. Charles Rosen, *Pivotal Season*; Chamberlain and Shaw, *Wilt*, 267–83; *Los Angeles Times*, 7 November 1971, 12 December 1971, 12 March 1972; *New York Times*, 10 November 1971, 29 April 1972, 12 May 1972; "Why L.A. Loves the Lakers," 73; Carry, "Getting Up and Going After a Title," 24–35; "Celtics Lakers," 51–52; "Lakers Roll On," 57–58; Carry, "Derailing the Laker Express," 12–15; S. Roberts, "Lakers Are Great," 18–30; L. Robinson, "Captain Wilt Leads L.A. Lakers," 114–21; "Court Choreography," 95–96; "One for the Dipper," 49–50; "Champagne and Peace," 67–68; Carry, "Bombs Away Out West," 14–17; Carry, "Swish and They're In," 26–27; Axthelm, "Year the Lakers Won," 54–57, 101–7.

51. Carry, "Where There's a Willis," 54–56; *Los Angeles Times*, 18 May 1973; *Washington Post*, 13 May 1973; Chamberlain, "My Impact Will Be Everlasting," 42.

52. M. Harris, *Lonely Heroes*, 33–34.

53. *Chicago Tribune*, 12 May 1973; *New York Times*, 12 May 1973; *Washington Post*, 12 May 1973 *Seattle Times*, 11–13 May 1973; *Seattle Post-Intelligencer*, 13 May 1973.

54. *Seattle Times*, 12–16 May 1973; *Seattle Post-Intelligencer*, 14 May 1973; *Chicago Defender*, 14 May 1973, 17 May 1973.

55. *Los Angeles Times*, 17 July 1973; *Chicago Defender*, 16 May 1973; *Seattle Times*, 15 April 1973, 3 May 1973, 4 May 1973, 7 May 1973, 12 May 1973, 13 May 1973.

56. Sale, *Seattle, Past to Present*, 201–4, 226–31. On relationships between cities and sports franchises, see Danielson, *Home Team*, 3–18; Riess, *City Games*, 237–38.

57. On course of expansion and realignment, see *New York Times,* 6 June 1969, 6 November 1969, 21 January 1970, 22 January 1970, 17 March 1970, 21 March 1970, 17 September 1971; "NBA's Big Mistake," 84. On expansion fees, see *Sporting News,* 7 February 1970; *New York Times,* 7 February 1970. On television, see Rader, *In Its Own Image,* 125–26; Sugar, "Thrill of Victory," 123–24; Arledge, *Roone,* 140–42; D. Halberstam, *Breaks of the Game,* 240–48. On NBA's popularity, see Fortunato, "Ultimate Assist," 182–83; Guttmann, *From Ritual to Record,* 142–45.

58. Pluto, *Loose Balls,* 125–271. On ABA's growing quality of play, see Embry, *Inside Game,* 211–15; *New York Times,* 3 October 1971, 30 January 1972, 26 May 1972, 27 May 1972, 17 June 1972. On Erving, see Pluto, *Loose Balls,* 25–29, 222–34, 317–22, 417–21; *New York Times,* 26 September 1972; *Sporting News,* 18 March 1972; Charley Rosen, "Dr. J Makes the Whole World Feel Good," 76, 84–88; Bell, *Legend of Dr. J,* 1–118. On competition and salaries, see "Basketball" 72; D. Fisher, "Instant Millionaires," 32–34"; Banks, "Take the Money and Run," 99–104; Michener, *Sports in America,* 370; *Chicago Tribune,* 18 October 1972. On Hawkins, see Wolf, *Foul!* 297–346; *Sporting News,* 26 October 1968, 28 December 1968, 22 November 1969. On Barry, see Barry, "Why I Want out of the ABA," 26–27, 72.

59. Robertson, *Big O,* 249, 276–80, 284–85; Staudohar, *Playing for Dollars,* 113–16; *New York Times,* 26 August 1969, 20 January 1970, 24 January 1970, 11 February 1970, 12 April 1970, 17 April 1970, 18 April 1970, 19 June 1970, 7 August 1970, 9 October 1970, 21 November 1970, 24 November 1970, 23 March 1971, 3 October 1971, 30 January 1972, 1 February 1972, 23 March 1972, 30 April 1972, 15 June 1972, 16 November 1972; *Sporting News,* 29 April 1972, 6 May 1972, 12 May 1973; Ronberg, "Tossing Bombs," 30–37; Deford, "Buy a Basketball Franchise," 40–43; Deford, "Merger, Madness and Maravich," 28–33.

60. Meschery, "There Is a Disease in Sports Now," 56–63; *New York Times,* 14 April 1972; Meschery, *Caught in the Pivot,* 19; D. Halberstam, *Breaks of the Game,* 8–16; Dickey, *Jock Empire,* 138–48. On Maravich, see Maravich, "I Want to Put on a Show," 39–46; Maravich and Campbell, *Heir to A Dream;* Kriegel, *Pistol.*

61. Watson, "Bill Russell Is Supposed to Put the Super Back in Sonics," 56; *History in Headlines of Sonics,* 16; B. Johnson, *What's Happenin'?* 40–41.

62. *New York Times,* 13 January 1971, 13 March 1971, 17 March 1971, 5 June 1971, 26 June 1971; Carry, "Anybody Else Care to Bid?" 54–55; W. Johnson, "Legal License," 34–41; Fields, "Odd Bedfellows," 193–206; Haywood, *Spencer Haywood,* 134–55; *History in Headlines of Sonics,* 11–16.

63. Watson, "Bill Russell Is Supposed to Put the Super Back in Sonics," 56; Ryan, *Celtics Pride,* 130–34; M. Harris, *Lonely Heroes,* 187–92; Meschery, *Caught in the Pivot,* 135–56; *Seattle Post-Intelligencer,* 21 January 1974; *History in Headlines of Sonics,* 6–17; Wilkens, *Lenny Wilkens Story,* 99–138; Wilkens, *Unguarded,* 122–40.

64. Carry, "High but No Longer Mighty," 48; *Seattle Post-Intelligencer,* 14 May 1973, 22 December 1973; *New York Times,* 12 January 1973, 28 March 1973, 11 December 1973, 12 December 1973, 22 December 1973; *Seattle Times,* 4 January 1974; Watson, "Bill Russell Is Supposed to Put the Super Back in Sonics," 56.

65. B. Russell, *Russell Rules,* 79–80; Watson, "Bill Russell Is Supposed to Put the Super Back in Sonics," 54.

17. SEATTLE'S NEW DICTATOR

1. Watson, "Bill Russell Is Supposed to Put the Super Back in Sonics," 54–62; Sale, *Seattle, Past to Present,* 144–49, 216–23; *Seattle Times,* 14 June 1973; *Seattle Post-Intelligencer,* 2 November 1973, 8 November 1973.

2. Carry, "High but No Longer Mighty," 48; *Chicago Defender,* 27 August 1973; *Seattle Times,* 2 September 1973.

3. Watts, *Slick Watts's Tales from the Supersonics,* 17; *Seattle Post-Intelligencer,* 29 February 1976.

4. *Sacramento Bee,* 3 May 1987; *Seattle Times,* 4 January 1976, 16 March 1978; Axthelm, "Why Pro Basketball Is Sick," 87.

5. *Chicago Defender,* 8 October 1974; Russell and Branch, *Second Wind,* 256–59; B. Russell, *Russell Rules,* 80–83.

6. *Boston Herald-American,* 5 March 1974; Watson, "Bill Russell Is Supposed to Put the Super Back in Sonics," 62; Watts, *Slick Watts's Tales from the Supersonics,* 9–10, 18–19, 27–28, 44–49, 58–60; B. Johnson, *What's Happenin'?* 10.

7. Carry, "High but No Longer Mighty," 48–49; Watts, *Slick Watts's Tales from the Supersonics,* 39–43.

8. *Seattle Times,* 10 October 1973, 18 October 1973, 29 October 1973, 3 November 1973, 12 November 1973, 16 November 1973, 2 December 1973, 5–7 December 1973, 10 December 1973, 13 December 1973, 20 December 1973; *Seattle Post-Intelligencer,* 12 November 1973, 23 December 1973; *Chicago Defender,* 15 November 1973, 8 December 1973.

9. *Chicago Defender,* 2 January 1974; *Seattle Times,* 8 February 1974; *New York Times,* 5 March 1974; *Los Angeles Times,* 19 October 1973; Carry, "High but No Longer Mighty," 48; Haywood, *Spencer Haywood,* 161–62.

10. *History in Headlines of Sonics,* 23; M. Harris, *Lonely Heroes,* 192.

11. Huey, "Who Is John Brisker?" 51–52.

12. Haywood, *Spencer Haywood,* 158–59; Watts, *Slick Watts's Tales from the Supersonics,* 24–25.

13. *Seattle Post-Intelligencer,* 18 January 1974, 19 January 1974; Huey, "Who Is John Brisker?" 50–53; *Seattle Times,* 24 October 1974, 17 October 1975; B. Johnson, *What's Happenin'?* 50–51; Capouya, "Bill Russell, Reconsidered," 37; *New York Times,* 5 March 1974.

14. *Seattle Post-Intelligencer,* 19 January 1974; *Seattle Times,* 17 January 1974, 27 October 1974, 15 December 1974, 29 December 1974, 26 January 1975, 19 January 1975, 18 February 1975, 9 November 1975, 15 February 1976, 7 November 1976; B. Johnson, *What's Happenin'?* 51.

15. *Seattle Times,* 2 February 1974, 4 February 1974, 18 February 1974, 28 March 1974, 29 March 1974; *Seattle Post-Intelligencer,* 18 March 1974, 28 March 1974; *Chicago Defender,* 9 March 1974.

16. For some "Take a Shot!" columns where Russell is asked about politics, see *Seattle Times,* 20 October 1974, 3 November 1974, 7 December 1975, 18 April 1976, 31 October 1976, 27 February 1977, On Russell as voice of franchise, see *Seattle Times,* 24 March 1974, 4 January 1975, 20 March 1975, 11 January 1976. On fans and attendance, see *Seattle Post-Intelligencer,* 26 December 1973; *Seattle Times,* 24 November 1973; *History in Headlines of*

Sonics, 24. On *Time* award, see "200 Faces for the Future," 35, 61; *Seattle Post-Intelligencer,* 8 July 1974, 11 July 1974.

17. *Chicago Defender,* 8 October 1974; *History in Headlines of Sonics,* 25; *Seattle Times,* 1 December 1974, 8 April 1975, 11 April 1975; *Seattle Post-Intelligencer,* 8 April 1975, 28 November 1976. As part of the Burleson trade, Seattle won the right to swap picks with Cleveland in the 1975 draft. Seattle ended up exercising that option, moving from the fifteenth to the twelfth pick. *Seattle Post-Intelligencer,* 6 February 1975.

18. Bob Hopkins, telephone interview with author, 13 October 2008; *Seattle Post-Intelligencer,* 28 November 1976.

19. *Seattle Times,* 19 October 1974, 26 October 1974, 8 November 1974, 11 November 1974, 14 November 1974, 29 November 1974, 9 December 1974, 12 December 1974, 13 December 1974, 1 January 1975, 20 January 1975, 21 January 1975, 3 February 1975, 10 February 1975; *Seattle Post-Intelligencer,* 6 January 1975, 26 January 1975, 30 January 1975, 6 February 1975, 12 February 1975, 19 February 1975.

20. *Seattle Times,* 9 March 1975, 12 March 1975, 17 March 1975, 29 March 1975, 30 March 1975, 8 April 1975; *Seattle Post-Intelligencer,* 20 March 1975, 29 March 1975, 31 March 1975, 8 April 1975; *History in Headlines of Sonics,* 27.

21. *Seattle Times,* 7–9 April 1975, 12 April 1975, 13 April 1975; *Seattle Post-Intelligencer,* 8–9 April 1975, 12 April 1975, 13 April 1975. On new play-off format, see *Seattle Times,* 21 March 1975. Lanier boosted his intensity and all-around game after Russell tutored him in the summer of 1972. M. Harris, *Lonely Heroes,* 150.

22. *Seattle Times,* 14 April 1975, 15 April 1975, 17 April 1975 18 April 1975; *Seattle Post-Intelligencer,* 14 April 1975, 15 April 1975, 17 April 1975, 18 April 1975, 25 April 1975.

23. *Seattle Times,* 2 March 1975, 20 April 1975, 20 April 1975, 22–23 April 1975, 25 April 1975; *Seattle Post-Intelligencer,* 22–26 April 1975.

24. *Seattle Post-Intelligencer,* 25 April 1975, 27 April 1975.

25. *Pittsburgh Courier,* 2 February 1974; *New York Amsterdam News,* 15 June 1974; *Los Angeles Sentinel,* 9 January 1975; "Best of All Worlds," 96–98; Lacy, *Fighting for Fairness,* 123; *New York Times,* 11 March 1972; *Sporting News,* 25 March 1972, 30 March 1972; Embry, *Inside Game,* 191–276; Watson, "Bill Russell Is Supposed to Put the Super Back in Sonics," 54. On Chamberlain coaching and retiring, see Cherry, *Wilt,* 294–99; Pluto, *Loose Balls,* 274–77; "Wilt's Big Leap," 67; Carry, "High but No Longer Mighty," 44–53; Chamberlain, "My Impact Will Be Everlasting," 36–47. Former Celtics also entered the coaching ranks in large numbers: Russell with Seattle, K. C. Jones with San Diego and Washington, Bill Sharman with Los Angeles, Bob Cousy with Cincinnati (later Kansas City), and Tom Heinsohn with Boston. Sam Jones was an assistant with New Orleans, and Larry Siegfried an assistant with Houston. Frank Ramsey coached the Kentucky Colonels of the ABA. Jim Loscutoff coached at Boston State. Tom Sanders coached at Harvard and later succeeded Heinsohn in Boston. *Washington Post,* 24 June 1973; *Seattle Post-Intelligencer,* 9 March 1975.

26. *New York Times,* 27 October 1973; *Boston Globe,* 24 January 2007; Al Attles, telephone interview with author, 8 May 2008; Dave Bing, telephone interview with author, 19 August 2008; Carey and McClellan, *Boston Celtics,* 161.

27. Robinson and Stainback, *Extra Innings,* 83; *Los Angeles Times,* 18 April 1974; *New York Times,* 18 March 1977.

28. *Washington Post*, 6 June 1973; *Los Angeles Times*, 6 June 1973; *Chicago Defender,* 6 June 1973; *Baltimore Afro-American*, 12 June 1973; *Boston Herald-American*, 6 June 1973, 8 June 1973. Regarding his comment about "too many black guys on the team," Russell evidently referred to a 1969 survey by the Celtics, in which more than 50 percent of the respondents voiced that opinion. B. Russell, *Red and Me*, 94.

29. On Boston's resurgent dynasty, see Ryan, *Celtics Pride;* M. Connolly, *Rebound!* 81– 174; *Sporting News*, 28 November 1970, 7 March 1970, 20 February 1971, 20 March 1971, 19 February 1972; Carry, "It Was a Brief Time Out," 22–23; Carry, "It's Just Like Old Times," 12–15; Carry, "They're Replaying the Sixth Man Theme," 26–27; "Rivals," 52; Carry, "In Seven, as in Heaven," 26–29; Carry, "Matter of Celtic Pride," 22–24; Axthelm, "Eternal Celtics," 45. On Russell and Cowens, see M. Harris, *Lonely Heroes*, 139–45. For attendance figures, see Bjarkman, *Boston Celtics Encyclopedia*, 117.

30. Lupo, *Liberty's Chosen Home*, 15, 79, 85–88; T. O'Connor, *Bibles, Brahmins, and Bosses*, 198–220; D. Taylor, *Public Opinion and Collective Action*, 44–91; Formisano, *Boston Against Busing*, 1–21, 75–80, 108–37; Transcript of Interview with Phil Donahue, Bill Russell File, Basketball Hall of Fame; *Seattle Times*, 24 November 1974.

31. *Los Angeles Times*, 6 June 1973; Q. Taylor, *Forging of a Black Community*, 3–10, 190– 240; Deford, "Ring Leader," 100–101; K. Russell, "Growing Up," 27.

32. K. Russell, "Growing Up," 27; Bobrow, "Bill Russell," 16–19, 52–54.

33. Bobrow, "Bill Russell," 18, 52.

34. B. Johnson, "Russell's Back in the Game," 8; Kenyon, "Very Private Bill Russell," 6– 10; Watson, "Russell on the Sonics and Seattle," 48, 68; *Los Angeles Sentinel*, 11 March 1976.

35. *Seattle Times*, 9 February 1975, 10 February 1975; *Seattle Post-Intelligencer,* 10 February 1975; *Springfield Union*, 10 February 1975, 13 February 1975; *New York Times*, 10 February 1975; *Chicago Defender*, 11 February 1975, 27 February 1975; *Chicago Tribune*, 10 February 1975, 13 February 1975; *New York Sun-News*, 16 February 1975; *Phoenix Gazette*, 20 February 1975; *New York Post*, 26 February 1975; *Tennessean Magazine*, 16 March 1975.

36. Press Release dated 24 March 1975, Bill Russell File, Basketball Hall of Fame; *New York Times*, 6 February 1972, 11 February 1975, 18 February 1975, 25 March 1975; *New York Post*, 28 February 1975; uncited column by Phil Pepe from February 1975, Bill Russell File, Basketball Hall of Fame; *Los Angeles Sentinel*, 13 February 1975, 27 March 1975; *Chicago Defender*, 18 February 1975, 30 April 1975, 7 May 1975; *Seattle Times*, 12 February 1975.

37. Russell and Branch, *Second Wind*, 210–14. The Harlem Rens got inducted in 1964 and Rens founder Bob Douglas entered in 1972, but Russell was the Hall's first black individual player.

38. *Springfield Union*, 12 February 1975; *Seattle Post-Intelligencer,* 11 February 1975; Undated Ray Fitzgerald column in *Boston Globe*, Bill Russell File, Basketball Hall of Fame; Russell and Branch, *Second Wind*, 210.

39. Michener, *Sports in America*, 157; *New York Amsterdam News*, 15 February 1975, 22 February 1975, 19 November 1977; *New York Times*, 9 March 1975. One Seattle resident had heard him called an "uppity nigger," but he admired Russell's "special kind of courage." *Seattle Times*, 23 February 1975.

40. W. Johnson, "Collision on the New Underground Railroad," 52–53; *Chicago De-*

fender, 1 February 1968; Edwards, *Revolt of the Black Athlete,* 80–81; Michelson, *Almost a Famous Person,* 4–123.

41. Michelson, *Almost a Famous Person,* 3–6, 124–246; Haywood, *Spencer Haywood,* 163–64.

42. Haywood, *Spencer Haywood,* 17–99; Libby and Haywood, *Stand Up for Something,* 1–4.

43. Donnelly, "Unknown Who Must Save Our Basketball Team," 44–45; *Sporting News,* 9 November 1968, 27 January 1973; Haywood, *Spencer Haywood,* 103–55.

44. Libby and Haywood, *Stand Up for Something,* 158–59, 210–13; Wilkens, *Unguarded,* 135–36.

45. Haywood, *Spencer Haywood,* 158; Libby and Haywood, *Stand Up for Something,* 39–40, 71–72.

46. Haywood, *Spencer Haywood,* 158–60; *Seattle Times,* 7 March 1974, 27 April 1975; *Seattle Post-Intelligencer,* 20 March 1974.

47. Haywood, *Spencer Haywood,* 158–67; Watts, *Slick Watts's Tales from the Supersonics,* 49; *Seattle Post-Intelligencer,* 7 March 1975.

48. Haywood, *Spencer Haywood,* 166–67; *Seattle Times,* 23 October 1975, 24 October 1975, 27 October 1975, 2 November 1975, 3 November 1975, 16 January 1976; *History in Headlines of Sonics,* 28. Ironically, Wilt Chamberlain figured into the Spencer Haywood trade. New York offered the Lakers compensation for Chamberlain, since the Lakers still owned his playing rights in the NBA. Chamberlain wanted to play in New York, but he remained in Hawaii, alienating the New York brass that flew to Los Angeles. The Knicks then pursued Haywood instead. Putnam, "Fortune Cookie Smiled," 77–79.

49. *Seattle Times,* 7 January 1976, 18 January 1976; *Boston Herald-American,* 9 January 1976; "Biggest Deal of All," 15–17.

50. *Seattle Times,* 27 October 1975, 7 January 1976; *Seattle Post-Intelligencer,* 23 November 1975; *History in Headlines of Sonics,* 29; B. Johnson, *What's Happenin'?* 42.

51. Papanek, "Slick's His Name," 30–33; Watts, *Slick Watts's Tales from the Supersonics,* 2–8, 65–88; B. Johnson, *What's Happenin'?* 14–22; Watson, "Slick Watts for Mayor???," 48, 72; *Washington Post,* 15 January 1974; *Seattle Post-Intelligencer,* 28 December 1973, 2 February 1975, 22 October 1975, 29 February 1976, 11 April 1976, 11 January 1977.

52. Barbieri, "Slick Watts Towers," 44–48; Papanek, "Slick's His Name," 30; *Chicago Defender,* 28 October 1975; *Seattle Times,* 15 October 1975, 22 October 1975, 25 October 1975, 28 October 1975, 13 December 1975, 31 December 1975, 5 January 1976, 16 February 1976, 22 February 1976, 9 April 1976; *Seattle Post-Intelligencer,* 19 October 1975, 22 October 1975, 24 October 1975, 14 December 1975, 15 February 1976; *New York Times,* 27 April 1976. On Gray, see *Seattle Times,* 28 February 1975, 16 November 1975; On Brown, see B. Johnson, "Great as He Wants," 15–16; *Seattle Times,* 21 January 1976, 7 March 1976; *New York Times,* 15 April 1976.

53. *Seattle Times,* 8 January 1976, 8 February 1976, 22 February 1976, 23 February 1976, 26 February 1976, 6 March 1976, 21 March 1976; *Seattle Post-Intelligencer,* 8 January 1976, 9 January 1976, 14 March 1976, 1 April 1976, 5 April 1976, 12 April 1976, 13 April 1976.

54. *Seattle Times,* 13 April 1976, 14 April 1976, 16 April 1976, 18 April 1976, 19 April

1976, 21 April 1976, 22 April 1976, 26 April 1976; *Seattle Post-Intelligencer*, 14 April 1976, 16 April 1976, 17 April 1976, 19–21 April 1976, 23 April 1976, 25 April 1976, 26 April 1976.

55. *Seattle Post-Intelligencer*, 20 April 1976; Russell and Branch, *Second Wind*, 257–59.

56. Pluto, *Tall Tales*, 421–34; Danielson, *Home Team*, 210–12; Cole, *Loose Game*, 55–64.

57. *Seattle Times*, 22 October 1976, 25 October 1976, 27 November 1976, 28 November 1976, 1 December 1976, 2 December 1976, 13 December 1976, 16 December 1976. On Wilkerson and Johnson, see *Seattle Times*, 23 November 1976, 12 December 1976, 2 January 1977; "Story Without an Ending," 20; *Boston Globe*, 11 October 1987.

58. *Seattle Times*, 8–10 December 1976, 19 December 1976; B. Johnson, *What's Happenin'?* 159–62, 168–70.

59. *Seattle Times*, 14 December 1976, 15 December 1976, 5 May 1977; Watts, *Slick Watts's Tales from the Supersonics*, 116–17; *Seattle Post-Intelligencer*, 26 December 1976.

60. *Seattle Times*, 26 December 1976, 19 January 1977; B. Johnson, *What's Happenin'?* 178–79.

61. Brewster, "Not-So-Super Sonics," 8–9; Russell and Branch, *Second Wind*, 259; *Seattle Post-Intelligencer*, 28 January 1977, 13 March 1977, 10 April 1977; Bob Hopkins, telephone interview with author, 13 October 2008.

62. *Seattle Times*, 16 January 1977, 6 February 1977; Brewster, "Not-So-Super Sonics," 9; *Seattle Post-Intelligencer*, 19 December 1976, 19 February 1977; Watts, *Slick Watts's Tales from the Supersonics*, 73–73, 172; Barbieri, "Slick Watts Towers," 44–48.

63. *Seattle Post-Intelligencer*, 20 February 1977, 24 February 1977, 27 February 1977, 1 March 1977, 5 March 1977, 10 April 1977; *Seattle Times*, 5 December 1976, 18 January 1977, 27 February 1977, 15 March 1977, 20 March 1977; Watts, *Slick Watts's Tales from the Supersonics*, 137–139; *Sacramento Bee*, 27 April 1987; B. Johnson, *What's Happenin'?* 103, 163, 181, 197–98, 200–205.

64. *Seattle Times*, 6–8 February 1977, 20 February 1977, 6 March 1977; *Seattle Post-Intelligencer*, 7 February 1977, 10 February 1977, 13 February 1977, 23 February 1977; *History in Headlines of Sonics*, 32; *Los Angeles Sentinel*, 10 February 1977; B. Johnson, *What's Happenin'?* 237.

65. *Seattle Post-Intelligencer*, 3 March 1977, 4 March 1977, 8 March 1977, 17 March 1977, 23 March 1977, 25 March 1977, 28 March 1977, 30 March 1977, 6 April 1977, 11 April 1977; *Seattle Times*, 3 March 1977, 4 April 1977, 6 April 1977; Bob Hopkins interview; Russell and Branch, *Second Wind*, 259; B. Johnson, *What's Happenin'?* 224.

66. B. Johnson, *What's Happenin'?* 224–25.

67. B. Johnson, *What's Happenin'?*; B. Johnson, "Russell's Back in the Game," 8. On the book, see *Seattle Times*, 10 December 1978; Watts, *Slick Watts's Tales from the Supersonics*, 136–37. For some of Johnson's profiles, see *Seattle Post-Intelligencer*, 16 November 1975, 30 November 1975, 21 December 1975, 4 January 1976, 8 February 1976, 4 April 1976, 18 April 1976, 24 October 1976, 21 November 1976, 26 December 1976.

68. B. Johnson, *What's Happenin'?* 226–33; *Seattle Post-Intelligencer*, 10 April 1977, 11 April 1977; *Seattle Times*, 7 March 1977, 10 April 1977, 11 April 1977; *Washington Post*, 7 April 1977; *Los Angeles Times*, 8 April 1977; *Chicago Tribune*, 11 April 1977.

69. *New York Times*, 5 May 1977; *Springfield Daily News*, 5 May 1977; *Seattle Post-Intelligencer*, 2 May 1977, 4 May 1977, 5 May 1977; *Seattle Times*, 4 May 1977, 5 May 1977.

70. *New York Times*, 5 May 1977; *Seattle Times*, 11 May 1977, 13 March 1977, 7 June 1979; *Sporting News*, 23 November 1987; *Boston Globe*, 12 May 1977. Sam Schulman and Gene Klein had paid a $1.8 million fee to enter the NBA in 1967. In 1984, Schulman bought out Klein and sold the franchise to Ackerly Communications for $21 million. Josza, *American Sports Empire*, 67.

71. *New York Times*, 14 May 1977; B. Johnson, *What's Happenin'?* 256–57; Papanek, "Add Super to the Sonics," 81–85; Kirkpatrick, "Down Goes Big Bill," 20–21; Kirkpatrick, "Ready for a Sonic Boom," 12–15; Papanek, "From Boom to Bust," 24–25; Papanek, "It Was Seattle, Handily," 16–19.

72. *Seattle Times*, 7 June 1979; *History in Headlines of Sonics*, 33–43; Watts, *Slick Watts's Tales from the Supersonics*, 145–51; Wilkens, *Unguarded*, 153–85; Axthelm, "Pity the Poor Coaches," 73.

73. *Boston Globe*, 3 May 1987; *Sacramento Bee*, 28 April 1987; B. Johnson, *What's Happenin'?* 263.

18. RUSSELL REDUX

1. *Seattle Post-Intelligencer*, 12 May 1977; B. Russell, *Russell Rules*, 130; *Seattle Times*, 31 December 1978; Russell and Branch, *Second Wind*, 93–118, 260–65.

2. *Seattle Times*, 8 June 1977; *Binghamton Press*, 9 June 1977; *New York Times*, 10 June 1977; Rein, "Catching His Second Wind," 78.

3. *Los Angeles Times*, 23 December 1980; *Los Angeles Sentinel*, 1 January 1981; Michaelson, *Almost a Famous Person*, 222; Russell and Branch, *Second Wind*, 261–62.

4. *Seattle Times*, 26 November 1978; *Sacramento Bee*, 6 November 1987.

5. Russell's columns date from at least 9 October 1977 to 25 January 1981. For columns on the mentioned subjects, see *Seattle Times*, 16 October 1977, 30 October 1977, 6 November 1977, 12 February 1978, 14 May 1978, 4 June 1978, 13 August 1978, 27 August 1978, 19 November 1978, 21 January 1979, 25 February 1979, 7 October 1979, 2 December 1979, 9 December 1979, 30 December 1979, 30 January 1980, 11 January 1981, 25 January 1981. On more of Russell's ideas, see *Seattle Times*, 27 October 1985.

6. "Author's Note" from Russell and Branch, *Second Wind*; *Seattle Times*, 11 May 1977.

7. *New Republic*, 20 October 1979; *New York Times Book Review*, 7 October 1979; *Washington Post*, 21 October 1979. For other positive reviews, see *Los Angeles Times*, 4 November 1979; *Library Journal*, 15 October 1979; B. Johnson, "Russell's Back in the Game," 8; J. King, "Accolade for Versatile Bill Russell," 14. For excerpt from *Second Wind*, see *New York Times*, 16 September 1979. For analysis of its literary tropes, see Pipkin, *Sporting Lives*, 53, 71, 76–78, 84–88, 95–96, 121–22.

8. Russell and Branch, *Second Wind*, 262–65.

9. K. Russell, "Growing Up," 23; Deford, "Ring Leader," 100–101. In 1983 police nabbed Arthur L. Trotter in Natchitoches, Louisiana, for running confidence schemes and posing as professional athletes, including Russell. Their only resemblance was black skin and a goatee. Reportedly, Trotter tried convincing one woman that he needed $2,500 to open a

restaurant while posing as Russell. He explained that he used to be 6'10", but doctors removed ten inches of bone from his legs so he could fit in his Mercedes. *Jet,* 8 August 1983; *Seattle Post-Intelligencer,* 20 July 1983.

10. Transcript of Interview with Phil Donahue, Bill Russell File, Basketball Hall of Fame; *Atlanta Daily World,* 29 May 1981; *Los Angeles Times,* 3 December 1980, 2 April 2007; John LoSchiavo, telephone interview with author, 13 April 2007; Tom Nelson, telephone interview with author, 11 July 2006. On all-time NBA team, see also *New York Times,* 31 October 1980, 2 November 1980; *Los Angeles Times,* 10 October 1980. Russell also participated in a Seattle fund-raiser for the American Federation of Television and Radio Artists, helping a legal challenge for a deposed local reporter. *Seattle Post-Intelligencer,* 29 January 1987.

11. Hill and Weingrad, *Saturday Night,* 309–11, 344–61; *Seattle Times,* 18 November 1979; *Washington Post,* 19 October 1979; www.imdb.com.

12. Production information from Twentieth Century Fox, Bill Russell File, Margaret Herrick Library of the Motion Picture Academy of Arts and Sciences; *New York Amsterdam News,* 16 May 1981; *Los Angeles Times,* 1 February 1981; www.imdb.com.

13. *Seattle Post-Intelligencer,* 21 August 1985; *Seattle Times,* 21 August 1985, 8 September 1985, 13 September 1985; Horovitz, *Sixteen Short Plays,* 258–87; *Variety,* 2 October 1985. Horovitz tried to reprise the production in a movie, but it never came off. *Boston Globe,* 9 November 1987.

14. Durslag, "He's on the Rebound from Basketball," 36–38; *Chicago Tribune,* 25 August 1978; *Los Angeles Times,* 18 July 1978, 26 October 1978; *Seattle Times,* 17 July 1978.

15. *Seattle Times,* 1 October 1978; *Chicago Tribune,* 18 January 1980.

16. Rader, *In Its Own Image,* 147–48; D. Halberstam, *Playing for Keeps,* 117–18; *Los Angeles Times,* 19 August 1980.

17. Feinstein, *Punch,* 3–16, 35–93, 208–15; Papanek, "There's an Ill Wind Blowing for the NBA," 20–27.

18. *Chicago Tribune,* 15 February 1980; *Jet,* 8 October 1984; *USA Today,* 20 September 1984; *Atlanta World,* 13 October 1981; *Los Angeles Times,* 29 May 1982; *Boston Herald,* 30 January 1983; *Washington Post,* 27 April 1980.

19. *Boston Globe,* 15 February 1980, 13 June 1982, 18 October 1983, 1 February 1985 5 November 1999; *Los Angeles Sentinel,* 21 February 1980; *Washington Post,* 27 April 1980; *New York Post,* 22 July 1971, 7 April 1982; *Binghamton Press,* 13 February 1982; *Chicago Tribune,* 28 April 1982; *Los Angeles Times,* 12 February 1983; Woolf, "This Coach Is Bleeping Good," 94–95; Taafe, "Good, the Bad, and the Ugly," 77; *Boston Herald,* 18 October 1983; *Springfield Republican,* 30 October 1983.

20. D. Halberstam, *Playing for Keeps,* 115–47; Ryan and Pluto, *Forty-Eight Minutes,* 202–3.

21. Wideman, *Hoop Roots,* 167–68; Lane, *Under the Boards,* 113–45; Boyd, *Young, Black, Rich and Famous,* 46–69. On Bird, see Deford, "Player for the Ages," 46–65; Bird, *Drive.*

22. *Boston Globe,* 29 March 1982, 27 October 1985, 4 June 1987, 15 June 1987, 26 September 1990, 2 February 1992, 17 December 1992; *Pittsburgh Courier,* 15 August 1987; *Boston Herald,* 13 August 1991; Araton and Bondy, *Selling of the Green,* 107–27, 157–69; "Scorecard," 1 October 1990, 9. See also M. Connolly, *Rebound!,* 203–87.

23. "Remembrance of Things Past," 35; Callahan, "Impressions in Black and White," 60; Ryan and Pluto, *Forty-Eight Minutes,* 66–67; Plimpton, *The X Factor,* 115–16. Auerbach also

hired K. C. Jones, first as an assistant coach and then as the head coach for Boston's 1984 and 1986 triumphs. For Jones, it was a satisfying rebound from depression, divorce, and alcoholism in the late 1970s. He believed that his association with the Celtics family saved him. See K. C. Jones, *Rebound,* 133–81.

24. *Boston Globe,* 21 September 1980; *Boston Herald,* 23 October 1984; *Sacramento Bee,* 17 January 1988.

25. K. Russell, "Growing Up," 23; *Boston Globe,* 5 January 1985; Auerbach, *On and Off the Court,* 12–13; Shaughnessy, *Seeing Red,* 244–45; Deford, "No. 2 in the Rafters," 40–44, 79–81.

26. *Sacramento Bee,* 27 April 1987; *New York Times,* 28 April 1987; *Boston Globe,* 28 April 1987; *Jet,* 18 May 1987; *Pittsburgh Courier,* 16 May 1987; McCormack, *Never Lose,* 91–129; J. Reynolds, *Reynolds Remembers,* 33–47.

27. *Sacramento Bee,* 9 March 1988, 24 April 1987–1 May 1987, 16 December 1987; McCallum, "King at His New Court," 37–42; Dickey, "Bill Russell," 18–23; Price, "Bill Russell," 42–46; *Seattle Post-Intelligencer,* 14 March 1988.

28. Capouya, "Bill Russell, Reconsidered," 33–38; *New York Times,* 20 October 1987; *USA Today,* 3 November 1987; *Seattle Times,* 4 November 1987, 18 December 1987; *Sacramento Bee,* 5 November 1987; *Sporting News,* 23 November 1987; *Washington Post,* 12 February 1988.

29. *Sacramento Bee,* 18 May 1987, 23 June 1987, 7 October 1987, 5 November 1987; J. Reynolds, *Reynolds Remembers,* 57–61.

30. *Sacramento Bee,* 7 November 1987, 30 November 1987, 7 December 1987, 8 December 1987, 13 December 1987, 27 December 1987, 1 January 1988, 10 January 1988, 13 January 1988, 4 February 1988; *Seattle Times,* 3 January 1988.

31. *Sacramento Bee,* 22 September 1987, 4 October 1987, 17 December 1987, 6 March 1988, 9 March 1988.

32. *Sacramento Bee,* 28 January 1988, 9 February 1988, 10 February 1988, 8 March 1988, 9 March 1988.

33. *Sacramento Bee,* 23 February 1990.

34. *Seattle Times,* 28 February 1988, 8 March 1988; *Sacramento Bee,* 26 February 1988, 3 March 1988, 6 March 1988, 8 March 1988, 9 March 1988; *Seattle Post-Intelligencer,* 8 March 1988, 14 March 1988; McCallum, "King for a Year," 15.

35. *Sacramento Bee,* 13 March 1988, 19 March 1988, 3 April 1988, 24 April 1988, 30 June 1988, 4 September 1988, 26 November 1988, 15 August 1989; Reynolds, *Reynolds Remembers,* 65, 73, 80–82.

36. *Sacramento Bee,* 18 November 1988, 26 November 1988, 24 February 1989, 26 February 1989, 25 April 1989.

37. *Sacramento Bee,* 28 June 1989, 29 June 1989, 27–29 September 1989, 27 October 1989, 29 October 1989.

38. *Sacramento Bee,* 6 December 1989, 20 December 1989, 24 December 1989; McCallum, *Unfinished Business,* 178.

39. Deford, "Ring Leader," 100.

40. *Sacramento Bee,* 20 December 1989.

41. *Los Angeles Times,* 2 November 1980, 6 January 1982; *Boston Globe,* 14 December

1980; *Binghamton Press and Sun Bulletin,* 8 November 1985; "Inside Track," 95–98; Deford, "Doing Just Fine, My Man," 62–76. In 1979, after Russell bought a subcompact Volkswagen Rabbit, his agent suggested an endorsement deal with the car manufacturer. Volkswagen had already contracted Chamberlain for the endorsement. *Los Angeles Times,* 18 April 1979; *Washington Post,* 20 April 1979.

42. On Chamberlain's potential comebacks, see *New York Times,* 12 July 1975, 13 September 1975, 9 December 1978, 15 December 1978, 2 February 1982; *Philadelphia Bulletin,* 9 December 1978, 16 November 1979, *Philadelphia Inquirer,* 5 December 1980; *Los Angeles Times,* 29 January 1982. On Chamberlain's good nature and celebrity, see Rosin, *Philly Hoops,* 46–47; Lupica, "Dipper's Lament," 53–56.

43. Chamberlain, *View from Above,* 251; *Boston Globe,* 6 November 1991; Fotheringham, "Could Wilt Really Count that High?" 84; Garrity, "Wilt Chamberlain," 24–28; Ashe and Rampersad, *Days of Grace,* 238–39. In the 1980s, Chamberlain also took myriad potshots at Kareem Abdul-Jabbar, who broke Chamberlain's all-time scoring title and won six NBA titles. Abdul-Jabbar responded in *Kareem,* his best-selling account of his final season, by labeling his former mentor a quitter in "An Open Letter to Wilt Chumperlame." Abdul-Jabbar, *Kareem,* 285–90. Chamberlain wrote another book in 1997 of even poorer quality and judgment. Among other absurdities, it claimed that Gheorghe Muresan was better than Shaquille O'Neal. Chamberlain, *Who's Running the Asylum?* 15.

44. Goldman and Lupica, *Wait Till Next Year,* 254–55; McCallum, "Basketball," 28–29; Montville, "Bill Russell," 102; Deford, "Ring Leader," 100–101; Shields, *Black Planet,* 98.

45. *New York Times,* 16 June 2000; Deford, "Ring Leader," 101.

46. Uncited article from 1992, Bill Russell File, Basketball Hall of Fame; *Seattle Times,* 21 June 1992; "Judgment Calls," 9; *Boston Globe,* 4 June 1994, 5 June 1994, 9 June 1995; *Boston Herald,* 7 June 1994, 7 January 1996.

47. J. Taylor, *Rivalry,* 363–64; B. Russell, *Russell Rules,* 5–6; *Boston Herald,* 5 January 1995; *Jet,* 30 January 1995; *New York Times,* 30 October 1996.

48. *Seattle Times,* 9 January 1995; *Boston Globe,* 8 January 1995; *Boston Herald,* 8 January 1995, 9 January 1995; "Scorecard," 16 January 1995, 11.

49. *New York Times,* 30 October 1996; *Boston Globe,* 30 October 1996; Cherry, *Wilt,* 360–61.

50. *New York Times,* 13 October 1999; *Boston Globe,* 14 October 1999; Levin, "Wonder of Wilt," 82; *New York Amsterdam News,* 14 October 1999, 21 October 1999; *Jet,* 1 November 1999; *Lawrence Journal-World,* 18 October 1999.

51. B. Russell, *Russell Rules,* 7.

52. Kellner, "Sports Spectacle, Michael Jordan, and Nike," 305–25; Dyson, "Be Like Mike?"; D. Halberstam, *Playing for Keeps;* 6–8, 11–12, 416–17; Wideman, *Hoop Roots,* 40–42; LaFeber, *Michael Jordan and the New Global Capitalism.* Between 1950 and 2000, the NBA had grown 71 percent in teams, 112 percent in games, and 1,446 percent in attendance. Josza, *American Sports Empire,* 2.

53. See Bascom, "Basketball"; Boyd and Shropshire, "Basketball Jones: A New World Order?" 1–11; Early, "Why Baseball *Was* the National Pastime," 29–32; Melnick and Sabo, "Sport and Social Mobility among African American and Hispanic Athletes," 221–41; Early, "Performance and Reality," 11–20.

54. On black sport fixation, see Hoberman, *Darwin's Athletes*, 3–95; McNutt, *Hooked on Hoops*; Gaston, "Destruction of the Young Black Male." On black masculinity and marketing, see Lane, *Under the Boards*, 1–112; Shields, *Black Planet*; Maharaj, "Talking Trash," 97–110; A. Baker, "Hoop Dreams," 215–39. On de-politicized athletes, see Rhoden, *Forty Million Dollar Slaves*, 147–217. See also Miles, "Basketball, Racial Authenticity, and Masculinity."

55. *Detroit Free Press*, 18 January 2002.

56. Frank Deford, telephone interview with author, 22 September 2008; Deford, "Ring Leader"; *New York Times*, 10 April 2000, 16 June 2000; *Bill Russell: My Life, My Way; Variety*, 17–23 April 2000.

57. *New York Times*, 16 June 2000.

58. *New York Times*, 16 June 2000; B. Russell, *Russell Rules*.

59. *New York Times*, 16 June 2000; www.vs-a.com.

60. *Boston Herald*, 18 January 2000; Rushin, "Doing Well and Doing Good," 19; *Jet*, 11 December 2006; *Harvard Gazette*, 7 June 2007; *USA Today*, 12 September 2007; *Boston Globe*, 8 February 2005, 17 November 2005, 13 May 2007, 20 May 2007; *Seattle Times*, 15 April 2001; *Slate*, 17 November 2005; B. Russell, *Red and Me; New York Observer*, 14 July 2008.

61. *New York Times*, 18 January 2006, 19 September 2007. The O'Neal-Bryant truce eroded when Bryant faced allegations of rape in Colorado and told investigators that O'Neal often bribed his way out of problems stemming from marital infidelity. O'Neal was later caught on video delivering a bawdy rap about Bryant. *Washington Times*, 25 June 2008.

62. *Boston Herald*, 6 April 1999; *Boston Globe*, 17 June 1999, 6 November 1999, 1 January 2000, 11 December 2000; Deford, "Ring Leader," 99.

63. Russell and Branch, *Second Wind*, 183; *Sacramento Bee*, 16 January 1988, 17 January 1988; *Boston Globe*, 16 January 1988, 15 January 1995, 22 January 1995; *Boston Herald*, 22 April 1995.

64. *Boston Globe*, 10 March 1999, 26–29 May 1999; *Boston Herald*, 17 May 1999, 27 May 1999; *Pittsburgh Courier*, 24 April 1999; Cherry, *Wilt*, 363; B. Russell, *Russell Rules*, 231–34; *Jet*, 14 June 1999; Dolph Schayes, telephone interview with author, 13 April 2007.

65. *Boston Herald*, 24 May 1999, 27 May 1999; *Boston Globe*, 6 November 1999; Bob Cousy, telephone interview with author, 23 April 2007.

66. *Boston Globe*, 12 May 2000; 8 November 2000, 12 April 2005; Pearson, "Green Giant," 240; *Charlestown Patriot-Bridge*, 19 April 2007; *Boston Herald*, 28 May 1999, 10 November 2000, 8 February 2001, 2 August 2002, 16 April 2005.

67. *Boston Herald*, 8 April 1999, 8 October 1999, 11 October 1999, 12 October 1999, 15 October 1999, 29 October 1999, 18 February 2000, 30 April 2000, 18 January 2002; *Sporting News*, 27 May 2002; *Boston Globe*, 8 October 1999, 12 October 1999, 8 November 1999, 25 April 2003, 31 October 2005.

68. McCallum, "Seems Like Old Times," 30–35.

69. *Boston Globe*, 18 June 2008.

70. Interviews available on http://www.youtube.com/watch?v = zc0a99xr2Rs&feature = related; www.youtube.com/watch?v = iy1y7-mUCTo&feature = related.

71. B. Russell, *Go Up for Glory*, 214.

BIBLIOGRAPHY

Aamidor, Abraham. *Chuck Taylor, All Star: The True Story of the Man Behind the Most Famous Athletic Shoe in History*. Bloomington: Indiana University Press, 2006.

"The ABA: Playing the Game Called Survival." *Sports Illustrated*, 23 October 1967, 46–47.

Abdul-Jabbar, Kareem, and Peter Knobler. *Giant Steps*. New York: Bantam Books, 1983.

———, with Mignon McCarthy. *Kareem*. New York: Warner Books, 1990.

———, with Raymond Obstfeld. *On the Shoulders of Giants: My Personal Journey Through the Harlem Renaissance*. New York: Simon and Schuster, 2007.

Adoff, Arnold. *Black on Black: Commentaries by Negro Americans*. Toronto: MacMillan Company, 1968.

"After Five Years." *Newsweek*, 2 April 1956, 84–85.

Alcindor Lew, with Jack Olsen. "My Story." *Sports Illustrated*, 27 October 1969, 82–88.

———. "UCLA Was a Mistake." *Sports Illustrated*, 3 November 1969, 34–40, 45.

———. "A Year of Turmoil and Decision." *Sports Illustrated*, 10 November 1969, 35–46.

Alfieri, Gus. *Lapchick: The Life of a Legendary Player and Coach in the Glory Days of Basketball*. Guilford, CT: Lyons Press, 2006.

"All the Credentials." *Time*, 29 April 1966, 104–6.

Allen, Forrest C. *Better Basketball: Techniques, Tactics and Tales*. New York: Whittlesey House, 1937.

"Along Came Bill." *Time*, 2 January 1956, 36–37.

"Americans Abroad." *Newsweek*, 6 July 1951, 85–86.

"And Still Champions." *Time*, 6 December 1963, 92–93.

Anderson, Carol. *Eyes Off the Prize: The United Nations and the African American Struggle for Human Rights, 1944–1955*. New York: Cambridge University Press, 2003.

Anderson, Dave. "Trials of the Tall Men." *Dell Sports*, February 1962, 4–7, 94.

Anderson, Kelli. "In Their Own Style." *Sports Illustrated*, 3 July 2006, 98–100.

Anderson, Lars, and Chad Millman. *Pickup Artists: Street Basketball in America.* New York: Verso, 1998.

"The Angry Black Athlete." *Newsweek,* 15 July 1968, 56–60.

Applin, Albert G. "From Muscular Christianity to the Market Place: The History of Men's and Boy's Basketball in the United States." PhD diss., University of Massachusetts, 1982.

Araton, Harvey, and Filip Bondy. *The Selling of the Green: The Financial Rise and Moral Decline of the Boston Celtics.* New York: HarperCollins, 1992.

"Are Some of Our Best Friends Gamblers?" *Life,* 22 September 1967, 8.

Arledge, Roone. *Roone: A Memoir.* New York: HarperCollins, 2003.

Arsenault, Raymond. *Freedom Riders: 1961 and the Struggle for Racial Justice.* New York: Oxford University Press, 2006.

Ashe, Arthur. *A Hard Road to Glory: A History of the African-American Athlete 1619–1918.* Volumes 1–3. New York: Amistad, 1988.

———, and Arnold Rampersad. *Days of Grace: A Memoir.* New York: Alfred A. Knopf, 1993.

Astor, Gerald. "Halfway Point in Pro Basketball." *Sports Illustrated,* 24 January 1955, 46–49.

Auerbach, Arnold "Red." *Basketball for the Player, the Fan, and the Coach.* New York: Pocket Books, 1953.

———, with Ken Dooley. *MBA Management by Auerbach: Management Tips from the Leader of One of America's Most Successful Organizations.* New York: Macmillan, 1991.

———, and John Feinstein. *Let Me Tell You a Story: A Lifetime in the Game.* New York: Little, Brown and Company, 2004.

———, with Joe Fitzgerald. *On and Off the Court.* New York: Macmillan, 1985.

———, and Joe Fitzgerald. *Red Auerbach: An Autobiography.* New York: G. P. Putnam's Sons, 1977.

———, with Irv Goodman. "Every All-American Doesn't Make a Pro." *Sport,* May 1955, 34–35, 76–77.

———, as told to Al Hirshberg. "How I Handle the Boston Celtics." *Saturday Evening Post,* 16 December 1961, 92–95.

———, and Paul Sann. *Red Auerbach: Winning the Hard Way.* Boston: Little, Brown and Company, 1966.

Axthelm, Pete. *The City Game: Basketball from the Garden to the Playgrounds.* Bison Books Edition. 1970. Reprint, Lincoln: University of Nebraska Press, 1999.

———. "The Eternal Celtics." *Newsweek,* 31 May 1976, 45.

———. "Pity the Poor Coaches." *Newsweek,* 1 May 1978, 73.

———. "Sports." *Vogue,* 15 November 1970, 76.

———. "Why Pro Basketball Is Sick." *Newsweek,* 22 November 1976, 87.

———. "Wilt Chamberlain: Victory in Our Time." *Los Angeles Times Magazine,* 27 October 1968, 42–47.

———. "The Year the Lakers Won the Championship." *Sport,* December 1972, 54–57, 101–7.

Baker, Aaron. "Hoop Dreams in Black and White: Race and Basketball Movies." In Boyd and Shropshire, *Basketball Jones,* 215–39.

———, and Todd Boyd, eds. *Out of Bounds: Sports, Media, and the Politics of Identity.* Bloomington: Indiana University Press, 1997.

Baker, William J. *Jesse Owens: An American Life*. New York: Free Press, 1986.

———. *Playing with God: Religion and Modern Sport*. Cambridge, MA: Harvard University Press, 2007.

———. *Sports in the Western World*. Rev. ed. 1982. Reprint, Urbana: University of Illinois Press, 1988.

Ballard, Chris. "Frank Ramsey, Celtics Sixth Man." *Sports Illustrated*, 26 February 2001, 14.

Banks, Lacy J. "Take the Money and Run." *Ebony*, February 1972, 99–104.

Barbieri, Ralph. "Slick Watts Towers over Bill Russell." *Sport*, January 1977, 44–48.

Barry, Rick, as told to Bill Gildea. "Why I Want out of the ABA." *Sport*, April 1970, 26–27, 72.

———, with Bill Libby. *Confessions of a Basketball Gypsy: The Rick Barry Story*. Englewood Cliffs, NJ: Prentice-Hall, 1972.

"Basketball: In the Money." *Newsweek*. 23 October 1972, 72.

"Basketball Bounces Back." *Time*, 24 March 1952, 66.

"Basketball: NBA v. ABA." *Ebony*, January 1968, 64–70.

"Basketball's All-Time All-America." *Sport*, April 1955, 20–23.

"Basketball's Best." *Time*, 14 March 1960, 52–53.

"Basketball's Leaning Tower." *Ebony*, April 1956, 50–51.

"Basketball's Little Big Shot." *Time*, 28 December 1953, 37.

Bass, Amy, ed. *In the Game: Race, Identity, and Sports in the Twentieth Century*. New York: Palgrave MacMillan, 2005.

———. *Not the Triumph but the Struggle: The 1968 Olympics and the Making of the Black Athlete*. Minneapolis: University of Minnesota Press, 2002.

Batchelor, Bob. *Basketball in America: From the Playgrounds to Jordan's Game and Beyond*. New York: Haworth Press, 2005.

Battema, Douglas L. "Going for the Gold: A History of the Olympic Games and U.S. Television, 1956–1988." PhD diss., University of Wisconsin, 2002.

Baumbach, Jonathan. "The Aesthetics of Basketball." *Esquire*, January 1970, 140–46.

Baylor, Elgin. "Elgin Baylor's Play-off Diary." *Sport*, July 1969, 34–37, 85–86.

Bee, Clair, and Ken Norton. *The Science of Coaching*. 2d ed. 1942. Reprint, New York: Ronald Press Company, 1959.

Bell, Marty. *The Legend of Dr. J*. 1975. Reprint, New York: New American Library, 1981.

Bellamy, Robert V., Jr. "Professional Sports Organizations: Media Strategies." In Wenner, *Media, Sports, and Society*, 127–28.

Belth, Alex. *Stepping Up: The Story of Curt Flood and His Fight For Baseball Players' Rights*. New York: Persea Books, 2006.

Berger, Phil. *Miracle on 33rd Street: The New York Knickerbockers' Championship Season*. New York: Simon and Schuster, 1970.

———. "Pro Basketball's Best Defenders." *Sport*, April 1966, 30–35.

———. "The *Sport* Interview: Red Auerbach." *Sport*, June 1979, 23–29.

Berkow, Ira. *Oscar Robertson: The Golden Year, 1964*. Englewood Cliffs, NJ: Prentice-Hall, 1971.

———. *Red: A Biography of Red Smith*. New York: Times Books, 1986.

———. *To the Hoop: The Seasons of a Basketball Life*. New York: BasicBooks, 1997.

Berry, Jason. *Amazing Grace: With Charles Evers in Mississippi*. New York: Saturday Review Press, 1973.

"Best Big Man on View." *Life*, 16 January 1956, 12–14.

"The Best of All Worlds for a Black Pro." *Ebony*, January 1975, 96–98.

"Better than the Best?" *Newsweek*, 25 November 1957, 88.

"Better to Die than Lose." *Time*, 3 May 1963, 85.

"Big, Big Men Cash in on League War." *Ebony*, December 1969, 164–73.

"Big Man, Big Business." *Ebony*, August 1964, 57–64.

"The Big Surprise of 1955." *Sports Illustrated*, 28 March 1955, 17–19.

"The Biggest Deal of All." *Sonics Magazine*, March–April 1977, 15–17.

Bill Russell: My Life, My Way. Home Box Office, 2000.

"Bill Russell—The Antenna with Arms." *Look*, 10 January 1956, 66–68.

"Bill vs. Wilt." *Life*, 1 December 1961, 51–55.

Bird, Larry, with Bob Ryan. *Drive: The Story of My Life*. New York: Doubleday, 1989.

Bjarkman, Peter C. *The Biographical History of Basketball*. Lincolnwood, IL: Masters Press, 2000.

———. *Boston Celtics Encyclopedia*. Champaign, IL: Sports Publishing, 2002.

Black Magic. ESPN, 2008.

Bloom, John, and Michael Nevin Willard, eds. *Sports Matters: Race, Recreation, and Culture*. New York: New York University Press, 2002.

Bluestone, Barry, and Mary Huff Stevenson. *The Boston Renaissance: Race, Space, and Economic Change in an American Metropolis*. New York: Russell Sage Foundation, 2000.

"Bob Cousy Examines Pro Basketball's Problems and Progress." *Sport*, February 1962, 24–27, 95.

Bobrow, Norm. "Bill Russell: A Private Man." *View Northwest*, October 1975, 16–19, 52–54.

Bogle, Donald. *Primetime Blues: African Americans on Network Television*. New York: Farrar, Straus and Giroux. 2001.

———. *Toms, Coons, Mulattoes, Mammies, and Bucks: An Interpretive History of Blacks in American Films*. New exp. ed. 1973. Reprint, New York: Continuum, 1993.

Bontemps, Arna. *Famous Negro Athletes*. New York: Dodd, Mead and Co., 1964.

Boskin, Joseph. *Sambo: The Rise and Demise of an American Jester*. New York: Oxford University Press, 1986.

Boston, Ralph. "Why They Should Not." *Sport*, March 1968, 42–43, 68–69.

"Boston's Old, Old Pros." *Newsweek*, 19 May 1969, 77.

Boyd, Todd. "The Day the Niggaz Took Over: Basketball, Commodity Culture, and Black Masculinity." In Baker and Boyd, *Out of Bounds*, 134–37.

———. *Young, Black, Rich and Famous: The Rise of the NBA, the Hip Hop Invasion, and the Transformation of American Culture*. New York: Doubleday, 2003.

———, and Kenneth L. Shropshire, eds. *Basketball Jones: America Above the Rim*. New York: New York University Press, 2000.

———, and Kenneth L. Shropshire, eds. "Basketball Jones: A New World Order?" In *Basketball Jones*, 1–11.

Bradley, Bill. *Life on the Run*. 1976. Reprint, New York: Vintage Books, 1995.

Branch, Taylor. *At Canaan's Edge: America in the King Years 1965–68.* New York: Simon and Schuster, 2006.

——. *Parting the Waters: America in the King Years 1954–63.* New York: Simon and Schuster, 1988.

——. *Pillar of Fire: America in the King Years 1963–65.* New York: Simon and Schuster, 1998.

Breslin, Jimmy. "Can Basketball Survive Chamberlain?" *Saturday Evening Post,* 1 December 1956, 33, 104–8.

——. "The Untold Facts Behind the Basketball Scandals." *Sport,* November 1961, 16–19, 78–80.

Brewster, David. "The Not-So-Super Sonics." *The Weekly,* 19–25 January 1977, 8–9.

Brody, Tom C. "Meet the New Wilt Chamberlain." *Sports Illustrated,* 2 March 1964, 24–25.

——. "Who Says You Can't Win 'Em All?" *Sports Illustrated,* 13 April 1964, 104–5.

Brokhin, Yuri. *The Big Red Machine: The Rise and Fall of Soviet Olympic Champions.* New York: Random House, 1978.

Brooks, Dana, and Ronald Althouse. *Racism in College Athletics: The African American Athlete's Experience.* 2d ed. 1993. Reprint, Morgantown, WV: Fitness Information Technology, 2000.

Broussard, Albert S. *Black San Francisco: The Struggle for Racial Equality in the West, 1900–1954.* Lawrence: University Press of Kansas, 1993.

Brown, Jim, with Steve Delsohn. *Out of Bounds.* New York: Zebra Books, 1989.

Brown, Jimmy, with Myron Cope. *Off My Chest.* Garden City, NY: Doubleday, 1964.

Brown, William Henry, Jr. "Class Aspects of Residential Development and Choice in the Oakland Black Community." PhD diss., University of California at Berkeley, 1970.

Bruns, Bill. "A Long Way with West—All the Way with Wilt?" *Life,* 13 March 1970, 46–50.

Bryant, Howard. *Shut Out: A Story of Race and Baseball in Boston.* Boston: Beacon Press, 2002.

Burnes, Bob. "Bob Pettit and the Hawks." *Sport,* February 1958, 24–25, 89.

Burstyn, Varda. *The Rites of Men: Manhood, Politics, and the Culture of Sport.* Toronto: University of Toronto Press, 1999.

Byers, Walter, with Charles Hammer. *Unsportsmanlike Conduct: Exploiting College Athletes.* Ann Arbor: University of Michigan, 1995.

"Café Society Rediscovers Harlem." *Ebony,* June 1962, 35–36.

Callahan, Tom. "Impressions in Black and White." *Time,* 23 December 1985, 60.

Campbell, John C. *Tito's Separate Road: America and Yugoslavia in World Politics.* New York: Harper and Row, 1967.

"Can't Anybody Here Beat These Guys?" *Time,* 29 January 1965, 60.

"Can't Miss." *Newsweek,* 12 March 1973, 61.

Caponi, Gena Dagel. "Introduction: The Case for an African American Aesthetic." In Caponi, *Signifyin(g), Sanctifyin, and Slam Dunking,* 2–41.

——, ed. *Signifyin(g), Sanctifyin, and Slam Dunking: A Reader in African American Expressive Culture.* Amherst: University of Massachusetts Press, 1999.

Caponi-Tabery, Gena. *Jump for Joy: Jazz, Basketball, and Black Culture in 1930s America.* Amherst: University of Massachusetts Press, 2008.

———. "Jump for Joy: Jump Blues, Dance, and Basketball in 1930s African America." In Bloom and Willard, *Sports Matters*, 39–74.

Capouya, John. "Bill Russell, Reconsidered." *Sport*, January 1988, 33–38.

Carey, Mike, with Jamie Most. *High Above Courtside: The Lost Memoirs of Johnny Most.* Champaign, IL: Sports Publishing, 2003.

———, with Jamie Most. *Voice of the Celtics: Johnny Most's Greatest Calls.* Champaign, IL: Sports Publishing, 2004.

———, and Michael D. McClellan. *Boston Celtics: Where Have You Gone?* Champaign, IL: Sports Publishing, 2005.

Carlos, John, with C. D. Jackson. *Why? The Biography of John Carlos.* Los Angeles: Milligan Books, 2000.

Carlson, Lewis H., with John J. Fogarty. *Tales of Gold.* Chicago: Contemporary Books, 1987.

Carry, Peter. "Anybody Else Care to Bid on Spencer Haywood?" *Sports Illustrated*, 25 January 1971, 54–55.

———. "Bombs Away Out West." *Sports Illustrated*, 24 April 1972, 14–17.

———. "Center in a Storm." *Sports Illustrated*, 19 February 1973, 16–19.

———. "Derailing the Laker Express." *Sports Illustrated*, 17 January 1972, 12–15.

———. "Getting Up and Going After a Title." *Sports Illustrated*, 13 December 1971, 24–35.

———. "Hey Look, Ma! Only One Hand." *Sports Illustrated*, 10 May 1971, 26–31.

———. "High but No Longer Mighty." *Sports Illustrated*, 29 October 1973, 44–53.

———. "In Seven, as in Heaven." *Sports Illustrated*, 7 May 1973, 26–29.

———. "It Was a Brief Time Out." *Sports Illustrated*, 11 January 1971, 22–23.

———. "It's Just Like Old Times." *Sports Illustrated*, 7 February 1972, 12–15.

———. "A Matter of Celtic Pride." *Sports Illustrated*, 20 May 1974, 22–24.

———. "Swish and They're In." *Sports Illustrated*, 15 May 1972, 26–27.

———. "They're Replaying the Sixth Man Theme." *Sports Illustrated*, 13 November 1972, 26–27.

———. "Where There's a Willis." *Sports Illustrated*, 21 May 1973, 54–56.

Carson, Clayborne. *In Struggle: SNCC and the Black Awakening of the 1960s.* Cambridge, MA: Harvard University Press, 1981.

Cave, Ray. "A Long-Neglected Art Is Now Flourishing Again." *Sports Illustrated*, 5 February 1961, 48–49.

"Celtics Climb on Cousy's Clever Coups." *Life*, 11 February 1957, 77–80.

Chafe, William H. *Civilities and Civil Rights: Greensboro, North Carolina, and the Black Struggle for Freedom.* New York: Oxford University Press, 1981.

Chalk, Ocania. *Black College Sport.* New York: Dodd, Mead and Company, 1976.

Chamberlain, Wilt. *A View from Above.* New York: Villard Books, 1991.

———. *Who's Running the Asylum? Inside the Insane World of Sports Today.* San Diego, CA: ProMotion Publishing, 1997.

———, with Roy Blount Jr. "My Impact Will Be Everlasting." *Sports Illustrated*, 7 October 1974, 36–47.

———, as told to Tim Cohane. "Pro Basketball Has Ganged Up on Me." *Look*, 1 March 1960, 55–58.

———, with Tim Cohane and I. R. McVay. "Why I Am Quitting College." *Look,* 10 June 1958, 91–101.

———, with Bob Ottum. "I Love the Game, Baby . . . But It Can't Go on this Way." *Sports Illustrated,* 19 April 1965, 39–41, 116–18.

———, with Bob Ottum. "I'm Punchy from Basketball, Baby, and Tired of Being a Villain." *Sports Illustrated,* 12 April 1965, 32–43.

———, and David Shaw. *Wilt: Just Like any Other 7-foot Black Millionaire Who Lives Next Door.* New York: Macmillan, 1973.

"Champagne and Peace." *Newsweek,* 22 May 1972, 67–68.

Chandler, Joan M. *Television and National Sport: The United States and Britain.* Urbana: University of Illinois Press, 1988.

Cherry, Robert. *Wilt: Larger than Life.* Chicago: Triumph Books, 2004.

Christgau, John. *The Origins of the Jump Shot: Eight Men Who Shook the World of Basketball.* Lincoln: University of Nebraska Press, 1999.

———. *Tricksters in the Madhouse: Lakers vs. Globetrotters, 1948.* Lincoln: University of Nebraska Press, 1999.

"The Celtics Lakers." *Time,* 27 December 1971, 51–52.

Clark, Kristine Setting. *Undefeated, Untied, and Uninvited: A Documentary of the 1951 University of San Francisco Dons Football Team.* Irvine, CA: Griffin, 2002.

Clay, Phillip L., ed. *The Emerging Black Community in Boston.* Boston: Institute for the Study of Black Culture, University of Massachusetts at Boston, 1985.

Cleaver, Eldridge. *Soul on Ice.* New York: Delta, 1968.

"Coach Russell." *Newsweek,* 2 May 1966, 72–73.

Cochran, Robert. "Folk Elements in a Non-Folk Game: The Example of Basketball." *Journal of Popular Culture* 10, no. 2 (1976): 398–403.

Cohen, Lizabeth. *A Consumers' Republic: The Politics of Mass Consumption in Postwar America.* New York: Alfred A. Knopf, 2003.

Cohen, Stanley. *The Game They Played.* New York: Farrar, Straus and Giroux, 1977.

Cole, Lewis. *A Loose Game: The Sport and Business of Basketball.* Indianapolis: Bobbs-Merrill, 1978.

Conley, Kathryn R. *One of a Kind: The Gene Conley Story.* Altamonte Springs, FL: Advantage Books, 2004.

Connolly, John F.X. *The University of San Francisco: A Credo—And a Commitment to Excellence.* New York: Newcomen Society in North America, 1960.

Connolly, Michael. *Rebound! Basketball, Busing, Larry Bird, and the Rebirth of Boston.* Minneapolis, MN: Voyageur Books, 2008.

Cook, Kevin. "The Rochester Royals: The Story of Professional Basketball." *Rochester History* 58, no. 1 (winter 1996): 1–20.

Cooper, Andrew. *Playing in the Zone: Exploring the Spiritual Dimensions of Sports.* Boston: Shambhala, 1998.

Cope, Myron. "A Last Cigar for a Last Hurrah?" *Saturday Evening Post,* 26 March 1966, 107–12.

———. "Life with Elgin Baylor." *Sport,* March 1963, 58–65.

————. "Unpredictable All-American." *Saturday Evening Post,* 9 January 1960, 28, 54–55.

Cosell, Howard. *Cosell.* Chicago: Playboy Press, 1973.

————. *Like It Is.* Chicago: Playboy Press, 1974.

————. "Wilt vs. Russell, No. 1." *Sport,* November 1963, 78.

Cosentino, Frank. *Almonte's Brothers of the Wind: R. Tait McKenzie and James Naismith.* Burnstown, Ontario: General Store Publishing, 1996.

"Court Choreography." *Time,* 8 May 1972, 95–96.

Cousy Bob, with Tim Cohane. "High Scoring Has Become Ho-Hum." *Look,* 12 February 1963, 53–56.

————, with John Devaney. *The Killer Instinct.* New York: Random House, 1975.

————, as told to Al Hirshberg. *Basketball Is My Life.* 2d ed. 1957. Reprint, New York: Lowell Pratt, 1963.

————, as told to Al Hirshberg. "Pro Basketball Needs a Bill of Rights." *Sport,* April 1956, 12–13, 68–69.

————, with Ed Linn. *The Last Loud Roar.* Englewood Cliffs, NJ: Prentice-Hall, 1964.

————, and Bob Ryan. *Cousy on the Celtic Mystique.* New York: McGraw Hill, 1988.

Crawford, Russell E. "Consensus All-American: Sport and the Promotion of the American Way of Life During the Cold War, 1946–1965." PhD diss., University of Nebraska, 2004.

Creamer, Robert. "Rough Night for Yuri and Jak." *Sports Illustrated,* 19 November 1962, 76–77.

Crosby, Emilye. "'God's Appointed Savior': Charles Evers's Use of Local Movements for National Stature." In Theoharis and Woodard, *Groundwork,* 165–92.

————. *A Little Taste of Freedom: The Black Freedom Struggle in Claiborne County, Mississippi.* Chapel Hill: University of North Carolina Press, 2005.

Crowe, Daniel. *Prophets of Rage: The Black Freedom Struggle in San Francisco.* New York: Garland Publishing, 2005.

Cunningham, Carson. "American Hoops: The History of United States Basketball from Berlin to Barcelona." PhD diss., Purdue University, 2006.

————. "The Russell Model: Melbourne 1956 and Bill Russell's New Basketball Standard." *Olympika* 15 (2006): 59–85.

Cyclops. "Eagle and Stork and Real Prince." *Life,* 25 February 1972, 8.

D'Agostino, Dennis. *Garden Glory: An Oral History of the New York Knicks.* Chicago: Triumph Books, 2003.

Daley, Arthur. "Education of a Basketball Rookie." *New York Times Magazine,* 24 February 1957, 22, 53–56.

Danielson, Michael N. *Home Team: Professional Sports and the American Metropolis.* Princeton, NJ: Princeton University Press, 1997.

David, Jay, ed. *Growing Up Black.* New York: William Morrow, 1968.

Davies, Richard O. *America's Obsession: Sports and Society Since 1945.* Fort Worth, TX: Harcourt Brace, 1994.

Davis, Laurel R., and Othello Harris. "Race and Ethnicity in U.S. Sports Media." In Wenner, ed., *Mediasport,* 155–69.

Davis, Lenwood G., and Belinda S. Daniels. *Black Athletes in the United States: A Bibliog-*

raphy of Books, Articles, Autobiographies, and Biographies on Black Professional Athletes in the United States, 1800–1981. Westport, CT: Greenwood Press, 1981.

"The Dazzling Knicks." Newsweek, 15 December 1969, 64–69.

DeBusschere, Dave. The Open Man: A Championship Diary. New York: Random House, 1970.

Deford, Frank. "And that Old Celtics Wheel Rolls Again." Sports Illustrated, 28 April 1969, 24–25.

———. "Another Big Bluff by Big Wilt." Sports Illustrated, 25 January 1965, 18-19, 52.

———. "At the End, It Was Up to the Two Big Men Underneath." Sports Illustrated, 21 April 1969, 66–71.

———. "Bill Russell—Center." In National Basketball Association, The Perfect Team, 217–33.

———. "Buy a Basketball Franchise and Join the War." Sports Illustrated, 2 February 1970, 40–43.

———. "The Changing Game." Sports Illustrated, 21 October 1968, 22–25.

———. "Comebacks All Over." Sports Illustrated, 14 April 1969, 28–31.

———. "Doing Just Fine, My Man." Sports Illustrated, 18 August 1986, 62–76.

———. "Eddie Is the Mogul." Sports Illustrated, 22 January 1968, 42–45.

———. "The Fans Get the Booby Prize." Sports Illustrated, 24 April 1967, 28–31.

———. "Follow the Bouncing Ball from Honolulu to Boston." Sports Illustrated, 4 May 1964, 81–84.

———. "How K. C. Won an Oscar in the NBA." Sports Illustrated, 20 April 1964, 58–61.

———. "In for Two Plus the Title." Sports Illustrated, 18 May 1970, 14–17.

———. "The Last Drop in the Bucket." Sports Illustrated, 12 May 1969, 22–29.

———. "Merger, Madness and Maravich." Sports Illustrated, 6 April 1970, 28–33.

———. "The New Spirit of the 76ers." Sports Illustrated, 17 April 1967, 28–31.

———. "New York Gets a Top Team at Last." Sports Illustrated, 23 October 1967, 28–32.

———. "No. 2 in the Rafters, No. 1 in Their Hearts." Sports Illustrated, 14 January 1985, 40–44, 79–81.

———. "On Top—But in Trouble." Sports Illustrated, 27 January 1969, 10–13.

———. "A Player for the Ages." Sports Illustrated, 21 March 1988, 46–65.

———. "The Playoff Was Child's Play." Sports Illustrated, 3 May 1965, 28–29.

———. "Push Comes to Shove." Sports Illustrated, 15 April 1968, 34–39.

———. "Razor-Cut Idol of San Francisco." Sports Illustrated, 13 February 1967, 32–35.

———. "The Ring Leader." Sports Illustrated, 10 May 1999, 97–114.

———. "Sarge Takes Philly to the Top." Sports Illustrated, 2 January 1967, 8–13.

———. "Some Old Pros Refuse to Die." Sports Illustrated, 9 May 1966, 30–33.

———. Sports People. New York: Harry N. Abrams, 1988.

———. "A Team that Was Blessed." Sports Illustrated, 29 March 1982, 58–75.

———. "A Teddy Bear's Picnic." Sports Illustrated, 7 February 1972, 46–56.

———. "Terror in the Air." Sports Illustrated, 3 April 1967, 16–21.

———. "This One Was Worth Shouting About." Sports Illustrated, 13 May 1968, 34.

———. "A Tiger Who Can Beat Anything." Sports Illustrated, 24 October 1966, 45–47.

———. "Two Guys on a Boston Hot Seat." Sports Illustrated, 3 November 1969, 22–25.

———. "Two Seconds Stretch for First." Sports Illustrated, 29 April 1968, 25–26.

———. "The Waiting Made It Sweeter." *Sports Illustrated*, 8 May 1967, 54–56.

———. *The World's Tallest Midget: The Best of Frank Deford*. Boston: Little, Brown and Co., 1987.

Devaney, John. "Chet Walker's Tug O'War." *Sport*, May 1967, 34–35, 84–86.

———. "Four Stars the NBA Wouldn't Touch." *Sport*, April 1968, 54–57, 84–85.

———. "Pro Basketball's Hidden Fear." *Sport*, February 1966, 32–33, 89–91.

———. "What Makes Havlicek Run . . . and Run . . . and Run." *Sport*, February 1969, 64–71.

Dexter, Charles. "Fabulous Predictions for the Sixties." *Sport*, April 1961, 25.

Dickey, Glenn. "Bill Russell." *Inside Sports*, January 1988, 18–23.

———. *The History of Professional Basketball Since 1896*. New York: Stein and Day, 1982.

———. *The Jock Empire: Its Rise and Deserved Fall*. Radnor, PA: Chilton Book Company, 1974.

Dittmer, John. *Local People: The Struggle for Civil Rights in Mississippi*. Chicago: University of Illinois Press, 1994.

"Dollars in His Legs." *Look*, 2 February 1960, 64.

Dolson, Frank. "Fiasco at the Foul Line." *Sports Illustrated*, 5 December 1960, 76.

Domer, Thomas Michael. "Sport in Cold War America: The Diplomatic and Political Use of Sport in the Eisenhower and Kennedy Administrations." PhD diss., Marquette University, 1976.

Donnelly, Joe. "The Unknown Who Must Save Our Basketball Team." *Sport*, October 1968, 44–45.

"Dons on Defense." *Time*, 14 February 1955, 50–51.

Du Bois, W. E. Burghardt. *The Souls of Black Folk: Essays and Sketches*. Chicago: A. C. McClurg, 1903.

Dudziak, Mary L. *Cold War Civil Rights: Race and the Image of American Democracy*. Princeton, NJ: Princeton University Press, 2000.

Dunnavant, Keith. *The Fifty-Year Seduction: How Television Manipulated College Football from the Birth of the Modern NCAA to the Creation of the BCS*. New York: Thomas Dunne Books, 2004.

Durslag, Melvin. "He's on the Rebound From Basketball." *TV Guide*, 4 March 1978, 36–38.

———. "The Man Who Gave Up $200,000 a Year Tells Why." *TV Guide*, 19 February 1972, 13–14.

Dyck, Noel, ed. *Games, Sports, and Cultures*. New York: Oxford University Press, 2000.

Dyreson, Mark. *Making the American Team: Sport, Culture, and the Olympic Experience*. Urbana: University of Illinois Press, 1998.

Dyson, Michael Eric. "Be Like Mike? Michael Jordan and the Pedagogy of Desire." *Cultural Studies* 7 (January 1993): 64–72.

Early, Gerald. "Performance and Reality: Race, Sports and the Modern World." *Nation*, 10–17 August 1998, 11–20.

———. *Tuxedo Junction: Essays on American Culture*. Hopewell, NJ: Ecco Press, 1989.

———. "Why Baseball *was* the National Pastime." In Boyd and Shropshire, *Basketball Jones*, 27–50.

"Easy Does It and Dons Do It." *Life*, 2 April 1956, 93–94.

Edelman, Robert. *Serious Fun: A History of Spectator Sports in the USSR.* New York: Oxford University Press, 1993.

Edwards, Harry. *The Revolt of the Black Athlete.* New York: Free Press, 1970.

———. *Sociology of Sport.* Homewood, IL: Dorsey Press, 1973.

———. *The Struggle that Must Be: An Autobiography.* New York: Macmillan, 1980.

———. "Why Negroes Should Boycott Whitey's Olympics." *Saturday Evening Post,* 9 March 1968, 6–10.

"Effortless Age." *Time,* 10 May 1968, 59.

Eig, Jonathan. *Opening Day: The Story of Jackie Robinson's First Season.* New York: Simon and Schuster, 2007.

Eisen, George, and David K. Wiggins, eds. *Ethnicity and Sport in North American History and Culture.* Westport, CT: Greenwood Press, 1994.

Eitzen, D. Stanley. *Fair and Foul: Beyond the Myths and Paradoxes of Sport.* Lanham, MD: Rowman and Littlefield, 1999.

"Elgin Baylor Comes Back." *Ebony,* February 1965, 35–37.

Ellis, Peter. "The Tall Boys of Summer." In Rudman, *Take It to the Hoop,* 139–44.

Ellis, Stephen. *The Mask of Anarchy: The Destruction of Liberia and the Religious Dimension of an African Civil War.* New York: New York University Press, 1999.

Embry, Wayne, with Mary Schmitt Boyer. *The Inside Game: Race, Power, and Politics in the NBA.* Akron, OH: University of Akron Press, 2004.

"End of the Affair." *Time,* 17 December 1956, 80.

Entine, Jon. *Taboo: Why Black Athletes Dominate Sports and Why We're Afraid to Talk About It.* New York: Public Affairs, 2000.

Erenberg, Lewis A. *The Greatest Fight of Our Generation: Louis vs. Schmeling.* New York: Oxford University Press, 2006.

Estes, Steve. *I Am a Man!: Race, Manhood, and the Civil Rights Movement.* Chapel Hill: University of North Carolina Press, 2005.

"Events and Discoveries." *Sports Illustrated,* 24 December 1956, 37.

Evers, Charles. *Evers.* New York: The World Publishing Company, 1971.

———, and Andrew Szanton. *Have No Fear: The Charles Evers Story.* New York: John Wiley and Sons, 1997.

"Eyeball to Eyeball Above Seven Feet." *Life,* 24 March 1972, 58–59.

Fairclough, Adam. *Race and Democracy: The Civil Rights Struggle in Louisiana, 1915–1972.* Athens: University of Georgia Press, 1995.

Falkenstein, Max, as told to Doug Vance. *Max and the Jayhawks: 50 Years On and Off the Air with KU Sports.* Wichita, KS: Wichita Eagle and Beacon Publishing Co., 1996.

"Faster, Higher, Farther." *Time,* 3 December 1956, 58–59.

Feinstein, John. *The Punch: One Night, Two Lives, and the Fight that Changed Basketball Forever.* Boston: Back Bay Books, 2002.

Festle, Mary Jo. " 'Jackie Robinson Without the Charm': The Challenges of Being Althea Gibson." In Wiggins, *Out of the Shadows,* 187–205.

Fields, Sarah K. "Odd Bedfellows: Spencer Haywood and Justice William O. Douglas." *Journal of Sport History* 34, no. 2 (spring 2007): 193–206.

Figone, Albert J. "Gambling and College Basketball: The Scandal of 1951." *Journal of Sport History* 16, no. 1 (spring 1989): 44–61.

Fisher, Dave. "Instant Millionaires from the Basketball War." *Life*, 23 April 1971, 32–34.

Fisher, Donald M. "The Rochester Royals and the Transformation of Professional Basketball, 1945–57." *International Journal of the History of Sport* 10, no. 1 (1993): 20–48.

Fisher, James. "Elgin Baylor: The First Modern Professional Basketball Player." In Batchelor, *Basketball in America*, 177–88.

Fitokova Connolly, Olga. "Love Made Me an American." *Saturday Evening Post*, 28 January 1961, 15–17, 52–54.

Fitzgerald, Joe. *That Championship Feeling: The Story of the Boston Celtics.* New York: Charles Scribner's Sons, 1975.

Fitzgerald, Ray. *Champions Remembered: Choice Picks from a Boston Sports Desk.* Brattleboro, VT: Stephen Greene Press, 1982.

Fitzpatrick, Frank. *And the Walls Came Tumbling Down: Kentucky, Texas Western, and the Game that Changed American Sports.* New York: Simon and Schuster, 1999.

Flood, Curt, with Richard Carter. *The Way It Is.* New York: Trident Press, 1970.

"For All the Marbles." *Time*, 24 February 1967, 57–58.

Formisano, Ronald P. *Boston Against Busing: Race, Class, and Ethnicity in the 1960s and 1970s.* Chapel Hill: University of North Carolina Press, 1991.

Fortunato, John Angelo. "The Ultimate Assist: An Agenda-Setting Study of Television's Influence in the Emergence of the National Basketball Association." PhD diss., Rutgers University, 1999.

Fotheringham, Allan. "Could Wilt Really Count That High?" *Maclean's*, 18 November 1991, 84.

Foulds, Alan. *Boston's Ballparks and Arenas.* Boston: Northeastern University Press, 2005.

Fox, Larry. "Presenting Lew Alcindor." *Sport*, September 1966, 72–73.

Fox, Stephen. *Big Leagues: Professional Baseball, Football, and Basketball in National Memory.* New York: William Morrow, 1994.

Fox, Tom. "Hal Greer: The Day I Slow Down I'm Finished." *Sport*, April 1965, 32–33, 103–4.

Frady, Marshall. *Jesse: The Life and Pilgrimage of Jesse Jackson.* New York: Random House, 1996.

France, Edward E. *Some Aspects of the Migration of the Negro to the San Francisco Bay Area Since 1940.* San Francisco: R. and E. Research Associates, 1974.

Frank, Stanley. "Basketball's Amazing Showboat." *Saturday Evening Post*, 18 December 1954, 25, 58–59.

———. "Basketball's Toughest War Horse." *Saturday Evening Post*, 28 December 1957, 61–62.

Frazier, Walt, and Joe Jares. *Clyde.* New York: Rutledge, 1970.

———, and Ira Berkow. *Rockin' Steady: A Guide to Basketball and Cool.* Englewood Cliffs, NJ: Prentice-Hall, 1974.

———, with Neil Offen. *Walt Frazier: One Magic Season and a Basketball Life.* New York: Times Books, 1988.

Freedman, Lew. *Dynasty: The Rise of the Boston Celtics.* Guilford, CT: Lyons Press, 2008.

Freeman, Mike. *Jim Brown: The Fierce Life of an American Hero.* New York: William Morrow, 2006.

Furlong, Bill. "Bob Cousy vs. Oscar Robertson: The Struggle to Remake the Royals." *Sport,* February 1970, 22–24, 81–83.
———. "Walt Bellamy vs. the NBA," *Sport,* 35–37, 68–69.
Fuse, Montye, and Keith Miller. "Jazzing the Basepaths: Jackie Robinson and African American Aesthetics." In Bloom and Willard, *Sports Matters,* 119–40.
Gaines, Kevin K. *American Africans in Ghana: Black Expatriates and the Civil Rights Era.* Chapel Hill: University of North Carolina Press, 2006.
Garrity, John. "Wilt Chamberlain." *Sports Illustrated,* 9 December 1991, 24–28.
Gaston, John C. "The Destruction of the Young Black Male: The Impact of Popular Culture and Organized Sports." *Journal of Black Studies* 16, no. 4 (June 1986): 369–84.
Gelman, Steve. "The View from the Locker Room." *Book Week,* 15 May 1966, 4.
Gemme, Leila B. *The New Breed of Athlete: 12 Star Athletes Who Shook the American Sports Establishment.* New York: Washington Square Press, 1975.
Gems, Gerald R. "Blocked Shot: The Development of Basketball in the African-American Community of Chicago." *Journal of Sport History* 22, no. 2 (1995): 135–48.
George, Nelson. *Elevating the Game: Black Men and Basketball.* New York: HarperCollins, 1992.
"The Giants of Schoolboy Basketball." *Life,* 21 February 1955, 59–62.
Gibson, Althea. *I Always Wanted to Be Somebody.* New York: Harper and Brothers, 1958.
Gladwell, Malcolm. "The Sports Taboo." *New Yorker,* 19 May 1997, 50–55.
Glickman, Marty. "All-America Basketball Preview." *Sport,* January 1955, 12–15, 91.
———. "The Night Stars Came out for the NBA." *Sport,* March 1981, 69–74.
"Go West, Tall Man." *Newsweek,* 22 July 1968, 48–49.
Goldman, William, and Mike Lupica. *Wait Till Next Year: The Story of a Season When What Should've Happened Didn't and What Could Have Gone Wrong Did.* New York: Bantam Books, 1988.
Goodman, Irv. "Arizin—The Pro Who Plays for Fun." *Sport,* February 1955, 40–41, 70–73.
———. "The Big Collision: Wilt vs. Russell." *Sport,* December 1959, 16–17, 76–77.
———. "Cousy, Sharman, Russell & Co." *Sport,* March 1958, 58.
———. "The High-School Kid Who Could Play Pro Now." *Sport,* March 1955, 30–33, 58–59.
———. "Hothead on the Boston Bench." *Sport,* February 1956, 28–29, 88–92.
———. "I Remember Basketball." *Sport,* September 1961, 104–5.
———. "Never a Dull Moment with the Hawks." *Sport,* December 1958, 32–35, 85–87.
———. "Royal Rookie." *Sport,* March 1956, 37–38.
———. "Second Chance for Lovellette." *Sport,* January 1958, 26–27, 66.
———. "Wilt vs. the NBA." *Sport,* April 1959, 20–21, 84–86.
———. "The Winning Ways of Red Auerbach." *Sport,* March 1965, 69–76.
Gorn, Elliott J., ed. *Muhammad Ali: The People's Champ.* Urbana: University of Illinois Press, 1995.
Gottehrer, Barry. "When Wilt and Russell Meet. . . ." *Sport,* March 1960, 38–41.
Goudsouzian, Aram. "'Ba-ad, Ba-a-ad Tigers': Crispus Attucks Basketball and Black Indianapolis in the 1950s." *Indiana Magazine of History* 96, no. 1 (March 2000): 5–43.
———. "Bill Russell and the Basketball Revolution." *American Studies* 47, no. 3/4 (fall–winter 2006): 61–85.

———. "Can Basketball Survive Chamberlain?: The Kansas Years of Wilt the Stilt." *Kansas History: A Journal of the Central Plains* 28, no. 3 (autumn 2005): 150–73.

———. " 'The House that Russell Built': Bill Russell, the University of San Francisco, and the Winning Streak that Changed College Basketball." *California History* 84, no. 4 (fall 2007): 5–25.

———. " 'My Impact Will Be Everlasting': Wilt Chamberlain in History and Memory." *Journal of Sport History* 32, no. 2 (summer 2005): 235–48.

———. *Sidney Poitier: Man, Actor, Icon.* Chapel Hill: University of North Carolina Press, 2004.

———. "Wilma Rudolph: Running for Freedom." In Wilkerson-Freeman and Bond, *Tennessee Women*, 305–32.

Gould, Todd. *Pioneers of the Hardwood: Indiana and the Birth of Professional Basketball.* Bloomington: Indiana University Press, 1998.

Gowdy, Curt, with John Powers. *Seasons to Remember: The Way It Was in American Sports, 1945–1960.* New York: HarperCollins, 1993.

"The Graceful Giants." *Time,* 17 February 1961, 54–61.

Grady, Sandy. "The Master Plan to Change Wilt Chamberlain." *Sport,* March 1962, 16–17, 67–69.

Graham, Tom, and Rachel Graham Cody. *Getting Open: The Unknown Story of Bill Garrett and the Integration of College Basketball.* New York: Atria Books, 2006.

Gray, Frances Clayton, and Yanick Rice Lamb. *Born to Win: The Authorized Biography of Althea Gibson.* Hoboken, NJ: John Wiley and Sons, 2004.

Green, Ben. *Spinning the Globe: The Rise, Fall, and Return to Greatness of the Harlem Globetrotters.* New York: Amistad, 2005.

Green, Tony. "Ali, Forman, Mailer, and Me." In Tate, *Everything but the Burden,* 158–59.

Greenberg, Cheryl Lynn. *Troubling the Waters: Black-Jewish Relations in the American Century.* Princeton, NJ: Princeton University Press, 2006.

Greenburg, Jan Crawford. "How Football Trumped Racism at Ole Miss." *The Journal of Blacks in Higher Education* 14 (winter 1996–97): 94.

Greene, Lee. "Bill Russell Is Better than Ever." *Sport,* January 1961, 25–26.

Greenfield, Jeff. "The Black and White Truth About Basketball." *Esquire,* October 1975, 170–71.

———. *The World's Greatest Team: A Portrait of the Boston Celtics, 1957–69.* New York: Random House, 1976.

Grenier, Mike. *Don't They Ever Stop Running?* Danvers, MA: Book Production Services, 1973.

Griffin, Edward M. "Hoops and Hurdles: The Unlikely Story of How I Learned How I Learn." University of Minnesota Faculty Memoir Group, 2003–2004.

Gross, Milton. "Basketball's Moody Marvel." *Saturday Evening Post,* 26 December 1959, 19, 60–62.

———. "Basketball's Unhappy Gunner." *Saturday Evening Post,* 20 December 1958, 30, 53–55.

———. "Gambling—Basketball's No. 1 Menace." *Look,* January 1950, 68–73.

———. "In Philadelphia Nearly Everybody Likes Gola." *Sports Illustrated,* 27 December 1954, 30, 62–63.

———. "The Pros Tell Their Favorite Bill Russell Stories." *Sport*, November 1969, 44–47, 88.

———. "Who Is the Best of Basketball's Superstars?" *Sport*, April 1962, 24–27, 93–95.

Grundman, Adolph H. *The Golden Age of Amateur Basketball: The AAU Tournament, 1921–1968.* Lincoln: University of Nebraska Press, 2004.

———. "The Image of Intercollegiate Sports and the Civil Rights Movement: An Historian's View." *Arena Review* 3, no. 3 (1979): 17–24.

Grundy, Pamela. *Learning to Win: Sports, Education, and Social Change in Twentieth-Century North America.* Chapel Hill: University of North Carolina Press, 2001.

Gutman, Herbert G. *The Black Family in Slavery and Freedom, 1750–1925.* New York: Vintage Books, 1976.

Guttmann, Allen. *Games and Empires: Modern Sports and Cultural Imperialism.* New York: Columbia University Press, 1994.

———. *The Games Must Go On: Avery Brundage and the Olympic Movement.* New York: Columbia University Press, 1984.

———. *The Olympics: A History of the Modern Games.* Urbana: University of Illinois Press.

———. *From Ritual to Record: The Nature of Modern Sports.* New York: Columbia University Press, 1978.

———. *Sports Spectators.* New York: Columbia University Press, 1986.

———. *A Whole New Ball Game: An Interpretation of American Sports.* Chapel Hill: University of North Carolina Press, 1988.

Guzzie, Tracie Church. "Courtside: Race and Basketball in the Works of John Edgar Wideman." In Bass, *In the Game,* 221–36.

Halberstam, David. *The Breaks of the Game.* New York: Ballantine Books, 1981.

———. *The Fifties.* New York: Villard, 1993.

———. *October 1964.* New York: Villard, 1994.

———. *Playing for Keeps: Michael Jordan and the World He Made.* New York: Random House, 1999.

Halberstam, Michael. "Are You Guilty of Murdering Martin Luther King?" *New York Times Magazine,* 9 June 1968, 27–29, 54–66.

Halliburton, Richard. *Complete Book of Marvels.* 1937. Reprint, Indianapolis: Bobbs-Merrill, 1960.

Hannum, Alex, with Frank Deford. "I've Barely Begun to Fight." *Sports Illustrated,* 18 November 1968, 34–48.

———, with Frank Deford. "Old Days and Changed Ways." *Sports Illustrated,* 25 November 1968, 36–44.

Hano, Arnold. "The Black Rebel Who 'Whitelists' the Olympics." *New York Times Magazine,* 12 May 1968, 32–33, 39–50.

———. "Elvin Hayes vs. Wilt: The Night the Rookie Became a Man." *Sport,* January 1969, 18–20, 86–88.

———. "The Fight to Remodel Wilt Chamberlain." *Sport,* February 1964, 24–26, 84–86.

———. "The Heart of Lew Alcindor." *Sport,* April 1967, 73–78.

———. "I Was Wrong About Jerry West." *Sport,* April 1966, 64–69.

———. "Jerry West's Burden." *Sport,* March 1962, 22–23, 72–73.

———. "Nate Thurmond at the Summit." *Sport,* March 1968, 54–62.

———. "On the Road with Wilt and the 76ers." *Sport*, April 1968, 68-73.

———. "Rick Barry's Drive to Greatness." *Sport*, February 1967, 66–71.

———. "Wilt, West, and Baylor: Do Three Superstars Make a Super Team?" *Sport*, March 1969, 62–69.

Hardy, Stephen. "Long Before Orr: Placing Hockey in Boston, 1897–1929." In Roberts, *The Rock, the Curse, and the Hub*, 267–72.

"Harlem Magicians." *Ebony*, February 1956, 51–52.

Harris, Cecil. *Breaking the Ice: The Black Experience in Professional Hockey*. Toronto: Insomniac Press, 2003.

Harris, Merv. *The Lonely Heroes: Professional Basketball's Great Centers*. New York: Viking, 1975.

Harris, Othello. "African American Predominance in Sport." In Brooks and Althouse, *Racism in College Athletics*, 37–52.

Hartman, Sid, with Patrick Reusse. *Sid!: The Sports Legends, the Inside Scoops, and the Close Personal Friends*. Stillwater, MN: Voyageur Press, 1997.

Hartmann, Douglas. *Race, Culture, and the Revolt of the Black Athlete*. Chicago: University of Chicago Press, 2003.

Hauser, Thomas. *Muhammad Ali: His Life and Times*. New York: Touchstone Books, 1991.

Havill, Adrian. *The Last Mogul: The Unauthorized Biography of Jack Kent Cooke*. New York: St. Martin's Press, 1992.

Havlicek, John, and Bob Ryan. *Hondo: Celtic Man in Motion*. Englewood Cliffs, NJ: Prentice-Hall, 1977.

———, with Bob Sales. "Behind the Celtics' Startling Comeback." *Sport*, August 1968, 18–20, 64.

———, with Bob Sudyk. "What Lucas Will Have to Learn." *Sport*, December 1963, 28, 76–77.

Hayes, Elvin, and Bill Gilbert. *They Call Me the Big E: The Elvin Hayes Story*. Englewood Cliffs, NJ: Prentice-Hall, 1978.

Haywood, Spencer, with Scott Ostler. *Spencer Haywood: The Rise, the Fall, the Recovery*. New York: Amistad, 1992.

Hearn, Chick, and Steve Springer. *Chick: His Unpublished Memoirs and the Memories of Those Who Knew Him*. Chicago: Triumph Books, 2004.

Heberle, Rudolf. *The Labor Force in Louisiana*. Baton Rouge: Louisiana State University Press, 1948.

Heinsohn, Tommy, and Joe Fitzgerald. *Give 'Em the Hook*. New York: Prentice Hall, 1988.

———, with Leonard Lewin. *Heinsohn, Don't You Ever Smile?: The Life and Times of Tommy Heinsohn and the Boston Celtics*. Garden City, NY: Doubleday, 1976.

———, with Bob Ottum, "Of Charley Horses and Little Old Ladies." *Sports Illustrated*, 26 October 1964, 38–49.

Heisler, Mark. *Madmen's Ball: The Inside Story of the Lakers' Dysfunctional Dynasties*. Chicago: Triumph Books, 2004.

Henderson, Russell J. "The 1963 Mississippi State University Basketball Controversy and the Repeal of the Unwritten Law: 'Something more than the game will be lost.'" *Journal of Southern History* 63, no. 4 (November 1997): 827–54.

"The Hidden Fear that is Not Our Fear." *Sport,* May 1966, 104.

Hietala, Thomas R. *The Fight of the Century: Jack Johnson, Joe Louis, and the Struggle for Racial Equality.* Armonk, NY: M. E. Sharpe, 2002.

Higgs, Robert J. *God in the Stadium: Sports and Religion in America.* Lexington: University Press of Kentucky, 1995.

Hill, Doug, and Jeff Weingrad. *Saturday Night: A Backstage History of Saturday Night Live.* New York: Beech Tree Books, 1986.

Hill, Lance. *The Deacons for Defense: Armed Resistance and the Civil Rights Movement.* Chapel Hill: University of North Carolina Press, 2004.

Hillson, Jon. *The Battle of Boston.* New York: Pathfinder Press, 1977.

Hirshberg, Al. *Bill Russell of the Boston Celtics.* New York: Julian Messner, 1963.

———. "Boston Gets a Winner." *Saturday Evening Post,* 16 March 1957, 36, 113–14.

———. "The Celtics' Cinderella Star." *Sport,* January 1962, 52, 70–71.

———. "Cousy Shoots Like Crazy." *Sport,* March 1953, 28–31, 82–83.

———. "Farewell to Bob Cousy." *Sport,* March 1963, 20–21, 75–76.

———. "It's Larry Siegfied." *Sport,* November 1968, 50–51, 86–87.

———. "Pro Basketball Needs a Bill of Rights." *Sport,* April 1956, 12–13, 68–69.

———. "Roommate: Bob Cousy." *Sport,* March 1956, 48–56.

———. "Sharman at the Crossroads." *Sport,* April 1952, 22–24, 89–90.

———. "A Visit with Bob Cousy." *Sport,* 12 December 1959, 30, 91–92.

History in Headlines of Sonics: The Complete Newspaper Account of the Making of a Championship Team 1967–1980. San Francisco: Celebrity Services, 1979.

Hoberman, John. *Darwin's Athletes: How Sport Has Damaged Black America and Preserved the Myth of Race.* Boston: Houghton Mifflin, 1997.

Hobson, Howard. "How to Stop Those Basketball Scandals." *Collier's,* 29 December 1951, 26–27, 65–67.

———. *Scientific Basketball.* New York: Prentice-Hall, 1949.

Hoch, Paul. *Rip Off the Big Game: The Exploitation of Sports by the Power Elite.* Garden City, NY: Doubleday, 1972.

Holman, Nat. *Holman on Basketball.* New York: Crown, 1950.

Holtzman, Jerome. "Sound Off! Wilt Chamberlain: 'No One Roots for Goliath.' " *Sport,* April 1963, 26–28, 82–84.

Holzman, Red, and Harvey Frommer. *Red on Red.* New York: Bantam Books, 1987.

———, with Leonard Lewin. *The Knicks.* New York: Dodd, Mead and Company, 1971.

———, with Leonard Lewin. *A View from the Bench.* New York: W. W. Norton, 1980.

Hoose, Phillip M. *Hoosiers: The Fabulous Basketball Life of Indiana.* 2d ed. 1986. Reprint, Indianapolis: Guild Press of Indiana, 1995.

———. *Necessities: Racial Barriers in American Sports.* New York: Random House, 1989.

Honey, Michael K. *Going Down Jericho Road: The Memphis Strike, Martin Luther King's Last Campaign.* New York: W. W. Norton, 2007.

Horger, Marc Thomas. "Play by the Rules: The Creation of Basketball and the Progressive Era." PhD diss., Ohio State University, 2001.

Horovitz, Israel. *Sixteen Short Plays.* Lyme, NH: Smith and Kraus, 1994.

"The House that Wilt Built." *Life,* 24 March 1972, 60–63.

"How Do You Stop Him?" *Time*, 25 January 1963, 40–41.

"How to Make Contact." *Time*, 8 May 1964, 58.

Huey, Lynda. *A Running Start: An Athlete, a Woman*. New York: Quadrangle/New York Times Book Company, 1976.

———. "Who Is John Brisker? And Why Did Bill Russell Do All Those Bad Things to Him?" *Black Sports*, April 1977, 51–52.

Hundley, Rod, with Tom McEachin. *Hot Rod Hundley: "You Gotta Love It, Baby."* Champaign, IL: Sports Publishing, 1998.

"Hungary's Heroes in Their Hour of Staggering Strain." *Sports Illustrated*, 3 December 1956, 22–23.

Hutchinson, George. "The Black Athletes' Contribution Toward Social Change in the United States." PhD diss., United States International University, 1977.

Hyman, Mervin. "The Case for the 12-foot Basket." *Sports Illustrated*, 78–83.

Iba, Henry P. "Defense Decides the Big Ones." *Saturday Evening Post*, 21 February 1959, 36, 71–73.

"The Inside Track: Wilt Chamberlain." *Inside Sports*, 30 November 1980, 95–98.

Isaacs, Neil D. *All the Moves: A History of College Basketball*. Philadelphia: J. B. Lippincott, 1975.

———. *Checking Back: A History of the National Hockey League*. New York: W. W. Norton, 1977.

———. *Vintage NBA: The Pioneer Era, 1946–1956*. Indianapolis, IN: Masters Press, 1996.

"It's Get Set and Go." *Newsweek*, 12 November 1956, 86.

"It's Still a Big Man's Game." *Ebony*, January 1973, 83–91.

Izenberg, Jerry. *How Many Miles to Camelot? The All-American Sport Myth*. New York: Holt, Rinehart and Winston, 1972.

———. "The Unpopular Star: How Much Does He Really Owe the Fans?" *Sport*, August 1966, 44–47, 81–82.

Jable, J. Thomas. "Jim Brown: Superlative Athlete, Screen Star, Social Activist." In Wiggins, *Out of the Shadows*, 241–62.

Jackson, Phil, with Charles Rosen. *Maverick: More than a Game*. Chicago: Playboy Press, 1975.

Jacobs, Barry. *Across the Line: Profiles in Basketball Courage: Tales of the First Black Players in the ACC and SEC*. Guilford, CT: Lyons Press, 2008.

Jacobson, Matthew Frye. " 'Richie' Allen, Whitey's Ways, and Me: A Political Education in the 1960s." In Bass, *In the Game*, 19–46.

Jares, Joe. "The Beard Moves into a New and Ticklish Pad." *Sports Illustrated*, 14 October 1968, 76–77.

———. "The Celtics Isn't Dead Yet." *Sports Illustrated*, 15 November 1965, 32–35.

———. "Four for the Bundle." *Sports Illustrated*, 24 February 1969, 14–19.

———. "Tiger in the House of Ivy." *Sports Illustrated*, 27 February 1967, 20–23.

Jay, Kathryn. *More than Just a Game: Sports in American Life Since 1945*. New York: Columbia University Press, 2004.

"Jerry West: Slicker from Cabin Creek," *Look*, 15 March 1960, 96–98.

Johnson, Blaine. "Great as He Wants." *Sonics Magazine*, October/November 1977, 15–16.

———. "Russell's Back in the Game." *The Weekly's Reader,* November 1979, 8.

———. *What's Happenin'? A Revealing Journey Through the World of Professional Basketball.* Englewood Cliffs, NJ: Prentice-Hall, 1978.

Johnson, James. *The Dandy Dons: Bill Russell, K. C. Jones, Phil Woolpert, and One of College Basketball's Greatest and Most Innovative Teams.* Lincoln: University of Nebraska Press, 2009.

Johnson, Marilynn S. *The Second Gold Rush: Oakland and the East Bay in World War II.* Berkeley: University of California Press, 1993.

Johnson, Rafer, with Philip Goldberg. *The Best that I Can Be: An Autobiography.* New York: Doubleday, 1998.

Johnson, Richard A., and Robert Hamilton Johnson. *The Celtics in Black and White.* Charleston, SC: Arcadia, 2006.

———, and Robert Hamilton Johnson. *A Century of Boston Sports.* Boston: Northeastern University Press, 2000.

———, and Brian Codagnone. *The Boston Garden.* Portsmouth, NH: Arcadia, 2002.

Johnson, William. "Collision on the New Underground Railroad." *Sports Illustrated,* 12 February 1968, 52–53.

———. "A Legal License to Steal the Stars." *Sports Illustrated,* 12 April 1971, 34–41.

———. "Triumph in Obscurity." *Sports Illustrated,* 22 April 1968, 68–80.

Jones, Jacqueline. *Labor of Love, Labor of Sorrow: Black Women, Work, and the Family from Slavery to the Present.* New York: Basic Books, 1985.

Jones, K. C., with Jack Warner. *Rebound.* Boston: Quinlan Press, 1986.

Joseph, Peniel E. *Waiting 'Til the Midnight Hour: A Narrative History of Black Power in America.* New York: Owl Books, 2006.

Josza, Frank P., Jr. *American Sports Empire: How the Leagues Breed Success.* Westport, CT: Praeger, 2003.

"Judgment Calls." *Sports Illustrated,* 29 June 1992, 9.

Kahn, Lawrence M., and Peter D. "Racial Differences in Professional Basketball Players' Compensation." *Journal of Labor Economics* 6, no. 1 (January 1988): 40–61.

Kahn, Roger. "Lew Alcindor's Life as a Pro." *Sport,* February 1970, 58–65.

———. "Preview: Great Season, Greater Star." *Sports Illustrated,* 13 December 1954, 20–21.

———. "Success and Ned Irish." *Sports Illustrated,* 27 March 1961, 39–46.

Kalinsky, George, and Phil Jackson. *Take It All!* New York: Collier Macmillan, 1970.

Kaliss, Gregory John. "Everyone's All-Americans: Race, Men's College Athletics, and the Ideal of Equal Opportunity." PhD diss., University of North Carolina at Chapel Hill, 2008.

———. "Un-Civil Discourse: Charlie Scott, the Integration of College Basketball, and the 'Progressive Mystique.'" *Journal of Sport History* 35, no. 1 (spring 2008): 98–117.

Kamp, David. "Only the Ball Was Brown." *GQ,* October 2001, 284–89, 343–47.

Kane, Martin. "An Assessment of 'Black Is Best.'" *Sports Illustrated,* 18 January 1971, 72–83.

Kaplan, Dick. "Bill Sharman, The Shooter." *Sport,* 54, 78–81.

Kashatus, William C. *September Swoon: Richie Allen, the '64 Phillies, and Racial Integration.* University Park: Pennsylvania State University Press, 2004.

Katz, Fred. "The Unknown Side of Bill Russell." *Sport,* March 1966, 24-26, 76-80.

Katz, Milton S. *Breaking Through: John B. McClendon, Basketball Legend and Civil Rights Pioneer.* Fayetteville: University of Arkansas Press, 2007.

Kellner, Douglas. "The Sports Spectacle, Michael Jordan, and Nike." In Miller and Wiggins, *Sport and the Color Line,* 305–25.

Kenyon, J. Michael. "The Very Private Bill Russell." *Seattle Post-Intelligencer NORTHWEST,* 23 January 1977, 6–10.

Keown, Tim. *Skyline: One Season, One Team, One City.* New York: Macmillan, 1994.

Kerkhoff, Blair. *Phog Allen: The Father of Basketball Coaching.* Indianapolis: Masters Press, 1996.

Kindred, Dave. *Sound and Fury: Two Powerful Lives, One Fateful Friendship.* New York: Free Press, 2006.

King, James. "Accolade for Versatile Bill Russell." *Seattle Times Magazine,* 18 November 1979, 14.

King, Mel. *Chain of Change: Struggles for Black Community Development.* Boston: South End Press, 1981.

Kirkpatrick, Curry. "The Celtics Stretch an Era." *Sports Illustrated,* 11 April 1966, 30–31.

———. "Down Goes Big Bill, Up Go the Sonics." *Sports Illustrated,* 1 May 1978, 20–21.

———. "A Place in the Big-City Sun." *Sports Illustrated,* 5 August 1968, 20–23.

———. "Ready for a Sonic Boom." *Sports Illustrated,* 22 May 1978, 12–15.

Kirshenbaum, Jerry. "Overdue Winner in New York." *Sports Illustrated,* 8 December 1969, 16–21.

Klein, David. *Rookie: The World of the NBA.* Chicago: Cowles Book Company, 1971.

Kline, John. *Never Lose: The Jumpin' Johnny Kline Story.* Detroit, MI: Papa Joe's Book Company, 1996.

Koppett, Leonard. *Championship NBA—Official 25th Anniversary.* New York: Dial Press, 1970.

———. "Does Pro Basketball Have a Future?" *Sport* 36, 81–84.

———. "The Celtics Look Better than Ever." *Sport,* December 1957, 42–45, 70–71.

———. "Does Pro Basketball Have a Future?" *Saturday Evening Post,* 6 December 1958, 36, 81–84.

———. *The Essence of the Game Is Deception: Thinking About Basketball.* Boston: Little, Brown and Company, 1973.

———. *Sports Illusion, Sports Reality: A Reporter's View of Sports, Journalism, and Society.* 1981. Reprint, Urbana: University of Illinois Press, 1994.

———. *24 Seconds to Shoot: The Birth and Improbable Rise of the National Basketball Association.* 1968. Reprint, Kingston, NY: Total/Sports Illustrated, 1999.

Kornheiser, Tony. "Bill Russell: Nothing But a Man." In MacCambridge, *ESPN Sports-century,* 184–89.

Korsgaard, Robert. "A History of the Amateur Athletic Union of the United States." PhD diss., Teachers College, Columbia University, 1952.

Kotlowski, Dean J. *Nixon's Civil Rights: Politics, Principle, and Policy.* Cambridge, MA: Harvard University Press, 2001.

Kriegel, Mark. *Namath: A Biography.* New York: Viking, 2004.

———. *Pistol: The Life of Pete Maravich.* New York: Free Press, 2007.

Kunstler, William M. "Bill Russell." *Sport,* December 1986, 39.

Kuska, Bob. *Hot Potato: How Washington and New York Gave Birth to Black Basketball and Changed America's Game Forever.* Charlottesville: University of Virginia Press, 2004.

Lacy, Sam, with Moses J. Newson. *Fighting for Fairness: The Life Story of Hall of Fame Sportswriter Sam Lacy.* Centreville, MD: Tidewater Publishing, 1998.

LaFeber, Walter. *Michael Jordan and the New Global Capitalism.* New and exp. ed. New York: W. W. Norton, 2002.

Laguerre, Andre. "World's Eye on Sport." *Sports Illustrated,* 3 December 1956, 13–14.

"The Lakers Roll On." *Time,* 10 January 1972, 57–58.

"The Lame and the Fat." *Newsweek,* 28 February 1966, 83.

Lane, Jeffrey. *Under the Boards: The Cultural Revolution in Basketball.* Lincoln: University of Nebraska Press, 2007.

Langley, Lester D. *The Americas in the Age of Revolution.* New Haven, CT: Yale University Press, 1996.

Lantz, Ragni. "Righteous Anger Need Not Be Silenced: LBJ at Rights Confab." *Jet,* 16 June 1966, 18–19.

Lapchick, Joe. *50 Years of Basketball.* Englewood Cliffs, NJ: Prentice-Hall, 1968.

———, with Tim Cohane. "The Toughest Big League of Them All." *Look,* 4 February 1958, 91–94.

Lapchick, Richard. *Broken Promises: Racism in American Sports.* New York: St. Martin's Press. 1984.

———. *Five Minutes to Midnight: Race and Sport in the 1990s.* Lanham, MD: Madison Books, 1991.

Lardner, John. "Letter from the Olympics." *New Yorker,* 8 December 1956, 137–44.

———. "We Hung in the Stretch." *Newsweek,* 17 December 1956, 98.

Lardner, Rex. "Can Basketball Survive Lew Alcindor?" *Saturday Evening Post,* 14 January 1967, 70-73.

Larner, Jeremy. "Basketball: The Graceful Game." *Holiday,* February 1966, 30–38.

———. "Just Too Much Giant." *Life,* 21 April 1967, 82–88.

Lawrence, Paul R. *Unsportsmanlike Conduct: The National Collegiate Athletic Association and the Business of College Football.* New York: Praeger, 1987.

Lawson, Earl. "The Tragedy of Maurice Stokes." *Sport,* February 1959, 18–19, 88–89.

Lawson, Hal A. "Physical Education and Sport in the Black Community: The Hidden Perspective." *Journal of Negro Education* 48, no. 2 (spring 1979): 187–95.

Lazenby, Roland. *The Lakers: A Basketball Journey.* New York: St. Martin's Press, 1993.

———. *The Show: The Inside Story of the Spectacular Los Angeles Lakers in the Words of Those Who Lived It.* New York: McGraw Hill, 2006.

Leab, Daniel J. *From Sambo to Superspade: The Black Experience in Motion Pictures.* Boston: Houghton Mifflin, 1975.

"The Leap that No One Can Stop." *Life,* 30 November 1959, 57.

Lee, Bruce. "Unstoppable San Francisco." *Sport,* April 1964, 37–39, 85–87.

Leggett, William. "Basketball at its Toughest." *Sports Illustrated,* 26 February 1963, 12–16.

———. " 'Cooz' and the Celtics." *Sports Illustrated,* 18 April 1960, 62–63.

———. "Growing to Greatness." *Sports Illustrated,* 29 October 1962, 41.

———. "The New Kid on the Block Takes on the Champ." *Sports Illustrated,* 14 November 1960, 24–25.

———. "Up to Their Old Tricks." *Sports Illustrated,* 6 May 1963, 54–55.

Lemann, Nicholas. *The Promised Land: The Great Black Migration and How It Changed America.* New York: Vintage, 1991.

Lemon, Meadowlark, with Jerry B. Jenkins. *Meadowlark.* Nashville, TN: Thomas Nelson Publishers, 1987.

"Letter from the Publisher." *Sports Illustrated,* 4 August 1969, 6.

"Letters." *Saturday Evening Post,* 15 February 1964, 4.

Levin, Bob. "The Wonder of Wilt." *Maclean's,* 25 October 1999, 82.

Levine, Lawrence W. *Black Culture and Black Consciousness: Afro-American Folk Thought from Slavery to Freedom.* New York: Oxford University Press, 1977.

Levine, Peter. *Ellis Island to Ebbets Field: Sport and the American Jewish Experience.* New York: Oxford University Press, 1992.

Lewin, Leonard. "The Wilt Chamberlain Controversy." *Sport,* August 1969, 16–19, 84.

Libby, Bill. "Bill Russell, Laughing that Laugh." *Los Angeles Times Magazine,* 18 April 1971, 19–21.

———. "The Courage and Splendor of Jerry West." *Sport,* March 1970, 26–29, 64–65.

———. *Goliath: The Wilt Chamberlain Story.* New York: Dodd, Mead and Co., 1977.

———. "Jerry West: Case Study of Desire in Pro Basketball." *Sport,* March 1965, 24–27, 101–3.

———. "Nate Thurmond: The World at His Fingertips." *Sport,* November 1965, 72–75, 107–8.

———, and Spencer Haywood. *Stand Up for Something: The Spencer Haywood Story.* New York: Grosset and Dunlap, 1972.

Liebling, A. J. *The Sweet Science.* 1956. Reprint, New York: North Point Press, 2004.

Linn, Ed. "Bill Russell's Private World." *Sport,* February 1963, 60–67.

———. "The Bill Sharman Story." *Sport,* 52–61.

———. "I Owe the Public Nothing." *Saturday Evening Post,* 18 January 1964, 60–63.

———. "Is the N.B.A. Big League?" *Sport,* 10–11, 82–85.

———. "Oscar Robertson at the Peak." *Sport,* April 1964, 57–63.

———. "There's No Telling How High He Can Go." *Saturday Evening Post,* 9 March 1968, 62–64.

———. "The Wonderful Wizard of Boston." *Sport,* January 1960, 52–60.

Lipsky, Richard. *How We Play the Game: Why Sports Dominate American Life.* Boston: Beacon Press, 1981.

———. *SportsWorld: An American Dreamland.* New York: Quadrangle/New York Times Book Company, 1975.

"Little Man, What Now?" *Time,* 22 February 1960, 73.

Litwack, Leon. *Trouble in Mind: Black Southerners in the Age of Jim Crow.* New York: Vintage, 1998.

Lomax, Michael E. " 'Bedazzle Them with Brilliance, Bamboozle Them with Bull': Harry Edwards, Black Power, and the Revolt of the Black Athlete Revisited." In Lomax, *Sports and the Racial Divide,* 55–89.

———, ed. *Sports and the Racial Divide: African American and Latino Experience in an Era of Change.* Jackson: University Press of Mississippi, 2008.

Lombardo, Ben. "The Harlem Globetrotters and the Perpetuation of the Black Stereotype." *Physical Educator* 35, no. 2 (May 1978): 60–63.

Love, Robert Earl, with Mel Watkins. *The Bob Love Story: If It's Gonna Be, It's Up to Me.* Chicago: Contemporary Books, 2000.

Lovellette, Clyde. "Pro Basketball Is Not for Me." *Sport*, February 1953, 30–31, 84.

Lovinger, Jay, ed. *The Gospel According to ESPN: Saints, Saviors, and Sinners.* New York: Hyperion, 2002.

Luisetti, Hank. "Racehorse Basketball Stinks!" *Sport*, February 1956, 10–11, 84–85.

Lukas, J. Anthony. *Common Ground: A Turbulent Decade in the Lives of Three American Families.* New York: Vintage, 1986.

Lupica, Mike. "The Dipper's Lament." *Esquire*, May 1988, 53–56.

Lupo, Alan. *Liberty's Chosen Home: The Politics of Violence in Boston.* 1977. Reprint, Boston: Beacon Press, 1988.

Lynch, Wayne. *Season of the 76ers: The Story of Wilt Chamberlain and the 1967 NBA Champion Philadelphia 76ers.* New York: Thomas Dunne Books, 2002.

MacCambridge, Michael. *America's Game: The Epic Story of How Pro Football Captured a Nation.* New York: Random House, 2004.

———, ed. *ESPN SportsCentury.* New York: Hyperion, 1999.

———. *The Franchise: A History of Sports Illustrated Magazine.* New York: Hyperion, 1997.

Maharaj, Gitanjali. "Talking Trash: Late Capitalism, Black (Re)Productivity, and Professional Basketball." *Social Text* 50 (spring 1997): 97–110.

Majors, Richard. "Cool Pose: Black Masculinity and Sports." In Messner and Sabo, *Sport, Men, and the Gender Order,* 109–14.

"The Making of a Legend: Towering Lew Alcindor." *Newsweek,* 27 February 1967, 59–62.

"Making the Giant Jolly." *Time,* 1 April 1966, 64–65.

Mallozzi, Vincent M. *Asphalt Gods: An Oral History of the Rucker Tournament.* New York: Doubleday, 2003.

Mandelbaum, Michael. *The Meaning of Sports: Why Americans Watch Baseball, Football, and Basketball and What They See When They Do.* New York: Public Affairs, 2004.

Mandell, Richard D. *Sport: A Cultural History.* New York: Columbia University Press, 1984.

Maraniss, David. *Rome 1960: The Olympics that Changed the World.* New York: Simon and Schuster, 2008.

———. *When Pride Still Mattered: A Life of Vince Lombardi.* New York: Simon and Schuster, 1999.

Maravich, Pete, and Darrel Campbell with Frank Schroeder. *Heir to a Dream.* Nashville, TN: Thomas Nelson Publishers, 1987.

———, with Curry Kirkpatrick. "I Want to Put on a Show." *Sports Illustrated,* 1 December 1969, 39–46.

Marecek, Greg. *Full Court: Stories of the St. Louis Hawks.* St. Louis, MO: Reedy Press, 2006.

Margolick, David. *Beyond Glory: Joe Louis vs. Max Schmeling, and a World on the Brink.* New York: Alfred A. Knopf, 2005.

Markus, Bob. "Who's the Greatest: Alcindor, Russell or Chamberlain?" *Sepia,* November 1971, 32–36, 38–41.

Martin, Charles H. "Integrating New Year's Day: The Racial Politics of College Bowl Games in the American South." In Miller, *The Sporting World of the Modern South*, 175–99.

———. "Jim Crow in the Gymnasium: The Integration of College Basketball in the American South." In Miller and Wiggins, *Sport and the Color Line*, 233–39.

Martin, Waldo E. *No Coward Soldiers: Black Cultural Politics and Postwar America*. Cambridge, MA: Harvard University Press, 2005.

Maule, Tex. "A Curtain Falls on a Long Run." *Sports Illustrated*, 25 July 1966, 18–24.

———. "Lew Turns Small Change to Big Bucks." *Sports Illustrated*, 9 March 1970.

———. "Rescued from Disaster by the Hard-to-Love Giant." *Sports Illustrated*, 14 April 1969, 32–33.

May, Lary, ed. *Recasting America: Culture and Politics in the Age of Cold War*. Chicago: University of Chicago Press, 1989.

May, Peter. *The Big Three*. New York: Simon and Schuster, 1994.

———. *The Last Banner: The Story of the 1985–86 Celtics, the NBA's Greatest Team of All Time*. Holbrook, MA: Adams Media Corporation, 1996.

McAdam, Doug. *Freedom Summer*. New York: Oxford University Press, 1988.

McCallum, Jack. "Basketball." *Sports Illustrated*, 22 October 1992, 28–29.

———. "The King at His New Court." *Sports Illustrated*, 16 November 1987, 37–42.

———. "King for a Year." *Sports Illustrated*, 21 March 1988, 15.

———. "Seems Like Old Times." *Sports Illustrated*, 30 June 2008, 30–35.

———. *Unfinished Business: On and Off the Court with the 1990–91 Boston Celtics*. New York: Summit Books, 1992.

McChesney, Robert W. "Media Made Sport: A History of Sports Coverage in the United States." In Wenner, *Media, Sports, and Society*, 60–63.

McConnell, John J. "A Chronology of Changes in Basketball Rules, 1915–16 to 1952–53." PhD diss., University of Iowa, 1953.

McCormack, Frank. *Never Lose: A Decade of Sports and Politics in Sacramento*. Rancho Cordova, CA: First Ink Publishing, 1989.

McGinniss, Joe. "One Celtic's Formula: Control . . . Contain . . . Curtail." *Sport*, February 1967, 46–47, 73–74.

McKenney, Joe. "Conley's on the High Road." *Sport*, April 1955, 42–45, 62–63.

McLaughlin, Thomas. "'Man to Man': Basketball, Movement, and the Practice of Masculinity." *South Atlantic Quarterly* 103, no. 1 (2004): 169–91.

McNutt, Kevin. *Hooked on Hoops: Understanding Black Youths' Blind Devotion to Basketball*. Chicago: African American Images, 2002.

McPhee, John. *A Sense of Where You Are: Bill Bradley at Princeton*. 1965. Reprint, New York: Farrar, Straus and Giroux, 1999.

McRae, Donald. *Heroes Without a Country: America's Betrayal of Joe Louis and Jesse Owens*. New York: Ecco Press, 2002.

McWhorter, Diane. *Carry Me Home: Birmingham, Alabama: The Climactic Battle of the Civil Rights Revolution*. New York: Simon and Schuster, 2001.

Meggyesy, Dave. *Out of Their League*. Berkeley, CA: Ramparts Press, 1970.

"Melbourne Concluded." *Newsweek*, 17 December 1956, 96.

Melnick, Merrill J., and Donald Sabo. "Sport and Social Mobility Among African American and Hispanic Athletes." In Eisen and Wiggins, *Ethnicity and Sport in North American History and Culture,* 221–41.

Meriwether, James H. *Proudly We Can Be Africans: Black Americans and Africa, 1935–1961.* Cambridge, MA: Harvard University Press, 2002.

Meschery, Tom. *Caught in the Pivot: The Diary of a Rookie Coach in the Exploding World of Pro Basketball.* New York: Dell, 1973.

———. *Over the Rim.* New York: McCall, 1968.

———. "There Is a Disease in Sports Now. . . ." *Sports Illustrated,* 2 October 1972, 56–63.

Messner, Michael A. *Power at Play: Sports and the Problem of Masculinity.* Boston: Beacon Press, 1992.

———, and Donald F. Sabo, eds. *Sport, Men, and the Gender Order: Critical Feminist Perspectives.* Champaign, IL: Human Kinetics, 1990.

Michelson, Herb. *Almost a Famous Person.* New York: Harcourt Brace, 1980.

———. "Confessions of a Basketball Groupie." *Esquire,* October 1974, 165–66, 318–20.

———. "Eagles and Priests." *View* (fall 1982): 10.

Michener, James A. *Sports in America.* New York: Random House, 1976.

Mikan, George, as told to Bill Carlson. *Mr. Basketball: George Mikan's Own Story.* New York: Greenberg, 1951.

———, and Joseph Oberle. *Unstoppable: The Story of George Mikan, the First NBA Superstar.* Indianapolis, IN: Masters Press, 1997.

Miles, La'Tonya Rease. "Basketball, Racial Authenticity, and Masculinity in African American Literature and Culture." PhD diss., University of California at Los Angeles, 2004.

Miller, Patrick B. "The Anatomy of Scientific Racism: Racialist Responses to Black Athletic Achievement." In Miller and Wiggins, *Sport and the Color Line,* 327–44.

———. "Muscular Assimilationism: Sport and the Paradoxes of Racial Reform." In Ross, *Race and Sport,* 146–82.

———, ed. *The Sporting World of the Modern South.* Urbana: University of Illinois Press, 2002.

———, and David K. Wiggins, eds. *Sport and the Color Line: Black Athletes and Race Relations in Twentieth Century America.* New York: Routledge, 2004.

Montville, Leigh. "Bill Russell." *Sports Illustrated,* 19 September 1994, 102.

———. "Blowin' Smoke." *Sports Illustrated,* 16 November 1992, 54–59.

———. *Ted Williams: The Biography of an American Hero.* New York: Doubleday, 2004.

Moretti, Anthony. "The Cold War and the Olympics: Coverage in the *New York Times* and *Los Angeles Times* of the United States' and Soviet Union's Pursuit of Athletic Supremacy, 1948–1988." PhD diss., Ohio University, 2004.

Mravic, Mark. "Fed Up." *Sports Illustrated,* 6 March 2000, 30.

Murray, James. "A Trip for Ten Tall Men." *Sports Illustrated,* 30 January 1961, 52–59.

Murray, Jim. *Jim Murray: The Autobiography of the Pulitzer Prize Winning Columnist.* New York: Macmillan, 1993.

———. "Wilt Chamberlain." *Sport,* December 1986, 49, 136.

Murray, Thomas J. "The Coming Boom in Pro Basketball." *Dun's Review,* November 1966, 52–53, 115–19.

Myerscough, Keith. "The Game with No Name: The Invention of Basketball." *International Journal of the History of Sport* 12, no. 1 (April 1995): 137–52.

Myler, Patrick. *Ring of Hate: Joe Louis vs. Max Schmeling: The Fight of the Century.* New York: Arcade Publishing, 2005.

Nack, William. "I've Made My Own Bed, Now I've Got to Lie in It." *Sports Illustrated,* 20 February 1984, 60–76.

Nadel, Eric. *The Night Wilt Scored 100: Tales From Basketball's Past.* Dallas, TX: Taylor Publishing, 1990.

Naismith, James. *Basketball: Its Origin and Development.* 1941. Reprint, Lincoln: University of Nebraska Press, 1996.

National Basketball Association. *The Perfect Team: The Best Players, Coach, and GM—Let the Debate Begin!* New York: Doubleday, 2006.

"The NBA is Big League—Almost." *Sport,* March 1956, 98.

NBA Dynasty Series—The Boston Celtics—The Complete History. Warner Home Video, 2004.

NBA Dynasty Series—The Los Angeles Lakers—The Complete History. Warner Home Video, 2004.

NBA Dynasty Series—The Philadelphia 76ers—The Complete History. Warner Home Video, 2005.

"The NBA's Big Mistake." *Sport,* May 1970, 84.

"Negro Athletes and Civil Rights." *Sepia,* June 1964, 35–39.

"The Negro in American Sport." *Sport,* March 1960, 28–35.

"Negroes in Pro Basketball." *Ebony,* February 1959, 55–58.

Nelson, Murry R. *Bill Russell: A Biography.* Westport, CT: Greenwood Press, 2005.

———. *The National Basketball League: A History, 1935–1949.* New York: McFarland, 2009.

———. *The Originals: The New York Celtics Invent Modern Basketball.* Bowling Green, OH: Bowling Green State University Press, 1999.

"New Role for Bill Russell." *Ebony,* January 1967, 60–68.

Newcombe, Jack. "Clumsy Sharpshooter." *Sport,* April 1954, 18–19, 74–75.

Newell, Peter, with Tim Cohane. "It's Time to Raise the Baskets." *Look,* 14 March 1961, 79–84.

"Nose to Chin Whiskers." *Time,* 13 January 1967, 51.

Novak, Michael. *The Joy of Sports: End Zones, Bases, Baskets, Balls, and the Consecration of the American Spirit.* New York: Basic Books, 1976.

Nucatola, John. "The Trouble with Pro Basketball." *Sport,* January 1955, 30–31, 66–69.

O'Brien, Sharon. "'We Want a Pennant, Not a White Team': How Boston's Ethnic and Racial History Shaped the Red Sox." In Bloom and Willard, *Sports Matters,* 169–84.

O'Connor, David K. "Wilt Versus Russell: Excellence on the Hardwood." In Walls and Bassham, *Basketball and Philosophy,* 116–28.

O'Connor, Thomas H. *Bibles, Brahmins, and Bosses: A Short History of Boston.* 3d ed. Boston: Trustees of the Public Library of the City of Boston, 1991.

———. *Building a New Boston: Politics and Urban Renewal 1950–1970.* Boston: Northeastern University Press, 1993.

"Off Again, On Again Chamberlain." *Sports Illustrated,* 22 August 1960, 8.

Ogbar, Jeffrey O. G. *Black Power: Radical Politics and African American Identity.* Baltimore, MD: Johns Hopkins University Press, 2004.

"Oh, Those Russian Gals!" *Sports Illustrated,* 7 December 1959, 20.

"Ol' Massa Russell?" *The Nation*, 1 March 1965, 211.

"Old Math." *Time*, 22 April 1966, 66.

Olderman, Murray. "Elgin Baylor: One-Man Franchise." *Sport*, April 1959, 24–26, 80–81.

———. "The Tom Gola Mystery." *Sport*, April 1960, 48, 72–73.

Olsen, Jack. "The Anguish of a Team Divided." *Sports Illustrated*, 29 July 1968, 20–35.

———. *The Black Athlete: A Shameful Story*. New York: Time-Life Books, 1968.

———. *Black Is Best: The Riddle of Cassius Clay*. New York: G. P. Putnam's Sons, 1967.

———. "The Cruel Deception." *Sports Illustrated*, 1 July 1968, 12–27.

———. "Hedonist Prophet of the Spartan Game." *Sports Illustrated*, 23 September 1968, 28–38, 58–61.

———. "In an Alien World." *Sports Illustrated*, 15 July 1968, 28–43.

———. "In the Back of the Bus." *Sports Illustrated*, 22 July 1968, 28–41.

———. "Pride and Prejudice." *Sports Illustrated*, 8 July 1968, 18–31.

"The Olympic Jolt: 'Hell No, Don't Go!'" *Life*, 15 March 1968, 20–27.

"Olympic War." *Time*, 19 November 1956, 65.

"One for the Dipper." *Time*, 22 May 1972, 49–50.

"One Last Smoke." *Time*, 6 May 1966, 54.

O'Ree, Willie, with Michael McKinley. *The Autobiography of Willie O'Ree*. New York: Somerville House, 2000.

Orr, Jack. "Magicians of the Basketball Midway." *Sport*, March 1954, 28–31, 68–71.

Ostler, Scott, and Steve Springer. *Winnin' Times: The Magical Journey of the Los Angeles Lakers*. New York: Macmillan, 1986.

Ottum, Bob. "The Panic Is on Again." *Sports Illustrated*, 9 November 1964, 18–19, 60–61.

"Our Flag on Wings." *Newsweek*, 10 December 1956, 98.

Owens, Jesse, with Paul G. Niemark. *Blackthink: My Life as Black Man and White Man*. New York: William Morrow, 1970.

Ozersky, Josh. "Felton X." *American Legacy* (summer 2003): 13–15.

"The Pack Closes on Boston." *Sports Illustrated*, 26 October 1964, 50–56.

Page, James A. *Black Olympian Medalists*. Englewood, CO: Unlimited, 1991.

Paino, Troy D. "Hoosiers in a Different Light: Forces of Change v. the Power of Nostalgia." *Journal of Sport History* 28, no. 1 (2001): 63–80.

Palmer, Bud. "The Six Best Shots in Basketball." *Sport*, April 1956, 44–47, 89.

Papanek, John. "Add Super to the Sonics." *Sports Illustrated*, 19 January 1978, 81–85.

———. "From Boom to Bust to Boom in the West." *Sports Illustrated*, 2 May 1979, 24–25.

———. "It Was Seattle, Handily." *Sports Illustrated*, 11 June 1979, 16–19.

———. "Slick's His Name—And His Game." *Sports Illustrated*, 23 February 1976, 30–33.

———. "There's an Ill Wind Blowing for the NBA." *Sports Illustrated*, 26 February 1979, 20–27.

"Parting in Melbourne." *Time*, 17 December 1956, 27.

"Parting Shots." *Newsweek*, 2 June 1969, 67.

Patterson, Floyd, with Milton Gross. *Victory over Myself*. New York: Scholastic Book Services, 1962.

Patterson, James T. *Brown v. Board of Education: A Civil Rights Milestone and its Troubled Legacy*. New York: Oxford University Press, 2001.

Paul, Joan, Richard V. McGhee, and Helen Fant. "The Arrival and Ascendance of Black Athletes in the Southeastern Conference." *Phylon* 45, no. 4 (4th quarter, 1984): 284–97.

Paxton, Harry. "Walter Kennedy Answers the NBA's Critics." *Sport,* February 1964, 40–41, 89–91.

Payne, Charles. *I've Got the Light of Freedom: The Organizing Tradition and the Mississippi Freedom Struggle.* Berkeley: University of California Press, 1995.

Pearson, Dan. "A Green Giant." *Boston,* December 2000, 240.

"People." *Sports Illustrated,* 8 May 1972.

Pepe, Phil. "Lew Alcindor Sounds Off!" *Sport,* October 1967, 34–37, 91–92.

———. *Stand Tall: The Lew Alcindor Story.* New York: Grosset and Dunlap, 1970.

Peterson, Robert W. *Cages to Jump Shots: Pro Basketball's Early Years.* New York: Oxford University Press, 1990.

Pettit, Bob, with Bob Wolff. *Bob Pettit: The Drive Within Me.* Englewood Cliffs, NJ: Prentice-Hall, 1966.

Pham, John-Peter. *Liberia: Portrait of a Failed State.* New York: Reed Press, 2004.

Phillips, Murray G., ed. *Deconstructing Sport History: A Postmodern Analysis.* Albany: State University of New York Press, 2006.

Pierce, Charles P. "Red Auerbach." *Esquire,* December 2000, 114–15.

Pierce, Richard B. "More than a Game: The Political Meaning of High School Basketball in Indianapolis." *Journal of Urban History* 27, no. 1 (November 2000): 3–23.

Pipkin, James W. *Sporting Lives: Metaphor and Myth in American Sports Autobiographies.* Columbia: University of Missouri Press, 2008.

"The Play that Won the Title." *Sports Illustrated,* 26 April 1965, 26–27.

Plimpton, George. *The Bogey Man.* New York: Harper and Row, 1967.

———. "Gods." In Lovinger, *The Gospel According to ESPN,* 227-28.

———. "My Team." In Sullivan, *The Boston Celtics,* 17–20.

———. *Out of My League.* New York: Harper and Row, 1961.

———. *Paper Lion.* New York: Harper and Row, 1965.

———. "Reflections in a Diary." *Sports Illustrated,* 23 December 1968, 40-44.

———. *Shadow Box.* New York: Putnam, 1977.

———. *The X Factor: A Quest for Excellence.* New York: W. W. Norton, 1995.

Pluto, Terry. *Loose Balls: The Short, Wild Life of the American Basketball Association—As Told by the Players, Coaches, and Movers and Shakers Who Made It Happen.* New York: Simon and Schuster, 1990.

———. *Tall Tales: The Glory Years of the NBA, in the Words of the Men Who Played, Coached, and Built Pro Basketball.* New York: Simon and Schuster, 1992.

Pomerantz, Gary M. *Wilt, 1962: The Night of 100 Points and the Dawn of a New Era.* New York: Crown, 2005.

Pope, S. W. "Decentering 'Race' and (Re)presenting 'Black' Performance in Sport History: Basketball and Jazz in American Culture." In Phillips, *Deconstructing Sport History,* 147–77.

———. *Patriotic Games: Sporting Traditions in the American Imagination, 1876–1926.* New York: Oxford University Press, 1997.

Povich, Shirley. "Basketball Is for the Birds." *Saturday Evening Post,* 8 December 1958, 24–27.

Powers, John. *The Short Season: A Boston Celtics Diary, 1977–1978*. New York: Harper and Row, 1979.

Powers, Richie, with Mark Mulvoy. *Overtime! An Uninhibited Account of a Referee's Life in the NBA*. New York: David McKay Company, 1975.

Price, S. L. "Bill Russell: The Center of Attention Again in Sacramento." *Hoop NBA Yearbook*, 1987, 42–46.

"Pro Basketball Roundup." *Ebony*, January 1964, 71–72.

"Pro Basketball's Dynasty." *Look*, 8 February 1966, 64–66.

"Professional Basketball's Dream Team." *Ebony*, March 1961, 54–56.

Putnam, Pat. "The Fortune Cookie Smiled." *Sports Illustrated*, 3 November 1975, 77–79.

Rader, Benjamin G. *In Its Own Image: How Television Has Transformed Sports*. New York: Free Press, 1984.

Rampersad, Arnold. *Jackie Robinson: A Biography*. New York: Alfred A. Knopf, 1997.

Ramsey, Frank, with Frank Deford. "Smart Moves by a Master of Deception." *Sports Illustrated*, 19 December 1963, 57–63.

Ransby, Barbara. *Ella Baker and the Black Freedom Movement: A Radical Democratic Vision*. Chapel Hill: University of North Carolina Press, 2003.

Rappoport, Ken. *The Classic: The History of the NCAA Basketball Championship*. Mission, KS: National Collegiate Athletic Association, 1979.

Rayl, Susan J. "The New York Renaissance Professional Black Basketball Team, 1923–1950." PhD diss., Pennsylvania State University, 1996.

Reed, Willis, with Phil Pepe. *A View from the Rim: Willis Reed on Basketball*. Philadelphia: J. B. Lippincott, 1971.

Rein, Richard K. "Catching His Second Wind, Ex-Celtic Legend Bill Russell Scores Now as a Social Critic." *People*, 14 January 1980, 78.

"Remembrance of Things Past." *Time*, 21 April 1980, 35.

Remnick, David. *King of the World*. New York: Vintage, 1998.

Report of the National Advisory Commission on Civil Disorders. New York: Dutton, 1968.

Reynolds, Bill. *Cousy: His Life, Career, and the Birth of Big-Time Basketball*. New York: Simon and Schuster, 2005.

———. *Our Game: The Story of New England Basketball*. Kingstown, RI: Hall of Fame Press, 2006.

Reynolds, Jerry, with Don Drysdale. *Reynolds Remembers: 20 Years with the Sacramento Kings*. Champaign, IL: Sports Publishing, 2005.

Rhoden, William C. *Forty Million Dollar Slaves: The Rise, Fall, and Redemption of the Black Athlete*. New York: Crown, 2006.

Rhomberg, Chris. *No There There: Race, Class, and Political Community in Oakland*. Berkeley: University of California Press, 2004.

Rice, Robert. "Annals of Crime: The Bewildered Fixer," *New Yorker*, 5 March 1955, 38-66.

Riesman, David, with Nathan Glazer and Reuel Denney. *The Lonely Crowd: A Study of the Changing American Character*. 1950. Reprint, New York: Doubleday Anchor Books, 1955.

Riess, Steven A. *City Games: The Evolution of American Urban Society and the Rise of Sports*. Urbana: University of Illinois Press, 1989.

———. *Sports and the American Jew.* Syracuse, NY: Syracuse University Press, 1998.

"The Rivals." *Newsweek,* 12 February 1973, 52.

Roberts, Gene, and Hank Klibanoff. *The Race Beat: The Press, The Civil Rights Struggle, and the Awakening of a Nation.* New York: Alfred A. Knopf, 2006.

Roberts, Michael. *Fans! How We Go Crazy Over Sports.* Washington, DC: New Republic Book Company, 1976.

Roberts, Randy. "The Battle of the Beards: Russell and Chamberlain." In Roberts, *The Rock, the Curse, and the Hub,* 293–315.

———. *"But They Can't Beat Us": Oscar Robertson and the Crispus Attucks Tigers.* Champaign, IL: Sports Publishing, 1999.

———. "Number 4 Is the One: The Emergence of Bobby Orr." In Roberts, *The Rock, the Curse, and the Hub,* 273–92.

———. *Papa Jack: Jack Johnson and the Era of White Hopes.* New York: Free Press, 1983.

———, ed. *The Rock, the Curse, and the Hub: A Random History of Boston Sports.* Cambridge, MA: Harvard University Press, 2005.

———, and James Olson. *Winning Is the Only Thing: Sports in America Since 1945.* Baltimore, MD: Johns Hopkins University Press, 1989.

Roberts, Steven V. "The Lakers Are Great, But Why Aren't They Champs?" *New York Times Magazine,* 5 March 1972, 18–30.

Robertson, Oscar. *The Big O: My Life, My Times, My Game.* New York: Rodale, 2003.

Robinson, Frank, with Al Silverman. *My Life Is Baseball.* Garden City, NY: Doubleday, 1968.

———, and Barry Stainback. *Extra Innings.* New York: McGraw-Hill, 1988.

Robinson, Jackie. *Baseball Has Done It.* Philadelphia: J. P. Lippincott, 1964.

———, as told to Alfred Duckett. *I Never Had It Made: An Autobiography.* 1972. Reprint, Hopewell, NJ: Ecco Press, 1995.

Robinson, Louie. "Captain Wilt Leads L.A. Lakers to Best Pro Sports Record Ever." *Ebony,* April 1972, 114–21.

———. "The High Price of Being Wilt Chamberlain." *Ebony,* January 1974, 94–101.

Rogin, Gilbert. "They All Boo When Red Sits Down." *Sports Illustrated,* 5 April 1965, 100–18.

———. "We Are Grown Men Playing a Child's Game." *Sports Illustrated,* 18 November 1963, 74–90.

———. "You're Looking at Success." *Sports Illustrated,* 24 October 1960, 48–49.

"A Romp in the NBA West." *Sports Illustrated,* 21 October 1968, 30–31.

Ronberg, Gary. "Tossing Bombs into the Hoops." *Sports Illustrated,* 22 September 1969, 30–37.

Rose, Ava, and James Friedman. "Television Sports as Mas(s)culine Cult of Distinction." In Baker and Boyd, *Out of Bounds,* 1–15.

Rosen, Charles. *God, Man and Basketball Jones: The Thinking Fan's Guide to Professional Basketball.* New York: Holt, Rinehart and Winston, 1979.

———. *The Pivotal Season: How the 1971–72 Los Angeles Lakers Changed the NBA.* New York: Thomas Dunne Books, 2005.

———. *The Scandals of '51: How the Gamblers Almost Killed College Basketball.* New York: Holt, Rinehart and Winston, 1978.

Rosen, Charley. "Dr. J Makes the Whole World Feel Good." *Sport,* March 1973, 76, 84–88.

———. *The First Tip-Off: The Incredible Story of the Birth of the NBA.* New York: McGraw Hill, 2009.

———. *The Wizard of Odds: How Jack Molinas Almost Destroyed the Game of Basketball.* New York: Seven Stories Press, 2001.

Rosenblatt, Roger. "The Way We Look at Giants." *Time,* 25 October 1999, 142.

Rosenthal, Harold. "Schayes Is a Hustler." *Sport,* February 1958, 40–41, 71–73.

Rosin, James. *Philly Hoops: The SPHAs and Warriors.* Philadelphia, PA: Autumn Road Publishers, 2003.

Ross, Charles K. *Outside the Lines: African American and the Integration of the National Football League.* New York: New York University Press, 1999.

———, ed. *Race and Sport: The Struggle for Equality on and off the Field.* Jackson: University Press of Mississippi, 2004.

Rowell, Charles H. "An Interview With John Edgar Wideman." *Callaloo* 13, no. 1 (winter 1990): 47–61.

Ruck, Rob. *Sandlot Seasons: Sport in Black Pittsburgh.* Illini Books Edition. 1987. Reprint, Urbana: University of Illinois Press, 1993.

Rudman, Daniel, ed. *Take It to the Hoop.* Richmond, CA: North Atlantic Books, 1980.

Rudolph, Wilma. *Wilma: The Story of Wilma Rudolph.* New York: New American Library, 1977.

Rupp, Adolph. *Rupp's Championship Basketball.* 2d ed. 1948. Reprint, Englewood Cliffs, NJ: Prentice-Hall, 1957.

Rushin, Steve. "Doing Well and Doing Good." *Sports Illustrated,* 14 November 2005, 19.

Russell, Bill. "A Tale of Two Very Big Men." *Newsweek,* 25 October 1999, 60.

———. "I Don't Have to Prove a Thing." *Negro Digest,* March 1964, 12–21 (adapted from Rogin, "We Are Grown Men Playing a Child's Game").

———, and Taylor Branch. *Second Wind: The Memoirs of an Opinionated Man.* New York: Random House, 1979.

———, as told to Al Hirshberg. "I Was a 6'9" Babe in the Woods." *Saturday Evening Post,* 18 January 1958, 25, 66–68.

Russell, Bill, as told to William McSweeny. *Go Up for Glory.* New York: Coward-McCann, 1966.

———, with Alan Hilburg and David Falkner. *Russell Rules: 11 Lessons on Leadership from the Twentieth Century's Greatest Winner.* New York: New American Library, 2001.

———, with Tex Maule. "I Am Not Worried About Ali." *Sports Illustrated,* 19 June 1967, 18–21.

———, with Bob Ottum. "The Psych . . . And My Other Tricks." *Sports Illustrated,* 25 October 1965, 32–39.

———, with Alan Steinberg. *Red and Me: My Coach, My Lifelong Friend.* New York: Collins, 2009.

"Russell Promises President He Will Play in the Olympics." *Ebony,* April 1956, 52–54.

Russell, Cazzie L. *Me, Cazzie Russell.* Westwood, NJ: Fleming H. Revell, 1967.

Russell, Charlie L. *Five on the Black Hand Side.* New York: Third Press, 1969.

Russell, Karen K. "Growing Up with Pride and Prejudice." *New York Times Magazine,* 14 June 1987, 22–28.

Russell, William F. "I'm Not Involved Anymore." *Sports Illustrated,* 4 August 1969, 18–19.
———. "Success Is a Journey." *Sports Illustrated,* 8 June 1970, 80–93.
Rust, Edna, and Art Rust Jr. *Art Rust's Illustrated History of the Black Athlete.* Garden City, NY: Doubleday, 1985.
Ryan, Bob, ed. *The Best of* Sport: *Classic Writing from the Golden Era of Sports.* Toronto: Sport Media Publishing, 2003.
———. *The Boston Celtics: The History, Legends, and Images of America's Most Celebrated Team.* Reading, MA: Addison-Wesley, 1989.
———. *Celtics Pride: The Rebuilding of Boston's World Championship Basketball Team.* Boston: Little, Brown and Company, 1975.
———. *The Pro Game: The World of Professional Basketball.* New York: McGraw Hill, 1975.
———, and Terry Pluto. *Forty-Eight Minutes: A Night in the Life of the NBA.* New York: Macmillan, 1987.
Sailes, Gary A. "The Myth of Black Sports Supremacy." *Journal of Black Studies* 21, no. 4 (June 1991): 480–87.
Sale, Roger. *Seattle, Past to Present.* Seattle: University of Washington Press, 1976.
Salzburg, Charles. *From Set Shot to Slam Dunk: The Glory Days of Basketball in the Words of Those Who Played It.* Lincoln: University of Nebraska Press, 1987.
Schaap, Dick. "The Real Wilt Chamberlain." *Sport,* March 1960, 54–57.
Schaap, Jeremy. *Triumph: The Untold Story of Jesse Owens and Hitler's Olympics.* Boston: Houghton Mifflin, 2007.
Schardt, Arlie W. "Too Much to Beat This Year." *Sports Illustrated,* 30 April 1962, 16.
Schayes, Dolph. "Wilt Chamberlain as We Knew Him." *Sport,* August 1960, 19, 66–68.
Schermeister, Phil. *The University of San Francisco.* Louisville, KY: Harmony House, 1987.
Schoenfeld, Bruce. *The Match: Althea Gibson and Angela Buxton: How Two Outsiders— One Black, the Other Jewish—Forged a Friendship and Made Sports History.* New York: Amistad, 2004.
Schumacher, Michael. *Mr. Basketball: George Mikan, the Minneapolis Lakers, and the Birth of the NBA.* New York: Bloomsbury, 2007.
Schwartz, Jonathan. "Me and Red See It Through." *Sports Illustrated,* 14 April 1980, 50–57.
"The 'Score' at Melbourne." *Newsweek,* 3 December 1956, 67–68.
"Scorecard." *Sports Illustrated,* 24 April 1961, 13.
"Scorecard." *Sports Illustrated,* 27 March 1967, 8.
"Scorecard." *Sports Illustrated,* 12 June 1967, 17.
"Scorecard." *Sports Illustrated,* 1 October 1990, 9.
"Scorecard." *Sports Illustrated,* 16 January 1995, 11.
Scott, Jack. *The Athletic Revolution.* New York: Free Press, 1971.
"Scouting Reports." *Sports Illustrated,* 24 October 1960, 50–53.
"Scouting Reports." *Sports Illustrated,* 28 October 1963, 32–39.
"Scouting Reports." *Sports Illustrated,* 24 October 1966, 48–57.
Self, Robert O. *American Babylon: Race and the Struggle for Postwar Oakland.* Princeton, NJ: Princeton University Press, 2003.
Senn, Alfred Erich. *Power, Politics, and the Olympic Games.* Champaign, IL: Human Kinetics, 1999.

"Seven-Foot Freshman." *Sports Illustrated,* 22 August 1955, 11.

Shainberg, Lawrence. "A Fan's Notes on the Amazing Knicks." *New York Times Magazine,* 25 January 1970, 28–48.

Shaughnessy, Dan. *Ever Green: The Boston Celtics: A History in the Words of Their Players, Coaches, Fans, and Foes, from 1946 to the Present.* New York: St. Martin's Press, 1990.

———. *Seeing Red: The Red Auerbach Story.* Holbrook, MA: Adams Publishing, 1994.

Shapiro, Leonard. *Big Man on Campus: John Thompson and the Georgetown Hoyas.* New York: Henry Holt, 1991.

Shapiro, Miles. *Bill Russell.* New York: Chelsea House Publishers, 1991.

Sharman, Bill. *Sharman on Basketball Shooting.* Englewood Cliffs, NJ: Prentice-Hall, 1965.

Shatzkin, Mike. *The View from Section 111.* Englewood Cliffs, NJ: Prentice-Hall, 1970.

Shaw, Gary. *Meat on the Hoof: The Hidden World of Texas Football.* New York: St. Martin's Press, 1972.

Shecter, Leonard. *The Jocks.* Indianapolis: Bobbs-Merrill, 1969.

———. "The Startling Change in Wilt Chamberlain." *Sport,* March 1967, 74–80.

Shields, David. *Black Planet: Facing Race During an NBA Season.* New York: Three Rivers Press, 1999.

"Shoot, Wilt." *Time,* 22 December 1967, 45.

"Shorties of the Court." *Newsweek,* 28 January 1957, 86–87.

"Should Negroes Boycott the Olympics?" *Ebony,* March 1968, 110–16.

Silverman, Al. "Bob Pettit: The Big Man of Pro Basketball." *Sport,* April 1957, 24, 84–86.

Simons, William. "Interview with Adolph Schayes." *American Jewish History* 74, no. 3 (1985): 287–307.

Singh, Nikhil Pal. *Black Is a Country: Race and the Unfinished Struggle for Democracy.* Cambridge, MA: Harvard University Press, 2004.

Smith, Joshua. "Boston: Cradle of Liberty or Separate but Equal?" *Theory into Practice* 17, no. 1 (February 1978): 54–66.

Smith, Marshall. "Basketball's Court Jester." *Life,* 9 March 1953, 91–99.

Smith, Maureen Margaret. "Bill Russell: Pioneer and Champion of the Sixties." In Wiggins, *Out of the Shadows,* 223–40.

———. "Identity and Citizenship: African American Athletes, Sport, and the Freedom Struggles of the 1960s." PhD diss., Ohio State University, 1999.

———. "New Orleans, New Football League, and New Attitudes: The American Football League All-Star Game Boycott, January 1965." In Lomax, *Sports and the Racial Divide,* 3–22.

Smith, Terry. "Basketball's Irish Czar." *Saturday Evening Post,* 8 February 1964, 54–55.

Smith, Thomas G. "Civil Rights on the Gridiron: The Kennedy Administration and the Desegregation of the Washington Redskins." In Miller and Wiggins, *Sport and the Color Line,* 251–67.

Smith, Tommie. "Why Negroes Should Boycott." *Sport,* March 1968, 40–41, 68.

———, with David Steele. *Silent Gesture: The Autobiography of Tommie Smith.* Philadelphia, PA: Temple University Press, 2007.

Snyder, Brad. *A Well-Paid Slave: Curt Flood's Fight for Free Agency in Professional Sports.* New York: Viking, 2006.

Sperber, Murray. *Onward to Victory: The Crises that Shaped College Sports*. New York: Henry Holt, 1998.

"The Spirited 76ers." *Newsweek*, 23 January 1967, 88.

Spitz, Bob. *Shoot Out the Lights: The Amazing, Improbable, Exhilarating Saga of the 1969–70 New York Knicks*. New York: Harcourt Brace, 1995.

Spivey, Donald. "The Black Athlete in Big-Time Intercollegiate Sports, 1941–1968." *Phylon* 44, no. 2 (2d quarter, 1983): 116–25.

Staff of the *Philadelphia Daily News*. *Philly Hoops: The Magic of Philadelphia Basketball*. Philadelphia, PA: Camino Books, 2003.

Starr, Kevin. *Embattled Dreams: California in War and Peace, 1940–1950*. New York: Oxford University Press, 2002.

"The Stars Are Ready." *Sports Illustrated*, 29 October 1962, 44–46.

Staudohar, Paul D. *Playing for Dollars: Labor Relations and the Sports Business*. Ithaca, NY: Cornell University Press, 1996.

"Story Without an Ending." *Sonics Magazine*, March/April 1977, 20.

Stout, Glenn. "Tryout and Fallout: Race, Jackie Robinson, and the Red Sox." *Massachusetts Historical Review* 6 (2004): 11–37.

Strom, Earl, with Blaine Johnson. *Calling the Shots: My Five Decades in the NBA*. New York: Simon and Schuster, 1990.

Stump, Al. "Bob Pettit: The Polished Pro." *Sport*, February 1965, 70–76.

Sugar, Bert Randolph. *"The Thrill of Victory": The Inside Story of ABC Sports*. New York: Hawthorn Books, 1978.

Sullivan, George. *The Boston Celtics: Fifty Years: A Championship Tradition*. Del Mar, CA: Tehabi Books, 1996.

———. *The Picture History of the Boston Celtics*. Indianapolis, IN: Bobbs-Merrill, 1981.

———. *Wilt Chamberlain*. Rev. ed. 1966. Reprint, New York: Grosset and Dunlap, 1970.

Sullivan, Thomas Robert. "A History of the National Association of Basketball Coaches in the United States." PhD diss., Ohio State University, 1981.

Susman, Warren. "Did Success Spoil the United States? Dual Representations in Postwar America." In May, *Recasting America*, 19–37.

Sydnor, Synthia. "Sport, Celebrity and Liminality." In Dyck, *Games, Sports and Cultures*, 221–37.

Taafe, William. "The Good, the Bad, and the Ugly." *Sports Illustrated*, 16 May 1983, 77.

Tait, Robin. "The Politicization of the Modern Olympic Games." PhD diss., University of Oregon, 1984.

"Talent, Inc." *Senior Scholastic*, 16 February 1956, 42.

Tang, Scott Harvey. "Pushing at the Golden Gate: Race Relations and Racial Politics in San Francisco, 1940–1955." PhD diss., University of California at Berkeley, 2002.

Tate, Greg, ed. *Everything but the Burden: What White People Are Taking from Black Culture*. New York: Broadway Books, 2003.

———. "Nigs R Us, or How Blackfolk Become Fetish Objects." In Tate, *Everything but the Burden*, 1–14.

Tax, Jeremiah. "All in the Mind." *Sports Illustrated*, 14 January 1957, 48–49.

———. "A Blessed Event." *Sports Illustrated*, 25 February 1957, 37–38.

——. "Bob Pettit." *Sports Illustrated*, 5 January 1959, 31.

——. "A Brave Man and a Good Friend." *Sports Illustrated*, 1 February 1960, 10–15.

——. "Bunyan Strides Again." *Sports Illustrated*, 6 April 1959, 18–19.

——. "Chamberlain's Big Mistake." *Sports Illustrated*, 4 April 1960, 58–59.

——. "The Facts About the Fixes." *Sports Illustrated*, 27 March 1961, 18–19.

——. "A Family Affair." *Sports Illustrated*, 10 December 1956, 40–42.

——. "Here Comes the Big Fellow at Last." *Sports Illustrated*, 26 October 1959, 16.

——. "The Man Who Must Be Different." *Sports Illustrated*, 3 February 1958, 29–32.

——. "Now Pitching for Boston." *Sports Illustrated*, 17 November 1958, 60–62.

——. "The Perfect Free Throw." *Sports Illustrated*, 17 February 1958, 44–45.

——. "Roundball Bounces Back." *Sports Illustrated*, 27 October 1958, 31, 58–61.

——. "Short, Sweet Series for Slick Celtics." *Sports Illustrated*, 20 April 1959, 66–68.

——. "The Tall Ones in Boston." *Sports Illustrated*, 16 November 1959, 28.

——. "This Vintage Year." *Sports Illustrated*, 4 November 1957, 38.

——. "Two Big Men in a Tight Pennant Race." *Sports Illustrated*, 22 February 1960, 46–49.

——. "What Price Glory for Oscar?" *Sports Illustrated*, 26 January 1959, 19–20.

——. "Wilt Knocks 'Em Dead." *Sports Illustrated*, 21 December 1959.

Taylor, D. Garth. *Public Opinion and Collective Action: The Boston School Desegregation Conflict*. Chicago: University of Chicago Press, 1986.

Taylor, John. *The Rivalry: Bill Russell, Wilt Chamberlain, and the Golden Age of Basketball*. New York: Random House, 2005.

Taylor, Quintard. *The Forging of a Black Community: Seattle's Central District from 1870 Through the Civil Rights Era*. Seattle: University of Washington Press, 1994.

Teitelbaum, Stanley. *Sports Heroes, Fallen Idols*. Lincoln: University of Nebraska Press, 2005.

Telander, Rick. *Heaven Is a Playground*. New York: St. Martin's Press, 1976.

Terrell, Roy. "Basketball." *Sports Illustrated*, 19 December 1955, 44.

——. "Basketball." *Sports Illustrated*, 23 January 1956, 45–46.

——. "Basketball Bounces In." *Sports Illustrated*, 12 December 1955, 22–25.

——. "Black Saturday." *Sports Illustrated*, 5 March 1956, 54–55.

——. "It's Dayton and the Dons." *Sports Illustrated*, 19 March 1956, 21, 46–47.

——. "NCAA Semifinals." *Sports Illustrated*, 26 March 1956, 47.

——. "The Tournaments and the Man Who." *Sports Illustrated*, 9 January 1956, 38–41.

——. "Victory No. 55: End of an Era." *Sports Illustrated*, 2 April 1956, 42–43.

Theoharis, Jeanne, and Komozi Woodard, eds. *Freedom North: Black Freedom Struggles Outside the South*. New York: Palgrave Macmillan, 2003.

——, and Komozi Woodard, eds. *Groundwork: Local Black Freedom Movements in America*. New York: New York University Press, 2005.

——. "'I'd Rather Go to School in the South': How Boston's School Desegregation Complicates the Civil Rights Paradigm." In Theoharis and Woodard, *Freedom North*, 125–51.

——. "'They Told Us Our Kids Were Stupid': Ruth Batson and the Educational Movement in Boston." In Theoharis and Woodard, *Groundwork*, 17–44.

Thernstrom, Stephan. *The Other Bostonians: Poverty and Progress in the American Metropolis, 1880–1970*. Cambridge, MA: Harvard University Press, 1973.

"They Said It." *Sports Illustrated*, 14 July 1986, 12.

Thomas, Damion Lamar. "'The Good Negroes': African-American Athletes and the Cultural Cold War, 1945–1968." PhD diss., University of California at Los Angeles, 2002.

Thomas, Ron. *They Cleared the Lane: The NBA's Black Pioneers.* Lincoln: University of Nebraska Press, 2002.

Thompson, Charles Herbert. "The History of the National Basketball Tournaments for Black High Schools." PhD diss., Louisiana State University, 1980.

"Those Big Galoots." *Senior Scholastic,* 13 December 1956, 22.

"Three in One." *Sports Illustrated,* 20 January 1958, 16–19.

"Tilting with Wilt." *Newsweek,* 30 December 1968, 48.

Toback, James. *Jim: The Author's Self-Centered Memoir on the Great Jim Brown.* Garden City, NY: Doubleday, 1971.

———. "What the NBA Playoffs Can Do to a Player." *Sport,* May 1970, 20–24, 78.

"The Toughest Job in Basketball." *Sport,* March 1961, 39.

Tuttle, Jeff Douglas. "High-Test Hoops: Industrial Basketball and the Phillips Petroleum Company." MA Thesis, University of San Diego, 1995.

Tygiel, Jules. *Baseball's Great Experiment: Jackie Robinson and His Legacy.* Exp. ed. 1983. Reprint, New York: Oxford University Press, 1997.

Tyson, Timothy. *Radio Free Dixie: Robert F. Williams and the Roots of Black Power.* Chapel Hill: University of North Carolina Press, 1997.

"The Ubiquitous Hands of Mr. C." *Sports Illustrated,* 5 February 1962, 28–35.

Underwood, John. "The Eye of an Eagle and a Big Wingspread." *Sports Illustrated,* 8 February 1965, 14–17.

———. "Last Fling for a Wizard." *Sports Illustrated,* 22 April 1963, 16–17, 58–60.

———. "The Non-Trial Trials." *Sports Illustrated,* 8 July 1968, 11–13.

———. "The True Moral Crisis in Sport." *Sports Illustrated,* 20 May 1963, 16–19, 83.

"Unstoppable." *Newsweek,* 5 February 1962, 81.

Van Deburg, William L. *Black Camelot: African-American Culture Heroes in Their Times.* Chicago: University of Chicago Press, 1997.

———. *Hoodlums: Black Villains and Social Bandits in American Life.* Chicago: University of Chicago Press, 2004.

———. *New Day in Babylon: The Black Power Movement and American Culture.* Chicago: University of Chicago Press, 1992.

———. "Villains, Demons, and Social Bandits: White Fear of the Black Cultural Revolution." In Ward, *Media, Culture, and the Modern African American Freedom Struggle,* 197–210.

Vande Berg, Leah R. "The Sports Hero Meets Mediated Celebrityhood." In Wenner, *Mediasport,* 134–53.

Vecsey, George. "Behind Oscar Robertson's Discontent." *Sport,* December 1967, 36–39, 71.

———. "Bill Russell's Most Trying Season." *Sport,* April 1967, 38–41.

———. "Unseld Makes the Difference." *Sport,* April 1969, 66–69, 81–83.

Von Eschen, Penny M. *Satchmo Blows Up the World: Jazz Ambassadors Play the Cold War.* Cambridge, MA: Harvard University Press, 2004.

Walker, Chet, with Chris Messenger. *Long Time Coming: A Black Athlete's Coming-of-Age in America.* New York: Grove Press, 1995.

Walls, Jerry L., and Gregory Bassham. *Basketball and Philosophy: Thinking Outside the Paint.* Lexington: University Press of Kentucky, 2007.

Walsh, George. "Jones & Jones at Court." *Sports Illustrated,* 20 March 1961, 49–52.

"War Threats Mess Up Olympics." *US News and World Report,* 23 November 1956, 55–56.

Ward, Brian. *Just My Soul Responding: Rhythm and Blues, Black Consciousness, and Race Relations.* Berkeley: University of California Press, 1998.

———, ed. *Media, Culture, and the Modern African American Freedom Struggle.* Gainesville: University Press of Florida, 2001.

Ward, Geoffrey C. *Unforgivable Blackness: The Rise and Fall of Jack Johnson.* New York: Alfred A. Knopf, 2004.

Watson, Emmett. "Bill Russell Is Supposed to Put the Super Back in Sonics." *Sport,* March 1974, 54–62.

———. "Elgin Baylor: Too Good for College Ball." *Sport,* February 1958. Reprinted in Ryan, *The Best of Sport,* 55–64.

———. "Russell on the Sonics and Seattle." *Sonics Magazine,* January/February 1977, 48, 68.

———. "Slick Watts for Mayor???" *Sonics Magazine,* March/April 1977, 48, 72.

Watterson, John Sayle. *The Games Presidents Play: Sports and the Presidency.* Baltimore, MD: Johns Hopkins University Press, 2006.

Watts, Slick, with Frank Hughes. *Slick Watts's Tales from the Supersonics.* Champaign, IL: Sports Publishing, 2005.

Webb, Bernice Larson. *The Basketball Man: James Naismith.* Lawrence: University Press of Kansas, 1973.

Weisbrot, Robert. *Freedom Bound: A History of America's Civil Rights Movement.* New York: Plume, 1991.

Wenner, Lawrence A., ed. *Media, Sports, and Society.* Newbury Park, CA: Sage Publications, 1989.

———, ed. *Mediasport.* New York: Routledge, 1998.

West, Jerry, with Bill Libby. *Mr. Clutch: The Jerry West Story.* Englewood Cliffs, NJ: Prentice-Hall, 1969.

Weyand, Alexander M. *The Cavalcade of Basketball.* New York: Macmillan, 1960.

Whalen, Thomas J. *Dynasty's End: Bill Russell and the 1968–69 World Champion Boston Celtics.* Boston: Northeastern University Press, 2004.

"What It Took to Get Wilt." *Life,* 28 January 1957, 113–17.

"Where the Negro Goes from Here in Sports." *Sport,* September 1966, 56–59, 87–88.

Whitfield, Stephen J. *A Death in the Delta: The Story of Emmett Till.* New York: Free Press, 1988.

"Who Won the Olympics?" *New York Times Magazine,* 23 December 1956, 13.

"Why L.A. Loves the Lakers." *Newsweek,* 13 December 1971, 73.

Wideman, John Edgar. *Hoop Roots.* Boston: Houghton Mifflin, 2001.

Wiggins, David K. *Glory Bound: Black Athletes in a White America.* Syracuse, NY: Syracuse University Press, 1997.

———, ed. *Out of the Shadows: A Biographical History of African American Athletes.* Fayetteville: University of Arkansas Press, 2006.

———. "Victory for Allah: Muhammad Ali, the Nation of Islam, and American Society." In Gorn, *Muhammad Ali,* 93–102.

———, and Patrick B. Miller. *The Unlevel Playing Field: A Documentary History of the African American Experience in Sport.* Urbana: University of Illinois Press, 2003.

Wigginton, Russell T. *The Strange Career of the Black Athlete: African Americans and Sports.* Westport, CT: Praeger, 2006.

Wilkens, Lenny. *The Lenny Wilkens Story.* New York: Paul S. Eriksson, 1974.

———, with Terry Pluto. *Unguarded: My Forty Years Surviving in the NBA.* New York: Simon and Schuster, 2000.

Wilker, Josh. *The Harlem Globetrotters.* Philadelphia, PA: Chelsea House Publishers, 1997.

Wilkerson-Freeman Sarah L., and Beverly Greene Bond, eds. *Tennessee Women: Their Lives and Times—Volume 1.* Athens: University of Georgia Press, 2009.

Wilkinson, J. Harvie III. *From Brown to Bakke: The Supreme Court and School Integration: 1954–1978.* New York: Oxford University Press, 1979.

Williams, Roger. "The Long Leap Forward of Jerry West." *Sports Illustrated,* 20 November 1961, 82.

Wilson, Wayne. "Wilma Rudolph: The Making of an Olympic Icon." In Wiggins, *Out of the Shadows,* 207–22.

Wilt Chamberlain: Larger Than Life. CBS Television, 2004.

"Wilt the Stilt." *Time,* 12 December 1955, 61–62.

"Wilt Talks Back." *Time,* 25 February 1966, 76.

"Wilt's Big Leap." *Newsweek,* 8 October 1973, 67.

Wind, Herbert Warren. "Bob Cousy: Basketball's Creative Genius." *Sports Illustrated,* 9 January 1956, 42–58.

———. "Bob Cousy: The Man and the Game." *Sports Illustrated,* 16 January 1956, 28–32, 56–58.

———. *The Gilded Age of Sport.* New York: Simon and Schuster, 1961.

———. "Hubbub in the Hub." *Sports Illustrated,* 22 April 1957, 17–19.

———. "The Sporting Scene: Farewell to Cousy." *New Yorker,* 23 March 1963, 146–66.

Wolf, David. *Foul! The Connie Hawkins Story.* New York: Warner Paperback Library, 1972.

"A Womb with a View." *Newsweek,* 13 March 1972, 55.

"The Wonderful Warriors." *Sport,* March 1956, 48–51.

Woodcock, Les. "One Hand Behind His Back." *Sports Illustrated,* 9 December 1957, 97–98.

Wooden, John, and Bill Sharman with Bob Seizer. *The Wooden-Sharman Method: A Guide to Winning Basketball.* New York: Macmillan, 1975.

———, as told to Jack Tobin. *They Call Me Coach.* Waco, TX: Word Books, 1972.

Woolf, Alexander. "This Coach Is Bleeping Good." *Sports Illustrated,* 24 May 1982, 94–95.

Woolpert, Phil. "Scene Behind the Scene on Dons." *USF Alumnus,* December 1955, 12.

Wright, Alfred. "For the Lakers, the Season Still Lies Ahead." *Sports Illustrated,* 16 March 1970, 42–47.

X, Malcolm, as told to Alex Haley. *The Autobiography of Malcolm X.* 1964. Reprint, New York: Ballantine Books, 1992.

Yaeger, Don. *Undue Process: The NCAA's Injustice for All.* Champaign, IL: Sagamore Publishing, 1991.

———, with Sam Cunningham and John Papadakis. *Turning of the Tide: How One Game Changed the South.* New York: Center Street, 2006.

"You Gotta Have Heart." *Newsweek*, 18 May 1970, 93–94.

Young, A. S. "Doc." *Negro Firsts in Sports*. Chicago: Johnson Publishing, 1963.

"Young Businessmen." *Newsweek*, 29 January 1951, 80–82.

Zang, David W. *SportsWars: Athletes in the Age of Aquarius*. Fayetteville: University of Arkansas Press, 2001.

Zanger, Jack. "The Better-Late-Than-Never Celtic." *Sport*, March 1969, 56–59, 81–83.

———. "The NBA Coaches Rate the Players." *Sport*, January 1969, 34–37, 94–96.

Zinkoff, Dave, with Edgar Williams. *Around the World With the Harlem Globetrotters*. Philadelphia, PA: Macrae Smith Company, 1953.

Zirin, Dave. *What's My Name, Fool? Sports and Resistance in the United States*. Chicago: Haymarket Books, 2005.

"The 7-Foot Man." *Newsweek*, 17 December 1956, 96.

"19th Hole." *Sports Illustrated*, 2 December 1963, 94.

"19th Hole." *Sports Illustrated*, 15 July 1968, 94.

"19th Hole." *Sports Illustrated*, 22 July 1968, 71–72.

"19th Hole." *Sports Illustrated*, 29 July 1968, 62–64.

"200 Faces for the Future." *Time*, 15 July 1974, 35–70.

COLLECTIONS

Basketball Hall of Fame, Springfield, Massachusetts
  Bill Mokray Scrapbook Collection
  Clippings files
Congressional Testimony (microform)
  Maurice Podoloff and Walter Kennedy Testimonies
Margaret Herrick Library of the Motion Picture Academy of Arts and Sciences, Los Angeles, California
  Clippings Files
Mississippi Sovereignty Commission Records (online at http://mdah.state.ms.us/arlib/contents/er/sovcom/)
  Clippings and correspondence
Museum of Television and Radio, New York City
  Footage of basketball games and television shows
Ouachita Parish Public Library Special Collections, Monroe, Louisiana
  Clippings Files
Papers of the NAACP (microform)
  Selected Branch Files
Spencer Research Library, University of Kansas, Lawrence, Kansas
  Clippings Files
University of San Francisco Archive Room, San Francisco
  Clippings Files
  Scrapbooks
Urban Archives, Temple University, Philadelphia
  Clippings and Correspondence Files

INDEX

TEXT
10/12.5 Minion Pro

DISPLAY
Minion Pro

COMPOSITOR
Integrated Composition Systems

PRINTER AND BINDER
Thomson-Shore, Inc.